Readings in
Modernity in Africa

Reviews of
Readings in African Popular Culture
Edited by Karin Barber

'...*likely to become the main source book for African culture studies*...' –
David Kerr in *African Theatre in Development*
'... *extraordinarily rich collection full of informative detail and excellent
interpretative analysis. There is not a single piece that fails to fascinate ...
The bibliographical information brought together is worth the price of the
volume alone.*' – Martin Banham, in *Leeds African Studies Bulletin*
'... *a critical testament of African popular culture. I strongly recommend it to
readers and libraries.*' – Tanure Ojaide in *African Studies Review*
'... *an impressive collection of inspiring and thought-provoking essays*' –
Francis B. Nyamnjoh in *Media Development*

Readings in Gender in Africa
Edited by Andrea Cornwall

'*Cornwall's* Readings in Gender in Africa *brings together existing work
in a number of key areas so placing the substantial growth of transdisciplinary
teaching and research in African gender studies during the last three decades
beyond refute. She is to be commended for including the work of leading
African scholars alongside that of their European and North American
counterparts, thus providing an excellent and long overdue teaching text that
works to remedy the overdetermination of African scholarship by Western
institutional and intellectual interests. African gender relations emerge as a
key arena of social transformation, which has inspired theoretical insights of
global import.*' – Amina Mama, African Gender Institute, Cape Town

Readings in African Popular Fiction
Edited by Stephanie Newell

'... *forces a reconsideration of the idea of "African literature".*' – Eileen
Julien, Indiana University
'*This is a rich and intelligently conceived anthology ... the examples presented
here also challenge the usual paradigms now taken for granted in postcolonial
studies, and demonstrate that "subaltern voices" so often assumed to be silent
or suppressed can be heard loud and clear if one cares to locate oneself outside
Western academies and networks. ...*' – Lyn Innes, Professor of
Postcolonial Literatures, University of Kent

Readings in African Politics
Edited by Tom Young

'*The introductory essay is very smart in the best sense. It does a very nice job
in a short space of both laying out the main themes in the evolution of
scholarship on African politics over the past forty years and of critiquing that
literature, and it does so in eloquent and witty prose*' – Leonardo Villalón,
Director of the Centre for African Studies at the University of
Florida

General Editors

Jocelyn Alexander is Lecturer in Commonwealth Studies at the
University of Oxford.

David Pratten is Lecturer in the Social Anthropology of Africa,
University of Oxford.

Tom Young is Senior Lecturer in Politics at the School of Oriental
and African Studies (SOAS), University of London.

Readings in ...

*This series makes available to students a representative selection of the best and
most exciting work in fields where standard textbooks have hitherto been
lacking. Such fields may be located anywhere across the full range of Africanist
humanities and social sciences. The emphasis is on newly emerging fields or
fields that cross older disciplinary or subject boundaries. It is in these areas that
the task of accessing materials is most difficult for students, because relevant
works may be scattered across a wide range of periodicals in different disciplines.
The aim is to bring together central, key works – classics that helped to define
the field – with other significant pieces that cut across established or conventional
positions from different angles. Within reasonable limits all the sub-regions of
sub-Saharan Africa is covered in each volume.*

*Each Reader includes materials from journals and books, condensed or
edited where appropriate. Work published or produced in Africa which, because
of the widening economic divide, may otherwise be unavailable in Europe and
the US, will be included wherever possible. The Readers also include new work
invited and hitherto unpublished where there are significant gaps in the field or
where the editors know of exciting developments that have not yet been represented in the literature.*

*The significance of the readings and the overall nature of the field they
contribute to, are discussed in an introductory essay in each volume. These
introductory essays aim to make significant contributions to the development of
the field in their own right. In all cases, they will provide a 'reading map' to
help students explore the materials presented.*

*The overall level is for for second- and third-year undergraduate and
postgraduate courses and the emphasis is on providing titles that can be used as
text books on these courses.*

**Edited by PETER GESCHIERE
BIRGIT MEYER & PETER PELS**

Readings in Modernity in Africa

*The International
African Institute
in association with*

INDIANA UNIVERSITY PRESS
BLOOMINGTON & INDIANAPOLIS

JAMES CURREY
OXFORD

UNISA PRESS
PRETORIA

First published in the United Kingdom by
The International African Institute
School of Oriental & African Studies
Thornhaugh Street
London WC1H 0XG

in association with
James Currey Ltd
73 Botley Road
Oxford OX2 0BS
www.jamescurrey.co.uk

in North America by
Indiana University Press
601 North Morton Street
Bloomington
Indiana 47404-3797
Tel: 1 800 842 6796
http://www.iupress.indiana.edu

and in South Africa by
Unisa Press
PO Box 392, Unisa
Muckleneuk 0003
www.unisa.ac.za/press

British Library Cataloguing in Publication Data
Readings in modernity in Africa
1. Africa − Civilization
1. Geschiere, Peter II. Meyer, Birgit III. Pels, Peter
960.3

ISBN 978-0-85255-898-0 (James Currey paper)

ISBN 978-1-86888-528-2 (Unisa Press paper)

Cataloging information is available from the Library of Congress.

ISBN 978-0-253-35176-0 (Indiana casebound)
ISBN 978-0-253-21996-1 (Indiana paper)

Typeset in 9.5/9.5 pt Bembo by Long House, Cumbria
Printed and bound in Malaysia

Contents

Part 2 Ethnographies of the Modern in Africa

Notes on Contributors

Kwame Anthony Appiah is Laurence S. Rockefeller University Professor of Philosophy at the Center for Human Values at Princeton University. His books include two monographs in the philosophy of language as well as the widely acclaimed *In My Father's House: Africa in the Philosophy of Culture* (1992) and, with Amy Gutmann, *Color Conscious: The Political Morality of Race* (1996). Together with Henry Louis Gates jr. he edited the *Dictionary of Global Culture* (1997). His recent books include, *Thinking it Through: An Introduction to Contemporary Philosophy* (2004), *The Ethics of Identity* (2005) and *Cosmopolitanism: Ethics in a World of Strangers* (2006).

Jean-François Bayart is Research Director at the CNRS/CERI (*Centre des Etudes et des Recherches Internationales* of the *Fondation Nationale des Sciences Politiques*) and professor at the IEP (*Institut d'Etudes Politiques*) in Paris. Main publications: *L'Etat en Afrique: La politique du ventre* (Fayard, 1989, translated as *The State in Africa: The Politics of the Belly*, Longman, 1993); *L'Illusion identitaire*, Fayard, 1996 (translated as *The Illusion of Cultural Identity*, Chicago University Press, 2005); *Le gouvernement du monde: Une critique politique de la globalisation* (Fayard, 2004).

Filip De Boeck is Professor of Social and Cultural Anthropology and Chair of the Anthropology Department of the Catholic University of Leuven. Since 1987 he has conducted extensive field research in both rural and urban settings in the Democratic Republic of Congo. Amongst his recent publications are *Kinshasa: Tales of the Invisible City* (Ludion/Royal Museum of Central Africa, 2004, in collaboration with the photographer Marie-Françoise Plissart) and *Makers and Breakers. Children and Youth in Postcolonial Africa* (James Currey, 2005, co-edited with Alcinda Honwana). In 2004, De Boeck co-curated an exhibition on Kinshasa with architect Koen Van Synghel for the ninth International Architecture Biennale in Venice. The exhibition was awarded a Golden Lion, and has travelled to Brussels and Johannesburg since.

Shmuel Noah Eisenstadt is an Israeli sociologist. He became a Professor of Sociology at Hebrew University, Jerusalem, in 1959, and retired in 1990. He held guest professorships at, among other places, Chicago University, Harvard, the University of Vienna, Stanford, and the University of Heidelberg. In his early career, he showed an affinity to American sociology and its commitment to modernization theory (*Modernization, Protest and Change*, 1966). He later concentrated on comparative historical research that provides a more critical view of the Eurocentric assumptions of early modernization theory (i.e. *European Civilization in Comparative Perspective*, 1987), and wrote prolifically on such alternatives and antinomies to modernity after his retirement (i.e. *Japanese Civilization: A Comparative View*, 1996; *Multiple Modernities*, 2007). He received a large number of awards and prizes for his work, and holds honorary positions at different universities worldwide.

James Ferguson is Professor of Cultural and Social Anthropology at Stanford University. He has also taught at the University of California at Irvine, the University of Michigan, and Harvard University. He has done research in Lesotho and Zambia, and has recently started working in South Africa. His most recent book, *Global Shadows: Africa in the Neoliberal World Order*, was published by Duke University Press, 2006. His current work in South Africa explores the emergence of new problematics of poverty and social policy under conditions of neoliberalism.

Mariane C. Ferme is Associate Professor of Anthropology at the University of California, Berkeley, and past chair of its Center for African Studies. She is the author of *The Underneath of Things: Violence, History, and the Everyday in Sierra Leone* (University of California Press, 2001). She also has written about secrecy, political practices and institutions, and post-conflict transitions and humanitarian governmentality in contemporary Sierra Leone.

Justin-Daniel Gandoulou obtained his doctorate in anthropology at the University of Paris V (Sorbonne) in 1988. Since 1990 he has been *Maître de Conférences* at the University of Rennes II where he teaches anthropology at the Department of Sociology. In 1997 he organized an exhibition on the Sapeurs (dandies from Brazzaville) at the University of Rennes II, in the context of the week *La Science en Fête*. His two books on these Sapeurs: *Au Coeur de la Sape* and *Dandies à Bacongo* (both 1989 with L'Harmattan, Paris) − brought the colourful role of these young Congolese men to the attention of the French public. At present he is studying issues of identity and territory with special reference to a family from Guadeloupe with Congolese ancestry.

Peter Geschiere is Professor of the Anthropology of Africa at the University of Amsterdam (earlier at Leiden University). He did historical-anthropological fieldwork in different parts of Cameroon and elsewhere in West and Central Africa. Recurrent themes in his work are: local effects of state formation; the impact of the market; cultural dynamics and processes of 'glocalization'; autochthony, citizenship and the politics of belonging. Key publications include: *Village Communities and the State: Changing Relations of Authority in Southeast Cameroon* (Kegan Paul International, 1982); *The Modernity of Witchcraft: Politics and the Occult in Postcolonial Africa* (University of Virginia Press, 1997); with Birgit Meyer, *Globalization and Identity: Dialectics of Flow and Closure* (Blackwell, 1999); with Bambi Ceuppens, 'Autochthony: Local or Global? New Modes in the Struggle over Citizenship and Belonging in Africa and Europe', *Annual Review of Anthropology* 34 (2005). He received the ASA's Distinguished Africanist Award in 2002.

Michael Lambek is Professor of Anthropology jointly at the London School of Economics and the University of Toronto at Scarborough where he also holds the Canada Research Chair in the Anthropology of Ethical Life. He has carried out fieldwork among Malagasy speakers since 1975, first in Mayotte and then also in northwest Madagascar. Publications include *Human Spirits* (Cambridge University Press, 1981); *Knowledge and Practice in Mayotte* (University of Toronto Press, 1993); *The Weight of the Past* (Palgrave, 2002); as well as *A Reader in the Anthropology of Religion* (Blackwell, 2002).

Brian Larkin writes on media and urbanization in Nigeria. Larkin is co-editor, with Faye Ginsburg and Lila Abu-Lughod, of *Media Worlds: Anthropology on New Terrain*, and has recently published, *Signal and Noise: Media, Infrastructure and Urban Culture in Nigeria* (Duke University Press, 2008). Currently his research focuses on the religious use of media by Islamic movements in Nigeria. He is Assistant Professor at Barnard College, Columbia University in New York.

Achille Mbembe is University Professor at the University of Witwatersrand (Johannesburg) and Senior Research Officer at WISER (Wits Institute for Social and Economic Research). He did his MA in History at the University of Yaoundé (1981) and his PhD at Paris I (1989). He taught history and philosophy at several American and French universities (Columbia, Pennsylvania, Chicago, Irvine, EHESS); from 1996 to 2000 he was Executive Director of CODESRIA (Dakar). Recent publications include: 'Sovereignty as a Form of Expenditure' in T. Blom Hansen and F. Stepputat, eds, *Sovereign Bodies: Citizens, Migrants, and States in the Postcolonial World* (Princeton University Press, 2005); with Sarah Nuttall, 'Writing the World from an African Metropolis', in *Public Culture* 16, 3, 2005; 'Essai sur la politique en tant que forme de la dépense' in *Cahiers d'Etudes africaines* 43, 4, 2004; and *On the Postcolony* (California University Press, 2001).

Birgit Meyer is Professor of Cultural Anthropology at the Department of Social and Cultural Anthropology at the Free University, Amsterdam. She has conducted research on missions and local appropriations of Christianity, Pentecostalism, popular culture and video-films in Ghana. Her publications include *Translating the Devil: Religion and Modernity Among the Ewe in Ghana* (Edinburgh University Press, 1999); edited with Peter Geschiere *Globalization and Identity: Dialectics of Flow and Closure* (Blackwell, 1999); edited with Peter Pels, *Magic and Modernity: Interfaces of Revelation and Concealment* (Stanford University Press, 2003); and edited with Annelies Moors, *Religion, Media and the Public Sphere* (Indiana University Press, 2006).

Basile Ndjio is a former Research Fellow at the ASSR, University of Amsterdam where he obtained his PhD in Social and Cultural Anthropology. He currently teaches Social and Cultural Anthropology at the University of Yaoundé. He has published widely on popular culture, African urban landscape, modernity of witchcraft, new forms of wealth, democratization processes in Africa, civil society, autochthony and ethnicity, corruption, modernity expectations, etc. His most recent works include 'Carrefour de la Joie: popular deconstruction of the African post-colonial public sphere' (in *Africa*, 2005) and 'Douala: inventing life in an African necropolis' in *Cities in Contemporary Africa* edited by M. Martin and G. Myers (Palgrave, 2006).

Isak Niehaus is Lecturer in Social Anthropology at the School of Social Sciences at Brunel University. He taught at various universities in South Africa. His current research interests are cosmology, masculinity, sexuality and HIV/AIDS in South African rural areas. He is the author with Kally Shokane and Eliazaar Mohlala of *Witchcraft, Power and Politics: Exploring the Occult in the South African Lowveld* (Pluto Press, 2001) and is currently engaged in writing the biography of a South African teacher.

Margaret Niger-Thomas is a social anthropologist who studied in Cameroon and the Netherlands. She was a Research Fellow at the CCCRW Oxford and the Afrika Studie Centrum in Leiden. She is the Founding President of the Manyu Women's Self-Reliance Foodstuff Co-operative and the Chairperson of the Women's Information and Co-ordination Forum (WICOF) Cameroon. She is the Provincial Delegate of Women's Empowerment and the Family in South West Cameroon and also lectures at the Department of Women and Gender Studies, University of Buea.

Mary Nooter Roberts is Deputy Director and Chief Curator of the UCLA Fowler Museum of Cultural History, and is Adjunct Professor in UCLA's Department of World Arts and Cultures. She holds a PhD in Art History from Columbia University with a specialization in African Art, and a BA in Philosophy and French Literature from Scripps College. From 1984 to 1994 Dr Roberts served as Senior Curator at the Museum for African Art, New York, where she organized numerous exhibitions and the accompanying books, including *Secrecy: African Art that Conceals and Reveals* (1993); *Exhibition-ism: Museums and African Art* (1994); and *Memory: Luba Art and the Making of History* (1996), which won the College Art Association's Alfred Barr Award for Outstanding Museum Scholarship. Her research focuses on the philosophical underpinnings of African visual arts, with emphasis on themes of the body and female representation; arts of divination and healing; and arts of memory, writing, and inscription. She has also written on issues of cultural representation and exhibitions as objects of knowledge. Her major research has been conducted in the Democratic Republic of the Congo and in Senegal, with archival and museum research throughout Europe.

Lungisile Ntsebeza is Professor and holder of the National Research Foundation (NRF) Research Chair in Land Reform and Democracy in South Africa in the Department of Sociology, University of Cape Town. He is also a Chief Research Specialist in the Democracy and Governance Research Programme of the Human Sciences Research Council (HSRC). Ntsebeza has conducted extensive published research on the land question in South Africa around themes such as land rights, democratisation, rural local government, traditional authorities and land and agrarian movements. His book, *Democracy Compromised: Chiefs and the Politics of Land in South Africa*, was published by Brill in 2005 and HSRC Press in 2006. Together with Ruth Hall, he has edited a volume: *The Land Question in South Africa: the Challenge of Transformation and Redistribution* (HSRC Press, 2007).

Francis B. Nyamnjoh is Head of Publications and Dissemination with the Council for the Development of Social Science Research in Africa (CODESRIA). He has taught sociology, anthropology and communication studies at universities in Cameroon, Botswana and South Africa, and has researched and written extensively on Cameroon and Botswana, where he was awarded the 'Senior Arts Researcher of the Year' prize for 2003. His most recent books include (with Piet Konings) *Negotiating an Anglophone Identity* (Brill, 2003); *Rights and the Politics of Recognition in Africa* (Zed Books, 2004); *Africa's Media, Democracy and the Politics of Belonging* (Zed Books, 2005); *Insiders and Outsiders: Citizenship and Xenophobia in Contemporary Southern Africa* (CODESRIA/Zed Books, 2006). Dr Nyamnjoh has published widely on globalization, citizenship, media and the politics of identity in Africa. He has also published three novels, *Mind Searching* (1991), *The Disillusioned African* (1995), and *A Nose for Money* (2006), and a play, *The Convert* (2003), of which his contribution to this volume is an excerpt.

Jean-Pierre Olivier de Sardan is Professor of Anthropology at the Ecole des Hautes Etudes en Sciences Sociales in Marseilles and Director of Research at the Centre National de la Recherche Scientifique (France). He lives and works in Niger where he is one of the founders of LASDEL, Laboratory for Study and Research on Social Dynamics and Local Development in Niamey. His *Anthropologie et développement* (Karthala, 1995) has recently been published in English (as *Anthropology and Development*, Zed Books, 2005). See also *Everyday Corruption and the State,* edited with G. Blundo (Zed Books, 2006). Earlier publications include: *Les sociétés songhay-zarma (Niger, Mali)* (Karthala, 1984); edited with T. Bierschenk and J.P. Chauveau, *Courtiers en développement. Les villages africains en quête de projets* (Karthala, 2000); and edited with Y. Jaffré, *Une médecine inhospitalière. Les difficiles relations entre soignants et soignés dans cinq capitales d'Afrique de l'Ouest* (Karthala, 2003). He is currently working on an empirical socio-anthropology of public spaces in West Africa.

Barbara Oomen is an Associate Professor in Law at the Roosevelt Academy, Utrecht University. As a lawyer and political scientist with a specialization in legal anthropology and human rights, she has a long-standing interest in issues of law and cultural diversity and has published widely on these topics. Her PhD research was published as *Chiefs: Law, Culture and Power in the Post-Apartheid Era* (James Currey/ Palgrave, 2005). A current research project concerns the globalization of (criminal) justice institutions and the way in which this relates to the legitimacy that these instititutions have in countries like Rwanda. Dr Oomen is a member of the Commission on Human Rights of the Dutch Advisory Council on International Affairs and the Science Committee of the Dutch Unesco Board.

Peter Pels is Professor of African Anthropology at the University of Leiden. He has published on critical anthropological theory, the anthropology of colonialism, the history of anthropology, modern African politics and religion, and material culture. He recently co-edited with Birgit Meyer, *Magic and Modernity* (Stanford University Press, 2003); with Lynn Meskell, *Embedding Ethics* (Berg, 2005); and with Romain Bertrand and Jean Louis Briquet, *Cultures of Voting: The Hidden History of the Secret Ballot* (Hurst, 2007) and is currently working on cyberculture and science fiction.

Allen F. Roberts is Professor of World Arts and Cultures and a former Director of the James S. Coleman African Studies Center at UCLA. He is also an affiliated Professor in the UCLA Department of French and Francophone Studies. His PhD and MA in Socio-Cultural Anthropology are from the University of Chicago, and BA in Anthropology from Amherst College; he also held a post-doc through the Michigan Society of Fellows. At Michigan he co-curated 'The Rising of a New Moon: A Century of Tabwa Art', a major NEH-funded exhibition and accompanying book based upon his doctoral research. Prior to UCLA, Roberts taught Anthropology and African Studies at the University of Iowa, where he was also director of the African Studies Program and co-founder and director of a Project for Advanced Study of Art and Life in Africa. Roberts has conducted field and archival research in thirty-four countries and has lived in Africa for over twelve years. His principal interests are in the visual cultures of mystical Islam, the efficacy of African material culture, vernacular architecture, cultural adaptations to radical social change, and the social history of local-level politics.

Janet Roitman is Associate Professor of Anthropology and International Affairs at the New School for Social Research in New York City. She is also a Research Fellow with the Centre National de la Recherche Scientifique (CNRS) and an associate of the research laboratories, Mutations africaines dans la longue durée (MALD) and the Groupe de sociologie politique et morale (GSPM) in Paris. Her recent publications include *Fiscal Disobedience: An Anthropology of Economic Regulation in Central Africa* (Princeton University Press, 2005); 'Productivity in the Margins: The Reconstitution of State Power in the Chad Basin', in Veena Das and Deborah Poole, eds, *Anthropology at the Margins of the State* (School of American Research Press/James Currey, 2004); 'Modes of Governing: The Garrison-Entrepôt' in Stephen Collier and Aiwha Ong, eds. *Global Assemblages: Technology, Governmentality, Ethics* (Blackwell, 2005); and 'The Ethics of Illegality in the Chad Basin', in Jean Comaroff and John Comaroff, eds, *Law and Disorder in the Postcolony* (University of Chicago Press, 2006).

AbdouMaliq Simone is an urbanist with particular interest in emerging forms of social and economic intersection across diverse trajectories of change for cities in the Global South. Simone is presently Professor of Sociology at Goldsmiths College, University of London and Visiting Professor of Urban Studies at the Wits Institute for Social and Economic Research, University of Witwatersrand. His work attempts to generate new theoretical understandings based on a wide range of urban practices generated by cities in Africa, the Middle East and Southeast Asia, as well as efforts to integrate these understandings in concrete policy and governance frameworks. Key publications include, *In Whose Image: Political Islam and Urban Practices in Sudan* (University of Chicago Press, 1994), and *For the City Yet to Come: Urban Change in Four African Cities* (Duke University Press, 2004).

Jojada Verrips is Emeritus Professor of European Anthropology at the University of Amsterdam. He has written and edited a number of books in Dutch and is currently working on a book entitled *The Wild (in the) West*.

Sources & Acknowledgements

The Editors of this volume wish to express their special thanks to Karin Barber and Tom Young, the Editors of this Series at the time of its inception; and to Elizabeth Dunstan and Robert Molteno at the International African Institute. They thank the Amsterdam School for Social Science Research for its financial assistance with the costs of translation. Also, and in particular, they are acutely aware that, without Lotte Hoek's stamina and creative diligence, this collection would never have taken final shape. And lastly, but by no means least, they are most grateful to Lynn Taylor at James Currey Publishers for her painstaking attention to detail in taking this volume through the press.

In relation to photographs other than those contained in the contributions listed below, the Editors are most grateful to the following persons for permission to reproduce their pictures in this volume: Heike Behrend, Philippe Boutté, Marie-Françoise Plissart, Allen F. Roberts & Mary Nooter Roberts, and Tobias Wendl.

Finally, the Editors and Publishers, as well as the International African Institute, are also most grateful to the following authors, journals and publishers for permission to republish the pieces in this volume.

Appiah, Kwame Anthony (1992) 'African Identities' in Kwame Anthony Appiah, *In My Father's House: Africa in the Philosophy of Culture*, London: Methuen. [Chapter 9, pp 280–293.] Courtesy of Oxford University Press and Kwame Anthony Appiah © Kwame Anthony Appiah.

Bayart, Jean-Francois (1998) 'Missionary Fact and Politics of the Belly: A Foucaultian Reading', *Le Fait Missionaire*, 6, pp. 9–38. [Translated by Luca Disanto and Peter Geschiere]

De Boeck, Filip (2002) 'Kinshasa: Tales of the "Invisible City" and the Second World', abridged version of a chapter in Okwui Enwezor et al. (eds), *Under Siege: Four African Cities: Freetown, Johannesburg, Kinshasa, Lagos*, Kassel: Hatje Cantz Publishers. Permission granted by documenta und Museum Fridericianum Veranstaltungs-GmbH.

Eisenstadt, S. N. (1966) *Modernization: Protest and Change*, 1st Edition © 1996, pp 1–7; pp 51–54]. Adapted by permission of Pearson Education Inc., Upper Saddle River, NJ.

Ferguson, James G. (1999) 'Global Disconnect: Abjection and the Aftermath of Modernism' (unpublished paper).

Ferme, Mariane (1999) 'Staging *Politisi*: The Dialogics of Publicity and Secrecy in Sierra Leone', in Comaroff, John L. and Jean Comaroff (eds), *Civil Society and the Political Imagination in Africa: Critical Perspectives*, Chicago: University of Chicago Press © 1999 by the University of Chicago Press.

Gandoulou, Jean-Daniel (1984 and 1989) Excerpts from *Entre Paris et Bacongo*, Paris: Centre Pompidou and *Dandies à Bacongo – Le culte de l'élégance dans la société congolaise contemporaine*, Paris: L'Harmattan. [Translated by Modeste Kemetia and Peter Geschiere]

Lambek, Michael (2003) 'Rheumatic Irony: Questions of Agency and Self-deception as Refracted through the Art of Living with Spirits', from *Illness and Irony*, Oxford: Berghahn, pp. 40–59.

Larkin, Brian (2004) 'Degraded Images, Distorted Sounds: Nigerian Video and the Infrastructure of Piracy', *Public Culture* 16 (2), pp. 289–314.

Mbeki, Thabo (1998) 'The African Renaissance, South Africa and the World'. Speech at the United Nations University, 9 April.

Mbembe, Achille (2002) 'The New Africans: Between Nativism and Cosmopolitanism', *Esprit*, pp. 1–10. [Translated by Peter Geschiere]

Ndjio, Basile (2006) '*Evolués* and *Feymen*: old and new figures of modernity in Cameroon' (unpublished paper).

Niehaus, Isak A. (1993) 'Witch-hunting and Political Legitimacy: Continuity and Change in Green Valley, Lebowa, 1930–91' *Africa* 63 (4), pp. 498–529. Courtesy of the International African Institute, London.

Niger-Thomas, Margaret (2000) Excerpts from '"Buying Futures": The Upsurge of Female Entrepreneurship – Crossing the Formal/Informal Divide in Southwest Cameroon', Ph.D. thesis, University of Leiden.

Nkrumah, Kwame (1964) 'Society and Ideology' and 'Conscientism' in Kwame Nkrumah, *Consciencism: Philosophy and Ideology for Decolonization and Development with particular reference to the African Revolution* (pp. 68–70, 78). London: Heinemann. Courtesy of Panaf Books, London.

Ntsebeza, Lungisile (undated) 'The Resurgence of chiefs: retribalisation and modernity in post-1994 South Africa' (unpublished paper).

Nyamnjoh, Francis B. (2003) *The Convert, A Two-Act Play* (Act One Scene III and Act Two Scene III), Gabarone: Mmegi Publishing House.

Nyerere, Julius Kambarage (1962) 'Ujamaa: The Basis of African Socialism' in Julius K. Nyerere, *Freedom and Socialism: Uhuru na Ujamaa*. Dar es Salaam: Oxford University Press.

Olivier de Sardan, Jean-Pierre (2005) Extracts from 'Introduction: The Three Approaches in the Anthropology of Development'; 'Socio-anthropology of Development'; and 'Development projects and social logic', in Jean-Pierre Olivier de Sardan, *Anthropology and Development*, London and New York: Zed Books.

Oomen, Barbara, 'Chiefs! Law, Power and Culture in Contemporary South Africa' (unpublished paper).

Pels, Peter (1996) 'The Pidginization of Luguru Politics: Administrative Ethnography and the Paradoxes of Indirect Rule', *American Ethnologist*, 23 (4), pp. 738–61. Copyright © 1996 by the American Anthropological Association.

Roberts, Allen F. and Mary Nooter Roberts (2003) 'Introduction: Aura and Icon in Contemporary Senegal' from Allen F. and Mary Nooter Roberts, *A Saint in the City: Sufi Art of Urban Senegal*, Los Angeles: UCLA Fowler Museum of Cultural History © Allen F. Roberts and Mary Nooter Roberts.

Roitman, Janet, 'A Successful Life in the Illegal Realm: Smugglers and Road Bandits in the Chad Basin' (unpublished paper).

Sarbah, John Mensah [1906] 'Administrative Questions', from *Fanti National Constitution: A Short Treatise on the Constitution and Government of the Fanti, Asanti and Other Akan Tribes of West Africa*. Republished by Frank Cass & Co. Ltd. (London, 1968).

Senghor, Léopold Sédar (1964) 'The African Road to Socialism' in Léopold Sédar Senghor, *On African Socialism*. New York and London: Frederick A. Praeger. Copyright © 1964. Reproduced with permission of Greenwood Publishing Group, Inc. Westport, CT.

Shepstone, Theophilus (1875) 'Report of the Expedition Sent by the Government of Natal to Instal Cetywayo as King of the Zulus...' British Parliamentary Papers, Colonies, Africa 30, Natal. HMSO.

Simone, AbdouMaliq (2001) 'On the Worlding of African Cities', *African Studies Review*, 44 (2), pp 16–41.

Verrips, Jojada and Birgit Meyer (2001) 'Kwaku's Car: The Struggles and Stories of a Ghanaian Long-distance Taxi-Driver' in Daniel Miller (ed.), *Car Cultures*, Oxford: Berg.

World Bank, Extracts come from Robert McNamara's Addresses to the Board of Governors, Washington, DC, 25 September 1972; Nairobi, 1973; Manila, 1976. Extracts from *Accelerated Development in Sub-Saharan Africa – An Agenda for Action* [The Berg Report], Washington, DC: The World Bank, 1981, pp. 2–8; 55–6; 124–5. Extracts from *Sub-Saharan Africa: From Crisis to Sustainable Growth: A Long-Term Perspective Study*, Washington, DC: The World Bank, 1989, pp 1, 3; 4–5; 10; 30; 54; 58–9; 60–61; 194.

PETER GESCHIERE
BIRGIT MEYER & PETER PELS[1]
Introduction

Throughout Africa, understandings of modernization and modernity have, in the twenty-first century, lost much of the innocent optimism that characterized them in the 1960s and 1970s, the first decades after independence. In 1971, on entering the District Office in a remote town in eastern Cameroon, Peter Geschiere could still be admonished by a notice underneath the President's portrait saying: 'Be brief, we have to do in decades what Europe achieved over centuries.' Since the 1990s, when the somber realities of what Structural Adjustment and neo-liberalism meant for everyday life became apparent, such an admonition would smack of irony, if not cynicism. Yet the term 'modern' seems to have lost little of its magic – it is just people's ideas about whether and how it can be achieved that seem to have changed. While some present-day Africans look for access to modern life through increasingly transnational forms of seeking wealth, others seem to feel trapped in downward spirals of deprivation and despair (Ferguson 1999; Weiss 2004). Even if grand narratives of modernization and development have lost credibility, among Africans as well as among those who study Africa, notions of being or becoming modern continue to wield tremendous power in everyday African life. 'Modern' became one of those 'words that fly'[2] – perhaps because its promise of a better life gives an illusory consistency to the often contradictory variety of its contents. In recent years, many scholars have felt the urgency to understand such ideas about modernity in present-day Africa, and have tried to make sense of these desires to move 'upward' or to 'develop', to cease being 'backward' or being held back by 'tradition'. Yet, people often regard 'modernity' as an abomination as much as a blessing, and yearn nostalgically for a vanished past (in a typically modern way). They form this ambivalence in widely divergent socio-cultural and historical trajectories, giving rise to a bewildering variety of often unexpected manifestations. These varied forms of modernity are the focus of this volume.

Ambivalence also lies at the heart of theoretical reflections and debates about modernity in Africa. While scholars were busy discrediting modernization theory, 'becoming modern' became part of contemporary African vocabularies, mobilized so as to articulate contemporary experiences (Spitulnik 2002). Thus, however ill-defined or confusing these terms may have appeared to scholars, it became difficult to ignore them. If a discourse on modernity became virtually unavoidable, the question of how to conceptualize modernity in relation to Africa remained. How can we talk and write about modernity without lapsing into discourses of modernization and their teleological views of world history? How do we avoid losing sight of the diversity of local expressive forms through which modernity is being negotiated or appropriated? Or, conversely: how, in studying such local appropriations, can we avoid sidelining the impact of Western-dominated power structures? Oscillating between, on the one hand, the urge to maintain a critical distance to discourses of modernization and development, and, on the other, the realization that these discourses generate powerful practices that do actually shape African people's lives, scholars still face the classical question: what is modernity?

Such considerations informed – if not haunted – the study of modernity in Africa that started to thrive since the early 1990s. By that

time, a new consciousness of 'globalization' – of the extent to which 'modernity' is 'at large' in the world (Appadurai 1996) – produced a variety of new theoretical attitudes and practical strategies with regard to questions of modernization and development. While, from the late 1960s onwards, academics increasingly discredited the simple model of unilinear progress from tradition to modernity, to be achieved by the transfer of technology and political systems from the West, it remained (and remains) a basic feature of the thinking and practice of international donor agencies, African elites, and people in the street (see Gendzier 1985; Leys 1996; Taylor 1973). In the context of globalization and neo-liberalism, however, intellectuals close to policy-making circles revived modernization theory in a different guise: one that focused on civil society reforming and developing the African state rather than the state developing (agricultural) society (Apter and Rosberg 1994; World Bank 1989).

In African studies, the term 'modernity' has become ubiquitous in the attempt to come to terms with the diverse forms through which modernity's attractions and discontents are being expressed (Comaroff and Comaroff 1993). Such studies aim at ways of gaining a critical distance towards the ideological constructs of modernization theorists and development bureaucrats, without thereby dismissing the cultural, political, social and economic effects of colonial and post-colonial policies implemented in the name of enlightenment, modernization and development (Comaroff and Comaroff 1993; Cooper 2005; Deutsch, Probst and Schmidt 1999; Donham 1999; Ferguson 1994, 1999; Geschiere 1997; Meyer 1999; Piot 1999). Often initiating and contributing to much wider multidisciplinary discussions,[3] these studies of modernity in Africa seek to move beyond the unilinear narratives of 'modernization' in which 'the West' provides the *telos* towards which all societies were in the process of moving. We already indicated above that such earlier teleological accounts were often rooted in the optimism of the post-war movements of decolonization and the building of 'new nations' – in Africa in particular. Today, such optimism appears increasingly unwarranted, as everyday life in Africa is increasingly marked by a gap between people's dreams of a better life, and their actual disconnection from the structures on which the materialization of this dream depends, as James Ferguson has brought out so well (1999; see also his contribution to this volume).

It is, therefore, important – particularly when we seek to picture and understand life worlds on the ground – to remain conscious of the teleological force of the notion of modernization and to resist its power to draw our understanding into meta-narratives that should be critically investigated instead of reproduced. However, it is no solution to avoid 'modernity' altogether, as argued by Englund and Leach (2000). Such a position foregrounds the local and particular at the expense of global power structures, which nevertheless impinge on local life worlds, and it thereby fails to address the gap that lies at the core of Ferguson's analysis. Yet another attempt to accommodate cultural particularity, which acknowledges the fact that people across the world share similar predicaments and dreams regarding modernity, can be found among those who explore the idea of the existence of 'alternative', 'other', 'local', 'parallel' or 'multiple' modernities different from the West (Gaonkar 2001; Hefner 1997; Larkin 1997; Piot 1999; Rofel 1999; Spitulnik 2002). This approach has been very valuable, and produced many detailed ethnographic studies that greatly enhanced our understanding of how people in a variety of contexts grapple with modernity's evils and attractions. But how can one invoke multiple modernities and yet reject, or at least circumvent, an understanding of modernity in the singular (see Gikandi 2002; Knobl 2002)? Doesn't the relativistic notion of an 'African' modernity imply the risk of, again, conceiving of Africans as being locked up in their own specific version of it?[4] Even worse, of ignoring the inequalities that differential access to modernity may imply (Ferguson, in this volume)? Many Africans might not be content with being placed in such a specific trajectory and would prefer admission to the same modern life that brought so much prosperity to the West. The proliferation all over the continent of decidedly un-African nicknames – like 'Santa Barbara' or 'Maison Blanche' for new wealthy suburbs, 'Nylon' for a shantytown, or 'Brooklyn' for a barbershop – seems to express a uniform view of what modernity should be about. Yet this does certainly not exclude cultural specificities. To the contrary, what we need to grasp is the 'paradox that people in different world areas increasingly share aspirations, material standards, and social institutions at the same time that their local definition of and engagement with these initiatives fuels cultural distinctiveness' (Knauft 2002: 2; see also Appadurai 1996).

This book intends to provide students of Africa with an overview of the variety of scholarly work stimulated by the question of modernity and to offer some tools for dealing with its intellectual paradoxes. It consists of two different parts: one providing both analytical and historical examples of the genealogies of modernity in Africa; the other a set of ethnographic sketches of current manifestations of modernity in Africa. Likewise, the first part of this introduction provides a rough sketch of the analytical methods and historical context in which to situate the four sections of Part One of the book, while its second part argues why we think that current research into modernity in Africa is best served by the ethnographic focus of the five sections of Part Two. This should provide students of Africa with two kinds of tools with which to research and manage the admittedly dazzling variety of manifestations of modernity in Africa:

- a selective but substantive sketch of the genealogies of modernity in Africa;
- and an – equally incomplete – research guide that provisionally catalogues some of the more important dimensions, trajectories and locations of modernity in Africa and beyond.[5]

Defining Modernity?

Before addressing these genealogies and manifestations of modernity in Africa, however, a word of caution: while we have tried to make our topic as accessible as possible, it remains fraught with contradictions, paradoxes and practical dilemmas. The term 'modernity' confuses, whether we want to or not, the analytical and the empirical levels, if only because the academic theories of yesterday have been cumulatively incorporated in African popular consciousness – whether as inventions of the tradition of colonialism, as the desire for national identity and autonomy of the 1950s and 1960s, or as the widespread faith in NGO-entrepreneurship of the 1980s and 1990s. There are no easy solutions available here: one only has to ask oneself whether we can think of improving people's lives without defining them as 'backward' or 'not yet developed' to see that these dilemmas are not merely theoretical. The term 'modern' can be used to merely refer to the 'contemporary', the 'present' or the 'now', or, more broadly, to 'innovation'. Nevertheless, a more substantive conception of the term seems to be more prevalent, one which forces us to consider the relative value of very different dimensions of the 'modern': processes of commodification and monetization; of instituting constitutional government, representative democracy, taxation and/or the civil service; of mass mediatization; of reconfiguring personal relationships towards the bourgeois nuclear family and/or the individual; of the

demise of religion and the rise of secularism; and so on. Whatever value one attributes to such dimensions and their interrelationships, in almost all contexts 'modernity' seems to refer to a basic sense of living in a new time, implying an opposition between 'us' as radically divorced from 'tradition', and 'others' who are still backward or not yet developed. True as this may seem, it is in itself insufficient for a substantial definition.

It is, of course, tempting nonetheless to try to design a comprehensive definition of modernity so as to transcend the contradictions, paradoxes and dilemmas that thrive in contemporary studies of modernity in Africa. In our view, however, the clarity promised by defining modernity is illusory. Rather than seeking to capture essential features of modernity in a universal frame, we propose to investigate modernity as a historical phenomenon that is still evolving, and to take into account the contradictions and ambivalences to which it gave rise. For this reason, we advocate a genealogical approach of modernity, that is aware of the different ways in which discourses of modernity – from colonial discourses of Enlightenment and education, to the hopeful striving for development and education in the 1960s, through to the increasing experiences of the failure of development now – have become deeply incorporated in African life worlds.

A definition of modernity poses a threat to our understanding of social dynamism and to our sensitivity to contradiction and ambivalence partly because it would require us to determine beforehand how the introduction of modern institutions such as state bureaucracy, schools, hospitals, churches, universities, and the policies and practices instigated by these institutions, on the one hand, are related to mental dispositions and forms of social behavior, on the other. To propose such a more or less strong alignment of these dimensions might lessen awareness of the disjunctures and contradictions between them. Definitions of modernity easily invoke a kind of internal balance, clarity and closure. It is, however, important to keep in mind that even with regard to the West, where modernity is supposed to have been generated as a pure form (but see below), thinkers view modernity as an unfinished project (Habermas 1981, see also Deutsch, Probst and Schmidt 2002) or even suggest that 'we have never been modern' (Latour 1993). Modernity is not a package deal but a set of powerful practices and ideas held together by 'family resemblances' (à la Wittgenstein), the different combinations of which may evoke a variety of responses. Instead of assuming the totalizing power of the project of modernity (and therefore the possibility of defining it), we advocate a 'relational' understanding (Knauft 2002: 32; further discussed below) that is aware of the contradictions and limits of this project.

'Africa' itself often was and is the 'other' – radically different, yet to be encompassed – in relation to which the project of modernity acquired meaning and was brought into play. As one of modernity's 'others', it is usually defined in *temporal* terms, and this goes together with a practice of defining people as unequal by placing them in a time other than that of 'developed' people (thus denying them 'coevalness': Fabian 1983: 31; see also Ferguson, this volume). Realizing how strategies of temporalization produce modernity's 'other' is a necessary step on the way of realizing why modernity so often promises solutions, yet produces embarrassment instead. We hope the rest of this introduction will clarify that point of view.

Genealogies of modernity in Africa and beyond

If the recent use of 'modernity' by scholars mostly manifests a late twentieth-century critique of a mid-twentieth-century ideal, the problematic of modernity stretches, of course, much further back. Intellectually, modernity was the central problem of founding fathers of social science like Marx, Weber and Durkheim. Their characterizations of modernity spawned modernization theory in the 1950s as well as its more recent critical alternatives. All of these took 'modernity' to be a feature of nineteenth- and twentieth-century Europe (or the 'West') seen in isolation from the world. Instead, our relational conception of modernity stresses that modernity developed some of its most characteristic features in the longer history of the relationship between Europe and its others: in the long-distance trade of mercantilism and the original accumulation of capitalism by slave labour in Caribbean agro-industry; in the colonial roots of nationalism in eighteenth-century America, nineteenth-century Ireland and twentieth-century Africa; in the emergence of statecraft or 'statistics' from eighteenth-century expeditions to Siberia or the nineteenth-century administration of India; in the orientalist imaginations of despotism against democracy, or tradition against individuality; in the European invention of racism; and so on.[6] The two parts of the present section will develop these two themes in relation to Africa, in an attempt to contextualize the chapters in Part One of this book.

The academic history of modernity

We do not have the opportunity here to do justice to the intellectual history of the term 'modernity' or its cognates.[7] For our purposes it is sufficient to start with the observation that, before the rise of modernization theory in the 1950s, the classical social thinkers cherished a far more ambivalent understanding of modernity. Karl Marx famously combined a vision of progress based on the increasing control of humanity over nature with a more pessimistic presentiment of the increasing alienation and fetishization of daily life under capitalism. Emile Durkheim saw a development from 'mechanic solidarity' to the superior division of social labour of 'organic solidarity', but was also concerned that modern society would fall apart without something like the collective representations of the Australian aborigines. If Max Weber saw a process of disenchantment in which the magic of tradition was replaced by the rationality of law, the latter was also threatened by the longing for charismatic leadership that was fuelled by the spiritless 'iron cage' of discipline. Modernity, in all these instances, remained haunted by ghosts of its own making. These ghosts – fetishism, religion, tradition and charisma – were clad in garments which modern people thought they had shed and left for their more 'primitive' or 'barbarian' neighbours.[8]

This ambivalent vision of modernity was, at least in his interpretation of Durkheim and Weber, erased by Talcott Parsons, whose *The Social System* (1951) fed and epitomized the optimism of post-1945 modernization theory. Parsons' seemingly empirical 'pattern variables' of action were dichotomous classifications of modern common-sense notions and could be used to juxtapose two ideal-typical societies: a 'modern' one characterized by universalism, functional specificity, achievement-orientation and collectivity-orientation, and a 'traditional' type combining particularism, diffuseness, ascription and self-orientation. Such dichotomies of societies based on reason, law and merit versus communities determined by religion, custom and birth recurred at the time in many guises: literate versus oral communication, constitutional versus personal politics, free versus fettered life – all varieties boiling down to an ideological distinction of the modern goal towards which all people should evolve, away from the traditional bondage in which everybody but the West 'still' found itself.

The empirical support for such theories was often sought in Africa, when political scientists turned to the continent in the atmosphere of the Cold War and the emergence of 'African studies' in the 1950s. 'Traditional' or 'tribal systems' – characteristically made up of hereditary chiefs, kinship relations, and 'personal' and 'diffuse' authority – could be modernized by 'political institutional transfer' of the secular authority thought to be characteristic of European parliamentary models (Apter 1963 [1955]). Not only did this conception rest on and legitimize the technocratic conception of 'development' as the transfer of appropriate (political) technology (Ullrich 1992: 275), it adopted much of this inspiration from British colonial development (Esteva 1992: 10) in the context of which these theorists did their research, often in collaboration with British colonial administrators (Almond and Coleman 1960; Apter 1963 [1955], 1965; Coleman 1958; Young and Fosbrooke 1960). Colonial administrators and modernization theorists basically agreed on the explanation of the emergence of modernity in these circumstances: it either happened through colonial conquest and subsequent technological transfer, or through an (usually elite) African individual's decision to become modern. This begged the question of how modernity – as a technology to be transferred or an example to be adopted – could emerge in the first place. Modernization theory itself rarely provided an answer: it was too busy typologizing 'secular-libertarian' and 'sacred-collective' models of political society (Apter 1965: 28–31) to bother with explanations of how the former could emerge from the latter. The modernist's conception of the birth of modernity remained immaculate (cf. Pels 2003b: 13).

This shows how much the opposition of modern and traditional was an ideological product of modernity itself, part of a 'modern constitution' that maintains 'pure' dichotomies by ignoring the necessary mediations and translations between these poles (Latour 1993). It underscores that one of the basic features of modern discourse and experience is a consciousness of temporal rupture (Habermas 1987), of there being two different, radically separated times – 'modernity' and 'tradition' – of which one is more advanced. One still finds this tautological and unilinear stance in sociological writing on modernity ('Modernity is essentially a post-traditional order' originating in 'post-feudal Europe': Giddens 1991: 15, 20), even among writers who have produced otherwise interesting views on the way modern society is constituted – such as the fact that it is characterized by the 'disembedding' of social relationships through abstract (monetary, legal, statistical) systems, generating a need for 'trust' in anonymous relationships and the concomitant consciousness of 'risk' that these relationships fail (Beck 1992; Giddens 1991). The interest in social processes of abstraction is perhaps better represented – in the sense of resting on a more sophisticated theory of history and method – by Michel Foucault's analyses of the modern forms of discipline in the interaction of technologies of domination and technologies of self (see Rabinow 1997), an approach that can be successfully adapted to the understanding of manifestations of modernity outside Europe (see Bayart, in this volume). The modern processes of abstracting relationships from their immediate locality have also increasingly become the topic of anthropological analyses of globalization and the development of the virtual worlds of finance and mass media, introducing a more pervasive role of the imagination in constructing social life (see, for example, Appadurai 1996; Carrier and Miller 1998; Ginsburg, Abu-Lughod and Larkin 2004). With the exception of such recent anthropological works, however, all of the academic perspectives mentioned locate the origins of modernity in Europe and do not allow for the possibility that some of 'modernity's' origins lay outside 'the West'. From Karl Marx, who failed to include the social organization of physical force – African slavery in Caribbean plantation economies in particular – into the history of capitalism proper (see Mitchell 2000: 10–11) to Michel Foucault, who did not acknowledge the imperial context of the emergence of 'state racism' based on the 'biopower' of disciplining human bodies (Stoler 1995), the vast majority of academic writings on modernity wrongly assumed that its sole source was the West, and that the West embodied modernity in pure form.

Genealogies of modernity in Africa

We can learn much about 'what it is to be modern' from the history of European and North American social theory, but will always run the risk of merely reproducing its ideological stance and its cultivated ignorance about its own origins if, as Appiah suggests, Africans and Westerners do not ask the question what it is to *be* modern together (1992: 172) – in other words, if we do not also understand modernity *from* Africa as well. This means that we have to look beyond the European Enlightenment or nineteenth-century industrialization and nation-building as the most obvious sources of modernity. We can see many of modernity's features emerge *before* the eighteenth century – this includes the popularization of the English word 'modern' itself[9] – and outside Europe. Proto-capitalist forms of commodification, for example, characterized the mercantile period, which not only changed European modes of producing knowledge, goods and wealth (see, for example, Mintz 1985; Pels 1998), but also changed West Africa by creating a transatlantic market for slaves (Rodney 1970), and, later, Eastern and Southern Africa when the Omani rulers of Zanzibar followed the French example of managing (clove) plantations by slave labour (Sheriff 1987). These modernizing influences had deep cultural reverberations: in what is now Sierra Leone, for example, the impact of the slave raids in the sixteenth and seventeenth centuries generated ritual techniques (of 'closure' and 'darkness') that were deemed essential for capture, concealment and survival in its violent landscape. Ironically, therefore, what some regard today as the 'primitive' magic of the Sierra Leonean civil war is in fact a ritual memory of an earlier phase of modernization in West Africa (Shaw 2003).

This seemingly exotic detail illustrates a general point, the importance of which cannot be exaggerated: that, looked at from Africa, one cannot but place modernity in the context of the transatlantic trading of human beings for money. It was and is impossible to be modern in Africa without drawing on this heritage of slavery, whether it appears as the Pan-Africanist sources of African nationalism or as the popularity of rap music among today's African youth. Both modern capitalism and the current meaning of the word 'Africa' derive in part from the 'Black Atlantic' (Gilroy 1993). '"[R]ace" was a central organizing principle', not only for the generation that theorized the decolonization of Africa (Appiah 1992: 13), but for the common focus of 'African studies' on 'sub-Saharan', that is, *black* Africa, as well. Thus, at the level of ideas, 'Africa' is usually an 'invention' based on the relationship between the West and the African continent (Appiah 1992: 1; Mudimbe 1988) and therefore always already 'modern'. At the level of practice, the violent modernization of African social life started at least when Europeans bought the 'biopower' required for the American plantations on the West African coast. It should be noted, however, that this violent modernization of social life did not imply that Africans were allowed to assume a modern identity. On the contrary, trapped in the trope of otherness, for a long time Africans were denied coevalness with Europeans and considered as ultimate embodiments of the primitive (Chidester 1996; Gikandi 2002). Contemporary attempts to redress the balance by articulating an African identity in non-Western terms often fall into the same trap.

This is an important example of how modernity should be understood relationally, and illustrates the central methodological principle that governs our approach: the *genealogical* principle that requires a sophisticated historical consciousness of the phenomena under study.[10] Genealogies are always plural: they show, in our case, the multiple trajectories that compose 'modern' life. If, for example, capitalism has to be understood as based on a European religious sensibility that promoted 'the spirit of capitalism' (Weber 1974) *as well as* on a practice of turning human beings into commodities for the triangular transatlantic trade (and these two early modern trajectories represent, of course, only a part of the genealogy of capitalism), it becomes obvious that a genealogical approach requires us to juxtapose the ideologically self-evident sources of modernity with those that have been historically and socially ignored. Hence the need, for example, to understand modernity through the 'counterculture' of the Black Atlantic (Gilroy 1993: 1) or, likewise, to bring modernity and ritual together in a 'methodological counterpoint' (Comaroff and Comaroff 1993: xxix). Genealogical research disaggregates phenomena and multiplies their origins, and allows us critically to assess how and why they survive. Analytically, modernity can be seen to originate from multiple trajectories, even if it gains its persuasive force by the ideological suggestion that it is a singular 'package deal' that every 'developed' person should have acquired.

Thus, it is vital to realize the historical depth and multiplicity of trajectories of modernity in Africa, and a considerable amount of research is still needed to do so. Whether or not we want to call them 'modern', we cannot ignore that the era of the slave trade and mercantilism has generated new cultural and social forms (of witchcraft, of slavery, of 'fetish', of Islamic organization; see Copans 1980; Pietz 1987; Shaw 2003) that are part of our 'modern' heritage. Early colonial commercial companies and missions generated the 'myth of the Dark Continent' in the mid-nineteenth century, setting the tone for what many still regard as an opposition of Enlightened modernity and African tradition (Brantlinger 1988) and co-producing modern forms of African Christianity and Islam (Fernandez 1982; Peel 2003; Cruise O'Brien 1975; Loimeier (nd); Larkin and Meyer 2006). The establishment of colonial states generated modern forms of chieftaincy and tradition, introduced state education, developed African nationalism, and developed conceptions of what it means to be African which guided postcolonial society up to the present. By zooming in on the themes of development, modernization, tradition and African personhood, the first part of this reader intends to show how such a relational concept of modernity can help us to understand these genealogies of modernity in Africa.

Modernity at large in Africa

If the first part of this book and the first part of our introduction focus on how to interpret modernity in Africa, the second parts of both deal with the modern in everyday life and the challenges it poses to ethnography. One of these challenges is how to come to terms with the widespread use of relational notions of the modern ('tradition'; 'development') as 'observers' *as well as* 'native' terms – with the explicit understanding that it becomes, at times, very problematic to distinguish observers from 'natives'. This is further complicated by the fact that our historically layered heritage of representations of Africa and understandings of modernity implies that one person's 'modernity' may become another's 'backwardness' – as when successful neo-liberal entrepreneurs in the 1990s could look 'back' on an older generation's belief in education and bureaucratic advancement with pity or scorn, or previously 'modern' African workers could feel 'left behind' by the deprivations of neo-liberal restructuring. The rapid popularization throughout Africa of development-by-civil-society and the concept of the 'non-governmental organization' since the 1980s should caution and worry us, since it illustrates the more general truth that most if not all analytical perspectives *on* African societies have been interventions *in* them as well (Pels and Salemink 1999). We need constant and vigilant reflexivity to recognize and understand how Africans creatively appropriated such 'modernization'.

As intimated already, this reflexivity invites skepsis about the conception of 'multiple modernities'. We certainly want to speak of multiple trajectories of modernity (this is what a genealogical approach requires), but to speak of 'modernities' in the plural creates an illusion of relativist equality, as if 'their' modernity exists at the same level as 'ours'. We insist that at both the analytical and the empirical level, 'modernity' is usually a way of defining *inequality* in temporal terms (Ferguson, this volume). One needs to remain critical of such master-narratives of temporal inequality, but even if they differ from time to time and place to place, this critique will, at most, allow us to 'provincialize Europe': we cannot rid ourselves of its 'modern' standards of development (however illusory or 'hyperreal' they are; Chakrabarty 2000). Once we try to do so, we risk losing sight of the most common and probably the most dominant way of articulating unequal access to power and authority: the way that, in Africa as elsewhere in the world, people classify others as being coeval with themselves, or not.

If impartial and valid research into modern African societies requires us to acknowledge as well as criticize such temporal constructions, we should also study the counterpoints to modernity's 'hyperreal' constructions of Europe or the West. The latter are commonly determined in an ideological sense by a 'package deal' that sweepingly lumps together capitalism and commodification by monetary exchange value, industrial production, impersonal bureaucracies, taxation and constitutional systems of popular representation, mass politics, state education, institutions of rational calculation, strategic surveillance and statistical discipline, individualist relationships of contract and property, reifications of 'culture', 'tradition' and 'nation', urban divisions of labour, commodified technology, mass media, and secularism paired to privatized or commercialized religion – as if they are necessarily interconnected functions of one indivisible institutional and psychological constitution. The essays in the second part of this book show that they are not. We need to unpack and disaggregate this modern package, and study alternative trajectories of its elements to see how they are creatively reconstructed in everyday life in Africa. This is why one requires, in addition to the genealogical/historical method of the first part of this book, an ethnographic study of how these elements of 'modernity' are disaggregated and recombined on and at various 'stages of modernity'.[11] Again, we do not 'sum up' this package as a definition of 'modernity', but as a way of identifying important ethnographic fields of study that, to our mind, have been insufficiently incorporated in research into everyday African life, because their 'modern' identification with Europe or the West was assumed to be self-evidently distinct from 'African tradition'. The second part of this book provides exemplars of how to conduct such critical research.

This book obviously does not allow us to elaborate on how to study all the different elements of modernity in Africa. The essays in Part Two, therefore, target a number of particularly important ethnographic counterpoints to it. We have not included such elements as have already been studied elsewhere – the ethnography of money (Guyer 1995), individualism (Piot 1999), political revolution (Donham 1999), the civil service (Anders 2005), witchcraft and ritual (Comaroff and Comaroff 1993; Geschiere 1997), to name just a few. Studies of Christian missions (Comaroff and Comaroff 1991, 1997; Meyer 1999; Pels 1999) or Islamic orders (Cruise O'Brien 1975, 2003) provide much insight into the mediations or translations of modernity in Africa beyond our scope here. Instead, Part Two of this volume targets variations on emblematic figures of modernity that have only recently been studied with the required ethnographic depth: issues of citizenship and democratization; of city life and new technology; of novel but 'enchanted' forms of political legitimacy and property; and the emergence of 'new figures of success' as alternative role models of advancement that Africans are imagining today and that are difficult to place in any traditional–modern opposition.

Conclusion

We hope that our case for a study of modernity in Africa that navigates between the illusory unity of a singular modern package exclusively transferred from the West and the denial or relativization of modernity's manifestations in Africa is convincing. A relational concept of modernity starts from the assumption that the extraordinary effectiveness and spread of notions of the modern in Africa have to be understood as an effect of the illusory unity of modernity, as it is supposed to manifest itself some time in the future, and that the power of these notions lies in their capacity to articulate temporal inequalities: of classifying some as modern and others as 'not yet'. Methodologically, this relational conception translates into genealogies of modernity that identify its historical origins in 'Europe' – real as well as 'hyperreal', (in the sense of illusory, yet extraordinarily effective) – but also in 'Africa', or even better, in 'Europe's' relationship with 'Africa' – and in ethnographies of how these relationships manifest themselves in local struggles over the denial of coevalness that is characteristic of developmental or modernist discourse. These genealogical and ethnographic studies should include, therefore, the study of expatriate Africans and other 'foreign bodies' (such as the World Bank, colonial administrators or missionaries, or expatriate experts), and, eventually, ourselves as (expatriate as well as African) scholars.

Thus, a relational study of modernity in Africa combines the awareness and empirical study of 'hyperreal' modernity in Africa with critical research into the forms of globalization, extraversion and appropriation by (temporary or permanent) inhabitants of the African continent and its 'others', and the creative recombinations of elements of the modern package with its local or global alternatives. To go further and *define* – that is, essentialize – 'Europe' and 'Africa', or 'modernity' and 'tradition', is to fail to do justice to both the power of the temporal ideal and the reality of its actual manifestations. As we indicated, this is a difficult position, full of paradoxes and contradictions, where often 'tradition' turns out to be modern, or 'development' contributes to making people more backward. It does not allow for easy solutions of practical predicaments: one cannot maintain, like many international donors do, that one simply hands over the required technologies of growth and good governance to African countries – a viewpoint that seems to enjoy an unexpected renaissance with the current presentation of the Millennium Development Goals as a panacea for Africa's crises – because that would deny the centuries-old genealogy of inequality between Africa and the West; nor can one simply say that Africa needs 'its own development' for that, too, implies a denial of Africa's coevalness with the 'developed' part of the world. Instead, we hope to have provided a critical, yet empirically adequate research perspective that will allow students of Africa to appreciate the alternatives and counterpoints to modernity as fully modern, and to counter the denials of coevalness that still govern its modern relationships in such a way that a more equitable shared trajectory towards a better future can be imaged and implemented.

Notes

1 See *Sources and Acknowledgements* for the names of the individuals and organizations we wish to express our special thanks to.
2 This was the title of a series of seminars organized by Seteney Shami and Itty Abraham for the SSRC (New York) in 2003/4.
3 To cite just some of the relevant works, see, in addition to those cited in the text, the discussions among anthropologists (Appadurai 1996; Englund and Leach 2000; Kahn 2001; Knauft 2002; Miller 1994, 1995; Rofel 1999), cultural studies scholars (Berman 1983; Gaonkar 2001; Gilroy 1993), historians (Breckenridge 1995; Conekin, Mort and Waters 1999; Daunton and Rieger 2001; Prakash 1999), feminists (Felski 1995), geographers (Harvey 1989; Pred 1995), political scientists (Chatterjee 1997; Mitchell 2000), philosophers (Gyekye 1997; Habermas 1987; Mbembe 2001; Taylor 1989, 2001), and sociologists (Beck 1992; Giddens 1990, 1991; Latour 1993).
4 A relativism that also undermines Englund and Leach's proposal to refrain from using 'modernity' (2000).
5 The necessary incompleteness of our genealogical sketch and our research guide is, of course, compensated for by the fact that modern politics, literature and art, and religion, are addressed in other books in this series at length.
6 See, among others, Anderson (1983), Cohn and Dirks (1988), Mitchell (2000), Pels (1999), Pels and Salemink (1999), Said (1978), Stoler (1995).
7 This would imply listing publications like Habermas (1987), MacPherson (1962), and Taylor (1989), to name just three seminal statements.
8 For an elaboration of (and references to) these arguments, see Pels (2003a: 17–29).
9 The word 'modern', however, mostly had an 'unfavourable' meaning until the nineteenth century (Williams 1983).
10 This methodology is inspired by Michel Foucault's genealogical method (1991 [1984]) and Walter Benjamin's notion of 'immanent critique' (see Caygill 1998: 34–79).
11 We borrow 'stages of modernity' from Tim Mitchell (2000), emphasizing that we are *both* talking about different periods in the history of the modern (rather than 'modern history', which implies a typically modernist temporal rupture) *and* about the differing performances, styles and representations of modernity in different places.

References

Almond, Gabriel A. and James Smoot Coleman, eds. 1960. *The Politics of the Developing Areas*. Princeton: Princeton University Press.
Anders, Gerhard. 2005. 'Civil Servants in Malawi: Cultural Dualism, Moonlighting and Corruption in the Shadow of Good Governance'. PhD thesis, Erasmus University Rotterdam.
Anderson, Benedict. 1983. *Imagined Communities. Reflections on the Origin and Spread of Nationalism*. London: Verso.
Appadurai, Arjun. 1996. *Modernity at Large. Cultural Dimensions of Globalization*. Minneapolis: The University of Minnesota Press.
Appiah, Kwame Anthony. 1992. *In My Father's House. Africa in the Philosophy of Culture*. London: Methuen.
Apter, David E. 1963. *Ghana in Transition*. [Rev. edition of *Gold Coast in Transition*, 1955]. New York: Athenaeum.
—— 1965. *The Politics of Modernization*. Chicago and London: The University of Chicago Press.
Apter, David E. and Carl G. Rosberg, eds. 1994. *Political Development and the New Realism in Sub-Saharan Africa*. Charlottesville and London: University

Press of Virginia.
Beck, Ulrich. 1992. *Risk Society*. London: Sage.
Berman, Marshall. 1983. *All That Is Solid Melts Into Air. The Experience of Modernity*. London: Verso.
Brantlinger, Patrick. 1988. 'A Genealogy of the Myth of the Dark Continent', in P. Brantlinger, *Rule of Darkness. British Imperialism and Literature, 1830-1914*. Ithaca: Cornell University Press.
Breckenridge, Carol, ed. 1995. *Consuming Modernity. Public Culture in a South Asian World*. Minneapolis: University of Minnesota Press.
Carrier, James and Daniel Miller. 1998. *Virtualism. A New Political Economy*. London: Berg.
Caygill, Howard. 1998. *Walter Benjamin: The Colour of Experience*. London: Routledge.
Chakrabarty, Dipesh. 2000. *Provincializing Europe. Postcolonial Thought and Historical Difference*. Princeton: Princeton University Press.
Chatterjee, Partha. 1997. *Our Modernity*. Rotterdam: SEPHIS.
Chidester, David. 1996. *Savage Systems. Colonialism and Comparative Literature in South Africa*. Cape Town: University of Cape Town Press.
Cohn, Bernard S. and Nicholas Dirks. 1988. 'Beyond the Fringe: the Nation State, Colonialism, and the Technologies of Power', *Journal of Historical Sociology* 1, 3: 224–9.
Coleman, James Smoot. 1958. *Nationalism in Nigeria*. Berkeley: University of California Press.
Comaroff, Jean and John Comaroff. 1993. 'Introduction', in *Modernity and its Malcontents: Ritual and Power in Postcolonial Africa'*. Chicago: The University of Chicago Press.
Comaroff, Jean and John L. 1991 and 1997. *Of Revolution and Revolution* vol. 1 and 2. Chicago: Chicago University Press.
Conekin, Becky, Frank Mort and Chris Waters. 1999. *Moments of Modernity. Reconstructing Britain, 1945–1954*. London: Rivers Oram Press.
Cooper, Frederick. 2005. *Colonialism in Question: Theory, Knowledge, History*. Berkeley and Los Angeles: The University of California Press.
Copans, Jean. 1980. *Les marabouts de l'arachide*. Paris: Le Sycamore.
Cruise O'Brien, Donal. 1975. *Saints and Politicians*. Cambridge: Cambridge University Press.
—— 2003. *Symbolic Confrontations: Muslims Imagining the State in Africa*. London: Hurst.
Daunton, M.J. and B. Rieger. 2001. *Meanings of Modernity: Britain from the Late Victorian Era to World War II*. London: Berg.
Deutsch, Jan-Georg, Peter Probst and Heike Schmidt, eds. 2002. *African Modernities. Entangled Meanings in Current Debate*. Oxford: James Currey.
Donham, Donald. 1999. *Marxist Modern: An Ethnographic History of the Revolution in Ethiopia*. Berkeley/Oxford: University of California Press/ James Currey.
Englund, Harri and James Leach. 2000. 'Ethnography and the Metanarratives of Modernity, *Current Anthropology* 41/2: 225–45.
Esteva, Gustavo. 1992. 'Development', in W. Sachs (ed.) *The Development Dictionary: A Guide to Knowledge as Power*. London: Zed Books.
Fabian, Johannes. 1983. *Time and the Other. How Anthropology Makes its Object*. New York: Columbia University Press.
Felski, R. 1995. *The Gender of Modernity*. Cambridge, MA: Harvard University Press.
Ferguson, James. 1994. *The Anti-Politics Machine: 'Development', Depoliticization, and Bureaucratic Power in Lesotho*. Minneapolis: University of Minnesota Press.
—— 1999. *Expectations of Modernity. Myths and Meanings of Urban Life on the Zambian Copperbelt*. Berkeley: University of California Press.
Fernandez, James. 1982. *Bwiti: An Ethnography of the Religious Imagination in Africa*. Princeton: Princeton University Press.
Foucault, Michel. 1991 [1984]. 'Nietsche, Genealogy, History', in Paul Rabinow (ed.) *The Foucault Reader*. New York: Pantheon Books.
Gaonkar, Dilip, ed. 2001. *Alternative Modernities*. Durham, NC: Duke University Press.
Gendzier, Irene. 1985. *Managing Political Change: Social Scientists and the Third World*. Boulder and London: Westview Press.
Geschiere, Peter. 1997. *The Modernity of Witchcraft. Politics and the Occult in Postcolonial Africa*. Charlottesville and London: University Press of Virginia.

Giddens, Anthony. 1990. *The Consequences of Modernity*. Cambridge: Polity Press.
—— 1991. *Modernity and Self-Identity. Self and Society in the Late Modern Age*. Cambridge: Polity Press.
Gikandi, Simon. 2002. 'Reason, Modernity & the African Crisis', in Jan-Georg Deutsch, Peter Probst, and Heike Schmidt (eds) *African Modernities. Entangled Meanings in Current Debate*. Oxford: James Currey. pp. 135–57.
Gilroy, Paul. 1993. *The Black Atlantic. Modernity and Double Consciousness*. London: Verso.
Ginsburg,, Faye, Lila Abu-Lughod and Brian Larkin, eds. 2004. *Media Worlds: Anthropology on New Terrain*. Berkeley: University of California Press.
Guyer, Jane I., ed. 1995. *Money Matters: Instability, Values and Social Payments in the Modern History of West African Communities*, Portsmouth, NH/London: Heinemann/James Currey.
Gyekye, Kwame. 1997. *Tradition and Modernity. Philosophical Reflections on the African Experience*. New York, Oxford: Oxford University Press.
Habermas, Jürgen. 1981. 'Die Moderne – ein unvollendetes Projekt', in J. Habermas, *Kleine Politische Schriften, vols I–IV*. Frankfurt am Main: Suhrkamp Verlag, pp. 444–64.
—— 1987. *The Philosophical Discourse of Modernity*. Cambridge, MA: MIT Press.
Harvey, David. 1989. *The Condition of Postmodernity*. London: Blackwell.
Hefner, Robert. 1997. 'Multiple Modernities: Christianity, Islam and Hinduism in a Globalizing Age', *Annual Review of Anthropology* 27: 83–104.
Kahn, Joel. 2001. *Modernity and Exclusion*. London: Sage.
Knauft, Bruce. 2002. 'Critically Modern: An Introduction', in B. Knauft (ed.) *Critically Modern. Alternatives, Alterities, Anthropologies*. Bloomington: Indiana University Press, pp. 1–54.
Knobl, Wolfgang. 2002. 'Modernization Theory, Modernization and African Modernities", in Deutsch, Jan-Georg, Peter Probst and Heike Schmidt (eds) *African Modernities. Entangled Meanings in Current Debate*. Oxford: James Currey, pp. 158–78.
Larkin, Brian. 1997. 'Indian Films and Nigerian Lovers: Media and the Creation of Parallel Modernities'. *Africa* 67 (3): 406–39.
Larkin, Brian and Birgit Meyer. 2006. 'Pentecostalism, Islam and Culture: New Religious Movements in West Africa', in Emmanuel Akyeampong (ed.): *Themes in West African History*. Oxford: James Currey; Athens, OH; Ohio University Press; Accra: Woeli Publishing Services. pp. 286–312.
Latour, Bruno. 1993. *We Have Never Been Modern*. Cambridge, MA: Harvard University Press.
Leys, Colin. 1996. *The Rise and Fall of Development Theory*. Nairobi/ Bloomington/Oxford: EAEP/Indiana University Press/James Currey.
Loimeier, Roman, nd, 'Is there Something Like "Protestant Islam"?' Unpublished ms.
MacPherson, C.B. 1962. *The Political Theory of Possessive Individualism. Hobbes to Locke*. Oxford: Oxford University Press.
Mbembe, Achille. 2001. *On the Postcolony*, Berkeley: University of California Press.
Meyer, Birgit. 1999. *Translating the Devil. Religion and Modernity Among the Ewe in Ghana*. Edinburgh: Edinburgh University Press.
Miller, Daniel. 1994. *Modernity, an Ethnographic Approach: Dualism and Consumption in Trinidad*. Oxford: Berg.
—— 1995. *Worlds Apart: Modernity through the Prism of the Local*. London: Routledge.
Mintz, Sidney. 1985. *Sweetness and Power. The Place of Sugar in Modern History*. New York: Viking Press.
Mitchell, Timothy. 2000. 'The Stage of Modernity', in T. Mitchell. ed.) *Questions of Modernity*, 1–34. Minneapolis: University of Minnesota Press.
Mudimbe, Valentin. 1988. *The Invention of Africa*. Bloomington/Oxford: Indiana University Press, James Currey.
Parsons, Talcott. 1951. *The Social System*, Glencoe, IL: Free Press.
Peel, J.D.Y. 2003. *Religious Encounter and the Making of the Yoruba*. Bloomington: Indiana University Press.

Pels, Peter. 1998. 'The Spirit of Matter: On Fetish, Rarity, Fact and Fancy', in P. Spyer (ed.) *Border Fetishisms. Material Objects in Unstable Spaces*. New York/London: Routledge, 91–121.
—— 1999. 'The Rise and Fall of the Indian Aborigines, Orientalism, Anglicism, and the Emergence of an Ethnology of India', in P. Pels and O. Salemink (eds) *Colonial Subjects. Essays in the Practical History of Anthropology*. Ann Arbor: The University of Michigan Press, pp. 82–116.
—— 2003a. 'Introduction: Magic and Modernity' in Birgit Meyer and Peter Pels (eds), *Magic and Modernity, Interfaces of Revelation and Concealment*, Stanford: Stanford University Press, pp. 1–39.
—— 2003b. *Het uitzonderen van 'Afrika'. Naar een antropologie van de politieke verbeelding*. Inaugural lecture, Leiden University.
Pels, Peter and Oscar Salemink. 1999. 'Introduction: Locating the Colonial Subjects of Anthropology', in P. Pels and O. Salemink (eds) *Colonial Subjects. Essays in the Practical History of Anthropology*, 1–36. Ann Arbor: The University of Michigan Press.
Pietz, William. 1987. 'The Origin of the Fetish', I, *Res* 9: 5–17.
Piot, Charles. 1999. *Remotely Global: Village Modernity in West Africa*, Chicago: Chicago University Press.
Prakash, Gyan. 1999. *Another Reason. Science and the Imagination of Modern India*. Princeton: Princeton University Press.
Pred, Allan. 1995. *Recognizing European Modernities: A Montage of the Present*. London: Routledge.
Rabinow, Paul, ed. 1997. *Ethics, Subjectivity and Truth. Essential Works of Michel Foucault, vol. I*. New York: Free Press.
Rodney, Walter. 1970. *A History of the Upper Guinea Coast, 1545–1800*. New York/London: Monthly Review Press.
Rofel, Lisa. 1999. *Other Modernities: Gendered Yearning in China after Socialism*. Berkeley: University of California Press.
Said, Edward. 1978 [1985]. *Orientalism*. Harmondsworth: Penguin.
Shaw, Rosalind. 2003. 'Robert Kaplan and 'Juju Journalism' in Sierra Leone's Rebel War: The Primitivizing of African Conflict', in Birgit Meyer and Peter Pels (eds) *Magic and Modernity*. Stanford: Stanford University Press, pp. 81–103.
Sheriff, Abdul. 1987. *Slaves, Spices and Ivory in Zanzibar*. London/Dar es Salaam/Nairobi/Athens, OH: James Currey/Tanzania Publishing House/ Heinemann Kenya/Ohio University Press.
Spitulnik, Debra A. 2002. 'Accessing "Local" Modernities: Reflections on the Place of Linguistic Evidence in Ethnography', in Bruce M. Knauft (ed.), *Critically Modern, Alternatives, Alterities, Anthropologies*. Bloomington: Indiana University Press. pp. 194–219.
Stoler, Ann Laura. 1995. *Race and the Education of Desire. Foucault's History of Sexuality and the Colonial Order of Things*. Durham, NC: Duke University Press.
Taylor, Charles. 1989. *Sources of the Self. The Making of the Modern Identity*. Cambridge, MA: Harvard UP.
Taylor, Charles. 2001. Two Theories of Modernity, in D. Gaonkar (ed.) *Alternative Modernities*. Durham, NC: Duke University Press.
Taylor, John G.. 1973. *From Modernization to Modes of Production. A Critique of the Sociologies of Development and Underdevelopment*. London: Macmillan.
Ullrich, Otto. 1992. 'Technology', in W. Sachs (ed.) *The Development Dictionary. A Guide to Knowledge as Power*. London: Zed Books.
Weber, Max. 1974 [1904/5]. *The Protestant Ethic and the Spirit of Capitalism*. London: Unwin University Books.
Weiss, Brad, ed. 2004. *Producing African Futures. Ritual and Reproduction in a Neoliberal Age*. Leiden: Brill.
Williams, Raymond. 1983. *Keywords. A Vocabulary of Culture and Society*. Revised edition. New York: Oxford University Press.
World Bank. 1989. *Sub-Saharan Africa: From Crisis to Sustainable Growth, A Long-Term Perspective Study*, Washington DC: The World Bank.
Young, Roland, and Henry Fosbrooke. 1960. *Land and Politics among the Luguru*. London: Routledge and Kegan Paul.

1 Genealogies of 'Modernity' in Africa

The first part of this Reader aims to document certain striking changes in the conception of the modern, notably in relation to Africa, over the last decades of the twentieth century. At issue is how we can capture an overall switch from the confident, unilineal metanarrative of 'modernization' in its different facets, to a more fragmented notion of 'modernity'. The first section highlights some important moments in this trajectory. Subsequent sections deal with three more specific themes that stand out in this transition: development, tradition and identity. A central issue in this first part of the reader is to what extent a 'relational' conception of modernity, as outlined in the introduction above, can help to understand these changes.

Section 1.A
From 'Modernization' to 'Modernity'

This section follows the transition from a unilineal view of 'modernization' that was so influential in African studies in the first post-Independence decades (roughly the 1960s and 1970s) to a much more uncertain vision of 'modernity' as following divergent trajectories and taking on unexpected shapes. However, we opted for a reversed order, starting from the present, in what might be an 'anthropological' take on history. James Ferguson's text on the cruel disappointment of 'expectations of modernity' is especially based on his fieldwork among Zambian miners and on their reactions to being disconnected from what seemed to be a promising path of modernization. However, their experiences have parallels in many parts of the African continent since the 1980s. S.N. Eisenstadt's chapter of 1966 is symptomatic for the heyday of the modernization dream and all the questions it raised of unilineality and Euro- or rather Americano-centrism. In the third text, from the early colonial period, John Mensah Sarbah, an intellectual from Gold Coast, offers an imaginative vision of an alternative path of development leaving more scope for African autonomy.

JAMES G. FERGUSON
Global Disconnect
Abjection & the Aftermath of Modernism

Reference
Unpublished paper, 1999

Introduction

In a recently completed book, I explore how mineworkers in the town of Kitwe on the Zambian Copperbelt have dealt with a long period of economic adversity. The book deals with a range of ethnographic questions: changing forms of labor migration; new patterns of urban-to-rural mobility; the dynamics of household formation and dissolution; the relation of urban cultural forms to the micro-political-economic relations linking urban workers to their rural kin and allies. In all of these domains, I have been less interested in constructing a developmental sequence of social and cultural forms than in exploring their temporal coexistence; less interested in a succession of 'typical' forms over time than in an understanding of the whole spread (what Stephen Jay Gould [1996] calls the 'full house') of diverse modes of getting by that may exist at any one moment, and how that spread is affected by political-economic shifts over time.

In arguing for non-linear, variation-centered models of social transformation (aiming to reconstruct what Gould calls the 'bush' of actual variation rather than an ideal tree or ladder of succeeding 'typical forms'), I have been concerned to demonstrate the inadequacy of what I call the modernist metanarratives through which urban life in Africa has so often been understood. Here, my target is not only the explicit Eurocentrism that allowed the Rhodes-Livingstone Institute anthropologists to see the Copperbelt as the new Birmingham of an African Industrial Revolution, but equally the still-ubiquitous use of a set of linear, directional concepts to frame scholarly understandings of urban Africa – what I call the '-izations': urbanization, modernization, proletarianization, commoditization, etc.

The last twenty-five years or so in Zambia pose a formidable challenge to such habitual ways of understanding the meaning of urban Africa. With declining terms of trade, increasingly worked-out mines, and the crushing burden of a debt crisis, Zambia's copper-based, urban industrial economy has seen a sustained and profound contraction. This had brought with it not only impoverishment and hardship, but also a strange flood of new '-izations'. What the Rhodes-Livingstone anthropologists used to call 'the Industrial Revolution in Africa' seems to have been called off: Industrialization has been replaced by 'de-industrialization'. The long-documented flow of migrants to the Copperbelt cities, too, is now running backwards, with urban-to-rural migration now outpacing rural-to-urban – a phenomenon for which the term 'counter-urbanization' has been coined. The apparently inevitable process of proletarianization, meanwhile, is now replaced by mass layoffs and 'back to the land' exercises – the 'unmaking', rather than the making, of a working class. And now, with the privatization of the state-held mining company, it seems that even 'Zambianization' (the nationalist policy of replacing white management with qualified black Zambians) is being replaced by what is now being called 'de-Zambianization', the rehiring of white, expatriate management.

A new generation of Zambians, then, has come of age in a world where the modernist certainties their parents grew up with have been turned upside down – a world where life expectancies and incomes shrink instead of grow, where children become less educated than their parents instead of more, where migrants move from urban centers to remote villages instead of vice-versa. It is the modernization story through the looking glass, where modernity is the object of nostalgic reverie, and 'backwardness' the anticipated (or dreaded) future.

In reflecting on this extraordinary turn of events, this paper will move between two levels. The first level is the lived experience of actual Zambian workers, who have seen the modernist story-line transformed, in their own lifetimes, from a marvelous promise to a cruel hoax. The second level is a set of global transformations that allow us to see the Zambian case as part of a much more general phenomenon, which I argue is nothing less than the collapse of the global modernist project that once seemed to define the future of what we used to call 'the developing world'. I have in mind here not only the collapse of the developmentalist vision of the world that saw the 'new nations' of the Third World as Western nation-states in embryo, and spoke breathlessly of the 'coming of age' of 'emerging' African nations that would one day soon – through the miracle of political and economic development – somehow resemble England and France. That was one side of the story. But the other was a vision of historical progress through a process of hooking citizens up into a national – and ultimately universal – grid of modernity. This paper will discuss specifically the 'grid' of electrical service, and the idea of a universal participation in modernity via copper connectivity as a metaphor for this. But we might think as well here of health care, where the post-war modernist ideal of a universal grid (epitomized in such things as the campaigns for universal vaccination against polio or small pox) can be contrasted against today's tendency to fragmentation and privatization (which gives us not the polio vaccine, but AIDS combo therapy – managing the disease for those who can pay, while the poor are bluntly notified that it is economically more rational for them to die). Or schooling, where the universal grid of public education is today under siege all over the world. Or public space and the rule of law, where walled communities and fortified private spaces increasingly undermine the social and political promise of a univer-salistic 'public'. (I note that recent figures show that private police in 'the new South Africa' now outnumber public police by a factor of three to one.)

By reflecting on Zambia's recent experience of decline and – in modernist terms – 'failure', I do not mean to suggest that this experience forms a template for an inevitable African future (or even an inevitable Zambian future). On the contrary, my analysis of recent Zambian history leads to an emphasis on non-linear trajectories, and multiplicities of pathways – to say that Africa is going 'down' today is as false and misleading as it was to say that it was going 'up' in the 1960s. But there is no disputing that the social experience of 'decline' (notwithstanding the variety of causes and contexts) is today of quite wide relevance across many areas of the African continent (and, indeed, in many other regions – e.g. Russia, or Indonesia – where recent political-economic restructuring has had comparable effects). For that reason, an analysis of the political and theoretical significance of that social experience may perhaps be of some wider relevance.

As an ethnographic point of entry into the social experience of decline on the Copperbelt, consider the following brief anecdote. One afternoon in 1989, I was chatting with a young officer of the mineworkers' union, who was expressing his dismay at how difficult it had become to find neckties of decent quality. Soon, we were talking about the two main retail shopping districts in Kitwe, one located in what had once been in colonial days the 'European' town center, the other in the former 'location' reserved for 'Africans'. What struck me was that these two shopping districts were still called (as they had been in colonial days) 'First Class' and 'Second Class', respectively. Why, I wondered, did people continue this usage? Wasn't this an embarrassing holdover of colonial thinking, and of the idea of 'second-class' status for Africans? Well, my companion replied, nobody really thought of it that way – it was just what the areas were called. Then he thought for a moment, and continued. 'Anyway,' he blurted with a bitter, convulsive laugh, 'now it's all "second-class", isn't it?'

I take this very particular way of experiencing one's own social world as having become 'second class' as a point of departure for what follows.

Abjection and the New World Society

When Godfrey Wilson wrote his 'Essay on the Economics of Detribalization in Northern Rhodesia' in 1940, he considered that the Africans of Northern Rhodesia had just entered into an economically and culturally interconnected 'world society', a 'huge world-wide community' within which they would soon find a place for themselves as something more than peasants and unskilled workers (Wilson 1941:12–13). The 'civilized' clothing and manners to which so many urban Africans attached such importance, he argued, amounted to a claim to full membership in that worldwide community. Indeed, Wilson suggested, it was for this very reason that many white settlers resented and feared the well-dressed African who politely doffed his hat in the street, preferring to see Africans in suitably humble rags. Fine formal evening wear, ballroom dancing, European-style handshaking – these, Wilson argued, were not inauthentic cultural mimicry, but expressed 'the Africans' claim to be respected by the Europeans and by one another as civilized, if humble, men, *members of the new world society*' (Wilson 1942:19–20, emphasis added).[1]

That claim to a full membership in 'the new world society', of course, was refused in a racist colonial society. The color bar explicitly distinguished between 'First Class' whites, who held the privileges of such membership, and 'Second Class' natives, who did not. But nationalism promised to change all that, by overturning the colonial system, and banishing forever the insulting idea that Zambians should be 'Second Class' citizens in their own land. The early years of Zambian Independence seemed on the verge of delivering on that promise. The color bar was indeed dismantled as educated black Zambians rose to unprecedented positions of power and responsi-bility; a booming economy and strong labor unions meanwhile helped even ordinary workers to enjoy a new level of comfort and prosperity. Zambia, as an 'emerging new nation', appeared poised to enter the world of the 'First Class'. It would be like other modern nations – right down to its state-of-the-art national airline. Zambia was no exception. With a rising standard of living, bustling urban centers, and such symbols of modern status as suits made in London and a national airline, membership in the 'new world society' seemed finally to be at hand.

It was the faltering of the 'industrial revolution' that changed all that. For no sooner had the blitzkrieg of industrialization turned the world upside down for millions of Central Africans, than rapid industrial decline set in motion another, even more devastating blitz. The economic hardships this has entailed have been staggering. But

Fig. 1 The dream of progress. *Une vie non ratée*, 1995. (Acrylic on canvas, 130 x 195 cm, C.A.A.C. – The Pigozzi Collection, Geneva. Photo Claude Postel © Chéri Samba)

equally important, if harder to measure, has been the sense of a loss of membership in that 'world society' of which Wilson spoke. Zambia, in the good times, had been on the map – a country among others in the 'modern world'. It was, older mineworkers reminded me, a place regularly visited by internationally known musical acts conducting world tours. One man recalled an early 1960s concert by the American Country-Western star Jim Reeves, for instance, and asked me with great feeling why such American acts no longer came to Zambia. But it is not just Country-Western acts that have stopped coming to Zambia. In the 1970s, international airlines like British Caledonian, UTA, Lufthansa and Alitalia connected Lusaka via direct flights to Frankfurt, Rome, London and other European centers; British Caledonian even offered a flight to Manchester. Zambia's own national airline, Zambia Airways, also flew an impressive fleet of planes, proudly piloted by black Zambian pilots, to international destinations both expected (London, Frankfurt, New York) and surprising (Belgrade, Bombay, Larnaca). But as the economic situation deteriorated, the European carriers one by one dropped Zambia from their routes. Finally, in 1996, it was announced that Zambia Airways itself would be liquidated. Like the 'industrial revolution', it had all apparently been a big mistake. Efficiency required that it be shut down. Today, a thrice-weekly British Airways plane to London is the only flight leaving Zambia for a non-African destination.

For many Zambians, then, as these details suggest, recent history has been experienced not – as the modernization plot led one to expect – as a process of moving forward or joining up with the world, but as a process that has pushed them out of the place in the world that they once occupied. The only term I have found to capture this sense of humiliating expulsion is 'abjection', which I adapt from Kristeva (1982); see also Borneman (1996). Abjection refers to a process of being thrown aside, expelled or discarded. But its literal meaning also implies not just being thrown out, but being thrown *down* – thus expulsion, but also debasement and humiliation. This, sad to report, captures quite precisely the sense I found among the Copperbelt mineworkers – a sense that the promises of modernization had been betrayed, and that they were being thrown out of the circle of full humanity, thrown back into the ranks of the 'Second Class',

cast outward and downward into the world of rags and huts where the color bar had always told 'Africans' they belonged.

With much talk today of 'globalization', of new forms of worldwide interconnection, and of yet another 'emerging' 'new world society', it is useful to consider briefly where Zambia fits in all of this, and what the story I have told here of decline and abjection might have to say about the nature of this 'new world order'. The Zambian case has something special to say about this, I will suggest, not simply because it illustrates a gloomy process of decline and disconnection that has had no place in many of the rosier accounts of the new global economy. Beyond simply illustrating the down side of the global economy, what has happened in Zambia reveals something much more fundamental about the mechanisms of membership, exclusion and abjection upon which the contemporary system of spatialized global inequality today depends.

When the color bar cut across colonial Africa, it fell with a special force upon the 'Westernized Africans' – those well-spoken, well-dressed, educated urbanites who blurred the lines between a so-called 'civilized', First Class white world, and a supposedly 'primitive', Second Class black one. It was they – the 'not quite/not white' (Bhabha 1997) – whose uncanny presence destabilized and menaced the racial hierarchy of the colonial social order. And it was they who felt the sting not just of exclusion, but of abjection – of being pushed back across a boundary that they had been led to believe they might successfully cross. In a similar way, when the juncture between Africa and the industrialized world that had been presented as a global stairway (leading from the 'developing' world to the 'developed') revealed itself instead as a wall (separating the 'First World' from the 'Third'), it was the Copperbelt and places like it – proud examples of just how modern, urban and prosperous an 'emerging' Africa could be – that experienced this boundary-fixing process most acutely, as a kind of abjection. The experience of abjection here was not a matter of being merely *excluded* from a status to which one had never had a claim, but of being *expelled*, cast out-and-down from that status by the formation of a new (or newly impermeable) boundary. It is an experience that has left in its wake both a profound feeling of loss as well as the gnawing sense of a continuing affective attachment to that which lies on the other side of the boundary. When Copperbelt workers of an older generation spoke to me with such feeling of having once, long ago, owned a fine tuxedo, or attended a concert by the Ink Spots, or eaten T-bone steak at a restaurant, they were registering a connection to the 'First Class' that they had lost many years before, but still felt, like the phantom pains from a limb long ago amputated.

When the Copperbelt mineworkers expressed their sense of abjection from an imagined modern world 'out there', then, they were not simply lamenting a lack of connection, but articulating a specific experience of *disconnection*, just as they inevitably described their material poverty not simply as a lack, but as a loss. When we think about the fact that Zambia is today disconnected and excluded in so many ways from the mainstream of the global economy, it is useful to remember that disconnection, like connection, implies a relation and not the absence of a relation. Dependency theorists once usefully distinguished between a state of being undeveloped (an original condition) and a state of being underdeveloped (the historical result of an active process of 'underdevelopment'). In a parallel fashion, we might usefully distinguish between being unconnected (an original condition) and being disconnected (the historical result of an active process of disconnection). Just as being hung up on is not the same thing as never having had a phone, the economic and social dis-

Figs 2 & 3 Photostudios & the art of imagining oneself as modern.
 Patrick Studio, Likoni, Mombasa, 1998 (courtesy Heike Behrend)

Mutokaa-Studio, Likomi, Mombasa, 1996
(courtesy Heike Behrend)

connection that Zambians experience today is quite distinct from a simple lack of connection. Disconnection, like abjection, implies an active relation, and the state of having been disconnected requires to be understood as the product of specific *structures and processes of disconnection*. What the Zambian case shows about 'globalization', I will suggest, is just how important disconnection is to a 'new world order' that insistently presents itself as a phenomenon of pure connection.

As Neil Smith has recently argued, in spite of aggressive 'structural adjustment' and a rhetorical celebration of 'free-market capitalism', 'what is remarkable about the last two decades [in Africa] is its virtual systematic expulsion from capitalism' (1997: 180). Indeed, a recent 35-page feature in *The Economist* on 'The Global Economy', made almost no reference to Africa at all, making only a passing note of the 'threat' to rich countries that may be posed by 'the 500 million or so people, most of them in Africa, who risk being left out of the global boom'. With private ventures in the continent falling by 25 per cent in the 1980s, and even further in the 1990s, Africa 'has been treated

to a crash course in the most vicious aspects of free-market capitalism while being largely denied any of the benefits' (Smith 1997: 180,181). Effectively 'red-lined' in global financial markets, and increasingly cut off from governmental 'aid' flows as well, most of sub-Saharan Africa today functions as 'a veritable ghetto of global capital' (1997: 179) – a zone of economic abjection that also makes a convenient object lesson for Third World governments in other regions that might, without the specter of 'Africanization' hanging over them, be tempted to challenge capital's regime of 'economic correctness' (Smith 1997; Ferguson 1994).

The very possibility of 'redlining' on such a massive scale reveals that the much-vaunted 'flexibility' of the new forms of global economy involves not simply new forms of connection, but new forms of disconnection as well. With increasing international wage competition and pressure on state welfare provisions, as Smith (1997: 187) notes, 'the global economy is ever more efficient at writing off redundant spaces of accumulation: the flexibility of investment and market options is matched by a wholly new flexibility in disinvestment and abandonment.' It is precisely this 'flexibility' that makes global 'red-lining' possible, and that makes Zambia's recent de-industrialization just as integral a part of 'globalization' as the appearance of Mexican car factories or Shanghai sky scrapers.

To speak of expulsion and abandonment here is not to suggest that Zambia is today somehow outside of the world capitalist system (and thus needs to be brought back into it). The mining industry, though shrunken, continues to dominate the Zambian economy, and may even (if the current plan for full privatization brings the new capital for exploration and development that its boosters promise) expand again in years to come; capitalists continue to profit from Zambia's copper. Other forms of capitalist production of course remain important as well. But the more fundamental point here is that the abjected, 'red-lined' spaces of decline and disinvestment in the contemporary global economy are as much a part of the geography of capitalism as the booming zones of enterprise and prosperity – they reveal less the outside of the system than its underbelly. Expulsion and abandonment (in Smith's terms), disconnection and abjection (in my own), occur within capitalism, not outside of it. They refer to processes through which global capitalism constitutes its categories of social and geographical membership and privilege by constructing and maintaining a category of absolute non-membership: a holding tank for those turned away at the 'development' door; a residuum of the economically discarded, disallowed, and disconnected – to put it plainly, a global 'Second Class'.

In its 'Industrial Revolution' era, it was copper that connected Zambia to the world. The world needed Zambia's copper, and it was copper that put the new nation on the economic world map, while bringing in the export earnings that financed everything from high wages for urban workers to state prestige projects like Zambia Airlines. But copper not only connected Zambia economically, it also provided a vivid symbol of a specifically modern form of world connection. The rolls of copper electrical wire produced by Zambian refineries literally did connect the world, via telephone and power cables that were forming a rapidly ramifying net across the globe. From the Soviet rural electrification program, to the United States' model Tennessee Valley Authority project, to the new South Africa's township electricity programs, electrification has provided the twentieth century with perhaps its most vivid symbol of modernization and development. Fusing a powerful image of universal connection in a national grid with the classical Enlightenment motif of illumination of the darkness, electrification has been an irresistible piece of symbolism for the modernist state (expressed perhaps most vividly in Lenin's suggestion that the 'backward' Soviet peasantry be uplifted by melting enough church bells into copper wire to permit the placing of a light bulb in every village [Coopersmith 1992: 154–5]).[2] It was no different in Zambia, where the electrification of the townships was a compelling symbol of inclusion, a sign that Africans, too, were to be hooked up with the 'new world society'.

Today, the Copperbelt mine townships are still wired for electricity. But the service is intermittent, as equipment often breaks down, and the copper power cables are from time to time stolen for sale as scrap. What is more, few township residents can afford to pay the monthly charges for the use of electricity, so electric appliances go unused as women huddle around charcoal fires preparing the daily meals and the township's skies fill with gray smoke each morning.

Nowadays, global interconnection does not depend so much on copper. The development of fiber optics and satellite communications technology, for instance, means that there is today much less need for copper-wired telephone cables. This 'advance' in global connectivity is actually one of the causes of Zambia's drastic economic marginalization; the world 'out there' can increasingly connect itself without relying on Zambia's copper (Mikesell 1988:40).[3] Ironically, then, the communication revolution that is generally thought of as 'connecting the globe' is playing a small but significant part in disconnecting Zambia.

There is a fundamental point suggested in this small detail. That is that what we have come to call 'globalization' is not simply a process that links together the world, but also one which differentiates it. It creates new inequalities even as it brings into being new commonalities and lines of communication. And it creates new, 'up-to-date' ways not only of connecting places, but of by-passing and ignoring them.

Most Zambians, let us remember, have never made a telephone call in their lives. Indeed, two out of three human beings alive today can say the same, according to one estimate.[4] With new technologies, will telecommunications now become more equally distributed, or even truly universal? One wonders. According to one recent report, at least, cellular telephone technology promises not to 'hook up' the African masses, but rather to make obsolete the very idea that they need to be 'hooked up': many of the poorest parts of the world, the article claims, may now *never* be wired for phone service (*Economist* 1993). For cellular technology allows businesses and elites to ignore their limited and often malfunctioning national telephone systems, and do their business via state-of-the-art satellite connectivity, bypassing altogether the idea of a universal copper grid providing service to all.

Wilson's 'new world society', for all its faults, implied a promise of universality and even ultimate equality that is strikingly absent from the current visions of the 'new world order'. In the plot-line of 'modernization', some countries were 'behind', it is true, but they were all supposed, and Zambia was no exception, to have the means to 'catch up' in the end. 'Second Class' countries could and (the story promised) surely would eventually rise to the ranks of the 'First Class'. Today, this promise is still mouthed by the ideologists of 'development' here and there. But it is without much conviction. More characteristic is *The Economist*'s casual casting aside of that troublesome 500 million 'or so' who have inexplicably missed the bandwagon of global growth. In the neo-liberal 'new world order', apparently, Zambia (along with most of the rest of Africa) is to be an exception.

Many of the people I spoke with on the Copperbelt understood this very well – understood that 'Africa', in the new global dispensation, was becoming a category of abjection. I noticed that whenever people were trying to convey their problems – to describe their suffering, to appeal for help, to explain the humiliation of their circumstances – they described themselves not as 'Zambians' but as 'Africans'. On the one hand, the term evoked all the images associated with 'Africa' in contemporary international media discourse – pictures of poverty, starvation and war; refugees, chaos, and charity. On the other, of course, it evoked the old colonial usage of 'African' as a stigmatized race category. Putting the two connotations together suggested (tragically, if accurately) a reimposition of the old, despised 'Second Class' status, but within a new macro-political order. As one old man put it, at the end of a wrenching narration of his country's downward slide: 'We are just poor Africans, now.' (See also Ferguson 1997).

The end of development?

A number of recent critical analysts have heralded 'the end of the development era'.[5] For Wolfgang Sachs, editor of the influential critical work, *The Development Dictionary* (1992), the whole project of 'development' today 'stands like a ruin in the intellectual landscape', a disastrous failure now made 'obsolete', 'outdated by history' (1992: 1,2). It is not only that 'development' has failed to deliver the economic growth and sociocultural 'modernization' that it promised; more fundamentally, the whole ideal of 'development' can no longer carry any conviction. Economically, Sachs argues, the very idea of the whole planet consuming at First World levels presents an ecological disaster if not an impossibility, while socially and culturally, 'develop-ment' offers only a thinly veiled Westernization, a colonizing global monoculture that must choke out the 'traditional' world's wealth of diverse local modes of life. To the extent that Third World people have themselves sought 'development', in this view, they have been misguided; the schemas of development have provided only 'the cognitive base for [a] pathetic self-pity' (1992:2) which has been self-defeating, and which must continue no longer.

Esteva argues in similar fashion that 'development' has led Third World peoples 'to be enslaved to others' experience and dreams' (Esteva 1992: 7). When United States President Harry Truman labeled two billion people as 'underdeveloped' in 1949,

> they ceased being what they were, in all their diversity, and were transmogrified into an inverted mirror of others' reality: a mirror that belittles them and sends them off to the end of the queue, a mirror that defines their identity, which is really that of a heteroge-neous and diverse majority, simply in the terms of a homogenizing and narrow minority (Esteva 1992:7).

According to Esteva, the world would be well advised to do without such a concept (which is in any case 'doomed to extinction' [1992:7]), and proceed to emulate the 'marginals' at the fringes of the capitalist economy who are rejecting the 'needs' imposed by the economic world view of 'development' and reinventing a world without scarcity (much like Sahlins' 'original affluent society' of hunters and gatherers) (Esteva 1992: 19–22).[6]

There is reason to be doubtful of such sweeping claims for the 'end of development'. Most obviously, it is clear that ideas of 'develop-ment' (often remarkably unreconstructed ones at that) hold great sway in many parts of the world today, perhaps especially in areas (notably, many parts of East and Southeast Asia) that have enjoyed recent rapid economic expansion (though the recent 'crash' that has stricken many countries in the region may yet shake that developmentalist faith). More theoretically, one might well be suspicious of criticisms of inevitable linear teleologies and progressive successions of epochs that proceed by constructing their own inevitable linear teleologies and progressive successions of epochs, as so many contemporary 'post-' and 'end of …' narratives seem to do.[7] But it remains true that some-thing has happened in recent years to the taken-for-granted faith in 'development' as a universal prescription for poverty and inequality. For Africa, at least, as for some other parts of the world, there is a real break with the certainties and expectations that made a 'development era' possible. The 'rolling back' of the state, the abandonment of the goal of industrialization, the commitment to what are euphemistically called 'market forces' and 'private enterprise', and the shattering of expectations for economic convergence with the West, all come together to create a very real end, at least at the level of perceptions and expectations, of at least the grander versions of the 'development' project in Africa.

Is this something to be celebrated? Critics like Sachs and Esteva give to this question an unequivocally affirmative answer. Develop-ment, they point out, has distorted people's understandings of their own histories, imposed Eurocentric values and ideals, and crowded out innumerable local ways of doing things. The sooner it disappears, they suggest, the better. There is much to recommend this view. Certainly, there is no reason why the people of former colonial territories should accept economic and cultural convergence with the West (whether it is owning a car, wearing suits made in London, or having a 'modern family') as the ultimate measure of achievement or progress; the critics are quite right to attack the ethnocentrism of such an assumption, and to point out its historical contingency (see Escobar's excellent critique [1995]). Moreover, the ecological and human degradation created by what have been termed 'overdeveloped' societies are only too evident; it is not obvious that such societies constitute a model to be emulated. It is also possible to show, as I have attempted to do in my own previous work (Ferguson 1994), that the conceptual problematic of 'development' has served, in concrete instances and through specifiable mechanisms, as what I have termed an 'anti-politics machine', systematically misrecognizing and depoliticizing understandings of the lives and problems of people living in what has long since come to be known as 'the Third World'.

But critics like Sachs and Esteva sometimes seem to forget that the post-World War II conceptual apparatus of 'development' did not create global inequality at a stroke, but only provided a new means of organizing and legitimating an only too real inequality that was already very well-established. It was not Truman's speech in 1949 that sent Africa and other colonial territories to the 'back of the queue', as Esteva implies; conquest, colonial rule, and centuries of predatory violence and economic exploitation saw to it that they were already there. 'Development' was laid on top of already-existing geopolitical hierarchies; it neither created North-South inequality, nor undid it, but instead provided a set of conceptual and organizational devices for managing it, legitimating it, and sometimes contesting and negotiating its terms (see Cooper 1997; Cooper and Packard 1997; Bose 1997; Gupta 1997, 1998). The subordinate position ascribed to 'the Third World' in 'development' discourse was therefore not a figment of the imagination or a mere Eurocentric illusion, but reflected an intractable political-economic reality that could not, and cannot, be wished or re-labeled away. 'Third World' people who have sometimes viewed themselves as located 'at the end of the queue' are therefore not victims of a self-destructive mystification, and they hardly require to be scolded for 'pathetic self-pity'.

Nor is there any reason to link the forecast 'end' of development with any general liberation or new autonomy, as many critics have tended to do. For if development did not inaugurate the inequalities it organized, neither can its demise be expected to make them suddenly disappear. Just as the end of one mode of organizing and legitimating a global hierarchy (colonialism) did not end inequality, but reconfigured it, so does the (very partial) disintegration of another ('development') inaugurate not a new reign of freedom from scarcity and global hierarchy, but a new modality of global inequality.

It is here, too, that we might register the ethnographic fact that 'the end of development' for Copperbelt workers (and, I suspect, for many others on the continent) has been experienced not as a liberation, but as a betrayal. The 'world society' that Godfrey Wilson anticipated has been taken out of play, and Zambians have been bluntly told that they are, and for the foreseeable future will remain, just so many 'poor Africans'. That the development story was a myth, and in some respects a trap, does not make the abrupt withdrawal of its promises any easier to take, or any less of a tragedy for those whose hopes and legitimate expectations have been shattered. If nothing else, 'develop-ment' put the problem of global inequality on the table, and named it as a problem; with the development story now declared 'out of date', global inequality increasingly comes to appear not as a 'problem' at all, but simply as a naturalized fact.

In this context, simply celebrating the end of development is a response that is neither intellectually nor politically adequate. For without a continuing engagement with the problems of global inequality, there is a real danger that what Watts (1995) has termed 'anti-development' critiques may aid and abet the current global abjection of Africa. The key questions in the present moment are less about the failures of Africa's developmentalist era than about what follows it. And here the celebration of 'social movements' in a 'post-development era' has sometimes seemed to obscure the fact that the new political and economic institutions that govern the global political economy today are often even less democratic and more exploitative than those which preceded them. Not only international organizations such as the IMF, World Bank, and World Trade Organization, but also NGOs, social movements, and 'civil society', today participate in new, transnational forms of governmentality that need to be subjected to the same sort of critical scrutiny that has been applied to 'development' in the past (Ferguson 1994; Ferguson, 2006; cf. Watts 1995).

At a more conceptual level, if the modernist story of development has lost its credibility, the most pressing question would appear to be not whether this fact is to be lamented or celebrated, but rather how the intellectual field can be reconfigured in such a way as to restore global inequality to its status as 'problem' without reintroducing the teleologies and ethnocentrisms of the development metanarrative. What, in short, comes after 'development' – both as an intellectual and cosmological framework for interpretation and explanation, and as a progressive political program for responding to its disastrous economic and social failures?

In seeking an answer to this question, we might do well to think seriously about the non-linear loops and reversals that have characterized recent Zambian history. Much that was understood as backward and disappearing seems today to be most vital. Moore and Vaughan, for instance, have shown in their study of Zambia's Northern Province that the method of shifting cultivation known as *citemene*, long understood as the very essence of agricultural 'backwardness', is alive and well in the 1990s, with most farmers continuing to incorporate it into their agricultural strategies – not as a way of trying to recreate the past, but as a mode of coping with the overwhelming uncertainties of the present (Moore and Vaughan 1994: 234). Indeed, as a symbol of flexibility and diversification, they argue, the 'old' *citemene* method appears especially well suited to the demands of both the present and the probable future.

I have made similar points in *Expectations of Modernity* (1999). Urban/rural labor mobility, once seen as a sign of incomplete or stunted modernity and a failure to attain 'full proletarianization', today seems better adapted than ever to present and likely future conditions, while the supposed 'main line' of permanent urbanization today appears as the anachronism (Chapter Two). Likewise, in the domain of urban culture, it is a supposedly 'old-fashioned' localism that prevails among today's Copperbelt mineworkers (Chapters Three and Four), while what was imagined to be an 'up-to-date' cosmopolitanism is pressed to the wall (Chapter Six). And the 'modern' nuclear family that was supposed to represent the inevitable future of urban domesticity is, I have shown, a rare bird, too, surrounded as it is by a range of supposedly 'backward' and 'pathological' domestic strategies that appear better suited to contemporary conditions (Chapter Five).

In the same spirit, one might wish to reappraise the place of the long-denigrated 'hangers-on' on the Copperbelt: the unemployed, 'useless' *lambwaza*. These are the heirs to the old Lamba 'loafers'[8] – originally, people of the 'Lamba' ethnic group from the sparsely populated rural countryside surrounding the Copperbelt, ethnically stereotyped as lazy and idle (Siegel 1989). The Lamba habit of hanging about the compounds 'unproductively' in the early days apparently earned them disdainful descriptions like the following (cited in Rhodesia 1956: 7):

> a degraded people on a degraded soil, a race of 'hangers on,' inhabiting the midden of the mines, hawkers of minor produce, vice, and the virtue of their women.

But the *lambwaza* of today – hawkers and hangers-on from every ethnic group – would seem to be as 'up to date' in their adaptation to contemporary urban conditions as anyone. To say this is not to join in the tendency I have criticized elsewhere of unreservedly celebrating the 'coping' abilities of the urban poor and the vitality of the so-called 'informal sector'; such a move can too easily end up whitewashing or romanticizing poverty and unemployment. But neither are we justified in assuming that this often stigmatized group constitutes a failed, marginal class peripheral to the 'main line' of a stable working class. For the urban people in this large and diverse category (who appear to have in common only their dependence upon one or another sort of social and economic improvisation) are not simply failures or victims; if anything, they seem to represent an especially viable and durable urban alternative in times like these (compare MacGaffey 1991; White 1990). Some, at least, seemed to be managing the hard times of the late 1980s more successfully than many who had 'real jobs'.[9]

In all of this, what emerges is a new respect for what Stephen Jay Gould (1996) would call the 'full house' of different urban strategies – that copiously-branching 'bush' of coexisting variation – and a corresponding revaluation of forms of life that a more linear, progressive narration might consign to the past (see the discussion of Gould's [1996] variation-centered alternative to teleological evolutionary narratives in Ferguson 1999: 42–3). For the 'dead ends' of the past keep coming back, just as the 'main lines' that are supposed to lead to the future continually seem to disappoint. It is this that gives the Copperbelt's recent history its 'recursive' quality (as Moore and Vaughan [1994] have remarked for Zambia's Northern Province), the sense of a continual reiteration of familiar themes, as old and supposedly bygone practices, patterns, and even policies sprout up again when least expected.[10]

A new way of conceptualizing urban life may be emerging in all of this, one which values multiplicity, variation, improvisation and opportunism, and distrusts fixed, unitary modes of practice and linear sequences of phases. For urban Zambians seem to have come, by their own paths, to an understanding at which scholars have recently arrived as well: the realization that global modernity is characterized not by a simple, Eurocentric uniformity but by coexisting and complex sociocultural alternatives (Appadurai 1996), and that the successful negotiation of it may hinge less on mastering a unitary set of 'modern' social and cultural forms than on managing to negotiate a dense 'bush' of contemporary variants in the art and struggle of living.

It may also be possible, it has occurred to me, to detect a fundamental mutation in the way that people are coming to talk about historical and economic change in the region. When I have heard Zambians in recent years talk about different parts of Africa, for instance, it seems to me that they no longer speak about this or that place as being ahead or behind, progressing well or too slowly. Instead, people are more likely to speak in terms of non-linear fluctuations of 'up' and 'down' (as in 'Mozambique is very bad right now, but I hear that Tanzania is coming back up' or 'Congo has been down so long, it is bound to come back up soon'), or in terms of particular niches and opportunities that might provide a bit of space here or there. Such usages evoke less the March of Progress than an up-to-date weather report – good times and bad times come and go, the trick is to keep abreast and make the best of it. 'Post-modernist' in a literal sense, this new style of understanding is driven by a pragmatic logic, the need to come to terms with a social world that can no longer be grasped in terms of the old scripts.

Scholars might learn from this example. One might well resist the idea that economic processes are really just like the weather: completely unresponsive to human purposes and beyond the control of human agency. To put matters thus would be to naturalize economic phenomena and to obscure the fact that they are always the products of human activity, always linked to political practices, and always subject to change (Ferguson 1994).[11] But the attempts of ordinary people to map the changes they have been living through in non-linear, non-teleological ways, and to take seriously the full range of multiplicity and variation in social life, might yet have much to teach us. In political terms, certainly, there would seem to be a compelling need to find new ways of approaching 'progressive' politics in an era when the term itself requires to be put in quotation marks. The linear teleologies on which virtually all conventional liberal and leftist political programs have rested simply will not take us very far in dealing with the sorts of challenges raised by the contemporary politics of global inequality, on the Copperbelt or elsewhere.

But to say that received ideas of 'progress' require to be critically interrogated is not to render the pursuit of equality or social improvement antique or laughable. Beyond the celebrations of the 'post-modern' or 'the end of development' lie profoundly challenging issues: How can democratic and egalitarian political movements address the transnational social and economic processes that by-pass the control of nation-states as they connect and enrich some regions and social classes, even while they disconnect, impoverish and abject others (Gupta 1998; Escobar and Alvarez 1992; Ferguson 2006). How can the responsibility of first-world citizens, organizations, and governments to impoverished and disaster-stricken regions and people be reformulated in a way that avoids the well-known limitations of developmental and humanitarian modalities of power (Malkki 1995b)? How can we acknowledge the historical and ethical obligations of connectedness, responsibility and, indeed, guilt that link Western wealth and security with African poverty and insecurity in an era when the modernist grid of universal copper connectivity has begun to disintegrate?

These formidable conceptual and political problems must be faced at the end of the modern era, as much by those who lament its passing as by those who celebrate it. As the people of the Copperbelt know only too well, the upending of the project of modernity is not a playful intellectual choice, but a shattering, compulsory socio-economic event. While the intellectual consequences are profound for all, such an event affects Copperbelt workers far more directly than it does First World scholars;[12] and viewed from the vantage point of the Copperbelt, it is about as playful as a train wreck. That the view from the Copperbelt is so different from that available from the academy gives it no automatic privilege; certainly no magic solutions to the daunting questions and problems listed here emerge from the experience of the men and women who saw 'the Industrial Revolution' come and go within the span of a single life-time. But at a time when First World academics are wont to speak perhaps a little too confidently of globalization or post-modernity, and a little too happily about 'the demise of metanarratives' or 'the end of development', there may be something to be gained from contemplating a place where the globalization of the economy has been experienced as disconnection and abjection, and where the much-celebrated end of the universalizing project of modernity has meant an end to the prospect of African equality, and the re-establishment of a global color bar blocking access from the 'First Class' world.

A return to modernist teleology, a new grand narrative that would trace the hopeful signs of an Africa once more 'emerging' out of the gloomy ashes of Africa's 'development' disaster, is neither plausible nor desirable. The modernization narrative was always a myth, an illusion, often even a lie. We should all learn to do without it. But if the academic rejection of modernization and development is not simply to reproduce at another level the global disconnects of capital, migration, and information flows, we must replace it with other ways of conceiving the relations of historical connectedness and ethical and political responsibility that link Africa and the rest of the world. If the people who have, in good faith, lived out the agonizing, failed plot-line of development and modernization are not to be simply disconnected and abjected from the new world order, it will be necessary to find new ways of thinking about both progress and responsibility in the aftermath of modernism.

Notes

[1] Hannerz (1996) has made a similar suggestion regarding the pursuit of 'international' popular culture by black artists and intellectuals in the Sophiatown district of Johannesburg in the 1950s.

[2] After a 1920 meeting, H. G. Wells reported that 'Lenin, who like a good orthodox Marxist denounces all 'Utopias', has succumbed at last to a Utopia, the Utopia of the electricians' (Coopersmith 1992: 154).

[3] I do not suggest that the changing requirements of communication technology are the major factor here; they are clearly but one among a number of factors leading to the decline of the copper industry in Zambia. I mention the association only as a way of pointing out some of the ironies associated with the apparently 'universal' process of globalization.

[4] The figure (obviously to be taken with a grain of salt, given the absence of direct evidence) appeared in *Harpers* (1997).

[5] In addition to the authors discussed here, see Escobar's important study (1995), which also heralds a 'post-development era', as well as the recent *Post-Development Reader* (Rahnema 1997); see also Marglin and Marglin (1990); and Nandy (1988).

[6] For the 'original affluent society' essay, see Sahlins (1972). For a telling critique, see Wilmsen (1989).

[7] Through such ironic reinscriptions of modernist teleology, the contemporary necessity of having to come to terms with the breakdown of modernism (i.e., post-*modernism* [an aftermath of modernism]) is routinely transmuted into a new evolutionary epoch ('postmodernity', the next rung on the ladder) with its own 'up-to-date' world view ('*Postmodern*-ism', a suitable 'latest thing' for the final chapter of the social theory textbook), and, indeed, its own triumphalist meta-narrative of emergence.

[8] Debra Spitulnik has suggested (personal communication) that the word, *lambwaza* probably derives from the stem, 'Lamba', in combination with the French 'ois', which is both a normal French word ending (as in chinois, bourgeois, etc.) as well as a French morpheme connoting idleness and laziness (as in *oiseux* [idle, pointless, useless] and *oisif* [idle, unemployed]). If this is correct, *lambwaza* would have an original meaning linked both to a specific ethnic group (the Lamba) and to a trait stereotypically associated with that group ('laziness'). It should be noted, however, that in my fieldwork, the term *lambwaza* was not taken to have any special relation to the Lambas, but referred generically to unemployed youth 'hanging around' the city.

[9] I cannot say more about this interesting group, as I did not study them in any systematic way (perhaps because I, too, carried in my head assumptions

about main lines and incidental peripheries).

10 Compare the deliberately 'recursive' exposition, particularly in dealing with the legacies of the Rhodes-Livingstone Institute, in Ferguson (1999).

11 Such a naturalization of the logic of a 'complex system' occurs in the uses of 'complexity theory' by economists, as shown in Maurer's critical review (1995).

12 I speak of 'First World' scholars here, because Zambian scholars, unfortunately, have experienced the economic crisis I have described here only too directly. One of the most vivid illustrations (at least for an academic) of the abjection and disconnection that I have tried to describe can be seen by visiting the University of Zambia library. Once a fine university library that could adequately support serious research in a range of fields, it resembled (at least when I last saw it) a kind of sad museum, with virtually no recent books or current periodical subscriptions at all. Salaries for university lecturers in Zambia, meanwhile, had by 1989 dropped so low that only by taking second and third jobs, and/or resorting to subsistence farming, were lecturers able to sustain themselves.

References

Appadurai, Arjun. 1996. *Modernity at Large: Cultural Dimensions of Globalization*. Minneapolis: University of Minnesota Press.

Bhabha, Homi K. 1997. 'Of Mimicry and Man: The Ambivalence of Colonial Discourse', in Fred Cooper and Laura Ann Stoler (eds) *Tensions of Empire: Colonial Centuries in a Bourgeois World*. Berkeley: University of California Press.

Borneman, John. 1996. 'Until Death Do Us Part: Marriage/Death in Anthropological Discourse'. *American Ethnologist* 23(2): 215–35.

Bose, Sugata. 1997. 'Instruments and Idioms of Colonial and National Development: India's Historical Experience in Comparative Perspective', in Frederick Cooper and Randall Packard (eds) *International Development and the Social Sciences: Essays on the History and Politics of Knowledge*. Berkeley: University of California Press.

Cooper, Frederick, ed. 1997. 'Modernizing Bureaucrats, Backward Africans, and the Development Concept', in Frederick Cooper and Randall Packard (eds) *International Development and the Social Sciences: Essays on the History and Politics of Knowledge*. Berkeley: University of California Press.

Cooper, Frederick and Randall Packard. 1997. 'Introduction', in Frederick Cooper and Randall Packard (eds) *International Development and the Social Sciences: Essays on the History and Politics of Knowledge*. Berkeley: University of California Press.

Coopersmith, Jonathan. 1992. *The Electrification of Russia, 1880–1926*. Ithaca: Cornell University Press.

Economist, The. 1993. 'Telecommunications Survey'. *The Economist* 329 (7834): 68ff (supplement).

Escobar, Arturo. 1995. *Encountering Development: The Making and Unmaking of the Third World*. Princeton, NJ: Princeton University Press.

Escobar, Arturo, and Sonia Alvarez, eds. 1992. *The Making of Social Movements in Latin America: Identity, Strategy, and Democracy*. Boulder: Westview Press.

Esteva, Gustavo. 1992. 'Development', in W. Sachs (ed.) *The Development Dictionary: A Guide to Knowledge as Power*. London: Zed Books.

Ferguson, James. 1994. *The Anti-politics Machine: "Development", Depoliticization, and Bureaucratic Power in Lesotho*. Minneapolis: University of Minnesota Press.

—— 1997. 'The Country and the City on the Copperbelt', in Akhil Gupta and James Ferguson (eds) *Culture, Power, Place: Explorations in Critical Anthropology*. Durham, NC: Duke University Press.

—— 1999. *Expectations of Modernity: Myths and Meanings of Urban Life on the Zambian Copperbelt*. Berkeley, CA: University of California Press.

—— 2006. *Global Shadows: Africa in the Neoliberal World Order*. Durham, NC: Duke University Press.

Gould, Stephen Jay. 1996. *Full House: The Spread of Excellence from Plato to Darwin*. New York: Harmony Books.

Gupta, Akhil. 1997. 'Agrarian Populism in the Development of a Modern Nation (India)', in *International Development and the Social Sciences: Essays on the History and Politics of Knowledge*. Frederick Cooper and Randall Packard, eds. Berkeley: University of California Press.

—— 1998. *Postcolonial Developments: Agriculture in the Making of Modern India*. Durham, NC: Duke University Press.

Hannerz, Ulf. 1996. *Transnational Connections: Culture, People, Places*. New York: Routledge.

Harper's. 1997. *Harper's* Index. Harper's 294 (1764): 15.

Kristeva, Julia. 1982. *Power of Horror: An Essay on Abjection*. New York: Columbia University Press.

MacGaffey, Janet. 1991. *The Real Economy of Zaire: The Contribution of Smuggling and Other Unofficial Activities to National Wealth*. Philadelphia/London: University of Pennsylvania Press/James Currey.

Malkki, Liisa H. 1995b. 'Speechless Emissaries: Refugees, Humanitarianism, and Dehistoricization'. *Cultural Anthropology* 11(3): 377–404.

Marglin, Frederique Apffel and Stephen Marglin, eds. 1990. *Dominating Knowledge: Development, Culture and Resistance*. New York: Oxford University Press.

Maurer, Bill. 1995. 'Complex Subjects: Offshore Finance, Complexity Theory, and the Dispersion of the Modern'. *Socialist Review* 25 (3&4): 113–45.

Mikesell, Raymond F. 1988. *The Global Copper Industry: Problems and Prospects*. London: Croom Helm.

Moore, Henrietta L., and Megan Vaughan. 1994. *Cutting Down Trees: Gender, Nutrition, and Agricultural Change in the Northern Province of Zambia, 1890-1990*. Portsmouth, NH/London: Heinemann/James Currey.

Nandy, Ashis, ed. 1988. *Science, Hegemony and Violence: A Requiem to Modernity*. Tokyo: The United Nations University.

Rahnema, Majid, with Victoria Bawtree, eds. 1997. *The Post-Development Reader*. London: Zed Books.

Rhodesia, Government of Northern. 1956. *Report of a Soil and Land-use Survey: Copperbelt, Northern Rhodesia*. Lusaka: Department of Agriculture.

Sachs,Wolfgang, ed. 1992. *The Development Dictionary: A Guide to Knowledge as Power*. London: Zed Books.

Sahlins, Marshall. 1972. *Stone Age Economics*. Chicago: Aldine Publishing Co.

Siegel, Brian V. 1989. 'The "Wild" and "Lazy" Lamba: Ethnic Stereotypes on the Central African Copperbelt', in Leroy Vail (ed.), *The Creation of Tribalism*. Berkeley: University of California Press.

Smith, Neil, 1997. 'The Satanic Geographies of Globalization: Uneven Development in the 1990s'. *Public Culture* 10 (1): 169–89.

Watts, Michael. 1995. '"A New Deal in Emotions": Theory and Practice and the Crisis of Development', in Jonathan Crush (ed.) *Power of Development*. New York: Routledge.

White, Luise. 1990. *The Comforts of Home: Prostitution in Colonial Nairobi*. Chicago: University of Chicago Press.

Wilmsen, Edwin N. 1989. *Land Filled with Flies: A Political Economy of the Kalahari*. Chicago: University of Chicago Press.

Wilson, Godfrey. 1941. *An Essay on the Economics of Detribalization in Northern Rhodesia (Part I)*. Rhodes Livingstone Paper, No. 5. Livingstone, Northern Rhodesia: Rhodes-Livingstone Institute.

—— 1942. *An Essay on the Economics of Detribalization in Northern Rhodesia (Part II)*. Rhodes-Livingstone Paper, No. 6. Livingstone, Northern Rhodesia: Rhodes-Livingstone Institute.

S.N. EISENSTADT
Excerpts from *Modernization*
Protest & Change

Reference
Modernization: Protest & Change
Englewood Cliffs, NJ: Prentice-Hall, 1966

The basic characteristics of modernization

Modernization and aspirations to modernity are probably the most overwhelming and the most permeating features of the contemporary scene. Most nations are nowadays caught in its web – becoming modernized or continuing their own traditions of modernity. As it spreads throughout the world, its common features as well as the differences between its characteristics in various countries stand out – and it is the purpose of this book to explore and analyze these common features and differences alike. Historically, modernization is the process of change towards those types of social, economic, and political systems that have developed in western Europe and North America from the seventeenth century to the nineteenth and have then spread to other European countries and in the nineteenth and twentieth centuries to the South American, Asian, and African continents.

Modern or modernizing societies have developed from a great variety of different traditional, premodern societies. In western Europe they developed from feudal or absolutist states with strong urban centers, in Eastern Europe from more autocratic states and less urbanized societies. In the United States and the first Dominions (Canada, Australia, etc.) they have developed through processes of colonization and immigration, some of which were rooted in strong religious motivations and organized in groups of religious settlers, while others were based mostly on large-scale immigration oriented mostly to economic opportunity and greater equality of status.

In Latin America more fragmentarily modern structures developed from oligarchic conquest-colonial societies, in which there existed strong division between the white conquering oligarchy and the indigenous subject population. In Japan the modernization process developed from a centralized feudal state of somewhat unique characteristics and in China from the breakdown of the most continuous Imperial system in the history of mankind, a system based on special types of 'literati-bureaucratic' institutions.

In most Asian and African societies the process of modernization has begun from within colonial frameworks, some (especially in Asia) based on preceding more centralized monarchical societies and elaborate literary-religious traditions, others (especially in Africa) mostly on tribal structures and traditions,

As we shall see, the different starting points of the processes of modernization of these societies have greatly influenced the specific contours of their development and the problems encountered in the course of it. And yet beyond these variations there also developed many common characteristics which constitute perhaps the major core of 'modernization' of a modern society, and it would be worth while to analyze these characteristics.

Social mobilization and social differentiation

The common characteristics of modernization refer both to what may be called socio-demographic aspects of societies and to structural aspects of social organization.

Karl Deutsch has coined the term 'social mobilization' to denote most of the socio-demographic aspects of modernization.[1] He has defined social mobilization as 'the process in which major clusters of old social, economic and psychological commitments are eroded and broken and people become available for new patterns of socialization and behavior,' and has indicated that some of its main indices are exposure to aspects of modern life through demonstrations of machinery, buildings, consumers' goods, etc.; response to mass media; change of residence; urbanization; change from agricultural occupations; literacy; growth of per capita income, etc. (These in themselves do not indicate, of course, whether the resources made available in this way will indeed be mobilized.)

Modern societies are also highly differentiated and specialized with respect to individual activities and institutional structures. Recruitment to these is not determined in characteristically modern societies in any fixed, ascriptive kinship, territorial caste, or estate framework. The specialized roles are 'free-floating' (i.e., admission to them is not determined by ascribed properties of the individual); similarly wealth and power are not ascriptively allocated – at least not as much as in non-modern societies. This is associated with institutions like markets in economic life, voting and party activities in politics, and instrumentally recruited bureaucratic organizations and mechanisms in most institutional spheres.[2]

Perhaps the most important aspect of this differentiation and specialization of roles in all the major institutional spheres is the *separation* between the different roles held by an individual – especially among the occupational and political roles, and between them and the family and kinship roles. This separation has taken place first, and perhaps most dramatically, between family and economic occupational roles during the industrial revolution, as has been so fully described by Marx in his studies of the Industrial Revolution and the emergence of the industrial system, by Tönnies in his classical studies of 'Community and Society,' and by Simmel in his studies of urban life.[3]

Such separation of roles meant, first, that the occupation of any given role within one institutional sphere – e.g., the occupational sphere – does not automatically entail the incumbency of a particular role in the political and cultural spheres. Second, within each institutional sphere (in the economy, polity, in the sphere of social organization, etc.) there developed distinctive units that were organized around the goals specific to each such sphere and that were not fused, as in more traditional societies, with other groups in a network based on family, kinship, and territorial bases.

In the economic sphere proper these developments have been characterized by the development of a very high level of technology (based on and combined with Newtonian science), fostered by the systematic application of knowledge, the pursuit of which became the province of specialized scientific institutions, and by the secondary (industrial, commercial) and tertiary (service) occupations, as against the primary extractive ones. In other words, by the development of industrial systems based on a high level of technology, on growing specialization of economic roles and of units of economic activity – production, consumption, and marketing – and on the growth of the scope and complexity of the major markets, the markets for goods, labor, and money.[4]

In the political sphere modernization has been characterized, first, by growing extension of the territorial scope and especially by the intensification of the power of the central, legal, administrative, and political agencies of the society. Second, it has been characterized by the continual spread of potential power to wider groups in the society ultimately to all adult citizens, and their incorporation into a consensual moral order.

Third, modern societies are in some sense democratic or at least populistic societies. They are characterized by the decline of traditional legitimation of the rulers with reference to powers outside their own society (God, reason) and by the establishment of some sort of ideological accountability, usually also institutional, of the rulers to the ruled, who are alleged to be the holders of the potential political power.

All these characteristics are, of course, connected with the greater fluidity of political support, with the large degree of 'interest-oriented,' nonideological political allegiance and with considerable weakening, sometimes almost total disappearance, of ascriptive political commitment to any given ruler or group. Thus the rulers, in order to maintain themselves effectively in power and receive support for the specific goals they propagate and the policies they want to implement, believe they must seek continually the political support of the ruled, or at least of large or vocal parts thereof, through elections, plebiscites, and acclamatory surrogates.[5]

Unlike the rulers of traditional autocratic regimes, the rulers of the totalitarian regimes accept the relevance of their subjects as the objects and beneficiaries, legitimators of policy. The difference between modern democratic or semidemocratic and totalitarian political systems lies not necessarily in the genuineness of these beliefs, but in the extent to which they are given institutional expression in pluralistic political organizations, in public liberties, and in welfare and cultural policies.[6]

In the cultural sphere, a modern society is characterized by a growing differentiation of the major elements of the major cultural and value systems, i.e., religion, philosophy, and science; the spread of literacy and secular education; a more complex intellectual institutional system for the cultivation and advancement of specialized roles based on intellectual disciplines.[7]

These developments have been very closely related to the expansion of media of communication, the growing permeation of such central media of communication into the major groups of the society, and the wider participation of these groups in the cultural activities and organizations created by the centrally placed cultural elites.[8]

The culmination of these developments has been the development of a new cultural outlook – perhaps the most pervasive aspect of modernization – even though its spread and permeation has been, in these societies, intermittent and very uneven. This outlook has been characterized by an emphasis on progress and improvement, on happiness and the spontaneous expression of abilities and feeling, on individuality as a moral value, and concomitant stress on the dignity of the individual and, last, on efficiency.[9] This has been manifest in the development of some new personality orientations, traits, and characteristics – greater ability to adjust to the broadening societal horizons; some egoflexibility; widening spheres of interest; growing potential empathy with other people and situations; a growing evaluation of self-advancement and mobility; and a growing emphasis on the present as the meaningful temporal dimension of human existence.[10]

Continuous structural differentiation and changes

In the societies that have made the journey, the movement to modernity has passed through a certain sequence of stages. Thus, to take the political field at different stages of the development of modern political systems, different problems became politically important and different types of political organization tended to develop. At certain stages of modernization, the problem of suffrage, of the definition of the new political community, of attainment of its independence, assumed central importance. In other societies or at other stages, problems of religious toleration or of so-called secularization of culture were most prominent. In still other stages of modernization the economic and social problems were most pertinent. The development of each of these problems was necessarily connected with the entrance of different new groups and strata into the political arena.

Similarly, new types of political organization have been developing. From small and parliamentary cliques, from varied, relatively restricted but fully articulated interest groups on the one hand, and from different types of social movements on the other, there developed more fully organized political parties, the mass parties. Later, especially in Europe and the United States from the late 1920s on, the relative importance of such parties and of the legislatures in which they were prominent became to some extent smaller, giving rise to more extensive and fully organized interest groups, on the one hand, and to the growing importance of the executive and administrative branches of the government, and especially to large-scale bureaucratic administration, on the other.[11]

In the economic sphere we witness the transition from relatively small-scale units of production, such as family firms, small factories, and commercial and banking enterprises operating for relatively restricted, local markets, to the more centralized, bureaucratized, and larger units of production such as the big corporations, trusts, cartels operating in more encompassing, large-scale new markets. Similarly, new techniques of production that greatly affected the structure of the economic process have been continually developing, giving rise to a growing and more complicated division of labor *within* each unit on the one hand and to growing complexity of the general market structure on the other.[12]

In the occupational system we witness, first, the continual development of new categories and groups. In the first stages of modernization the occupational structure might have been relatively uncomplicated and composed mostly of different manual occupations, unskilled and skilled, a small number of 'middle-class' occupations, such as trade and manufacture, and of some of the more traditional professions such as the ecclesiastical (religious), military, legal, and medical ones, including a much smaller proportion of population. Later, with continued economic development, each of these categories became divided into many subcategories. In addition, many new groups and categories – welfare service, scientific, technological, managerial – emerged and increased.[13]

The very development of new, more complex units of production, within each of which there increased the number of different categories of occupational manpower (i.e., technical, professional, administrative), has also given a push to the rise of new types of professional occupations and associations. These were no longer limited to the traditional professions – law, medicine, etc. – but spread out also to other occupational categories, such as scientific and technological research, nursing, social work, and business and managerial positions. In most of these one can discern a growing trend to professionalization, i.e., to the demand for higher educational qualifications as a prerequisite for engaging in them, on the one hand, and to some autonomous self-regulatory organization on the other. These developments tended to obliterate or weaken many of the older distinctions between different occupations.[14] They also give rise to continual new types of trade union organization and to different patterns of labor workers' relations. From the relatively simple union limited mostly to one factory, locality, or industrial branch, there developed the countrywide unions organized in different types of federations. These have spread into white and blue-collar occupations, creating within each new problems and demands. Hence the relations between the different units of production or consumption became enmeshed in a growing number of crosscutting allegiances and contacts between new organizations composed of different subgroups within each of these units.

In the demographic-ecological sphere we witness a continuous trend to the weakening of small, local rural and urban units in which any given population could take care of most of its needs within relatively narrow ecological confines.

The performance of such different functions – housing, work, schooling, entertainment, etc. – becomes more and more dispersed between different and far-apart ecological areas. At the same time there developed growing metropolitan areas within which new ecological sub-units tended to develop.[15]
[...]

Patterns developing in the first phase of modernization

Using the major variables in the analysis of modernization presented above – the various indices of modernization, its different historical starting points, the attitudes of modernizing elites, and the temporal sequence of processes of modernization – we proceed to the analysis of some of its major patterns, with the aim of understanding some of the reasons for their structural variety as well as, and especially, the conditions conducive to sustained growth as against conditions of regression and breakdowns.

It would, of course, be beyond the scope of this book to analyze even in a preliminary way all the major types or patterns of modernization and all the major elements that go into the construction of such types, but some general indications may not be out of place. These indications can be arranged according to the two major aspects of modernization – on the one hand the continuous structural differentiation, the impingement of broader groups on the center, and the problems arising out of these processes, and on the other the ability of the centers to deal with these problems, to develop adequate contractual and precontractual arrangements and symbols alike. It might be worth while to distinguish first between two phases of modernization according to the scope of mobilization, then to cross them with the nature of the existing or emerging centers.

The most important structural characteristics of the first, 'limited' phase, which developed in the late eighteenth and nineteenth centuries in Europe (especially western Europe, the United States, and to a smaller extent in Latin America and the Asian countries) are: the relatively small scale of the scope of various new organizations; the development of many relatively specific, goal-oriented organizations; the development of as yet restricted markets and for freefloating resources in the major institutional spheres; and the relative predominance of 'public' representation, communal, or professional–regulative and allocative arrangements.

At this phase the upper and middle classes have usually been predominant in the active process of modernization, which was gradually extended to the wider groups and strata, through the relatively slow and gradual tempo of urbanization and industrialization.

The most general problems arising at this phase of modernization have been the ways in which these broader groups and strata can be drawn into the central institutions of society, the ways in which their various problems crystallized into orientations of protest and political demands and then became 'translated' into various policies which extended the scope of the central institution of the society, and the extent to which at the center there did indeed develop cohesive

frameworks and new, flexible, collective identities.

These general problems can be subdivided into several areas. The first was the extension of political participation – both formal (i.e., franchise) and more general actual participation in the community in terms of access to various positions of power, on the one hand, and the ability to influence policy-making and decisions on the other.

Second were the various problems attendant on the growing transformation of the cultural-collective identity from a traditional ascriptive one to a more secular, differentiated civil and national one, and the consequent problems of the extent to which it was possible to incorporate the various traditions of different groups in the new symbolic center.

The third broad area of problems accrued from the first upsurge of industrialization and urbanization. It was here that the whole gamut of social problems, as well as more articulate social and political demands connected with them, developed.

The way in which these problems were dealt with varied greatly according to the orientation of the major modernization elites and the initial pushes to modernization – and were most evident in the structure, organization and symbols of the new center.

The center of the society which tended to develop at this stage of mobilization has usually, although not always, been characterized by the development of some strong, modern centralized political frameworks and sometimes also of relatively new differentiated central symbols, before the onset of industrialization and the rapid extension of political aspirations to wider groups and strata.

But such centers have differed greatly according to their strength and flexibility, according to the extent to which they tend to retain rigid traditional orientations, and according to their ability to deal with the various problems analyzed above. These differences have been, as we shall see in greater detail later, of great importance from the point of view of the whole process of modernization.

The characteristics and problems of the second phase of modernization differ in several important aspects from those of the first.

The most basic characteristics of this phase of modernization are the growing 'mass' aspect; i.e., the spread of participation in all the major spheres of society to broader groups and strata and a continuous direct and intensive impact of these broader groups on the various centers of society.

Structurally this phase of growing tempo of social mobilization was first characterized by the growth of large-scale and multi-purpose specialized – i.e., nonecological and nonkinship – groups and associations. Second, it is characterized by the continuous extension and interpenetration of the various internal markets in the institutional spheres of the society. Third, it is characterized by the continually growing and spreading urbanization and by the continual spread of mass media of communication.

At this stage there develop very important differences between societies – to no small degree identical with the distinctions between 'old-timers' and 'newcomers' to modernization. Structurally the major difference between these two types of societies was that between the *continuation* of relatively gradual, although often uneven, social mobilization, industrialization, and economic growth, and the consequent impingement of the broader strata into already existing and established frameworks, on the one hand; and the process of a relatively quick tempo of social mobilization and the direct intensive impingement of this process on the very establishment of the new centers, on the other.

In the latter case this process was often connected with a different pattern of the tempo of social mobilization and of the relative temporal development of the modernization in different institutional spheres. In most of the new states the process of differentiation and social mobilization was stronger in the political, ecological, and educational sphere than in the industrial or economic one. The phenomenon frequently found in many of these societies of over-urbanization unaccompanied by industrialization is a very important indication of this general trend.

Side by side with the older types of social problems and orientations of protest and political demands some new ones tend to arise, and their nature differs greatly between the relative 'old-timers' and 'newcomers' to modernization. In the older societies this second phase brought two interconnected problems. One was the possibility of the split-up of the center between different modernized groups and elites, the development of divisive symbols and orientations, and the consequent breakdown of relatively developed modernized frameworks. The other was the possibility of growing apathy of broader strata toward the center, and/or the withering away of the center under the pressure of various populist tendencies.

Among the relative newcomers there developed, in addition, the problem of their ability to establish effective central institutions and symbols under the impact of continually growing pressure of diverse groups that had not themselves undergone adequate processes of structural transformation and self-modernization. Moreover, among many of the new countries the problem of forging out a new national identity was very closely connected with problems of encounter between the impact of western European culture and the necessity to justify their national tradition in terms at least to some extent congruent with these new, modern Western orientations.

Here again the solutions to these problems and the consequent ability of the new centers to deal adequately with problems of sustained change varied greatly according to the internal cohesion and orientation of the major modernizing elites.

In the forthcoming chapters we shall start with the brief analysis of the early cases of modernization, especially in Europe and also in Japan, which were initially cases of relatively limited modernization, differentiating among them according to the flexibility and strength of their centers. We shall also deal briefly with some of the problems attendant on their transition to the second stage of modernization. We shall then proceed to analyze in somewhat greater length cases of the second phase of modernization, emphasizing especially, but not exclusively, the latecomers.

In each case we shall examine how the nature and orientations of the major modernizing elites and attitudes of the major strata and the structure of the center have influenced the process of modernization and its structural characteristics, and the extent of the ability of the emerging institutional structure to deal with the continually changing social problems and orientation of protest.

Notes

[1] K. W. Deutsch, 'Social Mobilization and Political Development', *American Political Science Review*, 55 (September 1961), 494–95.
[2] On these aspects of modernization, see T. Parsons, *Structure and Process in Modern Societies* (New York: Free Press of Glencoe, Inc., 1959), Chaps. 3, 4; D. Lerner, *The Passing of Traditional Society* (New York: Free Press of Glencoe, Inc., 1958); B. F. Hoselitz, 'Noneconomic Factors in Economic Development,' *American Economic Review*, 47 (May 2, 1957), 2871; and J. A. Kahl, 'Some Social Concomitants of Industrialization and Urbanization,' *Human Organization*, 18, 2 (Summer 1959).
[3] G. Simmel, 'The Metropolis and Mental Life', in P. Hatt and, A. Reiss, eds. *Cities and Society* (New York: Free Press of Glencoe, Inc., 1957); and F. Tönnies, *Community and Association*, trans. Charles P. Loomis (London: Routledge & Kegan Paul Ltd, 1955).
[4] W. Moore, 'The Social Framework of Economic Development', in R. Braibanti and J. Spengler (eds), *Tradition, Values and SocioEconomic Development* (Durham, NC: Duke University Press, 1961), pp. 57–82.
[5] S. N. Eisenstadt, 'Bureaucracy and Political Development', in J. La Polambara, ed., *Bureaucracy and Political Development* (Princeton, NJ: Princeton University Press, 1963), pp. 96–120.
[6] S. N. Eisenstadt, 'Political Modernization: Some Comparative Notes', *International Journal of Comparative Sociology*, 5, 1 (March 1964), 324.
[7] E. Shils, 'Political Development in New States', *Comparative Studies in History and Society* (Spring–Summer 1960), 265–92, 379–411; and K. Mannheim, *Man and Society in an Age of Reconstruction* (London: Routledge & Kegan Paul Ltd., 1940).
[8] Mannheim, *ibid.*; and L. Pye, ed., *Communication and Political Development* (Princeton, NJ: Princeton University Press, 1963).
[9] Lerner, *op. cit.*
[10] Shils, *op. cit.*; and A. Inkeles, 'Industrial Man: The Relation of Status to Experience, Perception and Value," *American Journal of Sociology*, 66, 1 (July 1960), 131.
[11] Shils, *op. cit.*; and Eisenstadt, *op. cit.*
[12] W. E. Moore, *The Impact of Industry* (Englewood Cliffs, NJ: Prentice Hall, Inc., 1965); and C. S. Belshaw, *Traditional Exchange and Modern Markets* (Englewood Cliffs, NJ: Prentice-Hall, Inc., 1965).
[13] Parsons, *op. cit.*
[14] Moore, *The Impact of Industry*.
[15] D. V. Class, *The Town in a Changing Civilization* (London: John Lane, 1935); Simmel, *op. cit.*; and L. Wirth, 'Urbanism as a Way of Life', in Hatt and Reiss, eds., *op. cit.*, pp. 46–63.

JOHN MENSAH SARBAH
Fanti National Constitution
Administrative Questions

Reference

Fanti National Constitution: A Short Treatise on the Constitution & Government of the Fanti, Asanti & Other Akan Tribes of West Africa
London: Frank Cass & Co. Ltd, 1968 [1906], pp. 225–56
(excerpts)

Administrative questions

There was a time when the declared policy of the British nation towards the West African protected territories was to encourage the inhabitants to train and qualify themselves, so as to make it possible for the administration of the settlements to be transferred to them. This policy was never heartily supported by British officials in West Africa. The new Imperialism of recent times, however, altered it, and declared these territories undeveloped estates, to be specially exploited with all expedition primarily, if not mainly, for the benefit and profit of Great Britain. While the policy was in vogue, much harm was done to British West Africa, for there were not a few Government officials, with more zeal than discretion and more assurance than knowledge, who thought it good policy to ridicule and try to break up the aboriginal institutions of the people, to undermine the authority of their natural rulers, and to subordinate everything possible to the paramount claims of what they called Imperial uniformity. In the minds of such persons, the doctrine of the individualism or distinct characteristics of each nation or race had no existence; to introduce English laws wholesale, abolish what is peculiar to Africans, and to treat them as subject races, saved them much trouble, patient study, and the effort of thinking. Thoughtful men realize that each of the colonies essentially British should develop her own individuality – political, social, financial, and intellectual. These men have had ample opportunities to acquire and study accurate information about those colonies where Britons and other Europeans have settled. But there are British possessions scattered the wide world over. The circumstances of each are different; they are inhabited by different races and peoples, whose national history and institutions radically differ from each other to such an extent, that it would seem as if the mind of his Majesty's Secretary of State for the Colonies must have as many facets as there are possessions, in order to direct or supervise the good government of each of them. The administration of British West Africa in general, and Gold Coast in particular, gives rise to certain questions, the satisfactory solution of which will not be made less easy by groping in the dark instead of acquiring some accurate knowledge, historical or otherwise, and endeavouring to appreciate, if not to view, things from the standpoint of the African whom Great Britain has undertaken to rule.

A few months ago, a governor of one of the British West African possessions, in the course of a speech in England about his administration, made certain remarks which one may consider to be an authoritative pronouncement of the policy of today. "It is far better for us,' said he, 'if we can rule the people through their chiefs, because they are ruled far more willingly in that way.' But he proceeded to add, 'We have a very hard task; we have to teach them in a few years the wisdom it has taken Europe centuries to acquire.' One discovers at once what many think is one of the weak spots in West African administration, the cause of numerous punitive expeditions, and the origin of such preventable incidents as the futile quest of the Asanti golden stool, with its sequel an inglorious campaign.

[…]

A short while ago, a Conservative Secretary of State for the Colonies said the British people were ignorant of many things, but there were few things they were so ignorant of as the Crown Colonies. This admission explains why tropical Crown colony administration is not up-to-date in these days of scientific knowledge and practice, and initiative in thought and action is more or less stifled or hindered by those rules officially called Colonial Office Regulations. The connection of the early British foreign plantations and colonies with Parliament was through a committee of the Privy Council, and, during the nineteenth century, the principal officer presiding over the destinies of these plantations was described as Secretary of State for War and the Colonies, which title was altered to the present one in 1854, when a department with a large clerical staff under a parliamentary and a permanent Under-Secretary was created. It will thus be seen that Maclean and the Gold Coast merchant government were under the Secretary of State for War.

The officer administering a Crown colony, whether called governor or administrator, is appointed by the Crown, and is under the authority of the Secretary of State for the Colonies, to whom he communicates all matters of importance. The governor alone is responsible for the colony's administration. His authority in the colony is practically autocratic. The position of the official members of the Legislative Council has been shown already. In the Executive Council, a member may freely express his opinion, and, if opposed to that of the governor, he may go so far as to record his reasons in writing, to be in due course forwarded to Downing Street. Human nature, however, does not encourage opposition; governors are but human. It is no wonder, then, to find the governor's opinion prevailing, the official members invariably supporting him, and uttering not a word of comment, or criticism, or suggestion of any kind, when the governor, introducing the annual estimates of revenue and expenditure, discusses subjects of general policy and questions of administration. One-man government has its advantages and defects, but in West Africa the defects have outweighed the advantages. Government appointments to Crown colonies by competitive examinations will serve to secure some promising officers, to whom better prospects should be held out, promotion being regulated not by favour but by merit. The necessity for improving the personnel of Government officers was recently impressed on the Government by more than one unofficial member at the sittings of the Gold Coast Legislative Council.

European residents, with some show of reason, complain that mere officialism is rampant in Gold Coast Colony; men in the Government services being too prone to look down on the white civilian engaged in commerce, from which the greatest part of the public revenue is derived. As for the African, he does not count in the estimation of these men, and, whether he remains as he is or no, is generally viewed with unconcern when he (the white official) is not otherwise engaged in his congenial task of securing Imperial uniformity. Thoughtful observers, moreover, think the most serious defect in Crown Colony rule of West Africa is the tendency to sow and disseminate amongst the inhabitants distrust and suspicion of each other, fostered by the employment or use of a large number of disreputable characters more than is required, perhaps, by the exigencies of the secret service, whose duty it is to give private information. Probably one of the principles of

Crown Colony rule is – *Divide et impera*, to be observed before an officer is expected to set about to gain the confidence of the governed and enlist their cooperation, which ought to be an easy matter if only the value of the popular Council were admitted and realized.

There is much, therefore, to commend and defend the policy to govern the African through his natural rulers under the direction of the British Government. In these days of scientific research, study, and experiments, the best means for carrying out this policy, will be evolved without doubt in due course. To climb steep hills requires slow pace at first. Direction in one form or another is a principle running through the operations of every human undertaking. Every one of us has been, and is still more or less, under direction of some sort. Up to a certain point it is good and necessary; nay, indispensable in the proper and successful conduct of human affairs. The State by sundry laws controls and directs the conduct of its citizens. Children are directed by their seniors. On the obedience or submission of the pupil to his teacher, while he instructs him and fills his mind with the knowledge of things, training him to think and act for himself, rests the whole success of education and the proper upbringing of the youth. He who cavils at a principle so universally at work has a great truth yet to learn. The chief difficulty in the proper appreciation of this important principle is, however, the extent to which it should be applied in the government of aboriginal nations, and what are called subject races. When the reasonable and legitimate demand of a people for some or greater control in the management of their affairs – political, municipal, or domestic – is met by the negative reply that they are not ripe, it is forgotten that only under favourable conditions do fruits and crops ripen quickly and to perfection; in other words, suitable environment is a controlling and essential factor. To smash up or gradually undermine aboriginal authority, to degrade or belittle African rulers, although professing to govern through them, can only end in the failure of European rule and the demoralization of Africans.

We repeat *direction* is a principle of universal application. When a child is taught to walk, it is guided by the hand, and such guidance is gradually relaxed, until at last its toddling footsteps are supported by just a little help; then it walks unaided, and finally it runs unrestrained. The parent is thoroughly acquainted with the child's condition, and is therefore in a position to encourage and direct its movements properly. The result is that at each stage of its growth the child gains confidence, and eventually realizes, or is conscious of, its individuality and capacity. The backward races are looked upon and treated as children, but they are not trained as children destined for some definite career in the future, and too often proper weight is not given to the fact that a sign of an intelligent and wise statesmanship is to train and develop a people to their utmost and highest state of usefulness. Limbs tied down or held under restraint for long become numb and useless; exercise and freedom of movement impart vigour and strength. Function creates structure; and the higher the structure the richer the flow of the life, healthy understanding, accurate judgment, and practical tact. The process is visible everywhere. True, the effort required to gain freedom is not without difficulties, and, in the impatience to teach in a few years the wisdom it has taken Europe centuries to acquire, there has been generally neglected the duty to understand the African – his life, habits, cast of mind, institutions, and history. Europe has not studied the African, nor understood him, but has preferred to carry him away to the slave-markets of America, or, latterly, to barter for or purchase at her own valuation such commodities as the African could offer. Europe is apt to forget that Africans are human beings, with human aspirations and instincts, and that they cannot for ever be treated like so many dumb-driven cattle.

The similarity of the constitution of town and village communities and of the principles regulating national public administration and government among the aboriginal tribes of Africa, is now admitted by students of jurisprudence and others who inquire into such matters. There are certain facts also which must be frankly admitted, and questions somewhat difficult resulting from them must be resolutely faced. The contact with Europeans and the advance of British ideas tend to change, if not to break up, some distinctive features of the African social system, which is communalistic. The discovery of new industries requiring skill and producing great rewards, gives scope for each individual member of the family to exercise his talents, skill, and ingenuity in the acquisition of wealth and private property. The result is that the authority of the head of the family is not as patriarchal as formerly, but gradually becomes weaker; and thus the basis of family government, on which African society rests, is undermined, causing no end of confusion, which, in the presence of an unsympathetic European direction, disconcerts and embarrasses the African, who, restrained from adjusting things, is filled with discouragement. It were undesirable, even if it were possible, to stay the operation of the natural laws of evolution. But were the Government sympathetic, it would not practically view with unconcern the widespread demoralization of the rising generation, which is mainly caused by the restraints against wrongdoing between the sexes becoming non-effective, through the absence of recognition and due enforcement of the customary laws relating thereto. It has been shown that these laws embody the convictions as well as the will of the community, whereby, for its protection, racial as well as individual, punishments for moral misconduct were adopted by common consent to regulate and govern the people in their relations with each other. An example or two will suffice: to say falsely of a single or married woman that she is incontinent is an actionable slander without proof of special damages. An unwedded girl who is unchaste is considered a dishonour to her parents and a disgrace to herself; and so particular are people about such behaviour, that in the country places, where the influence of European civilization is not much felt, any person offending in this respect is liable to be hooted around the village. Parents and guardians may bring an action in their aboriginal tribunals to restrain the unwelcome attentions of any person to their children or ward. British courts do not entertain such suits, and decline to support such a customary usage, which is pre-eminently suited to protect and safeguard the purity and sanctity of African family life.
[...]

The world moves on, the saying of Ansa the king still holds good: the sea and land are continually at variance and contending who shall give way; the sea with violence attempting to subdue the land, and the land with equal obstinacy resolving to oppose the sea. So far, tropical Africa – the land – has successfully opposed Europe – the sea. It seems that science and the scientific method alone can effect a successful and permanent reformation. The African must know himself, his country, and his destiny, and such knowledge within him will in due course permeate the possibilities outside until it fills his country with wonders. The horizon of his prospects will widen and become brighter from day to day as his mind is enriched.

To rule the people through their chiefs successfully demands knowledge, more or less intimate and accurate, of their country, and the principles of the constitution of their own government.
[...]

Travellers and writers of various attainments, and reports of Government commissions of inquiry in different parts of Africa, are now contributing largely to general knowledge some reliable information about the aboriginal races of East, West, South, and Central Africa. The absence of such knowledge has furnished many an excuse for errors committed during many past years. Had it been known that an African king or other ruler is not ordinarily a despot or other irresponsible person, but is, as a matter of fact. the first among his equals, and controlled by them in the Council which represents the whole people and expresses their will, possibly the deportation of African rulers would not have been a common occurrence. Were the gradation of authority, which is universal in African communities. properly recognized, and its uses fully appreciated and valued, civilization would, perhaps, make great strides, improvements of a permanent nature would doubtless be increased, and progress become better and more rapid. Some knowledge of the Council, whether of village, town, or district, of its nature, and the qualifications and duties of the councillors, is not only essential, but also of vital importance. Without a correct grasp of the principles of these things which pertain to the very foundation of the body politic, it will not be easy to give those whom Great Britain has taken under her rule and protection, all the facilities and such reasonable advantages in their spirit and effect which, as individuals or communities, as rulers or people, they would enjoy with proper and enlightened guidance under aboriginal conditions. The African, unfortunately for himself, is not always alive to his interest in safeguarding and protecting from neglect and discredit, when he comes under European jurisdiction, his greatest and priceless heritage – the *Council*. When men with suitable education and better training fully understand the invaluable nature of this popular assembly and its great possibilities, at present lying dormant or undeveloped, they will be as proud and jealous of its efficiency and good name, as the Briton is of the Houses of Parliament. It will be then impossible for any one but the best men in the community to have a predominant voice in the deliberations of the ruler and councillors; and the danger arising from certain characters capturing the Council, misguiding the other members to their undoing and to the serious detriment of the public welfare, will be minimized, even if unchecked. Properly looked after and gradually made to meet the needs of modern times, this will be found to be the means best suited and adapted for municipal or local self-government, thus becoming in due course the constituency upon whom the right shall be conferred to nominate as unofficial members of the Legislative Council men who by their good character, influence, capacity, acquirements, and the confidence they inspire in their fellow countrymen, are worthy of honour. When such a time arrives, the more important rulers should possess the right to elect two or three representatives of their order as members of the Legislative and Executive Councils. The promoter of the Fanti Confederation strove to put in practice the true patriot's highest ideal – giving the people good education, thorough industrial and agricultural training, with ample opportunities for self development and self-advancement. That ideal Japan has successfully kept in view to the admiration, if not the wonder, of Christendom. No Mary Kingsley, however, had arisen at that period to help Africans and explain such principles to England, and so they failed; but we are moving on. Even now, not a few discern dimly the possibilities that lie before their race. Past errors have generally been due, among other things, to the fact that the right path to the goal had not been discovered. Many short cuts in the pursuit of Anglo-Saxon ideas, more or less vague, have been tried, only to end in divers morasses. At one time, some reformers went so far as to advocate the suppression of the common language; they expressed the hope, that in the course of a few years, they would be able to bring thousands of the inhabitants into the habit of changing their own for European dresses. Although this hope was first expressed by Meredith in 1811, it

has not been realized, nor is likely to be for many a long day.
[...]

The masses take a keen interest in the actions of their European rulers, and do not the less feel the effects of misgovernment. Their legitimate complaints and grievances may not be as quickly expressed as those of their educated brethren, who are accordingly considered troublesome. It were well to give heed to these complaints and deal with them on their merits, but it were far better to remove all reasonable causes from which they spring. At any rate, it is absurd to ignore the fact, that on the educated African depends the successful administration of these tropical countries; nor should a greedy and selfish commercialism, which threatens to override every sense of justice and every principle of our common humanity, be permitted to inspire and create, what will defeat the high aims of the statesman.

The Government does not attempt by any means whatever to communicate to the people new legislation; information concerning acts of government finds its way as best it may to the public. Now and then a white officer goes on a tour of inspection, and is thus brought in touch with the principal men of his district; but inasmuch as he does not speak and understand the vernacular, and perforce depends on the services of an incompetent or indifferent interpreter, who is the medium of communication between these men and himself, he is unable to improve to the fullest extent these few opportunities.
[...]

Colonization in the true sense of the word has never been attempted in any part of British West Africa. Until the advent of railways, a few public works of general utility were erected; they are not conspicuous for their suitability, or any lasting benefits derived from them by the people. Here and there, one may find some attempts at improvements, but they are usually found in places where the European official is stationed; they are for his benefit and comfort, the people have no interest therein. Wherever you find a road in decent condition, it is sure to be in some Government station or its immediate neighbourhood. Contrast this state of things with what France insists on and what Japan has accomplished. The former inculcates the principles of hygiene, and gradually trains the natives of Madagascar and IndoChina to fill responsible posts in the civil service as well as in the social administration. In the French possessions may be seen, what one rarely, if ever, sees in any part of British West Africa, European subordinates serving under African officials, who are promoted by merit, recommended and guaranteed by long faithful service.

The Japanese method is similar to the French, and well repays study for its suggestiveness; it should stimulate and encourage the African, to disprove that theory of racial superiority, by reason of which he has been treated as a child, but with the onerous obligations of a man. Persons competent to judge; say, Japanese first attempt to govern a colony properly so called has been singularly successful, in spite of difficulties which at first seemed insuperable. Both Spanish and Dutch had given up in despair all attempts at colonizing Formosa. Neither France nor England cared to annex a savage and unruly country which the Chinese, its nominal owners, had absolutely neglected. On the conclusion of the Chino-Japanese war, 1894–5, Formosa was ceded to Japan. The lawless state of the country was remedied by military operations, and on the 31st March, 1896, a civil administration was established. The national customs of the inhabitants were not meddled with unless barbarous and inhuman. At the same time that she was introducing some of her own enlightened laws, Japan respected the prejudices of the people, and tried rather to guide than to drive and coerce them to civilization.
[...]

As a parent training his child, as a faithful guardian conscious of his obligation protecting his ward, so has Japan treated Formosa, Her officers were neither discouraged nor dismayed by difficulties; patiently and firmly they taught the Formosan to acknowledge the value of scientific methods and to follow the same. For administrators she had sent many of her ablest men, nor did she stint herself in spending and being spent. Her enlightened policy for that country is already justified by an encouraging economic progress shown in the general revenue, yielding nearly tenfold in 1905 more than what it did in 1896; but greater still, by the increased happiness of the aborigines, for, after all, the life and health, the intelligence and morals of a nation are its best assets, and count for more than mere riches.

The French in Madagascar have been training, for many years in the Government hospitals a large number of native medical assistants; so useful have they been found that this beneficial policy has been followed in their West African possessions, where the members of a recently formed class of such medical assistants have been largely increased; vaccination centres have been formed, and the grant for sanitation very considerably raised. A study of the Franco-Japanese system leaves the impression on one, that it seeks to raise up and make the aborigines efficient through their cooperation by scientific means.

On similar lines should Gold Coast be administered.

[…]

One has already thought proper to remind the educated inhabitant of Gold Coast of certain duties, and has gone so far as to tell him to review his mental equipment, and settle down to solve the hard task of adapting all the best features of his national institutions for use in the inspiring work of good government, for no person fully values or appreciates his rights, who neglects the calls of duty, and does not give heed to the pressing claims of a strenuous and useful life. Says the Bard of Avon, 'Our remedies oft in ourselves do lie, which we ascribe to heaven!' The educated African is at present like a pioneer in a forest primeval. Whatever visions he may have about the fair city that is to be, his present task is to cut down the trees, root up the stumps, clear the ground, and prepare the site for the city of the morrow. The yield of the harvest depends on the spadework now done, and on the deep ploughing of the furrows today. In the ranks of the educated Africans, one finds all grades of European learning and culture – the man who can only scrawl his name, and cannot without much labour struggle his way through the spelling primer; the petty clerk, who, having a fair knowledge of reading, writing, arithmetic, had received some Christian instruction of a superficial kind, thinking himself very high above the masses; he despises the dignity of labour, because he has not been taught a more excellent way; called by everybody a SCHOLAR, he has no ambition to acquire more learning. Next to the SCHOLAR are the intellectually ambitious men, who by assiduous application have mastered the English language, and attained proficiency in many subjects of commercial utility. By probity, integrity, and strict attention to business, and the exercise of those qualities which produce the most useful of men, most of them succeed in trade and gain wealth; many earn a fair competence; a few, however, fail; but every one of them is known and respected of all men. Persons of means from this class usually send their sons abroad, some to be trained in the British Universities, where a few graduate, and others to study the learned professions which they now practise with ability and generally with conspicuous success. When due weight is given to the fact, that the men so sent to Europe were not the most brilliant or promising of their schoolmates, that they were not picked students, but were sent because their parents or guardians had the means, the African himself should realize the great loss sustained by his race, whenever he neglects to support higher and improved education. These privileged persons themselves admit, there are many clever promising ones of sterling worth, who would do credit to themselves and nation, did they have similar advantages and opportunities. Ambitious to shine, they are by circumstances compelled to remain undiscovered in the depths of profound ignorance and surrounding superstition.

But the task before educated Africans is very much complicated by the failures and wastrels, who in some instances, starting life with the best advantages and with brilliant prospects, have become social and moral wrecks. The worst of them are lost to every sense of shame and infamy; they live by their wits; they are not ashamed to beg or steal; they look upon their untutored kith and kin as lawful prey to be flattered and threatened, bewildered and tricked, cheated and deserted, misguided and betrayed, as it suits their reprehensible purpose. The African's unfriends, never more candid than when referring to such men, declare the black man's education has proved a failure, to which statement one may correctly retort that it has never been properly tried. It is not one's intention to be engaged in mutual recrimination, a task as uncongenial as it is uninstructive; which serves no good purpose, only does much harm and causes more mischief. But were one so minded, instead of the hearsay yarns and other tittle-tattle and garbled stories which are related by some writers, one could from the records of the Law Courts show to what extent the simple African merchant has had his confidence in the honesty and rectitude of the European merchant abused to his undoing; and when such things are exposed in the course of a trial in Court, the excuse given is either in Gold Coast, 'they do not understand these things,' or, 'it is customary!' It is not wise to charge a class indiscriminately with wrongdoing. It is folly to indict a nation.

[…]

In speaking of the essentials of a successful administration, mention was made of a national character racy [sic] of the soil which can be properly moulded and guided only by suitable education. Now, education is a word very often misunderstood in West Africa. It means something better and higher than the mere passing of the low standards in elementary subjects set by West African Boards of Education. In its truest sense, it aims at the progressive and orderly development of all the faculties of the mind, to the intent that it may form good character and teach right conduct. In other words, it is a serious preparation for the business of life in the accomplishment of strenuous, useful, and congenial labour; for the work of really competent persons is generally distinguished and characterized by decisiveness and definiteness. What generally discloses the secret thoughts and opinions of men concerning public questions is their unconscious attitude. Public opinion of Gold Coast peoples has been dissatisfied with the rate of progress, and it is admitted on all hands that, as with the individual, so must it be with a nation, there are no short cuts to learning or fame. History teaches us, the ruler's influence and the work of the legislature are in no way equal to the combined effort of the individuals of the race, who, each in his place, or within his sphere of influence, shows strength, energy, initiative, and general uprightness.

Those who are not intimately acquainted with the African in his home are, by some irresponsible writers, made to believe that he lacks willpower; he is unable to take the initiative, his excitability and lack of reserve being two powerful integers in his mental makeup. To bolster up this nonsense, the black man's cranial capacity is compared with the Australian and Caucasian. These investigations are generally made in the United States of America, in the West Indies, and other places, where the African has been in bondage for ages, during which his natural powers, spirit of independence, and very manhood have been stunted, if not destroyed. So much have some lost self-confidence in their intellectual powers, so far have they lost all traces of pride of race, that, for every word or act, they unconsciously turn to the white man for his approbation, or to find out whether, in his opinion, they had spoken or acted correctly or properly. West Africans have not yet lost their manhood or manly qualities; and because they will not throw aside their self-respect, and cringe, bow, salaam, and grovel in the dust at the sight of a man merely because his skin is white, they are deemed to be incapable of any useful labour.

These few shortcomings have been mentioned candidly and without reservation. They must be corrected before real progress can be made. He who uses his opportunities to help raise the masses of his brethren to his own high level is following his destiny, and cannot be engaged in a nobler work. But when, from indifference or deliberate choice, an educated African becomes a tool of Europeans of the baser sort, and keeps back, directly or indirectly, the masses in ignorance and superstition, he becomes the greatest enemy of his downtrodden and long suffering race; and the greater his educational attainments and opportunities, the graver his fault and personal guilt. The legitimate demands of a united people, intelligent and educated, shrewd and self-respecting, is bound to carry weight within the confines of the British Empire. That being so, is it not the best and wisest policy for the educated children of the soil to take earnestly in hand the task of pioneers at once, and leave no stone unturned, until proper education is within the reach of every one in Gold Coast territories? The fact that a man cannot read or write a foreign language is not a proof positive, that he is not astute in business, or that he is ignorant, or possesses no natural intelligence or ability for any useful work. Placed as he is between the white man on the one side and his untutored brethren on the other side, the educated African has special difficulties to contend with; but at the same time, he is in a position to note and recognize such natural talent as should be brought to the knowledge of the well-disposed white man for encouragement, nurture, and proper training. Because the educated African has not in the past laid stress on the necessity for a general levelling-up of the masses, but shown a tendency at times to prefer the white man's food, dress, habits, tastes, and other ways, the latter has not hesitated to call him a self-seeker prepared to sacrifice his untutored brother for his own ends. As already stated, educated Africans have been, and still are, in a very small minority. Unwisely imitating and adopting the white man's style of living in every respect, they too often undergo a continuous struggle to support an Anglo-African position of spurious respectability, suffer no end of privations to keep up an appearance, which is as unsuitable in the tropics as it is unnecessarily expensive, leading to monetary embarrassments, which at times end in crime, with its concomitant disgrace and consequent sorrow. Now, when anyone of this class falls,he is pointed out as another example, proving the utter fatuity of negro education, which should therefore be suppressed; whilst latter-day apostles, in season and out of season, proclaim the African is best employed when forced to labour for the European, but deliberately ignore the other obligation, that the labourer is worthy of his hire.

[...]

Experience has shown over and over, that an African works as much as any one else of human kind, provided he is paid a fair price for his produce, he is not cheated of his wages. he is not knocked about and badly treated. Monthly engagements as practised by Europeans have proved demoralizing. Commonly called *Brofu edivuma*, i.e. white man's work, in practice it means regular pay, more days, more

dollars, leisurely activity. By hired labour under monthly engagements farming can hardly be profitable; contract work is more hopeful; piece work is the best thing.

To shun these pitfalls and snares, and to escape from such false position and the divers temptations connected therewith, is surely the highest wisdom. Righteousness exalteth a nation, but sin is a reproach to any people. Morals are of primary importance to the well-being of society. Humanity generally estimates a man's worth by his character, the value of institutions by the moral principles on which they are founded, and assigns to a nation its scale of importance in proportion to the purity of its morals. When we know the secret springs of a man's action, his knowledge of right and wrong, his principles, his motives, and his sense of duty, we can fairly tell his character.

The masses can be best taught by precept and example what their enlightened brother has proved by experience to be useful and beneficial for the race. They must not cease to possess and cultivate that self-respect which characterized their ancestors, and was such a trait in them as to win the admiration of high-placed European military officers, one of whom wrote to the War Office in London that 'they are a high-bred, aristocratic race.' Just as only the mere surface of Gold Coast territories has been scraped by alluvial washing, but the great deposits of precious gold and other minerals in quartz or banket formation have hardly been touched as yet, even so the mental capacity and capability of the African have not been probed, nor the vast store of his wisdom, natural powers, and other special gifts best fully disclosed to incredulous Europe.

It will thus be seen that what is of vital importance, and must be encouraged at all cost, is a system of national education, which shall build up a national character racy [sic] of the soil; character which makes men work for the sake of duty, which makes a man shun subterfuge and shirking, but keeps him truthful and self-respecting and jealous of his manhood, and, above all, a true servant of God.

[...]

On the 24th November, 1871, was published the Constitution of the Fanti Confederation to promote, *inter alia*, the public education of all children within the limits of the Confederation, to encourage agriculture, industrial pursuits, and development of the mineral resources of Gold Coast Protectorate. Provision was also made for the proper training and instruction of females. By a wonderful co-incidence, during the same month of November, 1871, the Emperor of Japan, addressing the nobles of his empire, is reported to have said in the course of his speech: 'After careful study and observation, I am deeply impressed with the belief that the most powerful and enlightened nations of the world are those who have made diligent efforts to cultivate their minds, and sought to develop their country in the fullest and most perfect manner. ... We lack superior institutions for high female culture. Our women should not be ignorant of those great principles on which the happiness of daily life frequently depends. How important the education of mothers on whom future generations almost wholly rely for the cultivation of those intellectual tastes which an enlightened system of training is designed to develop!'

Fanti patriots and Japanese Emperor with his statesmen were both striving to raise up their respective countries by the proper education and efficient training of their people. The same laudable object was before both. The African's attempt was ruthlessly crushed, and his plans frustrated. Japan was not under an unsympathetic protection; she has succeeded, and her very success ought to be an inspiration as well as an incentive to the people of Gold Coast Territories to attempt again, keep on striving, until they win in the twentieth century what was sought for thirty-five years ago.

With Great Britain is linked the destiny of the Akan nation as a whole – Asanti, Fanti, Twi, and all Gold Coast tribes. With the people there is no thought of any other European nation. They are proud of their inheritance, nor are they ashamed of their ancient history. Their kith and kin, taken away and sold in American slave-markets, were described as of superior physique and commanding highest prices. Even Gold Coast children showed an evident superiority, both in hardiness of frame and vigour of mind, over all the young people of the same age imported from other parts of Africa. An author has remarked that the same firmness and intrepidity distinguishable in Gold Coast adults were seen in their boys, at an age, which might be thought too tender to receive any lasting impression, either from precept or example. Their love of freedom and liberty was well known, hence some were described as desperate fellows who despised punishment, and even death itself. When certain men in a slave-ship were asked, why they had mutinied and attempted to escape, they boldly replied, that the captain was a great scoundrel to have bought them for the purpose of taking them away from their native land, and that they were resolved to obtain their liberty if they could.
[…]
Japan in seven years has transformed a savage island into a most promising possession. What she has done, surely, surely British statesmen can accomplish. Let us therefore frankly acknowledge our own limitations, not with an intention to rest and be thankful, but to make good our defects and press on to a higher level of usefulness. Let every one cultivate self-respect and have faith in his or her capabilities. Let us leave the gloomy shades of the lowly tamarisks, and, beneath the warm rays of the noonday sun, learn to sing somewhat higher strains befitting children of the tropics, for we are not destined to live as hewers of wood and water-carriers only. No matter the opposition of those who would like to use the African as a well-trained useful beast of burden, docile, manageable, and uncomplaining. Provided one is careful less to occupy high position than to perform his allotted task perfectly, even discouragements should stir up the flagged energy; taunts and revilings, merited or undeserved, nerve to greater efforts and the pursuit of higher and loftier ideals. The fleshpots should cease to be attractive any longer. To be God-fearing, truth-loving, and industrious ought to be the highest and noblest ambition of each of us. And in whatever positions of trust or honour one is placed, he ought to consider himself as put there to prove as well as to show the fitness of his class or tribe or nation; for, as he conducts himself and performs his duties and obligations, so does he create a precedent for or against the present or future prospects of the African.

Assisted by deftness and aim, perseverance and steady application assuredly increase one's talents, and strengthen his character. The ambition to excel in whatever is of good report is not insolence, neither is the determination to cultivate self-respect and to cherish a manly independent spirit impertinence, nor is pride of race in the African a sign of disloyalty. That the African can ever succeed once he sets his feet on the right path, is denied by his unfriends, and doubted by the sceptic; but, after all, could there be an answer more convincing and conclusive, than the chapels and conventicles, churches and cathedrals of Christendom to the cool, cynical challenge – Can any good thing come out of Nazareth?

Section 1.B
The Loss of
Development's Meta-Narrative

With Independence, the idea of 'development' became a forceful translation of modernization, especially where Africa was concerned. Originally, it was marked also by a strong emphasis on technocratic social engineering and unlinearity. The practical distinction between those who are 'developed' and those 'not yet so' – Africans usually being perceived as taking up the latter position – became fundamental to everyday life in the continent. Thus, development discourse offered its own version of a 'relative' concept of modernity emphasized in the Introduction to this reader. However, the last decades witnessed increasing doubts, both among elites and the wider population, about the feasibility of this meta-narrative. This does not preclude that the notion as such remains a powerful mobilizer. Our selection of World Bank texts from 1972 to 1989 highlights a changing focus, from a statist conception of development and reliance on 'modernizing elites' to determined efforts towards reaching out to 'civil society' through decentralization, by-passing the state and NGOs. Yet, the Bank's 1989 Africa report still maintains the developmental ideal, except that it now perceives the state bureaucracy, rather than rural society, as the object to be developed. Jean-Pierre Olivier de Sardan's chapter, a re-write of an innovative 1985 text, offers a completely different view of development, as an omnipresent local reality, imposed from outside, but deconstructed and 're-appropriated' by local actors. The third text by Margaret Niger-Thomas documents creative local adaptations of development, notably by female entrepreneurs, in a part of Cameroon that is close to the border with Nigeria and therefore offers special possibilities for smuggling and other informal practices.

THE WORLD BANK

The World Bank's Changing Discourse on Development
From Reliance on the State & 'Modernizing Elites' to 'By-passing the State'

Reference
Collage from World Bank texts, 1972–89

The days of hope: Extracts from the Bank's President Robert McNamara's speeches of the 1970s

In his address to the Board of Governors in Washington DC of 25 September 1972, McNamara argues:

Governments exist to promote the welfare of all of their citizens – not just that of a privileged few. Absolute egalitarianism is as chimerical as absolute laissez-faire, but what is certain is that

absolute human degradation – when it reaches the proportions of 30 to 40% of an entire citizenry – cannot be ignored, cannot be suppressed, and cannot be tolerated for too long a time by any government hoping to preserve civil order.

It would be naive not to recognize that that time in many quarters of the world is running out.

The task, then, for the governments of the developing countries is to reorient their development policies in order to attack directly the personal poverty of the most deprived 40% of their populations. This the governments can do without abandoning their goals of vigorous overall economic growth. But they must be prepared to give greater priority to establishing growth targets in terms of essential human needs: in terms of nutrition, housing, health, literacy, and employment – even if it be at the cost of some reduction in the pace of advance in certain narrow and highly privileged sectors whose benefits accrue to the few.

Such a reorientation of social and economic policy is primarily a political task, and the developing countries must decide for themselves if they wish to undertake it: it will manifestly require immense resolve and courage.

The task of political leadership in the wealthy world is to match that resolve and courage with a greater commitment to equity between their own affluent nations and the grossly disadvantaged developing nations.

I believe that no one within this forum would deny that the time for significantly greater social and economic equity both among nations and within nations has indeed come.

Given more than a million years of man's life on earth, it has been long in arriving.

Now that it is here we cannot escape asking ourselves where our responsibilities lie.

It seems to me that the character of our entire era will be defined by the shape of our response.[1]

The next year the Board of Governors meets in Nairobi. McNamara repeats his call to the governments of 'developing countries' but now with more urgency:

We should strive to eradicate absolute poverty by the end of this century. That means in practice the elimination of malnutrition and illiteracy, the reduction of infant mortality, and the raising of life-expectancy standards to those of the developed nations.

Essential to the accomplishment of this objective is an increase in the productivity of small-scale agriculture.

Is it a realistic goal?

The answer is yes, if governments in the developing countries are prepared to exercise the requisite political will to make it realistic.

It is they who must decide.

As for the Bank, increased productivity of the small, subsistence farmer will be a major goal of our program of expanded activity in the FY1974–78 period.

But no amount of outside assistance can substitute for the developing member governments' resolve to take on the task.

It will call for immense courage, for political risk is involved. The politically privileged among the landed elite are rarely enthusiastic over the steps necessary to advance rural development. This is shortsighted, of course, for in the long term they, as well as the poor, can benefit.

But if the governments of the developing world – who must measure the risks of reform against the risks of revolution – are prepared to exercise the requisite political will to assault the problem of poverty in the countryside, then the governments of the wealthy nations must display equal courage. They must be prepared to help them by removing discriminatory trade barriers and by substantially expanding Official Development Assistance.

What is at stake in these decisions is the fundamental decency of the lives of 40% of the people in the 100 developing nations which are members of this institution.

We must hope that the decisions will be the courageous ones. If they are not, the outlook is dark.

But if the courageous decisions are made, then the pace of development can accelerate.

I believe it will. I believe it will because I believe that during the remainder of this century people everywhere will become increasingly intolerant of the inhuman inequalities which exist today.

All of the great religions teach the value of each human life. In a way that was never true in the past, we now have the power to create a decent life for all men and women. Should we not make the moral precept our guide to action? The extremes of privilege and deprivation are simply no longer acceptable.

It is development's task to deal with them.

You and I – and all of us in the international community – share that responsibility.[2]

The same conviction that development can be realized in this manner, through further intensification of the collaboration with governing elites, is the Leitmotiv of McNamara's speech in 1976 when the Board of Governors meets in Manila:

Poverty tends to perpetuate itself, and unless a deliberate intervention is designed and launched against its internal dynamics, it will persist and grow.

The responsibility for such an effort lies first, of course, with the governments of the poorest countries themselves. Despite the fact that in the past decade they have financed almost 90% of their development investments out of their own meager incomes – a fact not often recognized in the developed world – they must make an even greater effort in the future. They have, after all, invested less than $5 billion annually in agriculture (only 3% of their GNP and only 18% of their total investment program), less than $100 million in population planning, and wholly inadequate amounts in essential public services. And much of what they have spent has benefited only a privileged few.

Yet whatever the degree of neglect the governments in the poorest countries may have been responsible for, it has been more than matched by the failure of the international community to assist them in the development task.

In recent years the poorest nations have received:

Only 6% of the total capital raised by all developing countries through long-term bonds;

Only 10% of the total borrowing by all developing countries in the Eurocurrency market;

Only 45% of the total concessional aid to all developing countries. As a result, the countries of South Asia, for example, received only one-third as much concessional assistance on a per capita basis as all other developing countries.

These instances could be multiplied.

But the central issue is that the plight of the poorest nations can be remedied only by deliberate decisive action, and that action must be taken at both the national and international levels. We must all accept two fundamental points.

The first is that the governments of the poorest nations have to redirect their own efforts to accelerate economic growth and reduce absolute poverty. A reasonable objective for them would be to meet the basic human needs of all of their peoples by the end of the century. They must begin by changing national investment priorities and by putting greater emphasis on assisting the poor to become more productive.

This will involve:
• Intensifying the effort to expand domestic food production;
• Taking more determined action to moderate population growth;
• And directing social services more equitably towards the poor.

The second fundamental point is that although nothing can be accomplished unless these governments themselves act, they clearly cannot meet such an objective without outside assistance. Therefore, the international community must help them, help them generously.[3]

The Berg report (1981): The state has to liberate the market

The confidence once held about development as a self-evident form of modernization wears progressively thinner during the 1980s, especially in relation to Africa. The well-known 'Berg report' of 1981 – written by the 'African Strategy Review Committee' led by Elliot Berg – is the first of a series of World Bank reports dealing specifically with Africa.[4] The writers emphasize that the prospects are grim and that a drastic reorientation is necessary. The report is mainly directed against administrative constraints. It sees the pricing policies adopted by governments as the main obstacles – notably the notorious 'marketing-boards' which allow for disastrous levies on the farmer's cash-crop production. Often these boards – with a national monopoly on commercializing the main cash-crops – channel more than half of the world market prices into the coffers of the State. Officially such levies are supposed to serve as protection for the farmers against years of lower prices. In reality these levies become a mainstay for State expenditure on prestige projects of private consumption. The Berg report insists on the need to leave free rein to the market. Striking, nonetheless, is that the solution is still sought in a close collaboration with those governments.

The present economic crisis

During the past two decades economic development has been slow in most of the countries of Sub-Saharan Africa. When, in the mid-1970s, the world economy experienced inflation and recession, nowhere did the crisis hit with greater impact than in this region.

The picture is not uniformly bleak. There are signs of progress throughout the continent. Vastly more Africans are in schools, and most are living longer. Roads, ports, and new cities have been built and new industries developed. Technical and managerial positions, formerly occupied by foreigners, are now held by Africans. Of the 45 countries in the region, nine posted annual growth rates of over 2.5% per capita between 1960 and 1979.

But for most African countries, and for a majority of the African population, the record is grim and it is no exaggeration to talk of crisis. Slow overall economic growth, sluggish agricultural performance coupled with rapid rates of population increase, and balance-of-payments and fiscal crises – these are dramatic indicators of economic trouble.

Between 1960 and 1979, per capita income in 19 countries grew by less than 1% per year, while during the last decade, 15 countries recorded a negative rate of growth of income per capita.

And by the end of the 1970s, economic crises were battering even high-growth countries like Kenya, Malawi and Ivory Coast – where per capita GNP growth had averaged an annual 2.7% between 1960 and 1979 – compelling them to design programs, supported by the Bank, to restructure their economies. Output per person rose more slowly in Sub-Saharan Africa than in any other part of the world, particularly in the 1970s, and it rose more slowly in the 1970s than in the 1960s.[5]

New priorities and adjustments in policy

A reordering of post-independence priorities is essential if economic growth is to accelerate. During the past two decades most African governments rightly focused on political consolidation, on the laying down of basic infrastructure (much of it tied to the goal of political integration), and on the development of human resources. Relatively less attention was paid to production. Now it is essential to give production a higher priority – without neglecting these other goals. Without a faster rate of production increase, other objectives cannot be achieved, nor can past achievements be sustained. Three major policy actions are central to any growth-oriented program: (1) more suitable trade and exchange-rate policies; (2) increased efficiency of resource use in the public sector; and (3) improvement in agricultural policies.

Exchange-rate and trade policies, addressed in Chapter 4, are especially critical for African economies, which are uncommonly 'open.' Exports account for a large share of marketed production, and imports constitute a significant share of consumption. Moreover, Africa has more frontiers per square kilometer than any other region, and they are highly permeable. The framework of incentives created by trade and exchange-rate policies is thus especially decisive. With respect to agriculture, for example, overvalued exchange rates discourage local production: farmers obtain less in their local currencies for their export crops, while the price of food imports is reduced. The situation is similar in the industrial sector. Also, direct controls over trade (for example, import bans and quotas), which are widely imposed to deal with balance-of-payments problems, have proved extremely costly to apply, as they require many trained people and an enlarged administrative apparatus. Moreover, they have freqently been ineffective.

Chapter 4 also considers policy issues which bear on the efficiency of resource use in the public sector. When African states won independence, they inherited unevenly developed economies with rudimentary infrastructure. Markets often functioned imperfectly and foreigners dominated trade and most modern businesses. To speed up development and make their economies more 'national,' the new governments expanded the public sector. It is now widely evident that the public sector is overextended, given the present scarcities of financial resources, skilled manpower, and organizational capacity. This has resulted in slower growth than might have been achieved with available resources, and accounts in part for the current crisis. Without improved performance of public agencies, stepped-up growth will be difficult to achieve. The organization and management of economic activity need to be reviewed to determine how the resources and energies of all economic agents can be better mobilized for development – for example, by improving government policy-making institutions and procedures; by giving the public sector's development-related agencies – 'parastatals' – clearer mandates and greater management autonomy; by giving wider responsibilities to the small-scale indigenous private sector; by allowing greater scope for decentralized cooperatives; and by defining an appropriate role for larger-scale private capital, domestic and foreign. Many governments have already acted in this area. In Guinea-Bissau, Mozambique, Senegal, Uganda, and Zaire, among others, governments have decided on efficiency grounds that the scope of private sector activity should be enlarged.[6]

Long-run strategy implications

The agriculture-based and export-oriented development strategy suggested for the 1980s is an essential beginning to a process of long-term transformation, a prelude to industrialization. It is not a permanent course for any country, but one that in Africa generates resources more quickly than any alternative and benefits more people. Without these resources, the foundations of future development cannot be established. The list of what must be done is formidable: administrative services have to be extended to the rural areas to increase social welfare and contribute to the building of a sense of national unity; critically needed social and economic infrastructure must be developed; roads must be built and maintained; suitable schooling must be offered to everyone; knowledge about the economy has to be increased by broader and deeper research and by pilot experiments on a wide front; and more people must be trained. Inter-African trade relations have to be developed and greater cooperation encouraged by means of joint programs. This will build mutual interests and the habit of common efforts, creating a sure basis for increased regional integration.

A strategy focused on agriculture and exports is thus open-ended, a necessary beginning. It will help generate the resources Africa needs to consolidate its political and administrative forces, educate and improve the health of its people, and find out what will work and what will not. It will bring forth human talent now neglected and uncover physical resources not yet imagined. And it will open the way to a future whose shape we cannot yet see.[7]

Both donors and African governments will have to change policies and attitudes if the large increases in aid recommended here are to come about, and if they are to have their desired effects. What is needed is a new kind of social compact, an agreement within the world community that the struggle against poverty in Africa is a joint concern which entails responsibilities for both parties. After all, foreign assistance has played a more substantial role in Africa than in most other developing regions, in terms of aid per capita, share of total investment, technical assistance, and project selection and design. Donors have thus contributed to some extent to the present crisis. Moreover, African states are among the world's newest and least developed. They face special economic problems handicapped by still-acute scarcities of trained and experienced people, fragile political systems, and untested institutions. They are, rightfully, a special concern of the community as a whole. On the donor side, therefore, assistance must not only be greater, but more effective. It will have to be accompanied by closer attention to project selection and design, by more flexibility in aid modalities (more financing of local and/or recurrent costs, for example), by more nonproject lending, and by greater attention to the policy environment. All of this also implies greater donor collaboration than in the past; no donor wishes to finance the recurrent costs of somebody's 'unsuitable' project. It means also that donors must engage in more systematic policy dialogue with their African partners.

On the African side, aid inflows have not always been used effectively; their development impact has been diluted by inadequacies in the domestic policy environment. African governments, therefore, must be willing to take firm action on internal problems, be more open to proposals to revise policies in the light of experience, and be willing to accept the proposition that without policy reform higher aid will be difficult to mobilize.[8]

Problems of pricing policy
It is now widely agreed that insufficient price incentives for agricultural producers are an important factor behind the disappointing growth of African agriculture. The importance of price policy comes out strongly in project experience. A recent review of 27 agricultural projects undertaken by the World Bank noted 'the almost overriding importance of producer prices in affecting production outcome and production levels, often cutting across the quality of technical packages and extension services. Seven out of nine projects implemented under favorable prices achieved or surpassed their production objectives; 13 of the 18 under unfavorable prices failed to do so.'[9] This idea is also borne out strongly in micro-level studies, which indicate substantial farmer responsiveness to price.

Despite this general appreciation of the importance of good prices, export crop producers have been heavily taxed, and prices of food crops have been systematically set at below-market levels for most of the past decade. These aspects of price policy are discussed below.[10]

Donor support for programs of policy reform
The level and pattern of donor assistance to a country must be determined in the framework of programs of action prepared by individual governments, which address the critical development policy issues outlined in this Report. In this way, donor financial assistance will effectively support the attainment of development objectives, and avoid financing projects that do not reflect a government's priorities or even run counter to these priorities.[11]

Conclusion
Despite their enormous advances since independence, particularly in developing institutions, human resources, and even nations, Sub-Saharan African countries are in a crisis that can only be surmounted by the joint efforts of African governments and the donor community. The increased aid and related technical assistance recommended in this Report can only be mobilized if they support deliberate and well formulated programs to reverse the downward trend of development in Africa. The policy reforms required in Africa will be technically difficult and politically thorny. African governments and the donor community will have to work out a relationship that recognizes these realities if the action program recommended in this Report is to be successful. But the rewards of taking these pains will be great. Policy action and foreign assistance that are mutually reinforcing will surely work together to build a continent that shows real gains in both development and income in the near future.[12]

The turning-point: The Africa Report of 1989[13]

The World Bank report on Africa of 1989 formulates a clear break with the earlier 'statist' approach to development – a break that signals also the shattering of the modernization perspective. In this report there is no question anymore of collaboration with 'modernizing elites', especially not with the governing elites. On the contrary 'by-passing the state' becomes a familiar slogan in development circles – together with 'decentralization' and 'strengthening civil society'. NGOs are now celebrated as an alternative to the state. The governing elites no longer constitute the obvious allies in the struggle for development but are rather seen as obstacles.

The populist character of this new approach to development is striking; the French anthropologist Jean-Pierre Olivier de Sardan even signals the return of Maoist ideas in this development-thought 'new-style'.[14]

Equally salient in this report is the advent of the term 'governance', which remains vaguely defined but perhaps because of this rises to prominence during the 1990s. Its meaning may be highly variable, but distrust of the state seems to be its common denominator – while in older visions it was precisely the state that had to play a pivotal role in modernization.

The recommendations of the Bank continue to assume the feasibility of strict social engineering. However, faith in modernization as an inevitable process has disappeared.

Introduction and overview
Africa entered independence with high expectations. Most people believed that rapid progress would be made in raising incomes and improving welfare. And indeed in the early years many African countries successfully expanded their basic infrastructure and social services. Much effort was spent too on consolidating the fragile new nation states.

After an initial period of growth, however, most African economies faltered, then went into decline. There were some exceptions, but Sub-Saharan Africa as a whole has now witnessed almost a decade of falling per capita incomes, increasing hunger, and accelerating ecological degradation. The earlier progress made in social development is now being eroded. Overall Africans are almost as poor today as they were 30 years ago. This situation has spurred many governments to undertake far-reaching reforms. More than half have embarked on structural adjustment programs. The countries that have persisted with reforms since the mid-1980s are showing the first signs of improvement. These give grounds for believing that recovery has started.

The experience of the first generation of Africans after independence raises some searching questions. Does Africa face special structural problems that have not been properly understood? Has the institutional dimension been neglected? Have the recent reform programs been too narrow or too shallow? Could the process of formulating and implementing reforms be improved? Has the effect of external factors been correctly assessed? Are external assistance and debt relief appropriate and adequate? More fundamentally, is there a long-term vision that is both credible and energizing? [...]

The post-independence development efforts failed because the strategy was misconceived. Governments made a dash for 'modernization,' copying, but not adapting, Western models. The result was poorly designed public investments in industry; too little attention to peasant agriculture; too much intervention in areas in which the state lacked managerial, technical, and entrepreneurial skills; and too little effort to foster grassroots development. This top-down approach demotivated ordinary people, whose energies most needed to be mobilized in the development effort.[15] [...]

A strategy for sustainable development and equitable growth
The long-term strategy proposed here envisages a move away from earlier practices. It aims to release the energies of ordinary people enabling them to take charge of their lives. Profits would be seen as the mark of an efficient business. Agricultural extension services would be responding to farmers, not commanding them. Foreign investors would be welcomed as partners, not discouraged. The state would no longer be an entrepreneur, but a promoter of private producers. And the informal sector would be valued as a 'seedbed for entrepreneurs, not a hotbed of racketeers. [...]

Africa needs not just less government but better government – government that concentrates its efforts less on direct interventions and more on enabling others to be productive. Every level of government should take measures to improve the performance of public administrations and parastatal enterprises. Institution building is a long-term endeavor that requires a clear vision and a specific agenda. Several countries have already embarked on major reforms of central government, for example, Central African Republic, Ghana, and Guinea. They aim to create a leaner, better disciplined, better trained, and more motivated public service, with competitive salaries for highly qualified officials. Special attention needs to be given to strengthening the policy analysis and economic management capabilities of governments. Public enterprises need to be given clear mandates, managerial autonomy, and monitorable performance indicators. Local governments also could play a greater role if allowed more autonomy and regular, independent sources of revenue, especially in managing the expanding urban networks that link the towns to their hinterlands. In rural areas local services, such as water supply, could be better run at the communal level. This too requires genuine delegation of responsibilities.[16]

Fostering African entrepreneurship
In the coming decades Africa's entrepreneurs face a monumental challenge – to find productive employment for a labor force that will surpass 600 million workers by 2020 – about three times the present number. These jobs are more likely to be created in a myriad of small and micro-enterprises than in a few large firms. Fortunately there is no shortage of entrepreneurship in Africa. During the recent years of economic crisis, small firms in the informal sector have provided a growing share of jobs and output. Estimates indicate that these enterprises currently provide more than half of Africa's urban employment and as much as one-fifth of GDP in many countries.

Unregulated and unrecorded, the informal sector is home to small firms in agriculture, industry, trade, transport, finance, and social services. It is not static and not necessarily traditional in its techniques, but it undertakes innovations and adaptations indicated by market forces. In the informal sector enterprises find a business environment that is competitive, free from unjustified regulatory constraints, and well-adapted to local resource endowments and demand. These enterprises are also supported by a system of grassroots institutions: on-the-job apprenticeships that provide training and small associations that can represent group interests and improve access to credit and other resources.[17]

Deteriorating government
At independence Africa inherited simple but functioning administrations. They were managed largely by expatriates and were not geared to the development role assigned to them by African leaders. The responsibilities of the state were enormously expanded. But at the same time the rapid promotion of inexperienced staff and the gradual politicization of the whole administrative apparatus led to declining efficiency. A combination of administrative bottlenecks, unauthorized 'fees' and 'commissions', and inefficient services imposed costs on businesses that have progressively undermined their international competitiveness. The gradual breakdown of the judicial systems in many countries left foreign investors doubtful that contracts could be enforced. The ones that did invest insisted on large profit margins to compensate for the perceived high risks. Authoritarian governments hostile to grassroots and nongovernmental organizations have alienated much of the public. As a result economic activity has shifted increasingly to the informal sector. Too frequently ordinary people see government as the source of, not the solution to, their problems.[18]

Public versus private institutions
The post-independence development strategy accorded the state a lead role in producing many goods and services. This approach foundered on the weak capacity of public institutions. At the same time, far from promoting the private sector the state often actively curbed private initiative, including cooperatives and grassroots organizations. These policies have been partly reversed, but where to draw the boundary between the private and the public sectors remains controversial and must be settled on a country-by-country basis.

The debate is not simply about the division of responsibilities between the state and the private sector, but also about the division among the central authorities, local government, and local communities. The goal is to reduce the number of tasks performed by central government and to decentralize the provision of public services. Many basic services, including water supply, health care, and primary education, are best managed at the local level – even at the village level – with the central agencies providing only technical advice and specialized inputs. The aims should be to empower ordinary people to take charge of their lives, to make communities more responsible for their development, and to make governments listen to their people. Fostering a more pluralistic institutional structure- including nongovernmental organizations and stronger local government – is a means to these ends.

The state has an indispensable role in creating a favorable economic environment. This should, in fact, be its primary concern. It is of the utmost importance for the state to establish a predictable and honest administration of the regulatory framework, to assure law and order, and to foster a stable, objective, and transparent judicial system. In addition it should provide reliable and efficient infrastructure and social and information services – all preconditions for the efficiency of productive enterprises, whether private or state-owned.

The division of responsibilities between the state and the private sector should be a matter of pragmatism – not dogma. Often public services can be provided by private contractors at very competitive rates – road maintenance, transport, water supplies, refuse collection, and public vehicle repair to name but a few. At the same time consumers have sometimes been exploited by private business monopolies. What matters is reliability and cost-effectiveness. There need be no preconceptions about the 'right' type of organization; appropriate incentives count for much more.

Most state enterprises have a poor performance record, although there are some notable exceptions. Managers have suffered from political interference. But it has also proved difficult to devise incentive systems to motivate employees and managers when entrepreneurship, commercial judgement, and risk-taking are needed. Increasing recognition of these problems has spurred a worldwide trend toward privatization, If Africa wishes to remain competitive, it should not resist this trend. State-owned enterprises will still be appropriate in many cases, especially in providing utilities and some public goods. In some cases the private sector lacks the capacity to take over, but in time and with imagination privatization can work.

Much can be done to strengthen the performance of those state enterprises that are retained. Efficiency has less to do with ownership than with the central conditions under which enterprises operate. Experience shows that state enterprises are more likely to succeed when they are given clear and attainable objectives, day-to-day managerial autonomy, and unambiguous performance indicators, which permit the supervisory body to monitor progress without undue interference. So far in Africa this has rarely been the case.

Development takes place through institutions, including markets, whether private or public. Institution-building in the widest sense is essential and must for the most part be nurtured by governments. But few African governments have paid much attention to the task. Agencies are created or disbanded without much attention to the inter-relationships and respective roles of the different institutions involved. Once created, they are often allowed to decay as their initiators move on. The turnover of senior staff is frequently kaleidoscopic; yet prolonged inaction in the face of urgent problems is also common, and equally damaging. Thus, to overcome these weaknesses during the next generation, governments need an explicit strategy for institution-building for both the public and private sectors. [19]

Better government
In the words of President Abdou Diouf of Senegal, Africa requires not just less government but better government. Despite reforms in the 1980s Africa's public administrations remain woefully weak. The principal causes are:

- The uncontrolled expansion of staff in the civil services and public enterprises, which have often functioned as welfare agencies for unemployed school-leavers
- The rapid promotion and turnover of poorly qualified staff who have little in-depth understanding of either the institutions they manage or of the broader context in which they are expected to function
- Difficulties faced by managers in motivating and disciplining their staff owing to the social and political context in which they operate
- Insufficient appreciation in government that public agencies work best if staffed and run by professionals according to objective rules and criteria
- In an increasing number of countries the compression of civil service pay scales at the expense of higher level staff.

Recognizing the urgency of this problem several governments – notably Central African Republic, The Gambia, Ghana, Guinea, Mauritania, and Senegal – have launched, although not yet completed, comprehensive programs of administrative reform. The key measures include:

- New and clearer mandates for the agencies, with staff planning based strictly on need
- Staff testing to help select the best qualified candidates and the release of redundant staff with compensation and assistance to enter the private sector
- Better personnel management, with competitive entrance examinations, regular staff appraisals as the basis for promotion based on merit (rather than patronage and longevity), and accurate personnel records that correspond exactly to the payroll
- Selective improvements in the pay structure to attract and retain highly qualified staff.

Public employment accounts for more than 50 percent of non-agricultural registered employment in Africa, compared with 36 per cent in Asia and only 27 per cent in Latin America. Chronic overstaffing has damaged performance severely, partly because staff are badly deployed and denied adequate material support and partly because idle staff undermine the morale of those who want to work. Many ministries in Africa would probably function better with a fraction of their present staff. Often the application of existing regulations – dismissing persistent absentees, requiring retirement at the mandatory age, laying off temporary staff when they have completed the task for which they were hired – would reduce staff substantially. Pressure on the wage bill can be eased by eliminating ghost workers, double payments, and automatic promotion. Merit-based pay systems, which relate bonus payments to performance and not status, and which pay a greater part of salary in that form, help to motivate staff. [20]

Strengthening local government
In most countries urban growth has far outstripped planning and administrative capacity at both the central and local levels. The task of meeting mounting infrastructure needs has increasingly fallen on local governments. This is as it should be. Although weak and underfunded, local governments are best suited to meet the needs of local communities. This is as true for the rural areas as it is for the towns. The initiative shown by Rwanda's communes in mobilizing citizens for road improvements, tree planting, and soil conservation illustrate the potential. Developing competent and responsive local governments is central to capacity-building. It implies stronger powers to raise revenue locally and a clearer delegation of authority and responsibility. Many of the problems of the towns and rural communities can only be solved locally; solutions imposed by central authorities are likely to fail. The objective should be to capitalize on the energies and resources of the local people.

Decentralization in Africa has so far mainly concentrated on strengthening the field agencies of central government. This has been justified by the fear of corruption and inefficiency in poorly supervised local governments. But a change of heart is now apparent. Francophone West African states have embarked on fresh efforts at decentralization; Nigeria is reappraising its local government systems; and Tanzania is in the midst of reviving local government. These are all moves in the right direction. They need to be extended and reinforced. [21]

Governance for development
Underlying the litany of Africa's development problems is a crisis of governance. By governance is meant the exercise of political power to manage a nation's affairs. Because countervailing power

has been lacking, state officials in many countries have served their own interests without fear of being called to account. In self-defense individuals have built up personal networks of influence rather than hold the all-powerful state accountable for its systemic failures. In this way politics becomes personalized, and patronage becomes essential to maintain power. The leadership assumes broad discretionary authority and loses its legitimacy. Information is controlled, and voluntary associations are co-opted or disbanded. This environment cannot readily support a dynamic economy. At worst the state becomes coercive and arbitrary. These trends, however, can be resisted. As Botswana has shown, dedicated leadership can produce a quite different outcome. It requires a systematic effort to build a pluralistic institutional structure, a determination to respect the rule of law, and vigorous protection of the freedom of the press and human rights.

Intermediaries have an important role to play; they can create links both upward and downward in society and voice local concerns more effectively than grassroots institutions. In doing this, they can bring a broader spectrum of ideas and values to bear on policymaking. They can also exert pressure on public officials for better performance and greater accountability. The National Christian Council of Kenya has played this role for some time. Others are now emerging in several countries. The intermediary's role can be politically controversial, yet it is essential for greater citizen involvement. In relating to the local organizations, it is the intermediary that must exercise restraint. A common mistake is to ignore local leadership, often on the grounds that it is exploitative, but there is little empirical evidence to support that view. On the contrary, studies show that working with existing leaders produces more effective development programs. Better information is crucial for generating greater public awareness. Too often political consciousness and participation are stymied – sometimes deliberately so – by lack of information about government policy.

The extent of corruption is largely determined by the example set by a country's leadership. And once bad habits have become entrenched, they are hard to undo. Unfortunately foreign aid has greatly expanded the opportunities for malfeasance exacerbated by the venality of many foreign contractors and suppliers. Hundreds of millions of dollars have been siphoned off to private bank accounts outside Africa. The cost is not just the waste of funds, but also more seriously the profound demoralization of society at large.

Corruption can be countered in several ways. The elimination of unnecessary controls greatly reduces the scope for 'rent seeking.' Transparent procurement procedures, scrupulous and prompt accounting, the publication of audits, and the vigorous prosecution of those misusing public funds all contribute to financial propriety. External agencies providing aid have a right to insist on such measures. Donor governments also have a responsibility to prosecute their own firms when they pay bribes to obtain business;

regrettably so far the United States is the only developed country that has outlawed such practices. A free and vigilant press – all too rare in Africa – is as important for good governance in Africa as elsewhere. The two countries with the best economic performance in Africa – Botswana and Mauritius – both have effective parliamentary democracies and a vigorous free press.[22]

The proposed global coalition for Africa would be a forum in which African leaders (not just from the public sector, but also from private business, the professions, the universities, and other NGOs) could meet with their key partners – the bilateral and multilateral agencies and major foreign NGOs – to agree on general strategies that would then provide broad guidance for the design of individual country programs. The coalition could seek agreement on actions to tackle the priorities identified in this report: environmental protection, capacity building, population policy, food security, and regional integration and cooperation. It could provide the impetus for channeling external assistance to programs in these areas and for monitoring programs. The creation of this coalition would be a decisive new step forward for Africa and its partners. It would mark a new resolve to work together for a better future.[23]

Notes

1 *The McNamara Years at the World Bank – Major Addresses of Robert S. McNamara 1968–1981*, Baltimore: Johns Hopkins University Press 1981, pp. 227–8.
2 *The McNamara Years at the World Bank*, 1981, pp. 259–61.
3 *The McNamara Years at the World Bank* 1981, pp. 342–4.
4 *Accelerated Development in Sub-Saharan Africa – An Agenda for Action*, Washington DC: The World Bank, 1981.
5 *Accelerated Development*, 1981, pp. 2–3.
6 *Accelerated Development*, 1981, pp. 4–5.
7 *Accelerated Development*, 1981, pp. 6–7.
8 *Accelerated Development*, 1981, pp. 7–8.
9 *Sixth Annual Review of Project Performance Audits*, September 1980, paragraph 3.71.
10 *Accelerated Development*, 1981, pp. 55–6.
11 *Accelerated Development*, 1981, pp. 124–5.
12 *Accelerated Development*, 1981, pp. 132–3.
13 *Sub-Saharan Africa: From Crisis to Sustainable Growth, A Long-Term Perspective Study*, Washington DC: The World Bank, 1989.
14 *Anthropologie et développement*, Karthala, 1995, p. 109.
15 *World Bank 1989 report, Sub-Saharan Africa*, pp. 1 and 3.
16 *World Bank 1989 report, Sub-Saharan Africaa*, pp. 4 and 5.
17 *World Bank 1989 report, Sub-Saharan Africa*, p. 10.
18 *World Bank 1989 report, Sub-Saharan Africa*, p. 30.
19 *World Bank 1989 report, Sub-Saharan Africa*, p. 54
20 *World Bank 1989 report, Sub-Saharan Africa*, p. 54.
21 *World Bank 1989 report, Sub-Saharan Africa* pp. 58–9.
22 *World Bank 1989 report, Sub-Saharan Africa* pp. 60–1.
23 *World Bank 1989 report, Sub-Saharan Africa*, p. 194.

JEAN-PIERRE OLIVIER DE SARDAN
Excerpts from *Anthropology & Development*[1]
Understanding Contemporary Social Change

Reference

Anthropology & Development:
Understanding Contemporary Social Change
London & New York: Zed Books, 2005 [1995], 1-3, 23-4, 137-48, 150-1

Introduction: The three approaches in the anthropology of development

This work was originally published in France in 1995 and had several objectives. Its primary aim was to develop a specific perspective, in the form of a non-normative approach to the complex social phenomena linked to development actions, grounded in a resolutely empirical (nonspeculative and based on enquiry) and 'fundamental' (situated upstream of 'applied' anthropology) practice of anthropology. A secondary objective was to take simultaneous account of works in English and in French dealing with the anthropology of development.

It is remarkable, on one hand, that the works published in English that approach the anthropology of development from one angle or another are, as a rule, completely oblivious of the works that exist in French, despite the fact that French-speaking Africa is as much a region where development policies and operations prevail as Anglophone Africa.[2] Conversely, most of the works published in French bear witness to a very unequal and impressionistic knowledge of the literature in English.[3] Thus, in France, the present work provided a linkage between two frequently disconnected scholarly universes. Its translation into English now offers the same opportunity to readers from English-speaking countries.

However, the main aim of this book is more general. I wish to propose a point of view on development that reintegrates development into mainstream anthropology as an object worthy of attention, a perspective that engages in a minute exploration of the various types of interactions which take place in the world of development, bringing into play conceptions and practices, strategies and structures, actors and contexts. This is therefore a project that intends to steer clear of both apology and denunciation, to avoid both prophecies and caricatures. However, another characteristic of the literature on development, in English and French alike, is that it is permeated with normative judgements arising from a variety of ideologies and meta-ideologies. The literature is the source of an endless stream of value judgements on development. Anthropologists are no exception to this rule: despite the fact that they readily denounce the ideologies in other people's work (especially those that are popular among development professionals), they fail to recognize those that abound in their own work – populism, for instance, or post-modernism and the 'politically correct'. Contrary to this, my conception of anthropology is that it is an empirical social science, but of course not a positivist one like the classic natural sciences. Social sciences have nothing to do with Popper's notion of falsification: their logic is based on plausibility on a basis of natural reasoning. But they are not hermeneutic sciences in the sense that epistemological relativism or radical subjectivism give to this term. Their hands are tied by the search for an empirical foundation.[4]

As far as this is concerned, my interest in development does not aim either at saving or condemning, deconstructing or reforming. It is rather a question of understanding, through development, a set of complex social practices: from this point of view, development is simply a set of actions of various types which define themselves as constituting development in one way or another (whether in the ranks of 'developers' or of 'developees'), notwithstanding the variations in their definitions, meanings and practices. The very existence of a 'developmentalist configuration'[5] – that is, a complex set of institutions, flows and actors, for whom development constitutes a resource, a profession, a market, a stake, or a strategy – is enough to justify the existence of a socio-anthropology[6] which takes development as an object of study or as a 'pathway'.

In fact, anthropology of development is merely a way of going about anthropology and sociology, that is, a way of carrying out empirical field enquiries leading to new ways of understanding social phenomena, based on contemporary objects. Development is just one of a range of topics, but one that presents some specific characteristics: in countries of the South, and in African countries in particular, it is omnipresent and inevitable.[7] It comprises considerable social stakes at the local and national levels, and is interwoven with interactions between actors originating in particularly heterogeneous social and professional worlds.

Anthropology of development is not an autonomous or independent discipline. Moreover, it is not necessarily 'applied' anthropology: the question of the relationship between research and action, whether in terms of the *relevance* of research to action, which is one thing, or of the *integration* of research into action, which is another, constitutes a different problem, which is certainly important, but different.[8] Anthropology 'applied' to development stands in need of what we may call *fundamental* anthropology of development, which provides it with problematics, concepts, methods and results. Our first step is to take into account some social realities of great importance to Africa such as development projects, the financing of development, development brokerage, and development associations, all of which intervene on a daily basis in even the smallest village, and to use these realities as pathways into political, economic, social and cultural anthropology, by making investigations into the practices and conceptions of the actors concerned, the interplay of the pragmatic and cognitive relationships, and the structural and institutional contexts in which all this occurs. If this type of research objective is pursued appropriately, we might be able to play a role in possible action, whether the role in question be operational, reformatory or critical, depending on the situation in question or on the options available. Hence, this work makes the appeal that development should be embraced by fundamental anthropology as an object that deserves scientific attention, methodological vigilance, and conceptual innovation.[9]

This perspective implies a break from or discrepancy with certain works dealing with the relationship between anthropology and development (especially the 'deconstructionist business'), and with a certain type of populist ideology encountered in the works of anthropologists and of development specialists alike. But I have also encountered many convergent viewpoints, not only during the writing of this book, but also in the years following its publication in French.

Independently of my own work, various authors, mostly from English-speaking countries, have developed research positions similar to mine in many regards, despite some differences of opinion. Other authors, mainly writing in French, have gone further afield or have opened up new perspectives. Consequently, I believe it will be useful to review the works in English and French that have appeared since the publication of the French version of the present work.[10]

Three main sets of writings can be distinguished: discursive approaches, populist approaches and entangled social logic approaches to development.

[...]

Socio-anthropology of development: Some preliminary statements

The matters dealt with in the present work can be summarized by a few simple theses.

- The processes and social phenomena associated with what is called development, development politics, development operations, development infrastructure, development projects, as regards countries of the South, constitute a specific domain within anthropology and sociology.

- In this field, in particular, anthropology and sociology cannot be separated, much less opposed. This is especially true in the case of a certain type of anthropology and a certain type of sociology, as long as we are willing to admit that these two closely related social sciences have nothing to do with essayism, philosophy, ideology or speculation, but are, on the contrary, the result of field enquiry, that is to say, the end product of rational procedures of empirical research.

- The dialogue and co-operation between operators and development institutions, on one hand, and anthropologists on the other, is necessary and useful, even though it is difficult and interwoven with almost inevitable misunderstandings, attributable to both parties. However, there is no 'applied' anthropology of development without 'fundamental' anthropology of development. Studies, evaluations and expert reports carried out at the request of development institutions should not be relegated to the ghetto of cut-rate research, to be dashed off simply to put bread on the table for researchers. They should be coupled, in ways yet to be invented, with anthropology 'in general' and with anthropology of social change and development in particular. In order to do this, their concepts, problematics and methodological requirements must be explored.

- 'Development' is just another form of social change; it cannot be understood in isolation. The analysis of development actions and of popular reactions to these actions should not be isolated from the study of local dynamics, of endogenous processes, of 'informal' processes of change. Hence, anthropology of development cannot be dissociated from anthropology of social change.

- Understanding development facts in their relation to facts of social change can contribute to a renewal of the social sciences. At any rate, anthropology of social change and development cannot exist as a separate discipline, truncated from sociology and anthropology as a whole. It calls on problematics situated at the heart of these disciplines, draws on the notions and concepts they provide, and makes use of their comparativist approach. Anthropology of development focuses in particular on the analysis of interactions between social actors belonging to different cultures or subcultures. It attempts to inventory the respective constraints to which all actors are submitted, and to decode the strategies actors deploy according to the room for manoeuvre available to them. It describes the conceptions and sense systems mobilized by the groups in interaction, and it studies the dynamics of transformation of these conceptions and sense systems.

- The context of domination and inequality in which development processes occur activates various types of 'populist' ideologies, rhetorics and practices in operators and researchers alike. Anthropology of development is not impervious to this, yet it must break away from 'ideological populism', to the benefit of what we may call 'methodological populism', if it is to produce reliable knowledge.

Let us rest the matter here. This brief inventory of some of the themes to be developed in the following pages requires the use of a number of terms whose meanings are somewhat ambiguous. *Development*, of course, but also *anthropology, comparativism, action, populism*. ... A few preliminary definitions must therefore be provided. The definitions proposed here are neither normative nor essentialist ones, aimed at defining the essence of things (for example what development 'really' is ...), but rather definitions in keeping with norms of convention and clarity. Their sole ambition is to provide the reader with stabilized meanings of these terms as used subsequently by me, within the perspective to be developed in the present work (for example the purely descriptive use of the word *development*).

[...]

Development projects and social logic

A development enterprise is always an arena in which various logics and strategies come into confrontation: those of the initiators of the development enterprise confront those of the so-called target population. Here I will take as the ideal type of development enterprise the development 'project', which is undoubtedly currently the most widespread and the most conspicuous type of development structure. But there are other institutional forms designed for improving development. Separate and apart from the classic project and its methods, there are different ways of organizing development: the 'game' public technical services usually play, the circulation of agricultural advisers or commercial agents, rural training, extension activities or the action of the social services, the creation of public or private infrastructure, the piloting of communication campaigns, the establishment of a banking network. These are all means of organizing development. However, regardless of the type of organization or the mode of intervention, a development action inevitably gives rise to interaction between social actors belonging to different worlds (developers/developees, for example) and whose behaviour patterns are regulated by a variety of logics. To this extent, our comments on projects also apply to other types of development enterprises, so long as we acknowledge that each development enterprise obviously has its own particular modes of organization and labours under specific constraints. At any rate, in the face of the resources, opportunities and constraints of which a particular development undertaking is composed, in interaction with the milieu (a 'project organization', in this instance), the social actors involved behave in various contrasting, sometimes contradictory ways. This is not only a matter of distinct personal choices; it is also a reflection of dissimilar interests, different norms of evaluation, a divergence in 'objective' positions occupied by individuals.

I will continue to use the term 'logic', while extending its field of application. It will be a question of pinpointing certain levels of coherence, surrounding the interaction between a project and a population, which allow us to explain similar types of behaviour (and their internal differences). In reality, despite the existence of an infinite variety of individual actions and reactions, the number of behaviour patterns is limited. I will attempt to define these in terms of 'logics' or 'strategies'. It would be a waste of time to propose formal definitions with the aim of distinguishing 'strategies' and 'logics': these two terms are usually employed as synonyms. For example, what Yung and Zaslavsky call a 'strategy' corresponds to what I will define here as a 'logic': 'By the strategy of agricultural producers, we mean the understanding put into practice by those for whose way of life agricultural and pastoral processes of production are central, and who bring agricultural means to bear as one element in achieving the maintenance, reproduction and growth of the family unit, in a context ever increasingly affected by uncertainty' (Yung and Zaslavsky, 1992: 24). This point of view even allows us to coin the expression 'strategic logics' in order to typologize the various 'arts' that actors deploy, as opposed to their 'notional logics', which is a category defining various ways of perceiving reality.

In fact, reference is sometimes made to a subsistence logic or to a strategy of reproduction as a mean of homogenizing a vast range of behaviour patterns by reducing them to the ulterior economic objectives actors set for themselves. Sometimes, too, reference is made to a security logic or a strategy aimed at minimizing risks as the means of enveloping another collection of modes of economic behaviour, which can be defined, more or less, as sub-sets of the former: the management of risk and security is one way of ensuring reproduction and subsistence. Sometimes, one speaks of an aid logic or of an aid-seeking strategy in order to designate another set of behaviour patterns (see also below), which intersects with the preceding: they may promote security but not exclusively. This variability in the use of the terms 'logic' or 'strategy' should not disturb us overmuch. If they cannot be stabilized at a single level of application this is simply because the behaviour patterns of the actors themselves occupy a variety of levels of overlapping coherence. Reference to actors' logics in general or to strategy *per se* is fruitless and even absurd.[11] A logic or strategy must always be specifically defined in order to make sense from a sociological point of view. On condition that one respects this imperative of clear definition, which is the only way of clarifying the level of coherence of the practices being investigated, the highlighting of overlapping or interfacing logics and strategies is merely a reflection of the complexity and diversity of social practices.

The context of interaction

Let us get back to the question of the interactions between a method of intervention and the population involved, seen from the angle of the impact of a development project. From the very outset, we need to bear in mind the fact that 'project/milieu' interactions take place in a particular context (whether ecological, economic, institutional or political) which deeply affects the outcome of this intervention. Developers and developees enter into relationship in the context of an environment that does not depend on them and that exerts a significant pressure on their relationship. Hence, a rural development project is faced with a variety of factors beyond its control, on which it is partially dependent: unpredictable climate, pricing systems, structures of securing and commercializing stocks, other interventions occurring in the same milieu (concurrent projects, taxation, administrative measures), opportunities existing outside the local system of production (migrations, schooling …). The way peasants react to a project depends to a great degree on external factors. This is one element that analysis must take into account.

Moreover, current projects all take place in a milieu that has already experienced previous interventions which have left their mark,[12] despite the fact that 'the natural tendency of any project is to assume that history begins with the project, to underestimate everything that came before and to overestimate its own impact' (translated from Gentil and Dufumier, 1984: 25). Peasant societies all have an economic history of trade (pre-colonial), of 'mise en valeur' (colonial) and of 'development'. They also have a history of rural training, of agricultural popularization, of co-operatives, of the one-party system, of projects small and large, of producers' associations, of the coming of NGOs, of the creation of village–member associations, etc. This history is also interlaced with tales of corruption, patron–client relationships, bureaucratic tyranny and incompetence − four fundamental themes which are factors in all long-term relationships between the African peasantry and the outside world of the state or of parastatal institutions. In this respect, 'projects' which strive to break away from the modes of state intervention and to substitute themselves, in part, for state interventions (or to short-circuit them), reproduce, often unwittingly, the state's methods of functioning, while contributing a few perverse effects of their own (see Daane and Mongbo, 1991: 65; Tidjani Alou, 1994).

Be that as it may, it is possible, everywhere, to bring to light a particular local history, which we could call a local history of contact with politico-economic interventionism, which necessarily structures current behaviour patterns, at least in part.

Consequently, the synchronic and the diachronic contexts should in no event be ignored or underestimated.

Levels of project coherence

A project always claims to have a specific coherence which justifies its existence, and which is often opposed to former or neighbouring projects, the development configuration being a world of fierce competition. However, this necessary declaration of coherence, which is one of the essential conditions of funding, and which is often expressed through a specific rhetoric (the 'project language'), is always undermined not only by the interaction between the project and the target population (see below) but also by the various elements that participate in the project itself. Let us take the example of the classic rural development project, which is still relatively prevalent (though it does not enjoy the same hegemony as before and has undergone certain transformations), and which derives its coherence from a production model arising from agronomy research, founded on clearly stated technical rationality.[13] In this perspective, which draws its inspiration from the 'green revolution' in India and from European experiences, it is a matter of importing a model of intensive production into the African peasantry, which also implies, over and beyond popularization and training, an in-depth transformation of peasant 'technical culture'. We could note, for example, the criteria that presided over the elaboration of the model and which regulate research in tropical agronomy: the creation of species and techniques that allow a high yield per hectare, adapted to average climatic conditions. These techniques are supposedly easily adoptable, and classified as 'simple', in terms of the technical culture of the Western peasantry, taken as the reference.

However, this technical rationality is confronted, within the developmentalist configuration itself, and therefore prior to any kind of interaction with the local populations, with other registers of coherence.

In fact, the technical model derived from agronomic research invariably promotes production goals intimately connected with the strategic considerations of national policies (balance of payments, structural adjustment, etc) which determine the general orientation that projects adopt. Thus technical coherence is overshadowed, if only nominally, by another level of coherence – economic policy or national planning – which has no direct relation with agronomy and its techniques. Notwithstanding, this declared coherence is sometimes in contradiction with the 'real' modes of functioning of public administration. As a result, this type of project is almost always short of at least some of the means required for action (see the comments on context on the previous page). In some cases, the problem concerns a lack of control over commercialization, in others it concerns the disastrous situation of the co-operatives in question and, everywhere there is the problem of corruption. These are a few examples that illustrate the extent to which the logics of action of certain mechanisms of the state apparatus or of the national economy, which totally escape the project's control, are liable to jeopardize its policy.

A third level of coherence, also independent of the two mentioned above, concerns the role of financiers and donors. Their influence is manifested indirectly, in the choice of technical agricultural models, in the national economic policy and the projects it approves. Moreover, in the context of the rapid decline of local administrations, financiers and donors claim an increased right to examine the exactitude in finances and accountancy on which, to a great extent, their norms of evaluation are based.

The structure of the project proper – that is, the project as an institution, apparatus, organization – constitutes the final level of coherence, which is also independent. It is a well-known fact that a project has its 'organizational logics', its specific constraints, its dysfunctions, its 'informal economy', which are quite different from the official flowchart. The hierarchical ladder, the collection and flow of information, the capacity of adaptation and self-correction are therefore parameters of primary importance. At this level, the 'professional culture' of development agents and the norms that regulate their training and career must be established as objects of anthropological investigation (see Koné, 1994). In more general terms, it is the project as an organization or as a system of interaction between employees and agents that inevitably leads to various types of sidetracking of the project as it exists 'on paper'. It will suffice to raise the example of the serious discrepancy that exists between the idea of a project, which is supposed to be temporary and whose intention is to provide the populations it assists with the means of carrying on on their own and freeing themselves from the project as soon as possible, and the project as an organization and as a system of resources whose agents intend, on the contrary, to prolong its existence as far as possible (see Berche, 1998; Koné, 1994).

In other words, all development projects – projects aimed at health, institutional or rural development, or otherwise – are connected, over and beyond the single level of coherence they are obliged to exhibit (the project 'on paper'), to several partially contradictory levels of compatibility:

(a) the internal coherence of the technical model

(b) the compatibility of the project with the national economic policy

(c) the conformity of the project with donors' norms

(d) the internal dynamic of the project itself.[14]

Thus, even if the problem of its contacts with the population is put aside, a project is still a partially incoherent entity, since it comprises various types of coherence. The fine coherent, technical and argumentative rationality around which projects are generally elaborated comes up against serious difficulties even before the project work begins.

Peasant reactions
The way in which the various categories of producers react obviously enhances the 'dismembering' of a project. This is an example of the 'sidetracking' mentioned above: it is the inevitable outcome of contact with reality. The question is whether or not everyday sidetracking can help us to learn a few lessons, even if they only illustrate the fact that 'developers' and 'developees', of necessity, do not have the same logics.[15] We could make a test based on two examples.

1. Dominant agronomic logics (those of research institutes, for instance) pay only scant or incomplete attention, in the process of research, to the range of 'non-technical' systems of constraint to which producers are exposed. The reactions of peasants are often linked to economic rationalities properly speaking, which integrate data on the economic and ecological environment (which is not the case with 'pure' agronomic researchers in laboratories): producers tend to take as the point of reference a year of insufficient rainfall rather than a year of average rainfall; to minimize on inputs if cash is limited; to avoid farming methods that rely on a workforce that is unavailable at a time when numerous tasks need to be performed; to preserve or gain access to land and to increase patrimonial land. Such preferences are in keeping with an economic logic familiar to peasants around the world.

2. The point of view of national planners and economists, whose problem is to increase the gross national product (GNP), to reduce reliance on foreign aid, to increase the inflow of foreign exchange, to obtains loans from the World Bank (depending on the case in point, on the region, on the historical period), is obviously different from the point of view of the head of a peasant household (or that of his junior brother or of his wife) whose problem is to find means of subsistence and reproduction (and of extension, wherever possible …). The criteria on which peasants and experts base their professional activity and the risks they respectively face are completely different: when a project fails, the professional in charge usually suffers no professional consequences, but the peasant gambles his security on each harvest.

As concerns rural development in general, the way peasants react to the proposals a project puts forward is usually, despite the variety of local situations, linked to a limited number of constraints. The following logics or strategies, more or less updated depending on the context, local situation or social groups, are the most frequently encountered:

• Maximizing workforce productivity as opposed to productivity per hectare (the option prescribed by agronomic research).

• Attempts at capturing land or staking off lots of land when the process of improvement begins.

• Placing priority on extensive farming whenever possible (that is, when land is relatively available) to the detriment of the intensification preached by projects. This is linked essentially to the two preceding points.

- Minimizing climatic risks. Hence frequent mistrust of selected seeds, which perform better in average years, but are more fragile in bad years.

- Minimizing of risks due to the dysfunctioning of official circuits of maintenance, of commercialization, and of provision of inputs. Hence the recourse to 'traditional' or 'informal' networks (local merchants and local artisans …).

- Annual revision of the choice of crops, and, in particular, of the ratio of subsistence crops to cash crops. This is not only a strategy of self-reliance, but also concerns the comparative profitability of both types of crops as speculative investments (food crops being cultivated also for profit).

- Control of the recruitment of the labour force (kinship or 'ethnic' network strategies).

- Modes of accumulation and use of an eventual surplus based on norms of ostentation and patron–client strategies.

- Use of non-agricultural resources (migration …).

- Making investments outside agriculture (schooling of children …).

- Personal appropriation of collective resources.

- Using credits obtained for ends other than those declared officially.

This list is not exhaustive. But the problem of enumeration might be simplified if an attempt is made to define 'types' of behaviour, or a few major alternatives. We might note, for example, that contemporary African peasants are faced with a series of more or less conflicting alternatives: safety versus risk; intensification versus extensive farming; agro-pastoral production versus non-agricultural resources; consolidating inheritance versus investment; redistribution (patron–client investment) versus savings (productive investment). However, the decisions peasants make at each of these levels appear to be connected essentially to context-related variables, and not to standard solutions or to the solutions that technical services and development operators usually prescribe. We could attempt to identify a number of these context-related variables: the gravity of the ecological crisis, the degree of reliability of circuits of civil service corruption, the degree of reliability of circuits of commercialization, the availability of opportunities outside agriculture, the amount of tension surrounding issues related to land, etc.

Other typologies could be used – for instance that of Yung and Zaslavsky (1992), mentioned above, who propose a more dynamic method of distinguishing between 'offensive strategies' and 'defensive strategies', in an attempt at summarizing peasant reactions, based on a corpus of Sahelian development projects.

As we will recall, the recurrence of similar behaviour patterns, encountered in a variety of situations, is by no means the result of discussion between the people involved. Peasant logics are expressed through fragmented, individual economic behaviour. They do not constitute a 'collective' (that is, deliberate, concerted) reaction of the peasantry in question (which is not a collective agent and does not constitute a relevant level of decision-making), but rather an aggregate or composite effect (the same causes – a given social logic – are likely to produce the same effects, at the level of a given set of relevant actors: women, seniors, juniors, leasers, etc.). Convergent, atomized actor behaviour should not be seen as the doing of a collective actor; hence our reference to actors' logics. The problem could be shifted to another level of abstraction at which recurrent behaviour empirically observed could be defined as the working out of a number of basic principles. These go beyond the framework of rural development,

since they appear to regulate various behaviour patterns in other domains.

Two principles

Two very general principles seem to be deducible from the infinite variety of concrete behaviour displayed by populations in the face of various types of development operations: the principle of selection and the principle of sidetracking.

The principle of selection

Technical messages, development projects and interventions are all 'packages' or sets of co-ordinated measures which claim to be coherent. The package proposed is never 'completely' adopted by the 'target' population: it is always picked apart, to a greater or lesser degree, by the selections that 'target' populations make among the elements proposed.

In this game the rule is neither 'take all' nor 'leave all'. The usual process is one of selective adoption. Certain themes 'work' while others do not. Thus the technical coherence presented by an agronomic project in the form of 'packages of techniques' is systematically disarticulated. This results in a number of 'perverse effects', which annul the effectiveness of the improvements proposed and might even induce outright negative results (see, for example, Yung, 1985). As for so-called 'integrated' development operations, which combine technical packages with other elements (training, management, literacy programmes, women's groups etc.) with a view to achieving 'horizontal coherence', these are even more subject to selective adoption. This is all the more paradoxical considering their ideology (liable to be interpreted as a 'totalitarian' and ineffective vision of development) which advocates complementarity between modes of intervention as a necessary requirement.

This principle also applies in the field of public health: doctors in the North will not be surprised by selective strategies as they are well aware that their patients never observe their prescriptions rigorously, that they make their own selections (of drugs or dosages) in keeping with the dominant family traditions, sub-cultures and networks to which they are affiliated, in consequence of factors such as finances or the pace at which they live, etc.

The principle of sidetracking

The reasons that motivate the adoption of a given development measure by potential users is generally at odds with the reasons cited by the experts who propose them. In other words, peasants exploit the opportunities at their disposal in keeping with their own particular objectives.

Credits granted by a development project for the acquisition of oxen and the promotion of animal traction are diverted to produce milk or fatten cattle; a vegetable farming co-operative proposed by an NGO with a view to ensuring self-sufficiency uses the proceeds to buy a minibus to conduct regular tourist visits to the village; the managers of a village pharmacy distribute drugs primarily to acquaintances, parents, close relatives and important men: there are endless examples of sidetracking.

Selective adoption and sidetracking can both be considered as ways in which a target group 'appropriates' a project. The paradox is that this appropriation, which in theory is the end sought by development operations, assumes shapes that often run counter to the project's objectives and methods.

These two very general principles aside, one can attempt to draw out some more specific logics encountered in a variety of practical situations. I will mention only three of these. There are many others.

Three logics, among many others

Seeking safety

Minimizing risk is a fundamental peasant strategy. One example is the resistance to high-yield seeds distributed by agricultural services (these thrive under average rainfall conditions, but are very vulnerable when rainfall is insufficient). Another example is the refusal to introduce new crops which might not sell well, or the choice of increasing a herd rather than selling meat on the market …

'Tried and proven methods' – the way local peasants practice agriculture is usually the result of a long history of adaptation to a given environment, an adaptation that has proven its worth in the long run[16] – are, logically, preferred to taking risks. And the proposals made by development agents usually entail a high degree of risk-taking on the part of peasants (risks which in no wise affect the development agents themselves – they have their salaries), and the experience of recent decades has too often confirmed the dangers involved.[17]

One could go even further and estimate that routine behaviour generally ensures safety for the peasantry (given the dominant mode of production based on the use of kin as the labour force and on a combination of self-sufficiency and commodity exchange) and for the development agents (who generally belong to bureaucratic organizations) who are not very flexible, as a rule, and who often propose innovations – to other people – in a very routine manner!

So far as the problems related to health are concerned, the situation is even more complex, despite the fact that, in the final analysis, the problems remain the same: peasant experiences confirm the fact that 'traditional' therapeutic procedures are uncertain and precarious, significantly more so than agricultural practices. Despite the fact that their effectiveness is not at all guaranteed, they also function as systems of meaning (modes of interpreting illness), which, for their part, have stood the test of time, in the sense that they allow those who use them to account for forms of suffering, for the vicissitudes of the individual condition, for possible therapeutic failures. In other words, popular health conceptions serve both in the quest for therapeutic methods considered locally to be 'effective' (seen from a strictly pragmatic angle) and in the construction of arguments that explain failure or success (seen from an essentially semiological point of view). This helps us to understand the paradoxical situation that Western medicine faces in rural Africa: in great demand as a therapeutic course (which is, nonetheless, often beyond the means of rural populations), it has not yet become an alternative to 'traditional' meaning systems (which partially belong to the register of 'magico-religious' beliefs, a universe peopled with spirits and sorcerers, but which also integrate the more prosaic universe of naming: see Olivier de Sardan, 1994). Time and again, rural populations have witnessed the relatively higher therapeutic effectiveness of Western medicine (even though, of course, it is not without uncertainties or risks). It also benefits from the prestige of Western knowledge and techniques. But it is not adopted as a credible system of interpretation, at least not in the popular classes, and it does not take the place of the dominant modes of interpretation of local cultures (despite the fact that these do evolve, but at their own pace). This is not specific to Africa: in Western countries as well, the awareness and widespread use of experimental medicine has not been enough to ensure the construction of a coherent system of meaning, and 'magico-religious' attitudes, in the broad sense of the term, to

medical practices – official or otherwise – are still common: we are well aware of the role 'rumour' plays in touting the effectiveness of a given therapy or of a particular practitioner.

In the final analysis, it would appear that the superposition of 'magico-religious' meaning systems and the strong demand for Western medicine observed in Africa, far from being a sign of cultural 'backwardness' or of 'ignorance', corresponds to a perfectly rational pursuit of security: it is a matter of combining the empirical search for therapeutic security all round (in Western and in more or less 'traditional' local practices) with the need for symbolic security (essentially guaranteed by the meaning systems associated with local therapeutic practices).

Aid seeking

The notion of self-sufficiency, or of 'self-reliance' (relying on one's own resources) has often been a key factor of recent development projects (we may observe, in passing, that such a notion is not as novel as it appears: certain local economic programmes dating back to the beginning of the colonial era were based on this principle, though couched in other terms[18]). The assumption is made, *a priori*, that the populations share this point of view and that it coincides with their best interests (but this is merely an ideological or moral point of view, which is praiseworthy in itself, but which cannot be attributed to or imposed on other people with impunity).

In fact, the opposite strategy, which we could qualify as aid seeking, since it aims at making the most of external aid, is extremely prevalent. There is nothing surprising about people attempting to gain as much as possible from the financial and material benefits that a project provides, while giving as little as possible in return. The development agent does exactly the same thing when he lays personal claim to the bike provided by the project that employs him. The expert with his *per diem*, the foreign technical assistant with his financial perks, act in the same way. And what can we say about our own case? As specialists in sociological research don't we spend our time searching around for external subventions?

It could, of course, be argued that these examples do not all fit in the same category. For some people (experts, foreign technical assistants, researchers), seeking subventions or obtaining *per diems* are legitimate procedures, in keeping with the rules of the game (regardless of what we might think about the morality of the game in question). One could say that others (peasants, project agents), do not respect the rules; their practices are therefore illegitimate. This objection needs to be taken into account: it is true that the peasants give their official consent to reimburse the loans they contract and that project agents know that they ought to distinguish between material belonging to the project and their personal belongings. The problem is that in the case in point the game is being played according to two sets of rules: legitimate rules, laid down by institutions (in this case development institutions); and pragmatic rules, which dictate the way in which actors behave. Legitimate and illegitimate rules sometimes coincide, as in the case of researchers and foreign technical assistants. Sometimes they don't, as in the case of peasants and project agents who play the game according to pragmatic rules, at variance with those they apparently accepted, but which they consider to be illegitimate and imposed from the outside. Thus, anthropology of social change and development, which takes into account practices as well as legitimacy, ends up classifying in the same category (the principle of aid seeking) behaviour patterns related to similar practices, which nonetheless have varying degrees of legitimacy, when compared to official rules.[19]

The health agent is not unfamiliar with aid-seeking strategies: the demands made on him or her usually translate as 'take care of me', rather than 'help me to take care of myself' … The attempts made to help rural populations to become 'responsible' in the face of health problems, to ensure 'sanitary self-reliance', as it were, at the village level, do not necessarily coincide with what the people concerned really want, that is – utterly understandably – to get 'help'. The paradox here is that the Western health system was essentially constructed, for its part, on a socialization of risks which ultimately resulted in a 'welfarism', at the other extreme from the 'responsibilization' strategy mentioned above. It therefore appears paradoxical that such a strategy is promoted as appropriate for those, in Africa, who are deprived of any form of social security whatsoever (this being reserved for a minority of urban wage earners).

Monopolizing aid opportunities

Development operations are sometimes 'appropriated' in ways their directors do not condone: specific groups within the 'target' population use development aid for their own ends (they appropriate it), in order to increase their privileges or simply to obtain privilege. This means that development actions can be seen as putting facilities, advantages and opportunities at the disposal of a population divided into groups, factions and networks. Development aid is also a stake in face of which certain persons or certain groups are better prepared or better armed than others when it comes to taking advantage.

[…]

Strategic logics and notional logics

[…]

Three conclusions can be deduced from the above reflections.

1. Resistance to an innovation has its motivations and its coherence, whether strategic or notional; this does not amount to mythologizing popular behaviour or to claiming that such kinds of 'resistance' are always inevitable or that they invariably produce positive effects. Not at all. What it implies is that they are 'normal', that is to say that they are explainable, understandable. It is only by explaining them 'from the inside' (from the users' perspective) that we can acquire the means of overcoming 'resistance' if necessary. A good comprehension-explanation 'from the inside' is the kind that allows us to say: 'In their position, I myself would act in the same way, and here's why!' Mastering this type of comprehension–explanation should figure among the central objectives of development institutions. However, comprehensions-explanations do not arise spontaneously. If this were the case, they would become mere stereotypes. They have to be sought out through enquiry, through appropriate enquiry: in other words, through field enquiry.

2. A successful (adopted) innovation is the product of 'invisible bargaining' and of a compromise between various groups of development actors and various groups of social actors. It does not imply that the technico-scientific and economic logics of its conceptors have prevailed.

3. Projects are subject to 'sidetracking'. What I mean by this is that there is a difference between what is expected and what really happens. Sidetracking is a sign that the actors involved have 'appropriated' the development project.

Notes

1. This chapter, written in 2001, does not appear in the French original version. My thanks to T. Bierschenk, G. Blundo, J.-P. Chauveau, P. Geschiere, J. Gould, J.P. Jacob, Y. Jaffré, P. Lavigne Delville, C. Lund, P.Y. Le Meur, E. Paquot, and M. Tidjani Alou for their remarks and suggestions on different chapters of this book. I would like to acknowledge in particular the close collaboration that I had for years on these topics with Thomas Bierschenk and Giorgio Blundo, and on the fact that my analyses in this book have been helped and supported by theirs.
2. This is why French-speakers need to publish in English, and why a book like Colin and Crawford's (2000), which provides in English a sample of the work done in French on the African peasantry, is interesting.
3. There are rare exceptions, e.g. Jacob, 1989, 2000, Jacob and Blundo, 1997.
4. For an explanation of this neo-Weberian epistemology, see Passeron, 1991. Deconstructionist development anthropologists, in a Manichaean view of the social sciences, systematically associate their own analyses with an alternative epistemology, and other people's analyses with a positivist epistemology (see Escobar, 1997, who considers anthropologists who do not make a radical critique of development, in other words who are 'associated with development', as following a 'realistic epistemology'). To the contrary, I believe that the (necessary and established) outmoding of yesterday's positivism does not mean that there is no means of escaping postmodern ideologies. Though its days of glory are over, post-modernism still exerts a strong influence on the literature of anthropology of development.
5. This term seems more neutral and more descriptive than the term 'field' (champs), which is preferred by authors like Lavigne Delville (2000), in reference to Bourdieu, and which implies an abstract and large system of power struggles and statutory positions. The term 'arena', on the contrary, evokes concrete interactions.
6. My use of this expression is meant to underline the convergence between anthropology and a certain type of sociology inherited from the Chicago School, often described as 'qualitative'.
7. In fact, this work concerns 'Africa and beyond', to borrow a phrase from the subtitle of the book edited by Fardon, van Binsbergen and van Dijk (1999): in Africa, the overriding importance and daily presence of development aid attain their peak, but the phenomena observed there also exist on other continents, albeit in different forms.
8. In his recent work (1998) on the process of monitoring, Mosse develops the same idea: that follow-up-evaluation and feedback procedures are perhaps the best practical contributions anthropology can make to development action.
9. Considering that anthropology of development is capable of renewing classic anthropology (see Bennett and Bowen, 1988: ix), I agree with Bates (1988: 82–83) who holds that anthropology of development makes four major contributions to academic anthropology: (a) it studies institutions and actors in real-life settings; (b) it does away with the vision of 'self-contained, autonomous, bonded communities'; (c) it opens the way for new themes of enquiry, including civil servants, elites, and administrators; (d) it provides linkages with other disciplines.
10. The chapters that comprise it were written between 1985 and 1993.
11. This is one of the reasons, among others, which explains the impasse in the dialogue between Bourdieu's sociology on one hand and the sociology of organizations on the other: both make abundant reference to logics and strategies, but only 'in general'. Bourdieu, for instance, never defines what he means by 'logic' or 'strategy': in fact, in his case, both terms are always combined, directly or indirectly, with the concept of 'habitus', which, by emphasizing the 'process of conditioning' (see Bourdieu, 1992: 105), refutes the various theories of rational choice or 'methodological rationalism' (Friedberg, 1993: 54). Hence, on one hand we have a sociology which insists on the immanent, unconscious, incorporated, inculcated, character of pragmatic logics, and on the other, a sociology which insists on the deliberate, explicit, calculated aspect of logics of action. It is not my intention to engage in this debate: 'logics' will simply mean lines of coherence which the observer can deduce based on empirical observation of sets and of specific differential practices, without casting judgement on any particular sociological theory of the subject, of rationality, or of 'habitus'.

[12] See the example provided by Crehan and von Oppen (1988: 118–22).

[13] For a general critical analysis of this dominant model, see, among others, Richards, 1985. For critical field analyses, carried out on specific cases in a perspective identical to the one we are using, see Yung, 1985; Pontié and Ruf, 1985. This model has also come in for criticism from agronomic research, and numerous attempts have been made to elaborate alternative research strategies connected with agro-pastoral development (see farming system research, development research) which make the most of peasant dynamics or place the priority on local varieties.

[14] Other considerations, connected to more specifically political stakes and which are generally unspoken truths, also come into play. One of the reasons that explain why Niger authorities finally approved the 'Maradi project' after a long-standing disagreement with the World Bank, concerning the contents of the project, has to do with the military putsch and the new ruler it brought into power: 'they proved much more amenable to the World Bank's approach … especially since they were turning away from a development strategy focused on rural facilitation, which the new masters of the country viewed with suspicion because of its "political" connotations' (Raynaut, 1989: 31).

[15] Sautter (1978: 242) had already made reference to the 'deviations' of 'programmed actions' in rural tropical Africa, which he saw as the result of the difference between the respective logics of suppliers of infrastructure – those of modern Western production-oriented agriculture – and of peasant users.

[16] Hence the problems that arise when, as often occurs in Africa nowadays, a brutal (demographic and/or ecological) imbalance is provoked, which annuls the effect of 'traditional' solutions adapted to the milieu, such as cultivation on burnt ground or extensive rainfall cropping (see Raynaut, 1986, 1989).

[17] The highlighting of safety logics is not a recent phenomenon. Scott's work *The Moral Economy of the Peasant* (1976) emphasized the 'safety first principle'. We might even go as far back as 1924, and refer to Chayanov as the original source (see Chayanov, 1966). The theme of the risk factor has recently been rediscovered as an important data entry in empirical pluri-disciplinary analyses (Eldin and Milleville, 1989). However, the limitation of risk factors, common to all peasant practices, should not be equated with a global refusal of all types of risk taking.

[18] See Chauveau 1992, 1994.

[19] Kintz (1987) proposes a beautiful empirical demonstration of the difference between official and pragmatic norms. It is true that she does not deal with questions of development, since she describes how adultery (reproved by official norms), is practised in the 'bush' Fulani milieu (here as elsewhere, and perhaps a bit more than elsewhere) while respecting certain pragmatic norms of decency.

References

Bates, R. 1988. 'Anthropology and Development: A Note on the Structure of the Field', in Bennett and Bowen (eds).

Bennett, J. and Bowen, J., eds. 1988, *Production and Autonomy: Anthropological Studies and Critiques of Development*. Lanham MD: Society for Economic Anthropology.

Berche, T. 1998. *Anthropologie et santé publique en pays dogon*. Paris: Karthala.

Boiral, P, Lantéri, J.F. and Olivier de Sardan, J.P. eds. 1985. *Paysans, experts et chercheurs en Afrique noire*. Sciences sociales et développement rural. Paris: Karthala.

Bourdieu, P. (with Wacquant, L.). 1992. *Réponses*. Paris: Seuil.

Chauveau, J.P. 1992. 'Du populisme bureaucratique dans l'histoire institutionnelle du développement rural en Afrique de l'Ouest', *Bulletin de l'APAD*, 4: 23–32.

— 1994. 'Participation paysanne et populisme bureaucratique. Essai d'histoire et de sociologie de la culture du développement', in J.P. Jacob and P. Lavigne Delville (eds) *Les associations paysannes en Afrique*. Paris: APAD-Karthala-IUED.

Chayanov, A. V. 1966. *The Theory of Peasant Economy*. Homewood: Irwin (1st edn 1924).

Colin, J.P. and Crawford, E., eds. 2000. *Research on Agricultural Systems: Accomplishments, Perspectives and Issues*. New York: Nova Science Publishers.

Crehan, K. and von Oppen, A. 1988. 'Understandings of "Development": An Arena of Struggle. The story of a Development Project in Zambia', *Sociologia Ruralis*, 28 (2–3): 113–45.

Daane, J. and Mongbo, R.1991. 'Peasant Influence on Development Projects in Bénin: A Critical Analysis', *Genève-Afrique*, 29 (2): 49–76.

Eldin, M. and Milleville, P., eds. 1989. *Le risque en agriculture*. Paris: ORSTOM.

Escobar, A. 1997. 'Anthropologie et développement', *Revue Internationale des Sciences Sociales*, 154: 539–59.

Fardon, R., van Binsbergen, W. and van Dijk, R., eds. 1999. *Modernity on a Shoestring: Dimensions of Globalization, Consumption and Development in Africa and Beyond*. London: EIDOS.

Friedberg, E. 1993. *Le pouvoir et la règle. Dynamique de l'action organisée*. Paris: Seuil.

Gentil, D. and Dufumier, M. 1984. 'Le suivi évaluation dans les projets de développement rural. Orientations méthodologiques', AMIRA, working paper no. 44 (mimeo).

Jacob, J.P. 1989. *Bibliographie sélective et commentée d'anthropologie du développement*. Geneva:IUED.

Jacob, J.P., ed. 2000. *Sciences sociales et coopération en Afrique: les rendez-vous manqués*, Geneva: Nouveaux Cahiers de l'IUED (10).

Jacob, J.P. and Blundo, G.1997. *Socio-anthropologie de la décentralisation en milieu rural africain*. Bibliographie sélective et commentée. Geneva: IUED.

Kintz, D. 1987. 'De l'art peul de l'adultère', *Bulletin de l'AFA*, 29–30: 119–43.

Koné, M. 1994. 'Être encadreur agricole en Côte d'Ivoire: principes et pratiques (le cas de Sakassou)', PhD thesis, École des Hautes Études en Sciences Sociales, Marseille.

Lavigne Delville, P. 2000. 'Impasses cognitives et expertises en sciences sociales. Réflexions à propos du développement rural en Afrique', in Jacob (ed).

Mosse, D. 1998. 'Process-oriented Approaches to Development Practice and Social Research', in D. Mosse, J. Farrington, and A. Rew (eds), *Development as Process: Working with Complexity*. London: Routledge/Overseas Development Institute.

Olivier de Sardan, J. P. 1994, 'La Logique de la nomination. Le representations fluides et prosaïques de deux maladies au Niger', *Sciences sociales et Santé*, 12 (3): 15–45.

Passeron, J.C. 1991. *Le raisonnement sociologique. L'espace non-poppérien du raisonnement naturel*. Paris: Nathan.

Pontié, G. and Ruf, T. 1985. 'L'opération de rénovation de la caféière et de la cacaoyère togolaises', in Boiral, Lantéri and Olivier de Sardan (eds).

Raynaut, C. 1986. 'Compte-rendu de "Seeds of famine" (Franke and Chasin, eds)', *Africa*, 56 (1): 105–11.

— 1989. 'L'opération de développement et les logiques du changement: la nécessité d'une approche holistique. L'exemple d'un cas nigérien', *Genève Afrique*, 27 (2): 8–38.

Richards, P. 1985. *Indigenous Agricultural Revolution*. London: Hutchinson.

Sautter, G., 1978, 'Dirigisme opérationnel et stratégie paysanne, ou l'aménageur aménagé', *L'Espace Géographique*, 4: 223–43.

Scott, J. 1976. *The Moral Economy of the Peasant: Rebellion and Subsistence in Southeast Asia*. New Haven, CT and London: Yale University Press.

Tidjani Alou, M. 1994. 'Les projets de développement sanitaire face à l'administration publique au Niger', *Santé Publique*, 4.

Yung, J.M., 1985, 'Evaluation de la filière arachide au Sénégal', in Boiral, Lantéri and Olivier de Sardan (eds).

Yung, J.M. and Zaslavsky, J. 1992. *Pour une prise en compte des stratégies des producteurs*. Montpellier: Cirad.

MARGARET NIGER-THOMAS
Excerpts from *'Buying Futures'*
The Upsurge of Female Entrepreneurship Crossing the Formal/Informal Divide in Southwest Cameroon

Reference
Ph.D. thesis, University of Leiden, 2000

Margaret Niger-Thomas analyses the striking resourcefulness of women in Southwest Cameroon in the face of increasing economic hardships resulting from the economic crisis and the application of Structural Adjustment Programmes. As in other parts of Africa, it is especially women, deploying a wide array of new forms of entrepreneurship, who are able to cushion at least to some extent the economic setbacks. Niger-Thomas started her research by focusing on women who were holding formal jobs (civil servants) but were increasingly involved in informal practices, varying from trade to private practice by nurses or teachers. However, in the course of her research she came to realize that there were also striking changes going on within the 'informal sector' itself, shifting its borders with the 'formal' economy. Not only were women traders involved in all sorts of activities – smuggling, new forms of trade – there was also a determined effort by these women to acquire some sort of formal recognition of their activities. This was facilitated be a series of new laws. Such formal recognition stimulated further 'informal' activities.

Chapter 2 of her study compares the changing balance between 'formal' and 'informal' activities by women in two towns in Southwest Cameroon (the Anglophone part of the country): Limbe and Mamfe. Limbe, a medium-sized town, is located on the coast. It is a minor port but also a centre for the anglophone part of Cameroon, with several schools and administrative institutions. Mamfe, much smaller and 250 kms. into the interior in a densely forested region, is situated on the Cross river, close to the Nigerian border which, especially recently, made it into a hub for cross-border trade. A subsequent chapter of Niger-Thomas' study describes how local women turn – with some success – to smuggling in order to cope with the onslaught of Structural Adjustment.
[Introductory Note by Editors]

Teachers' straddling strategies (pp. 40–51)

On Friday 9 February 1996 at about 11 am, my research assistant and I visited group one in the government primary school in Limbe. Preparations for the Youth Day celebrations were underway. Teachers as well as pupils seemed to be quite relaxed as no formal classes were being held. All the teachers were present at school, four male and eleven female teachers, including the headmistress. They were on the field with the pupils practising some activities for the Youth Day competitions. These included a march past, traditional dances, singing, etc. Meanwhile the headmistress of the school was sitting in one of the classrooms conversing with the other female teachers.

During this first contact, our aim was to carry out brief interviews with the teachers, especially the females either in groups or as individuals, and to appreciate the extent of their involvement in informal-sector activities. The headmistress and her teachers were quite willing to talk about their business activities outside of formal teaching. Their openness was surprising. About five years ago, it was still not common in Cameroon for formal-sector employees to expose their private activities. In the past, very few teachers or other professional employees would even have bothered to carry out income-generating activities beyond their normal public-service jobs.

None of these women described what they were doing as 'informal' but they gave various interpretations to such sideline activities. Phrases such as 'making ends meet', 'survival measures', 'self-help programme', and 'strategies to make up for the good old days', were commonly used. It was clear that each one of them was involved in one kind of activity or the other. 'Almost every woman now spends the greater part of her time thinking of all possible ways to make family ends meet,' commented one of them. Another explained: 'We teachers do what we call 'private jobs' (PJ) alongside other commercial activities so long as it can fetch an income'. This group of teachers explained that PJs was the name given to private classes organized by both male and female teachers in their homes, in the homes of pupils and students or on school premises in order to augment salaries earned from formal-sector jobs.

The female teachers stressed that even though men and women were both searching for a means of survival amidst salary cuts and economic hardship, the women have the greater responsibility to cater for their families. Some of the comments made by these female teachers help to illustrate the present trend in Cameroonian society:

> Today, women are the bread-winners not only where there are no men, but also in marital homes. Even though men still cling to the fact that they are the head, the tails are now taking over the responsibilities of the head. In my house, I spend more money than my husband, and my little business feeds everybody. My husband makes little or no contribution to the needs of the family. (E.S., aged 43, married, 1996)

Before the former speaker had finished expressing herself, two teachers simultaneously added: 'Women are now doing the thinking while men are doing the drinking and idling'.

This first contact with primary school teachers in Limbe set the pace for discussions with one of the main categories of informants, namely teachers, and led me to explore the various strategies they use in the informal sector to augment monthly salaries earned from public-service jobs.

The concept of private jobs (PJs)
Teachers involved in organizing private classes term their activity PJ, (Private Job), which conforms with the earlier definition of the informal sector. Even though skills and sometimes facilities from formal jobs are used by teachers in their PJs, these activities remain private and personal. In the sample of teachers interviewed, 67 out of 75 were involved in sideline activities, PJs included. PJs seemed to be the most vulnerable activity. Teachers had to negotiate either with parents, with pupils and students as a body, or with the Parent Teachers Association (PTA) to get children to attend private classes. Moreover, without the consent of parents, who are required to pay for services rendered to their children, PJs are not profitable. While some parents encourage their children to attend private classes to improve their academic progress, others saw PJs as a means for teachers to exploit parents and compensate for earlier salary cuts.

To a large extent, teachers are expected to work within the school timetable instituted by the Ministry of National Education and to impart as much knowledge as possible to pupils and students. The increasing number of PJs is partly attributed to the lack of monetary incentives for teachers. With a two-third cut in salaries, some teachers engage in PJs to make up what they believe is a state responsibility. Two types of PJs were identified in Limbe and Mamfe.

Firstly, there is the situation whereby individual teachers and parents or groups of parents living in the same neighbourhood jointly agree to organize private classes for their children in a parent's home or sometimes in the teacher's house. Such classes may be limited to children of a particular household or may include children from other households. In Limbe, private tuition fees per month varied from 1,000 F CFA to 5,000 F CFA per child. Classes would often be held three or four times a week depending on the child's level and the subjects involved. As one of the teachers noted:

> I have been carrying out PJs here in Limbe for the past four years. This year I have 8 pupils paying 2,500 F CFA each, and every month I am able to make an extra income of 20,000 F CFA This enables me to meet at least breakfast and taxi money. (B.S., aged 38, single, 1996)

A second type of PJ common to the Limbe area and collectively organized by secondary school teachers is what could be described as formal private evening and holiday classes. They are formal in the sense that the organisers obtain authorisation from the Minister of National Education. Thus, teachers who are ordinarily official state employees are able to give remedial private lessons (viewed by many as an informal job) with state authorisation. Teaching is done outside formal working hours and, in particular, during the long rainy-season vacation. The majority of these private evening classes make use of government infrastructure through arrangements with local school authorities and parent teacher associations.

Sale of polycops

As mentioned earlier, PJs are carried out by a limited number of teachers, as teachers carrying out informal-sector activities are involved in the marketing of diverse products, including commercial lecture notes or what are commonly called *polycops*.

The term *polycop* is derived from the word poly-copies.[1] These are teaching aids and complement prescribed textbooks in secondary and high schools. Without purporting to substitute the official textbook, polycops are lecture notes organized in a simplified and more systematic form and adapted to students' needs. The difference is that polycops are sold to students. While PJs are carried out by teachers in both primary and secondary schools, the production and sale of *polycops* are limited to secondary and high school teachers.

Although the Ministry of National Education does not officially approve the use of *polycops*, it has so far done nothing to discourage their production or use. Teachers are often cautioned not to force students to purchase them. Even though they may not openly compel students to buy these documents, teachers indirectly use various co-ercive strategies to encourage students to buy them. Many teachers constantly refer to their polycop during their lectures and it becomes a *de facto* textbook which students feel obliged to buy. Given such strategies, coupled with the lack of available finances to purchase prescribed textbooks, which have become very expensive, students tend to take advantage of *polycops* in those subjects where they are available.

Polycops are sold not only to students but also to other teachers and educationalists who might find such documents relevant. Marking centres where teachers congregate at the end of every academic year to correct the General Certificate of Education examinations have become a hypermarket for such lucrative business. Pedagogical meet-ings facilitate the marketing of *polycops* and private arrangements are also made with local booksellers and even recognized book shops for such sales. Another method of disposing of these lecture notes is by making private arrangements with colleagues from other schools who agree to sell them to their students and who receive commission on each copy sold.

Petty trading

One of the activities that characterizes the informal sector in Came-roon and elsewhere is petty trading and includes the sale of a variety of items notably assorted foods and other provisions. Petty trading is commonly carried out in front of certain homes, in the market, along the roadside in little kiosks and in open spaces. Although men do try their hand at it, it is mostly practised by women. One of the reasons given is that it does not require a very large start-up capital. Most women also find it convenient since household support can easily be used. Furthermore, business stocks and household stocks are easily merged. Unsold items can be consumed by the household.

The general observed trend is that poor women in both rural and urban areas are the main actors engaged in petty trading. However, recently, new entrepreneurs with a firm foothold in the formal sector have started entering the market. Our sample included eight teachers involved in petty trading. Some had trading stalls in front of their homes, in the market or along the roadside. While the old-timer entrepreneurs continue to trade in those items mentioned earlier, there is an added dimension to the activities of most newcomers carrying out petty trading. Household appliances such as refrigerators, deep freezers and grinding machines now have a dual function, serving both the household and the market. Items such as fresh fish, cold water, corn beer, *alaska*, fruit juice, etc. are preserved and sold within the area of residence, in market places and at formal work places. Ice boxes are used to carry fruit juice, yoghurt and *alaska* to sell at school. Advertisements such as 'BUY YOUR COLD WATER, FRUIT JUICE, *ALASKA* HERE' written on the walls of homes are a common sight in residential areas in Limbe. About seven years ago, this would have been very unusual. Then, few households would have thought of using the aforementioned electrical appliances for business purposes. To economise on electricity costs, heads of households turn the appliances off during certain hours of the day or night, which may jeopardise food safety. This, however, has never become a public issue.

Okrika business

The trade in second-hand goods (mostly clothing), popularly known as *okrika*, can be traced back to the late 1980s in the Mamfe area. Even though the economic crisis in Cameroon dates from 1986, the societal effects or what some women have described as 'the real crisis' began to be felt only in 1993 after salary cuts. The three female teachers who reported carrying out this trade in Mamfe said that they were not motivated by the crisis. They had started trading in 1991 taking advantage of their proximity to Nigeria. They were spurred on by what many women entrepreneurs at the time called 'big ventures', that is, the education of children abroad, building better houses, owning nice furniture, etc. (Niger-Thomas 1995).

Rotating savings and credit associations were already common at the time and they served as lucrative sources of business capital. Hence, these women took advantage of the situation to trade in second-hand goods as a form of investment. The demand for second-hand goods was increasing but still very few traders were involved in the trade and the female teachers involved enjoyed a virtual monopoly. During field research in 1996, I was determined to trace my earlier contacts in the *okrika* trade. Two of the three had been transferred, to Bafoussam and Limbe respectively. The only one left had given up cross-border trade and had taken up poultry farming.[2]

At the Treasury in Limbe, I met a teacher by the name of Lucy, who had traded in second-hand goods in Mamfe during the 1980s. Her husband had been transferred to Limbe and she had had to move with her family. When I met her, she was busy selling imported dresses and underwear in one of the offices and her first statement was: 'I have graduated from second-hand dresses in Mamfe and I am now dealing in new imported goods'. This statement brings to light the hierarchy of trade as perceived by female entrepreneurs. Trade activities can grow vertically or horizontally, even though most women prefer to diversify. Apart from this trade, Lucy also enjoyed formal contracts to supply blinds to government offices. Later on, during an in-depth interview, it became apparent that her informal-sector activities had greatly expanded in scope, forcing her to diversify, but she had not opened up a permanent store for retailing the imported goods. Her reasons were as follows:

> Having a permanent store means paying *patente*. This is what I have avoided over the years. After all, the government does not deserve the payment of taxes when they will not be used for the good of us all. What has happened with all the money that was paid over the years in the name of *patente*? See how much we suffer on the Mamfe-Kumba road. Why pay taxes when we can't even have good roads after 30 years of independence? Since I have left Mamfe, I am better off, at least I no longer push vehicles on the Mamfe road. (L.A., aged 44, married, 1996)

This statement raises a number of issues which will be discussed in greater detail. Suffice it to highlight the most obvious of such issues here, notably the fact that entrepreneurs have various ways of evading taxes. One common form of tax evasion is carrying out mobile sales, whereby the vendor moves from office to office. The problem of harassment is not solved by paying taxes. Those who are charged with enforcing tax regulations have little interest in collecting taxes for the state if they can receive bribes instead. Lucy was still maintaining her teaching job in the primary school but making three times her salary each month in her informal-sector business. However, she was reluctant to give me exact figures on her earnings.

Esther, Lucy's friend who kindled my interest in a formal/informal-sector study (Case 1) was still fully involved in this activity in Bafoussam, in Western Province. Bafoussam is one of the main centres for the distribution of second-hand goods apart from Douala. It must be noted that none of the teachers interviewed in Mamfe in 1996 were found engaged in the sale of second-hand goods, the reason being that crossing the Nigeria–Cameroon border had become very complicated especially for female entrepreneurs. Moreover, salary cuts had limited possibilities for raising capital. The devaluation of the CFA franc had also reduced what this money could buy in Nigeria.

In Limbe, developments did not reflect my earlier experiences in Mamfe. Contrary to expectations, interviews with teachers in Limbe in 1996 indicated that their participation in the sale of second-hand goods was relatively recent. About 80 per cent of those involved had been in the business for 2 to 4 years even though this activity had been an old line of trade for old-timer entrepreneurs in Limbe's main market.[3] Despite the number of entrepreneurs now involved in second-hand goods sales, the newcomers seem to be having their share of the trade. The case of the sale of second-hand goods in the government bilingual high school in Limbe gives a vivid picture of some of the strategies used by teachers to penetrate the informal sector.

Case 3: Sales of okrika at GBHS, Limbe. During an informal visit to the government bilingual high school in Limbe, we came across Caro who sold a variety of items but mostly *okrika*, especially women's clothes and shoes. It was break time (10.30–11 am) and most of the teachers were in the staff room. As we entered the staff room, we were struck by the items displayed on one of the large tables in the room. In one corner, another teacher was advertising Avon products from the United States including perfumes, cream sachets, deodorants, make-up, etc. I had a camera with me and thought I could take a picture of this interesting scene but my host felt it would be embarrassing for the teachers who did not know me. A number of teachers were bargaining and buying some of the items either paying on the spot (for those who had cash), or buying them on credit. After about 15 minutes, the school bell rang to mark the end of the break and the teachers went back to class. At this point, we had the opportunity to interview Caro about the nature of her business. She explained:

> I am an English language teacher in this school but today I have a free day so I decided to track down my colleagues and sell my goods to them. Now is 'payout' and civil servants are viable. Today one has to carry out self-help projects to make up for the chicken feed we now receive in the form of salaries. In the good old days, teachers of our grade, with a first degree, would not have dared to be identified with *okrika*, but today we have no choice. (C.M., aged 47, married, 1996)

Apart from second-hand goods, Caro once in a while receives and sells imported dresses and underwear from Europe. Even though she does not pay direct taxes to the government, she claimed to be paying indirectly by bribing policemen on the road and custom officials when she goes to clear her goods at the airport. She has a steady clientele, notably fellow staff members and colleagues in other nearby schools and in some offices. She limits her clientele to well-to-do women and makes sure that her goods are first grade *okrika*. She realises a profit of 30,000 FCFA to 50,000 FCFA per bale of *okrika*. This was her third year in the business which enables her to support a child at university and two children at high school, and supplement the household income generally.

Second-hand clothes are big business in Africa and the developing world (Wallman 1996) and this trade has become widespread in Cameroon in recent years. Teachers do not only sell to colleagues but to all kinds of buyers in the market and elsewhere. When we tried to find out from Caro how she managed to combine her teaching job, her business and her household activities, another teacher who overheard our conversation interrupted: 'Why not? We do manage, if you passed around the market on Tuesday (Limbe's main market day), you would have seen me selling *okrika* in the market.'

Secondary school teachers' work schedules are divided into discrete time periods, so they sometimes have free periods and even free days. This gives them time to carry out extra activities especially in the informal sector. It is partly for this reason that female teachers are the largest category on the list of newcomer entrepreneurs in the informal sector.

In Cameroon today, many people depend on second-hand clothing which is cheaper than making new clothes. As one of the tailors I talked to remarked: '*Okrika* has taken over our business and we no longer have customers who sew new dresses'. Local tailoring seems to be on the decline. In both urban and rural areas, the sale of second-hand goods has become a major source of income and therefore of key importance to the country's economy. These goods include dresses for all ages, shoes, handbags, socks, towels, panties, belts, etc. They are found in the main markets, along highways by day and at night, and also in fancy shops. Hawkers can also be seen moving with such goods from one quarter to another. It is not uncommon to find second-hand goods, mostly dresses and handbags, hanging on verandas in residential areas.

There are few gender discrepancies in most of the informal-sector activities discussed so far and carried out by formal-sector employees, with the exception of petty trading. However, it was noticed that only female formal workers were involved in the *okrika* trade. Caro explained why male teachers were not involved in this trade:

> We are all looking for a means of survival, but there is a limit to how far male colleagues can go. Some of them do own built-in provision stalls, barbers' salons, and other types of businesses. It is easier for women to try their hands at all kinds of odd jobs than men. Regardless of their qualifications and status in society, women are out to keep their families going. But working-class men will first of all think of their position in society and what their girlfriends will think of them before getting involved in any business. Moreover men are always looking for businesses with bigger profits unlike the women who do not mind smaller profits in the absence of bigger ones. (C.M., aged 46, married, 1996)

Female teachers seem to reap higher profits from informal activities than men. This disparity can be explained by the fact that, apart from carrying out activities hitherto reserved for men, they also engage in activities that men avoid. Women are less worried about status than men who perceive some of the women's activities as mean and degrading for their manhood or their status in society. This attitude can also be explained by the gender-based division of labour embedded in the norms of society and quite often imbued in boys and girls in early childhood.

Different types of food trade

According to female teachers in Limbe, trade in food remains one of the easiest businesses to initiate. The start-up capital required is small as household utensils can be used and support from household members is often available. Women's involvement in the food trade is linked to their traditional role in food cultivation, food processing and the daily feeding of the family. As one of the teachers explained:

> In the good old days, breakfast in my house for two children, a young relative, my husband and myself used to cost at least 700 F CFA. But now since the serious fall in my earnings, I can no longer afford 700 F CFA a day for breakfast alone. In my efforts to maintain the family's living standards, I now fry and sell puff-puffs and beans. My sales of puff-puffs and beans is not primarily for profit-making, but to subsidize the feeding of my household. What I prepare for the market each day serves my household for breakfast, while the rest is taken to school for sale. Sometimes there is a 'bad market', that is, very poor sales due to competition from other women selling the same food as myself. In such situations, I sell at give-away prices and what is left is consumed at home.

As in subsistence agriculture, there is no waste in the cooked food business, with the household consuming what is unsold. The food trade carried out by these newcomers includes the preparation and sale of lunch meals and sometimes raw foodstuffs. However, sales of a wide variety of snacks is most common among teachers in Limbe. These include the following:

puff-puffs (or *beignet* in French);
meat/fish rolls;
meat/fish pies;
akra balls (made of white beans, ground, spiced and deep-fried);
coconut sweets;
groundnut sweets;
parched groundnuts;
chinchin (fried pastry cut into thin pieces);
cakes;
plantain chips;
ice creams;
alaska (frozen water to which sugar and colouring is added);
yoghurt (this is prepared locally from dry milk); and
fruit juices.

While a few of the above-listed items need daily preparation, most can be prepared in large quantities once a week and preserved. Some teachers spend their weekends preparing snacks with the help of children and housemaids so that they can concentrate on their formal-sector jobs during the week. Teachers hire sales persons or make use of housemaids and relatives who hawk the food items around town, from office to office, in schools and hospitals. Such items are found in school canteens, sheds and even staff rooms following negotiations with the school authorities concerned. At the Government High School Mamfe, we noticed that the sale of snacks in the staff room is sometimes done on the basis of trust. Teachers selling fish pies and parched groundnuts would sometimes leave their wares on the table with price tags on, while they are in class teaching. Colleagues would leave the money on the table.

A marketing strategy frequently employed by primary school teachers is to entrust a quantity of assorted sweets to carefully selected pupils to sell during break with the middlemen usually receiving a few of the items entrusted to them as commission.

At the Government Domestic Science Centre, Mile One, Limbe, we came across what may be described as rotation sales by teachers. In the school shed where lunch meals and snacks are sold to pupils at break time, teachers are now the sole vendors of food, after having availed themselves of their formal status in the school to elbow out other vendors. Domestic science centres are staffed solely by female teachers and at the beginning of the school year in September, the teachers meet and agree on who will prepare and sell what to avoid duplication and competition among themselves. During the break (10– 11 a.m.), one teacher is in charge of the food stall selling food to pupils. By rotation, the teachers' role as traders stays relatively discreet, even though they are selling to their own pupils. Pedagogically, it is difficult for teachers to operate between these two spheres of activities, and one of the teachers we met was candid about the dilemma:

> Things are really tough, but we must survive. It doesn't really matter how we do it. What is important is how far we can keep our families going. In offices, almost everybody takes bribes to sign even a small official document. But teachers cannot collect bribes from pupils. We have to devise our own ways to raise extra income, that is why we can afford to teach and also sell at break time. Hiring somebody to sell means more expenditure, and less profit. We just want to ensure that our households can sometimes

feed on the items for sale. If we just recover the capital each day, then we are satisfied. (J.B., aged 30, married, 1996)

Impact of straddling on the teaching profession

The efforts made by female formal-sector workers to supplement their incomes definitely have a negative impact on their formal jobs. From the brief interviews and a general survey conducted, informants were selected for in-depth studies. Such interviews were often carried out in the evenings at the homes of informants. It was common to find teachers preparing *alaska* or other snacks for the following day's sales at a time when lesson notes could have been prepared or exercises corrected.

Some teachers go to bed late because the *puff-puff* mixture has to be prepared between 10 and 11 pm and then preserved for about 5 hours before frying it as early as 4 am. This was the case with Electa, one of the teachers at the Government High School Limbe, who revealed:

> When the country was economically viable, I could afford not to get up as early as 4 am every day to bake cakes for sale before going to school to teach. I am compelled to do what I am doing now, not out of a genuine wish, but through sheer necessity, even if my classes are affected as is the case on certain days, and I am bound to be late for school. Most often I have only about 4–5 hours of sleep because I have to prepare everything for baking before going to bed. (E.F., aged 35, separated, 1996)

Most of the teachers interviewed complained of a lack of time to keep up with all their activities, be they social or economic. It is clear that the time devoted to the preparation of teaching materials has become limited, since monthly earnings have to be supplemented. Some teachers take their private teaching jobs even more seriously than their official class work. In so doing, they encourage more pupils and students to enrol for private lessons. It has become commonplace to find pupils and students attending formal classes in the morning and informal classes taught by the same teachers in the evening.

In one of these primary schools in Mamfe, a teacher was observed collecting 500 F CFA from primary school pupils of classes four and five who had been grouped together for private classes at the school premises. She was making 15,000 F CFA on top of her salary every month in private tuition fees paid by 30 pupils. It should be mentioned that before the economic crisis began, only class seven pupils attended evening classes, which were officially recognized by the Ministry of National Education. They were meant to prepare the children for the First School Leaving Certificate examination, and no extra fees were paid for these classes. Today, private classes for income generation are organized at all levels from primary one to upper sixth. The quality of such tutorials is questionable given the teachers' divided interests.

Electa stressed the fact that her cake business was lucrative and helped a great deal. She made a good profit compared to her low monthly teaching salary. Weekly profits derived from the sale of cakes were about 20,000 F CFA. After deducting taxi fares for supplying cakes to various clients, she was left with 15,000 F CFA. In a month, Electa realised 60,000 F CFA in income generated from her sideline activity. She considered her business stressful but lucrative, remarking: 'I pay no taxes or dues to anybody.'

Both primary and secondary school teachers in Limbe urban centre had a wider informal market than their colleagues in Mamfe. Firstly, female teachers in Mamfe were not found carrying out PJs, nor were they involved in the production of *polycops*. These both seemed to be male domains. One of the reasons for the women's lack of participation in the production of polycops is that it is an intellectual exercise needing a lot of concentration, and thus is time-consuming. Material has to be collected from various sources and systematically organized. For carrying out more practical activities like trade, however, the help of family members can be enlisted. It was common in Limbe for female teachers to organize private classes at their homes but this form was not found in Mamfe.

About 70 per cent of the female teachers interviewed in Mamfe were involved in petty trading and trade in assorted foods, particularly the sale of snack items, just as in Limbe. Part-time farming also took up a good part of the time of some teachers after working hours. 'Rather than organize private classes and wait for income which may not always be available,' noted one of the teachers, 'I prefer to depend on the land which will never fail me and my family.'

The subsequent section of the chapter describes similar activities among nurses earning a lot more than their reduced formal salaries by 'PP' (private practice) [The Editors].

Government offices: the catalytic context for informal-sector activities (pp. 67–71)

Before the economic crisis there was a tendency for those, often male civil servants, in positions controlling substantial state resources to explore their working environment for individual benefits. But today it has become commonplace for all categories of workers in the public service, male and female, to adapt and transform their working environment to suit both their official and private pursuits.

Health workers capitalize on their skills as professionals and use diverse ways to explore the informal sector. Teachers, like health workers, have skills which they use to render services. However, the general tendency for the majority of female teachers is to turn to the market. The situation is slightly different with the third category, namely clerical workers. They have neither a 'shift' system of work nor a flexible work schedule, as is the case with health workers and secondary school teachers. Instead, they are expected to stay in their offices from 7.30 am to 3.30 pm, with only a short break of about 30 minutes. This one-shift system of work is not new in Southwest Cameroon as it was instituted during British colonial rule.

The case of the Provincial Treasury in Limbe illustrates the strategies used by clerical workers straddling the formal and informal sectors since nowhere else among all the offices visited did I find the level of informal market activity that goes on at this Treasury office. Moreover, female formal employees in offices that are involved in financial control seem to profit from some of the highest paid informal-sector activities when compared to other categories of formal workers. Besides, Limbe Treasury has the highest number of female clerical workers compared to other offices.

Formal work place and informal market

The Provincial Treasury in Limbe. My first impression as I entered the gate leading to the main entrance of the Treasury could be summarized thus: 'This is more of a market than an office'. In the open space that led to the main building of the Treasury, each visitor is welcomed by two rows of male and female entrepreneurs lined up with a variety of articles for sale. The Treasury is meant to pay salaries to workers as well as all types of government bills. Entrepreneurs who have made this environment a convenient market place do not only depend on treasury workers, but also target other formal workers whose wages are paid through the Treasury. Some go from one office to another advertising and selling their wares.

In the office of one Treasury staff member (Amy, aged 43), five different items were presented to her in less than 45 minutes. These included ready-made pleated skirts, underwear for men and children, wrist watches, different sets of dishes, and snacks (cakes and fruit juice). While I was there, I observed Amy buy one of the skirts for herself at 18,000 F CFA, some pants for her children at 3,000 F CFA, and some cake and juice for both of us at 1,000 F CFA. It was surprising that she was able to pay in cash (22,000 F CFA), even though salaries had not yet been paid. That amount of money, given the current salary scale, could have been more than the salaries earned by some state employees. It was all the more surprising since the majority of clerical workers are not known to earn very high salaries, considering their grades in the public service.

At the Treasury I saw extensive informal buying and selling. However, it was only possible to fully understand what went on at this office after several visits. I carried out structured interviews and in-depth studies with some of the workers during my third phase of field research in Limbe in August to September 1996. Our main concern at the Treasury was to find out how these women made extra income within their work environment. It was difficult to get an insight into the informal strategies of Treasury workers within their formal work places. Two women explained that they had taxis on the road through which they earned extra income. Two others had off-licence bars, and one owned a poultry farm. These activities were outside the work place. However, it was clear that these women needed more capital than women in other categories to invest in their businesses.

Out of 32 workers at the Treasury, 22 were female. I interviewed 20 of the women and 12 were reportedly carrying out different types of informal-sector activities. We further conducted three in-depth studies to get detailed life stories. One of the women did not carry out any informal activity as such, but earned extra income. I visited her at home three times. During the initial visit which was informal and friendly, a conducive atmosphere was created for further discussions.

This approach was necessary because most of the women working at the Treasury were not willing to talk about their strategies for income generation within their work places. During the second and third visits, Amy gave me her life story. My aim was to get a sense of her income, the relevant salary scales before and after the salary cuts, how she made extra income, and how she balanced household responsibilities and formal work. Here are some excerpts from Amy's story:

Most of us working at the Treasury fall within categories C and D of the public service. The government has reduced salaries drastically. Everybody is now looking for ways to close up the gaps. Like other office workers, our motto is 'a goat eats where it is tied'. Most of us use our offices to make extra money. After all, it is the government that has put us in this state; so if we can use government services to balance things up, it just goes to compensate for what we would have been receiving as our dues. All government *bons* (payment vouchers) pass through the Treasury, especially the blue *bons*, for advance salaries or arrears to be paid out. Government contractors are also paid through the Treasury and these are the big dealers. In every transaction a certain percentage is agreed upon between the individual and those of us who carry out the transaction to facilitate payments. The amount of money to be paid out determines the percentage we receive. However, for most *bons*, it is 20 per cent, especially when we deal with big contractors. For example, if 1m FCFA has to be paid out, our share of the deal will be 200,000 FCFA. At the end of the day, this amount is shared. Everyday I leave the office with money which is not part of my official monthly earnings. This enables me to meet my household needs, otherwise we couldn't survive. Some of my colleagues invest the money in their private activities like a taxi business, poultry farming, etc. (A.B., aged 43, married, 1996)

From A.B.'s story it is clear that the strategy of clerical workers and especially those controlling finances differs from that of other women. Even though salaries earned by clerical workers, most of whom fall within categories C and D, are lower than those of health workers and in particular those of teachers, the women at the Treasury seem to have an organized informal money-making strategy. This enables some to invest in more lucrative businesses, while others simply depend on extra amounts earned daily to sustain their families. If one considers the fact that on average the lowest amount earned from private daily transactions at the office by some Treasury workers is about 2,500 F CFA over 20 working days, the extra money would amount to 50,000 F CFA. These extra earnings coming from within the working environment are perceived by those concerned as a way of compensating for unfavourable measures taken by the state.

Unlike other offices I visited where attendance was irregular, I noticed that at the Treasury the offices were never empty. As an informant working at the Limbe post office observed: 'Treasury workers neither come late to work nor leave before time since they are always expecting kick-backs from their customers.'[4] This group of female formal employees were able to build up considerable capital for investment in sideline activities, unlike the smaller capital needed by most teachers and health workers for their informal activities.

Sale of services

While my case study dealt with a specific group of clerical workers, the situation differed in other offices where workers had no access to finance-control mechanisms. Workers in such offices tend to sell services in the form of private jobs. State jobs, for which they are paid, sometimes become 'favours' and they often expect tips or even levy charges on other civil servants. The system of compiling dossiers in Cameroon has become a lucrative avenue for some clerical workers. All kinds of forms needed are printed and sold in offices. These include forms for identity cards, and marriage and birth certificates. Each service has a format for the kind of documents to be compiled. Formerly, forms to compile all kinds of documents were made available by the state and given out free of charge. Today, individuals have to buy these same forms printed by those working in different services. Prices for forms range from 50 FCFA to 150 FCFA.

Sometimes state equipment such as telephones, typewriters and duplicating machines are used for private business transactions. As in other categories, a few of the clerical workers interviewed were engaged in petty trading, such as the sale of snacks and second-hand goods. Such workers were hardly ever in their offices because they had to move from office to office advertising the items for sale. Three of the female clerical workers studied owned market stalls where they sold various food items. Two had housemaids who carried out the household chores in the morning and stayed in the market to sell goods during the course of the day. After a day's work in the office, these women spent the evening period from 4 to 7 pm in the market monitoring the day's sales. One sold only on market days (Tuesdays and Fridays) due to the absence of a reliable salesperson and, based on private negotiations with her boss, she worked three days a week, using the other two days for her private business. As she noted:

My boss is very understanding. My present salary is so small that it would even be more profitable if I completely abandoned the so-called government job and concentrated on trade, but for the fact that though the salary is meagre, I am sure of something at the end of the month. With the trade, sometimes sales are very poor and irregular, and so I don't want to take the risk of giving up the government job as long as my boss remains understanding. (A.M., aged 50, married, 1996)

As in Limbe, clerical workers in Mamfe were not immune to the drive to make extra income. However, a difference was the limited population and the fact that the kind of activities differ somewhat. Petty trading and the sale of snacks from office to office were common among clerical workers in Mamfe. But it was unusual to find formal-sector employees having stalls or stands in the main market, as was the case in Limbe. Only one of my informants in Mamfe sold items such as vegetables, pepper, oil, etc. on Saturdays (the main market days), while two others owned off-licence bars in town. Due to its semi-urban nature, the activities that go on at the Mamfe Treasury are insignificant compared to those of the Limbe Treasury. There are fewer workers in Mamfe and thus fewer people make use of the Treasury. Only three female workers were found in the Mamfe Treasury yet transactions for kick-backs were common here as well, since salaries and government contracts are paid through the Treasury.

Conclusion

I have discussed a variety of patterns used by female formal-sector employees in combining formal and informal-sector activities. By using the census survey, I gained valuable insight into women's access to formal employment. Women, like men, were found working in almost all the ministries, although they were concentrated in the Ministry of Education, followed by the Ministry of Health. It was also in these two ministries that most of the women were found who penetrated the informal sector. The nature of their formal jobs and relaxed administrative control provided a conducive environment for formal-sector employees to become entrepreneurs in the informal sector. Moreover this sector easily absorbs women both in formal employment and those outside it. It is clear that formal employees are penetrating the informal sector on a large scale both for survival and capital accumulation. It is equally apparent that their fixed salary is an advantage vis-à-vis old-timer entrepreneurs who rely solely on trading to generate income.

Notes

[1] 'Poly-copies' is generally used by teachers and students to refer to mass production of certain academic documents.
[2] This teacher was present at a round-table discussion organized in April 1997 on 'Female Entrepreneurship in the Mamfe area'. In the course of our discussion, she recounted some of the constraints faced by female entrepreneurs on long-distance trade, especially across the Cameroon–Nigeria border.
[3] The figure was derived from the author's data.
[4] Kick-back refers to a type of bribe which is agreed upon by the parties concerned often based on a certain percentage. In the case of government contractors who receive payments through the Treasury, such money spent on bribes increases the cost of investment and reduces the profit margin.

References

Niger-Thomas, A.M. 1995. 'Women's Access to and the Control of Credit in Cameroon: The Mamfe Case', in S. Ardener and S. Brumen (eds) *Money Go Rounds*. Oxford: Berg Publishers.
Wallman, S. 1996. *Kampala Women Getting By: Wellbeing in the Time of AIDS*. Oxford: James Currey; Athens: Ohio University Press; Kampala: Fountain.

Section 1.C
The Modern Production of Tradition

'Tradition', in Africa as much as elsewhere, is a paradox: it is a product of modernity just as much as it tries to refer to something radically different from it. Whereas 'tradition' is the polar opposite of 'modernity' in an ideological sense, the historical and social scientific study of African tradition shows that its persistence relies on its constant (re)-invention by modern practices – and vice versa. This can only be understood when we adopt a relational conception of modernity (as developed in the introduction to this reader) which interprets most identifications of 'tradition' in Africa as saturated by cultural features of modernity. Minimally, even if many routines of 'traditional' behavior have much older roots (but some don't), people normally use the term to distinguish another, radically different temporality (of being modern or developed). Sometimes we classify something as 'traditional' that is really a product of modernity (such as the Pentecostalist perception of 'tradition' as diabolic). Sometimes, Africans feel compelled to distinguish and protect routines of survival, passed on by generations, from 'traditions' imposed on them by state authorities (Pels, this section). At yet other times, 'tradition' serves to hold up alternative social arrangements to modern eyes even while being reinvented by modern society. This section focuses mostly on political processes in order to provide students of Africa with three different sources of insights: first, Shepstone's report on the crowning of Cetshwayo in 1875 (one of the first reinventions of tradition in African indirect rule) can be compared to Julius Nyerere's invention of 'traditional African kinship' in Ujamaa in 1962, and Mbeki's reinvention of African tradition in his 'African Renaissance' of 1998. Secondly, Peter Pels shows how processes of inventing and transforming tradition exist simultaneously in his study of indirect rule in colonial Uluguru. Lastly, Lungisile Ntsebeza and Barbara Oomen argue how important, yet controversial and problematic, the reinvention of traditional chiefship in South Africa is today.

THEOPHILUS SHEPSTONE
Report of the Expedition Sent by the Government of Natal to Instal Cetywayo as King of the Zulus
Presented to both Houses of Parliament by Command of her Majesty, 6 February 1875

Reference
British Parliamentary Papers, Colonies, Africa 30,
Natal, Shannon: Irish University Press, 1971, pp. 6–22 (excerpt)

21. In 1861, the Government of Natal consented to my going to Zululand to endeavour to induce the King and his nobles to agree upon a successor, and to publicly nominate him or his house in my presence. I was attended by one of my sons, two other European companions, and a number of native followers from Natal. I found the task I had undertaken to be extremely difficult and somewhat dangerous, owing to conflicting interests and feelings and the bitter remembrance of the late deadly contest. I was fortunate enough, however, to be successful. Cetywayo's house was nominated, and I became chief witness to the formal act. The result was quiet to the Zulu country, and relief to this colony from continual apprehension of fresh disturbances; and with the exception of a serious alarm, which turned out to have real foundation, although it cost the colony a considerable sum of money, those benefits have continued to this day. [...]

28. It was an object of moment that an event which, when conducted by savages, such as the Zulus are, is invariably accompanied by the profuse shedding of blood, should, when taken in hand by a civilized Government show an exception to this savage rule, as marked as is the difference between the civilization and humanity of the two. The Lieutenant-Governor was anxious that the Zulus should understand also that we went to carry out the unanimous wish of the Nation as we understood it, and that we should take no part whatever in any dispute should that wish prove (contrary to our expectation) to be not unanimous. Before crossing the Tugela, therefore, I sent the following message to Cetywayo and the Zulu Nobles by Umnyembe and Gwilisa:

'I am about to enter the Zulu Country at the request of the Zulu Nation, to install Panda's son in the place of his deceased father. I cross the Tugela River today.

'I was the Chief Witness to the appointment and proclamation of that son twelve years ago. I was requested to convey the intelligence of those acts to the Government of Natal, and I did so. No word of the reversal of them has reached it since, and I now proceed to carry out what the Government I represent looks upon as the will of the Zulus. If I learn that this has been changed, my presence as Chief Witness will no longer be required, and I shall turn back.

'I cross the Tugela as the representative of the Government of Natal, with an escort befitting that position and the occasion that has rendered the visit necessary to the Zulus. I carry with me the dignity of the Government that has sent me; but the head of that Government has desired me to make a preliminary stipulation, namely, that its courtesy and condescension be not stained by one drop of blood. My own rank in Zululand entitles me to make another, and it is that, should any Zulu be adjudged to die for any political offence while I am in the country, such sentence be not carried out until the charges and evidence have been submitted to me. I shall expect, to meet on my way a decided acceptance of these conditions, or I shall refuse to proceed, as I cannot allow myself to be a witness to the spilling of blood, while I am deputed by my Government only to carry out a mission of peace.

'I have every hope that the result of this mission will be to show the Zulu people that their interests and those of Natal are in many respects one. Each can give what the other wants; and by arrangements mutually agreed upon, both can be served.

'I shall not condescend to contradict the foolish rumours that I am, bringing a rival heir to the Zulu authority. I leave these to be corrected by the Zulu messengers who travel with me. I come in good faith to carry out the wish of the Zulu people, and I must be looked upon as fully intending to keep my word.'

29. I must explain that the body of Umbulazi, Cetywayo's rival brother, was not found after the battle between them at the Tugela in 1856. And this fact, coupled with the accident that one of our magistrates was called by the same native name, led to the belief that this brother had not after all been killed as reported. Then it was rumoured that he had been sent by the Government to the Cape Colony; and that the delay in my proceeding to Zululand was being caused by the time necessary to get him back, and ultimately that he had arrived and was being kept strictly concealed and guarded until I should start.

These unfounded reports caused much uneasiness among the natives both in Zululand and in this Colony. Their dread of the consequences should they prove true was very great; and although Cetywayo tried to disbelieve them, his mind was evidently not at ease until his installation had actually taken place. The apprehension caused by them rendered more care and forethought necessary in the conduct of the expedition, and caused anxiety lest any accident should favour suspicion and bring about a catastrophe. Hence a direct reference to these reports in my first message was imperatively required, although I well knew that nothing but perseverance and a successful issue could furnish complete contradiction of them.

30. Upon our entering Zululand we found all the men, with few exceptions, absent from their kraals; they had been called up to the Royal Residence, and only women in most cases left in charge. Although this was a sign of confidence, there was the adverse fact, not observed at first, that many of the cattle had been removed. It soon became apparent, however, that our visit was heartily welcomed by the people, and that but for their anxiety as to the result, it gave them unmixed pleasure even on our upward journey. [...]

36. It should be understood that the fact of the 'King's head,' as it is called, having been presented to the Government of Natal, placed all arrangements for the succession absolutely, and theoretically the person of the successor, in its hands. The Government had deputed me to act on its behalf, and the Zulu people had unanimously requested that I should be allowed to act on behalf of themselves. I could not allow this position to be encroached upon. Cetywayo had for many years lived close to the Norwegian Mission Station nearest to the Colony; his people were as yet, in a measure, distinct from the bulk of the Zulu nation; he had hitherto governed the country in his father's name, and Zululand proper through his father's Prime Minister, Masipula. In theory the Zulus knew nothing of Cetywayo, except that he was *the* child. It had been arranged that I should travel the route that led past his residence, take possession of him, and present him to the assembled nation, and then proceed to install him as King.

37. Cetywayo had submitted himself to this programme, had assembled his young regiments which were to form the escort, and had held himself prepared to carry it out; but my leaving Natal was delayed from month to month, and he found it difficult to feed his large retinue of perhaps 15,000 men. He proposed, therefore, that he should precede me to where his force could support itself by hunting, and ultimately await my arrival at the Isirebe, in the valley of the White Imfolozi River. I had consented to this, and on our way could judge of the size of his escort by the large number of temporary shelters put up at each encampment. It appeared that when Cetywayo reached the Isirebe, he was there met by the heads of the Zulu people, led by Panda's Prime Minister, Masipula, and that on his address of welcome the royal salute had been either given or offered to the Prince.

38. It was known that Masipula represented the conservative feeling of the country; that he thought it derogatory to Zulu dignity to call in the assistance of foreigners to install a Zulu King, being of opinion that their own unaided authority was quite equal to the task, and that what could be done at home should not be allowed to pass into the hands of outsiders. But, although holding these opinions strongly, he had been compelled by the general wish to acquiesce in a contrary view.

39. The question, therefore, was whether this message was honestly what it professed to be, or whether it was intended to prepare me for the disclosure that Masipula, by a bold stroke of policy and a well-timed proposal, had got the national decision reversed by acclamation, and the services of the Natal Government declined unless it consented to render them as avowedly secondary and non-essential.

40. The situation was embarrassing. The possibility that the Expedition might have to turn back without doing what the Zulus had so long and so earnestly begged it might be sent to do; the loss of prestige to the Colony; the ill-feeling that such a result must create in, our future relations as neighbours, were considerations which caused much anxiety, to say nothing of the expenditure, which, however, I should have demanded and most probably received. I felt sure, also, that if such a step had been taken, it had been rendered possible only by the arrival of the Expedition in the country, and it would be Masipula's policy so to use the fact of its presence as to appear to the people to deny the obligation he was under to it.

41. To require full explanation seemed to be the only course: – 'How had the royal salute been given? Who had ventured to authorize it? If sufficient authority to do this existed in Zululand, my presence was not necessary, and the Government expenditure had been wasted; but I was there because the Zulus had themselves urged that such authority did not exist, or if it did, that the circumstances of the country prevented its being safely used. Unless I occupied the position allowed by my Government at the request of the Zulus, I could take no part in the matter. The sooner, therefore, I knew the truth the better, so that any further unnecessary expenditure might be prevented by the return of the Expedition.' These questions and suggestions were sent in reply to the message on the 15th August, on the day I received it. [...]

47. On the morning of the 18th, Capt. Escombe, of the Durban Artillery, fired a salute of seventeen guns to announce our arrival, and

the members of the Expedition made their arrangements to pass the days of the Zulu Court mourning at that Camp. On the same day Sidindi, Sirayo, and others brought the answer to my message of the 15th. They denied that at the meeting between young and old Zululand any act approaching to, or capable of being substituted for, any portion of the installation ceremony was either carried out or contemplated. No one, they said, could do that but myself. I came as Chaka. This reference to my representing Chaka is explained in my Memorandum of the 11th June, 1873, attached. I was commissioned by the Zulus, and by the Government that was superior to the Zulus, and I had my own special rank besides; no one could contest that right with me, and no one had ventured to contest it. What had taken place in sight of the spot where we then sat, at the meeting of the young section of the Zulus escorting their Prince with the old, was this – that Masipula had made a speech, in which he went into the history of Cetywayo's rank and public nomination. That Cetywayo had himself checked him when he thought he was going too far, but Masipula replied, 'I am only saying what Sonitseu (Mr. Shepstone) has already said. I am telling the young people that we are willing to accept this child of Panda, and to give him the Royal Salute, when we are authorized to do so by him whose arrival we expect. It is only he who can place the nation in possession of their King.' This, they protested, was all that had taken place, and that the Royal Salute had never been used by authority. The messengers brought a supply of seven oxen for the Expedition, and Cetywayo requested that we should proceed on our journey, and that our crossing Imfolozi should be reported to him. [...]

53. Shortly afterwards six of the leading men of the Country arrived as representatives of the Zulu people. They brought a tusk of ivory as an apology for what they now saw had been a want of respect. They admitted that the plan had been altered. 'The Zulus objected,' they said, 'to the ceremony being in anyway connected with the Isirebe,' for the reasons already explained, and that this change had not been, as it should have been, submitted to me on or before my arrival. But they assured me that the omission had been unintentional; that the master of ceremonies, Masipula, had died suddenly, and that this must be accepted as to some extent accounting for it. They begged, therefore, that I would overlook it, and proceed on my journey. I accepted their apology, and took the opportunity of saying that I should not regret what had happened if it should have the effect of showing how important it was that agreements should be kept, or, if broken, broken only by mutual consent; that to begin our relations with a new ruler by silently acquiescing in a decided departure from a well understood arrangement, might lead the Zulus to suppose that in other and more important matters hereafter the Government of Natal would be equally careless, and this again would tempt them to make promises which they never intended to fulfil, and so destroy confidence and produce disaster. The men left highly pleased with the result of their mission. [...]

63. On Monday, the 1st September, preparations were early commenced to carry out the installation. Mr. Consul Cato, assisted by Messrs. H. C. and G. Shepstone, went over and pitched a large marquee, brought for the purpose, in the central space of the Military Kraal. They decorated it inside with the shawls, blankets, and other showy articles which had been brought as presents. In the middle of one side stood a table covered with drapery, with a mirror, in front of which had been placed the head-dress; the design was taken from the Zulu war headdress, suggested by Mr. Dunn after consultation, I believe, with the Zulus, improved upon by the master tailor of the 75th Regiment, and signified the Zulu trappings of war subdued to a

peaceful purpose. There also stood his Chair of State, with the scarlet and gold mantle upon it, so that the Marquee presented a very tasteful appearance.

64. Cetywayo had not in any way interfered with, or suggested any portion of the programme; but he was anxious that, in accordance with the theory upon which we had hitherto acted, I should at some part of the ceremony take possession of him, and so transform him that his own people would not know him; it must not be done in public; the Zulus had given him over to me; I must take him from their sight a minor, and present him to them a man; I must take him as a Prince, and restore him to them their King. To save time and avoid accidents, always the danger in such cases, I had dispensed with the complimentary entrance of the Zulu regiments.

65. At noon we proceeded to the Umlambongwenya Kraal, where the ceremony was to be performed, leaving our Camp in sole charge of five or six natives. Major Giles organized the order of procession, in which we entered the lower gate with the band playing. I was accompanied by the officers and gentlemen already named, and others who were desirous of seeing what took place. The brilliant uniforms of the officers formed a contrast with the costume of the clergy and the miscellaneous dresses of some of my companions, and added much to the appearance of the procession. The Artillery, Mounted Volunteers, and the band of the Maritzburg Rifles formed on the right of the Marquee, my natives on the left, Cetywayo with his Councillors and my party formed a group in front. The Zulu people described three-fourths of a circle about fifty yards off, and may be estimated at from 8,000 to 10,000, mostly young men. These latter were forced into their position not by word of command so much as by the free use of sticks by their officers; it seemed to be many blows first and then a word, and some of them appeared to be severely hurt. I could not help thinking, as I sat and noticed this violence and the quiet manner in which it was taken, how different the condition of the natives in Natal was, and whether the extreme jealousy with. which our laws guard the infliction of corporal punishment on young natives is a good or an evil. The contrast seemed too great, and it appeared unreasonable to expect the same obedience from the same people under such different circumstances, although as necessary with one Country as with the other.

66. When the order desired was established, Cetywayo wished to examine the guns. Capt. Escombe caused the peculiarity of the breech-loading to be explained to him; he was surprised at the ability with which an open cylinder could be closed for firing, but seemed disappointed that they were not larger. On returning to our seats I stood up and explained in the Native language the nature and importance of the ceremony I had come to perform, the condescension and goodwill of the Government of Natal, shown by its allowing me to come, and by sending such a complimentary escort to accompany me; and after adding such introductory remarks as appeared necessary, I proceeded to the business I had in hand. I thought it would be best that all the points I wished to establish and impress should be presented in the shape of questions, and that I should require audible assent to each to be given by all the brothers of Cetywayo, and, the rulers and councillors of the country who formed my audience, for the common people were too far off to hear me speak.

67. To avoid mistake or omission I read from a paper I had prepared, and to every proposition I received audible and hearty assent. I then handed this paper to my eldest son, who acted as my secretary, and said I desired him to preserve it and to be the witness hereafter to the arrangements and laws it described, as I had been to

the arrangement made at Nodwengu (12 years before), and which we were completing that day. The questions and points were as follows:

'Have not I entered Zululand at the request of the Zulu nation to install their new King?'

'Have not I been requested to come because I was the chief witness to his nomination by his father at Nodwengu?'

'Is not Cetywayo the son that was then nominated, and is it not he whom the Zulus now wish me to install?'

'So say you all?' In addition to the general and vehement assent given to this, Uham said 'Yes, every woman and every child.'

'Have you not requested me to proclaim new laws to be administered under the New King, by means of which you hope that the New King will reign peaceably over a contented people and a prosperous country ?'

'Have not we agreed that the life of a man or woman, high or low, is the property of the Country, and that the King has vested in him that property on behalf of the Country?'

'Have not we agreed that for any man to take life, without the previous knowledge and consent of the King, is to take that which belongs to the Country without the Country's consent?'

'Have not we agreed that every man ought to be allowed to answer for himself before his immediate head, and, if he wishes, before the King any charges brought against him, and that he ought not to be condemned finally before he has had an opportunity of so doing?'

'Have not we agreed that the punishment of death for every crime destroys a people?'

'Do not I stand here in the place of Cetywayo's father, and so representing the Nation?'

'I proclaim therefore, –

'1st. That the indiscriminate shedding of blood shall cease in the land.

'2nd. That no Zulu shall be condemned without open trial and the public examination of witnesses for and against, and that he shall have a right to appeal to the King.

'3rd. That no Zulu's life shall be taken without the previous knowledge and consent of the King after such trial has taken place, and the right of appeal has been allowed to be exercised.

'4th. That for minor crimes the loss of property, all, or a portion shall be substituted for the punishment of death.'

68. One of the Councillors remarked that the practice of witchcraft by the people was the cause of their frequently being put to death, and that witch doctors from Natal were sometimes the accusers. This gave an opportunity for me to explain the evils and mischief brought about by these impostors, and the policy adopted by the Natal Government towards them. The Zulu idea is that, if they be suppressed, wizards and witches will have full swing, and destroy many victims. They were told that the suppression of witchdoctors in Natal, i.e., the fact that these practices were punishable, had not increased the rate of mortality, nor would it in Zululand; no law of a special nature, however, was laid down, seeing that accusations of witchcraft are included in Nos. 1, 2, and 3. Although all this was fully and even vehemently assented to, it cannot be expected that the amelioration described will immediately take effect. To have got such principles admitted and declared to be what a Zulu may plead when oppressed, was but sowing the seed which will still take many years to grow and mature.

69. I then led Cetywayo to the tent, followed by my own party of Europeans. When all had entered the door was closed and guarded by two sentries of the Durban Royal Artillery; and the Prince was now in our possession, unattended by any of his people, except one body-servant. He rapidly glanced at the different articles before him, but showed no sign of emotion. The transformation had now to be effected; and, after I thought a sufficient time had elapsed, I desired him to stoop that I might put on his head-dress and scarlet mantle, and we were ready to return to our position outside. In the meanwhile a carpet, presented to him by Capt. Macleod and Mr. Fairlie, had been spread, the chair of state we had brought him placed upon it facing the people, and another of a less pretentious character, but so disguised as to look suited to the occasion, was put alongside for me.

70. I then led him to his seat, and after a few minutes rose and presented him to his brothers and councillors as their King and desired the heralds to go round and make a proclamation to that effect in the face of the people. Thus he, who a few moments before had been but a minor and a Prince, had now become a man and a King; and, as if to suit the humour, one or two of his warriors pretended to doubt his identity, so complete was the change. The proclamation occupied perhaps a quarter of an hour, after which the Durban Artillery fired with great regularity and effect a salute of 17 guns, the Volunteers saluted also, and the band struck up.

71. The new laws had been made known to the councillors and great men, but not to the common people; and in my view it was important that they should be proclaimed to the latter in my presence, to prevent their being stifled by the nobles. Cetywayo agreed; but the difficulty was who should do it, his heralds or mine; I thought that his, and he that mine, should do it; so it was settled that both should go, his to make the actual proclamation, mine to correct and supply omissions. These latter processes were so frequently necessary that the people requested the Zulu heralds to leave the whole duty to mine, saying they wished what they heard to be authentic.

72. This operation took fully half an hour. The Volunteers had dismounted and left their horses standing in line linked in sections of fours, and one man to a section. The proclamation being ended, all the thousands of Zulus present lifted their shields, and struck them sharply with sticks in token of applause; the sound is strange and startling to one hearing it for the first time, and it terrified the horses; they wheeled suddenly to the left and seemed charging down upon where we were sitting. This belonged to a class of accidents that sometimes produce disasters, and for the moment one seemed likely to happen; the horses were fortunately however very soon under control again. Cetywayo at once saw what had taken place, and exclaimed 'they have left their horses and they are startled at the noise of the shields.' The quickness with which the accident was remedied soon changed the aspect of affairs, and turned adverse criticism into admiration at the smartness with which the mischief had been stopped.

73. The ceremony being now over, I addressed the brothers and councillors, pointed out to them their duties, and impressed upon them the new responsibilities laid upon them by the new laws, and their relations to their new King. I told the King that I well knew the difficulties of his position, and that he could overcome them only by moderation, and prudence, and justice, but without these they would certainly overcome him. He assented to what I said, and thanked us very heartily for what we had done for him. After paying a complimentary visit to his sisters, I bade him farewell, and we all left in the same order as we had entered, without serious accident or misunderstanding. The Marquee was handed over to him as it stood, and he immediately went to take possession of it. We were followed by crowds of Zulus, who were loud and extravagant in their expressions of satisfaction at what they had seen and heard. […]

98. The journey occupied between seven and eight weeks, and

was marred no sickness, danger, or other untoward event: and I trust that the recollection of it may be long perpetuated by the advantages which there is every reason to hope will flow from it to the Colony and to the Zulus themselves.

T. SHEPSTONE
Secretary for Native Affairs for the Colony of Natal

JULIUS KAMBARAGE NYERERE
Ujamaa
The Basis of African Socialism

Reference
Accessed 16/09/2004 at
www.nathanielturner.com/ujamaanyerere.htm
First published Dar es Salaam: Oxford University Press, 1966, pp. 1–11 (excerpts)

Since the appearance of millionaires in a society does not depend on its affluence, sociologists may find it interesting to try and find out why our societies in Africa did not, in fact, produce any millionaires – for we certainly had enough wealth to create a few. I think they would discover that it was because the organization of traditional African society – its distribution of the wealth it produced – was such that there was hardly any room for parasitism. They might also say, of course, that as a result of this Africa could not produce a leisured class of landowners, and therefore there was nobody to produce the works of art or science which capitalist societies can boast. But works of art and the achievements of science are products of the intellect – which, like land, is one of God's gifts to man. And I cannot believe that God is so careless as to have made the use of one of His gifts depend on the misuse of another!

[…]

Apart from the anti-social effects of the accumulation of personal wealth, every desire to accumulate it must be interpreted as a vote of 'no confidence' in the social system. For when a society is so organized that it cares about its individuals, then, provided he is willing to work, no individual within that society should worry about what will happen to him tomorrow if he does not hoard wealth today. Society itself should look after him, or his widow, or his orphans. This is exactly what traditional African society is doing. Both the 'rich' and the 'poor' individual were completely secure in African society.

Natural catastrophe brought famine, but it brought famine to everybody – 'poor' or 'rich'. Nobody starved, either of food or of human dignity, because he lacked personal wealth; he could depend on the wealth possessed by the community of which he was a member. That was socialism. That is socialism. There can be no such thing as acquisitive socialism, for that would be another contradiction in terms. Socialism is essentially distributive. Its concern is to see that those who sow reap a fair share of what they sow.

[…]

In traditional African society everybody was a worker. There was no other way of earning a living for the community. Even the Elder, who appeared to be enjoying himself without doing any work and for whom everybody else appeared to be working, had, in fact, worked hard all his younger days. The wealth he now appeared to possess was not his, personally; it was only 'his' as the elder of the group which had produced it. He was a guardian; the wealth itself gave him neither power nor prestige; the respect paid to him by the young was his because he was older than they, and had served his community longer; and the 'poor' Elder enjoyed as much respect in our community as the 'rich' Elder.

When I say that in traditional African society everybody was a worker, I do not use the word 'worker' simply as opposed to 'employer' but also as opposed to 'loiterer' or 'idler'. One of the most socialistic achievements of our society was the sense of security it gave to its members, and the universal hospitality on which they could rely. But it is too often forgotten, nowadays, that the basis of this great socialistic achievement was this: that it was taken for granted that every member of society – barring only the children and the infirm – contributed his fair share of effort towards the production of its wealth.

Not only was the capitalist, or the landed exploiter, unknown to traditional African society, but we did not have that other form of modern parasite – the loiterer, or idler, who accepts the hospitality of society as his 'right' but gives nothing in return! Capitalistic exploitation was impossible. Loitering was an unthinkable disgrace.

Those of us who talk about the African way of life, and, quite rightly, take a pride in maintaining the tradition of hospitality which is so great a part of it, might do well to remember the Swahili saying: '*Mgeni siku mbili; siku ya tatu mpe jembe*' – or, in English, 'Treat your guest as a guest for two days; on the third day give him a hoe!' In actual fact, the guest was likely to ask for the hoe even before his host had to give him one – for he knew what was expected of him, and would have been ashamed to remain idle any longer. Thus, working was part and parcel, was indeed the very basis and justification of his socialist achievement of which we are so justly proud.

[…]

The other use of the word 'worker', in its specialized sense of 'employee' as opposed to 'employer', reflects a capitalistic attitude of mind which was introduced into Africa with the coming of colonialism and is totally foreign to our own way of thinking. In the old days the African had never aspired to the possession of personal wealth for the purpose of dominating any of his fellows. He had never had laborers or 'factory hands' to do his work for him.

But then came the foreign capitalists; they were wealthy. They were powerful. And the African naturally started wanting to be wealthy too. There is nothing wrong in our wanting to be wealthy; not [nor] is it a bad thing for us to want to acquire the power which wealth brings with it. But it most certainly is wrong if we want the wealth and the power so that we can dominate somebody else.

Unfortunately there are some of us who have already learned to covet wealth for that purpose, and who would like to use the methods which the capitalist uses in acquiring it. That is to say, some of us would like to use, or exploit, our brothers for the purpose of building up our own personal power and prestige. This is completely foreign to us, and it is incompatible with the socialist society we want to build here.

Our first step, therefore, must be to re-educate ourselves; to regain our former attitude of mind. In our traditional African society we were individuals within a community. We took care of the community, and the community took care of us. We neither needed nor wished to exploit our fellow men.

And in rejecting the capitalist attitude of mind which colonialism brought into Africa, we must reject also the capitalist methods which go with it. One of these is the individual ownership of land. To us in Africa land was always recognized as belonging to the community. Each individual within our society had a right to the use of land, because otherwise he could not earn his living and one cannot have the right to life without having the right to some means of maintaining it. But the African's right to land was simply the right to use it: he had no other right to it, nor did it occur to him to try and claim one.

The foreigner introduced a completely different concept, the concept of land as a marketable commodity. According to this system, a person could claim a piece of land as his own private property whether he intended to use it or not.

[…]
We must not allow the growth of parasites here in Tanganyika. The TANU government must go back to the traditional African custom of land holding. That is to say, a member of society will be entitled to a piece of land on condition the [that] he uses it. Unconditional, or 'freehold,' ownership of land (which leads to speculation and parasitism) must be abolished. We must, as I have said, regain our former attitude of mind – our traditional African socialism – and apply it to the new societies we are building today. TANU has pledged itself to make socialism the basis of its policy in every field. The people of Tanganyika have given us their mandate to carry out that policy, by electing a TANU government to lead them. So the government can be relied upon to introduce only legislation which is in harmony with socialist principles.

[…]
European socialism was born of the Agrarian Revolution and the Industrial Revolution which followed it. The former created the 'landed' and the 'landless' classes in society; the latter produced the modern capitalist and the industrial proletariat.

These two revolutions planted the seeds of conflict within society, and not only was European socialism born of that conflict, but its apostles sanctified the conflict itself into a philosophy. Civil war was no longer looked upon as something evil, or something unfortunate, but as something good and necessary. As prayer is to Christianity or to Islam, so civil war (which they call 'class war') is to the European version of socialism – a means inseparable from the end. Each becomes the basis of a whole way of life. The European socialist cannot think of his socialism without its father – capitalism!

Brought up in tribal socialism, I must say, I find this contradiction quite intolerable. It give[s] capitalism a philosophical status which capitalism neither claims nor deserves. For it virtually says 'Without capitalism, and the conflict which capitalism creates within society, there can be no socialism!' This glorification of capitalism by the doctrinaire European socialists, I repeat, I find intolerable.

African socialism, on the other hand, did not have the 'benefit' of the Agrarian Revolution or the Industrial Revolution. It did not start from the existence of conflicting 'classes' in society. Indeed I doubt if the equivalent for the word 'class' exists in any indigenous African language; for language describes the ideas of those who speak it, and the idea of 'class' or 'caste' was nonexistent in African society.

The foundation, and the objective, of African socialism is the extended family. The true African socialist does not look on one class of men as his brethren and another as his natural enemies. He does not form an alliance with the 'brethren' for the extermination of the 'non-brethren.' He rather regards all men as his brethren – as members of his ever extending family. That is why the first article of TANU's creed is 'Binadamu wote ni ndugu zangu, na Afrika ni moja'. If this had been originally put in English, it could have been 'I believe in Human Brotherhood and the Unity of Africa'.

'Ujamaa,' then, or 'familyhood,' describes our socialism. It is opposed to capitalism, which seeks to build a happy society on the basis of the exploitation of man by man; and it is equally opposed to doctrinaire socialism which seeks to build its happy society on a philosophy of inevitable conflict between man and man.

We, in Africa, have no more need of being 'converted' to socialism than we have of being 'taught' democracy. Both are rooted in our own past – in the traditional society which produced us. Modern African socialism can draw from its traditional heritage the recognition of 'society' as an extension of the basic family unit. But it can no longer confine the idea of the social family within the limits of the tribe, nor, indeed, of the nation. For no true African socialist can look at a line drawn on a map and say, 'The people on this side of that line are my brothers, but those who happen to live on the other side of it can have no claim on me.' Every individual on this continent is his brother.

It was in the struggle to break the grip of colonialism that we learned the need for unity. We came to recognize that the same socialist attitude of mind which, in the tribal days, gave to every individual the security that comes of belonging to a widely extended family, must be preserved within the still wider society of the nation. But we should not stop there. Our recognition of the family, to which we all belong must be extended yet further – beyond the tribe, the community, the nation, or even the continent – to embrace the whole society of mankind. This is the only logical conclusion for true socialism.

THABO MBEKI
The African Renaissance, South Africa & the World

Reference
Accessed 30/06/2004 at www.unu.edu/unupress/mbeki.html
Speech by the South African Deputy President
at the United Nations University, Japan, 9 April 1998

We must assume that the Roman, Pliny the Elder, was familiar with the Latin saying, 'Ex Africa semper aliquid novi!' (Something new always comes out of Africa). Writing during the first century of the present millennium [sic], Pliny gave his fellow Romans some startlingly interesting and supposedly new information about Africans. He wrote:

Of the Ethiopians there are diverse forms and kinds of men. Some there are toward the east that have neither nose nor nostrils, but the face all full. Others that have no upper lip, they are without tongues, and they speak by signs, and they have but a little hole to take their breath at, by the which they drink with an oaten straw … In a part of Afrikke be people called Pteomphane, for their King they have a dog, at whose fancy they are governed … And the people called Anthropophagi which we call cannibals, live with human flesh. The Cinamolgi, their heads are almost like to heads of dogs ... Blemmyis a people so called, they have no heads, but hide their mouth and their eyes in their breasts. (Cited in John Reader, *Africa: A Biography of the Continent*, Hamish Hamilton, London, 1997)

These images must have frightened many a Roman child to scurry to bed whenever their parents said, 'The Africans are coming! The strange creatures out of Africa are coming!'

Happily, fifteen centuries later, Europe had a somewhat different view of the Africans. At the beginning of the sixteenth century, Leo Africanus, a Spaniard resident in Morocco, visited West Africa and wrote the following about the royal court in Timbuktu, Mali:

The rich king of Timbuktu ... keeps a magnificent and well-furnished court ... Here are great store of doctors, judges, priests, and other learned men, that are bountifully maintained at the king's cost and charges. And hither are brought diverse manuscripts or written books out of Barbarie, which are sold for more money than any other merchandise. (Reader, *op cit*.)

Clearly, this was not the Dog King of which Pliny had written at the beginning of [his] millennium, but a being as human as any other and more cultured and educated than most in the world of his day. And yet five centuries later, at the close of our millennium, we read in a book published last year:

I am an American, but a black man, a descendant of slaves brought from Africa... If things had been different, I might have been one of them (the Africans) – or might have met some... anonymous fate in one of the countless ongoing civil wars or tribal clashes on this brutal continent. And so I thank God my ancestor survived that voyage (to slavery) ... Talk to me about Africa and my black roots and my kinship with my African brothers and I'll throw it back into your face, and then I'll rub your nose in the images of the rotting flesh (of the victims of the genocide of the Tutsis or Rwanda)... Sorry, but I've been there. I've had an AK-47 (automatic rifle) rammed up my nose, I've talked to machete-wielding Hutu militiamen with the blood of their latest victims splattered across their T-shirts. I've seen a cholera epidemic in Zaire, a famine in Somalia, a civil war in Liberia. I've seen cities bombed to near rubble, and other cities reduced to rubble, because their leaders let them rot and decay while they spirited away billions of dollars – yes, billions – into overseas bank accounts ... Thank God my ancestor got out, because, now, I am not one of them. (Keith B. Richburg. *Out of America: A Black Man Confronts Africa*: Basic Books, New York, 1997.)

And this time, in the place of the Roman child, it is the American child who will not hesitate to go to bed when he or she is told, 'The Africans are coming! The barbarians are coming!'

In a few paragraphs, quoted from books that others have written, we have traversed [2 millennia]. But the truth is that we have not travelled very far with regard to the projection of frightening images of savagery that attend the continent of Africa.

Images of hope and despair

And so it may come about that some who harbour the view that as Africans we are a peculiar species of humanity pose the challenge: How dare they speak of an African Renaissance? After all, in the context of

the evolution of the European peoples, when we speak of the Renaissance, we speak of advances in science and technology, voyages of discovery across the oceans, a revolution in printing and an attendant spread, development and flowering of knowledge and a blossoming of the arts.

And so the question must arise about how we – who, in a millennium [sic], only managed to advance from cannibalism to a 'blood-dimmed tide' of savages who still slaughter countless innocents with machetes, and on whom another, as black as I, has turned his back, grateful that his ancestors were slaves – how do we hope to emulate the great human achievements of the earlier Renaissance of the Europe of the fifteenth and sixteenth centuries?

One of our answers to this question is that, as Africans, we recall the fact that as the European Renaissance burst into history in the fifteenth and sixteenth centuries, there was a royal court in the African city of Timbuktu which, in the same centuries, was as learned as its European counterparts.

What this tells me is that my people are not a peculiar species of humanity! I say this here today both because it is true, but also because I know that you, the citizens of this ancient land, will understand its true significance. And as we speak of an African Renaissance, we project into both the past and the future. I speak here of a glorious past of the emergence of *homo sapiens* on the African continent.

I speak of African works of art in South Africa that are a thousand years old. I speak of the continuum in the fine arts that encompasses the varied artistic creations of the Nubians and the Egyptians, the Benin bronzes of Nigeria and the intricate sculptures of the Makonde of Tanzania and Mozambique. I speak of the centuries-old contributions to the evolution of religious thought made by the Christians of Ethiopia and the Muslims of Nigeria.

I refer also to the architectural monuments represented by the giant sculptured stones of Aksum in Ethiopia, the Egyptian sphinxes and pyramids, the Tunisian city of Carthage, and the Zimbabwe ruins, as well as the legacy of the ancient universities of Alexandria of Egypt, Fez of Morocco and, once more, Timbuktu of Mali. When I survey all this and much more besides, I find nothing to sustain the long-held dogma of African exceptionalism, according to which the colour black becomes a symbol of fear, evil and death.

I speak of this long-held dogma because it continues still to weigh down the African mind and spirit, like the ton of lead that the African slave carries on her own shoulders, producing in her and the rest a condition which, in itself, contests any assertion that she is capable of initiative, creativity, individuality, and entrepreneurship. Its weight dictates that she will never straighten her back and thus discover that she is as tall as the slave master who carries the whip. Neither will she have the opportunity to question why the master has legal title both to the commodity she transports on her back and the labour she must make available to ensure that the burden on her shoulders translates into dollars and yen.

An essential and necessary element of the African Renaissance is that we all must take it as our task to encourage the one, who carries this leaden weight, to rebel, to assert the principality of her humanity – the fact that she, in the first instance, is not a beast of burden, but a human and African being.

But in our own voyage of discovery, we have come to Japan and discovered that a mere 130 years ago, the Meiji Restoration occurred, which enabled your own forebears to project both into their past and their future. And as we seek to draw lessons and inspiration from what you have done for yourselves, and integrate the Meiji Restoration into these universal things that make us dare speak of an African

Renaissance, we too see an African continent which is not 'wandering between two worlds, one dead, the other unable to be born.'

'A rediscovery of ourselves'

But whence and whither this confidence? I would dare say that that confidence, in part, derives from a rediscovery of ourselves, from the fact that, perforce, as one would who is critical of oneself, we have had to undertake a voyage of discovery into our own antecedents, our own past, as Africans. And when archaeology presents daily evidence of an African primacy in the historical evolution to the emergence of the human person described in science as *homo sapiens*, how can we be but confident that we are capable of effecting Africa's rebirth?

When the world of fine arts speak to us of the creativity of the Nubians of Sudan and its decisive impact on the revered and everlasting imaginative creations of the African land of the Pharaohs – how can we be but confident that we will succeed to be the midwives of our continent's rebirth? And when we recall that African armies at Omdurman in the Sudan and Isandhlwana in South Africa out-generalled, out-soldiered and defeated the mighty armies of the mighty and arrogant British Empire in the seventies of the last century, how can we be but confident that through our efforts, Africa will regain her place among the continents of our universe?

And in the end, an entire epoch in human history, the epoch of colonialism and white foreign rule, progressed to its ultimate historical burial grounds because, from Morocco and Algeria to Guinea Bissau and Senegal, from Ghana and Nigeria to Tanzania and Kenya, from the Congo and Angola to Zimbabwe and South Africa, the Africans dared to stand up to say the new must be born, whatever the sacrifice we have to make – Africa must be free!

We are convinced that such a people has a legitimate right to expect of itself that it has the capacity to set itself free from the oppressive historical legacy of poverty, hunger, backwardness and marginalization in the struggle to order world affairs, so that all human civilization puts as the principal objective of its existence the humane existence of all that is human!

And again we come back to the point that we, who are our own liberators from imperial domination, cannot but be confident that our project to ensure the restoration not of empires, but the other conditions in the sixteenth century described by Leo Africanus: of peace, stability, prosperity, and intellectual creativity, will and must succeed! The simple phrase 'We are our own liberators!' is the epitaph on the gravestone of every African who dared to carry the vision in his or her heart of Africa reborn.

The conviction therefore that our past tells us that the time for Africa's Renaissance has come, is fundamental to the very con-ceptualization of this Renaissance and the answer to the question: Whence this confidence? Unless we are able to answer the question 'Who were we?' we will not be able to answer the question 'What shall we be?' This complex exercise, which can be stated in simple terms, links the past to the future and speaks to the interconnection between an empowering process of restoration and the consequences or the response to the acquisition of that newly restored power to create something new.

[…]

And so we must return to the question, 'Whence the confidence that we, as Africans, can speak of an African Renaissance?'

What we have said so far is that both our ancient and modern history as well as our own practical and conscious deeds convey the same message: that genuine liberation, in the context of the modern world, is what drives the Africans of today as they seek to confront the problems which for them constitute a daily challenge.

Defining liberation

The question must therefore arise: What is it which makes up that genuine liberation?

The first of these (elements) is that we must bring to an end the practices as a result of which many throughout the world have the view that as Africans, we are incapable of establishing and maintaining systems of good governance. Our own practical experiences tell us that military governments do not represent the system of good governance which we seek.

Accordingly, the continent has made the point clear that it is opposed to military coups and has taken practical steps, as exemplified by the restoration to power of the elected government of Sierra Leone, to demonstrate its intent to meet this challenge when it arises. Similarly, many governments throughout the continent, including our continental organisation, the OAU, have sought to encourage the Nigerian government and people to return as speedily as possible to a democratic system of government.

Furthermore, our experience has taught us that one-party states also do not represent the correct route to take towards the objective of a stable system of governance, which serves the interests of the people. One of the principal demands in our liberation struggle, as we sought to end the system of apartheid, was: 'The people shall govern!' It is this same vision which has inspired the African peoples so that, during the present decade, we have seen at least 25 countries establish multi-party democracies and hold elections so that the people can decide on governments of their choice.

The new South Africa is itself an expression and part of this African movement towards the transfer of power to the people. At the same time, we are conscious of the fact that each country has its particular characteristics to which it must respond as it establishes its democratic system of government.

Accordingly, none of us seek to impose any supposedly standard models of democracy on any country, but want to see systems of government in which the people are empowered to determine their destiny and to resolve any disputes among themselves by peaceful political means.

[…]

Popular rule and political rebirth

What we are arguing therefore is that in the political sphere, the African Renaissance has begun. Our history demands that we do everything in our power to defend the gains that have already been achieved, to encourage all other countries on our continent to move in the same direction, according to which the people shall govern, and to enhance the capacity of the OAU to act as an effective instrument for peace and the promotion of human and people's rights, to which it is committed.

Such are the political imperatives of the African Renaissance which are inspired both by our painful history of recent decades and the recognition of the fact that none of our countries is an island which can isolate itself from the rest, and that none of us can truly succeed if the rest fail.

The second of the elements of what we have described as the genuine liberation of the peoples of Africa is, of course, an end to the tragic sight of the emaciated child who dies because of hunger or is ravaged by curable diseases because their malnourished bodies do not have the strength to resist any illness.

What we have spoken of before, of the restoration of the dignity of the peoples of Africa itself, demands that we deal as decisively and as quickly as possible with the perception that as a continent we are condemned forever to depend on the merciful charity which those who are kind are ready to put into our begging bowls.

[…]

These economic objectives, which must result in the elimination of poverty, the establishment of modern multi-sector economies, and the growth of Africa's share of world economic activity, are an essential part of the African Renaissance. We are certain that the movement towards their achievement will also be sustained precisely because this movement represents an indigenous impulse which derives from our knowledge of the mistakes we have made in the past and our determination to put those mistakes behind us.

I say this to emphasize the point that necessarily the African Renaissance, in all its parts, can only succeed if its aims and objectives are defined by the Africans themselves, if its programmes are designed by ourselves and if we take responsibility for the success or failure of our policies.

[…]

It is our hope and conviction that this important member of the world community of nations, Japan, will see itself as our partner in the practical promotion of the vision of an African Renaissance. By acting on the variety of matters we have mentioned and others besides, we trust that Japan will continue to place herself among the front ranks of those who are driven to act not only within the context of a narrowly defined national interest, but with the generosity of spirit which recognizes the fact that our own humanity is enriched by identifying ourselves especially with those who suffer.

When once more the saying is recalled, '*Ex Africa semper aliquid novi!*' (Something new always comes out of Africa!), this must be so, because out of Africa reborn must come modern products of human economic activity, significant contributions to the world of knowledge, in the arts, science and technology, new images of an Africa of peace and prosperity.

Thus shall we, together and at last, by bringing about the African Renaissance depart from a centuries-old past which sought to perpetuate the notion of an Africa condemned to remain a curiosity slowly grinding to a halt on the periphery of the world. Surely those who are the offspring of the good that sprang from the Meiji Restoration would not want to stay away from the accomplishment of so historic a human victory!

Thank you.

PETER PELS
The Pidginization of Luguru Politics
Administrative Ethnography & the Paradoxes of Indirect Rule

Reference
American Ethnologist, 23, 4, 1996: 738–61

The study of 'colonialism' faces a paradox: while its object is increasingly recognized as crucial to any understanding of the practice of anthropology, it has at the same time lost the meaningful unity of a systematic and intentional project of rule (Dirks 1992: 7; Thomas 1994: ix).[1] While the term *colonialism* suggests that one can outline a certain order imposed by colonizers on colonized societies, the study of this order unveils 'tensions of empire' among colonizers (Cooper and Stoler 1989). When the balance between strategies of coercion, persuasion, collaboration, and resistance employed by both colonizers and colonized is drawn up, 'colonialism' fragments into contingencies (Guha 1989: 230). It turns out that the concept of 'hegemony' has too often lent a spurious unity to the power relationships between colonizer and colonized, perpetuating the failure of both colonialist and anticolonialist historiography 'to discern the anomalies that made colonialism into a figure of paradox' (Guha 1989: 213).

The contradiction in terms of 'indirect rule' exemplifies the tensions of empire (Cooper and Stoler 1989: 616), and an echo of its paradoxicality can be heard in its description as an 'invention of tradition' (Ranger 1983). But if an 'invented tradition' is taken to be a successful transformation of a politics of 'competition, movement and fluidity' into a rigid code of unchanging custom (1983: 248–51), one may doubt whether the terms cover the full range of imperial tensions, negotiations, manipulations, and paradoxes that characterized indirect rule. In the following study of the implementation of indirect rule in the Uluguru Mountains of Eastern Tanganyika in the 1920s and 1930s, I hope to show that it did not completely 'invent' Luguru standards of legitimate leadership and that its reified concept of Luguru 'tradition' masked a number of shifts and renegotiations, sometimes directly occasioned by the flexible use Luguru authorities made of these 'traditions.' The fact that Waluguru, to this day, distinguish between 'traditional' headmen (*wakubwa wa jadi*) and the headmen appointed by British administrators (*wandewa*) makes one doubt whether the legitimacy of the invented tradition was ever accepted and should lead us to reconsider the premises of both 'invention' and 'tradition' and the hegemony that is often ascribed to them. I hope to show that, as elsewhere in Africa (cf. Fields 1985), and perhaps in all administrative ethnography (Pels and Salemink 1994: 18), indirect rule did, indeed, add a more rigid dimension to local politics. This reification of Luguru political discourse, however, did not give British administrators a stable hegemony and was used by both Waluguru and administrators in flexible ways. I shall argue that the construction and use of a reified concept of Luguru custom can be better understood as a process of 'pidginization' in circumstances of large power differences between substrate and superstrate political languages.

Representation and pidginization

In Africanist historiography, 'invented traditions' were first identified in order to distinguish 'authentic' ones: 'invented traditions' were things against which students of African history had to 'defend' themselves in order to reach the 'really pivotal' traditions of, in this case, Lozi history (Prins 1980: 8, 12). This led Prins to support Horton and Soyinka by saying that the colonial factor was a mere 'catalytic incident' in African history (1980: 15), a denial of historical change and a further reification of culture that few students of colonial history will accept. Terence Ranger also sees invented traditions as 'false models of colonial codified African tradition,' but – adding that they became colonial realities (1983: 212) – clearly thinks they were more than incidental. He also interprets them, however, as an inauthentic 'ideology' imposed by colonizers and shared, against their interests, by the colonized (1983: 229, 236).

The issue of the (in)authenticity of 'traditions' may be more important than the emphasis on their reification. The latter often fails to integrate analytically the interactions between colonizers and colonized (Thomas 1992: 213). It also fails to address the historical impact of a (Western) discourse on the truth or falsity – the 'authenticity' – of knowledge of other cultures within these interactions. Contemporary apologists of indirect rule generally emphasized the necessity of 'true' representations of indigenous institutions to create legitimate rule (Cameron 1937; Fortes and Evans-Pritchard 1940: 1, 15; Malinowski 1929; Perham 1934). Critics of indirect rule stressed the way in which European government on African lines created 'false' representations of indigenous tradition (Graham 1976; Ranger 1983). These opposed interpretations of colonial history both rely on a discourse of representation – that is, a discourse on the truth, or falsity, of ethnographic statements about 'others'.[2]

I submit that to understand the involvement of Waluguru and British in the implementation of indirect rule, one should not focus on the authenticity of the content of colonial representations but on the institution of representation (both political and textual) as such. In an important contribution to the debate, Timothy Mitchell has argued that a Western discourse of representation transformed Egyptian political discourse from a shifting play of difference into an attribution of certain, unambiguous, and stable meanings to political concepts (1991: 138): a step toward the reification of custom and culture mentioned above. This effect is achieved through an ordering discipline of 'enframing', a method of dividing up and containing social practices in a 'neutral' space that creates the illusion of an independent, objective, or natural system of magnitudes (1991: 44–5). Enlisting Foucault in the service of Derrida, Mitchell writes that in its way, 'political power, however microphysical in its methods, operates *always* so as to appear as something set apart from the real world' (1991: 160; emphasis added). It does this by creating the 'theological effect' of an absent, objective referent that conceals its author and its political authority at the same time (1991: 146, 154).

Mitchell's account contains much of value, particularly when he points out the redundancy of widely dispersed ordering and classifying activities that under colonial rule were condensed in statistical surveys and the census (Anderson 1991; Cohn 1987; Rafael 1994). But his theory presupposes a kind of hegemony that contains all modes of resistance 'within the organizational terrain of the colonial state' (Mitchell 1991: xi). Mitchell cannot conceive theoretically of the interaction between a Western discourse on representation and the forms of production of meaning that it transforms: the latter are only addressed as fundamentally 'other' to the former, which reproduces an essentialization of otherness upon which the colonial discourse that he criticizes also relied.[3] Mitchell's account perhaps incorporates a microphysics of European discipline as it was intended to be imposed on Egyptian society, but he leaves out the microphysics of colonial contact that mediated the transformation of indigenous social practice by European 'representation' and 'discipline' (Hirschkind 1991).

Thus, despite Mitchell's innovative stress on the dominance of a discourse of representation, as in many accounts of indirect rule (e.g., Fields 1985; Graham 1976; Ranger 1983),[4] he seems unable to conceive of an interaction between dominant and subordinate discursive practices. If we want to maintain a focus on the reifications and restrictions of indigenous political discourse produced by the ethnographic representations of indirect administration, it might be better to follow the lead of Johannes Fabian (1978: 317) and regard this ethnography as a 'pidgin' constructed in the interaction between substrate and superstrate political languages. The pidgin, while being a creative proliferation of meaning in the context of linguistic interaction as a whole, may appear as a 'restricted' development when measured against either the substrate or the superstrate language.

The study of pidgins and creoles has departed from the evolutionary model that posited the transformation from an unstable, restricted, artificial second language – the pidgin – into a stable, elaborated, more natural 'mother tongue' – the creole (Jourdan 1991: 192, 194). The model of a restricted and artificial language development broke down in the face of research emphasizing the importance of substrate languages, the social contexts in which pidgins and creoles are produced, and the diversity of speakers' linguistic praxis (1991: 188–9). Christine Jourdan concludes that one can distinguish between pidgins, creoles, and other languages by taking as criteria the nature of the contact situation and the type of language transmission to other generations (1991: 190). On that basis, a pidgin can be identified as a second language to speakers from both substrate and superstrate languages (Jourdan 1991: 194). It is created by eliminating those forms of the sub- and superstrate languages that speakers regard as anomalous to the functioning of the pidgin as a communicative system (1991: 195).

All this is remarkably like the invented traditions of administrative ethnography. Poised between the superstrate discourse on (political) representation and the substrate indigenous political language, administrative ethnography developed on the basis of creative negotiation between agents of both discursive communities. Like a pidgin, however, it is also the product of a balance of power and of global and local inequalities between languages (see Asad 1986). This administrative ethnography can be identified by its contact situation – the *préterrain* (forefield) of British administrative anthropology and Luguru political practice, as it became discursively realized at the ethnographic occasion of the baraza or council meeting – and by its transmission by bureaucratic reproduction.[5] This pidgin of Luguru politics was 'restricted' because it realized only selected elements from British administrative doctrine and Luguru politics, yet in practical interaction it complicated and fractured both and therefore also enriched both.

In the following pages, I first describe the superstrate political discourse of tribal representation characteristic of Tanganyikan indirect rule (its administrative anthropology) and show that it was internally fractured by suppositions about 'good' and 'other' government. Second, I hope to show that the substrate or subaltern political discourse of Waluguru was also internally divided between a stable lineage politics and discourse on initiation and a more fluid negotiation of 'big man' positions based on rainmaking and other magical capacities (a reversal of the situation in Usambara so aptly recorded by

Feierman [1990]). Finally, I hope to show through what kind of social mediations the pidgin – the administrative ethnography of Uluguru – was brought into being, how its paradoxical development depended on both the substrate and superstrate political discourses, and why the latter can be interpreted (but not understood) as a prophylactic device that tried to ensure the *absence* of the administrator from Luguru politics – a paradoxical situation eminently characteristic of indirect rule.

Indirect rule as administrative anthropology

It has been argued that the decision to rule through indigenous authorities in Africa was an economical one based on the scarcity of personnel and that, in consequence, the doctrine of indirect rule had little impact when adopted (Fields 1985: 32, 41). But in Tanganyika, if not elsewhere, the introduction of indirect rule enabled the state to penetrate society far deeper than before (Iliffe 1979: 325). This was the result of a language of 'tribal' representation that, although it had roots in British Indian colonial society, had developed into a distinct, British–African, political anthropology by the time Donald Cameron implemented it as governor of Tanganyika in 1925.

Although Cameron partly learned his trade when acting as chief secretary to Frederick Lugard in Nigeria, he departed from the latter's policy of calculated noninterference. Lugard's first interest was to extend military rule – rule by conquest – in a downward direction, that is, to delegate his own authority to native chiefs rather than incorporate theirs (Lugard as quoted in Kirk-Greene 1965: 45). In Nigeria, Lugard did not advocate 'ruling on African principles,' the benevolent protection of native life and the institution of Native Treasuries characteristic of later forms of indirect rule; these were added by subordinate officers inspired by British Indian examples and were vehemently opposed by Lugard (Flint 1978: 302–4; Gailey 1974: 11; Kirk-Greene 1965: 9–11).[6] Instead, Cameron's propensity for anthropological research stems from Lugard's successor as governor of Nigeria, Hugh Clifford, who inherited it from Malayan exemplars, the indirect rule of Rajah Brooke, and Hugh Low in particular.[7] When Cameron was appointed governor of Tanganyika in 1925, he insisted, like Clifford, on the necessity of guiding African political evolution, a task that rarely occupied Lugard during his Nigerian years (Gailey 1974: 115).

Thus Cameron arrived in Tanganyika in April 1925 with an administrative anthropology largely derived from South (East) Asian colonial rule, a tradition that was both at the roots of and in tension with the budding anthropological profession in Britain.[8] His predecessor, Horace Byatt, left Cameron with sufficient staff and revenue for the large-scale administrative reform (Gailey 1974: 36) which was thought necessary for the purpose of undoing Byatt's ambiguous policy of nominally instituting indirect rule through 'tribal' chiefs while at the same time retaining the 'non-tribal' *akida* appointed by the Germans. This gave Cameron the additional opportunity to centralize the administration (Ingham 1965: 547–52) and wrest the initiative from a group of senior officers, accustomed to the velvet glove of Byatt, who had already started to implement indirect rule after Byatt's departure.[9] The most forceful personality among them was Charles Dundas, who was as dedicated as Cameron to the promotion of African interests.[10] Dundas was appointed the first secretary of native affairs of Tanganyika, but he did not get along very well with Cameron. Both agreed on the necessity of ethnography for native administration, but Cameron was dogmatic in his insistence on a theory of 'tribes' held together by chieftainships, while Dundas argued that 'chiefs' were hard to find in many Tanganyikan societies.

To appreciate this conflict in the administrative hierarchy, and its

influence on indirect rule in Uluguru, it is necessary to emphasize again that Cameron substituted the Lugardian delegation of authority to chiefs by the incorporation of mechanisms of tribal cohesion. The political evolution that this implied was to be achieved by a process of development from the tribal constitution of the past to local government on British lines in the future, under the advice and control of British officers. In this process the recognition of the *present* ruler was less important than research into the *past* tribal constitution, and interference by the political officer was necessary.[11] The latter emphasis was a result of his commitment to two specific ideas: the akida myth and his theory of tribal cohesion. Cameron thought the Germans had intentionally destroyed indigenous institutions by imposing rule through an akida, who was an alien to the tribe concerned and therefore lacked a traditional position of authority. Lugard preserved chiefship by deposing the rulers of Northern Nigeria only to reinstate their relatives later on, but Cameron did not expect to find institutions worth preserving in existence. While his dogmatic view of Tanganyikan history made it imperative to do research, not all of Cameron's officers agreed with it (Gailey 1974:79).[12] The akida myth provided a scapegoat to which the 'defects or weaknesses' of indirect rule could be attributed.[13] It also emphasized the urgency with which it had to be instituted: to counter the threat of leaderless and uncontrolled, detribalized natives, Cameron's subordinates had to work, to work fast, and on the lines set out by him. This sense of urgency was created by the theory of tribal rule in which Cameron believed and that forms the core of his anthropology.

Unlike the early Lugard, Cameron did not legitimate rule by conquest.[14] Conquest, including the imposition of purely British standards of government, would create the desire among Africans to take over government. This would turn them into 'bad imitations' of Europeans, a phenomenon that Cameron thought was the cause of nationalist troubles in Egypt and India. To Cameron, the 'Good African' was an African 'from the bottom,' still in touch with traditional ways of life and giving his allegiance to his 'natural leaders,' the chiefs. If the chiefs were incorporated into the system of administration and Africans given an immediate share in their own government, they would perhaps seek more independence – but not on the side of the modern political agitator.[15]

Although Cameron would later acknowledge that chieftaincy was not the only principle of Tanganyikan politics, in 1926, when he published his Native Authority Ordinance, he was convinced that the office of a Native Authority '*normally* consists of a hereditary tribal chief, almost invariably in association with certain elders and other persons who occupy positions of dignity and responsibility.' Despite Dundas's conviction (in 1925) that there were societies in Tanganyika that had never developed institutions of chiefship and were only 'democratic and patriarchal,' Cameron was at that time far from acknowledging the 'essential democracy' of Bantu society that the Tanganyika government claimed before the Permanent Mandates Commission in 1929 (Ingham 1965: 567). Tribal consent was, in the words of the East Africa Commission, to be based on the acknowledgment that 'hereditary right to authority is an idea still generally recognized in the African mind.' Thus Cameron and his officers could switch at will from 'tribal institutions' to 'tribal constitutions,' because institutions were conceived in a legalist sense, as ideas or laws shared by all members of the tribe.[16] The customs of the tribe were the laws of succession and the laws of succession were hereditary. If Africans did not have their legitimate, hereditary chiefs, tribal organization would be destroyed. Therefore every improvement the administration wanted to make in native society depended on the quality of the chiefs. That meant that the sons of chiefs had to be educated in order to modernize native society; moreover, 'extra-tribal' forms of organization such as those created by missionaries had to be guarded so as not to develop into something 'political.'[17]

It is crucial to realize the paradoxical aspects of this attempt to find a baseline for political evolution (compare to Flint 1978: 301). By formulating a conception of an 'other' politics, Cameron implicated himself in a hierarchy of standards different from that of British politics (Fields 1985). 'Representation' of the majority, for instance, could not be the result of elections on European lines – this would merely give room to the agitator. Instead, the chief was supposed to represent his people by their recognition of his hereditary authority.[18] But that implied that Cameron had to caution his officers not to insist on 'the highest standards of English public life,' because, were they to do so, they could urge measures that threatened tribal organization. For the appointment of chiefs three principles applied: personal ability, hereditary or traditional right and custom, and the will of the people. The first had to be ignored most often, for 'nothing short of republican government will ensure that a ruler is always a capable man.'[19] Deposition of a chief on the grounds of incompetence meant nothing less than that hereditary or lawful succession was disallowed. 'Therewith the foundation of the tribal organization is undermined and Chiefs become purely government servants. Therefore rejection on this score must be based on stronger grounds than mere inferiority of intellect and character not amounting to absolute incapacity.' Because 'hereditary and traditional right substantiates personal claim and warrants the assumption that the people approve,' it was clear that of the three principles 'hereditary or traditional right' had to be the major one.[20]

Hereditary succession was, of course, not foreign to British politics: it was part and parcel of the aristocratic discourse surrounding the cult of the gentleman. A second aspect of the accommodation to the 'African' atmosphere was derived from British public school practice: the emphasis on the 'responsibility' of and the 'delegation of authority' by the chiefs resembled the ideology of the prefect system. As teachers supervised the prefects, so chiefs had to supervise their subchiefs and administrators their chiefs (Heussler 1963: 96–98; Ranger 1983: 216). A third aspect of accommodation – and a most successful one – was the fusion of legislative, executive, and judicial functions of government in the office of the chief, another aspect of colonial rule that had been previously tested in India and that was perceived as a pre-Montesquieuian phase of political evolution. Cameron dismissed Chief Justice Russell's protests against severing the connection between native courts and the High Court. Chiefs became the judges of the native courts, in which no barristers (even Africans) could appear in a professional capacity (Moffett 1952: 19).[21]

The urgency Cameron felt on account of this theory of tribal representation is made clear by the institution of indirect rule in Uluguru: Chief Muhina Goso Kingo of Northern Uluguru and Chief Kingalu Mwanamfuko of Southern Uluguru were both installed (replacing the akida of their territory) in June 1925, *before* Cameron asked his District officers to compile notes on the 'original constitution' of the tribes in their districts (in September 1925). Although Dundas, supported by the Morogoro District Officer, E. E. Hutchins, proposed a different arrangement after some research had been done, Cameron ignored the anomalies posed for his theory by the fact that Kingo was a conqueror of Northern Uluguru, while Kingalu was in no sense a hereditary chief of South Uluguru. Kingalu was to continue as chief until his deposition in 1936.[22] Eventually, Dundas had to pay for his opposition to Cameron's theory: his career suffered considerably and lagged behind that of his former assistant, Philip Mitchell.[23]

Administrative communication was not only hampered by dogmatism at the top but also by (mis)interpretation further down the administrative hierarchy. Many of the subtleties introduced by Cameron in indirect rule doctrine did not reach the lower levels of the administration. F. J. E. Bagshawe, as Provincial Commissioner of the Southern Highlands, issued the following instructions to his subordinates:

> Each tribe must be considered a distinct unit.... Tribal boundaries must be settled. Each tribe must be under a chief.... The wishes of the whole people must be taken under consideration.... Remember always that a chief is a native, with a native's partially developed sense of right and wrong, passions and temptations. Remember that he is your principal weapon in your work and that if he breaks you will have to make another.... Chiefs must be made to understand that we are increasing their power and paying them salaries and in return we expect a great deal more from them. [Graham 1976:4]

The martial analogies, the sense of European superiority, and the clear emphasis on chiefs as collaborators with the administration, instead of hereditary representatives of their people, show that sometimes there was not much difference between the chief and the akida (Graham 1976: 4) and that Lugard's conceptions of authority might still recur among Cameron's subordinates. This was partly the result of the exigencies of administration, which asked for hurried 'either-or' decisions instead of painstaking ethnography. As we will see, however, it was less a lack of knowledge as such than the absence of reflection on the way in which ethnographic representations were constructed that made a crucial difference for the construction of indirect rule in Uluguru.

Clans and big men in Uluguru political discourse

To understand how indirect rule transformed Luguru political discourse, it is necessary to construct an image of the substrate or subaltern political language that can be contrasted with the 'traditional' politics invented by the British. This contrast is more complex than Ranger's juxtaposition of 'competition, movement and fluidity' with a rigid administrative code (1983:248). Administrators usually talked of the Luguru 'clan system,' while later ethnographers used Evans-Pritchard's 'segmentary lineage system' (Young and Fosbrooke 1960: 39) or one of its modifications (such as the 'sub-clan' system [Brain 1973: 114]) to conceive of the unity of Luguru society. These conceptions were legalistic and reified descent categories predicated, for instance, on the argument that lineage discourse leads to ever-increasing segmentation (Young and Fosbrooke 1960: 70–71) or to straightforward progression, without choice or political struggle, to a lineage headmanship (Brain 1973: 114). These administrators ignored Evans-Pritchard's idea that talk of lineages was also a way to discuss other principles of organization (1940: 143) – that, in other words, descent categories were a *discourse* through which political and economic relations were organized and discussed.

Luguru lineages are traced back 15 generations at most, and these genealogies legitimize the position of the present lineage head, who embodies the power of these ancestors. Descent categories also help to organize relations of production and the exchange of labor.[24] This does not exclude that some lines of descent are fictitious, and Waluguru clearly distinguish between tracing descent through the female line and tracing it through classificatory kinship (in particular through adopted sister's sons, the *wapwa wa kukaribisha*). There is therefore room for political maneuvering within lineage relationships – for struggles between parallel lines of descent, between generations, and between men and women – but relationships are never only decided by the skills of the Machiavellian political entrepreneur central to transactionalist analyses (see Thoden van Velzen 1973). Beyond the realm of lineage discourse, however, a political entrepreneur's economic, military, and magical sources of power could well stake out a temporary 'big man' position.

This small-scale form of political organization evidently fits a society that, in very recent history, had been composed of small groups of travelers. Threatened by drought, famine, or war, the people who during colonial times were to be named 'Waluguru' fled into the mountains in the beginning of the nineteenth century.[25] Even there they were harassed by Wambunga warriors, Arab slavers, or internecine warfare often caused by the intervention of one or both of these groups. Waluguru commonly refer to the period before the Germans both as *wakati wa Wambunga* and as *wakati wa Waarabu*, as Wambunga raids and alliances between Luguru headmen and slave-raiding Arabs took place at the same time. Waluguru seem to have come from all points of the compass (Mzuanda 1958: 7 *et passim*), but their linguistic similarity to coastal peoples suggests that a majority came from the Eastern plains of Uzaramo and Ukwere.[26] In the process those Waluguru who possessed cattle lost them through east coast fever, and they settled down to a purely agricultural economy. District Commissioner Hutchins's encounter with the Waluguru in 1925–26 took the following ethnographic form:

> The tribal system is a clan system (UKOO), which is the strongest I have met with. The people have always paid more attention to their clan-heads than to the German-imposed *Jumbes*. Marriage within a clan is absolutely forbidden....Feeling between the various clans is still very strong and is mainly caused by jealousy. It is this interclan antagonism that has been so difficult to contend with in our efforts to re-establish the old system of tribal administration. It seems as if the family unit were the basis of organization, the elder of the family being appealed to in any matter requiring arbitration. This would also seem to be the foundation unit of the village and the latter to have grown round it. As descent in the tribe is matrilineal the growth of the family into the villages has been a natural outcome of the spread of family trees. Thus the family-head also grew into the village head, and, from arbitrating in purely family affairs he came to be the judge upon all village matters.
>
> This practice still continues and would appear to suit the immediate needs of the people. It would be a grave mistake to deprive these elders of their powers within the villages, nor would the people wish them to be so deprived. Over each group of villages is an hereditary Ndewa [*sic*] who rules a small district and is the head of the people living within its boundaries, but further than this tribal organization did not originally go. There seem to have been no cohesion amongst the various Wandewa, nor any of a higher standing than the others. Later on, as the successful rainmaker became more powerful, he gradually took over the control of the Wandewa in his particular sphere of work and this appears to have been the way that the families of Kingalo [*sic*], Hega and Mwanambago gradually became chiefs in their respective areas.[27]

Hutchins was correct in stating that the largest formal unit of organization was the area under the nominal authority of an original landholder (*mwenye saku* or *mndewa*, plural: *wenye saku*), and that none of them was capable of exercising substantial authority over the others.

His description, however, strongly oversimplified the situation. Moreover, his statement is framed by Cameron's theory of political evolution, according to which the family unit evolved gradually, by the logical extension of family trees and the growth of numbers, into a village, while a group of villages would eventually submit (by consent or by force) to a chief, whose prominence was based on martial and rainmaking powers.[28] The theory suggested that an emerging rainmaker would eventually occupy a position as politically stable and secure as that of the existing, less-powerful headmen.

When asked, 'Who is your chief?' a Mluguru would name a lesser headman, the landholder (*mwenye issi* [Kiluguru]; *mwenye nchi* [Swahili]) of the area around one or several hamlets, an area often inhabited by people belonging to one lineage (*tombo* [Kiluguru], 'breast'; *ziwa* [Swahili]) and some of their affines. The *mwenye issi* was a first among equals, and his position was legitimated by the genealogy of his ancestors, counted from the first to settle in that specific area. The recitation of the genealogy of landholders (all of whom took the name of the first upon accession to office) was first of all a claim to land; second, it was a claim to prominence in that area of a specific lineage or clan; and only in the last resort was it a claim to authority over all people occupying that land. In a larger unit of territory, usually a mountain valley, several wenye issi would be the nominal inferiors of the original landholder (*mwenye saku* or *mndewa*),[29] the one whose ancestor cleared the first patch of land and thereby established the claim of his clan (*lukolo* [Kiluguru]; *ukoo* [Swahili]) to that valley; but in practice, they were both advisors and competitors. The people settling on that land, however, were never merely (bio)logical extensions of the family that had settled there first. The concept of lukolo allowed the landholder to accept nominal sister's sons and their families and give them room to settle in the valley.[30] Thus, contrary to Hutchins's view, the authority of an original landholder was never merely authority over his direct descendants, and lineage discourse could be used both to subdivide territorial groups (in lineages) and to enlarge them (by adoption into the clan).

The order of succession to a landholder's name was never a fixed and logical matrilineal form of descent. Figure 1 displays the possibilities for negotiation. Supposing (1) is the ruling mwenye issi, (2) would be the ideal heir after his death or deposition, or (3) when there are no brothers. Generally, however, a group of women of the lineage – (a) or her mother the most prominent among them – decided whether a candidate was really suitable for the post. They could bypass (2) and (3) and give the name to (4) if he was old enough. An important consideration in this decision was whether the wife of the candidate was also suitable for high office, as she received the same rank as her husband. If (5) inherited the name, however, the chance for fission would increase because of the possibility that the eldest lineage (*tombo dikulu* [Kiluguru], or 'big breast') would at some point in time claim back the right to the name from a middle lineage (*tombo magati,* or 'breast in between') or the youngest (*tombo dudogo,* or 'little breast'). This essential negotiability of descent categories is also apparent from the fact that, at some points in Luguru history, one finds the sons of important headmen taking up a temporary post of prominence and even attempting to change matrilineal into patrilineal descent (and thus to objectify their right to rule).[31]

The integration of these political bodies was further enhanced by the practice of initiation. For Luguru boys, the entrance into the adult world was organized by the inhabitants of the valley or a smaller unit, depending on the power of the landholding clan. Girls were initiated individually or in twos and threes, emphasizing the prominence of the lineage (Pels, 1999: chs. 3 and 4). Access to valley politics was also

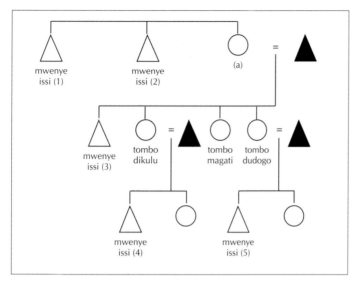

Fig. 1 Luguru kinship discourse. The diagram represents an ideal sequence of succession to male lineage and/or clan headmanship and some alternatives in the selection of suitable candidates. The black symbols indicate a member of a different clan. The order of birth is from left to right.

determined by initiation into the local society of *wenye mlunga* ('those who possess ancestral emblems'), a group of elders (male and female) that included members of other clans, a practice that acknowledged the local influence of the other clans while at the same time tying them to the landholding clan by the magical secrets shared among these initiates.[32] In this way, the tenants on another clan's land (*wapangaji*) could enter the political arena.

Landholders were the judges in matters of land and other disputes. They guarded relationships with the ancestors and, through them, regulated agricultural affairs in order to ensure a good harvest (always, however, in consultation with other elders). While a mwenye issi of a specific hamlet would guard the land of his own lineage, the mwenye saku would allocate land to newcomers in the valley as a whole, serve as a court of appeal, and be called upon to act in cases of lack of rain, locust plagues, epidemic illnesses, and other disasters due to the wrath of ancestors. (Before Europeans intervened he also made war medicine.) The secrets of his magical capabilities would be passed on to him when he took the name of his ancestor and received his regalia on accession to office. Since the settlement of the Uluguru mountains, several of the wenye saku had built up reputations bigger than others: the most important of these were Bambarawe in Matombo, Kingalu in Kinole, Hega in Kolero, and Mbago in Mgeta area (see Figure 2). This was partly due to their claim of possessing a place of reconciliation with ancestral or nature-spirits (*tambiko*) that had far more power for making war- or rain-magic than did others. They nonetheless never attained a position that gave them direct authority over another clan, or another lineage, except when it was of the same clan in the same area.

Hutchins called these big rainmakers 'chiefs' and in the autumn of 1925 suggested that both Mbago and Hega should be enthroned as equals to Kingalu, who was already chief of the former *akidat* of Mkuyuni. (Hutchins seems to have forgotten Bambarawe, possibly because he thought that Bambarawe no longer exercised his rain-

making functions after having become a Catholic – which was not the case.) But these influential headmen can be better understood as big men (*wakubwa*) who had risen to prominence by the successful manipulation of the magical, economic, and military sources at their command. Some of them drew on resources from outside the mountains: Mbago MwanaMatolola and Kingalu Fimbombili are on record as using their traffic with the coastal Arabs to their advantage (Mzuanda 1958: 27–31; Wendelini n.d.: 43–44).[33] Two different stories of the original settlement of Kinole area by the first Kingalu, however, will show what indigenous political strategies were available to Waluguru beyond lukolo discourse. The two versions of the story share the same outline: Mleke MwanaMsumi and his sister Mkirindila were on their way from the Nyingwa-Kibungo area to look for new land in the Kinole area (see Figure 2).[34] When they camped in that area, they were discovered by the local leader, Magoma, who was of a different clan.[35] Magoma immediately suspected evil intentions and went out to meet Mleke with a force. Mleke, however, managed to convince him of his peaceful intentions, they became friends, and, while Mleke got a piece of land from Magoma, Magoma married Mkirindila. Mkirindila, however, was asked by Mleke to spy on Magoma. When Mleke's army was ready and he knew all secrets of Magoma, he treacherously attacked him and drove him from Kinole. Subsequently, Mleke changed his name to Kingalungalu, the fickle one, which was later shortened to Kingalu. Kingalu continued with warfare, attacking his brother or, alternatively, his father, who still lived in the Nyingwa-Kibungo area, but he was killed, also through treason, and his people were driven back to Kinole.

The meeting between Mleke and Magoma is of great interest because the two versions of the story differ considerably. In the Kibungo version, told to an African priest (see Mzuanda 1958) by people of that area, Mleke says he wants to be friends and Magoma naively believes him and gives him a piece of land. Only after two years does Magoma decide to take a Mlambena (daughter of the Bena clan, Iike Mkirindila) as his wife.[36] In the other version, which James Brain got from one of the sons of Kingalu Mwanarubela at Kinole, the interaction is pictured rather differently. On his arrival at Mleke's camp, Magoma first inquires whether he has evil intentions and, after Mleke's denial, spends some time talking. The next day he returns and is given maize beer – a considerable gift, because beer (*pombe*) has a pivotal role in ritual and social action. The story emphasizes that to Magoma and his people maize beer is an innovation. Magoma spends the night at Mleke's camp and during the next day sees Mleke's sister Mkirindila and asks for her hand in marriage. Mleke consents (another gift); after staying for some time with Mleke, Magoma leaves with his bride. Just before their departure, Mleke instructs his sister to spy on Magoma.

Significantly, in the Kibungo version (which derived from a group hostile to the imperial claims of Kingalu and his supporters), Magoma is an innocent who gives a gift and gets treason in return. In the Kinole version, it is Mleke who starts giving (first a novel way of preparing beer, then his sister) and Magoma responds by allowing him to stay on his land. Like a good son-in-law, Magoma stays with Mleke – uxorilocally – but then anomalously departs for his own home. It is only when Magoma departs with his bride that Mleke starts his treason. Moreover, in the Kinole version Kingalungalu starts making war on his brother only after the latter had insulted his sister's son's wives (who are, nominally, Kingalu's wives), while, in the Kibungo version, he makes war on his father, headman of Kibungo, without any reason – an unforgivable act of disrespect.

Essential to an understanding of Luguru political process is that

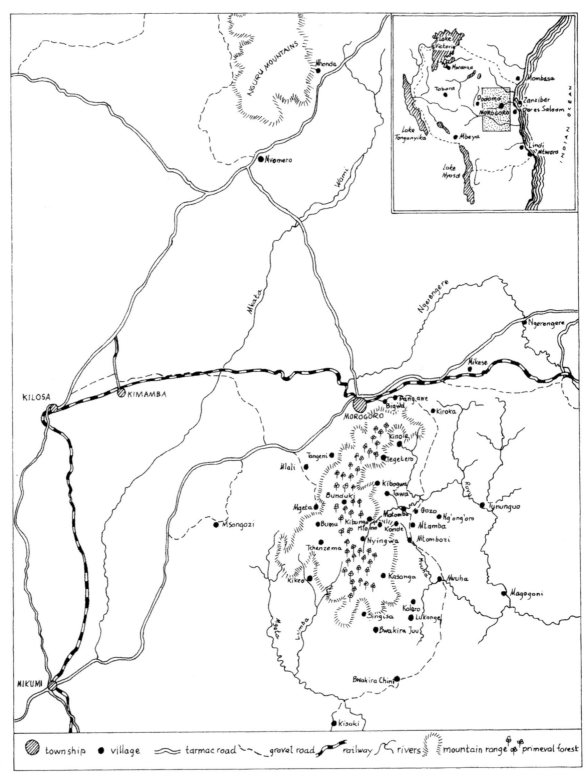

Fig. 2 Uluguru
Mountains and environs

both versions of this story relate a form of contact between members of different clans. The clans have no necessary relationship with each other, and it is significant that in this interclan context Kingalungalu, the fickle one, becomes a *nom de guerre*. Brain rightly remarks that among Waluguru cunning (*ujanja*) is something to be admired (1971: 831).[37] Although someone who gains his objectives by cunning alone does not deserve respect, many Waluguru are conscious that, in political realms where relationships of descent and respect no longer provide a more or less sufficient check on individual initiative, no one is to be trusted.

F. G. Bailey's treacherous 'clever leader' (1969: 61), however, is not simply the 'norm' for Luguru politics outside the politics organized by the discourse on clans and lineages. There are many examples of different clans that coexist peacefully. Lukolo discourse could also serve to co-opt new members into a body politic: the majority of landholders in the valley of Konde had once been adopted by the mwenye saku, Lwango, as nominal sister's sons, perhaps to strengthen the Mwenda clan against attacks by its powerful neighbor, Bambarawe.[38] Moreover, it would be naive to think that the politics of give-and-take, threat, and treason were restricted to relationships between people who did not share a line of descent: members of the same clan, (but different lineages) or members of the same lineage, also had to consider gift giving, magical threat, or physical power among themselves. If such internal quarrels were usually addressed in the idiom of witchcraft, that idiom itself shaded imperceptibly into the idiom of war- and rain-magic of interclan rivalry (Pels, 1999: ch. 6). The difference between intraclan and interclan politics arose mainly from the dominance established by elders – men in particular – in education, initiation, and marriage negotiations. This dominance found its most concentrated expression in the practices of initiation specific to a certain group, and it was legitimated by lukolo discourse.

Thus we can distinguish two registers of Luguru political discourse: one characterized by the concepts of lukolo authority, and another that allowed for the Machiavellian machinations of big men. As the story of Kingalu I makes clear, the latter register was also discursively regulated (by the right ways of giving a gift, of granting hospitality, and of marriage exchange) although it was not stabilized by the magical sources of clan and lineage authority that underpinned the position of a landholder – which, if violated, would incur the wrath of the ancestors to the detriment of the whole hamlet. Beyond the influence of ancestral authority, no enduring vertical relationships were maintained, and those landholders who managed to rise above their fellows can be designated as 'big men.' Their superior status was firmly tied to their personal initiative and could not easily be objectified to such an extent that it could be passed on to their successors. Ironically, the British directed most of their efforts at introducing hereditary chiefship into the latter sphere, where Luguru ideas about hereditary power did not apply.

The safari method and the pidginization of Luguru politics

In order to assess the interaction of the languages of indirect rule and Luguru politics, it is insufficient to concentrate on the texts of Luguru administrative ethnography alone (Pels 1994). To identify the latter as a pidgin in relation to its substrate and superstrate languages, one must focus on the practice of the production of administrative knowledge about Uluguru. What can be called a 'safari method' underlay both major efforts in the administrative ethnography of Uluguru, Hutchins's 'Tribal History and Legends,' and F. J. E. Bagshawe's 'Land Development Survey Report.' Fortunately, Bagshawe kept a diary,

recording his tour of Uluguru in minute detail.[39] The tour was a common practice of all Cameron's officers, who administered a district while traveling through it, calling together a council meeting (*baraza*), and, when finished, packing up and leaving for the next rural center. For ethnographic work, the administrators simply had to invert the council meeting: during a normal meeting, the Officer spoke and the Africans (chiefs, subchiefs, headmen) asked questions or nodded assent, while during ethnographic study it was the officer who asked questions and nodded assent when and where the answers to his questions confirmed what he wanted to hear.

A council meeting proceeded in Swahili, not Kiluguru; thus, to be able to speak Swahili was a *sine qua non* for administrative office, a criterion not explicitly recognized by the British. Despite any hereditary claim to authority, widespread popularity, or proven competency, a headman who spoke only Kiluguru could not get a government job. Like Kingalu Mwanarubela, Bagshawe's main conversation partner in the following account, Waluguru who were successful in government jobs were usually former servants of Europeans, proficient in Swahili, and inured to a routine of command and obedience. When Bagshawe set off on his tour in December 1929, his assignment was to find out whether, given the nature of Luguru land tenure, land could be alienated and sold to nonnative settlers. Moreover, he wanted to check the ethnographic material that District Commissioner Hutchins (according to Bagshawe 'an over-stalwart fellow running to fat which has penetrated to his brain') had gathered in the Morogoro District Book since 1925, and on which the implementation of indirect rule in Uluguru was based.

His first stop was the resthouse in Mkuyuni, headquarters of Kingalu Mwanarubela, then Chief (*sultani*) of South Uluguru. Kingalu, together with his son Omari, the subchief (*mtawala*) of Mkuyuni and several headmen (*wandewa*), soon joined Bagshawe in a council meeting. Although Bagshawe did not record in his diary the talk during that first baraza, after another talk with Kingalu and Omari the next day he wrote: 'Most disappointing, as I find that most of what I wrote yesterday is wrong! I took for granted a lot in the district record book & Kingalo [*sic*] said 'ndio' (*yes*/pp) to everything! Curse it.' Kingalu had obviously been on his guard on that first day, probing Bagshawe's mind and trying to ascertain what it was that he wanted to hear. After the previous day's chat about his work as a servant to a German official and his voicing complaints about traveling allowances, Kingalu must have found out that Bagshawe was out for something new and that he did not merely want to reproduce the district book's statements. On this second day, unencumbered by the presence of headmen who might dispute his claims, he told Bagshawe the story of his ancestor Kingalu I's conquest of Kinole (as recorded in the previous section), and added that the whole of Southern Uluguru–including Mgeta, Matombo, and Kolero – submitted to Kingalu I.

Bagshawe recognized Kingalu's strategy ('[his claims], I think, will be disputed'), probably assisted by Hutchins's account of the equal status of the chiefs of Kolero (Hega) and Mgeta (Mbago).[40] Despite his doubts about Kingalu's claims, Bagshawe nevertheless wrote that Kingalu's appointment 'was wise. It is accepted cheerfully by the people and there is no apparent friction with any of the Sub-chiefs though possibly his appointment was accepted grudgingly by Hega and Mbago in the beginning.'[41] But Bagshawe was taking a snapshot of a political process that had been in motion for some time, and Kingalu skillfully manipulated Bagshawe's safari method in order to set the frame and contents of the picture. Just as speakers from substrate and superstrate languages creatively construct a pidgin in specific contact situations and by specific means of transmission to other generations, so Kingalu and Bagshawe cooperated (albeit for different reasons) to select a number of political representations by means of a contact situation (the safari method) and a form of transmission of its results (bureaucratic writing). Part of the result, however, was to keep large chunks of Luguru political practice out of the administrator's eye.

In the mountains a political struggle went on that largely escaped Bagshawe's method of gathering information. Kingalu Mwanarubela had, shortly after succeeding his deceased uncle in August 1927, attacked the positions of his potential rivals by subordinating his subchiefs Mbago and Hega to the control of an assistant and by diminishing the headmanship of subchief Bambarawe's son to half its size.[42] Moreover, only six years after Bagshawe's survey, District Commissioner Hutchins had to ask for sanction from the Governor to depose Kingalu:

> The Chief is greedy and unscrupulous and the sole reason why his subjects have accepted his abuses without complaint for so long is because of the power he holds over them as a rain-doctor, which practice he has never abandoned, Whilst little could be definitely proved against him, whispers of his malpractices are becoming increasingly audible, and I have little doubt but that the majority of his subjects will breathe a sigh of relief when his reign comes to an end.[43]

The Governor agreed, and the process of assessing the administrative capacities of Kingalu's heir, his nephew Gungurugwa, and the claims of his rivals was started. Kingalu's subchiefs were very diffident about having to express their preferences, and, although they chose Gungurugwa, Hutchins could not but feel that it was not 'in agreement with the wishes of the majority.' Gungurugwa, on the other hand, knew that, when appointed, he would be no more than a figurehead for his deposed uncle.[44] Hutchins proposed to his Provincial Commissioner to amalgamate North and South Uluguru under the Chief of North Uluguru, Muhina Goso Kingo, and went on leave. The Provincial Commissioner encountered the same confusion in trying to assess who really represented the wishes of the majority, and, after a number of unsatisfactory and mutually contradicting council meetings, the majority of subchiefs and headmen expressed themselves in favor of the government's choice; in due time Kingo became the first Chief of the whole of Uluguru.[45]

The British attempts to second-guess at the whispers of the majority, and the hesitation of Waluguru to choose between 'hereditary' claims to office and the wishes of the government, indicate an element of the substrate or subaltern politics that helped to construct – yet did not appear in – administrative ethnography. Waluguru often told me of the necessity of having a 'cool heart' (*moyo baridi*) in dealing with other people. A responsible leader had been taught to suppress *moto* ('fire,' but also 'anger,' 'desire,' or 'aggression'), because it could neither lead to agreement in relations with others, or, more significant, to harmony with the ancestors (*mizimu*), who prefer coolness, tranquility, and shade to sun and exertion. Contradicting another person was a gesture of moto that befitted neither leaders nor their subordinates. Kingalu, Bambarawe, Mbago, and Hega embodied some of the most important spirits in Eastern Uluguru and could anger them – their source of power and authority – in contradicting each other. They might provoke a showdown of power, unleashing magical forces that none of them wanted to confront.[46] And, of course, it was neither necessary nor advisable to unveil one's political strategies for a chief or his white superior – they were better kept to oneself. We only have to think of Kingalu saying 'ndio' to everything Bagshawe

suggested on the first day of the visit to understand how elementary this reticence was in Luguru politics.

Kingalu adroitly manipulated this tendency not to complain about one's leader except behind his back: he hardly left Bagshawe's side during his survey safari.[47] Conversely, the superstrate language of representation guaranteed that Bagshawe never tried to speak to Kingalu's subordinates in Kingalu's absence, despite the fact that Kingalu himself had shown how Waluguru guarded their statements in the presence of superiors. Issues of hereditary representation constituted the council meetings: at a later baraza, Bagshawe discussed the subchiefship of Kasanga, in the presence of the Kingalu, the Matombo subchief Bambarawe, some headmen, and several candidates for the post. Headmen not appointed by the British were automatically excluded. More important, there were no women present, despite the fact that the leading women of a lineage exerted formal political power beyond the selection of suitable successors to a lineage headmanship. The former subchief of Kasanga, Chambandewa, was a son of the prewar Hega, and Kingalu had taken hereditary, matrilineal succession as an excuse to replace him with his own candidate. The latter, however, was soon deposed for embezzlement, and Bagshawe had to resolve who was to succeed him, sandwiched as he was between Kingalu's manipulation of 'hereditary' succession and Chambandewa's attempts to resist it. In this context, it is significant that Bagshawe had no time for Chambandewa when the latter tried on a later occasion to talk to him alone: Chambandewa was no longer 'representative.' Thus Luguru avoidance of moto and British ideas of representation combined to pidginize Luguru politics.

Kingalu was absent from Bagshawe's council meetings on only one other occasion, and this may indicate another way in which a discourse of representation pidginized Luguru politics. Bagshawe sent Kingalu to Morogoro to settle the boundaries of Northern and Southern Uluguru with Kingo, chief of the North, and went alone to Matombo, where he had a long talk with Bambarawe and his wandewa:

> [Bambarawe] does not claim that the ancient Mbambalawe's[48] were 'over' the local Wandewa, but they were respected & were rain and war doctors, his uncle, especially, having defeated Wambunga invaders. All Wandewa ruled their clans in ordinary affairs independently. The Germans made his uncle chief; he says that if anyone was chief in pre-German days, it was Kingalo [*sic*]. No one has replaced his (Bambarawe's/pp) family as rain-makers since he became a Christian.[49]

Before his wandewa (including powerful men like Moto, Lwango, Gugulu, and Chamlungu) and without the presence of Kingalu, Bambarawe stated that they were independent. Then follows an interesting sentence: 'If anyone was chief in pre-German days, it was Kingalo.' This probably helped to convince Bagshawe of Kingalu's 'representativeness,' but the written sentence does not give any indication as to how it was spoken. Information gathered in writing divorces the content of knowledge from its performance. By emphasizing communication as writing and reading, it elevates visual activity over the oral/aural and tactile production of knowledge. It thereby reinforces a European language ideology that takes writing as the model for semiotics, and thereby privileges a discourse of representation (Fabian 1983; Tyler 1984).[50] When we add oral/aural activity, however, by emphasizing intonation, the sentence that begins with '*If* anyone was chief …' may as well be read as a guarded statement about the absence of chiefs in Uluguru before the German period. (My guess is that Bambarawe did not like to add, 'But no one was.') Speculative as it may be, the example indicates the possibility that the language of representation intervened even more deeply in the performance of the baraza than merely determining who should be present.

This is not the only way in which pidginization from a position of power can occur: others have pointed to the 'brutal' use of the expressive function of language and its tendency to limit conversation to expressions of command (Samarin 1984: 449–50; see also Cohn 1985; Fabian 1986: 112–34). 'Brutal' expression is related to coercion, however, whereas the privileging of the referential function in Luguru administrative ethnography enabled collaboration. The two forms of pidginization could work together: the hesitation and lip-service to government displayed by Walugurubela during the barazas held after the deposition of Kingalu Mwanarubela show that they found it hard to distinguish between British questions, exhortations, and commands. But it was the language of tribal representation, translated into the pidgin of 'true' Luguru chiefs, subchiefs, and headmen, that enabled indirect rule to penetrate Luguru society far more deeply than before.

This penetration was made possible initially by the contact situation of the baraza. In a 'traditional' Luguru council meeting the number and variety of positions of the people present guaranteed a certain practical democracy. The women were there, and although the women did not speak, the men certainly felt their presence. When someone whose opinion was deemed important was absent, the meeting was often postponed. An administrative baraza, however, ignored all these 'unofficial' or unrepresentative political positions; it had to be concluded in a single session. The language of hereditary chieftaincies and headmanships convinced British administrators that this was how such sessions should be performed, a conviction actively sustained by those Waluguru who, like Kingalu, profited by that language and tried to keep their political struggles out of the government's eye. In this way, the discourse on representation created both its representation (the ethnography of Uluguru) and its referent (the appointed 'chief') in one single move.

In addition, the penetration of Luguru society by the language of tribal representation was sustained through transmission to both Waluguru and future administrators by bureaucratic reproduction (see Schulte Nordholt 1994). Once identified, the chief or headman was subject to a hierarchy of command and communication that made him responsible for the accuracy of the information given to the British official and for the implementation of the policies dictated by that official. In the practice of the Luguru Native Administration, this implied a constant repetition of the central tenets of administrative ethnography, reinforcing the hierarchy of headmen, subchiefs, and chiefs. Most administrators subordinate to or succeeding Hutchins and Bagshawe never took care to check the earlier ethnography, an oversight that indicates the power mediated by the written word. The fundamental tendency of bureaucratic thought 'to turn all problems of politics into problems of administration' (Mannheim 1960: 105) required stable representations, which were provided by both the written reifications of administrative ethnography and the 'chief' as the personified, nonarbitrary sign of Luguru authority.

The stability of this administrative pidgin was nevertheless an illusion, if only because its contents were interpreted by different groups in different ways. While Bagshawe seemed to think of the appointed chiefs and headmen as representative of their people (owing to either the laws of hereditary succession or a simple absence of complaints), subordinate Waluguru probably thought of the chief as the employee of the government. The stability of 'true' or legitimate political representation as perceived by British administrators, might, instead, be a stability based on fear of the powerful, for, as I was told

in 1990, 'we should be afraid of the government' (*tuogope serikali*). That brings us, in conclusion, to the systematic instability of indirect rule.

The paradoxes of pidgin politics

Indirect rule in Uluguru was characterized by a strong tendency toward the reification of ethnographic representation along legalistic and bureaucratic lines. But no bureaucracy can keep out politics by decree alone, and this was further complicated by the paradoxes and contradictions existing among and within substrate, superstrate, and pidgin political discourses. Above, I have already noted the tension between the standards of hereditary succession and those of 'good government' within administrative anthropology, as well as the tension within Luguru political discourse between lukolo discourse and the realm of the exchange of violence, magic, and gifts. In conclusion, I would like to consider how these tensions reappeared in the practical implementation of pidgin politics, which created a proliferation of political possibilities comparable in effect to the addition of a pidgin to the linguistic world of both substrate and superstrate languages.

As I have demonstrated, the implementation of indirect rule in Uluguru was based, on the one hand, on the invented offices of chief and subchief (which reified the fluid and transitory 'big man' positions of Kingalu, Hega, Bamabarawe, and Mbago on the grounds of a theory of political evolution through war- and rainmaking powers) and on the other on the incorporation of selected Luguru landholders at a lower level of the administration. The instability of the standards by which appointments were made is evident from the fact that the 15 headmen appointed in the Matombo area in 1926 had been increased to 21 in 1947.[52] The appointed headmen often ruled an area much larger than their previous sphere of influence, partly because headmen who could not speak Swahili were ineligible for office. Moreover, many Waluguru tried to keep pidgin politics – the representations of administrative ethnography – at a distance because they were afraid to see their leader, who had to protect clan and land fertility through a tenuous relationship with his ancestors, compromised by direct subordination to the white man. Often, sons or cousins of wenye saku were appointed as headmen in the place of their fathers or uncles. In some places, a rival managed to stage a coup (like Moto – the name is significant – who displaced his nominal uncle Lwango in Konde). In others, a former jumbo (headman under German rule) who had settled in the area as a Christian teacher managed to retain his post (like Marie Pauli in Tawa) with no hereditary rights whatsoever. Bambarawe joined Kiswira (his own valley) with Gozo into one single headmanship and gave it to his son, who remained in office until 1928, when Barnbarawe's rival Mgombelwa got Gozo back with Kingalu's help. The seemingly stable representations of Luguru authority by the British thus often merely covered a series of desperate political fights.

But this stability was also threatened from within the discourse of administrative anthropology. Its standard of hereditary succession was the core of its theory of tribal representation and topped the hierarchy of standards of government. As I have shown, however, hereditary succession had to be weighed against the suitability of the candidate and the will of the people. In practice this combination turned out to be difficult to maintain. The history of Native Administration in Uluguru shows a constant recurrence of warnings and depositions of chiefs and subchiefs, and at each occurrence the standards of chiefship had to be renegotiated. The deposition of Kingalu Mwanarubela and the amalgamation of Uluguru under Chief Kingo in 1936 was rationalized by Hutchins, who argued that 'Kingalu was never more than a clan head (Ndewa [sic]) who had acquired additional powers locally through the sacerdotal functions of a rain-maker,' while Kingo was the 'only real chief' of Uluguru because of his grandfather's conquest of the Morogoro plains.[53] Thus, Cameron's evolutionary theory, in which rain-making powers were part of the development of chiefship from the clan stage, gave way to the more Lugardian conception of rule through conquest. When a successor to Kingo had to be chosen after his death in 1943, the 1936 conception of chiefship was again reinterpreted; by this point the chief had not been appointed by right of succession or of conquest but because he was 'the only Chief of any standing in Uluguru.' As the appointment had been reinterpreted as meritocratic, it no longer followed that his heir should necessarily become chief.[54]

This occasion marked the demise of Cameron's standards of otherness: despite the incessant protests of the heirs of Kingo and Kingalu.[55] the former was succeeded by Sabu bin Sabu, the subchief of Mkuyuni, who, as the most efficient native administrator, was appointed on merit only. Such renegotiation of standards of rule was widespread: the only subchief to continue in office until his death in 1950 was Bambarawe. His hereditary successors were deposed for maladministration, tax fraud, or other forms of 'corruption,' and the next subchief was appointed on merit. All other incumbents of subchief positions suffered the same fate. What happened at the level of headmanships was rarely recorded, but the few instances that were suggest similar processes.[56] Indirect rule, therefore, was caught in the paradox that the standards of good government along pidginized Luguru lines created bad government along British lines. This paradoxicality of British standards of colonial rule was probably the cause of the oft-repeated complaint by Waluguru that while the German rulers were tough (kali) but explicit, the British were difficult to understand and ambiguous.[57] The British administrator, drawing on a heterogeneous discourse of colonial rule, was not the social engineer of Cameron's policy of political evolution but a bricoleur reinventing the criteria of good government from occasion to occasion and thereby giving Africans reason to reflect on the 'White Man's Madness' (wazimu wa wazungu [Liebenow 1971: 143]).

However paradoxical, standards of rule still had to apply, and this was partly achieved by shifting the burden of representation to Luguru shoulders.[58] Often Waluguru had to do the work of replacing the predominantly horizontal relationships of magical, political, and economic exchange among lineages with the vertical lines of bureau-cratic command and obedience. When Sabu bin Sabu, the successor to Sultan Kingo, displayed ill feeling against his former rival Kingalu by refusing him a pension, he was warned by the Provincial Com-missioner not to be concerned with 'old political jealousies' but to stick to the 'present practical issue' – that is, to be above, not in, politics.[59] Two aspects of Luguru politics were, in contrast to hereditary succes-sion, particularly inadmissible to British administration: gift giving and magical exchange. They were kept out, or kept quiet, by defining them negatively as 'corruption' or by a more ambiguous bricolage around the positive, magical, sources of Luguru power.

Gift giving was crucial to Luguru inter- and intraclan relationships and, by implication, to the position of mwenye saku, but the positions of headman and chief in the Native Administration were not meant to be reciprocal.[60] Although Kingalu Mwanarubela certainly used his office to enrich himself and his family, it is probable that in many other cases the 'corruption' of British standards of rule was occasioned by adherence to Luguru standards of obligation and good relationship. Tax collection and the implementation of agricultural campaigns – the

main tasks of the headman – were projects foreign to most Waluguru. Many Waluguru must have felt that the headmen's salaries were earned over their backs and presumably expected something in recompense. This may have been more difficult, in lukolo terms, for the legitimate landholder than for a usurper or alien because the former would have to consider all his existing obligations as well as what the British asked of him. If the salary of an incumbent subchief without hereditary rights was, in one case, surrendered to the rightful mwenye saku,[61] we can presume that more of the spoils of government position were divided in this way. The fact that after 1945 'corruption' became scarcer may not mean that it disappeared but merely that Waluguru had accommodated to British desires about the public performance of government servants.

Magical powers were even more ambiguous for indirect rule. Steven Feierman has shown how persistent and necessary rain-making powers were in Usambara politics (1990). In Uluguru, Kingalu's status as a rain doctor was first an (evolutionist) argument for, and then against, his appointment to the chiefship. Uganga ('medicine' or 'benevolent magic') was close to witchcraft and not admissible to the British government; yet it was an important ingredient of Luguru power relationships (as Hutchins's comments on Kingalu's rainmaking capacities make clear). The British were forced to deal with its ramifications but preferred to do so offstage. For instance, the District Commissioner asked the African mayor of Morogoro to accompany sultan Sabu when the latter toured Uluguru, because the mayor did not believe in magic and could therefore strengthen the morale of his friend who feared the magic of his political rivals.[62] Fields (1982) has shown to what extent British officials themselves were implicated in the practice of magic, a practice to which their disbelief was peripheral.

Judging from the memoirs of an Agricultural Officer, the number of times British officials went to a mganga (witch doctor) for divination to find a thief or for medicine to cure a mysterious disease that did not respond to European treatment was considerable.[63] Most of the work in the realm of unseen political powers, however, had to be done by Africans themselves, and in particular by traveling medicine hunters. Administrators' initial fear that these large-scale political movements might imply a recurrence of the Maji Maji rebellion of 1905–06 was overcome by the early 1940s and laid to rest by labeling them 'religious.'[64] In this way, political magic could continue to function under indirect rule, perhaps bothering Christian missionaries but causing little practical anxiety to British administrators (Pels, 1999: ch. 6).

Conclusion

Thus, while I agree with Timothy Mitchell that a European discourse of representation created an 'appearance of order' that tried to mask its own authorship of, and authority over, a 'Luguru tribe,' I hope to have shown that it was not an 'order that works by appearance' (Mitchell 1991: 60; emphasis added). While administrative ethno-graphy and its bureaucratic reproduction may sometimes have given British administrators the feeling that they could absent themselves from political struggle, they had to work hard to keep up the appear-ance of 'indirect' rule, and they did not succeed without regularly subverting the 'tribal' representation of administrative anthropology by their evolutionist notions about progress toward good government. Conversely, many Waluguru attempted to defend their existing political routines against the encroachment of the written represen-tations and embodied representatives of administrative ethnography.

For both parties, administrative ethnography remained a second language, a pidgin that could not carry the full range of political possibilities of the discursive practices from which it was derived but that nevertheless complicated and enriched these possibilities. In the end, the paradoxes and contradictions of indirect rule led to a grave political crisis in the 1950s when the Luguru Native Administration was attacked directly by those it claimed to 'represent' (see Brain 1979). Shortly afterward, Luguru political life was swept into the channel of African nationalism, a 'shift to the superstrate' of representative democracy that it is tempting to describe as a political form of 'creolization' (cf. Hannerz 1987; Jourdan 1991: 202). But that story must be addressed elsewhere.

Notes

Acknowledgments. Research for this article was supported by the Amsterdam School for Social Scientific Research and by a grant from the Netherlands Foundation for the Advancement of Tropical Research (WOTRO). I thank Johannes Fabian for his comments and editorial work on an earlier version, and three anonymous reviewers of the *American Ethnologist*, and the previous editor, Don Brenneis, for their valuable and productive comments. Mr. H. Streefkerk kindly drew the map, a task he has performed for so many other Dutch anthropologists.

1 The archival sources referenced in this article are as follows:

CS – Chief Secretary to the Governor of Tanganyika

DAM – Diocesan Archives Morogoro, in the Bishop House, Morogoro, Tanzania

DC – District Commissioner of the Tanganyikan Administration

PC – Provincial Commissioner of the Tanganyikan Administration

RH – Rhodes House Library, Oxford, United Kingdom

TNA – Tanzania National Archives, Dar es Salaam, Tanzania. The 'Morogoro District Book' is accessible on microfilm no. 19

UDSM – University of Dar es Salaam library, Dar es Salaam, Tanzania

2 A similar emphasis on true and false representation can be identified in both critical and apologetic studies of colonial missions (Pels, 1999: ch. 1).

3 See Hirschkind 1991: 285. See also Mitchell's treatment of Bourdieu's account of the Kabyle house (Bourdieu 1977: 90-91), which makes it into the 'other's' play of difference and ignores it was originally meant as an illustration of a general, rather than culturally specific, theory of practice (Mitchell 1991: 48-53).

4 John Iliffe discusses the mutual implication of colonizers and colonized in indirect rule politics, but his territory-wide focus prevents him from studying its mediations in detail (1979: 318-41). Feierman provides one of the few subtle analyses of the colonized's reception of indirect rule, but his account of the British is disappointing (1990: 134-37).

5 For an elaboration of these terms, see Pels 1994; Pels and Salemink 1994; and Schulte Nordholt 1994.

6 Lugard's main contribution to Tanganyikan indirect rule was to support, after his return to England in 1918, missionary activists who formulated the principle of colonial trusteeship in terms of the 'primacy of African interests' in opposition to (predominantly Kenyan and South African) settler polities, a principle on which Cameron and his Labour allies drew during their own struggles in the late 1920s (Bennet 1960: 357; Cell 1989; Gailey 1974: 40).

7 Clifford was a good researcher and an expert on the Malay language. He introduced the post of secretary of native affairs to the Nigerian administration, an innovation that Cameron also adopted in Tanganyika to coordinate ethnography (Gailey 1974: 49). Clifford wrote in 1922:

> Knowledge, sure and unerring knowledge of the people, of their character, of their point of view, of their customs, habits, modes of thought, is needed as the solid foundation upon which alone really sound political work can be reared up; and this has to be garnered slowly, patiently, painfully, little by little. [as quoted in Kirk-Greene 1965: 179]

8 Anthropological professionalization in Britain was first propagated by both academics and former Indian administrators (see Kuklick 1991: 196-99;

Pels and Salemink 1994). The debate between Malinowski and Cameron's Chief Secretary, Philip Mitchell, shows the potential tension between the two groups (Malinowski 1930; Mitchell 1930). While both drew on similar exemplars, professional anthropology was more influenced by the zoological field expedition and the psychological laboratory (Stocking 19831, while administrative anthropology's 'field' was a bricolage of public school playing field (Heussler 1963), the hunter's safari (Mackenzie 19871, and the amateur naturalist's scientific interests (Pels 1995). For an admirable description of how these different influences made a late colonial anthropological 'field,' see Schumaker 1996.

9 Cameron claimed that this problem convinced him to institute indirect rule (Gailey 1974: 391; also Ingham 1965: 552, 571). Dundas, however, wrote that Cameron had already decided upon this policy before arriving in Tanganyika (Dundas 1955: 132).

10 As District Commissioner of Kilimanjaro, Dundas persuaded Wachagga to grow coffee (Ingham 1965: 556) and was instrumental in forming the Kilimanjaro Native Planters Union. In due time Dundas became 'Wasahuye-O-Wachagga,' an elder of the Chagga; he returned the favor by publishing a history *of* the Wachagga *for* the Wachagga, a highly unusual gesture at the time (Dundas 1955: 117-28).

11 Compare Cameron's 1934 reformulation of Lugard's 'cardinal principle' of indirect rule to the original (Cameron as quoted in Kirk-Greene l965: 193; Lugard 1970 [1919]: 296). This reformulation was a product of Cameron's later years, and less dogmatic on the primacy of chiefs than he had been in his Tanganyikan dispatches (see Cameron 1937).

12 'There is a great deal of work to be accomplished in the way of ascertaining the history of the tribe affected, their traditional organization, their traditional rulers, their proper boundaries, etc.' (TNA 7777: CS to All Senior Commissioners and Administrative Officers, 5-18-95). This was a form of colonial empiricism that had rather different, because historicizing, consequences from an earlier, British Indian, form (see Ludden 1993). Among the dissidents, F. J. E. Bagshawe thought that Western influence had been present for too long to be erased from the minds of the Africans, while Dundas (who knew the German records better than Cameron) said that the absence of chiefs was a good reason for the institution of the akidas (RH s.285: Bagshawe diary, 8-24-27; TNA 7777: Dundas to Scott, 7-3-25). Cameron repeatedly opposed the view that the Germans had also used some form of indirect rule (TNA 11 6011): Oldham to Cameron, 2-27-29, Mitchell to CS, 4-5-29, KastI to Scott, 10-9-28).

13 TNA 7777: Note for Officer Commanding Troops on Native Administration by C. C. Dundas, probably 1927.

14 Cameron's 1934 comments on the Hausa-Fulani chiefs installed by Lugard show that he thought this medieval stage, which emphasized conquest rather than legitimacy, should be skipped by political engineering (as quoted in Kirk-Greene 1965: 193, 195, 205-206).

15 TNA 7777: 'Tanganyika Territory. Native Administration,' by D. Cameron, 1-3-27; CS to all Senior Commissioners and Administrative Officers, 5-1 8-25; Minute Cameron, no. 28, 6-25-25; Confidential Circular, Native Administration, 7-16-25; TNA 1733/6: Tanganyika Territory Annual Report, 1925; TNA 61/6: Instruction on Native Administration, in Dundas to All PCs, 8-20-26.

16 Cameron, in Kirk-Greene (1965:193); TNA 61/6: Dundas to All PCs, 2-23-26; TNA 7777: Dundas to Scott, 7-3-25, Secretary of State for the Colonies to Cameron, 9-1 6-25, CS to all Senior Commissioners and Administrative Officers, 11-26-25.

17 Therefore, an alien 'native agent' could not try the cases at a Native Court (TNA 7777: Minute Cameron no. 28, 6-25-25; on 'extra-tribal' forms, see TNA 7777: Secretary of State for the Colonies to Cameron, 9-16-25).

18 Compare with Public School ideology (see Heussler 1963: 95 on the inadvisability of elections in Tanganyika; TNA 61/6: Dundas to All PCs, 2-23-26). Cameron refused to have Africans on the Legislative Council because he felt that none of the chiefs were educated enough to participate and that no educated African sufficiently represented his people (Gailey 1974:47).

19 TNA 7777: Minute Cameron no. 28, 6-25-25; Confidential Circular on Native Administration, 7-16-25.

20 The 'will of the people' seems to have been an addition typical of Dundas, who drafted the circular (C. Dundas, Draft Circular no. 50, TNA 7790: 7-9-25).

21 The third pillar of native administration, the native treasuries (the first and second being the native authority and the native court), was more clearly propagandistic: it should create the impression that people paid for their own native authority, with only 'minor intervention' by the Officer to prevent waste and corruption. Most Waluguru seem to have thought, however, that the British simply took most of the loot (TNA 7777: Confidential Circular on Native Administration, 7-16-25; TNA 1733/6: Tanganyika Territory Annual Report, 1926; Mzee Paulo Josefu Mgundukano, Konde, 11-7-89).

22 See below (and TNA, Morogoro District Book: 'The Akida System,' by E. E. Hutchins, 1930; 'Tribal History and Legends, Luguru and Kami Tribe,' by E. Hutchins; TNA 7777: CS to Administrative Officer Morogoro, 8-7-25; TNA 173311 3: Morogoro Annual Report, 1925; TNA 7777: Dundas to Scott, 7-3-25). Graham mentions that Mitchell, as secretary of native affairs, decided upon the (faulty) constitution of the Njombe Native Authorities in 1926, which implied bypassing CS Dundas and PC Bagshawe (1976:5). Something similar may have happened in Morogoro.

23 Dundas was made CS (and succeeded by Mitchell as secretary of native affairs), but under Cameron (who did most work himself) that post did not carry the weight of the formally lesser post of secretary of native affairs. In 1928, there was animosity between Cameron and Dundas (RH s.287: Bagshawe diary, 8-10-28). Contrary to Philip Mitchell, Cameron's favorite, Dundas was not promoted after his tour as CS, and, while Mitchell became governor of Uganda in 1935, Dundas had to wait until 1937 to get a minor governorship, that of the Bahamas. Dundas succeeded Mitchell in Uganda in 1940 (Gailey 1974: 138-40).

24 Clans (lukolo [Kiluguru]; ukoo [Swahili]) and lineages itombo [Kiluguru]; ziwa [Swahili]) are too important in Luguru society to accept that we should refrain from using the term 'lineage' because it does not represent folk models and because lineages do not organize 'vital political or economic activities' (Kuper 1982: 92; he uses the term lineage model, the 'model' aspect of which he fails to explain). Kuper does not mention Peters (1967), who had formulated Kuper's doubts about the term 'lineage' 15 years earlier.

25 The Agricultural Department dated the settlement of Uluguru later (in 1884) to emphasize the speed with which soil erosion took place (TNA, Morogoro District Book: 'Soil Erosion in the Uluguru Mountains,' A. H. Savile, 4-24-47). Waluguru list up to 15 successors to a lineage headmanship, which makes this unlikely. Fosbrooke, taking 20 years for one generation, arrived at 1660 as the approximate year of entry (Young and Fosbrooke 1960: 21), but ignored succession by brothers. In Kingalu's genealogy, Hutchins listed six instances of brotherly succession (TNA, Morogoro District Book: 'Tribal History and Legends, Luguru and Kami Tribe'). Of the 12 Kingalus (Fosbrooke: ca. 240 years) that could be listed in 1960, therefore, six generations disappear (minus 120 years), which would put the time of Kingalu I at around 1840. He, however, was a latecomer. Cory's guess (no evidence supplied) of approximately 1800 seems to be closest to the truth (UDSM: Cory Paper 430).

26 I cannot go into this history in detail. For further information see Mzuanda 1958; UDSM: Cory paper 430; Wendelini n.d.

27 TNA, Morogoro District Book: 'Tribal History and Legends: Luguru and Kami Tribe,' by E. Hutchins.

28 The theory was shared by Cameron, Dundas, Mitchell, and others (TNA 7777: CS to Senior Commissioners Dar es Salaam, Tanga, Lindi and Administrative Officers Bagamoyo and Pangani, 1-26-26; Dundas to Scott, 7-3-25). It was still held in substantially the same way in the 1950s, although by then Evans-Pritchard's 'segmentary lineage systems' further legitimated its theoretical underpinnings (Young and Fosbrooke 1960:41-43).

29 I will use mwenye saku for traditional authority, reserving mndewa for the neotraditional bureaucratic positions created by the British. Waluguru still follow the same usage.

30 This was the case in the valley of Konde (Mzee Mahumbo, Konde, 10-15-89).

31 An example was Shenekambi, son of Kingalu Mwanashaa (the sixth; TNA 61/1/3: Hutchins to PC, 7-15-31).

32 All wenye issi and wenye saku were wenye mlunga, but not all wenye mlunga were members of the landholding clan; some earned their titles on merit.

33 Hutchins (RHs. 1059: 'The Waluguru,' p. 2) mentions Mbago's tricks with a looking glass acquired in Bagamoyo. Debenham mentions an alliance, around 1860, between Kingalu I and Mwinyimkuu of Bagamoyo (TNA, Morogoro District Book: 'Tribal History and Legends, Luguru and Kami Tribe'); it is more likely, however, that this is Kingalu Fimbombili IV who, according to Fosbrooke, died on the coast (Young and Fosbrooke 1960: 48).

34 Brain provides two versions of the story (1971), one from Mzuanda (1958: 9-16) and the second, recorded by himself in Kinole. Unfortunately, his amalgamation of euhemerist, functionalist, and structuralist approaches misses the historical and dysfunctional importance of the two versions.

35 Mleke was a Mbena and Magoma, according to the second version of the story recounted by Brain, a Mnyagatwa. The present Magoma of Tegetero calls himself Mnyani; according to Mzuanda, Wanyagatwa and Wanyani are the same (1958: 78-80).

36 Mzee Magoma Mwanamtali (Tegetero, 1-16-90) said that Kingalu could not have betrayed Magoma, as he was Magoma's mjukuu (grandchild). Given the fact that Magoma married the first Kingalu's sister (who only had daughters, which meant that the name of Kingalu could only go to her grandchild), Mzee Magoma may have wanted to convince me of his seniority over Kingalu in terms of kinship discourse.

37 When I had been cheated out of a considerable sum by my first research guide, I was rather taken aback by the admiration with which my best friends alluded to him: amefaulu, 'he has succeeded.'

38 Mzee Mahumbo, Konde, 10-15-89.

39 The Matombo Mission diary shows that DC Hutchins used the same method, using the mission as base (DAM: Matombo Diary, 11-18-25; for Bagshawe's work, TNA 1891 3: Uluguru Land Development Survey Report, 1931; RH s.288: Bagshawe diary).

40 RH s.288: Bagshawe Diary, Vol. XI, December 1929 -January 1930.

41 TNA 18913: Land Development Survey report, Uluguru Mountains, 1931 :4.

42 TNA 11676/1: Ann. Rep. Eastern Province, 1927; TNA 11676/11: Ann. Rep. Eastern Province, 1928; TNA, Morogoro District Book: 'Tribal History and Legends, Luguru tribe,' by E. Hutchins, notes of 2-17-28 and 7-7-28; DAM: Matombo Diary, 10-27-28.

43 TNA 23841: PC Eastern Province to CS, 2-14-36.

44 TNA 23841: PC Eastern Province to CS, 2-14-36.

45 TNA 23841: PC Eastern Province to CS, 6-30-36; PC Eastern Province to CS, 9-4-36; CS to Attorney General, 9-14-36.

46 Hutchins relates how in 1925, when Kingalu and Hega first met each other during a government baraza, they covered their faces, because looking at each other would have meant instant death. Although Hutchins wrote that they were later persuaded to give up the 'superstition,' it is more likely that they reinterpreted the efficacy of their magic (RH s.1059: 'The Waluguru', E. Hutchins).

47 In addition, Kingalu took the opportunity to emphasize his importance in his subordinates' eyes by being carried in a chair, heralded by drums and pipes, into each location visited by Bagshawe. This earned Kingalu's retine the name of 'Alexander's Rag Time Band' from Agricultural Officer Hill.

48 This is Bagshawe's usage; most of my informants spelled it 'Bambarawe.' (The 'l' and 'r,' different in Swahili, are not distinguished in Kiluguru.)

49 RH s.288: Bagshawe Diary, vol. XI. January 20, 1930.

50 For an overview of language ideology, see Woolard and Schieffelin 1994, particularly the references listed under literacy (1994: 65) and European ideologies of referentiality (1994: 71).

51 For the political role of Luguru women see Pels, 1999: chapter 4.

52 Cf. Bates's remark about the proliferation of 'tribes' in Tanganyika (1965: 631), and Thomas's observation that the ethnographic genre, by 'localizing questions' (1991: 312) leads to a similar proliferation (cf. Fardon 1990; for Luguru headmanships: Mzee Morisi Martini, Kiswira, 8-14-89; Mzee Zongera, Mtamba, 2-8-90; TNA 31 347: Page-Jones to CS, 5-9-47).

53 TNA 23841: Hutchins to PC Eastern Province, 3-19-36.

54 TNA, Morogoro District Book: 'The appointment of Mzee Sabu as Sultan of Uluguru,' by D.S. O'Callaghan, 5-9-44.
55 In this they kept drawing on the standard of hereditary office, often by claiming the example of the British royal family (see Feierman 1990:135; Ranger 1980; TNA 26/220/II, passim).
56 For subchiefs: TNA, Morogoro District Book: passim; an example of successive headmen is the Mgombelwa's lineage in Kisem: TNA 26/220/11: passim.
57 For the Germans, in the succinct words of Chief Patrick Kunambi's father, 'black was black and white was white' (Patrick Kunambi, Dar es Salaam, 4-12-89).
58 The expression is borrowed from Tagg (1988).
59 The missionary Otto Raum (supported by Charles Dundas) made a similar observation in Uchagga: he said that a salary made a chief independent of the horizontal obligations maintained by a politics of tribute. Philip Mitchell dismissed the issue by saying he did 'not understand the fuss' (TNA 11601/1: Dundas to Cameron, 12-14-28, Mitchell to Cameron, 12-29-28; for Sabu, see TNA 26/220/II: PC Eastern Province to D.C. Morogoro, 8-9-48).
60 This is confirmed by the clear distinction that Waluguru make between (government) wandewa and 'traditional' wenye issi or wenye saku, while recognizing that mndewa was their traditional term for both.
61 RH s.288: Bagshawe Diary, Vol. XI, December 1929; January 1930.
62 Mzee Sharif Dossi Salim, Morogoro, 2-11-90.
63 A. H. Savile, 'Recollections, 1928-1954' (RH s.1840). At least one administrator believed in the magic of the medicine hunter Ngoja bin Kimeta (TNA 12333: Dundas to Cameron, 6-2-28). Missionaries had a similarly ambiguous relationship with magic (see Pels 1999: chapter 6).
64 Compare the fears about Maji Maji in the papers on Ngoja (TNA 12333: passim) with the Mahenge's District Officer's comparison of Christianity and witch finding in 1943 (TNA 61/128/11: DC Mahenge to PC Eastern Province, 3-22-43).

References

Anderson, Benedict. 1991. Imagined Communities. Reflections on the Origin and Spread of Nationalism. 2nd ed. London/New York: Routledge.
Asad, Talal. 1986. 'The Conception of Cultural Translation in British Social Anthropology'. In Writing Culture. James Clifford and George Marcus, eds. Pp. 141-64. Berkeley: University of California Press.
Bailey, Frederick G. 1969. Stratagems and Spoils. Oxford: Blackwell.
Bates, Margaret L. 1965. 'Tanganyika: Changes in African Life, 1918-1945'. In History of East Africa, 2. Vincent Harlow and Ernest M. Chilver, eds. Pp. 625-40. Nairobi: Oxford University Press.
Bennet, George. 1960. 'Paramountcy to Partnership: J. H. Oldham and Africa'. Africa 30: 356-60.
Bourdieu, Pierre. 1977. Outline of a Theory of Practice. Cambridge: Cambridge University Press.
Brain, James L. 1971. 'Kingalu: A Myth of Origin from Eastern Tanzania'. Anthropos 66:817-38.
— 1973. 'Tales from Uluguru in Eastern Tanzania'. Anthropos 68: 113-36.
— 1979. 'The Uluguru Land Usage Scheme: Success and Failure', Journal Dev. Areas 14: 175-90.
Cameron, Donald. 1937. 'Native Administration in Nigeria and Tanganyika'. Supplement to the Journal of the Royal African Society 36.
Cell, John W. 1989. 'Lord Hailey and the Making of the African Survey'. African Affairs 88: 481-505.
Cohn, Bernard S. 1985. 'The Command of Language and the Language of Command'. In Subaltern Studies IV. Ranajit Guha, ed. Pp. 276-329. Delhi: Oxford University Press.
— 1987. 'The Census, Social Structure and Objectification in South Asia'. In An Anthropologist among the Historians and Other Essays. Bernard Cohn, ed. Pp. 224-254. Delhi: Oxford University Press.
Cooper, Frederick, and Ann Laura Stoler. 1989. 'Introduction: Tensions of Empire: Colonial Control and Visions of Rule'. American Ethnologist 16: 609-621.
Dirks, Nicholas B. 1992. Colonialism and Culture. Ann Arbor: University of Michigan Press.
Dundas, Charles C. F. 1955. African Crossroads. London: Macmillan.
Evans-Pritchard, E. E. 1940. The Nuer. A Description of the Modes of Livelihood and Political Institutions of a Nilotic People. Reprint. New York and Oxford: Oxford University Press.
Fabian, Johannes. 1978. 'Popular Culture in Africa: Findings and Conjectures'. Africa 48: 315-34.
— 1983. Time and the Other: How Anthropology Makes its Object. New York: Columbia University Press.
— 1986 Language and Colonial Power. The Appropriation of Swahili in the Former Belgian Congo, 1880–1938. Cambridge: Cambridge University Press.
Fardon, Richard, ed. 1990. Localizing Strategies. Regional Traditions of Ethnographic Writing. Edinburgh/Washington, DC: Scottish Academic Press/Smithsonian Institution Press.
Feierman, Steven. 1990. Peasant Intellectuals. Anthropology and History in Tanzania. Madison: University of Wisconsin Press.
Fields, Karen. 1982. 'Political Contingencies of Witchcraft in Colonial Central Africa: Culture and State in Marxist Theory'. Canadian Journal of African Studies 16:567-93.
— 1985 Revival and Rebellion in Central Africa. Princeton, NJ: Princeton University Press.
Flint, John E. 1978. 'Frederick Lugard: The Making of an Autocrat (1858–1943)'. In African Proconsuls: European Governors in Africa. Lewis Gann and Peter Duignan, eds. Pp. 290-312. New York: Free Press.
Fortes, Meyer, and E. E. Evans-Pritchard. 1940. 'Introduction'. In African Political Systems. Meyer Fortes and E. E. Evans-Pritchard, eds. Pp. 1-23. London: Oxford University Press.
Gailey, Harry A. 1974. Sir Donald Cameron: Colonial Governor. Stanford, CA: Hoover Institution Press.
Graham, John D. 1976. 'Indirect Rule: The Establishment of "Chiefs" and "Tribes" in Cameron's Tanganyika'. Tanzania Notes and Records 87:l-9.
Guha, Ranajit. 1989. 'Dominance without Hegemony and its Historiography'. In Subaltern Studies VI. Ranajit Guha, ed. Pp. 210-309. Delhi: Oxford University Press.
Hannerz, Ulf. 1987. 'The World in Creolisation'. Africa 57: 546-59.
Heussler, Robert. 1963. Yesterday's Rulers. The Making of the British Colonial Service. London/Syracuse, NY: Oxford University Press/Syracuse University Press.
Hirschkind, Charles. 1991. 'Egypt at the Exhibition: Reflections on the Optics of Colonialism. A Review of Timothy Mitchell's Colonizing Egypt'. Critique of Anthropology 11: 279-98.
Iliffe, John. 1979. A Modern History of Tanganyika. Cambridge: Cambridge University Press.
Ingham, Kenneth. 1965. 'Tanganyika: The Mandate and Cameron, 1919-1931'. In History of East Africa, 2. Vincent Harlow and Ernest Chilver, eds. Pp. 543-93. Nairobi: Oxford University Press.
Jourdan, Christine. 1991. 'Pidgins and Creoles: The Blurring of Categories'. Annual Review of Anthropology 20:187–209.
Kirk-Greene, Anthony H. M., ed. 1965. The Principles of Native Administration in Nigeria. Selected Documents, 1900–1947. London: Oxford University Press.
Kuklick, Henrika. 1991. The Savage Within. The Social History of British Anthropology, 1885–1945. Cambridge: Cambridge University Press.
Kuper, Adam. 1982. 'Lineage Theory: A Critical Retrospect'. Annual Review of Anthropology 11 :71-95.
Liebenow, J. Gus. 1971. Colonial Rule and Political Development in Tanzania. The Case of the Makonde. Nairobi: East African Publishing House.
Ludden, David. 1993. 'Orientalist Empiricism'. In Orientalism and the Postcolonial Predicament. Carol Breckenridge and Peter van der Veer, eds. Pp. 250-78. Philadelphia: University of Pennsylvania Press.
Lugard, Frederick Dealtry. 1970 [1919]. Political Memoranda, 1913–1918. Plymouth and London: Frank Cass.
Mackenzie, John. 1987. The Empire of Nature. Hunting, Conservation and British Imperialism. Manchester: Manchester University Press.
Malinowski, Bronislaw. 1929. 'Practical Anthropology'. Africa 2: 22-38.
— 1930. 'The Rationalization of Anthropology and Administration'. Africa 3:405–23.

Mannheim, Karl. 1960. *Ideology and Utopia. An Introduction to the Sociology of Knowledge*. Edward Shils, trans. London and Henley: Routledge and Kegan Paul.

Mitchell, Philip E. 1930. 'The Anthropologist and the Practical Man. A Reply and a Question'. *Africa* 3: 217-23.

Mitchell, Timothy. 1991. *Colonizing Egypt*. 2nd ed. Berkeley: University of California Press.

Moffet, John P. 1952 'Native Courts in Tanganyika'. *Journal of African Administration* 4: 17-25.

Mzuanda, Rev. Fr. Canute. 1958. *Historia ya Uluguru*. Morogoro: Diocese of Morogoro.

Pels, Peter. 1994. The Construction of Ethnographic Occasions in Late Colonial Uluguru. *History and Anthropology*. 8: 321-51.

— 1995. 'The Politics of Aboriginality: Brian Houghton Hodgson and the Making of an Ethnology of India', *Yearbook of the International Institute for Asian Studies* 1994:147-68.

— 1999. *A Politics of Presence: Contacts between Missionaries and Waluguru in Colonial Tanganyika 1930–1961*. Chur, Switzerland: Harwood Academic Publishers, 1997.

Pels, Peter, and Oscar Salemink. 1994. 'Introduction: Five Theses on Ethnography as Colonial Practice'. *History and Anthropology* 8: 1-34.

Perham, Margery. 1934. 'A Re-Statement of Indirect Rule'. *Africa* 7: 321-34.

Peters, Emrys L. 1967. 'Some Structural Aspects of the Feud among the Camel-Herding Bedouin of Cyrenaica'. *Africa*. 37: 261-82.

Prins, Gwynn. 1980 *The Hidden Hippopotamus. Reappraisal in African History: The Early Colonial Experience in Western Zambia*. Cambridge: Cambridge University Press.

Rafael, Vicente L. 1994 'White Love: Census and Melodrama in the United States Colonization of the Philippines'. *History and Anthropology* 8: 265-97.

Ranger, Terence O. 1980. 'Making Northern Rhodesia Imperial'. *African Affairs* 79:349-73.

— 1983 'The Invention of Tradition in Colonial Africa'. In *The Invention of Tradition*. Eric Hobsbawm and Terence O. Ranger, eds. Pp. 211-62. Cambridge: Cambridge University Press.

Samarin, William J. 1984. 'The Linguistic World of Field Colonialism'. *Language in Society* 13: 435-53.

Schumaker, Lynette. 1996. 'A Tent with a View: Colonial Officers, Anthropologists, and the Making of the Field in Northern Rhodesia, 1937–1960', *Osiris*, 2nd series, 11: 237-58.

Schulte Nordholt, Henk. 1994. 'The Making of Traditional Bali: Colonial Ethnography and Bureaucratic Reproduction', *History and Anthropology* 8:89-127.

Stocking, George W., Jr. 1983. 'The Ethnographer's Magic: Fieldwork in British Anthropology from Tylor to Malinowski'. In *Observers Observed. Essays on Ethnographic Fieldwork*. George W. Stocking Jr., ed. Pp. 79-120. Madison: University of Wisconsin Press.

Tagg, John. 1988. *The Burdens of Representation: Essays on Photographies and Histories*. London: Macmillan.

Thoden van Velzen, H. U. E. 1973. 'Robinson Crusoe and Friday: Strength and Weakness of the Big Man Paradigm'. *Man* (n.s.) 8: 592-612.

Thomas, Nicholas. 1991. 'Against Ethnography'. *Cultural Anthropology* 6: 306-322.

— 1992. 'The Inversion of Tradition', *American Ethnologist* 19: 213-232.

— 1994. *Colonialism's Culture. Anthropology, Travel and Government*. London: Polity Press.

Tyler, Stephen. 1984. 'The Vision Quest in the West, or What the Mind's Eye Sees'. *Journal of Anthropological Research*. 40: 23-40.

Wendelini, Mzee Pius. n.d. 'Milango ya History ya Uluguru. Zamani Mpaka Siku Hizi'. Unpublished manuscript.

Woolard, Kathryn, and Bambi Schieffelin. 1994. 'Language Ideology'. *Annual Review of Anthropology*, 23: 55-82.

Young, Roland, and Henry Fosbrooke. 1960. *Land and Politics among the Luguru of Tanganyika*. London: Routledge and Kegan Paul.

Two texts on Chiefs in Present-day South Africa: A Renaissance of Tradition

We are happy to include two quite different texts by Lungisile Ntsebeza and Barbara Oomen on this issue since it is such a striking example of the constant reconstruction of 'the traditional' or 'custom' as an antipode to modernity. The resurgence of 'customary chiefs' under African National Congress (ANC) rule in South Africa – even though during most of the twentieth century they were seen as stooges of the apartheid regime – is a topic that fascinated (and worried) many observers. Moreover, it lends itself to quite different interpretations, as these two texts show.

LUNGISILE NTSEBEZA
The Resurgence of Chiefs
Retribalization & Modernity in Post-1994 South Africa

Reference
Unpublished paper

Introduction

For almost ten years, the ANC-led government was ambivalent about the precise roles, functions and powers of traditional authorities in South Africa's democracy. The Constitution merely recognized the institution of traditional leadership. It was up to legislation to define the roles, functions and powers of the institution and its incumbents. After many hesitations, the South African Parliament eventually passed two pieces of legislation in 2003 and 2004 that would give some degree of clarity to the position of traditional authorities in South Africa's democracy. These laws make concessions to traditional authorities, effectively resuscitating the powers they enjoyed under the notorious Bantu Authorities Act of 1951. As will be seen below, the Traditional Leadership and Governance Framework Act of 2003 establishes what it refers to as Traditional Councils. The apartheid-created and much-hated Tribal Authorities will be the foundation for the establishment of these Councils. On the other hand, the other piece of legislation, the Communal Land Rights Act of 2004 recognizes these Traditional Councils as having the authority to administer and allocate land in the rural areas.

In other words, after 10 years of prevarication, the ANC-led government has ended up giving powers to traditional authorities on pretty much the same lines as its predecessor, the apartheid state. During the apartheid epoch, rural governance in South Africa's former Bantustans was controlled by Tribal Authorities. These structures were dominated by traditional authorities and their appointees. Tribal Authorities were unaccountable, undemocratic and despotic. They were imposed on unwilling rural residents. In areas such as Phondoland (Mbeki 1984), Sekhukhuneland (Delius 1996) and Xhalanga (Ntsebeza 2002), the imposition of these institutions often led to bloody conflicts between apartheid state supporters and those in resistance. To the extent to which traditional authorities could claim legitimacy, this has been based on their control of the land administration and allocation process at the local administrative and Tribal Authorities level. The powers they will enjoy under the Communal Land Rights Act perpetuate this legacy.

In this chapter, I will examine how, despite their notorious role during the apartheid era in particular, an ANC-led government is endorsing the authority of traditional authorities. I will do so by tracing the evolution of the policies of the ANC towards traditional authorities from the time of the formation of the organization in 1912 to the present. The reason for this focus on the ANC is that since 1994, this political party has been and continues to be the dominant political party in government and indications are that this position will remain in the foreseeable future. Particular attention will be given to the processes leading to the promulgation of the two controversial pieces of legislation referred to above. In this regard, a number of factors, including the political and economic context within which the ANC came to power will be highlighted, in particular the interplay between the global, national and local. This interplay is critical for a comprehensive understanding of what seemingly are national and local processes.

A key argument of this chapter is that recognizing and giving unprecedented powers to unelected traditional authorities amounts to compromising the democratic project to which the post-1994 ANC-led government has committed itself. The legitimacy of traditional authorities is highly suspect and it is dangerous and inappropriate to assume it.

Retribalization

As indicated, two pieces of legislation, the Traditional Leadership and Governance Framework Act (TLGFA) of 2003 and the Communal Land Rights Act (CLRA) of 2004, set the platform for retribalization in post-1994 South Africa. An objective of the TLGFA that is pertinent to the purposes of this chapter is the provision for the establishment and recognition of Traditional Councils. A traditional council, according to section 3(1) will be established in an area which has been recognizd by the Premier as a 'traditional community'. This would take place, in terms of the preamble, within the context of transforming 'the institution of traditional leadership ... in line with constitutional imperatives ... so that democratic governance and the values of an open and democratic society may be promoted'. The Act provides for a role for traditional leadership, not only in the local government sphere, but in all three spheres of government. In the vital area of land administration though, the Act does not specify a role for traditional authorities. This is dealt with in the Communal Land Rights Act of 2004.

It is important to note that despite the Act's declared commitment to transforming the institution of traditional leadership, the introduction of the Act and the establishment of traditional councils raise the question of the meaning of democracy and citizenship in rural areas. How should we understand this notion of transformation, particularly if one takes into account that the Act recognizes existing apartheid era Tribal Authorities as the foundation for setting up Traditional Councils? Although a four-year transition period for the transformation of Tribal Authorities is allowed, there is no provision, as Cousins and Claassens have pointed out, for sanctions in the event that the Tribal Authorities have not been transformed.[1] Secondly, the Traditional Councils are undemocratic in their nature, resembling the Tribal Authorities they are meant to replace. Although there is provision for a minimum of 30 per cent representation of women in the councils, the majority of the members are not popularly elected. Initially, there was a recommendation that a mere 25 per cent of members should be elected. After strong protests from NGOs and other civil society organizations, this number was increased to 40 per cent. This, however, still gives unelected traditional authorities and their appointees a majority and a decisive role in the vexed issue of land allocation.

The Communal Land Rights Act of 2004 makes Traditional Councils supreme structures when it comes to land administration. Section 21(2) of the Act: 'If a community has a recognized traditional council, the powers and duties of the land administration committee may be exercised and performed by such council.' It must be noted that this clause came about as a result of a last minute amendment by the Cabinet on 8 October 2003 to the Communal Land Rights Bill of 2002. This was at more or less the same time that the TLGFA was being considered. According to reporter Christelle Terreblance, the amendment was made shortly after a meeting involving the then Deputy President Jacob Zuma, King Zwelithini of KwaZulu-Natal and the President of the Inkatha Freedom Party (IFP), Chief Buthelezi, leading to speculation that the amendment was a deal (*Cape Times*, 28 January 2004). Whatever the circumstances, this decision gave enormous and unprecedented powers to a structure with a majority of unelected members.

It is worth noting that this was an amendment to a much more progressive and radical draft Communal Land Rights Bill which was gazetted on 14th August 2002. On land administration, the Bill divested traditional authorities of their land administration functions, including land allocation, in favour of democratically elected administrative structures, even in areas where traditional authorities existed. In such areas, traditional authorities were accorded *ex officio* representation not exceeding 25 per cent. The draft Bill clearly attempted to strike a balance between the constitutional obligation to extend democracy to all parts of the country, including rural areas, and accommodating the institution of traditional leadership, which is recognized in the constitution. But traditional authorities had rejected the August 2002 draft Bill, with some apparently threatening bloodshed (*Daily Dispatch*, 2 November 2002).

Despite the protest, the controversial Bill was bulldozed through and passed unanimously by parliament on 27 January 2004. It was later signed as an Act by the President in July 2004.

For the first time in more than ten years traditional authorities have given their overwhelming support to the Communal Land Rights Act.[2] In a *Business Day* article dated 2 December 2003, the chairperson of the National House of Traditional Authorities, Chief Mpiyezintombi Mzimela, supported the second draft of the Communal Land Rights Bill with these words: 'The Communal Land Right Bill aims to restore to rural communities ownership of the remnants that they occupy of land that the colonial and apartheid government took from them by force – giving the communities registered title, so that it cannot happen again.'

My argument in this chapter is that the two Acts can be seen as some kind of compromise, given the tension arising out of the constitutional recognition of a hereditary institution of traditional leadership in the context of an acceptance of liberal principles of democracy based on representative government. When municipalities were introduced in rural areas as part of extending democracy to rural areas, traditional authorities vehemently protested against this move and insisted that they should be the only structure in rural areas. In many ways, the TLGFA attempts to avoid the constitutional amendment and still recognizes municipalities made up of elected councillors as the primary form of local government in rural areas. On the other hand, the recognition of apartheid era Tribal Authorities as a basis for establishing Traditional Councils and giving these structures (which are dominated by traditional authorities and their appointees) powers in land administration amounts to a trade-off. In the totality of things, especially given the centrality and importance of land notably for residential purposes in rural areas, traditional authorities seem to enjoy more powers than elected councillors.

Historical and theoretical background

As already noted, rural governance in South Africa's former Bantustans was dominated by traditional authorities operating within apartheid-created structures – these were unaccountable and authoritarian and were referred to as Tribal Authorities. The system of land allocation arguably presents the best example of how these structures operated. In many instances, traditional authorities and their appointees did not adhere to the letter of the law. The main problem was how to monitor the system and make those charged with authority accountable. In the majority of cases, traditional authorities were upwardly accountable to the government, rather than to the rural residents. This was made possible by the fact that the apartheid and Bantustan regimes gave traditional authorities such powers that they were feared, rather than respected, by their communities (Ntsebeza 1999). This made it extremely difficult for ordinary, elderly rural residents to hold traditional authorities accountable.

Traditional authorities exploited this lack of 'checks and balances'. There were basically two forms of violations: allocating land without going through the correct procedure, and illegal taxation. Traditional authorities abused their power by charging unauthorized fees, in the name of the 'rights of the great place' (iimfanelo zakomkhulu), to applicants. These included alcohol, poultry, sheep, and even an ox. This practice reached its zenith in the early 1990s when, for instance, some cottage sites were illegally allocated to some 'whites' along the Wild Coast in the old Transkei. These sites were dubbed 'brandy sites', as it was imperative that applications be accompanied by a bottle of brandy. It was standard practice in some parts that ordinary rural residents present the sub-headman with a bottle of brandy (or some suitable gift) (De Wet and McAllister 1983: 50). Further, in a number of cases, traditional authorities allocated land to rural residents by-passing the formal system by which the district commissioner or magistrate issued the final legal document called permit to occupy (PTO). These rural residents consequently occupied land without any legal documentation.

Research in which I was involved along the Wild Coast of the Eastern Cape Province in the late 1990s showed that the above abuse of power continued well into the new democracy (Ntsebeza 1999). Traditional authorities and their appointees/representatives continued to illegally allocate land along the coastal area even at a time when a special investigative unit, the Heath Special Investigative Unit, was set up to investigate corruption in land allocation along the Wild Coast. A major part of the problem was that well into the South African democracy, the issue of whose function it was to administer land had not been resolved. For as long as this state of affairs continued, Tribal Authorities, unaccountable as they have been shown to be, remained the official structures.

As noted, from their inception, rural residents resisted Tribal Authorities. However, the resistance to these structures was crushed in the early 1960s as part of a countrywide clampdown on political opposition in South Africa. When resistance against apartheid re-emerged from the late 1960s and early 1970s initially in the urban areas, but later shifting to rural areas in the late 1980s and early 1990s, Tribal Authorities were in almost all cases the target. These were areas where evidence abounded of cases where chiefs and headmen abused their authority in the land allocation process. In these instances Tribal Authorities were challenged. In the former Ciskei Bantustan, these structures were toppled and replaced by Residents Associations made up of elected representatives. At the centre of these struggles was control over land, in particular, land allocation. By 1994, land administration in many rural areas, especially in the Eastern Cape, had virtually collapsed, and there was no clarity as to who ruled in these areas.

Mahmood Mamdani (1996), in his book, *Citizen and Subject*, has correctly, in my opinion, characterized Tribal Authorities as a South African version of what he refers to as 'decentralized despotism' similar to what countries on the African continent went through under colonialism. As Mahmood Mamdani has noted, a key problem that confronted colonialists was how to stabilize 'alien rule', or how to deal with the 'native question'. Here is how he formulates the question: 'How can a tiny and foreign minority rule over an indigenous majority?' The colonial answer to this was 'indirect rule', or rule by association. Thus, while this policy purported to preserve the pre-colonial structures, in reality, it was established as a means of controlling black Africans in the rural areas.

Very briefly, Mamdani's thesis is that the colonial state in Africa was 'bifurcated', with different modes of rule for urban 'citizens' and rural 'subjects' (1996). The colonial strategy of 'divide and rule' took two related forms: an enforced division of Africans along ethnic lines, on the one hand, and an enforced division between town and countryside. According to Mamdani, the African was 'containerised', not as a native or indigenous African, but as a 'tribesperson'. Colonialists justified indirect rule on the basis that 'tradition' and 'custom' were indigenous forms of social organization. However, colonialists themselves reinforced these identities and used them to divide and manage rural Africans. In order to enforce their dual policy of 'ethnic pluralism' and urban–rural division, colonialists, Mamdani asserts, exercised 'force to an unusual degree'. In this way, colonial despotism was highly decentralized (1996: 22-4). In this project, Mamdani argues, the 'chief' was cardinal, especially in the local state, the Native Authority.

Mamdani argues that the colonial legacy was reproduced after independence. Post-colonial African states, whether conservative or radical, deracialized the colonial state, but, according to him, did not democratize it. On democratic transformation, Mamdani proposes 'nothing less than dismantling' the 'bifurcated state'. This will entail 'an endeavour to link the urban and the rural – and thereby a series of related binary opposites such as rights and custom, representation and participation, centralisation and decentralisation, civil society and community – in ways that have yet to be done' (1996: 34).[3]

Why the recognition of traditional authorities?

Given conditions on the ground in the early 1990s in particular, and the struggles waged by rural residents against Tribal Authorities and their incumbents, the recognition of the institution of traditional leaders in the Interim Constitution in 1993 (and the Final Constitution in 1996) must have come as a great shock to many observers. More surprising was why it is that an organization such as the ANC which fought for a democratic unitary state after apartheid would embrace the institution of traditional leadership and its incumbents with their notorious record under apartheid, and end up in 2003 and 2004 giving traditional authorities more powers than they enjoyed under apartheid in the administration of land. These questions become all the more relevant when one takes into account that the legitimacy of traditional authorities continued to be contested even after the advent of democracy in 1994.

Conditions on the ground after 1994 in many rural areas under traditional authorities demonstrated just how difficult it would be to accommodate traditional authorities in a democracy. This was complicated by the fact that the Constitution recognized the institution of traditional leaders but the roles, functions and powers of traditional authorities were not spelt out. This led to a great deal of confusion and tensions on the ground. As already noted, these tensions were evident even before the advent of democracy in 1994. At the time, the tensions were between traditional authorities and groups in civil society, especially those organized under the South African National Civic Organisation (SANCO). At the centre of these struggles was control over land, in particular land allocation.

After the 1995/6 local government elections, these tensions manifested themselves as between elected rural councillors and SANCO on the one hand, and traditional authorities, on the other hand. Elected councillors were introduced following the local government elections in 1995 and 1996 as part of the attempt to extend democracy to rural areas. In terms of the Constitution, municipalities were to be introduced in all parts of the country, including areas falling under the jurisdiction of traditional authorities. This meant that new structures based on elected councillors were introduced in these areas, too. The majority of rural councillors were drawn from SANCO activists. Some of the functions of these democratically elected structures, such as the promotion of state-led development in rural areas, used to be performed by traditional authorities. In the absence of clear-cut functions for traditional authorities, taking some functions from them was surely going to be a recipe for chaos and confusion.

It is, above all, confusion over the land allocation function that most of the tension revolved around. This was particularly true in the case where civic structures and traditional authorities had more or less equal support. There are two levels at which this dilemma could be understood and explained: the law and practice. Before the promulgation of the Communal Land Rights Act, the laws governing the allocation of land in the rural areas of the former Bantustans had not been repealed. In this regard, the South African Constitution is clear that existing laws will remain in force until such time as they have been replaced by appropriate legislation. In terms of the existing laws, an application for land would only get legal recognition if it bore the stamp of the relevant Tribal Authority and was signed by the appropriate signatories.

Reality on the ground, though, was different. Many rural residents, rural councillors, and indeed South Africans assumed that the newly elected councillors would take over the vital function of land allocation. After all, control over land was the cardinal issue in rural struggles in the early- to mid-1990s. An example, drawn from the Xhalanga district in the Eastern Cape will highlight this point. When the Integrated Development Plan (IDP) for this area was developed in 1999, the issue of who is responsible for land allocation cropped up.[4] Although interviews and the minutes of meetings suggest that on the whole there were no tensions between elected rural councillors and the representative of traditional authorities, there were animated discussions when it came to the question of land administration. It appears that the representative of traditional authorities pointed out that Tribal Authorities were still responsible for land administration. This claim was strongly challenged by rural councillors. The explanation of the representative of traditional authorities was simple and highlighted the lack of clarity regarding land administration in the countryside: 'Nothing is clear. Government has indicated that land allocation will be the function of the TRCs. However, at the moment this has not happened. Most areas still use the old method.'[5] The IDP committee never resolved this issue. One of the committee members pointed out that one of the reasons why the matter was not discussed further was that 'it was seen as divisive'. Of course, the committee could not resolve the issue, given the government's ambivalence regarding the role, functions and powers of traditional authorities shown above. However, residents and rural councillors in particular, got a rude shock when it turned out that the old apartheid laws were still in place. Above all, government officials still use, with minor adjustments, the apartheid procedure and do not recognize elected councillors as having the powers to allocate land.

In the light of the above, the question that forces itself upon us is how to explain not only the recognition of the institution of traditional leadership and its incumbents in the Constitution but also the powers they enjoy in South Africa's democratic dispensation. To answer this question, I propose that there is a range of matters which, taken together throw light on this apparent puzzle. I elaborate on these more fully below.

The continental and global context

The recognition of traditional authorities in South Africa cannot be divorced from the general re-emergence of traditional and customary authorities on the African Continent in particular. This resurgence is often associated with the advent of multi-party democracy and decentralization in the early 1990s. Countries such as Mozambique which were initially hostile towards and even abolished traditional authorities, ended up recognizing them in the 1990s. Some scholars and commentators argue that, by marginalizing traditional authorities the ruling party in Mozambique, FRELIMO, drove most of them to the camp of the opposition RENAMO which waged a civil war against FRELIMO in the 1980s and early 1990s. When FRELIMO succumbed under the pressures of neo-liberalism and accepted multiparty democracy and decentralization in the 1990s, it recognized the institution of traditional leadership, although, like the ANC, the party was ambivalent about the status of traditional authorities (for the Mozambican case see Dinerman 2001; Bowen 2000; Libombo 2000; Pitcher 1996).

It is important to note that at the time of the struggle between FRELIMO and RENAMO, the ANC, which had offices in Mozambique, was closely watching developments. This emerged in discussions within the ANC when the issue came up of how the ANC would relate with the Congress of Traditional Leaders in South Africa (CONTRALESA), the organization of traditional authorities. The ANC tried to draw some lessons from the Mozambican experience. However, what the ANC leadership did not do was to situate their reading of the Mozambican experience within the specific context of South Africa. While similarities between the two countries cannot be denied, it is equally short-sighted to overlook the differences. If it was true in the case of Mozambique that rural residents supported traditional authorities; for whatever reasons, there was clear evidence in South Africa by the late 1980s and early 1990s that the legitimacy of these authorities was seriously questioned.

Apart from developments on the Continent in the early 1990s, the global context within which the ANC entered into the political negotiating project in the early 1990s must also be taken into account. There is a sense in which it is true to say that the late 1980s and early 1990s was a triumph for the forces of global neo-liberal capitalism. The Cold War had come to an end with the demise of the Soviet Empire and capitalism became the only system dominating the world. This left organizations such as the ANC, which drew its support and inspiration from the Soviet-bloc, almost stranded. At the time of the start of the political negotiations, the Freedom Charter, a programme with socialist aspirations, including the notion of nationalization of the main means of production, was the main programme of the ANC. In an age dominated by neo-liberal capitalism, the Freedom Charter was an anachronism. By 1994, the ANC had succumbed to neo-liberal pressures. Its election manifesto for the 1994 election was based on the Reconstruction and Development Programme (RDP), a contradictory document that incorporated elements of neo-liberalism and social democracy. When the ANC came to power in 1994, it pushed to the back burner the developmental aspects of the RDP and gradually leaned more heavily on neo-liberal principles, culminating with the introduction in 1996 of Growth, Employment and Redistribution (GEAR). There were, as Marais (1998) argues, tensions within the ANC, but the conservative forces won the day.

Additionally, traditional authorities in South Africa gained recognition in the Interim Constitution largely as a result of political expediency. On the one hand, the ANC was keen to gain the support of CONTRALESA and its supporters, while, on the other hand, it simultaneously confronted and made concessions to the Inkatha Freedom Party (IFP). By this time, it was clear that democratic elections were going to be held in South Africa, something which made consideration of the vote important. These concessions had very little to do with the situation on the ground. On its part, the ANC seemed to think that the co-existence between democracy and traditional authorities was possible in a democratic South Africa.

Ambivalence of the ANC

Another factor which could help explain how traditional authorities succeeded in gaining concessions in a democratic South Africa, was their ability to exploit the ambivalence and hesitations of the ANC towards traditional authorities. The position of the ANC towards traditional authorities has always been ambivalent. The fact that the ANC never really had a stronghold in rural areas is a critical part of the explanation. The organization tended to adopt seemingly desperate and naïve positions of collaborating with traditional authorities. Mbeki quotes Oliver Tambo (1987) as having confessed from exile: 'We have not done and are not doing sufficient political work among the millions of our people who have been condemned to the Bantustans' (quoted in Mbeki 1996: 95).

When the ANC was approached by a group of traditional authorities who were opposed to the declaration of apartheid-style independence in KwaNdebele in 1987, it had to define its position on traditional authorities. In the final analysis, the ANC played a critical role in the formation of CONTRALESA, which was officially launched on 20 September 1987. The thinking of the ANC leadership was that 'the institution should be allowed to exist in future but under "our" control.' The ANC had hoped that CONTRALESA and 'the other formations of the mass democratic movement' would 'play an important role in the mobilisation of the rural masses' (Zuma 1990: 75). In practice, this was not to be the case. As will be seen below, CONTRALESA rejected a secondary, subordinate position. At the same time, the chiefly organisation did not organize rural masses, nor

did it collaborate with 'the other forces of the mass democratic movement'. In the first place, members of CONTRALESA were an elite and not the traditional authorities that are permanent residents in their rural constituencies. They were 'conference-oriented'. These conferences were held in hotels, and, as Zuma observes, 'the most unlikely places to find a patriotic chief' (1990: 70).[7]

An ANC policy on traditional authorities after its unbanning in 1990 was, as before, difficult to pin down. Oomen has argued that traditional authorities have never been officially denigrated in ANC documents. Oomen quotes Mandela, on the occasion of his release from prison on 11 February 1990, to support this position: 'I greet the traditional leaders of our country – many of you continue to walk in the footsteps of great heroes like Hintsa and Sekhukhune.' By 1991, according to her, it was common to hear traditional authorities mentioned by some ANC leaders as part of the coalition of forces struggling for national liberation, alongside 'black workers, students, the rural poor, professionals and black business-people' (1996: 101). An attempt to clarify the role of traditional authorities was, however, made in 1992, when the ANC formulated its policy guidelines:

> The institution of chieftainship has played an important role in the history of our country and chiefs will continue to play an important role in unifying our people and performing ceremonial and other functions allocated to them by law. The powers of chiefs shall always be exercised subject to the provisions of the constitution and other laws. Provision will be made for an appropriate structure consisting of traditional leaders to be created by law, in order to advise parliament – on matters relevant to customary law and other matters relating to the powers and functions of chiefs. Changes in the existing powers and functions of chiefs will only be made by parliament after such consultation has taken place. (Quoted in Oomen 1996: 103)

The ANC guidelines were clearly informed by the notion of the co-existence of democratic and traditional authority structures in a democracy. In this regard, the powers of traditional authorities are defined as unifying 'our people' and to perform 'ceremonial and other functions allocated to them by law'. The guidelines clearly limit the powers of 'chiefs' by subjecting them 'to the provisions of the constitution and other laws'. The guidelines further limit the participation of traditional authorities to an advisory capacity, advising Parliament 'on matters relevant to customary law and other matters relating to the powers and functions of chiefs' (quoted in Oomen 1996: 103). The implications for traditional authorities were that they would lose the substantial powers they enjoyed under the apartheid regime in particular.

The ANC guidelines on traditional authorities were formulated in the midst of the political negotiations of the early 1990s that led to the first democratic election in 1994 on the one hand, and at the height of a bloody conflict involving the ANC and IFP in KwaZulu-Natal. Both the then ruling National Party (NP) and the ANC were keen that traditional authorities and the IFP in particular be part of the political negotiation process that was unfolding. However, despite these attempts traditional authorities were, by March 1993, not an integral part of the negotiation process. Chief Buthelezi proved to be critical on the non-involvement of traditional authorities. He demanded separate delegations for his KwaZulu government on the one hand, and his King, on the other. When this was not granted, Buthelezi and the King pulled out of the process. Where traditional authorities participated, they did so as part of the delegations of the former Bantustans.

By March 1993, though, both the National Party and the ANC considered that 'the institution of traditional leaders is still relatively widely supported, especially in rural areas where they fulfill an important government function at local level' (Henrard 1999: 397). According to Oomen, the ANC and the NP saw traditional authorities as 'important vote brokers' (1996: 56). The broader context of this statement is that by this time, the question of non-racial elections was squarely on the cards and votes counted. Given my discussion above about rural dynamics, I challenge the ANC and NP assumption that traditional authorities were 'widely supported'. What cannot be disputed, though, is that in areas where traditional authorities were feared, some rural residents could be intimidated to vote for a candidate preferred by a traditional authority.

At the same time there were important developments taking place in CONTRALESA. The organization rejected the ANC's vision that the institution of chieftainship be a ceremonial and advisory body. The election of Chief Phathekile Holomisa seems to have been critical in this rejection. Chief Holomisa became president of CONTRALESA following the murder on 25 February 1991 of its first president, Chief Maphumulo.[8] According to Gevisser, Chief Holomisa was a student at the University of Natal in the mid-1980s. He sought out the ANC in exile to canvass its opinion as to whether he should take up his hereditary position as a chief in the Transkei legislature. Chief Holomisa was recruited by the ANC underground, which set him up in lawyers' offices in Umtata. Holomisa, according to Gevisser, played a key role in bringing chiefs on board.[9] Chief Holomisa's standing in the ANC was demonstrated by the fact that he became a Member of Parliament after the first democratic elections in 1994. After the third democratic election in 2004, he was again returned to Parliament for the third time.

It is, indeed, during the reign of Holomisa that CONTRALESA pushed for the recognition of traditional authorities and their institutions as the primary level of government in rural areas. Even by the early 1990s, CONTRALESA under chief Holomisa rejected the notion that, in the rural areas of the former Bantustans, municipalities and elected councillors be the primary level of local government.[10] It is arguably due to this uncompromising stand of CONTRALESA as well as the unresolved issue of KwaZulu-Natal that there was no provision in the 1993 Local Government Transition Act for the form local government would take in rural areas.

It is thus a combination of the Inkatha factor, the assumption that traditional authorities were 'vote brokers' and CONTRALESA's resistance to accepting a secondary and subordinate role in rural governance that led to the ANC and NP's wooing of traditional authorities. In the final analysis, traditional authorities, particularly those in CONTRALESA, were party to the adoption of Resolution 34 of the National Negotiating Council that was unanimously adopted on 11 December 1993.[11] Thus, traditional authorities managed to secure guarantees, albeit of a subordinate position to that of the elected bodies, in the Interim Constitution. Some commentators see the ANC's support for the recognition of traditional authorities in the Interim Constitution as *quid pro quo*, as a reward for their political support. Henrard cites Richard Sizani, at the time Deputy Director General of the Department of Provincial Affairs and Constitutional Development, as having asserted that traditional authorities managed to secure significant guarantees in the Interim Constitution (cited in Henrard 1999: 398). On close analysis, however, the guarantees obtained in the Interim Constitution are not as strong as they initially appear. The recognition of existing traditional authorities and their practices applies only in situations where they are not repugnant to the provisions of the Constitution and existing legislation. In addition Resolution 34 has a strong bias in favour of elected local government and traditional authorities would only be *ex officio* members of the local government.

How traditional authorities exploited the ambivalence and hesitations of the ANC

A third factor that seems relevant in our understanding of the phenomenon of the resurgence of traditional authorities in South Africa is how they have managed to exploit the ambivalence and hesitations of the ANC. Since 1994, the ANC-led government has attempted, in a rather ambiguous manner, to extend democracy to rural areas. A significant step that the government took in this regard was to separate the functions of local government and land administration, thus undoing a major legacy of apartheid of concentrating and fusing power in one authority, the Tribal Authority. With regard to local government, the division between the rural and the urban was abolished in the sense that municipalities made up of elected councillors were extended to all parts of the country, including rural areas under traditional authorities where municipalities did not exist before. This was in line with the 1993 Interim Constitution and the 1996 Constitution, which stipulated that municipalities made up of elected councillors be established throughout the country.

With regard to land administration, the Department of Land Affairs (DLA) had by 1998 developed principles that would guide its legislative and implementation framework. The principles emphasized that where land rights 'to be confirmed exist on a group basis, the rights holders must have a choice about the system of land administration, which will manage their land rights on a day-to-day basis'. In addition,

> the basic human rights of all members must be protected, including the right to democratic decision-making processes and equality. Government must have access to members of group-held systems in order to ascertain their views and wishes in respect of proposed development projects and other matters pertaining to their land rights. (Thomas et al. 1998: 528)

It seems quite clear from the above that both the Departments of Provincial and Local Government and Land Affairs intended to subject traditional authorities to a system that would make them more representative and accountable to their communities.

Not surprising, the moves by the ANC-led government towards democratizing rural local governance drew fierce criticism and resistance even from CONTRALESA. The post-1994 government policies and laws were closing the ideological gap between members of CONTRALESA and those traditional authorities who are sympathetic to the IFP (Ntsebeza 2005; 2004; 2002). In the run-up to the first democratic local government elections in South Africa in 1995/1996, the IFP and CONTRALESA began to work together. Traditional authorities in both CONTRALESA and IFP took the ANC-led government to the Constitutional Court, challenging the government over the issue of establishing municipalities throughout the country, including rural areas under their jurisdiction. The president of CONTRALESA, Chief Phathekile Holomisa, who is also an ANC Member of Parliament, took an increasingly defiant stand towards the ANC. He called for a boycott of the first democratic local government elections.[12]

While the initial collaboration was around local government, it is quite clear that the main issue that brought traditional authorities together was their opposition to the notion of introducing new democratic structures. They would be happy to be the only primary structure in rural areas and insist on preserving the concentration of functions they enjoyed under apartheid, in particular land administration. Not only were they opposed to the idea of a separation of powers, they were also opposed to any attempt to introduce alternative structures that would compete with them. For example, in the case of local government, traditional authorities rejected the introduction of municipalities in 'their' areas. They argued that they should play a central role in rural development, and by implication, they rejected the democratic principles upon which post-1994 developmental local government is based. Traditional authorities adopted a similar stand with regard to land tenure reform. While they agreed with the government that land in the rural areas of the former Bantustans should not be the property of the state, they rejected the notion that where land is held on a group basis, the administration thereof should be transferred to democratically constituted and accountable structures. Traditional authorities strongly argued that the land should be transferred to Tribal Authorities that, as has been argued, are undemocratic and unaccountable. Transferring land to Tribal Authorities would legally exclude ordinary rural residents from vital decision-making processes, including land allocation.

Initially, the ANC-led government appeared to have been committed to extending participatory and representative notions of democracy to rural areas. An expression of this radicalism was the promulgation of the Regulation of Development in Rural Areas Act, 1997 by the Eastern Cape Legislature. This Act sought to divest traditional authorities of all their development functions and transfer these to elected councillors. This, of course, was in line with new functions of local government. However, since the end of 1997, the pendulum seems to have swung in favour of traditional authorities (Ntsebeza 2005). The first indications of this were in the White Paper on Local Government published in March 1998 which made broad and sweeping statements about the possible role that traditional authorities can play. Traditional 'leadership' is assigned 'a role closest to the people'. On the issue of development, a task that has been added to local government by the Constitution, the White Paper (Department of Constitutional Development 1998: 77) boldly asserts: 'There is no doubt that the important role that traditional leaders have played in the development of their communities should be continued.'

The issue of the role of traditional authorities was the subject of much discussion and negotiation in the run-up to the second democratic local government election in December 2000. It was instrumental in causing the postponement of announcing the date for the election. The position of the government was, in the run-up to the election, still ambivalent. After a series of meetings between the government and traditional authorities, the government made some concessions. The first significant concession was the amendment of the Municipal Structures Act that was successfully rushed through Parliament just before the local government elections. The amendment increases the representation of traditional authorities from ten to twenty per cent of the total number of councillors. Further, traditional authorities would not only be represented at a local government level, but also at a District and, in the case of KwaZulu-Natal, Metropolitan level. Traditional authorities, though, would not have the right to vote.

This concession seemed to have encouraged traditional authorities to ask for more. They rejected the twenty per cent increase. They wanted nothing short of amendments to the Constitution and legislation flowing from it regarding municipalities in rural areas in the former Bantustans. They wanted municipalities to be scrapped in these areas in favour of apartheid era Tribal Authorities as the primary

local government structures. Traditional authorities have claimed that the President had promised them, in word and in writing, that their powers would not be tampered with. If anything, they would be increased.[13] On his part, the President has neither denied nor endorsed the traditional authorities claim.

With regard to land administration, similar shifts in favour of traditional authorities were taking place in the Department of Land Affairs. We have seen above that the guiding principles of this department towards land administration were that where land was held on a group basis, the land rights holders would have a choice about the system of land administration. However, by August 2002, there was no clarity as to how the question of land administration would be resolved in rural areas. Neither was it clear how the issue of the role of traditional authorities in local government would be handled. In the end, as has been seen at the beginning of this chapter, this matter was resolved, at least in legislative terms, by the promulgation of the Traditional Leadership and Governance Framework Act of 2003 and the Communal Land Rights Act of 2004.

It is worth noting that the manner in which this vexed issue of the role of traditional authorities in a post-1994 democratic South Africa has been handled and negotiated is intriguing. In so far as local government issues are concerned, traditional authorities fall under the Department of Provincial and Local Government. In practice, though, traditional authorities did not seem to be recognizing this Department. They preferred that the President and the Deputy President handle their matters. For example, traditional authorities have submitted almost all their requests to the Office of the President. They seem to think that the Minister of Provincial and Local Government is not as favourably disposed towards them as the President. Alternatively, this might be a deliberate strategy to pit the President against the Minister.

To sum up this section, there is little doubt that since the early 1990s, traditional authorities have exploited the ambivalence and hesitations in ANC thinking and practice on the role of traditional authorities in a democracy. They have waged concerted campaigns and lobbied government, including, as I have shown, by-passing official channels, to ensure a place in the emerging South African democracy. Ironically, traditional authorities have used resources the government has made available to them to achieve their objectives. For example, the government has established Houses of Traditional Leaders in all the six provinces that have traditional authorities, as well as the National Council of Traditional Leaders. Traditional authorities have used these resources to consolidate their position. Those who are in Parliament, for example chiefs Holomisa and Nonkanyana, have also ensured that they use their positions as Members of Parliament of the ANC to advance the interests of their constituency.[14]

In addition, the collaboration between traditional authorities in CONTRALESA and in Inkatha has further strengthened their positions. The ANC finds itself in a position where it has to nurse the relationship with CONTRALESA in order not to lose the support of traditional authorities in this organization, and presumably their followers. At the same time, the ANC seems to be reluctant to strain relations with Inkatha especially given the history of political violence in KwaZulu-Natal in the 1980s and early 1990s referred to above. In this regard, Lodge has argued that government accommodation of traditional authorities was

a compromise to avert a threatened boycott of the first general elections by the Inkatha Freedom Party if the institution was not recognized and protected in the constitution. If it was not for the pressure from the IFP, the institution would have been destroyed by now … Rather than abolishing it, the ANC is creating legislation conditions through local government that will allow for the gradual phasing out of the institution which is done to avoid resistance from traditionalists … the ANC has become more tactful and has recognized that abolishing the institution will cause serious political conflict in the country. (quoted in Dladla 2000:15)

Given the passing of the two pieces of legislation in 2003/4 as discussed above, it is difficult to see how these laws are creating legislative conditions for the gradual phasing out of the institution and its incumbents. Further, it is a moot point whether winning over the support of traditional authorities in practice does ensure winning over their rural constituency. Moreover, it is not clear whether the strategy of resorting to violence on the part of Inkatha would work in conditions where the organization is no longer getting support from the police and army.

The poor performance of elected councillors
Poor performance of elected councillors over the last 10 years appears to have strengthened the position of traditional authorities and headmen. This poor performance should be viewed against expectations that rural people had that a developmental local government would transform their lives. Some of these expectations were fuelled by election promises. As early as the second local government elections in 2000, rural councillors had lost the confidence of ordinary rural residents who initially supported them. The run-up to the 2006 local government elections has again been marred by various incidents of protests against municipalities, including those which are supposed to deliver services to rural areas. The burning issues in most rural areas in the former Bantustans, apart from the demand for land for residential purposes, are poor services especially for the basic necessities of water and infrastructure.

However, the apparent neglect of rural councillors cannot be dissociated from the neo-liberal, macro-economic policies pursued by the ANC-led government especially since 1996. It can be argued that macro-economic policies, with their tight fiscal discipline, substantially constrain the government from setting up and monitoring new structures. As Hart has lamented: 'GEAR sits uneasily astride the emancipatory promises of the liberation struggle, as well as the material hopes, aspirations, and rights of the large majority of South Africans' (2002: 7). The low budgets for rural programmes, land reform and local government make it difficult for government to employ new and competent staff that would enhance government capacity (see Mingo 2002; Lahiff 2001; Adams, Cousins and Manona 2000). In this regard, it could be argued that the government sees supporting Tribal Authorities as less demanding than setting up new structures. The big question is where this puts rural residents regarding democracy, and how, in wooing traditional authorities, the ANC would dismantle tribalism and the Bantustans. Indeed, tribalism is inherent in the recognition of separate chieftaincies (Hendricks and Ntsebeza 1999).

The weak structures of civil society in rural areas
In contrast to the organization displayed by traditional authorities, not forgetting the resources at their disposal, land-based and rural development non-governmental organizations (NGOs) and social movements in South Africa appear to be weak. Part of this weakness could be attributed to the stance that they adopted towards the democratic government, particularly between 1994 and 1999. Most of these organizations aligned themselves with and gave support to the new ANC-led democratic government. Some of their leading activists took up positions in government departments. The Department of Land Affairs (DLA), with a Minister, Derrick Hanekom, who had liberation struggle credentials, was especially targeted. The Director-General of DLA in the first six years or so of South Africa's democracy, Geoff Budlender, was a leading lawyer from a public interest NGO, the Legal Resources Centre. Other senior officials of the Department were drawn from leading NGOs at the time such as the National Land Committee (NLC). Apart from releasing activists to work in government, organizations such as the NLC played a supportive role in helping the DLA develop and implement land policies and laws. The thinking, it appears, was that by collaborating with government, these movements would influence policies.

It is worth noting, though, that poor delivery in terms of the land reform programme in South Africa, in particular land redistribution, has divided the NGOs and social movements into two broad categories: those who do not want to rock the boat and prefer to continue working within the existing government policies, on the one hand, and those who argue that the limits of the existing policy should be exposed and pressure should be put on government to re-visit existing policies and change them where necessary. The spectrum in each of these broad categories is wide. More research needs to be done in this area. What seems clear is that without a strong and organised voice, rural inhabitants are going to find it hard to contest the emerging influence of traditional authorities on government.

Conclusion

This paper has put the spotlight on traditional authorities, in particular how, despite their collaborative role in the apartheid state, the ANC-led government has embraced them and given them unprecendented powers which have been enacted in the Traditional Leadership and Governance Framework Act of 2003 and the Communal Land Rights Act of 2004. I have traced this development by focusing, amongst others, on the evolution of the policies of the ANC towards traditional authorities paying particular attention to the period from the transition to democracy in South Africa to the promulgation of the two laws referred to above. As explained in the introduction to this paper, the reason for this focus is that the ANC has been and remains the dominant political party in South Africa.

A substantial part of the paper has been devoted to attempting to understand why the ANC took the positions that it did. In this regard, I have considered a number of factors including the global political and economic context since the time of the transition, the active role of traditional authorities in defining a place for them in South Africa's democracy, and the weakness of local government and civil society in South Africa. In the final analysis, the ANC has gradually shifted from its earlier hope that traditional authorities would accept a secondary, ceremonial role after 1994 to conceding to traditional authorities powers which effectively resuscitate the powers they enjoyed under the notorious Bantu Authorities Act of 1951. I have shown that the Traditional Councils set up in terms of the Traditional Leadership and Governance Framework Act are dominated by unelected traditional authorities and their appointees and thus unrepresentative and unaccountable, as was the case with apartheid-era Tribal Authorities. What this means is that, in one respect, namely, local government, rural residents enjoy the same citizenship rights that are enjoyed by their urban counterparts, in the sense that they elect their councillors.

However, on the vital issue of land allocation, rural people become 'subjects' in the sense that decisions are taken by Traditional Councils which are, as indicated, dominated by unelected traditional authorities and their appointees.

This raises critical questions about citizenship and the nature of democracy in South Africa. Mamdani (1996) has proposed that 'dismantling' the 'clenched fist' of Tribal Authorities entails 'an endeavour to link the urban and the rural – and thereby a series of related binary opposites such as rights and custom, representation and participation, centralization and decentralization, civil society and community – in ways that have yet to be done' (1996: 34). To what extent has post-1994 South Africa succeeded in 'dismantling' the apartheid-created 'clenched fist' of unaccountable Tribal Authorities? In the end, it has been shown that the ANC-led government opted, despite internal differences and the dubious history of traditional authorities particularly during the apartheid period, for the co-existence of traditional authorities with elected representatives. I have, however, demonstrated what this means for democratizing land administration in South Africa's countryside.

Notes

[1] Ben Cousins and Aninka Claassens, 'Looming land disaster', in *Mail and Guardian*, 31 October to 6 November 2003.

[2] As we have seen, disagreements between traditional authorities and government about their role in a democracy go back to the political negotiation period in the early 1990s.

[3] While agreeing with Mamdani that Native Authorities were despotic, mimicking their colonial masters, I, however, question whether they were decentralized, and that the colonial state could be viewed as bifurcated. Decentralization implies some degree of devolution of powers and autonomy. My research (Ntsebeza 2005) suggests that Tribal Authorities, while despotic, were not decentralized in the sense that they were autonomous and had significant powers devolved to them. Magistrates, who were representatives of the colonial state at a district level, assumed tight control over Tribal Authorities.

[4] IDPs will be explained below.

[5] Interview with headman Zantsi, Manzimahle, 9 September, 2000.

[6] Interview with Liwani, Cala, 11 September 2000

[7] It is worth noting that this orientation on the part of CONTRALESA has not changed. The leadership spends more time at airports and conference centres, than in their constituencies.

[8] After prior attempts on his life, Chief Maphumulo was shot and killed at his home in Pietermaritzburg by assassins. No one was apprehended.

[9] Mark Gevisser 'The other Holomisa', http://web.sn.apc.org/wmail/issues/960913/NEWS66.html.

[10] The author has shared numerous platforms with Chief Holomisa, debating the question of the role of traditional authorities in a modern democracy.

[11] In terms of this resolution, the following points, *inter alia*, were agreed upon: Traditional authorities shall continue to exercise their functions in terms of indigenous law as prescribed and regulated by enabling legislation; there shall be an elected local government, which shall take political responsibility for the provision of services in its area of jurisdiction; the (hereditary) traditional leaders within the area of jurisdiction of a local authority shall be *ex officio* members of the local government; and the chairperson of any local government shall be elected from amongst all the members of the local government

[12] Mark Gevisser 'The other Holomisa', http://web.sn.apc.org/wmail/issues/960913/NEWS66.html.

[13] I have not been in a position to get a copy of this statement by the President.

[14] This is from various conversations I have had with them from 1996. However, as pointed out in the foreword, it has not been possible to have formal interviews with these chiefs, except Nonkonyane in 1996.

References

Adams, M., Cousins, B. and Manona, S. 2000. 'Land Tenure and Economic Development in Rural South Africa: Constraints and Opportunities'. In: Cousins, B. (ed), *At the Crossroads: Land and Agrarian Reform in South Africa into the 21st Century*. Cape Town: Programme for Land and Agrarian Studies and National Land Committee.

Bowen, M.L. 2000. *The State Against the Peasants: Rural Struggles in Colonial and Postcolonial Mozambique*. Charlottesville: University Press of Virginia.

Delius, P. 1996. *A Lion Amongst the Cattle: Reconstruction and resistance in the Northern Transvaal*. Johannesburg: Ravan Press.

Department of Constitutional Development and Local Government. 1998. *The White Paper on Local Government*. Pretoria.

De Wet, C.J. and McAllister, P.A. 1983. *Rural Communities in Transition: A Study of the Socio-Economic and Agricultural Implications of Agricultural Betterment and Development*. Grahamstown: Department of Anthropology in collaboration with the Institute of Social and Economic Research, Rhodes University, Working Paper no. 16.

Dladla, S. 2000. 'Slow Fall of the House of Chiefs', *Land & Rural Digest*, March/April.

Dinerman, A. 2001. 'From "Abaixo" to "Chiefs of Production": Agrarian Change in Nampula Province, Mozambique, 1975–87', *The Journal of Peasant Studies*, 28 (2): 1–82.

Hart, G. 2002. *Disabling Globalization: Places of Power in Post-Apartheid South Africa*. Pietermaritzburg: University of Natal Press.

Hendricks, F. and Ntsebeza, L. 1999. 'Chiefs and Rural Local Government in Post-Apartheid South Africa', *African Journal of Political Science: New Series*, 4 (1): 99–126.

Henrard, K. 1999. 'The Interrelation between Individual Human Rights, Minority Rights and the Right to Self-determination for an Adequate Minority Protection', Leuven: Leuven University, unpublished Doctor of Law thesis.

Lahiff, E. 2001. *Land Reform in South Africa: Is it Meeting the Challenge?* Policy Brief No. 1: Debating land reform and rural development. Cape Town: Programme for Land and Agrarian Studies.

Libombo, A. 2000. 'Mozambique's Bitter War between Chiefs and Liberation Government', *Land & Rural Digest*, March/April 2000.

Mamdani, M. 1996. *Citizen and Subject: Contemporary Africa and the Legacy of Late Colonialism*, Princeton/Cape Town/Oxford: Princeton University Press/David Phillip/James Currey.

Marais, H. 1998. *South Africa, Limits to Change: The political economy of transformation*. London: Zed Books.

Mbeki, G. 1984. *South Africa: The Peasants' Revolt*. London: International Defence and Aid Fund.

Mbeki, G. 1996. *Sunset at Midday: Latshon' ilang' emini!* Braamfontein: Nolwazi Educational Publishers.

Mingo, C. 2002. *The 2002 Land Affairs Budget: Is Land Reform on Track?* Cape Town: Idasa (Budget brief No. 89).

Ntsebeza, L. 1999. *Land Tenure Reform, Traditional Authorities and Rural Local Government in Post-apartheid South Africa: Case studies from the Eastern Cape*. Bellville: Programme for Land and Agrarian Studies, Research Report No. 3.

— 2002. 'Structures and Struggles of Rural Local Government in South Africa: The Case Study of Traditional Authorities in the Eastern Cape'. Grahamstown: Rhodes University, unpublished PhD thesis.

— 2004. 'Rural Governance and Citizenship in Post-apartheid South Africa: Democracy compromised?' In: Daniel, J. Southall, R. and Lutchman, J. (eds), *The State of the Nation: South Africa 2004–2005*. Cape Town: HSRC Press and Michigan State University Press.

— 2005. *Democracy Compromised: Chiefs and the Politics of Land in South Africa*. Leiden: Brill Academic Publishers

Oomen, B. 1996. 'Talking Tradition. The Position and Portrayal of Traditional Leaders in Present-day South Africa'. Leiden: University of Leiden, unpublished MA thesis.

Pitcher, M.A. 1996. 'The Politics of the Countryside: Democracy and Economic Liberalisation in Northern Mozambique'. Paper presented to the annual meeting of the African Studies Association, 23–26 November.

Thomas, G., Sibanda, S. and Claassens, A. 1998. *Current Developments in South Africa's Land Tenure Policy*. Proceedings of the International Conference on Land Tenure in the Developing World with a focus on Southern Africa. University of Cape Town, 27–29 January.

Zuma, T. (1990), 'The Role of Chiefs in the Struggle for Liberation'. *The African Communist*, 121.

BARBARA OOMEN
Chiefs! Law, Power & Culture in Contemporary South Africa

Reference
Unpublished paper

Introduction

'*Re buswitše!* We are being ruled again!', shrieked a praise-singer in animal skins, his feet kicking up the red Sekhukhune sand. It was 19 December 1998, and in front of him sat the newly enthroned Billy Sekwati Mampuru III, king of the important Pedi lineage of Mamone. Behind him thousands of people roared in agreement, women in colourful attire ululated shrilly, the trumpets of the khaki-clad Zionist marching band sounded, old men hymned songs from the initiation schools, disco music pulsed, and against the clear blue sky a helicopter carrying VIPs prepared to land. The whole cacaphony of sound seemed to add up to one message, voiced by an old man later that evening: 'It is time to go back to our history.'

A similar spirit seemed to permeate the inauguration of another leader, half a year later. In contrast to Sekwati's coronation, Thabo Mbeki's ascent to the presidency was world news, with press, presidents and royalty gathered to hear how the new leader intended to build on the policies of his already legendary predecessor, Nelson Mandela. Thousands listened breathlessly as Mbeki sketched how South Africa was at the time of the '*mahube a naka tsa kgomo* – the dawning of the dawn, when only the tips of the horns of cattle can be seen etched against the morning sky'. He said these times were characterized by the need to rediscover and claim the African heritage, and to redefine South Africa as an 'African nation in the complex process simultaneously of formation and renewal'. The time had come for an African Renaissance, the new president declared amid a storm of applause.

One striking aspect of this African Renaissance forms the subject-matter of this contribution: the surprising resurgence of traditional authority and customary law within South Africa's democratic dispensation. Approaching this issue from a socio-legal perspective, I concentrate on three questions: What was the relation between the changing legal and socio-political position of traditional authority and customary law in post-apartheid South Africa? Why was this so? And what does this teach us about the interrelation between law, politics and culture in the post-modern world? In answering these questions, this article will start with a brief discussion of the theoretical relevance as well as methodological approach of the research it summarizes: a legal-anthropological PhD project concerning the position of chieftainship in the post-Apartheid era, conducted by myself at the end of the twentieth century.[1] This research called for a specific methodology that combined extensive and in-depth fieldwork with a more multi-sited and ethnographic approach. This is why, in addition to a total of 15 months spent on classic qualitative and quantitative field research in the Northern Province, I also spent five months of research interviewing policy-makers and parliamentarians, visiting conferences on the future of traditional leadership and generally recording South Africa's 'struggle for the soul of custom'.

This contribution will first discuss the causes and consequences of the return of 'chiefs and customs' in national and international policy discourse, and subsequently turn to the implications of this phenomenon in one particular locality, Sekhukhune. Finally, it will briefly look at the implications of this case-study for general theory on the relations between law, politics and culture.

Background

What is the relevance of a study on traditional leadership and customary law in South Africa to a reader on modernity in Africa? For one, the reappraisal of 'chiefs and customs' within South Africa's first democratic dispensation seems to exemplify a much wider trend at the end of the twentieth century described in other articles in this volume: a widespread challenge to the nation-state, once considered to be the only vehicle to progress. Instead, a number of alternative sub-, supra- and transnational polities, some vintage, others virgin, seemed eager to take over some of the state's practical and symbolic functions. A striking aspect of this renegotiation of the nation-state was how it was often played along the lines of culture, with communities claiming political autonomy on the basis of their cultural uniqueness. One manifestation of this 'culturalism', and the way in which it knitted together law, politics and culture, was the ubiquitous rise of 'rights to roots', with indigenous peoples claiming and receiving more autonomy.[2] A second example was the revival, all over Africa, of traditional leadership, not only informally but also in laws and policy documents.

For all the newness of this cultural rights discourse, there was also something disturbingly familiar about it. Often, it seemed to rest on the idea that society consisted of a tapestry of distinct cultures, and that the – ascertainable – normative and governmental systems of these cultures were worthy of official legal recognition. While these images and notions were presented as new postulates of post-modern times, they nonetheless at times bore a striking resemblance to the paradigms of both colonial and apartheid policies. Both policies made use of notions of cultural difference in order to legitimate discriminatory systems of indirect rule. A bureaucratized chieftaincy, for instance, was frequently incorporated into the colonial state, and transformed beyond recognition in the process. Customary law suffered a similar fate: an essentially flexible system was chiselled into 'the austerity of tabulated legalism', and made subject to colonial laws and so-called repugnancy clauses. A substantial amount of literature has pointed out how this was hardly a top-down exercise, how those versions of chieftaincy, custom and culture that made it to law were often determined in a dialogue between government officials and traditional leaders, and were thus foremost the versions in their interest.[3]

It is at the juncture of these two sets of givens – the enthusiastic embracing of chiefs, custom and culture in a new world and the lessons customary law studies hold about their artificial origins – that the set of key theoretical challenges arises to which this article seeks to provide part of an answer. First, now that an increasing number of states are drawing their legitimacy from associations with traditional leaders, and other polities – chiefdoms, first nations – are relying on 'cultural difference' to attain autonomy from states, there is a need to rethink the relation between law, power and culture. What is law in these situations, what does it reflect? A second topic concerns the constitutive effects of cultural rights legislation: what does state recognition of chiefs and customs do locally? Finally, and related to all this, there is a challenge in rethinking the connections between the state recognition of traditional leadership and its resurgence all over Africa – not only in constitutions and parliaments, but also in villages like Mamone, seemingly far from the wider world. What legitimacy do these chiefs have? Is their revival locally driven; the local adoption of a bureaucratic myth (as deconstructivists would have us believe) or is there an alternative, more balanced explanation?

For a number of reasons, South Africa is an ideal case-study for examination of both the empirical resurgence of traditional leadership and its theoretical implications. For one, there is the starkness of the contrast between the abuse of notions of cultural difference under apartheid, and their unexpected comeback in the post-apartheid era. The struggle against apartheid was above all against this imposition of cultural diversity, which caused even the even-tempered Bishop Tutu to fulminate in the 1980s: 'We blacks – most of us – execrate ethnicity with all our being.'[4] Yet, less than two decades later, the country's constitution re-recognized chieftaincy and customary law, and the country's vice-president advocated an 'African Renaissance [...] where all communities are free to explore, explain, reflect and rejoice in that which makes them unique....'[5] Another reason why South Africa, of all countries, turned out to be such an interesting case-study for analysis of the changing position of chieftaincy, culture and custom was the period in which the research for it was conducted. There was the titillating excitement of the 'dawning of the dawn', the daybreak of democracy which seemingly opened all positions, made them debatable. In considering these issues, this study thus forms an explicit attempt to link the local to the national and even the global, and to focus on the dialectical interactions between these polities. Even though it describes the position of chiefs and customary law in one place – Sekhukhune in South Africa's Northern Province – its concern is with the complex dialogue between this locality and the wider world.

The patchwork democracy

What were the outcomes of the national discussion on the future of traditional leadership and customary law after 1994? Those observers who, in the 1980s, had expected chieftaincy to 'melt away like ice in the sun' noted with surprise how the strong formal position of chiefs under apartheid did not diminish after South Africa's democratization.[6] If anything, the position of chiefs was strengthened. Six years after the elections, practically all the institutional arrangements that singled out the former homelands as separate spheres of rule, largely under chiefly jurisdiction, were still in place. This legal and institutional legacy consisted of over 1500 pieces of legislation, many of them based on the 1927 Black Administration Act and the 1951 Black Authorities Act, which had turned traditional leaders in the former homelands into 'decentralised despots', with wide-ranging powers in local government, land allocation and dispute settlement. Other authors have labelled this legacy 'bifurcated', but the number of different laws and regulations passed in individual homelands, regional authorities and traditional authorities led to and comprised proof of so many different scenarios of governance that the term 'patchwork democracy' seems to be a more suitable description of the situation.[7]

Of course, much did change in the new South Africa. For one, the

system of racial segregation was officially replaced by a 'sovereign and democratic constitutional state in which there is equality between men and women and people of all races'. Ever since Nelson Mandela, in his first speech after 27 years of imprisonment, explicitly saluted the traditional leaders of the country, it had been clear that they too would somehow have to be granted a place in this egalitarian constitutional order. A strong presence of traditional leaders in the constitutional negotiation process, combined with Inkatha Freedom Party (IFP) leader Buthelezi's threat not to participate in the elections if chieftaincy was not recognized, ensured that a constitutional principle on the recognition of traditional leadership and customary law was adopted even before the 1994 elections. Like an alimony agreement from a former marriage, this principle would tie the hands of the democratically elected Constitutional Assembly when it was drawing up the final constitution. Thus, this final constitution, adopted in 1996, declared:

> 211. 1) The institution, status and role of traditional leadership, according to customary law, are recognised, subject to the Constitution

Nevertheless, the real decisions concerning the future of these institutions still had to be taken. The years that followed showed how difficult this process would be. For instance, a Traditional Authorities Act to replace the still-valid apartheid legislation concerning chieftaincy was originally planned for 1998 but was nowhere near adoption in 2002. Likewise, the patchy institutional legacy persisted in the key policy areas of local government, land allocation and dispute resolution. Concerning local government, elected municipalities were installed in the rural areas, but traditional leaders protested vehemently against this situation of 'two bulls in one kraal'.[8] This caused President Mbeki to promise in 2000 that he would, if necessary, amend the constitution to ensure 'a dual system (providing) for the retention of traditional leadership, while at the same time allowing local communities to elect public representatives'. Similarly, little changed in land allocation: a Bill seeking to democratize access to land in traditional authority areas was shelved, and the responsible minister was dismissed to make place for a staunchly pro-traditionalist colleague. And in the field of customary law, traditional leaders managed to retain civil and criminal jurisdiction over 'their' subjects, perpetuating duality in this area as well.

The pressing question is, of course, why? Why did that legal and institutional web designed to perpetuate social and economic inequality, and based on ethnicity and patriarchy, prove so hard to unravel? The answer lies in the interplay of the actors and the more structural conditions at work. One of the central actors, for instance, was the very active and able body representing the traditional leaders, CONTRALESA, which ranked among its members chiefs who combined law degrees with political agility and popular support. These traditional leaders were able to profit from the indecisiveness of the ANC, which was ripped apart over this issue of identity, as well as from the willingness of other parties to endorse their position. In addition, the wilting of activist organizations after democratization made alternative voices representing 'rural communities' less strong than they used to be. And then there was the staunch support of government departments like Traditional Affairs, which considered its main challenge to be to 'restore the traditional nature and respectability of the institution of traditional leadership'.[9] But all these actors operated in, drew on and contributed to, a wider set of conditions favourable to a resurgence of traditional leadership. The South African party-political landscape, for one, made the ANC feel that it somehow had to co-opt the chiefs, if only as 'voter brokers'. Also, there was apartheid's heritage, which made it so easy to slip into familiar discourses, representations and ideas about rural reality. But there was more, like the deeply and widely felt need to reconnect with the roots, to rediscover an African identity, to relive an African Renaissance. This quest for cultural revival reflected, as we have seen, a global mood of recognizing culture within law and politics, and of 'rights to roots'.

The power of definition

The post-apartheid political constellation was thus not only one which favoured a strong formal position for 'chiefs and customs', but also one which allowed traditional leaders themselves to take centre stage in discussions that, essentially, affected not only them but also the at least 13 million people considered to be their 'subjects'. Because it was a central presupposition in policy debates that South Africa had a cultural diversity that needed to be 'recognized', what was essentially at issue in these debates was the contents of culture, custom and tradition. And because traditional leaders played such a central role in the policy debate, they had the power of definition and virtually monopolized knowledge on the rural condition, the popularity of traditional authority and the character of customary law. To give one example: when the national Department of Traditional Affairs embarked on a research project concerning the popularity of traditional leadership, it only sent out questionnaires to the Houses of Traditional Leaders, and not to chiefly subjects.

All this led not only to a strengthening of the legal and socio-political position of traditional leaders in the national power landscape, but also to an acceptance of a certain understanding, a specific definition of the character and the value of traditional leadership. This understanding seemed to rest on four – all too familiar – assumptions that made it to policy debates and, finally, into law. The first assumption concerned the popularity of traditional leadership and the immutability of support for the institution. The second, perpetuated by government officials and traditional leaders, was that rural society consisted of coherent communities, which could be represented as such. A third assumption pertained to the existence of coherent systems of customary law, ready to be ascertained and 'recognized'. Finally, there was the idea of an irreconcilable difference, in terms of needs and aspirations, between the 'rural' and the 'urban'.

The institutional landscape

How did these assumptions, which determined the extent to which, as well as how, traditional leaders received recognition at the national level, compare with the locally lived reality of Sekhukhune?

One central reason for this study was the often-signalled lack of empirical information on 'what occurs on the ground', people's perspectives on the legitimacy of traditional leadership. Here, possibly surprisingly, the data from Sekhukhune, an impoverished area in the Northern Province with a long history of famous traditional rulers, show that there was as much a call for 'retraditionalization' locally as there was nationally. The freedoms of democracy, and the chances it offered to rethink and re-express identities, led to the revival of Pedi dancing, the zealous reinstallation of chiefs and calls for the reanimation of 'traditional' systems of dispute resolution. Not only did 80 per cent of the people we interviewed say that they supported a traditional leader,[10] but many of them also underlined the changes that this support had undergone: 'During the struggle we'd fight like dogs

with our chief, but now we're back together again.'

Even though there was a revival of chiefly popularity in Sekhukhune, there seemed to be a large fissure between the national assumptions of culture, custom, communities and chieftaincy, and the rural realities. While there was general support for institutions such as traditional leadership and customary law, the *character* of this support differed drastically from the ideas held, circulated and perpetuated in national discourse.

Let us start with the assumed popularity of traditional leadership. While the national image was one of a sole representative institution, with a fixed set of functions and responsibilities and an immutable support base rooted in tradition, even the briefest of visits to Sekhukhune would reveal a rather different picture. We find an institutionally plural landscape in which a variety of actors compete, or sometimes co-operate, over local power. In each village, a different constellation of actors, such as the widely influential vigilante organization *Mapogo*, the civic organizations, elected representatives, Churches, and business and migrants' organizations, worked with or against the traditional authorities in order to attain control over resources, boundaries, people and meaning. It was precisely the ability of traditional leaders to form a 'hegemonic bloc' with the more conservative of these actors over the need to restore law and order that facilitated their comeback in many places. Also, traditional leaders themselves were surrounded by a variety of other actors, be they the royal family, a wider group outside the family, or the Tribal Council. Successful traditional leaders were those that could operate in three different spheres – party politics, bureaucracy and palace politics – belying the notion of solitary rulers.

Additionally, the functions and responsibilities of traditional leaders appeared to be far from fixed, and subject to permanent discussion. Even if most people theoretically approved of the notion of traditional leadership, there was a permanent tussle to make the institution more accountable, to ensure that it delivered, to open it up (or keep it closed) to women, to redefine its contents. Of course, the way in which this was done differed from place to place: In Madibong, for instance, a progressive chief decided to replace some of the royals in the Tribal Council with elected members, among which were women. In Mamone, on the other hand, villagers embarked on a process to write a 'Tribal Constitution', circumscribing and redefining the powers of the traditional authority. But in every village support for chieftaincy depended not only on individual and village characteristics, but also on the governance of the chief concerned: wise, accountable, assertive and 'obedient' traditional leaders who 'delivered' – projects, spoils – could count on increase in support. Many Bapedi, for instance, related their support for traditional leadership to the failure of local councils to deliver: 'As these boys have brought us nothing, for now let's keep the *magoši*.'

A look at local 'living law' revealed a similar discrepancy between the assumption held nationally – that of a legitimate, coherent and distinct system of customary law – and the dynamic and discursive local filling-in of the concept. While many Sekhukhune citizens acknowledged the importance of *melao*, law, this did not at all mean that its contents were fixed. Rather, law as lived in day-to-day life – under thorn trees, in rickety school buildings – and the values and norms it drew on were the outcome of an ongoing series of negotiations, firmly embedded in local power relations, in which actors could draw on a wide variety of resources. 'The loosely constructed repertoire' of custom was one, as were constitutional and developmental values, Biblical wisdom, force, common sense, and information from outside sources, for instance, that received over the radio. Even in cases where norms were clear, those interested in predicting outcomes were better off looking at power relations than the rules involved.

A third assumption held nationally was that rural society consisted of communities coherent enough to be represented by a single institution such as traditional leadership. Again, a superficial glance at Sekhukhune reality would have confirmed this assumption: people identified strongly with their *setšaba* (community/nation) and related community identity to the presence of a chief: *setšaba ke setšaba ka kgoši* – a community is a community because it has a traditional leader. This, however, did not imply homogeneity, or even that people considered the chief to be the ideal spokesperson in dealings with the outside world. Far from it. For one, communities were rife with gender and generational disputes, expressed in and fed by dark undercurrents of jealousy and witchcraft accusations. Also, practically every Sekhukhune community was torn apart by – often violent – succession disputes.

The fourth assumption, that of rural–urban difference, was also at variance with the multi-layered local reality. Indeed, many rural people interviewed cherished traditional leadership and customary law. And yes, Sekhukhune residents (particularly the migrants) felt that Bopedi was governed by other rules, a different pace and even a different normative order than *makgoweng* – the world of the whites. But this did not preclude most Bapedi from holding the same democratic and materialist aspirations as the rest of the population: support for traditional leadership was not exclusive, but combined with wide backing of democractic governance or any other institutional arrangement that could ensure realization of the ANC's promise – 'a better life for all'.

The constitutive effects of cultural rights legislation

There were thus two sets of givens concerning the legal position of traditional authority and customary law. On the one hand, there were the official, codified versions of culture, custom and chieftaincy: laws departing from notions of chiefly sovereignty, communal coherence and rural–urban difference. On the other hand, there were the permanently shifting dynamics of local law, the fluctuating and contested character of ideas on chiefly functions and authority and the ongoing debates on what local custom and culture were, and what they should be. The question arises, of course, as to how these two sets are interlinked, what all these official laws mean and do locally. To express it in another way: What are the constitutive effects of cultural rights legislation?

I discuss this issue from two angles: the legitimacy of traditional leadership and the debates on customary law. But before turning to a brief description of the outcomes of this approach, it is necessary to put forward a caveat concerning the impossibility of neatly measuring the impact of the 'legal' on the 'local'. As law is hardly an independent variable, I prefer to take a *constitutive* approach to the question of 'how law matters'. Such an approach sees law 'as the way of organizing the world into categories and concepts which, while providing spaces and opportunities, also constrains behaviour and serves to legitimate authority'.[11] As such, it recognizes that law cannot be separated from wider social forces. In Sekhukhune, for instance, the formal, legal affirmation went hand-in-hand with political statements on the importance of chieftaincy, NGOs singling out traditional leaders as their main counterparts in development programmes, companies like Coca-Cola and Douglas Colliery sponsoring royal coronations, and the ANC executive telling local cadres that the time had come to make peace with the chiefs.

Nevertheless, the law did matter. A first perspective through which this became clear was that of the legitimacy of both individual traditional leaders and the institution of traditional leadership. In Sekhukhune, we not only looked at who supported traditional leaders (more the elderly than youngsters, more lower-educated and lower-income Bapedi than the higher educated, and rich and – surprisingly – more women than men) and how these people supported chiefs – in a dynamic, limited, issue-related and not exclusive way. A large part of our investigation also concerned the why of popular support for traditional leadership. Here it turned out that people generally quoted four equally important sources of legitimacy: tradition, chiefly performance, lack of alternatives and ... government support. There were thus just as many people who supported chiefs because 'they are the eyes and ears of the government' as there were people who gave reasons like: '*bogoši* is our culture as black people and should therefore be protected and promoted'; 'at least they are doing some good things for us'; and 'who else is there to rule us?'

This government recognition as an important source of chiefly legitimacy contrasts sharply with all the literature that considers traditional leaders as alternatives to the state system, their powers rooted purely in an alternative, traditional morality. Nevertheless, it should also not be overestimated. Case material from three different villages – the tiny under-developed Hoepakranz, the apartheid artefact Ga-Masha and the fast-developing Mamone – demonstrated how government recognition was far from the only source of legitimacy. Strikingly, the more 'developed' the community concerned, the more support for chieftaincy was legitimated in terms of 'tradition'. Development, it appears, does not so much reduce support for chieftaincy as it alters the character of this support.

A second prism through which to look at the local constitutive effects of cultural rights legislation was that of customary law. Local everyday law, as stated above, is far from the coherent, ascertainable system that national discourse would have it. It is negotiated, within local power relations, by actors who can draw on a wide variety of resources. One of these resources is official customary law as recognized by the state: the constitutional recognition of chiefs, the still-applicable Black Authorities Act and Black Administration Act, and the thousands of ensuing regulations. Far from local, living law and state law being two distinct systems, state law was often pulled in as a resource, even if it always had to be validated and reappropriated locally. And it was especially there where there was widespread legal uncertainty, such as with the overlapping and contradictory official land legislation, that state law sided with the more powerful, those with privileged access to information.

One particularly telling example was the role that official, codified customary law played in local succession disputes. Even though the formal rule here was that the oldest son of one of the chief's wives – the *mmasetšaba* – would always inherit the throne, reality proved to be otherwise: in the majority of cases, chiefs were succeeded by someone else, often someone who was better equipped for the function. It would seem as though the Sekhukhune system of succession contained a built-in vagueness and uncertainty that allowed the best candidate out of a limited pool not only to ascend to chieftaincy, but also to argue this claim in terms of customary law.[12] The state appointment of traditional leaders thwarted this subtle local system. By rigidly applying the principle of the eldest son, state anthropologists often helped highly unpopular candidates to the throne and sowed the seeds of heated succession disputes.

State law categorizes, demarcates subjects, defines powers and draws lines. And once they are singled out and defined in law, categories like 'a traditional leader', 'a tribal resolution' and 'a customary marriage' can have important local consequences, if not causatively then at least by structuring both 'thought and action'.

Categories have consequences

It is time to return to the three main questions that this article has briefly addressed: what was the relation between the legal and sociopolitical position of traditional leadership and customary law in post-apartheid South Africa, why was this so, and what does this teach us about the relation between law, politics and culture in the post-modern world? A first striking finding is how the reappraisal of traditional leadership in South Africa was not confined to policy documents and parliamentary plush, but also took place on the dusty plains of Sekhukhuneland. A second noteworthy outcome is the role played by state law in this reappraisal, in many different ways and in conjunction with a multitude of other resources. State law and its categorizations impacted on how Bapedi constituted themselves and their relations with the wider world, on local political formations and on who could claim access to resources. It strengthened political positions, rendered some scenarios less logical than others and thus functioned as a resource in the negotiations on the local order and people's place in it. For all the local creativity in accepting, rejecting or redefining legal categorizations, the law did matter.

How, then, can we extend these findings to wider studies of the relation between law, power, culture and modernity? The most important implication is that they (once again) refute two of the central ideas to which lawyers and social scientists debating cultural rights cling with surprising doggedness. The first is 'the myth of the mirror': the notion that within a given nation there exists such a thing as an amalgam of coherent cultures, separate coloured blotches neatly shimmering on a painter's palette, ready to receive state recognition. However, reality shows a murky and smudged picture of blending lines and uncertain textures. Drawing certain features of 'culture' and 'custom' out of this blend for neat classification in legal categories is in essence a political act, certain to privilege some voices, visions and versions while silencing others. Second, it belies the equally tenacious belief that there are, in countries like South Africa, isolated and traditional communities with systems of sociopolitical and legal order free from interactions with the outside world, and draws attention to the dialectic, mutually constitutive dialogue between polities.

These lessons also contain the seeds of some alternative approaches to the legal recognition of culture. They demonstrate the importance of the 'power to define' culture and custom, and thus of granting this power of definition to the people concerned instead of to their leaders. Similarly, they show the need to drop the notion that customary law and human rights, tradition and modernity, chiefly rule and democracy, would somehow be antithetical. Finally, they show how the law can act as a weapon of not only the mighty but also the weak, and how knowledge of the law can empower the marginalized in their struggle for a better life.

Notes

1 Barbara Oomen, 2005, *Chiefs in South Africa. Law. Power and Culture in the post-Apartheid era.* Oxford/New York: James Currey/Palgrave.

2 The term 'culturalism' was coined by Appadurai, who defined it as the conscious mobilization of cultural differences in the service of a larger national or transnational politics; see A. Appadurai. 1996. *Modernity at Large: Cultural Dimensions of Globalization.* Minneapolis: University of Minnesota Press. The term 'rights to roots' is used in: B. De Sousa Santos, 'State, Law and Community in the World System: An Introduction.' *Social & Legal Studies* 1 (1992): 131–42.

3 Three seminal works are: M. Chanock,1985, *Law, Custom and Social Order: The Colonial Experience in Malawi and Zambia,* Cambridge: Cambridge University Press; Mahmood Mamdani, 1996, *Citizen and Subject: Contemporary Africa and the Legacy of Late Colonialism.* Princeton Studies in Culture/Power/History, Princeton: Princeton University Press; and Kristin Mann and Richard Roberts, eds, 1991, *Law in Colonial Africa.* Portsmouth, NH/Oxford: Heinemann Educational Books/James Currey.

4 Quoted in Arend Lijphart, 1995, 'Self-Determination Versus Pre-Determination of Ethnic Minorities in Power-Sharing Systems.' In Will Kymlicka (ed.), *The Rights of Minority Cultures.* Oxford: Oxford University Press, pp. 275–87.

5 South African Press Agency, 2001, 'Address by Deputy President Jacob Zuma to the Opening Ceremony of the National Khoisan Consultative Conference', www.sapa.com

6 Cf. an article in the official ANC bulletin, which stated that 'there can be no compromise with our perspective of a unitary, democratic South Africa where there shall be no bantustans' ANC. 'The Bantustan Question: A New Approach?' *Sechaba* 24, no. 4 (1990): 13–14. The quote 'In the new South Africa, chiefs will melt away like ice in the sun' comes from Eddy Maloka, 1996, 'Populism and the Politics of Chieftaincy and Nation-Building in the New South Africa', *Journal of Contemporary African Studies*, 14, 2: 173–96.

7 M. Mamdani. 1996. *Citizen and Subject: Contemporary Africa and the Legacy of Late Colonialism.* Princeton/Cape Town/Oxford: Princeton University Press/David Philip/James Currey.

8 K. Mamaila. 2000. 'Chiefs Happy at Steps Taken to Resolve Municipality Dispute', *The Star.* Johannesburg, 17 May: 1.

9 Department of Constitutional Development, 2000, 'A Draft Discussion Document Towards a White Paper on Traditional Leadership and Institutions.' Pretoria: Government Printer.

10 N = 607, of which 52 % female and 48 % male; 5% under 20, 28% 20–30, 22% 30–40, 19% 40–50, 1% 50–60 and 12% 60 +; 20% no education, 21% up to standard 6, 42% standards 6–10, 7% matric, 7% technicon, 3% university; only 27% formally employed. This is more or less representative of the Sekhukhune *adult* population as a whole, and based on Probability Proportionate to Size samples in the three fieldwork areas (N= 367) and other Sekhukhune traditional authority areas (N=240). The interviews were conducted by Tsepo Phasha, Patson Phala and myself or by two of us, usually in Sepedi, in personal, face-to-face interviews based on a Sepedi questionnaire with 45 closed and open-ended questions, which would typically take 1–2 hours and have been translated into English by the interviewers. The data used derive from uni-, bi- and multivariate analysis in SPSS.

11 B.G. Garth and A. Sarat. 1998. 'Studying How Law Matters: An Introduction.' In B. Garth and A. Sarat (eds), *How Does Law Matter?* 259. Evanstown, IL: Northwestern University Press, p. 239.

12 Cf. John L. Comaroff. 'Rules and Rulers: Political Processes in a Tswana Chiefdom', *Man* 13, no. 1 (1978): 1–20.

Section 1.D
Identity & Personhood
in Africa

Ever since African peoples' encounters with Western traders, missionaries and colonial officials in the late nineteenth century, the traditional–modern opposition played a crucial role in organizing discourses about the specificity of African identity. Africans were marked as traditional not only by Westerners, the notion of tradition also pervaded African modes of self-description. African intellectuals and activists perceived Africans to have acquired a problematic split personality in the course of their submission to Western colonial power – a theme that has kept informing reflections about African identity until today, be it in the context of Christianity or attempts to venture an African Renaissance. While a great variety of such reflections exists, they converge in grounding the distinctiveness of 'the African person' in an essential – and indeed essentializing – difference with regard to the Western person. Salient examples of such an inverted dialectics in which the West features as Africa's 'Other' can be found in Kwame Nkrumah's African personality, and Léopold Senghor's négritude. Both views, excerpts of which are reprinted below, converge in taking race as the prime factor in producing a distinct African personhood that is primarily emotional rather than rational, spiritual rather than materialistic, and socialist rather than individualistic. In his book *In My Father's House*, the Ghanaian philosopher Kwame Appiah has critiqued and refuted such groundings of African identity on race. In the chapter reproduced here he makes a plea for deconstructing the mystifications and mythologies on which race-based understandings of African identity and personhood thrive, without, however, denying their actual power and political efficacy. Arguing that the value of identities is relative rather than natural, he advocates dismissing the project of a racialized Negro nationalism in favor of a new kind of Pan-Africanism based on shared experiences. Jean-François Bayart shares this non-essentializing understanding of personhood and identity. Based on Michel Foucault's thinking about governmentality, he places missionaries' initiatives to invigorate a new type of religious person, identified by a distinct modern life style, material culture and mindset, in broader processes of subjectivation through which Africans became part of colonial modern regimes. In an ethnographic study of Ali, 'one of the most "modern" people' in his village and yet possessed by spirits that make his engagement with modernity increasingly problematic, Michael Lambek highlights how the relational quality of personhood in Mayotte impinges on people's agency vis-à-vis the modern.

LEOPOLD SEDAR SENGHOR
The African Road
to Socialism

Reference
On African Socialism
New York & London: Frederick A. Praeger, 1964, pp. 73–5

Let us then consider the Negro African as he faces the object to be known, as he faces the Other: God, man, animal, tree or pebble, natural or social phenomenon. In contrast to the classic European, the Negro African does not draw a line between himself and the object; he does not hold it at a distance, nor does he merely look at it and analyze it. After holding it at a distance, after scanning it without analyzing it, he takes it vibrant in his hands, careful not to kill or fix it. He touches it, feels it, *smells* it. The Negro African is like one of those Third Day Worms,[1] a pure field of sensations. Subjectively, at the tips of his sensory organs, his insect antennas, he discovered the Other. Immediately he is moved, going centrifugally from subject to object on the waves of the Other. This is more than a simple metaphor; contemporary physics has discovered universal energy under matter: waves and radiations. Thus the Negro-African *sympathizes*,[2] abandons his personality to become identified with the Other, dies to be reborn in the Other. He does not assimilate; he is assimilated. He lives a common life with the Other; he lives in a symbiosis. To use Paul Claudel's expression, he 'knows[3] the Other.' Subject and object are dialectically face to face in the very act of knowledge. It is a long caress in the night, an embrace of joined bodies, the act of love. 'I want you to feel me,' says a voter who wants you to know him well. 'I think, therefore I am,' Descartes writes. The observation has already been made that one always thinks something, and the logician's conjunction 'therefore' is unnecessary. The Negro African could say, 'I feel, I dance the Other; I am.' To dance is to discover and to recreate, especially when it is a dance of love. In any event, it is the best way to know, just as knowledge is at once discovery and creation – I mean, re-creation and recreation, after the model of God.

Young people have criticized me for reducing Negro-African knowledge to pure emotion, for denying that there is an African 'reason' or African techniques. This is the hub of the problem; I should like to explain my thought once again. Obviously, there is a European civilization and a Negro-African civilization. Anyone who has not explained their differences and the reasons for them has explained nothing and has left the problem untouched.

Thus, I explain myself. However paradoxical it may seem, the vital force of the Negro African, his surrender to the object, is animated by reason. Let us understand each other clearly; it is not the *reasoning-eye* of Europe, it is the *reason of the touch*, better still, the *reasoning-embrace*, the sympathetic reason, more closely related to the Greek *logos* than to the Latin *ratio*. For *logos*, before Aristotle, meant both reason and the word. At any rate, Negro-African speech does not mold the object into rigid categories and concepts without touching it; it polishes things and restores their original color, with their texture, sound, and perfume; it perforates them with its luminous rays to reach the essential surreality in its innate humidity – it would be more accurate to speak of subreality. European reasoning is analytical, discursive by utilization; Negro-African reasoning is intuitive by participation.

Young people in Black Africa are wrong to develop a complex and to believe the latter inferior to the former. 'The most beautiful emotion that we can experience,' wrote the great scientist Einstein, 'is mystic emotion. It is the germ of all art and all true science.' To return to Negro-African speech, I refer you to two significant articles. The first, 'Ethnologie de la parole,' is by Maurice Leenhardt,[4] the second, 'Introduction à l'étude de la musique africaine,' is by Geneviève Calame-Griaule and Blaise Calame.[5] Leenhardt studies the New Caledonians, who are blacks; he contends that the New Caledonian meaning of the word is related to that of Negro Africans; the Calame article confirms this. For him, therefore, the black word, 'uttered under the shock of *emotion*' (my italics) surpasses that emotion. Coinciding with the real, it is not only an expression of knowledge, but knowledge itself, ready for action, already action. 'The word,' he concludes, 'is thought, speech, action!' Now you will understand why, in my definition of Negro-African knowledge, I rejected abstract analysis on the European pattern, why I preferred to use analogous imagery, the metaphor, to make you feel the object of my speech. The metaphor, a symbolic shortcut in its sensitive, sensual qualities, is the method par excellence of Negro-African speech.[6]

Today, it is also, quite often, the style of European speech, as Gaëtan Picon indicates. So, our young people should not repudiate the Negro-African method of knowledge since, once again, it is the latest form of the European method. *Participation* and *communion* – those are Picon's words; they are the very words that ethnologists specializing in the study of Negro-African civilizations have used for decades.

Does this mean, as certain young people would like to interpret my remarks, that the Negro African lacks discursive reason, that he has never used any? I have never said so. In truth, every ethnic group possesses different aspects of reason and all the virtues of man, but each has stressed only one aspect of reason, only certain virtues. No civilization can be built without using discursive reason and without techniques. Negro-African civilization is no exception to this rule. Witness the astonishment of the earliest European navigators disembarking in Africa to discover well-organized states, with government, administration, justice, and army, with techniques (remarkable for that date) for working in wood, ivory, bronze, iron, basketry, weaving, and terra cotta, with medical and agricultural techniques worthy of Europe.

From all that, I will conclude that we must maintain the Negro-African method of knowledge, but integrate into it the methods Europe has used throughout his history – classical logic, Marxian dialectics, and that of the twentieth century. Negro-African reason is traditionally dialectical, transcending the principles of identity, noncontradiction, and the 'excluded middle.' Let us merely be careful not to be led astray by the narrow determinism of Marxism, by abstraction. Let us hold firmly to the concrete, and we shall find, underlying the concrete, beyond the discontinuous and the undetermined, the liberty that legitimates not only our faith but the *African Road to Socialism.*

Notes

[1] An allusion to the Age of Reptiles. [TRANS.]
[2] In the French text, *sympathise*, literally, 'feels with'. [TRANS.]
[3] Here again the word is separated, *con-naît*, literally, his born with'. [TRANS.] See Arthur Koestler, *The Lotus and the Robot* (New York: The Macmillan Co., 1961) p. 43:
The traditional Eastern way of looking at things is to deny that there *are*

things independently from the act of looking. The objects of consciousness cannot be separated from the conscious subject; observer and observed are a single, indivisible, fluid reality, as they are at the dawn of consciousness in the child, and in the cultures dominated by magic. The external world has no existence in its own right; it is a function of the senses; but that function exists only in so far as it is registered by consciousness, and consequently has no existence in its own right.

[4] Maurice Leenhardt, 'Ethnologie de la Parole', *Cahiers internationaux de sociologie* 1 (1946).
[5] Geneviève Calame-Griaule and Blaise Calame, 'Introduction à l'étude de musique africaine', *La Revue musicale*, p. 238.
[6] For the importance of word and symbol in Black Africa, see Marcel Griaule, *Dieu d'eau*, pp. 15, 25, 27–8, 34, 46, 60, 73, 80. See also Leo F Frobenius, *Histoire de la Civilisation africaine* (Paris: Gallimard, 1936), and Tempels, *La Philosophie bantoue* (Paris: Présence africaine, 1949).

KWAME NKRUMAH
Society
& Ideology

Reference
Consciencism: Philosophy & Ideology for Decolonization & Development with Particular Reference to the African Revolution
London: Heinemann, 1964, pp. 68–70 and 78–9

The need for subtle means of social cohesion lies in the fact that there is a large portion of life which is outside direct central intervention. In order that this portion of life should be filled with order, non-statutory methods are required. These non-statutory methods, by and large, are the subtle means of social cohesion. But different societies lay different emphases on these subtle means even if the range of conformity which they seek is the same. The emphasis which a particular society lays on a given means depends on the experience, social-economic circumstances and the philosophical foundation of that society.

In Africa, this kind of emphasis must take objective account of our present situation at the return of political independence. From this point of view, there are three broad features to be distinguished here. African society has one segment which comprises our traditional way of life; it has a second segment which is filled by the presence of the Islamic tradition in Africa; it has a final segment which represents the infiltration of the Christian tradition and culture of Western Europe into Africa, using colonialism and neocolonialism as its primary vehicles. These different segments are animated by competing ideologies. But since society implies a certain dynamic unity, there needs to emerge an ideology which, genuinely catering for the needs of all, will take the place of the competing ideologies, and so reflect the dynamic unity of society, and be the guide to society's continual progress.

The traditional face of Africa includes an attitude towards man which can only be described, in its social manifestation, as being socialist. This arises from the fact that man is regarded in Africa as primarily a spiritual being, a being endowed originally with a certain inward dignity, integrity and value. It stands refreshingly opposed to the Christian idea of the original sin and degradation of man.

This idea of the original value of man imposes duties of a socialist kind upon us. Herein lies the theoretical basis of African communalism. This theoretical basis expressed itself on the social level in terms of institutions such as the clan, underlining the initial equality of all and the responsibility of many for one. In this social situation, it was impossible for classes of a Marxian kind to arise. By a Marxian kind of class, 1 mean one which has a place in a horizontal social stratification. Here classes are related in such a way that there is a disproportion of economic and political power between them. In such a society there exist classes which are crushed, lacerated and ground down by the encumbrance of exploitation. One class sits upon the neck of another. In this sense, there were no classes in traditional African society.

In the traditional African society, no sectional interest could be regarded as supreme; nor did legislative and executive power aid the interests of any particular group. The welfare of the people was supreme.

But colonialism came and changed all this. First, there were the necessities of the colonial administration to which I referred in the Introduction. For its success, the colonial administration needed a cadre of Africans, who, by being introduced to a certain minimum of European education, became infected with European ideals, which they tacitly accepted as being valid for African societies. Because these African instruments of the colonial administration were seen by all to be closely associated with the new sources of power, they acquired a certain prestige and rank to which they were not entitled by the demands of the harmonious development of their own society.

In addition to them, groups of merchants and traders, lawyers, doctors, politicians and trade unionists emerged, who, armed with skills and levels of affluence which were gratifying to the colonial administration, initiated something parallel to the European middle class. There were also certain feudal-minded elements who became imbued with European ideals either through direct European education or through hobnobbing with the local colonial administration. They gave the impression that they could be relied upon implicitly as repositories of all those staid and conservative virtues indispensable to any exploiter administration. They, as it were, paid the registration fee for membership of a class which was now associated with social power and authority.

Such education as we were all given put before us right from our infancy ideals of the metropolitan countries, ideals which could seldom be seen as representing the scheme, the harmony and progress of African society. The scale and type of economic activity, the idea of the accountability of the individual conscience introduced by the Christian religion, countless other silent influences, these have all made an indelible impression upon African society.

But neither economic nor political subjugation could be considered as being in tune with the traditional African egalitarian view of man and society. Colonialism had in any case to be done away with. The African Hercules has his club poised ready to smite any new head which the colonialist hydra may care to put out.

With true independence regained, however, a new harmony needs to be forged, a harmony that will allow the combined presence of traditional Africa, Islamic Africa and Euro-Christian Africa, so that this presence is in tune with the original humanist principles underlying African society. Our society is not the old society, but a new society enlarged by Islamic and Euro-Christian influences. A new emergent ideology is therefore required, an ideology which can solidify in a philosophical statement, but at the same time an ideology which will not abandon the original humanist principles of Africa.

Such a philosophical statement will be born out of the crisis of the African conscience confronted with the three strands of present African society. Such a philosophical statement I propose to name *philosophical consciencism*, for it will give the theoretical basis for an ideology whose aim shall be to contain the African experience of Islamic and Euro-Christian presence as well as the experience of the traditional African society, and, by gestation, employ them for the harmonious growth and development of that society.
[...]
Practice without thought is blind; thought without practice is empty. The three segments of African society which I specified in the last chapter, the traditional, the Western, and the Islamic, co-exist uneasily; the principles animating them are often in conflict with one another. I have in illustration tried to show how the principles which inform capitalism are in conflict with the socialist egalitarianism of the traditional African society.

What is to be done then? I have stressed that the two other segments, in order to be rightly seen, must be accommodated only as experiences of the traditional African society. If we fail to do this our society will be racked by the most malignant schizophrenia.

Our attitude to the Western and the Islamic experience must be purposeful. It must also be guided by thought, for practice without thought is blind. What is called for as a first step is a body of connected thought which will determine the general nature of our action in unifying the society which we have inherited, this unification to take account, at all times, of the elevated ideals underlying the traditional African society. Social revolution must therefore have, standing firmly behind it, an intellectual revolution, a revolution in which our thinking and philosophy are directed towards the redemption of our society. Our philosophy must find its weapons in the environment and living conditions of the African people. It is from those conditions that the intellectual content of our philosophy must be created. The emancipation of the African continent is the emancipation of man. This requires two aims: first, the restitution of the egalitarianism of human society, and, second, the logistic mobilization of all our resources towards the attainment of that restitution.

The philosophy that must stand behind this social revolution is that I have once referred to as philosophical consciencism; consciencism is the map in intellectual terms of the disposition of forces which will enable African society to digest the Western and the Islamic and the Euro-Christian elements in Africa, and develop them such a way that they fit into the African personality. The African personality is itself defined by the cluster of humanist principles which underlie the traditional African society. Philosophical consciencism. is that philosophical standpoint which, taking its start from the present content of the African conscience, indicates the way in which progress is forged out of the conflict in that conscience.

KWAME ANTHONY APPIAH
African
Identities

Reference
In My Father's House: Africa in the Philosophy of Culture
London: Methuen, 1992, pp. 280–93

It is, of course, true that the African identity is still in the making. There isn't a final identity that is African. But, at the same time, there is an identity coming into existence. And it has a certain context and a certain meaning. Because if somebody meets me, say, in a shop in Cambridge, he says, 'Are you from Africa?' Which means that Africa means something to some people. Each of these tags has a meaning, and a penalty and a responsibility.[1]

Chinua Achebe

The cultural life of black Africa remained largely unaffected by European ideas until the last years of the nineteenth century; and most cultures began our own century with ways of life formed very little by direct contact with Europe. Direct trade with Europeans – and especially the slave trade – had structured the economics of many of the states of the West African coast and its hinterland from the mid-seventeenth century onwards, replacing the extensive gold trade which had existed at least since the Carthaginian empire in the second century BC. By the early nineteenth century, as the slave trade went into decline, palmnut and groundnut oils had become major exports to Europe, and these were followed later by cocoa and coffee. But the direct colonisation of the region began in earnest only in the later nineteenth century; and European administration of the whole of West Africa was only accomplished – after much resistance – when the Sokoto caliphate was conquered in 1903.

On the Indian Ocean, the eastward trade, which sent gold and slaves to Arabia, and exchanged spices, incense, ivory, coconut oil, timber, grain and pig iron for Indian silk and fine textiles, and pottery and porcelain from Persia and China, had dominated the economies of the East African littoral until the coming of the Portuguese disrupted the trade in the late fifteenth century. From then on European trade became increasingly predominant, but in the mid-nineteenth century the major economic force in the region was the Arab Omanis who had captured Mombasa from the Portuguese more than a century earlier. Using slave labour from the African mainland, the Omanis developed the profitable clove trade of Zanzibar, making it, by the 1860s, the world's major producer. But in most of East Africa, as in the West, extended direct contact with Europeans was a late nineteenth-century phenomenon; and colonisation occurred essentially only after 1885.

In the South of the continent, in the areas where Bantu-speaking people predominate, few cultures had had any contact with Europeans before 1900: by the end of the century the region had adopted many new crops for the world economy, imports of firearms, manufactured in the newly industrialised West, had created a new political order, based often on force, and European missionaries and explorers – of whom David Livingstone was, for Westerners, the epitome – had travelled almost everywhere in the region. The administration of Southern Africa from Europe was established in law only by the ending, in 1902, of the Boer War.

Not surprisingly, then, European cultural influence in Africa before the twentieth century was extremely limited. Deliberate attempts at change – through missionary activity or the establishment of Western schools – and unintended influence – through contact with explorers and colonisers in the interior, and trading posts on the coasts – produced small enclaves of Europeanised Africans; but the major cultural impact of Europe is largely a product of the period since the First World War.

To understand the variety of Africa's contemporary cultures, therefore, we need, first, to recall the variety of the precolonial cultures. Differences in colonial experience have also played their part in shaping the continent's diversities; but even identical colonial policies identically implemented working on the very different cultural materials would surely have produced widely varying results.

No doubt we can find generalizations at a certain abstract level, which hold true of most of black Africa before European conquest. It is a familiar idea in African historiography that Africa was the last continent in the old world with an 'uncaptured' peasantry, largely able to use land without the supervision of feudal overlords and able, if they chose, to market their products through a complex system of trading networks.[2] While European ruling classes were living off the surplus of peasants and the newly developing industrial working class, African rulers were essentially living off taxes on trade. But if we could have travelled through Africa's many cultures in those years – from the small groups of Bushman hunter-gatherers, with their stone-age materials, to the Hausa kingdoms, rich in worked metal – we should have felt in every place profoundly different impulses, ideas and forms of life. To speak of an African identity in the nineteenth century – if an identity is a coalescence of mutually responsive (if sometimes conflicting) modes of conduct, habits of thought, and patterns of evaluation; in short a coherent kind of human social psychology – would have been 'to give to aery nothing a local habitation and a name'.

Yet there is no doubt that now, a century later, an African identity is coming into being. I have argued throughout these essays that this identity is a new thing; that it is the product of a history some of whose moments I have sketched; and that the bases through which it has largely so far been theorized – race, a common historical experience, a shared metaphysics – presuppose falsehoods too serious for us to ignore.

Every human identity is constructed, historical; every one has its share of false presuppositions, of the errors and inaccuracies that courtesy calls 'myth', religion 'heresy', and science 'magic'. Invented histories, invented biologies, invented cultural affinities come with every identity; each is a kind of role that has to be scripted, structured by conventions of narrative to which the world never quite manages to conform.

Often those who say this – who deny the biological reality of races or the literal truth of our national fictions – are treated by nationalists and 'race-men' as if they are proposing genocide or the destruction of nations, as if in saying that there is literally no Negro race one was obliterating all those who claim to be Negroes, in doubting the story of Okomfo Anokye one is repudiating the Asante nation. This is an unhelpful hyperbole; but it is certainly true that there must be contexts in which a statement of these truths is politically inopportune. I am enough of a scholar to feel drawn to truth-telling, though the heavens fall; enough of a political animal to recognize that there are places where the truth does more harm than good.

But, so far as I can see, we do not have to choose between these impulses: there is no reason to believe that racism is always – or even usually – advanced by denying the existence of races; and, though there is some reason to suspect that those who resist legal remedies for the history of racism might use the nonexistence of races to argue in the United States, for example, against affirmative action, that strategy is, as a matter of logic, easily opposed. For, as Tzvetan Todorov reminds us, the existence of racism does not require the existence of races; and, we can add, nations are real enough, however invented their traditions.[3]

To raise the issue of whether these truths are truths to be uttered is to be forced, however, to face squarely the real political question: the question, itself as old as political philosophy, of when we should endorse the ennobling lie. In the real world of practical politics, of everyday alliances and popular mobilizations, a rejection of races and nations in theory can be part of a programme for coherent political practice, only if we can show more than that the Black race – or the Shona tribe or any of the other modes of self-invention that Africa has inherited – fits the common pattern of relying on less than the literal truth. We would need to show not that race and national history are falsehoods, but that they are useless falsehoods at best or – at worst – dangerous ones: that another set of stories will build us identities through which we can make more productive alliances.

The problem, of course, is that group identity seems to work only – or, at least, to work best – when it is seen by its members as natural; as 'real'. Pan-Africanism, black solidarity,. can be an important force with real political benefits; but it doesn't work without its attendant mystifications. (Nor, to turn to the other obvious example, is feminism without its occasional risks and mystifications either.) Recognizing the constructedness of the history of identities has seemed to many incompatible with taking these new identities with the seriousness they have for those who invent – or, as they would no doubt rather say, discover – and possess them.[4] In sum, the demands of agency seem always in the real world of politics to *entail a misrecognition of its genesis*; you cannot build alliances without mystifications and mythologies. And this chapter is an exploration of ways in which what is productive in Pan-African solidarity can be fruitfully understood by those of us whose positions as intellectuals – as searchers after truth – make it impossible for us to live through the falsehoods of race and tribe and nation; and whose understanding of history makes us sceptical that nationalism and racial solidarity can do the good that they can do without the attendant evils of racism – and other particularisms; without the warring of nations.

Where are we to start? I have argued often in these pages against the forms of racism implicit in much talk of Pan-Africanism. (And in other places, especially in 'Racisms' and 'Racism and Moral Pollution', I have offered further arguments against these racist presuppositions.) But these objections to a biologically-rooted conception of race may still seem all too theoretical: if Africans can get together around the idea of the Black Person, if they can create through this notion productive alliances with African-Americans and people of African descent in Europe and the Caribbean, surely these theoretical objections should pale in the light of the practical value of these alliances. But there is every reason to doubt that they can. Within Africa – in the OAU, in the Sudan, in Mauritania[5] – racialisation has produced arbitrary boundaries and exacerbated tensions; in the Diaspora alliances with other peoples of colour, as victims of racism – people of South Asian descent in England, Hispanics in the United States, 'Arabs' in France, Turks in Germany – have proved essential.

In short, I think it is clear enough that a biologically-rooted conception of race is both dangerous in practice and misleading in theory: African unity, African identity, need securer foundations than race.

The passage from Achebe with which I began this essay continues in these words: 'All these tags, unfortunately for the black man, are tags of disability.' But it seems to me that they are not so much labels of disability as disabling labels; which is, in essence, my complaint against Africa as a racial mythology – the Africa of Crummell and Du Bois (from the New World) and of the *bolekaja* critics (from the Old); against Africa as a shared metaphysics – the Africa of Soyinka; against Africa as a fancied past of shared glories – the Africa of Diop and the 'Egyptianists'.

Each of these complaints can be summarised in a paragraph.

'Race' disables us because it proposes as a basis for common action the illusion that black (and white and yellow) people are fundamentally allied by nature and, thus, without effort; it leaves us unprepared, therefore, to handle the 'intraracial' conflicts that arise from the very different situations of black (and white and yellow) people in different parts of the economy and of the world.

The African metaphysics of Soyinka disables us because it founds our unity in gods who have not served us well in our dealings with the world – Soyinka never defends the African World against Wiredu's charge that since people die daily in Ghana because they prefer traditional herbal remedies to Western medicines, 'any inclination to glorify the unanalytical [i.e. the traditional] cast of mind is not just retrograde; it is tragic'. Soyinka has proved the Yoruba pantheon a powerful literary resource: but he cannot explain why Christianity and Islam have so widely displaced the old gods, or why an image of the West has so powerful a hold on the contemporary Yoruba imagination; nor can his myth-making offer us the resources for creating economies and politics adequate to our various places in the world.

And the Egyptianists – like all who have chosen to root Africa's modern identity in an imaginary history – require us to see the past as the moment of wholeness and unity; tie us to the values and beliefs of the past; and thus divert us (this critique is as old as Césaire's appraisal of Tempels) from the problems of the present and the hopes of the future.

If an African identity is to empower us, so it seems to me, what is required is not so much that we throw out falsehood but that we acknowledge first of all that race and history and metaphysics do not enforce an identity: that we can choose, within broad limits set by ecological, political and economic realities, what it will mean to be African in the coming years.

I do not want to be misunderstood. We are Africans already. And we can give numerous examples from multiple domains of what our being African means. We have, for example, in the Organisation of African Unity and the African Development Bank, and in such regional organisations as the Southern African Development Coordination Conference (SADCC) and the Economic Community of West African States (ECOWAS), as well as in the African caucuses of the agencies of the United Nations and the World Bank, African institutions. At the Olympics and the Commonwealth games, athletes from African countries are seen as Africans by the world – and, perhaps, more importantly, by each other. Being African already has 'a certain context and a certain meaning'.

But, as Achebe suggests, that meaning is not always one we can be happy with; and that identity is one we must continue to reshape. And in thinking about how we are to reshape it, we would do well to remember that the African identity is, for its bearers, only one among many. Like all identities, institutionalised before anyone has permanently fixed a single meaning for them – like the German identity at the beginning of this century, or the American in the latter eighteenth century, or the Indian identity at independence so few years ago – being African is, for its bearers, one among other salient models of being, all of which have to be constantly fought for and refought. And indeed, in Africa, it is another of these identities that provides one of the most useful models for such rethinking; it is a model that draws on other identities central to contemporary life in the subcontinent, namely, the constantly shifting redefinition of 'tribal' identities to meet the economic and political exigencies of the modern world.

Once more, let me quote Achebe:

> The duration of awareness, of consciousness of an identity, has really very little to do with how deep it is. You can suddenly become aware of an identity which you have been suffering from for a long time without knowing. For instance, take the Igbo people. In my area, historically, they did not see themselves as Igbo. They saw themselves as people from this village or that village. In fact in some places 'Igbo' was a word of abuse; they were the 'other' people, down in the bush. And yet, after the experience of the Biafran War, during a period of two years, it became a very powerful consciousness. But it was real all the time. They all spoke the same language, called 'Igbo', even though they were not using that identity in any way. But the moment came when this identity became very very powerful … and over a very short period.

A short period it was; and also a tragic one. The Nigerian Civil War defined an Igbo identity: it did so in complex ways, which grew out of the development of a common Igbo identity in colonial Europe, an identity which created the Igbo traders in the cities of Northern Nigeria as an identifiable object of assault in the period that led up to the invention of Biafra.

Recognising Igbo identity as a new thing is not a way of privileging other Nigerian identities: each of the three central ethnic identities of modern political life – Hausa-Fulani, Yoruba, Igbo – is a product of the rough-and-tumble of the transition through colonial to postcolonial status. David Laitin has pointed out that '[t] he idea that there was a single Hausa-Fulani tribe … was largely a political claim of the NPC [Northern Peoples' Congress] in their battle against the South' while '[m]any elders intimately involved in rural Yoruba society today recall that, as late as the 1930s, 'Yoruba' was not a common form of political identification'.[6] Nnamdi Azikiwe – one of the key figures in the construction of Nigerian nationalism – was extremely popular (as Laitin also points out) in Yoruba Lagos, where 'he edited his nationalist newspaper, the *West African Pilot*. It was only subsequent events that led him to be defined in Nigeria as an *Igbo* leader.'[7] Yet Nigerian politics – and the more everyday economy of ordinary personal relations – is oriented along such axes; and only very occasionally does the fact float into view that even these three problematic identities account for at most seven out of ten Nigerians.

And the story is repeated, even in places where it was not drawn in lines of blood. As Johannes Fabian has observed, the powerful Lingala and Swahili-speaking identities of modern Zaire exist 'because spheres of political and economic interest were established before the Belgians took full control, and continued to inform relations between regions under colonial rule'.[8] Modern Ghana witnesses the development of an Akan identity, as speakers of the three major regional dialects of Twi – Asante, Fante, Akuapem – organise themselves into a corporation against an (equally novel) Ewe unity.[9]

When it is not the 'tribe' that is invested with new uses an meanings it is religion. Yet the idea that Nigeria is composed of Muslim North, a Christian South and a mosaic of 'pagan' holdovers i as inaccurate as the picture of three historic tribal identities. Two ou of every five Southern Yoruba people are Muslim; and, as Laitin tell us: '[M]any northern groups, especially in what are today Benue Plateau, Gongola, and Kwara states, are largely Christian. When th leaders of Biafra tried to convince the world that they were oppresse by northern Muslims, ignorant foreigners (including the pope believed them. But the Nigerian army … was led by a northern Christian.'[10] It is as useless here as in the case of race to point out i each case that the tribe or the religion is, like all social identities, base on an idealizing fiction, for life in Nigeria or in Zaire has come to b lived through that idealization: the Igbo identity is real becaus Nigerians believe in it, the Shona identity because Zimbabweans hav given it meaning. The rhetoric of a Muslim North and a Christian South structured political discussions in the period before Nigerian independence; but it was equally important in the debates abou instituting a Muslim Court of Appeals in the Draft Constitution o 1976; and it could be found, for example, in many an article in th Nigerian press as electoral registration for a new civilian era began i July 1989.

There are, I think, three crucial lessons to be learned from these cases First, that identities are complex and multiple and grow out of history of changing responses to economic, political and cultural forces, almost always in opposition to other identities. Second, tha they flourish despite what I earlier called our 'misrecognition' of thei origins; despite, that is, their roots in myths and in lies. And third, tha there is, in consequence, no large place for reason in the constructio – as opposed to the study and the management – of identities. On temptation, then, for those who see the centrality of these fictions i our lives is to leave reason behind: to celebrate and endorse thos identities that seem at the moment to offer the best hope of advancin our other goals, and to keep silence about the lies and the myths. But as I said earlier, intellectuals do not easily neglect the truth, and, al things considered, our societies profit, in my view, from the institu tionalization of this imperative in the academy. So it is important fo us to continue trying to tell our truths. But the facts I have been rehearsing should imbue us all with a strong sense of the marginality o such work to the central issue of the resistance to racism and ethnic violence – and to sexism, and to the other structures of difference tha shape the world of power; and they should force upon us the clea realization that the real battle is not being fought in the academy Every time I read another report in the newspapers of an African disaster – a famine in Ethiopia, a war in Namibia, ethnic conflict i Burundi – I wonder how much good it does to correct the theorie with which these evils are bound up; the solution is food, o mediation, or some other more material, more practical step. And yet as I have tried to argue in this book, the shape of modern Africa (th shape of our world) is in large part the product, often the unintende and unanticipated product, of theories; even the most vulgar o Marxists will have to admit that economic interests operate *through* ideologies. We cannot change the world simply by evidence and reasoning, but we surely cannot change it without them either.

What we in the academy *can* contribute – even if only slowly and marginally – is a disruption of the discourse of 'racial' and 'tribal' differences. For, in my perfectly unoriginal opinion, the reality o these many competing identities in Africa today plays into the hand of the very exploiters whose shackles we are trying to escape. 'Race' in Europe and 'tribe' in Africa are central to the way in which the objective interests of the worst-off are distorted. The analogous point for African Americans was recognized long ago by Du Bois.[11] Du Bois argued in *Black Reconstruction* that racist ideology had essentially blocked the formation of a significant labour movement in the US; for such a movement would have required the collaboration of the nine million ex-slave and white peasant workers of the South.[12] It is, in other words, because the categories of difference often cut across our economic interests that they operate to blind us to them. What binds the middle-class African-American to his dark-skinned fellow citizens down town is not economic interest but racism and the cultural products of resistance to it that are shared across (most of) African-American culture.

It seems to me that we learn from this case what John Thompson has argued recently, in a powerful but appreciative critique of Pierre Bourdieu: namely, that it may be a mistake to think that social reproduction – the processes by which societies maintain themselves over time – presupposes 'some sort of consensus with regard to dominant values or norms'. Rather, the stability of today's industrialised society may require 'a pervasive *fragmentation* of the social order and a proliferation of divisions between its members'. For it is precisely this fragmentation that prevents oppositional attitudes from generating 'a coherent alternative view which would provide a basis for political action'. 'Divisions are ramified along the lines of gender, race, qualifications and so on, forming barriers which obstruct the development of movements which could threaten the *status quo*. The reproduction of the social order may depend less upon a consensus with regard to dominant values or norms than upon a *lack of consensus* at the very point where oppositional attitudes could be translated into political action.'[13]

Thompson allows us to see that within contemporary industrial societies an identification of oneself as an African, above all else, allows the fact that one is, say, not an Asian, to be used against one; and in this setting – as we see in South Africa – a racialized conception of one's identity is retrogressive. To argue this way is to presuppose that the political meanings of identities are historically and geographically relative. So it is quite consistent with this claim to hold, as I do, that in constructing alliances *across* states – and especially in the Third World – a Pan-African identity – that allows African-Americans, Afro-Caribbeans and Afro-Latins to ally with continental Africans, drawing on the cultural resources of the Black Atlantic world – may serve useful purposes. Resistance to a self-isolating black nationalism *within* England or France or the United States is thus theoretically consistent with Pan-Africanism as an international project.

Because the value of identities is thus relative, we must argue for and against them case by case. And given the current situation in Africa, I think it remains clear that another Pan-Africanism – the project of a continental fraternity and sorority, *not* the project of a racialized Negro nationalism – however false or muddled its theoretical roots, can be a progressive force. It is as fellow Africans that Ghanaian diplomats (my father among them) interceded between the warring nationalist parties in Rhodesia under UDI; as fellow Africans that OAU teams can mediate regional conflicts; as fellow Africans that the human rights assessors organized under the OAU's Banjul Declaration can intercede for citizens of African states against the excesses of our governments. If there is, as I have suggested, hope, too, for the Pan-Africanism of an African Diaspora, once it, too, is released from bondage to racial ideologies (alongside the many bases of alliance available to Africa's peoples in their political and cultural struggles), it is crucial that we recognize the independence, once

'Negro' nationalism is gone, of the Pan-Africanism of the Diaspora and the Pan-Africanism of the continent. It is, I believe, in the exploration of these issues, these possibilities, that the future of an intellectually reinvigorated Pan-Africanism lies.

Finally, I would like to suggest that it is really unsurprising that a continental identity is coming into cultural and institutional reality through regional and sub-regional organizations. We share a continent and its ecological problems; we share a relation of dependency to the world economy; we share the problem of racism in the way the industrialized world thinks of us (and let me include here, explicitly, both 'Negro' Africa and the 'Maghreb'); we share the possibilities of the development of regional markets and local circuits of production; and our intellectuals participate, through the shared contingencies of our various histories, in a discourse whose outlines I have tried to limn in this book.

'Ɔdɛnkyɛm nwu nsuo-ase mma yɛmmefrɛ kwakuo sɛ ɔbɛyɛ no ayie,' goes an Akan proverb: the crocodile does not die under the water so that we can call the monkey to celebrate its funeral. Each of us, the proverb can be used to say, belongs to a group with its own customs. To accept that Africa can be in these ways a usable identity is not to forget that all of us belong to multifarious communities with their local customs; it is, not to dream of a single African state and to. forget the complexly different trajectories of the continent's so many languages and cultures. 'African' can surely be a vital and enabling badge; but in a world of genders, ethnicities, classes and languages, of ages, families, professions, religions and nations, it is hardly surprising that there are times when it is not the label we need.

Notes

1. Chinua Achebe, Interview.
2. See, for example, Robert Harms, *Times Literary Supplement*, 29 November 1985, p. 1343.
3. Tzevetan Todorov, '"Race", Writing and Culture' in Henri Louis Gates Jr, 1986, ed., *'Race', Writing and Difference*, University of Chicago Press. You don't have to believe in witchcraft, after all, to believe that women were persecuted as witches in colonial Massachusetts.
4. Gayatri Spivak recognizes these problems when she speaks of 'strategic' essentialisms. See p. 205 of her *In Other Worlds: Essays in Cultural Politics*.
5. The violence between Senegalese and Mauritanians in spring 1989 can only be understood when we recall that the legal abolition of racial slavery of 'Negroes', owned by 'Moorish' masters, occurred in the early 1980s.
6. David Laitin, 1986, *Hegemony and Culture: Politics and Religious Change Among the Yoruba*, University of Chicago Press, pp. 7–8.
7. Laitin, *Hegemony and Culture*, p. 8.
8. This passage continues: 'Increasingly also Lingala and Swahili came to divide functions between them. Lingala served the military and much of the administration in the capital of the lower Congo; Swahili became the language of the workers in the mines of Katanga. This created cultural connotations which began to emerge very early and which remained prevalent in Mobutu's Zaire. From the point of view of Katanga/Shaba, Lingala has been the undignified jargon of unproductive soldiers, government clerks, entertainers, and, recently of a power clique, all of them designated as *batoka chini*, people from down-river, i.e. from Kinshasa. Swahili as spoken in Katanga was a symbol of regionalism, even for those colonials who spoke it badly.' Johannes Fabian, 1986, *Language and Colonial Power*, Cambridge University Press, pp. 42–3. The dominance of Swahili in certain areas is already itself a colonial product (p. 6).
9. Similarly, Shona and Ndebele identities in modern Zimbabwe became associated with political parties at independence, even though Shona-speaking peoples had spent much of the late pre-colonial period in military confrontations with each other.
10. Laitin, *Hegemony and Culture*, p. 8. I need hardly add that religious

identities are equally salient and equally mythological in Lebanon or in Ireland.

[11] That 'race' operates this way has been clear to many other African-Americans: so, for example, it shows up in a fictional context as a central theme of George Schuyler's *Black No More*; see, e.g., p. 59. Du Bois (as usual) provides – in *Black Reconstruction* – a body of evidence that remains relevant. As Cedric Robinson writes, 'Once the industrial class emerged as dominant in the nation, it possessed not only its own basis of power and the social relations historically related to that power, but it also had available to it the instruments of repression created by the now subordinate Southern ruling class. In its struggle with labour, it could activate racism to divide the labour movement into antagonistic forces. Moreover, the permutations of the instrument appeared endless: Black against white; Anglo-Saxon against southern and eastern European; domestic against immigrant; proletariat against sharecropper; white American against Asian, Black, Latin American, etc.' C. Robinson, 1983, *Black Marxism: The Making of the Black Radical Tradition*, Zed Books, p. 286.

[12] Robinson, *Black Marxism: The Making of the Black Radical Tradition*, p. 313.

[13] John B. Thompson, 1984, *Studies in the Theory of Ideology*, University of California Press, pp. 62–3. Again and again, in American labour history, we can document the ways in which conflicts organized around a racial or ethnic group identity can be captured by the logic of the existing order. The financial support that Black Churches in Detroit received from the Ford Motor Company in the 1930s was only a particularly dramatic example of a widespread phenomenon: corporate manipulation of racial difference in an effort to defeat labour solidarity. See James S. Olson, 'Race, Class and Progress: Black Leadership and Industrial Unionism, 1936–1945', in M. Cantor (ed.), 1969, *Black Labor in America*, Negro Universities Press, pp. 141–3; and David M. Gordon et al, 1982, *Segmented Work, Divided Workers*, Cambridge UP, pp. 141–3, and Fredric Jameson, *The Political Unconscious*, Cornell UP, p. 54.

JEAN-FRANÇOIS BAYART
Fait Missionnaire
& Politics of the Belly
A Foucaultian Reading[1]

Reference
Le Fait missionnaire, 6, 1998: 9–37, trans. of pp. 21–34 by Luca Disanto & Peter Geschiere

In the first two sections of this article, the author elaborates upon Michel Foucault's concept of *gouvernementalité* – in relation to the latter's earlier notions of *gouvernement* and *pouvoir* – in order to show that this concept not only applies to the ascent of bio-politics and the 'panopticon' State in Europe since the seventeenth century, but also offers interesting perspectives for a broader comparative approach to politics. Crucial to this notion of 'governmentality' is that it is focused on 'subjectivation' as a historically contingent process.

The author proposes a Foucaultian reading, in terms of governmentality and subjectivation, of the *politique du ventre* (politics of the belly, a concept he developed in his earlier writings on the state in Africa (Bayart 1989a, 1993b) – even though the term does apply elsewhere also.[2] A Foucaultian approach suggests analysing these politics of the belly in terms of the constitution of the self as moral subject, not only through being submitted to an external rule which imposes an unequivocal relation of domination, but

also as a form of 'belonging'. 'Becoming a subject means also to belong – that is to intervene both as element and as actor in broader processes....' (Bayart 1998, p.18). [Introductory Note by Editors]

For a genealogy of the politics of the belly

It may be apt to recall that the 'politics of the belly', with its specific historicity, deeply rooted in a bundle of continuities from the contemporary state back to pre-colonial societies, emerged in the 'accidental context of the event', and that this type of emergence 'is always produced in interstices', and 'in the hazards of the struggle', to use Michel Foucault's terms (DE, II: 144, 148).[3] The different ideological strands of Africanism were not spared by what Foucault more generally called 'a tradition of history, whether theological or rationalist, which tends to dissolve the singular event into an ideal continuity – a teleological movement or a natural chain of events' (DE, II: 148). Yet, state formation south of the Sahara has been a perfectly contingent and confused process. The struggles that mediated this process took place mostly at the level of 'historical terrains' (Bayart 1989b) whose extreme fragmentation does not facilitate the task of the scholar – certainly not if the latter wants to avoid the meta-narratives of colonialism and independence. In my view, one of the great qualities of the journal *Le Fait missionnaire* is precisely to have given priority to this analytical framework (Monnier 1995; Péclard 1995).

In view of what we know concerning the structuring role of bureaucratic power and its position at the heart of the state and of society, a realist approach – and a very Foucaultian one in that it would imply doing research in archives – would consist in the study of great institutions that supply 'discipline' and especially subjectivation. Among these would certainly be the colonial administration, but before this probably the trading post, the school, the hospital, and the Christian missionary station. Even more than the colonial state and its bureaucracy, whose intervention often came later and to some extent was limited (J. and J. Comaroff 1997: 21), each of these 'social institutions'– to use Max Weber's term (1996 [1992]: 142) – put into operation discourses, procedures, rules, and prescriptions, in other words 'technologies of power' for which the body was a privileged 'target' (SS: 138), sometimes imprisoned, submitted to forced labour, whipped, deported and put to death; but sometimes also healed, educated, clothed and reshaped. In this way, these social institutions sheltered and developed true 'cultures of the self' which allowed for a 'constitution of the self as a "moral subject",' (UP: 30), and grounded the indigenous people's sense of belonging in the emerging configuration. The *ethos* of work, which was inculcated into salaried workers and in new converts through the reinforcement of incentives, admonitions, preaching and blows, and intended to counter the innate 'laziness' of the natives, was a dominant factor in this process, with all that this entailed in transforming people's relationship with time and space (Monnier 1995: 42–5). From this perspective, the teaching delivered to nursing students of the Swiss mission in South Africa, or the exhortations of an Arthur Grandjean at the station of Antioka and of a Heli Chatelin in Lincoln – to stick to data assembled by *Le Fait missionnaire* (Monnier 1995; Péclard 1995; Egli and Krayer 1997) – are very revealing.

Of course, I am not the first scholar to shed a Foucaultian light on the social institutions of colonization. However, very often these institutions are interpreted in a quite mechanical fashion, like control machineries of a more or less totalitarian 'disciplinary society' (SS). By contrast, the 'micro-physics of power' which they put in place, while still replete with coercive procedures, was at the same time a range of modes of subjectivation whose attraction has been largely under-estimated. Apparently political correctness left its mark!

First of all, recall that colonization was an experience of subjectiva-tion for the Europeans themselves. Soldiers, administrators, traders and missionaries had to situate themselves in relation to both their own representations of the metropole – which was in the midst of the industrial revolution's decadence, of materialism, and communism – and the savagery of Africans to whom they had come to deliver the emancipatory message of civilization, paradoxically starting with a conquest, and despite their often tempered ideas about the West. Despite this web of contradictions, they nonetheless constituted themselves as 'moral subjects', affirming a specific 'life-style' such as the Catonism of British administrators (Berman and Lonsdale 1992: 234-235), or the missionaries' path to redemption (J. and J. Comaroff 1991, 1997; Elphick and Davenport 1997: 31 ff; Péclard 1995).

Later, numerous Africans adhered sincerely to these 'conducts of life' that were both proposed and imposed on them. If we fail to admit this we will be unable to understand how the European occupation was able to perpetuate itself with such derisory military and administrative means; it would make us reduce the collaboration of vast segments of the autochthonous elites to narrow motivations of self-interest or to pure 'alienation'; it would mean to deny the sincerity of the Christian faith of the subcontinent's converts and block any understanding of the 'subjections' of Africans to the State and the 'politics of the belly'. Thus, Martina Egli and Denise Krayer (1997: 70–2) show well how the prestigious career of nursing in South Africa was at the same time a synonym of social dignity and a guarantee of financial income – a double professional dream symbolically con-densed in the white uniform.

At the same time, the Africans' adherence to new 'conducts of life' implied that these conducts were re-invented through creative deviations. Writing about the 'civilizing mission' of non-conformist evangelizers to Bechuanaland, the Comaroffs object to 'any narrative of remorseless subjection':

[…] neither processes of commodification nor technologies of rationalization ever advance in so totalizing, mechanical a fashion as to make human consciousness a mere cipher of 'power' or 'profit'. […] the mundane became an area of complex exchanges rarely reducible to the zero-sum of domination or resistance. The landscape of the lived world was slowly reshaped in the image of colonial capitalism, it is true. However, that image was constantly ruptured and refigured, yielding half-caste currencies, playful synthetic styles, and mixed modes of production. They were indeed converts, both to the church and to the ethos of the market. Yet they were never mere mimics of their mentors. (J. and J. Comaroff 1997: 34–5)

One of the manifestations of this appropriation of the missionary institution and its 'conducts of life' were the numerous conflicts that divided not only the foreign evangelizers from their auxiliaries or their autochthonous followers, but also African believers among themselves. For example, women invested massively in the churches in order to advance their condition, even though these were dominated by men (Elphick and Davenport 1997: 102, 253 ff.). And among the latter, young men never ceased to attack the cultural Malthusianism of their elders, who in their turn were determined to confine the young within the respectability of neo-traditional social and material practices, for example in the domain of clothing.

Actually, this *politique du ventre*, little one might grasp it in all its complexity, did not only draw on a regime of economic accumulation and social inequalities, but also on what we might call a 'moral economy.'[4] Institutions like the administration, the school, or the mission became the site for the 'emergence' of a 'moral subject' whose bodily and ethical practices became constitutive of a new cité [in the sense of the society of citizens – *civitas*] characterized by bureaucratic management by the State, specific economic activities, but also by special forms of religious expression and political mobilization – in terms of both collaboration with the colonizers as well as of resistance or nationalist negotiation. Moreover, they generated the 'social strata' which would become the 'bearers' (*Träger*) of those 'conducts of life', to speak Weberian language; or, in Foucaultian language, the 'class' which would turn these 'modes of subjectivation', these 'stylistics of existence', into an 'affirmation of the self'. These catechists, teachers, nurses, administrators and clerks of trading houses were cornerstones of the colonial edifice, and later of the nationalist movement. And as wage earners, they laid the foundations of the contemporary dominant class and its processes of primitive accumulation (Kitching 1980; Bayart 1989a).

To be sure, this mode of 'subjection' remains heterogeneous, especially because of numerous confessional, philosophical, political, social and material contradictions which deeply divided colonial actors themselves, as well as their universal legatees. Thus this subjection mode has its limits, which tend to make all the work on 'discipline' in colonial and postcolonial contexts redundant. Notorious illustrations of the limits of such 'subjection' are: phenomena of religious dissi-dence or proliferation – for example, of independent churches, prophetic movements, and sects; the telescoping of the redistributive moral economy of families and villages into the bureaucratic ethos; the conflict between practices of the 'politics of the belly' and the critique of 'corruption'; and, finally, the divergence between ethno-substantialist and universalist definitions of citizenship. All this often led to major convulsions, such as the confrontation between the liberal-modernist vision of the ANC, the seeds of which were sown in the nineteenth century by the non-conformist preachers of the London Missionary Society or of the Wesleyan Methodist Missionary Society, and the ethno-nationalist vision of the Inkhatha and other leaders of Bantustans, inherited from the same imperial culturalism from which these missionaries themselves had not escaped (J. and J.Comaroff 1997: 79–80 and 401).

The 'paradoxes' inherent in such 'inventions of modernity' (Bayart 1994a and 1996a: 231 ff.) are equally numerous. The diffusion of the bureaucratic approach, vector of a well known 'mode of subjection', was carried out on a large scale, particularly (and paradoxically) through political, social and cultural movements of dissidence against the colonial order, like the Beni dance in East Africa (Ranger 1975), the nationalist parties, or the independent churches born out of the schisms of Western missions. In a similar perspective, 'prophets' (Anderson and Johnson 1995; Dozon 1995), as much as catechists, require specific attention, especially since the former as well often began their careers as assistants to missionaries, before entering into competition with them by denouncing the latter's cultural or even 'racial' domination, but also out of a desire for social or material advancement (McCracken 1977). As another 'paradox' of modernity, evangelizers preaching on the 'frontier of the Word' in South Africa dreamed of contributing to the emergence of an independent peasantry, to be initiated to the bourgeois respectability of Victorian customs. In practice, however, they helped to create an agrarian proletariat who would eventually become the 'reserve army' of the pitiless universe of the mines (J. and J. Comaroff 1997:162–3) and develop a workers' culture far removed from the rural 'irenism' of the non-conformists. Often these missionaries tried also to 'civilize' the natives by 'traditionalizing' them (J. and J. Comaroff 1997: chapter 5).

In general, state formation south of the Sahara appears to be inseparable from the emergence of what Max Weber calls 'a type of man (*Menschentum*), created by the articulation of elements of a religious origin and elements of an economic origin' (Weber, 1986 [1922]: 138) – that is, a ' type of man' who operated by jointly defining his relationship to God, his political relationships with society, and his own strategy of wealth accumulation. The mission – even more than the colonial administration, the trading post, or the school with which it partly overlapped – was a major institution in manufacturing this specific 'type of man', even though it produced him in multiple ways, given the great differences in philosophical or theological vision (J. and J. Comaroff 1991 and 1997), and the organizational, confessional, or national rivalries among churches (Monnier 1995; Péclard 1995; Elphick and Davenport 1997: 112).

First of all, the mission represented a site for the territorialization of power. In its relations to local authorities and socially subordinated categories (such as the young, prisoners, or women), but also to white settlers and even to European administrators, it was part and parcel of the general 'strategic situation' of colonization. Nicolas Monnier (1995: 5 and 32–5) characterizes the missionary movement very well as 'the deployment of a "strategy"' which first of all attempted to construe 'visibility' that was especially cartographic. The missionary stations assured for themselves 'a mastery of the place by sight' (Certeau 1980: 85); they constituted 'machines for seeing' (Deleuze 1989: 186). Their 'panopticism' is sometimes literal: thus Chatelain (a Swiss missionary in Angola, cited by Didier Péclard 1995: 39–40) rejoices: 'From my windows on the upper floor of the new house, I can survey all the cultivated areas; thanks to my binoculars, I can just see how people work, and through the foghorn I can give them orders without having to run all the time and in all directions in the fields.' Missionary territorialization expressed itself ever more systematically through a reification of social flows, and especially of identities along the lines of an 'ethnicization' of the subcontinent (Monnier 1995; Harries 1988). This was done through the introduction of private property (J. and J. Comaroff 1997: 374 ff.), the delegitimization of pastoralism and the celebration of the achievements of agriculture (J. and J. Comaroff 1997: *passim*), the settling of nomads, and the modification of spatial relations of power within societies or between them – for example under the guise of protecting them (of course with fairly ambiguous implications) against the abuses of settlers, government officials or slave-traders.

Moreover, with its religious and social teaching, the mission became the main manufacturer and protagonist of 'practices of the self' through which the 'moral subject' was constituted: European missionaries were concerned with the body of their flock as much as with their soul. The Comaroffs (1997: 67 ff., and 71 ff.) note that missionary preaching was itself, in the first instance, a technique of relating the Self to itSelf, and the Self to the Other, entailing a gestuality and a passion – think of the image of the evangelist delivering the Word from his carriage in Southern Africa! – and privileging certain senses (hearing) over others (sight), tending, moreover, toward criminalizing indigenous modes of subjectivation. From this point of view, the 'missionary fact' consisted of a series of procedures – the sermon, the confession, the pastoral visit, putting natives to work – but also of a whole range of behaviors of the preachers themselves. Thus, Chatelain 'never moved away from the station without singing one of the songs he had composed in Umbundu, and always rejoiced whenever he heard them sung by the Africans to

whom he had taught them' (Péclard 1995: 37, footnote 69). Such practices had an impact of their own as models of subjectivation, around which expectations crystallized with retro-active effects on the relations between foreigners and natives, working eventually in the mode of an 'operational misunderstanding' (Salamone 1985). Missionaries preached by example, in the literal sense of the term. But they did not hesitate to have recourse to coercion, driven as they were by a holy fury against the superstition and depravation within their flock, even though they – in contrast to administrators and colonizers – could not make widespread use of the whip, except perhaps in their schools. The condemnation of clitoridectomy by some missions in Kenya in the 1930s is a well-documented case (Spencer 1985: 71 ff.). Throughout the continent the controversial status of dance in evangelized societies, especially in the propagation and enculturation of faith, was another major theme of moral disputation between foreign religious personnel and their autochtonous followers. However, subsequently a progressive rehabilitation of dancing took place, also in the Catholic Church, which constituted a non-negligible ingredient in defining a Christian mode of subjectivation. In contrast, certain fundamentalist North American missions impose, up to this day, an especially constraining mode of life full of prohibitions – like, for instance, the Presbyterian *Rules of the Church* and *Hymn Book* implanted among the Uduk of southern Sudan, which in addition to dance also condemn the consumption of beer and cigarettes (James 1988: 207 ff.). More or less restrictive, this fashioning of the self through the white people's religion took the form of a true 'epic of the everyday', to use the excellent formulation of the Comaroffs: the everyday was like an 'epiphany', the 'privileged terrain of the missionary movement' as the medium of both European civilization and of salvation (J. and J. Comaroff 1997: 29–35). At a later stage, independent churches and sects in turn assumed this 'type of man' as their own, and contributed in their own way to the reproduction of this type. Some scholars argue that the role of such churches and sects in the propagation of Christianity was much more decisive than that of Western evangelizers, especially in South Africa (Elphick and Davenport 1997).

Finally, the mission was an instance of 'government' (still in the Foucaultian sense of the word) insofar as it banalized the 'pastoral' conception of power (Monnier 1995: 45–52) – paradoxically while discrediting pastoral societies (J. and J. Comaroff 1997: 123–4). It benefited, too, from multiple 'discharges' of the state (Max Weber), especially in the realms of health-care and education, and never ceased its efforts in the economic sphere, thus confusing at least at first the divulgation of the Word with trading activities – in conformity with David Livingstone's vision – as well as developing agriculture and wage labour (Péclard 1995: 38 ff.).

To evaluate the historical impact of the 'missionary fact' in the emergence of this 'governmentality of the belly' – as a 'meeting between technologies of domination exercised on others and technologies of the self' (DE, IV: 785) – it is sufficient to consider such widely different examples as the commercial establishment of the Basel Mission on the coast of the Gulf of Guinea; the role of Christian elites in the leadership of several nationalist movements; the recurrence of pastoral and messianic statements in the discourse of postcolonial States; the ideological representation of 'development' among national political classes and international donors; and the importance of ecclesiastical positions in the provision of social services – especially the capacity of the Catholic Church to take the place of failing States as in the case of Zaïre/Congo from the 1980s to this day. Hence the conflicts that have opposed states to churches after independence – *Kulturkämpfe* of which Eric Morier-Genoud (1996) analysed an exemplary case, that of Mozambique, in *Le Fait mission-naire* – did not involve antagonists confronting each other in a relation of exteriority, but rather protagonists in the emergence of a same governmentality, who were attempting to 'structure the eventual field of action of the others' to their own advantage (DE IV: 237). The harshness of these struggles derived from the fact that they were largely fratricidal. Whatever the real philosophical or religious differences between their actors, they came largely from the same social institutions – often the mission itself – and fought over resources, competences, styles and powers of a same 'government'.

It seems to me, then, that a Foucaultian problematization of the missionary 'event' offers a royal road for deepening our understanding of the historicity of the political in Africa, understood both as manifestation of the State and as movement of subjectivation. But the success of such an inquiry presupposes that one pays special attention to a dimension of social life that was neglected by Foucault, even though nothing in his approach would deny its relevance – quite the contrary (SP: 154–5; SS; UP). This is the dimension of material culture that was at the heart of the constitution of the 'moral subject' in Sub-Saharan Africa. In recent years, post-modern anthropology – while often quite disappointing when treating the question of 'discipline' – made a decisive breakthrough in showing to what extent practices of consumption, far from limiting themselves to a logic of Westernization and alienation, contributed to the appropriation of modernity by autochthonous actors, and took the form of a 'reinvention of difference' (Clifford, 1988), inherent in the very process of globalization (Appadurai 1986; Miller 1994; Warnier 1994 and 1997; Burke 1996; Weiss 1996). The condensation of the political imagination, the constitution of a 'moral subject', and finally the historicity of the State cannot be separated, especially in Africa, from material practices – for example, concerning clothing – which mediate relations self-self, as well as self-Other, beginning with the authorities. The emergence of the 'governmentality of the belly' too played itself out around conflicts over the wearing of wrappers and of short or long trousers – certainly not marginal issues from the point of view of the general economy, be it moral or political (Bayart 1996: chapter 4).

It bears repeating that the mission was a privileged site for such symbolic and material confrontations (Ranger 1975: 126–32), in addition to often being a great distributor of Western consumer goods, especially on the early evangelization 'front', and later at the beginning of colonization. The first contacts between preachers and natives were often mediated by material gifts, which sanctioned, for example, the 'settlement contract' for the station (Monnier 1995: 55), and which sometimes epitomized in itself the *Weltanschauung* (world view) underlying Christianization – like the mirrors distributed by 'non-conformist' missionaries among the Tswana: fetish objects of nineteenth-century industrial modernity in Europe, but also vehicles of individuation and self-reflexivity (J. and J. Comaroff 1991: 186 ff.). I have already pointed out that a long-standing missionary tradition equated the development of trade to the spreading of the Christian faith (Elphick and Davenport 1997: 36, 109, 340–1; J. and J. Comaroff 1997: passim). For Chatelain, for example, 'every mention of the work of evangelization was accompanied by commercial considerations,' the pastoral tour being simultaneously a commercial tour:

After we announced our arrival through the foghorn, or rather the 'Urihorn', just like our old Swiss folks of the Waldstätten, I immediately unpacked my stuff and started calling out for corn, string beans, flour, cassava, and potatoes. My stuff included as much as possible everything the natives could desire, except for schnaps (brandy). In order to buy 50 francs worth of beans, it is necessary to bring a sufficient quantity of goods and often much more. It might be good to give you an idea. This time I had: sugar, salt, oil, dry meat, soap, a few padlocks, locks, shovels, hoes, axes, brass wire, traps for rats and wild animals, knives of several prices, pocket knives, forks, spoons, plates, cups, pots, bowls, gilded nails, buttons for shirts and suits, ten types of glass jewelry, rings, necklaces, earrings, belts, cotton fabric and handkerchiefs of all colors, blankets, shirts, trousers, coats, hats, powder, lead, medicines, flint, remedies, paper, mirrors, needles, thread, matches, bracelets, music-makers, and other things that escape me at the moment: a complete bazaar, as you can see. (Péclard 1995: 76)

Chatelain also counted on those 'missionary wagons' to ensure the further spread of his philo-African work:

With our wagons and ox teams, a trading evangelist could bring goods to the Ganguella and announce the 'Good News' to the crowds that will stick to the wagons to trade. […] The traffic will attract around the evangelist thousands of blacks, who would never come just to hear the evangelical songs, and even less for preaching of any kind. (cited by Péclard, 1995: 80–1)

All men of religion were not that comfortable with this link between evangelical message and the commodification of societies which were to be converted: 'People are happy to see us come back, but their thoughts are for the textiles and trinkets rather than the Word of God,' complained a certain Arthur Grandjean (cited by Monnier 1995: 61–2). Nonetheless, the mission, whether it wanted or not, was indeed like a bazaar – in the words of Chatelain – in the literal sense, and the Christian imaginary partially embraced that of commodities, if only because the process of Christianization, very often explicitly, fused with the 'civilizing mission' of the White man (the main colonial metaphor then in use – which was, of course, not innocent). The recent volume by the Comaroffs rightly insists on this point and shows how the 'epiphany of the ordinary' allied itself with 'a conquest by way of consumption', whose prime target was the body:

For the colonial evangelists in South Africa, the most crucial realm of enlightened consumption hinged on the human shape. It was on the body that the commodity came into physical contact with, and enclosed the self. To a nineteenth century religious sensibility […] the treatment of the domesticated physique was an everyday sacrament. In cleaning it, housing it, curing it, and clothing it lay the very essence of civility. (J. and J. Comaroff 1997: 219–20)

As a historically situated material culture, the 'missionary fact' was ultimately a formative process of economic as well as moral values, since it was a vehicle of commodification and monetarization, and also since the religious conversion for which it worked was inseparable from other effects of conversion in various spheres of the societies concerned, whether in the domain of the invisible or in that of materiality (J. and J. Comaroff 1997: chapter 4; Weiss 1996: 220 ff).

The future of the 'politics of the belly'

Clearly then, the Foucaultian problematization of 'governmentality' is useful for understanding the genealogy of the politics of the belly. It can help us equally well to decipher its unfolding in the present. Its contribution seems to me to be threefold: it easily deconstructs the ideology of international donors to which an increasing number of scholars shamelessly adhere, mostly because the latter have become practically monopolistic funders of their work; it is capable of identifying the technology of 'privatization' for what it is, namely a simple mode of 'governance' which imposes itself at a specific historical moment, and with equally specific effects; and it allows us to understand how different processes of subjectivation can co-exist and compete in a given society.

I shall not insist on the first point because James Ferguson has already demonstrated, in a remarkable book of Foucaultian inspiration, how the discourse of development functions as a machine for depoliticizing an eminently political question, that of the centralization of the state apparatus, of social inequality, and of poverty (Ferguson 1990). I would like merely to suggest, once again, that the statements of international donors and the procedures of their realization lead to the multilateralization of a 'passive revolution': development institutions – particularly the Bretton Woods ones – have taken up the process of co-optation of counter-elites inside African States, making the latter recite the theme of depoliticization, which is all the more easy since they have structurally 'adjusted' the continent's universities and research institutions, all along exerting their hegemony over African studies in America and Western Europe (Bayart 1993b, critiqued in Banegas 1998). From this perspective, the notion of 'civil society' has become central in the pidgin of structural adjustment and of the 'transition' to 'a democracy of the market'. On the one hand, this notion pleads in favour of a minimal state and privileges the 'alternative path' of the informal sector; on the other hand, its vitality is supposed to guarantee the consolidation of democracy. Reality is obviously much more complex: the informal sector is not the Other of the formal economy, the state, or its partisans (Hibou 1996); neither does it seem to stimulate a process of primitive accumulation of a capitalist nature (Kitching 1980). Moreover, it works against the structuring of a true 'economic society', which might be more needed for a democratic consolidation than the greatly exaggerated virtues of 'civil society' (Linz and Stepan 1996).

This notion of 'civil society' is all too clearly linked to 'a form of schematization associated with a specific technology of government', to quote from Foucault's analysis of liberalism (RC: 113). The churches participate directly in such a schematization of 'government', since they often constituted de facto the civil society – for instance at the beginning of colonization (J. and J. Comaroff 1997: 385); or in contexts of monopolistic power, as in Mozambique in the years immediately following independence (Morier-Genoud 1996); or by playing a key role during the 'democratic transition' of the 1990s and embodying an 'alternative' concept of development – more socially sensitive, and closer to the perspective of the 'lowest of the downtrodden', the people 'without a voice'.

The Foucaultian analysis of liberalism thus leads to my second point. As a statement and as a procedure, the theme of 'civil society' neutralizes all critical discourse on what is labeled the 'transition'. It goes together with a moralizing celebration of an abstract 'good governance', which one cannot emphasize enough is a historical heritage of the 'missionary fact' (Bayart 1989c; George and Sabelli 1994; Hibou 1998). It offers an ideological justification of the distribution of development assistance credits, set up in such a way that representatives of State power can create their own NGOs, thus becoming full members of civil society and legitimately benefiting from this. However, such a schematization in the form of an allegory that sets 'society' against the 'state', and the technology of power that

follows from this, refer to a decisive mutation of the 'governmentality of the belly', along the lines of its 'privatization'. Such an evolution, by now beyond the sector of public enterprise alone, has affected the regal functions of the state, specifically the levying of taxes, and the management of internal security and national defence (Hibou 1996 and 1998). On the one hand, this evolution inscribes itself in a novel context of a general liberalization of the international economy and of globalization; on the other hand, it reconnects with forms of 'discharge' (Max Weber) or of 'government' that Africa experienced during the last century, already under colonialism (Bayart, Ellis and Hibou 1997). Its political operators – businesses, private security or surveillance companies, NGOs, militias and armed movements – are often new actors, but in many ways they follow the footsteps of the trading posts, the concessionary companies, the missions and the war-chiefs of the economy of the slave trade, predation and evangelization that characterized the second half of the last century.

The advantages of a Foucaultian problematization to account for these recompositions lie in sparing us a teleological and historicist reconstruction, by focusing instead on institutions and identifiable procedures that possibly modify the structuration of 'the potential field of action of the others' (DE IV: 237). We should be able to escape in this way the debate over the 'responsibilities' of Christianization in Africa's misfortunes, which has so frequently confused reflections within the churches, and especially within the missions. By contrast, we can see clearly that the multiple 'discharges' and derogations attributed to them, even formally, in the realms of health-care, education or trade,[5] nowadays confer upon them a specific place in the 'strategic situation' engendered by the privatization process. Moreover, missions were and remain one of the main matrixes creating a distinction between private and public south of the Sahara – as institutions which stimulated a neo-Victorian subjectivation, thus introducing the very idea of 'privacy', particularly through new housing patterns (J. and J. Comaroff 1997: chapter 6); as instruments for women's affirmation in the public sphere (Elphick and Davenport 1997: 253 ff.); and as vectors of commodification, since the consumption practices of material culture have direct implications for the definition of the boundary between private and public, and for the contours of emerging forms of subjectivity (Breckenridge 1995).

In fact – and this is my third point – this transformation of a power configuration that is constitutive of the 'governmentality of the belly' directly effected the process of subjectivation. For example, Richard Banégas (1998) suggests that the democratization of the 'passive revolution' in Benin translated into changes in its 'moral economy', including in the sphere of the invisible: the qualities one expects from a deputy or from the president of the Republic are no longer exactly the same as under the single party regime; similarly the 'type of man' valued by citizens has changed. One may similarly point out that economic liberalization itself has repercussions on the mode of subjectivation of its principal protagonists, specifically in the domain of clothing or eating practices, in the domain of athletic and nutritional education of the body, and in the domain of ethical norms or intellectual competences: the man (or woman) of 'privatization' flaunts a specific 'lifestyle'.

Nevertheless, there are other movements of subjectivation in contemporary Africa: in particular – and by and large in mutual contradiction – the so-called 'independent' religious movements and armed movements, both of which propose to their members that they constitute themselves as 'moral subjects' according to different 'conducts of life' and recurrent (but unstable) figures of the imaginary affecting 'a stylistics of existence' that is manifest as much among young combatants as among adepts of neo-Christian or neo-Islamic sects and organizations. The future of the 'governmentality of the belly' will follow from the 'complex strategic situation' that is emerging from such an articulation of the Word of God, the voice of the People, and the crackling of firearms. Nowadays, the latter sound is naturally the more audible. It covers a silent labour of political and state re-organization, changes in ontological representations of life, death and kinship, and of the monetarization and commodification of societies. It allies itself with the 'privatization' of economic circuits and sovereignty. Finally, at least in the Great Lakes region, it punctuates without doubt the emergence of racialist ethno-nationalisms, which echo certain pages of Foucault's lectures in *Society Must Be Defended*, and put on the scholarly agenda of researchers a new political operator, so very Foucaultian in its working: the refugee camp, 'disciplinary' source of a terrible pastoral message of power, messianic and deadly at the same time, which found in the Hutu exodus an especially tragic experience of subjectivation (Malkki 1995).

And yet, war, whatever its horrible impact on state formation – rather than on state disintegration (Bayart, Ellis and Hibou 1997) – and despite its potential affinities with religion, 'privatization', or 'democracy', should not blind us to other trajectories, sometimes less gloomy, in the interstices of African societies. These are far too complex and diverse to be caricatured in a few pessimistic sketches. The very strong religious mobilization that accompanies the urbanization of these societies – in contrast with what happened in Western Europe – is inevitably inscribed in the continuity of the 'missionary fact', be it in terms of conflict and rupture; it is also representative of a social experience which cannot be reduced to a univocal orientation. One cannot exclude that it will be capable of shaping new conceptions of citizenship and political freedom (Devisch 1996).

Conclusion

In the final analysis, a judicious use of Foucault for better grasping the missionary 'event' would look at the analytical differentiation of the 'modes of subjection' at the heart of a 'governmentality' that is relatively coherent in historical respect, namely that of the 'belly'. The comparative advantage of such a problematization in relation to that of Max Weber is no doubt not obvious if the point is merely to grasp the historicity and contingency of the political in Africa or the lifestyle of the social actors involved. By contrast, there seem to me to be real advantages if the task is to think through the relationship between these two phenomena or to follow the process of subjectivation, understood as an ambivalent relation of power (Bayart 1996: chapter 3).

At this level, the mission, as a major social institution of the 'politics of the belly', is far from having said its last word. It continues to play a key role as a reservoir of imaginary representations, an organizational model, a site for territorializing historical fields, a network of elite and popular socialization, an economic actor, and a place of social and material struggles. It remains also one of the great sites in which the insertion of Africa in the maelstrom of globalization is negotiated – one of the pivots of the 'glocalization' of the continent (Gifford 1993; Ter Haar 1992). To be brief: one should not underestimate its place in the different processes of subjectivation of Africans in the sense in which I have used this concept, as both a mode of 'subjection' and the constitution of a 'moral subject' – as a meeting-point between techniques of domination exerted on others and techniques of the self (DE IV: 785). Perhaps it would be an exaggeration to speak, with regard to the 'governmentality of the

belly', of a *cité missionnaire* as one speaks for classical Greece and Rome of a *cité évergétique*, even though the State in Africa is without doubt a *cité culturelle* (Bayart 1993a).[6] The social institution of the mission has lost some of its pride and, precisely because of its fanning out, no longer controls the totality of the Christian religious field. Nevertheless, it is still sufficiently central for the team behind Le Fait missionnaire to have a lot on its plate!

Notes

[1] This article continues and elaborates upon a presentation at the seminar '*Pratiques politiques et usages de Michel Foucault*', organized by the Centre d'études et de recherches internationales (Paris, 13–14 November 1997).

[2] The notion *politique du ventre* (politics of the belly), commonly used in Africa south of the Sahara and notably in Cameroon, is particularly rich in all sorts of evocative meanings. It refers to a situation of economic precariousness, notably to lack of food; but also to practices of economic accumulation by politicians and bureaucrats; to the pompous ways of the powerful and the rich; to corpulence, appreciated as a special political quality; to the social realities of lineage and kinship; and to the invisible forces, notably witchcraft. Thus, the *politique du ventre* is a total social fact, in the sense of Marcel Mauss, which has to be grasped in its full historicity (Bayart 1989a).

[3] A list of the abbreviations used to refer to the writings of Michel Foucault is to be found at the end of this text.

[4] See the writings of E. P. Thompson on the British working class (1963 and 1993), and also the works by Bruce Berman and John Lonsdale, two historians of Kenya who, more than others, knew how to reconstruct the ethical foundations of colonial society; in this way they showed, for example, that the Mau Mau movement of the 1950s was not a 'class war', but a moral war' (Berman and Lonsdale 1992: 453; cf. Bayart 1994b).

[5] Such 'discharges' were effected right from the beginning of the conquest era: in the Cape Province, during the 19th century, the British had exempted missionaries from prohibitions against exporting goods beyond colonial borders, except for guns, ammunition and alcohol (Comaroffs 1997: 182).

[6] Translators' note: *cité* is used here in the classical sense: *civitas*, or *polis*; in Greece and Rome the city/*cité* is characterized by some as *évergétique* (of 'good works', charitable); for Africa one might speak in parallel of a 'cultic' (*culturelle*) rather than a 'missionary' city.

Works cited by Foucault

DE: *Dits et Ecrits. 1954–1988*. Paris: Gallimard, 1994.
RC: *Résumé des cours. 1970-1982*. Paris: Julliard, 1989.
SP: *Surveiller et punir. Naissance de la prison*. Paris: Gallimard, 1975.
SS: *Le souci de soi*. Paris: Gallimard, 1984.
UP: *L'usage de plaisirs*. Paris: Gallimard, 1984.
VS: *La volonté de savoir*. Paris: Gallimard, 1976.

Bibliography

Anderson, David M. and Johnson, Douglas H. 1995. *Revealing Prophets. Prophecy in Eastern African History*. London: James Currey.

Appadurai, Arjun, ed. 1986. *The Social Life of Things. Commodities in Cultural Perspective*. Cambridge: Cambridge University Press.

Banégas, Richard. 1998. *La démocratie 'à pas de caméléon'. Transition et consolidation démocratique au Bénin*. Paris Institut d'études politiques.

Bayart, Jean-François. 1989a. *L'état en Afrique: La Politique du ventre*. Paris: Fayard.

— 1989b 'Les églises chrétiennes et la politique du ventre: le partage du gateau ecclésial', *Politique africaine* 35: 3–26.

— 1989c 'La Banque mondiale, un libéralisme à visage humain', *La Croix-L'Evènement* 18, October.

— (ed.), 1993a. *Religion et modernité politique en Afrique noire. Dieu pour tous et chacun pour soi*. Paris: Karthala.

— 1993b. 'Preface to the English edition' in *The State in Africa. The Politics of the Belly*. London: Longman.

— (ed.), 1994a. *La réinvention du capitalisme*. Paris: Karthala.

— 1994b, 'Hors de la "vallée malheureuse" de l'africanisme', *Revue française de science politique*, 44 (1).

— 1996, *L'illusion identitaire*. Paris: Fayard.

Bayart, Jean-François, Ellis, Stephen, Hibou, Béatrice. 1997. *La criminalisation de l'Etat en Afrique*, Bruxelles: Complexe. Published in English (1999) *The Criminalization of the States in Africa*. Bloomington/Oxford: Indiana Press/ James Currey, in association with the International African Institute.

Berman, Bruce, and Lonsdale, John. 1992. *Unhappy Valley. Conflict in Kenya and Africa*. Portsmouth, NH/Oxford: Heinemann Inc/James Currey.

Breckenridge, Carol A., ed., 1995. *Consuming Modernity. Public Culture in a South Asian World*. Minneapolis: University of Minnesota Press.

Burke, Timothy. 1996. *Lifebuoy Men, Lux Women. Commodification, Consumption and Cleanliness in Modern Zimbabwe*. Durham, NC: Duke University Press.

Certeau, Michel de, 1980. *L'invention du quotidien. Vol. 1: Arts de faire*. Paris: UGE.

Clifford, James. 1988. *The Predicament of Culture*. Cambridge, MA: Harvard University Press.

Comaroff, Jean and John, 1991. *Of Revelation and Revolution. Vol. 1: Christianity, Colonialism and Consciousness in South Africa*. Chicago: University of Chicago Press.

— 1997. *Of Revelation and Revolution. Vol. 2: The Dialectics of Modernity on a South African Frontier*. Chicago: University of Chicago Press.

Deleuze, Gilles. 1989. 'Qu'est-ce qu'un dispositif?' In *Michel Foucault, philosophe. Rencontre internationale. Paris 9, 10, 11 janvier 1988*. Paris: le Seuil.

Devisch, René. 1996. 'Independent churches heal modernity's violence in Zaire', in B. Kapferer, ed., *Peripheral Societies and the State*. Oxford: Berg.

Dozon, Jean-Pierre. 1995. *La cause des prophètes. Politique et religion en Afrique contemporaine*. Paris: Le Seuil.

Egli, Martina and Krayer, Denise. 1997. 'Mothers and Daughters': The Training of African Nurses by Missionary Nurses of the Swiss Mission in South Africa', *Le Fait missionnaire*, no. 4, March.

Elphick, Richard and Davenport, Rodney, eds. 1997. *Christianity in South Africa. A Political, Social and Cultural History*. Berkeley/Cape Town/ Oxford: University of California Press/David Philip/James Currey.

Ferguson, James. 1990. *The Anti-Politics Machine. 'Development', Depolitization and Bureaucratic Power in Lesotho*. Cambridge: Cambridge University Press.

George, Susan and Sabelli, Fabrizio. 1994. *Crédits sans frontiers: la religion séculaire de la Banque mondiale*. Paris: La Découverte.

Gifford, Paul. 1993. *Christianity and Politics in Doe's Liberia*. Cambridge: Cambridge University Press.

Harries, Patrick. 1988. 'The roots of ethnicity: discourse and the politics of language construction in south-east Africa', *African Affairs*, 87 (346): 25-42.

Hibou, Béatrice. 1996. *L 'Afrique est-elle protectionniste? Les chemins buissonniers de la libéralisation extérieure*. Paris: Karthala.

— 1998. 'Economie politique du discours de la Banque mondiale en Afrique subsaharienne. Du catéchisme économique au fait (et méfait) missionnaire', *Les Etudes du CERI*, 39.

James, Wendy. 1988. *The Listening Ebony. Moral Knowledge. Religion and Power Among the Uduk of Sudan*. Oxford: Clarendon Press.

Kitching, Gavin. 1980. *Class and Economic Change in Kenya. The Making of an African Petite-Bourgeoisie*. New Haven, CT: Yale University Press.

Linz, Juan and Stepan, Alfred. 1996. *Problems of Democratic Transition and Consolidation. Southern Europe, South America and Post-Communist Europe*. Baltimore, MD: Johns Hopkins University Press.

Malkki, Liisa H. 1995. *Purity and Exile. Violence, Memory and National Cosmology Among Hutu Refugees in Tanzania*. Chicago: The University of Chicago Press.

McCracken, John. 1977. *Politics and Christianity in Malawi. 1875–1940. The Impact of the Livingstonia Mission in the Northern Province*. Cambridge: Cambridge University Press.

Miller, Daniel. 1994. *Modernity. An Ethnographic Approach. Dualism and Mass Consumption in Trinidad*. Oxford: Berg.

Monnier, Nicolas. 1995. 'Stratégie missionnaire et tactiques d'appropriation indigènes. La mission romande au Mozambique, 1888–1896', *Le Fait missionnaire*, no. 2, December.

Morier-Genoud, Eric. 1996. 'Of God and Caesar: the Relation between Christian Churches and the State in Colonial Mozambique, 1974–1981', *Le Fait missionnaire*, no. 3, September.

Péclard, Didier. 1995. 'Ethos missionnaire et esprit du capitalisme. La mission philafricaine en Angola. 1897–1907', *Le Fait missionnaire*, no. 1, May: 1–53.

Ranger, Terence. 1975. *Dance and Society in Eastern Africa. 1890-1970. The Beni Ngoma*. London: Heinemann.

Salamone, Franck A. 1985. 'The Social Construction of Colonial Reality: Yauri Emirate', *Cahiers d'études africaines*, 98, XXV, 2.

Spencer, John. 1985. *The Kenya African Union*. London: KPI.

Ter Haar, Gerrie. 1992. *Spirit of Africa: The Healing Ministry of Archbishop Milingo of Zambia*. London: Hurst.

Thompson, E.P. 1963. *The Making of the English Working Class*. London: Victor Gollancz.

— 1993. *Customs in Common. Studies in Traditional Popular Culture*. New York: The New Press.

Warnier, Jean-Pierre, ed. 1994. *Le paradoxe de la marchandise authentique. Imaginaire et consommation de masse*. Paris: L'Harmattan.

— (ed.). 1997. *Authentifier la marchandise. Anthropologie critique de la quête d'authenticité*. Paris: L'Harmattan.

Weber, Max. 1996 [1922]. *Sociologie des Religions*. Paris: Gallimard.

Weiss, Brad. 1996. *The Making and Unmaking of the Haya Lived World: Consumption, Commoditization, and Everyday Practice*. Durham, NC: Duke University Press.

MICHAEL LAMBEK
Rheumatic Irony
Questions of Agency & Self-Deception as Refracted through the Art of Living with Spirits

Reference
Illness & Irony
Oxford: Berghahn, 2003, pp. 40–59

... unresolved – that is life and humanity, and it would betray a dreary lack of subtlety to worry about it. (Thomas Mann, *The Magic Mountain*, as quoted by Nehamas 1998: 19)

Something that anthropology can be and is about, though it is almost never phrased as such, is the art of living. I borrow this phrase (along with much else) from a recent book of that title by Alexander Nehamas (1998). Nehamas's subject is philosophy and in particular certain heroic philosophers who have seen the artful, and at times agonizing, creation of their own lives as exemplary (his subtitle is *Socratic Reflections from Plato to Foucault*). Anthropologists sometimes discover characters among their subjects who stand out for their genius or the style or emphasis with which they lead their lives, cutting a swathe through convention. But perhaps we learn more by exploring how ordinary people draw on local conventions and idioms in the living of their individual and interrelated lives. Their actions can prove exemplary or edifying when they illustrate the potential of local idioms for generating or articulating insight and movement of general relevance.

I have gradually come to see that one of the things that I have been exploring over the years is the art of living as practised and demon-strated by spirit mediums in the Malagasy-speaking world of northwestern Madagascar, Mayotte, and, increasingly, France. What has intrigued me is less the ritual of spirit possession or the temporary state of trance than the integration of other voices, other persons, with the self in the construction of a life for oneself and with others – a life (as we say) for better and for worse, in sickness and in health, in good times and bad. That is to say, I have been intrigued with tracing the place of spirits in the lives of mediums over time; with the ways in which spirits are entwined with the biographies of people and families (and sometimes whole communities); with the ways they figure in informal autobiography and memory as people construct and reflect on their lives in narrative and practice, in retrospection and in prospect; and thus with the art of living with spirits, or rather, with spirit possession as an art of living.[1]

Here I do not wish to individualize my subjects too strongly both because spirits can be shared among people and form a vehicle of connection between them, and because possession cannot help but draw attention to itself, becoming a display that draws, engages, and provokes an audience much as Socrates did (Nehamas 1998), much as a written text does. Insofar as the events of lives lived with possession become public, so they become objects of contemplation, interroga-tion, identification, and edification for those around them. Possession thus becomes a vehicle with respect to which the non-possessed or soon-to-be-possessed also reflect on and live their lives, if only by resisting its form, messages, or imprecations.[2] The salience of other lives is heightened through spirit possession, not only because possession is simply noisy and disruptive but because virtually everything about possession calls attention to itself as an artifact.

I see the accomplished spirit medium somewhat like a Western artist or craftsman. An acclaimed violinist needs her instrument in order to create beautiful music; a great philosopher needs the texts of his predecessors. The analogy is rough, but in the Malagasy world the spirits are likewise vehicles, instruments in a technology for creative expression and building, for that dimension of human activity Aristotle referred to as polesis. But much more clearly than the violin, spirit possession is also a vehicle or instrument for a second dimension of human activity, what Aristotle called phronesis, practical wisdom, that is, the exercise of situated moral judgment, being a decent, dignified, virtuous person, acting on behalf of what is considered right and good. Here there appears a stubborn paradox, or at least a place of resistance, with respect to dominant contemporary Western notions of personhood and of direct, unmediated consciousness in moral judgment. How can the evidently impassioned spirit medium be simultaneously a moral agent? How can she be acting virtuously when she is evidently temporarily displaced by another voice, another person? And in speaking about her agency, do I thereby risk importing an ethnocentric Western concept into a situation of non-Western personhood? Or conversely, by declining to speak of agency in this context, would I collude in a picture of disempowered, less than fully realized moral selves?

I would rather turn the question around and ask what an account of spirit possession can contribute to revising dominant Western views of autonomous selfhood and agency. To speak convincingly, such an account must engage with Western theory, especially by drawing upon those streams of thought that have challenged extreme individualism. I begin with brief reference to one of the strongest of these, the object-relational – or now simply relational – school of psychoanalysis, which recognizes, as Joan Rivière put it, that "[e]ach personality is ... a company of many ... We are members of one

another' (as cited by Chodorow 1989: 158). Such mutual membership is the product of a dialectic of introjection and projection that begins in infancy. Our psychic reality is thus relational as well as individuated. An excessive weighting or over-reliance on either pole creates a problematic personality, and each pole may be seen as a kind of defense against the other.[3]

For Stephen Mitchell, who was a major spokesman for relational psychoanalysis, 'Being a self with others entails a constant dialectic between attachment and self-definition, between connection and differentiation, a continual negotiation between one's wishes and will and the wishes and will of others, between one's own subjective reality and a consensual reality of others with whom one lives' (1988: 149). Likewise, Nancy Chodorow states: 'If a person is to develop at all, the self must come to include what were originally aspects of the other and the relation to the other ... We become a person, then, in internal relation with the social world ... People inevitably incorporate one another; our sociality is built into our psychic structure and there is no easy separation of individual and society or possibility of the individual apart from society' (1989: 149). It may be, then, that Marilyn Strathern's Melanesian 'dividual' (1988), or something quite like it, is universal at the level of psychic structure. The question is whether cultural idioms and social practices recognize, articulate, and enable – or disclaim, constrain, and mystify – these processes and where, in a given social world, and with respect to given social statuses, the balance between autonomy and connection lies or is expected to lie. The following discussion of spirit possession will demonstrate the point.

Among Malagasy speakers, to gain (most kinds of) spirits is also to become increasingly connected to others. While relative to their hosts spirits are in one sense originally alien beings, non-selves, they are also social persons, and as such they carry with them the prior histories of their relations with humans. To become impassioned by a spirit is to introject aspects of this history. A woman who becomes possessed by a spirit who previously possessed and spoke through her mother or grandmother is identifying deeply with them, not only acknowledging her prior identification but introjecting another aspect of their persons (Lambek 1993). A break in the unity of the conscious self is thus at the same time a bridge to the identities of others. In this respect, I think, spirit possession is radically different from multiple personality disorder, in which dissociation is generally private, alienating, disruptive, fragmenting, and socially distancing.

Spirit possession is thus not entirely beyond the range of at least one Western conception of selfhood. Concomitantly, possession is markedly resilient in the face of social change, accommodating itself to Western contexts and accommodating those contexts to itself. The story I now tell will exemplify these points while raising the question of how a relational perspective can address agency and accountability. The central figure, both narrator and character, is not a spirit medium. He is, nevertheless, someone in whose life a spirit has intervened, sharply and strikingly, and in a manner relevant to and for others, at least for the kind of moral tale anthropologists like me like to tell.

Ali's brief military career

This is a story about a friend of mine, a young man of the very first cohort in the once remote village in Mayotte, which I have studied since 1975, to receive a full French education and subsequently to become a member of what his cousin referred to as the small set of village intellectuals. 'We were the ones,' said Ali, 'who discovered school.'[4]

Ali is a very sweet guy and someone who is attempting to make a difference in his community. In August 2000 he was the director of the new elementary school and was very concerned to keep it running well. He was proud that, unlike a cousin who directed the school in a neighboring village, he did not allow his relatives to deplete his supplies. He showed me a cupboard filled with notebooks, pens, and other implements ready for the new school year. He had plans to seek subsidies in order to start a school snack program of bread and cheese that would minimize the hardship of poorer families. Ali was also very involved in music, not only as the conductor of a local young people's choir. As a board member of the islandwide *Association des Jeunes*, he tried to enable participation for talented youngsters in music competitions in the metropole. However, he said he preferred teaching to administration and was hoping to return to school for a specialist degree in music education.

Ali thus took his civic responsibilities very seriously. We could, if we wanted to use the term, consider Ali one of the most 'modern' people in the village. While his wife is away working on a higher degree in La Réunion, Ali, unlike almost everyone else in his community, eats dinner alone and late. He explains he is usually too busy to eat with his in-laws and children. For similar reasons, he rarely gets to the mosque. Time has become a scarce resource and more precious than informal sociality or religious practice.[5]

In the last decade an ever increasing number of people, most of them youths, have begun to move from Mayotte to La Réunion and metropolitan France. In many instances these moves are temporary, but they can last several years. One of the first people from the village to do so was Ali. After completing his *3ième*,[6] Ali first went to continue his studies in La Réunion. But his older sister, who was married to a navigator in the French navy, asked him to join her in France to keep her company during her husband's long absences. So Ali moved to Nantes in 1987, when he was around twenty years old. He finished *2ième* in France and then began to work as an electrician. From photos I could see that his sister's family lived in a tall apartment building. They were dressed in French clothing, and in one picture there is an elaborate Christmas tree set up for the children.

In retrospect, Ali says he prefers life in Mayotte to that in France, especially now that he has a family. The only way France would be better than Mayotte would be if he had a really good job. In Mayotte, the vast majority of people older than Ali had been subsistence cultivators who supplemented cash-cropping when the market made it worthwhile and who are now largely unemployed. In contrast, Ali earned a salary of over 10,000 FF per month when living in Nantes. As he says, money counts.

In fact, Ali was able to save a good deal of money in France. He returned home in 1992 with a car, a lot of luggage, and the cash for a splashy wedding. The wedding, which cost several thousand francs and which he paid for himself, included what he called a *sirop d'honneur* and a *diner-dansant*, in conscious and expensive mimesis of French affairs. The bride wore a white dress. Before this, while he was in France, his mother had been busy setting up the engagement. On a visit to France, Ali's mother had found him in a relationship with a Malagasy woman. She wanted him to marry in Mayotte and preferably within the village. She brought videos of eligible girls from which he made a selection agreeable to his mother, began correspondence, received a photo with the reply, and knew it was on. Ali's fiancée was in any case a close cousin (*mushemwananya*) through both her parents, and her father was a good friend, though with nowhere near the education of Ali. She was nine years Ali's junior, and he wanted to wait until she had finished high school and was 'up to his

intellectual level' before marrying. But the wedding was held in 1995 after his fiancée found him with another woman. She said if he was going to sleep with someone, it should be her. It was still important for a bride to be a virgin at marriage, and Ali and his wife ensured this was the case. During the dance celebrating her virginity, his mother's (male) *trumba* spirit rose briefly to express his joy.[7]

Ali's wife soon surpassed him in education by earning her *bac* and equaled him in modern outlook. In a community where most people have between eight and a dozen children, they planned to have three because, as his wife put it to Ali, 'If we have four we won't be able to rent a car on family vacations!' (The French have strongly enforced their driving code, including seat belt regulations.) In sum, then, we can say that Ali appears successfully and self-consciously 'modern' (bourgeois?) in outlook and practice.

Although physically and mentally very active, Ali's life has not been free of illness. He says he was a victim of sorcery from his father's other wife, with whom he was sent to live as a child because at the time his home village was without a school. He had a short acute illness and something remained, bothering his stomach for years so that he became very thin. When his mother visited him in France, her trumba spirit rose and said he would need to have sorcery removed when he returned to Mayotte. This eventually took place, and he has felt better since though he has never regained his weight. In secondary school he suffered from headaches, and he gave this as a reason he withdrew before achieving the *bac*.

Ali's life might have turned out very differently were it not for another experience of ill health. During his stay in France, Ali eagerly embarked on a military career. He enrolled in the army and was happily in training at the base in Nantes when his mother arrived on a visit in order to help his sister, who had just given birth. She was not happy with Ali's new direction, and, more to the point, neither was the trumba spirit that had long inhabited her and recently become quite active. To begin with, the trumba made her stay in the apartment difficult. Being very sensitive to bad smells, it took offense at the indoor toilet, and at first Ali's mother refused to use it. They placed her bed as far from the lavatory as they could, but the trumba would rise crying 'Mantsing! Mantsing! [Stinky].' In fact, said Ali, it rose much more often in France than since her return home.

But the worst thing was that Ali began to feel sick every time he put on his uniform or set foot on the military base. He suffered terribly. He couldn't bend his legs and could barely walk. 'It was rheumatism,' said Ali. 'It took me five minutes to pull on my socks.' And it took him some 30 minutes just to get over to the canteen for meals.

To add insult to injury, he was persecuted by his commanding officer, who accused him of malingering and deception. This was not altogether an unreasonable deduction because on weekend leaves Ali felt fine. The moment he reached the bus stop he was well: he walked normally. As he said, 'As soon as I left the base, my symptoms disappeared.' But each time he returned to base, he was sick and could barely move.

Ali's condition lasted for some three months. Finally, he requested a medical discharge because he was suffering from both the illness and the anger of his commanding officer. He was placed in the hospital for three days and given x-rays over his whole body, but they showed nothing.

So, much to his disappointment, Ali was forced to quit the army. Ali's mother, who, remember, was visiting at the time, had explained to him that it was the family spirit, the *trumba ny razaña*, who sent the symptoms. It was said (*ary*) that the spirit didn't like him in the army.

Military clothes are dirty: spirits don't like them [*tsy tian' trumba*].' His mother said she too was upset and couldn't accept his career decision ('*rohu nakahy tsy mety izy mandeha militaira*'); she was afraid for him.

I was not able to put two and two together when Ali spoke to me in 1995, but the second time Ali told me the story (in 2000), he made the point explicit. His mother's visit to France had coincided with the beginning of the Gulf War. She confirmed this. Not only was she frightened he would be sent to the Gulf, she said, but from watching the televised reportage, she realized that he would be placed at high risk: 'And I could see they were putting black people [*ulu mainting*] in the front lines.'

At the time, Ali got angry with the trumba (not with his mother). He said he was a man and wanted to take risks. He was even hoping to train as a submarine diver. On base it was part of Ali's duties to call the ambulance whenever a recruit was injured during training exercises. The trumba said to him, 'So can't you see that people in the military get hurt?'

Ali's agency

Ali's story provides the gist of the issue that anyone interested in understanding personhood across cultures must face. If our own concepts and idioms of personhood come with moral entailments, as they must, how are we to evaluate the conduct of persons whose identity is construed somewhat differently? How are we to understand agency, avowal, and accountability in a universe in which the relational quality of personhood is granted value alongside individual autonomy?

There is perhaps not much in the actions of Ali's mother or the trumba that needs direct explanation. Their interests and arguments are perfectly rational, their agency and observations only too clear, and their fears realistic. Whereas many of my previous analyses of instances of spirit possession entail interpreting the double and ostensibly conflicting voices (messages and desires) of spirit and host, this is a case in which not only their underlying interests but also their stated motives coincide. But the case is more complex with respect to Ali who, several years later, still felt regret that he was coerced by the spirit into giving up something dear to him.

Although Ali is adamant that he himself has never been possessed by the trumba spirit, and never will be, when Ali was on the base, his actions were formally like those of possession. He acted, or rather his body acted, contrary to his conscious intentions. It was as though his body spoke with one voice and Ali with another. His body, if not his mind, was evidently in the grip of the spirit.

Ali's situation thus nicely illustrates a point I have long made, namely, that in thinking about the incidence of possession (at least, in Mayotte), one cannot take account of only the mediums themselves (Lambek 1981, 1989). While it is true that the majority of mediums in Mayotte are women, the spirits nevertheless interact with men as well. Spirits engage with those around them, and neither their presence nor their significance can be explained reductively in terms of trance or the intentions and personalities of the mediums alone.

Ali's mother is, of course, an interesting and powerful woman in her own right. She had the courage and foresight to send away her children for the sake of their education and later followed them intrepidly to France. I remember her pride and her enthusiasm for what she had seen after one of her returns to Mayotte. She has handled the experience of rapid social change with grace, her first encounter with indoor plumbing notwithstanding, but she also sees herself as representative of an older way of life. She has appointed herself my

primary raconteur of folktales. She is what I would describe as a classy lady in terms of comportment and self-esteem, but also, because of an implicit elitism, the assurance of coming from one of the 'best' local families.

Yet this is not simply a kind of mother-son story either. As a trumba, the spirit has a personal identity as an individual member of the Sakalava royal descent line. Moreover, the spirit is identified not specifically with the mother but as a *trumba ny razaña*, a trumba of Ali's family, ancestry, or descent line. It is a trumba which has long possessed members of this family that has a sense of its own importance. For many years the trumba was particularly associated with Ali's mother's mother's brother (the same man who happens to be the grandfather of Ali's wife), who himself spent part of World War II in the French army, but stationed in Madagascar.[8] Before any important event, such as a circumcision or a journey, the spirit would be informed and its assistance requested. It has since gone on to inhabit several younger members of the family – including not only Ali's mother and his wife's father's older brother, but several of Ali's older sisters – and it thus serves, in part, as a sign of the unity, distinctiveness, and continuity of the family (Lambek 1988a). It speaks with the voice of someone who has an enduring association with the family and has long been concerned with its welfare. What Ali hears, therefore, is not simply a transformation of his mother's voice, but a voice that condenses the weight of several generations of ancestors and collateral kin. The spirit acts with the authority of a Sakalava king, but equally with the force of ancestrality and the established commitment to intergenerational continuity and reproduction.[9]

The distinction, then, between the voice of Ali's mother (the host) and the voice of the spirit here lies less in the content of what each is saying in this instance than in the rhetorical force of their respective presence. As the mother tells the story, she and the spirit were in complete agreement. But where her remonstrances might have been ineffective, the trumba's intentions were realized in their effects. In the face of the urgency of the spirit's concern, Ali could scarcely remain impassive. And he did not. He acquired the symptoms of acute rheumatism.

The next question is whether Ali's mother and the trumba were able to enunciate a wish that Ali is unable to acknowledge is also his own. Did he want, on his own account, to retract his decision to enter the army, and should we therefore see Ali's action (or inaction) as a product of his own fear or instinct for self-preservation? Is it a kind of *pre*-traumatic stress disorder? Or should we take a different approach and see it, in Mitchell's terms, as part of the 'constant dialectic between attachment and self-definition' (1988: 149), or as representative of the psychic internalization of sociality described by Chodorow (1989: 149)? Did Ali come, to a degree, to internalize the family's wishes as his own? Did he come to take their part? We could let the psychoanalysts fight this out among themselves,[10] but I think that I have already given enough evidence to make the relational argument highly plausible. At least I have shown how spirit possession as a practical idiom exemplifies, articulates, and enables the processes of which the relational theorists speak. But let us move from the murky realm of the psyche to the more sociological concept of agency. In what sense is Ali responsible for his rheumatism?

Here we have something of a double task: how to understand spirit possession as a form of human agency and how, in turn, to rethink agency so that it can take account of possession. In what follows I omit from discussion Marxist conceptions of agency with their emphasis on grasping hegemonic social relations so as to gain a purchase on radical change. I am concerned with action on a less grand scale, as it functions in the day-to-day tasks of taking control of events concerning work, family, and the living of one's life in some meaningful, dignified, and authentic fashion.

In the general social sciences literature, 'agency' is sometimes applied in a rather idealized fashion, ignoring much of what philosophers, psychoanalysts, and anthropologists have taught us about human intentionality and mind. Agency is a naive or romanticized concept insofar as it implies: (a) that acts are transparent to their agents, that they are always the product of deliberate plans with specific ends in mind or of calculation among means and ends in a rational choice model; (b) that agents fully understand the consequences of their acts or the relationships between acts and consequences; (c) that agents' intentions are not often dense, complex, and possibly even contradictory; that agents do not routinely suffer from ambivalence and possibly from self-deception; (d) that agents – or we as observers – can fully and objectively recognize what constitutes their interests: (e) that agency is a capacity of fully autonomous individuals rather than relationally constituted social persons: and (f) that action occurs without respect to convention and commitment, that is, as if agents were not specifically located social persons operating within moral universes, with respect to prior and binding commitments both to specific liturgical orders (Rappaport 1999) and to specific other persons. For example, a person's sexual agency may be informed by prior commitment both to a certain form of marriage that he or she has undergone and to a specific partner.

While all these points are relevant for interpreting Ali's situation, I will focus in particular on the issue of deception. Is his rheumatism a case of simple, outright, knowing deception? If we disagree with his commanding officer on this question, which I think we must, we are faced with a second question: Is it a case of self-deception? If so, how are we to understand and evaluate such self-deception?

I want to argue that although Ali does not avow his agency in the immediate acts of getting sick or choosing to get discharged, in fact he acts responsibly and in terms of an acceptance of responsibility within a wider frame of references – as a son, as a member of an ancestry, and as a member of a community. His withdrawal from the military is ultimately not very different from his acquiescence to marrying in the direction and manner that his parents wish. In both cases his agency is evident: in neither case is it autonomous. In getting sick he accedes to the will of the trumba. The difference is that in this case he does so apparently self-deceptively, that is, without acknowledging to himself that this is what he has done.

Self-deception often implies denying what is authentic and thus in some sense harming oneself or living a less than fully realized life. But arguably in this case, the consequences for Ali have been a more fully realized life than he could have held in the military, and probably a longer one. Moreover, at exactly which phase can we assert that Ali was more fully self-deceived? Perhaps the brunt of Ali's self-deception lay in his idealization of a military career with dreams of heroic underwater feats rather than the brute realities of the battlefield. As the trumba spirit said to Ali, 'Can't you see that soldiers get hurt?'

In an insightful discussion, Fingarette analyzes self-deception as 'the disavowal of a continuing engagement' (2000: 137). He distinguishes avowal of personal agency (identity) from acceptance of moral agency (responsibility). A sociopath can acknowledge his act (avowing that it was he who committed it) while refusing to take responsibility for it, that is, without any moral concern about it. The self-deceiver, however, does not avow his act, and this may be precisely because,

What is threatened is some aspect of integrity rooted in moral concern. The less integrity, the less is there motive to enter into self-deception. The greater the integrity of the person, and the more powerful the contrary individual inclinations, the greater is the temptation to self-deception ... It is because the movement into self-deception is rooted in a concern for integrity of spirit that we temper our condemnation of the self-deceiver. We feel he is not a mere cheat. We are moved to a certain compassion in which there is awareness of the self-deceiver's authentic inner dignity as the motive of his self-betrayal. (Fingarette 2000: 139)

Ali's case is virtually the complete inverse of the sociopathic personality. He does not avow his agency, but he does accept responsibility insofar as he is the victim. He is very concerned about the illness and its implications, and he realizes that as a result he must request a discharge. He understands that his responsibility is inevitably bound up in his relationship to his mother and to the family trumba.[11]

Another strand of Fingarette's approach is the argument that self-deception occurs all the time, that it is 'as ordinary and familiar a kind of mental activity as one can imagine' (2000: 162), if only because our attention cannot be focused everywhere at once. In this view, self-deception is frequently morally neutral, such as when we walk home without being able to recall the route we took, but even in stronger cases Fingarette's inclination is to follow Freud and be nonjudgmental. This is obviously not the case for Sartre's analysis of the specific form of self-deception he termed 'bad faith'. Can Ali be said to have acted in bad faith?

Bad faith can be described as follows:

Inauthentic and self-deceptive refusal to admit to ourselves and others our full freedom, thereby avoiding anxiety in making decisions and evading responsibility for actions and attitudes. (Sartre, 1956 [1943])

One self-deceiving strategy identified by Sartre is to embrace other people's views in order to avoid having to form one's own: another is to disregard options so that one's life appears predetermined to move in a fixed direction. (Audi 1999: 70)

In sum, bad faith is the dishonest and cowardly refusal to take responsibility for one's choices and actions. Is Ali's disavowal a matter of cowardice or dishonesty? It may be true that Ali has refused to accept his full freedom. But this is not necessarily out of a refusal to confront an unpleasant truth that he cannot admit to himself. What is difficult for him to reconcile is the discrepancy between his courage, enthusiasm, and skill as a man, an adventurer, and a soldier (as far as he understands what being a soldier entails) and his obligations to his family and to himself as a family man. Choice in favor of the latter is seen by the military as cowardice, laziness, or retreat, attributions that are simply not acceptable to Ali. Indeed, there is no reason to assume that he is either cowardly or lazy, and much evidence to the contrary. However, Ali is left with the dilemma of finding a face-saving way of making his choice, of withdrawing from the military, one in which, for reasons of moral integrity as described by Fingarette, he will not reveal to himself his abrogation of the commitment he engaged in by signing up.

It seems apparent that the existential emphasis on the freedom of the individual self is very different from the moral questions facing the relationally embedded person. There is a difference between exercising one's judgment and claiming absolute freedom of choice.[12] Moreover, Ali's case differs from most discussions of self-deception precisely because he is not the sole agent of his deception, and, in a sense, his way out of the dilemma is imposed upon him. The suggestion of the trumba plays a large role, and the explanation for the illness is reinforced by the family. The means are there at hand for disavowal, for letting the rheumatism take over. From the standpoint of the family, as opposed to that of the military, it is the socially correct thing to do.

We could reconstruct the whole story as one of resistance to French hegemony, or we could say that following his mother's intervention, Ali made the choice to fall under the spirit's influence. Not to have fallen sick would have been to reject his mother's and the elders' persuasion as well as the force of culture and tradition and the ends to which he had been raised and had already committed himself.[13] Ali knows that the spirit is tricking the commanding officer; the latter is right, after all, to be suspicious, though what he can never suspect is precisely whom he is dealing with.

Finally, whether we call this self-deception or bad faith or not depends, of course, on how we understand spirits and spirit possession, how we understand their social reality for people from Mayotte, and how people themselves attribute agency to spirits. Ali was subject to the spirit's grip, and he suffered for it. Suffering may be a sign of truth (Lambek 1998). At least it is self-evident; you cannot argue with it. Thus, an attribution of Sartrean bad faith has to be relative to how compelling we take the social reality of spirit possession to be for people of Mayotte in general and here for Ali in particular.[14]

But the fact that Ali's illness is precipitated by the cultural institution of spirit possession enables us to take the analysis to another level.

Rheumatic irony

So far I have been pushing the case for Ali's sincerity. But Ali's personal sincerity has to be counterposed to the inherently poletic and ironic qualities of spirit possession. Let me begin with irony. In a well-known statement, Becker (1979) argues that spirit possession transforms the ordinary communicative event so that the presupposition of the identity of the speaker is challenged.

> Trance speaking can be defined as communication in which one of the variables of the speech act (I am speaking to you about x at time y in place z with intent a) is denied, most frequently the variable I is paradoxically both speaking and not speaking, or speaking involuntarily or nonintentionally. Trance is a kind of incongruence between statement and intent (I/not I am speaking to you/not you ...), and covers a wide spectrum of linguistic experiences, from the minor trance of singing the national anthem – or any song you *believe* – to the major trance of hypnosis and schizophrenia. (Becker 1979: 232–33)

Disregarding Becker's provocative examples, his analysis clearly holds for the institution of spirit possession as found in Mayotte and many other parts of Africa. What is striking is how close this picture comes to the analysis by certain literary theorists and philosophers of irony.

In a brilliant discussion of Socratic irony, Nehamas quotes Lionel Trilling to the effect that 'irony implies "a disconnection between a speaker and his interlocutor, or between the speaker and that which is spoken about, or even between the speaker and himself"' (Nehamas 1998: 57, citing Trilling 1971: 120). 'Irony,' Nehamas writes, 'is acknowledged concealment' (1998: 67); 'irony allows you simply to refuse to let your audience know what you think and to suggest simply that it is not what you say' (ibid.: 55). And so '[i]rony allows us to pretend we are something other than our words suggest. It enables

us to play at being someone, without forcing us to decide what we really are or, indeed, whether we really are anyone ... Irony always and necessarily postulates a double speaker and a double audience' (ibid.: 59–60). Finally, to bring home the connection I am making, Nehamas says that '[t]hrough his irony, Socrates *dissociates* himself from his words' (ibid.: 61, my emphasis).

If Ali has not deceived his commanding officer, he suspects that the spirit has. But where does the agency of Ali leave off and that of the spirit begin? Whose agency is at issue? Who is communicating through the signs and symptoms of Ali's body? Ali is ostensibly speaking sincerely, but he is speaking about, with, and through an idiom that is intrinsically ironic. For Nehamas, irony understood as concealment moves interpretation away from the question of truth versus deceit. 'Like truthfulness, concealment does not distort the truth: like lying, it does not reveal it' (Nehamas 1998: 62). But in addition, '[i]rony often insinuates that something is taking place inside you that your audience is not allowed to see, but it does not always entail that you see it yourself. Irony often communicates that only part of a picture is visible to an audience, but it does not always entail that the speaker sees the whole. Sometimes, it does not even imply that a whole picture exists. Uncertainty is intrinsic, of the essence' (ibid.: 67).

Once we accept the irony intrinsic to any invocation of spirit possession, the question of self-deception becomes more complex, murkier. There is always in possession a hint that things are not what they seem. Possession is asserted and established as real, but at the same time there is a knowing glint in the spirit's eye (though not in that of the host or, as in Ali's case, in that of the object of the spirit's attention), as though to say, 'After all, *I* am not deceived.' At some level, Ali, too, is not deceived. His self-deception lies only with the sincerity with which he protects himself from his knowledge. But not deceived about what? It is we who deceive ourselves if we mistake the essential uncertainty of human selfhood, or ambivalence, for some substantial core or definitive choice.

Thus, I have been asked how I can call Ali ironic in the absence of conscious intentionality. My response is twofold. First, the irony lies in the recognition of the very ambiguity of intentionality. Second, how can one help being ironic when one takes up, or is taken up by, a discursive form that is itself intrinsically ironic?

I hope you will now not find me unduly ironic if I refer to Ali's condition as one of an *ironic illness*. I do not mean that it is ironic that Ali fell sick, or ironic that his illness was rheumatism, but rather that the very illness is constituted through irony. Ali was sick in an ironic mode. Much better to speak of rheumatic irony than of rheumatic hysteria.

Indeed, embodied irony might prove a fruitful redescription of the condition suffered by the women recorded by Freud and Breuer (1955 [1893–1895]). The tension between Freud's diagnoses and his consistently positive descriptions of his patients' high moral character and lively intelligence could be reread in this light. This would also fit Susan Bordo's (1989) interpretation and comparison of hysteria with agoraphobia and anorexia as caricatures of dominant modes of femininity. In referring to the illness or mode of illness as irony, I am suggesting that the irony is embodied and intrinsic and precisely not that it is conscious or reflective. I am not denying the authenticity of the suffering. Rather, I am suggesting that however real the symptoms, they cannot be reduced to a single, clear-cut cause or that, if there were such a cause, we could never know it with complete certainty. The irony of the illness is precisely an expression of its evasion at being pinned down by sufferer, observer, or therapist.

Self-textualizing acts

The final part of my argument concerns acknowledging spirit possession not only as something done, but as something made – that is, not only as a practice or as an idiom of practice, but as poiesis, as artful creation, and specifically attending to the way in which such creation draws attention to itself. What I am suggesting is that if Ali's condition is one of self-deception, insofar as it involves a spirit, it is self-deception that subtly but inevitably draws attention to itself as concealing something. And insofar as it does this, can it be self-deception after all?

That spirit possession is an aesthetic artifact to be engaged with should come as no surprise; it is the point at which analysis of possession rituals could start (Boddy 1989; Kapferer 1983; Lambek 1981). Spirit possession is simultaneously a part of life, something that really happens, that hurts, harms, or heals and establishes relationships, and an artistic production and performance, a lens or drama through which life is inspected, highlighted, reshaped, reflected upon, and responded to (often with explicit, theatrical irony or satire, as with the spirit's complaints about the smell of the toilet). It is serious business and aesthetic commentary, simultaneously part of the texture of life, the portrait of that life, and the gazing over the shoulder at the portrait. This kind of space for spectatorship, for theorizing (to draw on the original meaning of the word) is available not only for us or for Ali's friends and family, but for Ali himself (cf. Boddy 1988). This is true not only of full-blown possession ceremonies with their costumes and music, but of every appearance of possession in daily life.

What happened to Ali was not something that simply happened and was over, but action that contained the seeds of its own textualization (cf. Barber 1999; Ricoeur 1971; Silverstein and Urban 1996). Indeed, perhaps possession can be described more broadly as composed of self-textualizing acts. I cannot pursue this here except to suggest that through the framing and marking qualities of possession, ordinary people simultaneously become characters in dramas that are immediate and social but are also at arm's length from their immediate context, having historical associations or allegorical qualities, and that always contain the leavening of irony. [15]

Although Ali is never directly possessed by a spirit, both what happened to him and his narrative of the events have a heightened, created quality. Ali tells a good story. His symptoms have a kind of extravagance, and he describes his condition with verve. There is a dramatic tension as he doggedly hangs in at the military base, suffering and yet trying to convince his superiors of his will to work and stay on, determined to have his condition medically diagnosed and treated. When the x-rays came back negative, he says he was 'disappointed' (déçu). He wanted his condition medicalized, even though presumably that would have been harder to cure than the effects of the spirit. And yet there are signs – the way the illness started and stopped each time he entered or left the precinct – that he knew all along this was no ordinary illness.

Ali's self-narrative is itself ironic. At one level the story is about whether Ali suffered from ordinary rheumatism or was in the hands of the spirit. But there are multiple levels of ambiguity. One suggests that Ali was self-deceived to hope he could be free of the spirit. Another asks if he was not after all in some agreement with the spirit. Was not his ostensible resistance the space of his self-deception? Can we not hear Ali saying: 'if I had only had sufficient critical distance, I might have recognized my own collusion.' Or is he saying: 'What difference would it have made? The ending was inevitable from the start.'

Ali tells a story in which he appears doubly self-deceived. Relatively explicit is his deception in thinking his condition might be ordinary rheumatism. Relatively implicit is his deception in attempting to resist the spirit and his illness. But in thinking he is self-deceived, he may be deceiving himself, and we, too, may be deceiving ourselves. Would we have remained healthy in Ali's situation? Would we have asked for an immediate discharge? Would we have gone to the front? Could we have exercised some Sartrean existential ideal of freedom? Would to claim that we (or Ali) could have done so not be evidence of our own bad faith?

Whatever we would have done in his place, the point is that Ali's story is there before his eyes, but also before ours – to enable us to be presumptuous about our own ostensibly more sovereign agency, to ask the question of ourselves, and, very possibly, to recognize the limits of autonomy in the face of an exigent mother, a determined spirit, and a relationally constituted self. Those people in or from Mayotte who hear about what happened to Ali must reflect on their own knowledge of the force of other persons in their lives – and of course on the delicious fact that their spirits are able to overcome the lure of French military heroism and even the power of military discipline.

The textualization of acts of possession also enables us to expand our appreciation of irony from the playful, rhetorical, and dialogical Socratic version to the tragic Sophoclean one. Ali and others can observe the effects of human agency against or with the tide that fate (structure, determinism) plays in their lives. [16]

My account owes not a little to Nehamas's reflections on *The Magic Mountain*, in which Thomas Mann 'shows that the attribution of self-deception to others is one of the surest paths to the deception of oneself' (Nehamas 1998: 32). In a fashion similar to Mann, possession 'relentlessly undermines our ability to make unconditional judgments in the same process that it tempts us to keep doing so' (ibid.: 30). [17]

As they become textualized, the events in which spirits intervene in people's lives become objects of contemplation, much as literature can move in the opposite direction to intervene in people's lives. We can read *The Magic Mountain* and be deceived by Mann, much as the hero of the novel deceives himself; so, too, with possession. I am all too well aware that to posit the intrinsic irony of possession and its textualization makes it an object of interpretation and moral pleasure for *me* (I have made my living from it) and that literary theory offers familiar instruction in the appreciation of texts. I have also begun to wonder whether the relationship of anthropologists to their subjects is not intrinsically ironic in much the same way that I have described spirit possession. [18] In sum, if irony is to be attributed like illness, it may be contagious! But I think that through irony and textualization, spirit possession also becomes an object of edification and pleasure for those who engage with it on a more intimate and regular basis. Ali's encounter with the spirit was immediate, painful, and deeply embodied. But it was also distanced and objectified sufficiently to be available to Ali and others in the form of a narrative. The nature of his illness, as artfully enshrouded in ambiguity as that of the hero of *The Magic Mountain*, invites all who encounter it to contemplate agency and its limits, dignity and its vicissitudes, individuality and its relational entailments, hope and contingency, the essential uncertainty of life.

Earlier in the essay I asked what spirit possession might teach us about agency. The answer I propose is akin to Mann's depiction of the ironic saturation of his characters' situation. Any invocation of 'agency' must itself be tinged with irony. Agency is to be taken seriously, but not always literally.

Forward

Let us remember the relational quality of personhood in Mayotte exemplified by spirit possession. We have seen how Ali's agency is harnessed to realize the intentions of another. That other, as his mother, is also a part of himself. And his mother's own other, her self-object, the spirit, is in part a refraction of her parents in turn, and beyond them, of a deeper ancestry for which she is just a contemporary vehicle or trustee.

Earlier I mentioned Ali's comfortable assertion that he would never become host to the spirit himself. I do not know whether to interpret this as a refusal to extend the relational boundaries of the self, as a limit on his ironic self-recognition, or whether to interpret it as a sign of strength, weakness, or realism, or as undecidable.

Near the end of my stay in Mayotte in 2000, Ali and I were talking about the return of his wife from her year at university and her choice of a career; she had chosen education over medicine. He mentioned that while they were enjoying a drive in the countryside, his wife became rigid in the seat beside him, her arms and legs outstretched so that he had to lift her out of the car. In some concern, I asked whether she had seen a doctor. I should have known better. 'Oh,' he laughed, 'It's not worth going to a doctor. We know already that it is trumbas.' He added, 'and that's why she didn't want to study medicine. The trumbas can't stand dirty things like blood.'

Of course, one of the trumbas who has entered his wife and wants to establish a permanent relationship with her is the very spirit who is to be found in Ali's mother and who accompanied her on her fateful visit to France. As his cross-cousin, Ali's wife, too, is in line to succeed to the spirit, and in her case the marital and affinal connections are probably equally compelling. As for Ali, he will find that the spirit is never too far away.

Acknowledgements

This essay was inspired by an invitation to speak at the seminar on 'Personhood and Agency in African Studies,' at the African Studies Center, Leiden, and was duly delivered 27 September 2000. I am grateful to Rijk van Dijk, Peter Geschiere, Peter Pels, and Robert Ross for the invitation, to the audience for their responses, and to Paul Antze, Janice Boddy, Peter Geschiere, Carol Greenhouse, and Andrew Walsh for insightful comments on the written text, not all of which I have followed. A revised version has benefited from the scrutiny of departmental seminars at McGill, University of California San Diego, Yale, Oxford, and Wilfrid Laurier Universities. As usual, I am indebted to the Social Science and Humanities Research Council of Canada for supporting my research and writing, and of course to the people in Mayotte who have shared their lives, especially 'Ali'.

Notes

[1] See Lambek (1988b, 1996. 2000, 2002, and 2003).

[2] It is true, in any case, that the lives of our friends and contemporaries, insofar as we know them, become the objects of our contemplation – John falling sick when and as he did, Mary having a child, John and Mary raising their children as they do. The ways in which the lives of our friends, colleagues, and consociates become available to us as objects of moral contemplation, and the questions they raise for us, are intensified in 'life term' communities (Moore 1978).

[3] Unlike ego psychology, the focus of object-relations is not primarily on individual autonomy so much as on growth through relationships and on the necessary permeability of selves. I believe this psychic basis to be universal – and to be universally recognized – insofar as I can easily empathize with Malagasy friends and they with me, and we can agree about our descriptions and our likes and dislikes of other persons or our interpretations of motivation (even when we are mistaken). I assume this to be true, with a little mutual effort and good will, anywhere in the world. With sufficient acquaintance of cultural frames and forms of personal expression, one can discriminate among people who appear overly dependent, assertive, aggressive, and so forth and people whose quiet autonomy is impressive.

[4] His name and some of the incidental details have been changed. Since my original fieldwork, Mayotte has been increasingly integrated into the French state and has become the object of rapid development. In 2000 a referendum was held to change its status from that of *collectivité territoriale* to that of *collectivité départementale*. An African island in the Comoro Archipelago of the Western Indian Ocean, it is now using the euro. While most citizens of Mayotte speak Shimaore, a Bantu language, the members of Ali's village are Malagasy speakers. Their antecedents arrived before the French conquest in 1841 or during the early colonial period.

[5] Ali says that since his stay in France, he no longer has the patience to sit through night-long religious recitations of the kind frequently performed in the village. However, like others of his social status and education, Ali is by no means opposed to Islam. He willingly joined in rebuilding the village mosque, and he helped pay for his father's participation in a pilgrimage circuit in Madagascar. He assures me he will pray consistently when he gets older.

[6] According to the French system of calculating high school education, completion of *3ième* is three years prior to the *bac* degree, which is the prerequisite for university. La Réunion is a French *département d'outre-mer* in the Indian Ocean east of Madagascar and some 1,700 kilometers from Mayotte. The two islands were connected in 2000 by numerous direct flights. Metropolitan France is some 9,000 kilometers from Mayotte and was reached via La Réunion.

[7] In fact, not all new brides are virgins (Lambek 1983). Trumbas (*tromba* in Malagasy spelling) are Malagasy spirits, usually members of the royal Sakalava descent group, whose genealogy stretches back to before 1700 and who rise in and speak through specific mediums (Lambek 1981, 1993, 2002; Sharp 1993).

[8] The trumba never fully rose in this man (he never went into full trance), but he would shake when the spirit was manifest and had purchased all of its clothing. The military connection may hold significance for the recurrence and knowledge of the individual spirit, but I have not been able to discover it.

[9] The situation is a bit more complex than this in that the expensive ceremony in which the spirit announces its name has not yet been held for Ali's mother, nor was it ever held for her mother's brother. The name of the spirit should thus not be uttered (Lambek 1981), and its common identity among family members remains latent. There is also some conflict and competition over the production of the ceremonies. Succession to specific spirits marks segmentation no less than family unity (Lambek 1988a).

[10] As Donald Tuzin noted (personal communication), Freudian ego psychologists might speak of the 'secondary gains' of Ali's illness and the way his 'somatic conversion' provided a face-saving way of submitting to his mother's will. Mel Spiro (personal communication) has suggested simply that part of Ali wanted one outcome and part, the other.

[11] For Fingarette 'avowal is a necessary condition of responsibility' (2000: 147), yet this does not appear to hold for Ali's case. However, Fingarette also acknowledges that 'the issue [of acceptance of responsibility] is complicated by the fact that a person is responsible, in spite of unconcern with respect to a specific engagement, if there are other concerns of the person's by virtue of which he has indirectly committed himself to be concerned for the engagement at issue' (146).

[12] However, Sartre's argument was an important ethical and political intervention in postwar France.

[13] The argument here is essentially the same as that used to describe the role of suggestion and illocutionary acts in therapy.

[14] We might also ask whether *spirits* are portrayed as acting individualistically or relationally, exercising free choice or social judgment. One of the

themes of *Human Spirits* (Lambek 1981) is that the possession 'cure' entails socializing the spirit and thus moving it from the former position to the latter. The drama of the cure, including vociferous interchanges between the spirit and the healers, provides instruction for everyone. But equally, the socialization of the spirits remains inconclusive and ambiguous: spirits can always utilize means, such as sending rheumatism, that would be illegitimate were they applied by humans. This contrast between humans and spirits is itself one of the edifying features of possession.

15 Such textualizing is incomplete insofar as the indexical qualities never completely disappear. Were they to do so, the intrinsically ironic quality of possession would be lost.

16 Marxian structure (via Hegel) and Freudian unconscious both derive from the Sophoclean version of irony. I am indebted to Paul Antze for these points (cf. Fortes 1983 [1959]).

17 I have been criticized for undertaking to judge Ali's motives and for shifting to an experience-distant mode of understanding, but my aim has been neither to judge nor to criticize Ali, but rather to expose, as Nehamas says of Plato's dialogues, 'our ignorance of our own ignorance' (1998: 44).

18 I owe this idea to Andrew Walsh's suggestion (personal communication, 1 October 2000) that when Ali was reciting the story to me, he, too, was doing so ironically – not lying, but not revealing everything either. The anthropologist's stance is also at issue. I am ironic insofar as I hold two sets of beliefs or hold one of them back. 'Is it possible,' asks Walsh, 'that any invocation of an ethnographic encounter (like that between you and Ali) is ironic in the way that any invocation of possession is?' Crapanzano (1980) provides sustained reflection on these issues. See also Fernandez and Huber (2001).

References

Audi, R., ed. 1999. *The Cambridge Dictionary of Philosophy*. 2nd ed. Cambridge: Cambridge University Press.

Barber, K. 1999. 'Quotation in the Constitution of Yorùbá Oral Texts.' *Research in African Literatures* 30, no. 2: 17–41.

Becker, A. 1979. 'Text-Building, Epistemology, and Aesthetics in Javanese Shadow Theatre' in *The Imagination of Reality*, edited by A. Becker and A. Yengoyan. Norwood NJ: Ablex, pp. 211–43.

Boddy, J. 1988. 'Spirits and Selves in Northern Sudan: The Cultural Therapeutics of Possession and Trance.' *American Ethnologist* 15, no. I:4: 27.

— 1989. *Wombs and Alien Spirits*. Madison: University of Wisconsin Press.

Bordo, S. 1989. 'The Body and the Reproduction of Femininity.' in *Gender/Body/Knowledge: Feminist Reconstructions of Being and Knowing*, edited by A. Jaggar and S. Bordo. New Brunswick, NJ: Rutgers University Press, pp. 13–33.

Chodorow. N. J. 1989. *Feminism and Psychoanalytic Theory*. New Haven: Yale University Press.

Crapanzano. V. 1980. *Tuhami: Portrait of a Moroccan*. Chicago: University of Chicago Press.

Fernandez, L and M. T. Huber, eds, 2001. *Irony in Action: Anthropology, Practice, and the Moral Imagination*. Chicago: University of Chicago Press.

Fingarette, H. 2000. *Self-Deception*. 2nd ed. Berkeley: University of California Press.

Fortes, M. 1983 [1959]. *Oedipus and Job in West African Religion*. Cambridge: Cambridge University Press.

Freud, S. and J. Breuer. 1955 [1893–1895]. 'Studies on Hysteria' in S. Freud *Standard Edition of the Collected Works*. Vol. 2.

Kapferer, B. 1983. *A Celebration of Demons: Exorcism and the Aesthetics of Healing in Sri Lanka*. Bloomington: Indiana University Press.

Lambek, M. 1981. *Human Spirits: A Cultural Account of Trance in Mayotte*. Cambridge: Cambridge University Press.

— 1983. 'Virgin Marriage and the Autonomy of Women in Mayotte.' *Signs Journal of Women in Culture and Society* 9, no. 2: 264–81.

— 1988a. 'Spirit Possession/Spirit Succession: Aspect of Social Continuity among Malagasy Speakers in Mayotte.' *American Ethnologist* 15, no. 4: 710–731.

— 1988b. 'Graceful Exits: Spirit Possession as Personal Performance.' *Cultur* 8, no. 1: 59–69.

— 1989. 'From Disease to Discourse: Remarks on the Conceptualization of Trance and Spirit Possession' in *Altered States of Consciousness and Mental Health: A Cross-Cultural Perspective,* edited by C. Ward. Thousand Oaks CA: Sage Press, pp. 36–61.

— 1993. *Knowledge and Practice in Mayotte. Local Discourses of Islam, Sorcery, and Spirit Possession*. Toronto: University of Toronto Press.

— 1996. 'The Past Imperfect: Remembering as Moral Practice' in *Tense Past Cultural Essays in Trauma and Memory*, edited by P. Antze and M. Lambek New York: Routledge, pp. 235–54.

— 1998. 'The Sakalava Poiesis of History: Realizing the Past through Spirit Possession in Madagascar.' *American Ethnologist* 25, no. 2: 106–127.

— 2000. 'Nuriaty, the Saint, and the Sultan: Virtuous Subject and Subjective Virtuoso of the Post-Modem Colony'. *Anthropology Today* 16 no. 2: 712.

— 2002. *The Weight of the Past: Living with History in Mahafanga, Madagascar* New York: PalgraveMacrnillan.

— 2003. 'Memory in a Maussian Universe' in *Regimes of Memory*, edited by K. Hodgkin and S. Radstone. London: Routledge, pp. 202–16.

Mann, T. 1995 [1924]. *The Magic Mountain*. Translated by J. E. Woods. New York: Knopf.

Mitchell, S. A. 1988. *Relational Concepts in Psychoanalysis: An Integration*. Cambridge, MA: Harvard University Press.

Moore, S. F. 1978. 'Old Age in a Life-Term Social Arena' in *Life's Career – Aging*, edited by B. Myerhoff and A. Simic. Beverly Hills: Sage, pp. 23–76.

Nehamas, A. 1998. *The Art of Living: Socratic Reflections from Plato to Foucault*. Berkeley: University of California Press.

Rappaport, R. A. 1999. *Ritual and Religion in the Making of Humanity*. Cambridge: Cambridge University Press.

Ricoeur, P. 1971. 'The Model of the Text: Meaningful Action Considered as a Text.' *Social Research* 38: 529–562.

Sartre, J. P. 1956 [1943]. *Being and Nothingness*. Translated by H. Barnes. New York: Philosophical Library.

Sharp, L. 1993. *The Possessed and the Dispossessed*. Berkeley: University of California Press.

Silverstein, M. and G. Urban, eds. 1996. *Natural Histories of Discourse*. Chicago: University of Chicago Press.

Stathern, M. 1988. *The Gender of the Gift: Problems with Women and Problems with Society in Melanesia*. Berkeley: University of California Press.

Trilling, L. 1971. *Sincerity and Authenticity*. Cambridge, MA: Harvard University Press.

2 Ethnographies of the Modern in Africa

If modern changes on the African continent cannot be interpreted as self-evidently fitting into the framework of the meta-narrative of modernization, the challenge is how we can grasp these changes in all their surprising variety and unexpected turns. Only over the last two decades the fragmented realities of the modern have been studied with the required ethnographic depth. This part offers a first overview of different directions in these 'ethnographies of the modern'. Five foci were selected since they represent nodal points in the crystallization of modern expectations and experiences, but also because seminal interpretations emerged from these fields.

Section 2.A., 'Dynamics of Governmentality', epitomizes that we need a considerable amount of imaginative ethnography to understand the divergence of modern politics in Africa from the ideological focus on impersonal constitutional systems and the congruence of national belonging and citizenship. Achille Mbembe discusses the tensions between nativism, cosmopolitism and citizenship in the African context. Mariane Ferme analyses special implications of the first democratic elections after a long period of civil war in Sierra Leone.

Section 2.B., 'The City', explores how urban life in Africa has departed radically from the model of the city as the source of modernity that we find with modernization theorists like Eisenstadt (see section 1.A.). Filip de Boeck evokes the different reflections that shape city life in Kinshasa and the penetration of the invisible in everyday life. Abdou-Maliq Simone shows that the 'worlding' of the African cities follows unexpected trajectories.

Section 2.C., 'Technology' counters the commodified conception of technological transfer that was so central to early, technocratic discourses of 'development'. Instead these studies show how technology has to be reconfigured so as to work once it travels to Africa. Brian Larkin discusses how video technology and the infrastructures on which its circulation depends assume new aspects in a context of piracy in northern Nigeria. Jojada Verrips and Birgit Meyer tell a story of technological creativity that will be familiar to anyone who has had to struggle with the precariousness of cars in Africa.

Section 2.D., 'Modernity's Enchantment' provides critical counterpoints to modernist expectations of what would happen with religion and magic in Africa and elsewhere. Instead of the disenchantment and enlargement of cosmic scale, expected by Robin Horton and others, magico-religious repertoires are becoming entwined with modern ways of life (just as in Europe or America, we would like to stress). Isaac Niehaus analyses the outbreak of witch-hunts that marked the promising transition to post-apartheid in the northern parts of South Africa. Francis Nyamnjoh's theatre play offers vivid scenes of how Pentecostalism grafts itself upon modern developments. Allen Roberts and Mary Nooter discuss how a modern city, Dakar, is pervaded by the rich imagery of an Islamic saint, the Mourides' Sheikh Amadou Bamba.

Finally, section 2.E., 'New Figures of Success: Beyond the Modern?' offers examples of new role models, emerging in many parts of present-day Africa. The emblematic figure of modernity used to be the civil servant, who due to his educational certificates made a prosperous career in government service. However, with structural adjustment and economic crisis, the benefits of such a career have become less and less impressive. Instead new figures of success emerged, marked by fashion, highly volatile performances of trust and risk, and a refined straddling of the formal and the illicit. Gandoulou's *sapeurs* (Congolese dandies), Roitman's *coupeurs des routes* (bandits from the Chad basin) and Ndjio's *feymen* (Cameroon's trans-national swindlers) can hardly be termed 'modern' in the classical sense of the word. Yet it is quite clear that they do not epitomize 'tradition' either. Do they represent new ways of exploring modernity?

Section 2.A
Dynamics
of Governmentality

ACHILLE MBEMBE
The New Africans
Between Nativism & Cosmopolitanism

Reference
Esprit, 2002: 1–10, trans. by Peter Geschiere

By insisting too much on the crisis, numerous analysts end up attributing to Africa such a particular character that this continent would no longer be comparable to any other region of the world. Even more serious is that, thus, they seem to lose sight of the recompositions that are underway in the continent. These recompositions take quite different forms in various countries; yet, they have in common that it is clear from their political, economic and cultural structures that they reflect not a state of anomy but rather a process of transnationalization. This process obeys specific logics and takes place on multiple scales. Yet, nearly everywhere, it highlights the conflict between a cosmopolitan vision and a nativist vision of African identity and culture.

Since structural events of a global nature have aggravated this cultural conflict, there is first of all a direct link to important shifts in the modalities of Africa's insertion in the world economy. Indeed, during the last quarter of the twentieth century, an atomized capitalism, without agglomerating effects or a giant pole of growth, developed on the remainders of a rent economy formerly dominated, on the one hand, by parastatals under the control of the regime and, on the other, by monopolies dating mostly from the colonial period and operating on controlled markets. The dichotomy between the urban and the rural economy imploded and so did the separation between the formal and the informal economy, characteristic of the immediate post-colonial period. This was replaced by a fractured economy, composed of various closely related nodes, maintaining changing and extremely complex relations with international circuits.

From the extreme fragmentation emerged often within one and the same country a multiplicity of economic territorialities, sometimes interrelated but more often in disjunction. It is in this context that enclaves for mining, oil concessions or fishing have become of decisive importance. Whether they are on the sea or on land, these enclaves have in common that they are of an extractive nature. They are in practice disconnected from the rest of the national territory, or they are at most related to it by informal and precarious networks. In contrast, they are closely linked to the circuits of international trade and in many cases contradict the current supposition that the continent is being marginalized. Even when they do not become the object of open warfare or conflict, these enclaves as such form contested spaces. Sometimes controlled by multinationals to whom the state extends – or in practice delegates – its sovereignty, sometimes allied with armed formations of dissidents, these enclaves and their economy express symbolically the osmosis of warlike and commercial activity. Trade and militarism in their turn feed on international flows.[1]

Another aspect of the transnationalization of the African economies is the emergence of free zones and corridors, the aim of which is to allow for the implantation of firms in protected and fiscally privileged spaces.[2] As in the case of the enclaves, the economy of these corridors is completely oriented towards export and, in this respect, particularly vulnerable to the shocks of the world market and the volatility of conjunctures. The fragmentation of economic space in Africa manifests itself also in the growing importance of nature parks and reserves – which often get a (semi-)official status as some sort of concession – or even the forest in general, exploited as it is by tourist companies and international firms. Between these spaces, zones of flow develop, hotbeds for the kind of informal networks that everywhere accompany the emergence of several big regional metropoles.

This process of an atomization of capitalism has numerous effects on the formation of identities. On the one hand, two configurations of violence, that in former days were relatively disparate, are now combined and become ever more closely linked: the violence of the market, aggravated by the struggles over the privatization of resources, and social violence that is no longer under control because the public powers have lost their monopoly. On the other hand, because of the transnationalization of the economies, African actors, both private persons and officials, have been obliged to search new sources of rent further away – or even more simply, new means of survival.

New dynamics of profit-making have thus emerged. They have led to an unprecedented revival of imaginaries of the faraway. This revival has expressed itself by an equally unprecedented increase of migratory practices and experiences of displacement (forced displacement, or linked to the search for work or to religious considerations). Due to this phenomenon of expatriation, numerous diasporas are born. In economic respects, flows of migrants have also contributed to the emergence of new financial circuits animated by diasporas in foreign countries. In cultural respects, these long journeys – being constantly in transit, the crossing of borders, the negotiations of risks in the place of arrival – have become structuring aspects of the identity of youth.

In parallel ways, the society re-composes itself around a labyrinth of commercial and religious networks with their related institutions and associations, some of which claim to form the 'civil society'. This is especially manifest in the urban context. Most of these networks result from the intertwinement of the state and the informal. Some are screens for political parties or local satellites of international organizations. Others, notably armed formations, are linked to war and violence. They contribute to the consolidation of a culture of banditry and robbery, of which the symbolism and methods are inspired by international movies. Yet others participate in healing movements and new religious cults which promise especially to keep evil and misfortune in check by an uncompromising struggle with new figures of the devil. The heterogeneity of the logics that these different actors follow explains the dispersed character of their interventions and the brutality of the struggle over the access to external financial resources. This testifies also to the accelerated pluralization of African societies.

Identity, autochthony and citizenship

Another factor behind the social recompositions of the last quarter of the twentieth century and the emergence of changing identities is war, which is the consequence of the intertwinement of various processes. Most wars that go on at present are the results of controversies that can be classified as constitutional since they concern the division of power and privileges in the countries concerned. Other wars originate from fundamental controversies over the conditions for the enjoyment of citizenship in a context of growing scarcity of the advantages distributed by the state and, paradoxically, increasing possibilities to claim these openly (democratization) or even try to appropriate them by force. All these wars have re-launched, on an unprecedented scale, old struggles over autochthony, citizenship and ownership.

Indeed, in the aftermath of Independence, the authoritarian post-colonial regimes succeeded in de-politicizing the double construction of state and nation by setting it up as a categorical imperative. In accordance with this, they developed a conception of the nation resting on the affirmation of collective rights, which the new leaders preferred to oppose to individual rights. Development, as the regime's central metaphor and utopia for social transformation, was presented as the locus for the realization of these rights and of collective happiness. It had to be realized through the establishment of an ensemble of institutional apparatuses (a single party, an overarching labour union that was strictly controlled, a national army) and by resorting to a broad spectrum of practices supposedly inspired by autochthonous traditions of communalism. This post-colonial communalism strongly favoured, even if only verbally, the search for consensus, regional and ethnic balance, the 'reciprocal assimilation' of various segments of the elite and the constitution of a communal space by strong social control and, if necessary, by coercion. These tactics and apparatuses aimed to prevent the outbreak of conflicts or the constitution of factions on an ethnic basis. The state (and the party) became thus, at least formally, the only basis for belonging and identity, of privileges and prosperity.

It is this consensus that was broken in the early 1990s. The market model and the idea of liberal democracy destroyed this ideological construction by insisting on individual rights and by re-kindling the debate on private property and inequality. This did not necessarily result in a re-appropriation or a local translation of the crucial philosophical principles of the state and the law (political recognition of the individual as rational citizen, capable of making independent choices; affirmation of individual liberty and the rights following from this; fundamental equality between individuals and recognition of their dignity). One of the ambiguities of democratization under the special circumstances of atomized capitalism, as it is now taking place on the African continent, is therefore the re-launching – but now on an unprecedented scale – of disputes over the private accumulation of wealth and its corollary, social exclusion.

Due to these disputes new currents of thought emerged concerning the state and the nation. Two merit our attention in particular. The first one tries to resolve the apparent contradiction between citizenship and identity by proclaiming a philosophy of a reconstitution of the state, based on the constitutional recognition of autochthonous community and distinct traditions. This line of thought denies the existence of individuals in Africa. In this view, the only individuality existing would be that of entire groups. The nation would define itself not by what unites it, but by the total sum of its differences and the particularities of each of its cultures seen in separation. On top of the distinction between nationals and strangers, internal differences are set up; the most decisive of these is supposed to be the opposition within the same country between autochthons and *allogènes*. Due to the principle of anteriority, only autochthons would be entitled to access the local civic space and its citizenship. Only they could enjoy collective rights, such as special access to the resources coming from the soil.[3] At the national level, this line of thought proclaims that the access to the advantages and privileges that follow from the control over the state's apparatus should be simply organized on a rotating basis between each autochthonous community.

Cosmopolitism

Next to these nativist approaches to identity and citizenship, an ensemble of cosmopolitan practices develops. At least two versions of cosmopolitism emerged in the course of the last quarter of the twentieth century. The first one is a practical cosmopolitism, of a vernacular brand, carried by *petits migrants* (small migrants). Most of these migrants are involved in the spatial strategies of various networks built around trade, religion or prostitution. They travel to and fro between their country of origin and their new locations; thus they contribute to an urban mesh that links Africa to pivotal places outside the continent. Such links developed notably between West and East Africa on the one hand, and territories across the Sahara, the Gulf states and the Indian Ocean country at the other.

This cosmopolitism of 'small migrants' rests certainly on the obligation to belong to a specific cultural or religious entity; but it leaves scope for intensive exchanges with other parts of the world.[4] Such exchange is at the same time religious (pilgrimage), economic (importation of commodities such as textiles, carpets, household appliances, electronic equipment, cars and car-parts) and cultural. From this trade emerged hybrid cultural formations and accelerated forms of creolization. This is in particular the case in the Soudanian-Sahelian part of Islamic Africa where migrations and long-distance trade continue age-old practices. But now they imply the peddling of identities and a clever use of modern technologies.[5] This is also the case for pentecostalist movements in Christian countries or for the creole formations in Central Africa.[6] All these movements are carried by the emergence, in urban settings, of cybercafés and the ubiquity of the fax and the mobile phone.

This 'small migrants' cosmopolitism has led to a proliferation of clandestine spaces. Extensive informal towns have emerged through irregular forms of access to land. Illegal migrants adopted increasingly fluid practices in their new countries in order to maintain themselves there. Yet, this triggered ever more blatant forms of xenophobia which further contributed to keeping these migrants in the shadows. In these domains of illegality, marginalization favours the reconstruction of communal frameworks. In extreme cases, these zones outside the law introduce significant ruptures in the urban mesh. A criminal economy, functioning at the interface of the institutional and the informal, allows for a geographical implantation of exchange systems on a local as much as an international scale. Its social actors are obliged to create resources under permanently unstable conditions, almost absolute uncertainty, and within an extremely short time span.

The elites have developed another kind of cosmopolitism which

Fig. 1 Bill Clinton in Dakar, mural by Papito Boy (courtesy of Allen F. Roberts & Mary Nooter Roberts)

Fig. 2 The slave house, Gorée Island, mural by Papito Boy (courtesy of Allen F. Roberts & Mary Nooter Roberts)

strives to reconstruct an African identity and a public space following the universal rules of reason. This reconstruction works in two directions. One consists, paradoxically, of an effort towards a re-enchantment of tradition and custom. This is expressed, for instance, in the transfer of powers from the central states to new territorial collectivities (in other words: decentralization) and in the local re-appropriation of symbolic resources of globalization.

Indeed, the trend towards decentralization was complemented by important shifts in territorial divisions in relation to multiple political and cultural stakes. These re-divisions have been accompanied in general by changing attributions of services and employment. Even more important is that, in the context of the ongoing transnationalization of African societies, the control over local resources has proved to be a powerful factor for getting access to international resources, which the elites use, inversely, to concoct a sentiment of local belonging. Due to administrative and territorial re-divisions, local elites are able to reinforce their position as brokers between the locality, the state and international networks. The mobilization of local resources remains indispensable to the negotiations at the international level; thus, it becomes self-evident that the logics of the locality and those of globalization are not opposed, but on the contrary reinforce each other.

Moreover, since the grip on local resources is based on the control over public, political and financial positions, many social actors (customary chiefs, notables, holy men, professional elites, different associations, political parties, brokers, D.O.s and other civil servants, associations of relief and solidarity) tried to mobilize traditional solidarities in order to prevail in the competition opened up by this inter-twinement of positions.[7] This is one of the reasons why – far from favouring the emergence of a legal subject – decentralization and democratization contributed so clearly to a revival of solidarities with a genealogical-territorial basis, to the resurgence of conflicts over autochthony, and to the aggravation of tensions between the natives of a locality, on the one hand, and migrants and *allogènes*, on the other.[8]

These processes, at the same time cultural, political and economic, are not only promoted by private local actors. They are also encouraged by the state, the international financial institutions and the non-governmental organizations, involved in struggles over the safeguarding of the environment, the promotion of women's rights or the protection of 'indigenous peoples'. Thus, in several countries, the transfer of the management of sustainable resources from the state to rural communities not only led to the creation of new municipalities and districts, most of them corresponding to ethnic or lineage divisions; it also caused the proclamation of new laws, and sometimes the *de facto* recognition of customary rights.

Land-law is one of the fields in which a certain recognition of customary law has taken place – notably in the context of the formation of reserves and nature parks, or in the delimitation of logging concessions or protected areas.[9] The confiscation of supposedly customary land and the attribution of these domains to individuals, who are planning to exploit it, are no longer the main factors that direct the state's interventions. On the contrary, the latter no longer seeks to undermine the force of custom or to weaken the authorities who are meant to affirm it.[10] The result is a highly complex inter-twinement and unsolvable interlocking between the law of the state and that of the local communities.[11]

The other form of cosmopolitism among elites is based on distancing themselves from tradition, their main concern being the emergence of a modern and de-territorialized self. In this trend, there is a heavy emphasis on questions of civil government and the creation of institutions that could favour egalitarian participation in the exercise of sovereignty and representation. At a philosophical level, this current is focused on those aspects that show Africans to be identical to other human beings.[12] Thus, questions of ownership and individual rights get priority over racial, cultural or religious individualities or the philosophy of the non-reducibility of Africa, its people and its culture.[13]

The second form of cosmopolitism is closely interlinked with the difficult emergence of a private sphere. Different factors push towards the constitution of such a sphere. The first one is linked to the special possibilities for migration open to elites. Thus, they can withdraw from the demands of the immediate family and liberate themselves from the social control by the community. The other factor is related to new opportunities to enrich themselves outside the control of the state – opportunities legitimized by the ideologies of privatization.

Inevitably, the enjoyment of individual rights, especially when these are linked to private ownership, becomes a critical element in the new imaginations of the self.

'Metropolization' and new life-styles

Changing life styles remain one of the most obvious sites where the new African identities manifest themselves. In the context of strong economic fluctuations and the intense volatility that characterized the last quarter of the twentieth century, a process of social fragmentation deeply affected the familial structures. This is notably the case in the big metropoles.[14] The main social mutations in this domain are linked with the (decreasing) access of the young to employment, the increasing importance of women's economic activities due to the crisis, and to changes in the patterns of cohabitation and sexuality.

The relative weakening of the socio-economic status of young men constitutes in this respect a novel phenomenon. Unemployment levels have risen significantly for this social category. The passage from adolescence to adulthood is no longer automatic, and in some countries the average age of the household heads is clearly rising. Often, a man's first marriage no longer coincides with the moment that he assumes male tasks. The social distance between social seniors and juniors deepens, while the distribution of roles and resources between generations becomes more complex. Henceforth, for numerous young men various forms of dependence are prolonged; the only escape is to migrate or to have themselves recruited as soldiers in military formations.

The relations between men and women are being re-defined, just as the parental roles. The composition of households has deeply changed. The ubiquity of conjugal families without children, polygamic families without collateral relatives or one-parent families signals that a greater diversity of family forms is emerging. Nearly everywhere, the mobility of men has incisive consequences for the control over the household. Since so often men and women within a marriage no longer live together, many families have a female head.[15] Male and female roles within the marriage change also in other respects, due to increasing irregularity of employment and ever sharper social exclusion. There is an emerging levelling process of existing differences in the status of women and young men.

All this encourages a proliferation of micro-strategies among social actors. Changes in polygamic arrangements, for instance, allow for novel strategies both for men and women in order to appropriate resources within the domestic structure in a context in which women's activities contribute ever more to the family's income. Systems of solidarity based on lineage and customary idioms are henceforth combined with mercantile relations with often brutal impact, next to traditional networks of support and clientelism.

The other major re-composition of the last quarter of the twentieth century is the gradual emergence of a private sphere which borrows its symbols from global culture. There are no other domains that highlight so vividly the impact of such transnationalization as those of clothing and fashion, sport and body care in general.[16] However, the same drive to open up to the world is to be found in music, dance and sexuality.[17] Musical creativity is now ever more dominated by a métissage principle. From this viewpoint, three categories of experimentation seem to have been decisive: first efforts to produce 'world music', starting from an exploration of old heritages, whether African or not (following the examples by Ray Lema, Wasis Diop or Lkua Kanza); secondly the grafts and transfers between ancient rhythms (*soukous* and others) and the music of the islands; and finally the local re-appropriations of black Atlantic sonorities (for example the rap in Senegal or the *kwaito* in South Africa). These phenomena are carried by a general movement of privatization and new cultures of the self which cannot be reduced to individualism or narcissism.[18]

Notes

1. Achille Mbembe, 'At the Edge of the World: Boundaries, Territoriality, and Sovereignty in Africa', *Public Culture* 12, 1, 2000.
2. See Sarah Nuttall, Françoise Vergès, AbdouMaliq Simone, 'Diasporic Economies and Cultural Corridors in the Southern African Indian Ocean', mimeo, IRD-CODESRIA, 2000.
3. John Biye Ejobowah, 'Who Owns the Oil? The Politics of Ethnicity in the Niger Delta of Nigeria', *Africa Today*, 37, 1999: 29-47.
4. Mamadou Diouf, 'The Murid Trade Diaspora and the Making of a Vernacular Cosmopolitanism', *CODESRIA Bulletin*, I, 2000.
5. Robert Launay, 'Spirit Media: The Electronic Media and Islam among the Dyula of Northern Côte d'Ivoire', *Africa* 67,3, 1997: 441-53.
6. See Janet MacGaffey and Rémy Bazenguissa, *Congo-Paris. Transnational Traders on the Margins of the Law*, Oxford: James Currey, 2000.
7. Thomas Bierschenk and Jean-Pierre Olivier de Sardan, eds, *Les Pouvoirs au village*, Paris: Karthala, 1998.
8. Peter Geschiere and Francis Nyamnjoh, 'Capitalism and Autochthony: The Seesaw of Mobility and Belonging', *Public Culture* (Chicago), vol. 12, no. 2, 2000: 423-52.
9. Jocelyn Alexander and JoAnn McGregor, 'Wildlife and Politics: CAMP-FIRE in Zimbabwe', *Development and Change*, vol. 31, 2000: 605-27.
10. François Ekoko, 'Balancing Politics, Economics and Conservation: The Case of the Cameroon Forestry Law Reform', *Development and Change*, vol. 31, 2000: 131-54.
11. See Emile Lebris, ed., *L'Appropriation de la terre en Afrique noire*, Paris, Karthala, 1991; Etienne Leroy, ed., *La Sécurisation foncière en Afrique noire,. Pour une gestion viable des ressources renouvelables*, Paris: Karthala, 1996.
12. See Achille Mbembe, 'À propos des écritures africaines de soi', *Politique africaine* 77, 2000: 16-43.
13. See Njabulo S. Ndebele, 'Of Lions and Rabbits: Thoughts on Democracy and Reconciliation', *Pretexts: Literary and Cultural Studies*, vol. 8, no. 2, 1999: 147-58.
14. See the studies by Antoine Philippe et al., *Trois générations de citadins au Sahel. Trente ans d'histoire sociale à Dakar et à Bamako*, Paris: L'Harmattan, 1998; A.Philippe et al., *Les Familles dakaroises face à la crise*, Dakar: ORSTOM-IFAN-CEPED, 1995.
15. J.Bisillial, *Femmes du Sud, chefs de famille*, Paris: Karthala, 1996.
16. See the collection *The Art of African Fashion*, Trenton, NJ: Africa World Press, 1998.
17. Adam Ashforth, 'Weighing Manhood in Soweto', *CODESRIA Bulletin*, 3-4, 1999.
18. See S.Nuttall and C.A.Michael, eds, *Senses of Culture*, Cape Town: Oxford University Press, 2000.

MARIANE FERME
Staging *Politisi*
The Dialogics of Publicity & Secrecy in Sierra Leone

Reference

Comaroff, John L. and Jean Comaroff (eds) *Civil Society & the Political Imagination in Africa: Critical Perspectives* Chicago: University of Chicago Press, 1999, pp. 160-91

In this chapter, I explore the vicissitudes of postcolonial politics in Sierra Leone and their articulation within a public sphere, through an examination of elections that appeared to contradict their democratic potential. Sierra Leonean participants in the 1986 ballot considered the management of ambiguity and the coexistence of covert and public strategies to be central elements in electoral politics, and their ultimate goal was to build consensus through processes of consultation designed to eliminate public opposition. This, in the view of many participants, was the only viable avenue to a peaceful project of democratization. By contrast, the distinction between winners and losers at the ballot generated resentment, and hence the potential for violence. This feature of electoral politics in turn was linked in the local social imaginary to the historical development of the colonial and postcolonial nation-state.

An alternative logic of power to that of public debate and competition was at work, one of dissimulation. Individual success and political effectiveness were seen as being predicated on the ambiguous and sometimes illicit cohabitation with different powerful agencies. The ever-present possibility of politicians resorting to covert politics and the occult to attain power by unconventional means shaped how people decoded events in public, and made these very events unpredictable and potentially violent. The point here is not to romanticize an authentically 'African' political idiom of consensus building and ambiguous outcomes, or to minimize the violent elements embedded in these processes. On the contrary, autocratic Sierra Leonean regimes have appropriated this indigenous idiom of consensus in pursuit of their own ends, through the skillful manipulation of symbols rooted in local and regional history. In modern Sierra Leonean politics, the idiom of consensual 'hanging heads' (*ngu hitɛ* in Mende) articulated with that of competitive elections to create tension and ambiguity, and these together – not as dialectical stages alternating with peace and clarity – produced outcomes that were remarkably democratic in spirit, even under single-party rule.[1] The case I examine here underscores the different ways a society's membership can be counted, and count, at the ballot, and make a difference in a collective act of self-construction.

I also raise questions about the relationship between covert strategies and principles of publicity, transparency, and open rational debate, which are central to normative definitions of democratic processes and of the public sphere. For if a defining feature of the public sphere is its accessibility to the broadest possible spectrum of citizens, then its existence in the Sierra Leone case is beyond doubt – except that the conditions under which so many can participate in creating 'a public opinion' are that debates be as much secret as they are public, and that outcomes remain ambiguous. A central tenet to the continued existence of a public sphere in Sierra Leone is that its deliberations remain partly secret, especially when these deliberations concern the ballot, given the modem history of electoral abuses in the country. Only through the careful and sometimes unpredictable management of rumors of secret gatherings and strategies can the abuses of the electoral system be kept in cheek. At the same time, these covert strategies open the way to those very abuses. Both state agents and social actors opposed to them share a view of these shifting idioms and strategies of political culture, a complicity that has been identified as one of the defining features of postcolonial subjectivity under autocratic regimes in Africa (see Mbembe 1992). These shared terms of engagement further complicate the distinction between state and civil society – and the public sphere's mediating role between them – challenged by other contributors to this volume and by previous critical assessments of civil society in an African context (e.g., Harbeson, Rothchild, and Chazan 1994). An understanding of this complicity is at the heart of the African project of political modernity.

Public events in Sierra Leone must be seen in the context of polysemic symbols from the past, symbols whose open character makes them fundamentally appropriable for a variety of purposes. These events unfold on the terrain of a long history of earlier sedimentations. They are 'built on the ruins of earlier symbolic edifices and use their materials – even if it is only to fill the foundations of new temples, as the Athenians did after the Persian wars' (Castoriadis 1987, 121). In this patently pre-postmodern world, political actors inherit cultural forms that shape their practices and visions of a moral community, even when these are aimed specifically at subverting a particular legacy (in which case the past is often consciously addressed), or when this legacy is relatively unconscious and emergent.

It is indeed the practices that most explicitly link societies to their past, such as rituals, that also bear within them the 'experimental technology' necessary to make sense of, and respond to, novel and contradictory circumstances of modernity (Comaroff and Comaroff 1993, xxx). Thus, for example, Peter Geschiere (1995) has shown that 'traditional' Cameroonian witchcraft beliefs and practices – because they potentiate *both* individualistic accumulation and social leveling – have become a potent idiom in national politics. The intrinsic ambiguity of witchcraft mimics the opacity of the affairs of the Cameroonian state. However, the unprecedented speed and scale of modern forms of enrichment in Cameroon have tested the fluid limits of existing witchcraft idioms, and have warranted the introduction of new ways of operating in the domain of the occult, a domain in which the Cameroonian state itself has become an actor (Geschiere 1995, 157–62, chap. 5). Hence the need to analyze the ways in which existing cultural idioms may also be mobilized, and transformed, to articulate unbridgeable gaps between past and present, albeit in the guise of a mediation between them.

Public consensus, secret competition

In the rural Wunde chiefdom, the 1986 parliamentary elections were fraught with ambiguity and violence. These were widely perceived by participants to be common features of the political process in Sierra Leone at large. By contrast, the same elections were characterized by Western observers as among the least violent and the most 'democratic' of the post-independence period (Hayward and Kandeh 1987, 27); for social scientists, of course, the *absence* of physical coercion, the presence of rational debate, and the peaceful exercise of free individual choice are the hallmarks of liberal democratic forms of participation.

Habermas ([1962] 1989), for example, links democracy in Europe, and the displacement of the absolutist state, to the rise of a bourgeois public sphere and its cultural institutions (the theater, the literary salon, the café, and especially the press), in which communities of interest can negotiate their differences. For Habermas, the substitution of physical force – which he sees as a symptom of the irrational – with the force of discursive argument is central to the emergence of modern political forms. So, too, is the presence of public spaces and procedures for transacting different interests – such as eighteenth-century English parliamentary and press debates – after the secrecy that had characterized court politics (52). Indeed, Habermas perceives the potential demise of the bourgeois public sphere in the return to greater political secrecy in nineteenth- and twentieth-century European states, exemplified by the shift of deliberations and negotiations back to the restricted domains of ministerial cabinets and committees – while political institutions of the public sphere, such as parliament, were only left with a 'rubberstamping' role. This shift coincided with the transformation of public debate in the nineteenth century from an earlier focus on the *principle* of publicity, to the problem of the *enlargement* of the public sphere through electoral reform and the extension of the franchise beyond the property-owning, literate bourgeoisie (133).

From an anthropological perspective (e.g., Hann 1996; Rabo 1996; Spülbeck 1996), and especially from an Africanist one (e.g., Ekeh 1975; Woods 1999) Habermas's theory of political modernity appears partial and Eurocentric. The experience of colonialism, where European political and social institutions were applied in situations of racialized hierarchies of difference, often made 'the bourgeois legal fiction of citizenship ... a farce' (Chakrabarty 1992, 9). At best, it was a fiction applied to an emerging African urban bourgeoisie and not to the majority of rural 'native' subjects: 'civil society, in this sense, was presumed to be civilized society, from whose ranks the uncivilized were excluded.'[2] In Africa and elsewhere in the postcolonial world, the colonial state has left a bifurcated legacy, where a hybrid juxtaposition of direct and indirect rule separates urban citizens from rural subjects governed by 'native authorities' (Mamdani 1996, 16). More generally, indirect rule facilitated the practice by European and indigenous agents of the colonial state of 'straddling' between administration and business, between 'official duties and lucrative activities' (Bayart 1993, 70–71). The fusion of public and private spheres upon which these straddling practices were predicated has led to the privatization of many state functions in postcolonial Africa (Bayart 1993, 97–98). Indeed, an outright 'criminalization' of the state has occurred: police prey on the civilian population they are supposed to protect; financial institutions falsify the extent of their insolvency, and so on (Bayart, Ellis, and Hibou 1997).

While these developments in postcolonial Africa seem to contradict Habermas's normative definition of the public sphere, they have also produced critical spaces where 'public opinion' has taken shape, albeit in hybrid, covert forms.[3] Habermas himself saw in modern politics a return to covert, secretive practices, linked to the dramatic rise of the public sphere since the nineteenth century – a process marked by the growth of competing interests within the public sphere in such a way as to limit its critical role vis-à-vis the state; and, in the twentieth century, by a breakdown of the separation between the state and the institutions of civil society. Note that, for Habermas, it is the expansion of voting privileges, above all else, that enlarged and multiplied the institutions of the public sphere in the nineteenth century, and that dramatically limited their 'publicity'. At the same time, the separation between state, civil society, and the public sphere began to be redefined; the state took on 'private roles' (e.g. the oversight of social welfare), while societal institutions assumed statelike functions in the domain of economic activity

([1962] 1989, 142–60). These transformations, though, were not necessarily reflected in the public's continued self-image as a critical body – an image or fiction that, according to Habermas, was (and continues to be) an equally important element in the historical constitution of a public sphere. This is especially evident in the context of elections, which are at the core of participatory democracy and underpin the very idea of a free, transparent political society; party platforms, public debates, and critical press scrutiny are, after all, conventions that perpetuate 'the liberal fiction of a public sphere in civil society' (211).

In the Sierra Leonean instance examined here, this fiction was called into question, even when it was invoked. The rituals and events of the electoral process were not articulated through the contestation and debate that constitute the main 'periodic staging of a political public sphere' (Habermas [1962] 1989, 211). Rather, what was staged during the 1986 national ballot in Sierra Leone, and in others before it, was a performance of consensus and unity, which on the surface seemed inimical to democratic competition. Struggles for power and political argument did occur. But they took place elsewhere: in domains whose restricted access made them antithetical to those normally associated with institutions of the public sphere. Political debates straddled public and secret settings, but the general awareness that this was the case makes possible an argument that a public opinion of sorts was nonetheless being formed, one whose straddling techniques – in the interest of avoiding violence – owed its origins to the violent, alien logic of 'outvoting'. Like other intergroup negotiations,

> voting, too, is a projection of real forces and of their proportions upon the plane of intellectuality; it anticipates, in an abstract symbol, the result of concrete battle and coercion. This symbol, at least, does represent the real power relations and the enforced subordination which they impose on the minority. (Simmel 1950, 242)

The electoral process might be an ill-adapted, alien political institution in Sierra Leone. And its introduction here may have been deformed by the single-party state. Yet, as its outcome suggests, the 1986 ballot produced unexpected results that seemed, indeed, to coincide with the will of the majority.[4] Where they occurred, public displays of consensus were usually framed *both* in the idiom of traditional political culture and as shared values of modern national politics. Some rural people questioned the part played by competition in elections and decried the relationship between public and secret politics. But they saw them as an inevitable aspect of *politisi*, of national electoral politics, and of the violence engendered by this process.

The General Election of 1986: Kpuawala

The 1986 general elections were held a few months after the installation of a new president, Maj. Gen. J. S. Momoh, to succeed Siaka Stevens. At the time, the peaceful transition from the aging Stevens – who had led the country for most of its post-independence years – to his handpicked successor was hailed by the international media and by political observers as a rare event in Africa. All the more so because political and economic life in Sierra Leone was at a particularly low point. Hopes for real change were reflected in the high percentage of contested seats in this ballot – 90 percent compared to about 71 percent in 1982 – the first held after the declaration of a single-party state under the All Peoples' Congress (APC) in 1978 (Hayward and Kandeh 1987, 36). The electoral campaign and vote canvassing, the process of finalizing candidate lists, the elections, and their outcome were fraught with anxiety and ambivalence in the rural village of Kpuawala (see Ferme 1992, 66–82).

In addition to the public appearances and speeches made by politicians and their supporters at regular intervals, another kind of politicking was at work: in secretive, nocturnal conclaves. Initially these two domains existed in parallel to each other, the one shadowing the other. Open gatherings in the central communal spaces during daytime hours were followed by night-time meetings known to only a few. These were held inside darkened houses or in the secluded forest enclosures of the men's Poro society; open, verbal allegiance to a candidate was often followed by private avowals of support to his opponent. Occasionally, however, the articulation of these different arenas became apparent through unexpected circumstances, highlighting the implicit connections between them.

The ambivalence about the elections among village people in Kpuawala was brought on, in part, by the configuration of a particular struggle. The incumbent member of Parliament (M.P.) for the area, who was the paramount chief's (P.C.'s) brother and a Freetown physician, was challenged by the brother of the local section chief. In Sierra Leone, rural villages and hamlets are grouped into sections, several of which make up a chiefdom, and each of these nesting administrative units are represented by a chief and his or her speaker, in addition to select elders. In sparsely populated rural areas, a political constituency may encompass multiple chiefdoms. Here, in Bo South I, it included two: Wunde and Jaiama-Bongor. The candidates, however, came from the same chiefdom, Wunde, and, in fact, from neighboring sections and communities. Kpuawala was roughly equidistant from the chiefdom and section headquarters that were, respectively, to be identified with the opposing contestants. As a result, it would be caught in the middle.

Both candidates had close, overlapping kinship and social ties to all communities in Wunde. The challenger was a civil servant in the chiefdom administration known as 'V.J.' (for Vandi Jimmy, his surname). He had been begged not to run against Dr Dabo, the P.C.'s brother, who was his elder. This happened at a public meeting in early February 1986, when leaders and representatives of the chiefdom were called ostensibly to discuss the implementation of a national price regulation program. The introductory speech was given by the central chiefdom administration clerk, who stressed 'our' need to 'make sacrifices' in accepting price reductions and in resisting the temptation to hoard goods. 'We,' he told the audience, 'are the government.' This speech was delivered in English and translated simultaneously into Mende for the benefit of a member of the national press who had accompanied Dr Dabo from Freetown to follow his campaign. The imprecise rendering of expressions such as 'making sacrifices' with *saa gbua* (the vernacular term for ritual sacrifices of food and animals) must have given a somewhat surreal quality to the discussion of price controls and international loans. In any event the assembled audience seemed not to pay much attention to the official speeches. It only perked up when the list of commodities and prices was introduced. After having reached an agreement on a uniform price list for locally produced goods, the gathering turned to other political matters.

Visiting dignitaries were introduced. These included B. A. Foday Kai, the elderly but energetic paramount chief from Jaiama-Bongor, the other chiefdom in the constituency. Foday Kai was also a figure of national renown and a member of the APC's central committee, and was thus asked to chair the proceedings.[5] On this occasion, he wore his usual attire: blue jeans with a 'Pierre Cardin' belt, a 'Wisconsin' T-shirt emblazoned with his own initials, a 'Miller Beer' baseball cap, and thick prescription spectacles. The chain-smoking Foday Kai cut a very different figure from the Wunde P.C., whose long, white robe, round skullcap, and abstention from smoke and drink identified him as a 'praying', or practicing, Muslim. However, Foday Kai also had a leather whip casually draped around his neck, a traditional marker of Mende chiefship that complicated his cosmopolitan appearance. This blend of imported and locally manufactured commodities, of new and old, and of cosmopolitan fashion and the historic symbols of indigenous rule underscored Foday Kai's carefully crafted identity as a cultural broker. Widely respected for his knowledge of Mende tradition and his interest in and patronage of vernacular arts and crafts, he was consulted in matters relating to local culture and history by rural people as well as by foreigners and urban Sierra Leoneans.[6] His roles as paramount chief and a member of the APC's central committee, as native ruler, and as one of a handful of chiefly representatives on the national scene extended his brokerage skills into the political domain as well. Foday Kai was a powerful reminder of the integral role played by 'traditional' rulers in modern African politics, especially in bridging the gap between state and civil societal institutions, between democratic and lineage politics (whose idiom he always employed).

The political meeting had begun with a cheering drill, orchestrated from the dais by men wearing matching white trousers and red caps. These men incited the crowd to shout each letter of the ruling APC party logo, followed by slogans about unity The attire of these cheerleaders, later referred to by Dr Dabo as his 'Unity Force,' corresponded to the party's flag, or 'symbol,' a red rising sun against a white background. Their opening ritual set the stage for the official proceedings, situating them within the purview of the ruling national party. Then there was an announcement that the educated descendants of the chiefdom – those who had migrated to urban areas or abroad and who held white-collar jobs – had formed the 'Sewa Descendants Association', which recently had met in Bo, the provincial headquarters.

At that gathering, they had discussed the upcoming parliamentary elections. Their secretary had told those present that two men had expressed a desire to run: the incumbent, Dr Dabo, and V.J., the section chief's brother, who was a government clerk in the neighboring Sherbro district. The meeting was not able to reach a consensus on a single candidate to support, nor could it manage to convince either one to drop out of the race; so it decided to put the matter to the constituency itself. Members of the association in the audience, which included professionals, civil servants, and businessmen, were identified by their T-shirts silkscreened with the organization's acronym which had been sent by a chapter in the United States. The composition of such associations in Sierra Leone further confuses the division between the state and civil society, and emphasizes the increasing importance in political processes at home of the wealthier and better educated expatriates in Europe and the United States. In the wake of the hardships brought about by previous economic policies, the financial support given by these foreign groups to the grass roots, and the networks they have established, has made them an important factor in constituting a transnational civil society.[7]

Following the announcement about the association, and its earlier meeting, V.J., the challenger, made a theatrical, late entry, conspicuously taking up a position with his followers at the back of the audience. By contrast, Dr Dabo, the incumbent, was seated on the dais in front of the assembly, with the other dignitaries – many of whom were his relatives. P.C. Foday Kai stood up and spoke forcefully, saying that he disliked the gossip and the vicious rumors

($sɔlɛ$, literally 'noise') that might be generated by a contested election. He expressed fears about the infighting to which it would lead. It would have been bad enough if the candidates had been from two different chiefdoms in the constituency. But with both coming from nearby areas of Wunde, there was sure to be trouble. Foday Kai asked the interested parties and their supporters to 'hang heads' ($ngu\ hitɛi$): to engage in consultations until they reached 'one voice', or unity ($ngo\ yila$), and agreed on a candidate.

In making this request, Foday Kai was not merely rejecting competitive electoral politics out of a regressive attachment to tradition. He was affirming a principle central to single-party rule in Sierra Leone since 1978; the principle that also underlay the ritual display of unity at the start of the meeting. The move away from a multi-party constitution had been justified on the ground that it was inconsistent with the consensus building implied in the customary practice of 'hanging heads.' This, President Siaka Stevens had argued at the time, was a more 'African' approach to the democratic process and would prevent the widespread violence and corruption that had characterized earlier elections (see Kpundeh 1995; Reno 1995, 66; Scott 1960, 187; Zack-Williams 1989, 125). Significantly, he had called a referendum to pass the constitutional change, to show that the process of transition had itself been consensual; that hanging heads had occurred on a national scale (see Hayward and Dumbuya 1983, 663–64). With this creative reading of 'tradition,' Stevens and his supporters implied – as other Africans have done – that democratization might be better served by being grounded in vernacular political styles, rather than in liberal theories without local resonances (see Haugerud 1995; Karlström 1996). But this modern appropriation of hanging heads could also be seen as anti-democratic: its fundamental premise, to enable participation in decision-making processes in a relatively egalitarian setting, was easily subverted by exclusionary strategies aimed at eliminating threatening political opponents. Simply put, Stevens had appealed to consensus politics as a preliminary step toward instituting a single-party state, because his APC party had barely won the 1977 elections. During that ballot, the APC's strong-arm tactics against candidates of the largely Mende-based Sierra Leone People's Party (SLPP) had gained the latter considerable popular sympathy. As a result, many believed that the SLPP would have won in future contests (see Hayward and Dumbuya 1983, 663). More immediately, in Kpuawala in 1986, the paramount chief sought to achieve an uncontested election by building on a modern use of his own role in politics; from the very first elections at the eve of independence, in 1957, local rulers used the strategy of 'hanging heads' to run unopposed in their own local ballots and to support their favorite candidates on the national stage (Scott 1960, 185–87).

Unlike those early, uncompetitive elections, the move now to 'hang heads' in search of consensus, and the fears expressed by Foday Kai of the consequences of a contested race, belied the very high percentage of contested seats fought in all Sierra Leonean elections since independence. Indeed, Foday Kai's concern may have been prompted by a recent ballot closer to home: in 1982, in the neighboring Pujehun district, the division of the constituency between two candidates from the same area resulted in unprecedented violence, deaths, destroyed property, and the burning of entire villages (see Kandeh 1992, 96; Hayward and Dumbuya 1985, 80–81). Many refugees from those events were now living in Wunde and were among Foday Kai's audience. Thus the search for consensus in this setting might be read both as a response, by the APC leadership, to recent experiences of similar electoral contests *and* as an evocation of an older, more encompassing political culture. Local political practices always carry a multiplicity of meanings and symbolic articulations.

After Foday Kai, virtually every one of the dignitaries from his chiefdom gave speeches openly supporting Dr Dabo, even though some used ambiguous language suggesting that they did not oppose the challenger either. In following their P.C., these speakers exemplified exactly the consensus they were trying to elicit from the two candidates. They intimated that having an open contest would be embarrassing, and that it would be a disgrace if the matter could not be settled 'in the chiefdom family'. The reference to family immediately triggered a response from V.J.'s close relatives. They protested against the assumption that they had encouraged him to stand. The audience around Alhaji Vandy Jimmy, V.J.'s brother and the local section chief, murmured in agreement; it was well-known to them that the latter had tried to 'sweet talk' his brother out of running (*i ngi ma nɛnɛa*). The very fact that Alhaji Vandy Jimmy – to whom no direct reference was made – presumed that he was being called into question is itself instructive. It suggests that political speech is always thought to comprise multiple, often concealed messages. The exchange offered a glimpse into that other, less visible domain of politics, as Chief Vandy Jimmy articulated what would normally have remained unsaid in public. At that point, various friends of the challenger scrambled to chronicle their efforts to dissuade him from his candidacy – acknowledging, in effect, that the hanging heads process had not succeeded at that level.

All through this discussion, V.J. stood in stone-faced silence on the margins of the gathering, conspicuously unaffected by efforts to provoke his participation. Then he was asked again, in front of everyone, if he still intended to run. He replied in the affirmative. This gesture indicated his unwillingness to go along with what was in effect a performance. Recall that the meeting had begun with a theatrical cheering session, a ritual expression of unity; also, the protestation of the section chief, which suggested that real political negotiations ought to be concealed, never more than partially enacted in public. English, a language well understood by only a handful of the audience's members, was used earlier in the meeting, which added to the notion that substantive deliberations were a secondary aspect in this kind of open political gathering. Indeed, the proper domain for hanging heads and reaching consensus here is never the public arena, whose oppositional, competitive dynamics underscores the authoritarian logic of 'open,' rational debate. With his statue-like posture and his refusal to be drawn into the discussion, V.J. underscored the staged character of these proceedings, whose sparrings were a mere *overture* to both the electoral campaign and the negotiations characteristic of any political process (see Murphy 1990). The tension was palpable, until the P.C. changed the subject with a formal speech that made no reference to what had just transpired.

This last intervention signaled a shift. Negotiations over the issue of political elections would now move to another register, away from the public domain to the parlors and backrooms of village compounds. Accordingly, the gathering adjourned. Later, young men discussing the day's events in Kpuawala seemed quite skeptical of the public expression of support for the incumbent: 'That's what they said, but who knows what is in their hearts?' They speculated that the backing for V.J. was much greater than was apparent – even if he was a newcomer with relatively few patronage networks in the area. Some criticized the M.P. for never having set foot in the villages of his constituency since his election; his rare visits had been confined to the chiefdom headquarters. They pointed out that his challenger had built a beautiful, modern cement house in his hometown (the most attractive house in the community), and took this to indicate that he would

spend more time locally than his opponent did. Eventually, however, it was announced that the two candidates had come to an agreement. V.J. had withdrawn from the race.

The (Body) Politics of Ambiguity

V.J.'s change of mind turned out not to have been, in Mende terms, a change of heart. Nor had most people thought so. In the days following the February meeting, casual conversations in the village turned to the dangers of *politisi*, and to the 'bad medicine' (*hale nyamui*, also 'unattractive, ugly') often deployed to acquire power and wealth. One man remembered a court case in the neighboring chiefdom some years before; he described the metal claws found on an alleged member of the leopard medicine society indicted for murder. Members of this society and a handful of other banned secret cults were thought to mimic the attack techniques of wild animals to procure human bodies, whose parts were used to make amulets or substances that endowed their wearers or consumers with special capacities (Kalous 1974; Richards 1996a, 143–45). Women and children were said to be the most common victims of bad medicine, as they were easier prey. The covert manner in which these substances were thought to work under ordinary clothes and appearances was analogous to the way in which political speech was assumed to evoke hidden meanings and to project its significance to the outside world. When politicians or performers displayed unusual oratorical skills, when they seemed particularly charming and persuasive, Kpuawala bystanders often wondered what made them so attractive. Jokes about things hidden under clothes or inside bellies revealed the preoccupation with potency medicines, and brought the issue of bodily substance to the forefront of their evaluation of people.

Beyond the practices they address, such public discussions of bad medicine have political effects as well. Rumors, suspicions, accusations, and denials of witchcraft activities in the national media as well as village gossip circuits are the discursive extensions of power medicine's strategic, concealed deployment. Politicians enhance their reputations by circulating rumors of their own occult powers, while attempting to undermine their rivals with suspicions of consorting with much worse concealed agencies (see MacCormack 1983); public accusations of involvement in bad medicine may trigger reactions of horror and fear toward the accused, but they also add to their power, especially when there is no evidence with which to prosecute in a court of law.

Not a week had passed after the February political meeting when it was rumored that V.J. was again a candidate. According to local gossip, as soon as the gathering had ended, the Jaiama-Bongor people who had publicly opposed V.J.'s candidacy had written to his brother, the section chief, declaring their secret support. Those who reported this rumor found nothing strange in this shift from a vocal public stance against somebody to surreptitious support for him – or vice versa. The backing for Dabo at a meeting of all the constituency notables, where even the national press had been present, was thus countered by a personal letter to V.J.'s brother; what is more, the latter was seen to reflect real loyalties more than the former. This domain of concealed actions and relations carried greater weight than did the open debate of political meetings.

The months leading up to the May ballot saw visits from both candidates and their supporters, who extolled the virtues of their man and the shortcomings of his opponent. At one point, V.J. reported the P.C. to the national electoral commission in Freetown for publicly backing his own brother and intimidating his subjects, instead of

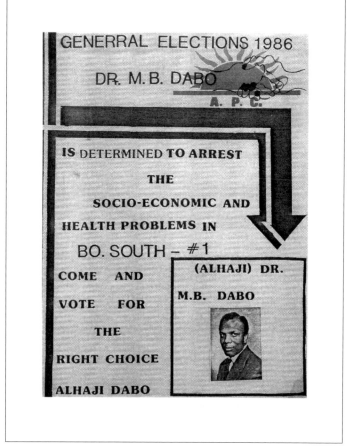

Fig. 1 Incumbent M.P. (Alhaji) Dr Dabo candidate poster.
Bo South I constituency general elections, 1986.

Fig. 2 Challenger Vandi Jimmy (V.J.) candidate poster.
Bo South I constituency general elections, 1986.

keeping out of the campaign. V.J. also mentioned being harassed by his opponent's allies when he went to Freetown to collect the party 'symbol' that was necessary to stand in the election, and which would grace official candidate posters (see Figures 1 and 2). Supporters of each side gave speeches saying that people should follow their hearts in 'dropping the paper,' in voting (*a wu kɔlɔ gula wu li woma*), but then tried to turn those hearts in a particular direction through gifts of cash, food, and even drugs. On one occasion, a group of young men said that V.J. had brought a big bag of *jamba* (marijuana) for his followers. This substance was consumed mostly by young men, who made up the bands of escorts/thugs that protected the candidates and threatened their adversaries. V.J. courted this constituency most openly, thus reinforcing his image as the candidate for change and youth and against the status quo. In this aspect, this political struggle conformed to a generational conflict evident throughout Africa (e.g., Hutchinson 1996; Marchal 1993; Richards 1995, 1996b).

In addition to its formal public appearances, each camp held unannounced, 'secret' meetings. One April day, I dropped by without advance warning at the section chief's house and found him surrounded by local notables and Kpuawala men, who were obviously embarrassed to be seen with him. Among those eating at his table were some of the most eloquent supporters of his brother's political opponent. Like the Jaiama-Bongor elders, these people seemed to be backing one candidate in public and another in private. Turning surprise to advantage, the section chief approached the man accompanying me – a known follower of his brother's opponent and a brother-in-law of the P.C. – and began 'sweet-talking' him into changing his mind. In a context in which it was assumed that loyalties were often multiple and dissimulated, and where special attributes were thought to endow political figures with irresistible powers of persuasion, it was always worthwhile to sow the seeds of alliance. And, concomitantly, to court *all* potential voters.

Courting the voter is characteristic of democratic elections, where the undecided, who lack a strong commitment to any side, may determine the outcome. In Kpuawala voters are courted for a different reason: because an eloquent campaigner, aided by concealed powers, can always entice followers with *multiple* loyalties to turn – if only long enough to effect the desired result. The notion that unusual personal attributes, or persuasive ways, can alter political balances at any time also suggests that political contests remain undecided until the last.

When sweet talking was not enough, more or less open threats of action followed. A group of elders from the chiefdom headquarters visited Kpuawala in May to beg the gathered community to vote for the incumbent. Insisting that they had come at their own initiative, without the P.C.'s knowledge, they at first repeated the familiar litany that they were not there to campaign and that everyone should vote according to their hearts. But, on two separate occasions during the meeting, speakers reminded the audience that votes would be counted by village. It would be obvious, therefore, whether they had 'followed' Dr Dabo or V.J. This thinly veiled threat was also one of the few open acknowledgements that despite public declarations, the M.P.'s backers were aware that secret machinations might be afoot to put an end to his long political career.

The candidates' platforms shared common elements: both Dr Dabo and V.J. focused on 'development', on the benefits that would accrue to their constituencies from their election, and on their kinship ties to the chiefdom. But significant contrasts were apparent as well. The two men could not have been more different, nor could the symbolism invoked by them. While they both ran under the same party icon, a red rising sun, each had a distinctive set of allegiances to its colors. The incumbent belonged to the country's educated elite: a European-trained physician who had spent many years abroad, he had a private practice in Freetown and traveled upcountry in a Mercedes. His electoral poster portrayed him in suit and necktie (Figure 1). His pilgrimage to Mecca had also earned him the title of *Alhaji*, but this was bracketed in his poster, which privileged the 'Dr'. Nonetheless, Dr Dabo's Muslim identity helped bridge the distance between his European education and his political reliance on the religious rural leadership in the constituency.

Despite the kinship rhetoric in Dr Dabo's speech and his appeal to a common Muslim faith, he remained for many constituents a distant, foreign relative. Much was made by his opponents of the fact that he did not own a house in the chiefdom or spend much time there; also that his family was of Mandingo origin, from neighboring Guinée. Dr Dabo's speeches emphasized the public works projects he had steered toward the chiefdom, but whispered comments from the audience suggested that, by living in the capital, he distanced himself from his constituency. A story circulated about how, when the local men had helped clear a large farm for the M.P. after his previous election, they were fed 'white people's food' – sweets and finger food instead of the customary rice meal – and had left hungry.

By contrast, his opponent was said always to feed people generous meals when they assisted him in major farming tasks. 'At least with V.J. we will eat rice and fill our stomachs', declaimed his supporters. In his campaign, the challenger exploited the rich political symbolism of his populist appeal to earthiness and full stomachs. V.J. also capitalized on the fact that he had not received a sophisticated education, or traveled abroad. He labeled himself a 'son of the soil,' whose closeness to his homeland and its problems was demonstrated by his having built a house there (Figure 2). Another strand of V.J.'s strategy to claim the higher moral ground was in the very domain of religious symbolism in which the opposing camp appeared to have its most solid credentials. In contrast with the urban, professional attire of Dr Dabo in his campaign poster, V.J. chose to be portrayed in the white gown worn by the P.C, and all other local Muslim clerics.[8] His followers presented him as a candidate for change, one who would spend more time locally than his opponent ever did. As evidence, they stressed the difference between V.J.'s section chief brother, who worked on his farm every day, and the paramount chief, who 'stayed in town'. While Dr Dabo's identification with the APC regime was brought home by the constant presence of an escort wearing the party logo and chanting its 'unity' routines, V.J.'s campaign bore no such markers; to wit, his distance from the ruling party took on even more radical overtones as events unfolded.

The campaign came to a fever pitch with the approach of the elections in May, and the fear of slander and violence in local communities increased apace. People from the neighboring chiefdoms – where the 1982 elections had been marked by assault and destruction – had begun to arrive over the preceding weeks. Carrying their possessions and settling in with local friends and relatives, they hoped to avoid the worst political turmoil. It was said that at times like these, such places as Kpuawala, being in the 'bush,' were far safer than the big towns.

The isolation of these bush communities was not accidental. The work to maintain roads and bridges within the chiefdom was scheduled by the P.C. and local authorities, and depended on voluntary cooperation. Thus one of the ways in which political sympathies in the various areas could be gauged at election time was through the willingness of people to participate in such communal labor. For a long time now, the palm log bridges and paths leading to Kpuawala had been left to deteriorate, and things were getting worse with the onset of the rains. Residents complained about the state of the road every time a vehicle tried to get through. But no effort was made to clear the vegetation engulfing it, I was told, in order to limit the risk of thugs coming in from outside to cause trouble. Kpuawala, in short, had deliberately pushed itself farther into the bush through the strategic neglect of road maintenance. This tactic also bespoke the political factionalism that divided the chiefdom, cutting off the village, now increasingly opposed to Dr Dabo, from the P.C. and his headquarters, which had come to be identified with the incumbent.

Three days before the elections, two rotting bridges were finally repaired so that a vehicle carrying the electoral commission and ballot boxes could get through. The voters' roll was wildly inaccurate. It included over twice the number of people recorded by the national census five months earlier. No attempt was made to update the lists by dropping duplicate entries and by deleting the names of the deceased and departed or by registering immigrants and those too young to vote at previous elections. As before (see Scott 1960, 197–200, 245–51), the lists were treated as inviolable documents. As a result, several young men and women were not mentioned in the roll call preceding election day. After some objection, the commissioner said that people on the list who were still in Kpuawala would vote first; those not on it could do so later.

Election day saw people converge on Kpuawala from the four other communities that were to vote at this polling station. Crowding around the meeting place where their names were read, voters received a blue marble and had their fingers marked in green to prevent them from casting more than one ballot. They went alone to a nearby house, where two boxes were placed. Each was marked by a photographic portrait of a candidate, and voters were instructed to drop the marble into the box of their choice. Nobody left the village for the whole day. Despite these arrangements, which were intended to guarantee the secrecy considered crucial to 'free and fair elections' – and the fact that nobody openly discussed their ballots – everyone seemed to assume that voting preferences would be known to the opposing camp. When asked how this could happen, people said that there were ways in which what went on inside the closed room could be ascertained. Some seemed particularly uneasy about having the candidates' portraits looking on. These pictures were alluded to as indexical symbols of the human beings they represented, rather than being neutral icons to differentiate ballot boxes.

At the end of the day, when the polls closed, the electoral commissioners were besieged by complaints about irregularities; some people even refused to let them leave with the ballot boxes. After arguments and physical struggles, they were allowed to depart in a vehicle sent to fetch them – but with an escort of young male leaders who went along to register their objections and to prevent further irregularities. The following two days were spent in almost unbearable anticipation of the results, and hardly anyone went off to their fields. Slanderous speculation began even as we were waiting, when one local man said loudly – to nobody in particular – that, if V.J. won, the Kpuawala chief was sure to be replaced; that nobody would ever listen to him or respect him again. This chief had never wavered in his support of the M.P., whose brother, the paramount chief, was his son-in-law.

Finally, at daybreak on 2 June, the third day after the elections, the arrival of a crowd of shouting people from the path to the section headquarters made plain that V.J. had won. Most of the community broke into song and dance. The losing M.P.'s most prominent supporters were slandered – including the village chief. Piles of palm branches were left in front of his house – the first public display of a different party symbol in a supposedly single party election. The palm tree had been the symbol of the Sierra Leone People's Party (SLPP), which had led the government in the pre- and post-independence years, and had then been the APC's main opposition until its suppression (discussed in the following section). The crowd intoned a song addressing the local chief by his first name rather than the respectful *maada* ('grandfather') and the Dabo surname, and he was told that he was now an 'ordinary person' and would soon be replaced. The song went on to say the same of the paramount chief; also that a new chief would sit in Wunde. This was a play both on the word for chief (*mahei*, 'he who sits upon') and on the fact that Wunde is, at once, the name of the chiefdom and the name of the particular village where V.J. was from and where his brother lived. The implication was that the section chief was being put forth as a likely successor to the P.C. Other local people were accused of having acted as spies for Dr Dabo's campaign during the preceding months, and they were beaten or driven out of town over the following days. The same happened in neighboring communities.

Later, a large crowd gathered in the section chief's village to celebrate his brother's victory. His compound was surrounded by palm tree branches planted in the ground, and palm fruits were hung on strings from the eaves of his house. The section chief proclaimed, publicly, that palm trees had been the source of his wealth, adding: 'This is where I found money for my brother's campaign. The Dabos are rich [from diamonds and trade and politics], but [palm] oil is what made *me* rich.'[9] People ate and collected the palm fruits throughout the day. One Kpuawala man came back from the celebration proudly displaying what by his own reckoning were 150 palm fruits: he said that he would plant them and begin his own palm tree nursery. Thus it was that palm fruits, the symbol and instrument of V.J.'s election, became a tangible expression of political and economic patronage, helping others to reproduce wealth elsewhere.

Palm trees against the sunset: political symbols and their transformation

Alhaji Vandy Jimmy's victorious display of palm leaves and fruits was more than a celebration of hard work and honestly gained wealth. It also tapped into political symbolism with deep historical roots in Mendeland. The palm tree, as I mentioned, was the symbol of the

illegal, mostly Mende-based Sierra Leone People's Party (SLPP), which dominated the national scene from before independence to 1969, when it became the opposition. During the 1973 general elections, the SLPP was marginalized by the APC; it was formally outlawed with the establishment of single-party rule five years later. Thus Alhaji's celebratory display could also be interpreted as an assertive resuscitation of the SLPP, as a challenge to the process of 'hanging heads' associated with decades of oppressive APC rule, and as a rejection of the leadership of the likes of Dr Dabo. Indeed, V.J.'s campaign, beginning with his defiant stance at the margins of the APC-dominated meeting in February, might be read as the symbolic reenactment of a suppressed oppositional politics, appealing specifically to Mende ethnicity.

The periodic evocation of ethnic sentiment has been an increasingly common feature of modern party politics in Sierra Leone (Kandeh 1999) and elsewhere in Africa. In particular, it has been linked to political dynamics in single-party states, where ethnicity 'became the home of the opposition' in the absence of other unifying factors such as a developed class consciousness (Vail 1989, 2). Ironically, oppositional ethnic politics have been exacerbated by calls in the early 1990s for multi-party elections across Africa on the part of international donors (e.g., Moore 1996, 589–92).[10]

In sum, the 'son of the soil' rhetoric accompanying that display of palm leaves went beyond a generic opposition against the foreign values and cosmopolitan lifestyle of Dr Dabo, whose wealth was based both on professional and political activities and on family mercantile enterprises. It also had a more specific link to modern party politics in Sierra Leone, pointing toward the emergence of an opposition. In addition, the image of V.J.'s generously nurturing roots in Mendeland invoked a specific local history. Among the claims made by some of his relatives was that they were 'warriors' descended from the legendary Ndawa of Wunde, founder of their village. A century earlier, Ndawa had led a blockade against the coastward transport of commodities on demand by European merchants – a move that resulted in the intervention of British colonial authorities (Abraham 1978, 37, 85; Fyfe 1962, 483).[11] Their connections to a lineage of landowners and warriors was contrasted with the alien origin of Dr Dabo and his brother, the P.C. It was pointed out that being tall and fair, the Dabo family even *looked* different from real Mende, and still spoke among themselves the Manding language of their Guinée homeland, which none of the local villagers could understand.

The palm leaf also carried another yet deeper historical significance in this Mende setting. It was said to have been the signal sent among communities by leaders of Poro, the men's secret society, to organize a rebellion against the imposition of taxes, in 1898, in the Sierra Leone Protectorate (Abraham 1978, 159; Chalmers 1899). Thus its association with unity and consensus went back a long way, much longer than the red-and-white 'Unity Force' of the APC. By appropriating this symbol to express discontent with the government, V.J.'s supporters recast their victory as continuous with those century-old events. The secret role of Poro and other esoteric societies in orchestrating political outcomes has long been a preoccupation in modern Sierra Leone (e.g., Cohen 1981; Kilson 1966; Little 1965, 1966; Scott 1960, 174); this was underscored in a comment made by a still-furious Dr Dabo several months later. After referring to the palm leaves, he said that the election turnout had been secretly arranged by the Poro initiation chapters in the villages of the chiefdom. '*They* kept on meeting in the bush,' he said, and promised that this was not the end of the story. His meaning was clear: he, too, had recourse to covert ways of getting even.

Of bees, warriors, and politics by other means

The official vote count in the Bo South I constituency was reported in Kpuawala a few days after the ballot. A representative from the electoral commission toured the chiefdom villages accompanied by the P.C.'s messenger, and posted a typed copy of the vote breakdown by polling station near the main meeting places (see the Appendix to this chapter). V.J. had won a majority of votes in all polling stations of both Wunde and Jaiama-Bongor chiefdoms, with the exception of the headquarter towns, Gboyama and Telu, and of P.C. Foday Kai's hometown of Bendu. In other words, despite the ambiguity surrounding Chief Foday Kai's political loyalties, and his followers' covert support for V.J., both P.C.s and their closest allies ended up backing the incumbent candidate. This outcome underscores the strategic linkages between traditional authorities and politicians at the national level in modern Sierra Leone. The profile of the two candidates in this election suggests why this is the case: there is no fundamental discontinuity between these two kinds of political elites, their formation, and the sites they inhabit. Within the same family, close brothers may hold 'traditional' or national political office, or, as in the case of P.C. Foday Kai both at the same time. Though the continuity between 'traditional' and modern educated elites has been seen to be especially strong in postcolonial Sierra Leone (see Bayart 1993, 148; Kilson 1966, 71–79), and their political alliances a feature of single-party states elsewhere in Africa, this linkage also owes much to the institutional legacy of the colonial state and its role in shaping 'native authorities' (see Geschiere 1995; Mamdani 1996, 16–23). In particular, Mamdani has seen a major obstacle to the development of a modern African civil society in the racist exclusion of rural peoples from full citizenship in the colonial state, and their subjection to traditional authorities and 'customary' laws that differed from the citizenship rights of urban dwellers. However, this chapter points to a more optimistic future for civil society, given that in practice the same social actors can straddle the two domains of traditional and national politics, and of rural and urban locations.

During the weeks between the elections and the inaugural celebrations for the new M.P. on 15 July, supporters of Dr Dabo, relatives of the paramount chief, and local authorities were harassed, insulted, and threatened. Some relocated to the chiefdom headquarters, which had become isolated from all other communities despite its prominent location on the main road. Bush paths and back roads connecting villages suddenly came alive with travelers, thus opening up an alternative geography – one previously concealed – to that associated with the out-of-favor regime. On inauguration day itself, the 'unity' conveyed by the uniform attire of the crowd – *ashɔbis*, clothes made especially for the occasion from a single fabric pattern – belied the uneasiness of the new M.P.'s followers. They were less than delighted to hold the festivities, according to protocol, at the political center of the chiefdom, right 'at the feet' of the losing M.P.'s constituency; many of them stayed away. But a large gathering, with masked dancers and a variety of other entertainments, took place anyway. As was customary, these were accompanied by licentious language and political and social satire.[12] Chiefdom officials and visiting dignitaries spoke about mending old enmities and forgiving each other, to general applause and vigorous nodding in the audience. But, at the high point of the festivities, a war dance was performed by P.C. Foday Kai and some of the elders. On this, his first visit to the chiefdom since the February meeting, Foday Kai put aside his jeans and baseball cap. Along with his cohort, he wore 'traditional' warrior garb: a rust-colored, kolanut-dyed tunic, breeches, and a cap made from strip-woven local cotton, on which were sewn amulets and animal horns filled with protective medicines. In this attire, the handful of elders performed one of the carefully choreographed dances for which Foday Kai was known, waving swords over their heads and staging mock duels.

Although intended as a form of celebratory entertainment, this dance seemed to speak of political battles of another time and kind, and to relate them to the contest just concluded. In the event, the dancing warriors' protective garb was put to the test not by bullets or blades, but by a swarm of dangerous killer bees, which suddenly descended on the crowd in the midst of this performance. In a few minutes, the village's open spaces were deserted as people ran shouting in all directions, shutting doors and windows behind themselves. Amid the eerie silence, the only sound was the drone of insects and the running engine of a single abandoned car: its doors were open and its white interior was alive with bees.

One of the paramount chief's brothers said that the bees must have been nesting in the roof of a an abandoned kiosk nearby, a building whose fading sign read 'Post Office'. Perhaps it was fitting that the bees had chosen this site. It stood as a reminder of the collapse of state services and of the severed communication links between outlying rural areas, the country's urban centers, and the world beyond. The man argued, quite reasonably, that the commotion from the unusually large crowd must have disturbed the nest. His sister, however, seemed skeptical of this explanation. Eventually the swarm began to lift and people emerged from hiding, many with multiple stings on their bodies. Visitors were anxious to get away as fast as possible. Few doubted that this attack had been the work of witches (*hɔnabla*), unleashed by vengeful, disappointed Dabo supporters.

'*Hɔnabla mia a tie, kpɛlɛ!*' 'They are all witches!' one woman said excitedly, adding that she just *knew* she should have stayed away. An alternative gathering was held in the new M.P.'s hometown, where the main topic of songs, speeches, jokes, and other performances was the bee attack, whose meaning was interpreted with variable degrees of explicitness. All along, most people seemed to think, there had been intentions other than reconciliation in the minds of the P.C., the losing candidate, and their supporters. They had tricked people into coming to their territory, only to unleash their evil medicines on them, even to try and kill them. Thus the unpredictable, terrifying bee attack that put an end to the 'celebration' hosted by the losing candidate's brother spawned an open discussion about the relationship between public and secret political practices. Among its recurring themes was the impossibility that the losing party would accept the results. This followed the assumption that it was driven by witchcraft. But the violence was also seen as an inevitable consequence of electoral politics in general, a process that produced winners and losers rather than consensus through negotiation.

Because it played into a long history of oppositions, and called upon powerful symbols, the conflict continued for a long time after the elections. Seven months later, when I left Sierra Leone, followers and relatives of the P.C. and Dr Dabo were still being harassed and ostracized; in extreme cases they had abandoned their home villages. Procedures were under way to depose chiefs who had been too openly supportive of the losing candidate, and others were made to apologize profusely with gifts, money, and public humiliation. Then my farewell party in Kpuawala turned into a political confrontation, in which Foday Kai had yet again to intervene as peacemaker in order to avoid open violence. This was the fate of most major gatherings in the chiefdom thereafter. The bee attack came to be accepted as conclusive proof that the losers were not going to resign themselves gracefully and were planning to use witchcraft to even scores. It should be said, however, that some people in the P.C.'s compound at the time of the attack interpreted the event in very different terms: as a covert punitive action by V.J.'s supporters. Secret strategies and connections were seen to have been a major factor in his victory; hence Dr Dabo's comment about V.J.'s meetings in the Poro bush.

In March 1987, only a few months after his inauguration, the new M.P. was implicated with five others in an alleged coup attempt against President Momoh, supposedly mounted by a Mende anti-smuggling agent with the support, among others, of Vice President Minah. A prominent Mende politician from the neighboring Pujelum district, Minah was also considered responsible for the violent *ndɔgbɔsui* attacks there following the 1982 elections. The accused men were imprisoned and most of them were executed. V.J. managed to get his sentence converted to house arrest in Freetown, where he died in 1990, apparently from complications from diabetes (Paul Richards, personal communication, London, March 1997). In Wunde, however, his death was imputed to more mysterious agencies.

These events turned politics inside the chiefdom upside down, as the persecuted supporters of Dr Dabo regained control of the local scene and began to exact their own revenge. Some of those who had been chased from their villages as spies were installed as village chiefs, albeit very unpopular ones. The section chief was deposed and heavily fined by the P.C., with the backing of police sent in by the national government. The police also helped track down, imprison, and mistreat many elders who had followed V.J. Had Dr Dabo been prophetic when he had said, in 1986, that the political fallout of the election was far from over? Or had he been at work behind the scenes, marshaling his own resources and networks to bring all this about? Many Kpuawala people felt they knew the answer as soon as the bees attacked.

In light of the conflict, the president of Sierra Leone, Momoh, decided to pay a visit to the chiefdom to settle the land (*a ndɔlɔ hugbatɛ*), arriving by helicopter with the inspector general of police, Bambay Kamara. But resentment continued to brew over the crackdown by the P.C. after V.J.'s death. Rumors began again to circulate about gatherings in the Poro bush. As it happened, the civil war overtook the affairs in the chiefdom. The military regime that seized power in 1992 weakened the authority of all P.C.s installed under the APC government, accusing them of having been corrupt. When elections were held again in February 1996 to establish a civilian government, they were open to more than one party for the first time in twenty years. Among those fielding candidates were several with names harking back to 'pre-APC times,' including the SLPP, which won the ballot.

Conclusion

I began this analysis of the 1986 elections outlining some of the challenges posed by the straddling strategies and bifurcated historical legacies that make the application of normative models of the public sphere and civil society problematic in the context of the postcolonial Sierra Leonean state. The permeability in Africa between spheres that might arguably have limited autonomy elsewhere, if only under specific circumstances, is also an aspect of the 'illicit cohabitation' between authority and its subjects in postcolonial regimes (Mbembe 1992, 4). In the Sierra Leonean case, this cohabitation was exemplified by the shared idiom of covert power at different levels of state and civil society. Regardless of the implications for struggles in local, national, or even transnational political arenas of any electoral

reforms in Sierra Leone, the continued link between these domains i also ensured by a shared political culture among their actors. One o the defining features of postcolonial subjectivity in Sierra Leone is the fundamental ambiguity of political intentions, practices, and agencies Modern politics and life also presume the coexistence of multiple public and covert dimensions of reality. That 'numerous contents o life cannot even emerge in the presence of full publicity' (Simmel 1950, 330) is taken for granted; but this, as Habermas himself ha noted, has come increasingly to characterize the democratic formations of late capitalist societies as well.

The potent social imaginary of ambiguity, rumors, and occult forces deployed in the more 'ordinary' political setting of the 1986 ballot and its aftermath also provides a context for understanding the extraordinary forms of violence that took place at the outbreak of civil war some five years later.[13] Both events drew on symbols linked to the historical genealogy of the modern state, its violent genesis in colonialism and its more recent history under the corrupt, sometime brutal APC regime. This genealogy includes previous instances o belligerent resistance, such as the 1898 'tax war'; and of bitterly oppositional party politics, such as those evoked by the silent deploy-ment of SLPP icons during the 1986 elections, itself a protest agains single-party rule.

The SLPP's rapid transition from banned party to majority government in the 1996 elections was foreshadowed by the continued invocation of its key symbols in major political events during the year of its suppression. Its existence in people's memories and desires, a they lived through the excesses of what came to be known as the 'APC time,' conforms to Mende notions of how power operates Power is seen to work in secret, covert spheres, whose existence i tantalizingly evoked by the use of polysemic symbols in the public domain, such as the palm branches displayed by the section chief o the rhetoric of hanging heads. These symbols are sufficiently rich in their resonances to conjure up many other meanings as well. Palm branches speak of ancestral links to the land, of a commitment to feed one's followers, of Mende political history in both postcolonial and colonial times. Hanging heads may be understood, generically, as a means to achieve unified, concerted political action through consul-tation and compromise; but it is also associated with the introduction of a single-party constitution, and with the APC era. Furthermore the polysemy of political symbols like the palm leaf – as icons o authority in some contexts and as oblique calls to resistance in other – challenges any simple antinomy between hegemonic and counter-hegemonic signs.

After V.J.'s involvement in the 1987 coup attempt, his brother wa not reinstated as section chief, although he commanded a loya personal following. By contrast, the paramount chief displayed remark-able staying power. He continued to hold office, despite periodic threats to his authority posed by changes in government and by the civil war that has displaced him and many of his subjects. However the 1996 (multi-party) elections did not resolve the issue of the M.P for the constituency, and the post did not return to its previous holder

On the face of it, the discourse of democratization and reform that has engulfed Sierra Leone and other African states seems to favor the concentration of electoral politics in urban centers. In Sierra Leone the civilian government elected in the 1996 multi-party elections, and restored to power in 1998, ran on a platform that included electora reform proposals. Future elections might restrict voters to a choice o parties, not individuals, and this might shift competition for politica patronage and office from the local constituency to the party headquarters in Freetown. At the same time, multi-party election may also facilitate the politicization of ethnic identities; witness, for example, the formation of new, ethnic-based parties in the 1995 Tanzanian elections (see Moore 1996).

What is most striking, finally, about the 1986 elections in Wunde is the remarkable democratic spirit at their core. And this in spite of real anxieties and fears of violence; in spite, too, of the foreignness of the idiom of government and of the electoral process embodied in *politisi*. The counter pressures to conform and compete, to renounce political ambitions in favor of consensus and yet to struggle to the very end, is embedded in the logic of covert politics. While electoral politics enact the fiction of free and fair competition, many Sierra Leoneans are uncomfortable with the way in which this creates winners and losers; for them, it is a process, more akin to court cases, that inevitably causes resentment and potential violence. Throughout the relatively short history of elections in Sierra Leone, therefore, efforts have been made to transform political institutions and practices inherited from the colonial state through their integration with local political idioms, like that of hanging heads. While the autocratic potential of these idioms was demonstrated both by their appropriation on the part of the APC and by the role of paramount chiefs in national politics during the early post-independence years, they remain a powerful symbolic resource. In any event, recourse to covert strategies, to the occult, and to the rumors that amplify their potency in public domains provide a powerful check to political excesses.

Together, these features of modem Sierra Leonean political culture give voice to another kind of civility. It is one — and here is the crucial point — that resituates civil society and moral discourse at the very center of national politics; that treats these things as inseparable in the first place. This, to be sure, is the corollary of a public sphere based, in the local imagination, on a dialogics of compromise, of consensus forged through both overt and covert consultation, of communal and sectarian interest, of civility.

Appendix

The first half of the polling stations on this list are located in Jaiama-Bongor chiefdom, the remaining ones in Wunde. Note that the only places where Dr Dabo won a majority of votes were the chiefdom headquarter towns of the constituency, namely Telu (16) and Gboyama (23–25). Also notable is the disparity of votes cast in each chiefdom, especially compared to figures from the national census carried out only a few months earlier. The December 1985 census of Wunde chiefdom reported a total population figure of 6,973 inhabitants, while the Jaiama-Bongor population was roughly three times as large. However, the table shows that Wunde voters outnumbered those from Jaiama-Bongor.

Several factors may account for this discrepancy. Seasonal population movement is one: the census was conducted in early December, a dry season month during which many people visit relatives and attend social occasions. This is also the season in which younger men travel to alluvial diamond-mining areas to supplement their income during a gap in the farming cycle. By the time elections were held at the end of May, the dry season was at its end, and most people returned home. Furthermore, the fact that Jaiama-Bongor chiefdom was itself the site of significant diamond-mining operations, which accounted for its larger population, also meant that it contained a greater number of strangers, including non-Sierra Leoneans. The latter, although not entitled to vote in elections, would have been counted in a census.

Despite these factors, the discrepancies remain significant. It suggests that, at the very least, a large number of people not normally resident in Gboyama (Dr Dabo's hometown) — where by far the largest number of votes were cast — were encouraged to return home to vote. The results may give substance to accusations of vote tampering, but if improprieties did occur in Gboyama, it is remarkable that they did not succeed in obtaining a victory for the home candidate.

1986 Sierra Leone General Election Results for Bo South I Constituency

Polling Station Number	Polling Station Name	Votes for Dr Dabo	Votes for V.J. (Vandi Jimmy)
1	Mendekelema	162	245
2	Mano	31	234
3	Pelewahun	75	179
4	Ngelehun	45	239
5	Largor	62	205
6	Koribundu I	64	131
7	Koribundu II	53	137
8	Koribundu III	50	220
9	jombohun	13	249
10	Kpetema	48	214
11	Bendu	219	129
12	Kandor Old	128	162
13	Mamboma I	153	282
14	Mamboma II	42	152
15	Mamboma III	130	277
16	Telu	268	75
17	Bawomalum	114	379.
18	Gbaama I	222	309
19	Gbaama II	230	274
20	Hegbebu	77	172
21	Ngogbebu	39	130
22	Kponima	94	219
23	Gboyama I	1,050	19
24	Gboyama II	746	31
25	Gboyama III	504	14
26	New Dia	180	445
27	Klmawala	112	199
28	Fanima	137	189
29	Wunde I	22	537
30	Wunde II	8	259
31	Yengerna	81	358
32	Yanihun	68	151
33	Niagorehun	99	18o
34	Pelewahun	70	161
Total		5,396	7,132

Note: Roman numerals following a location's name indicate that these are larger towns encompassing several polling stations.

Notes

My fieldwork in Sierra Leone was carried out in 1984–86, 1990, and 1993. A Hellman Family Faculty Grant (through the University of California, Berkeley) supported a leave in 1997 during which this essay was written. I am grateful to John Comaroff and Luca D'Isanto for their editorial input, though I am responsible for selectively following their advice. Helpful comments on earlier versions were also given by two anonymous readers, by colleagues in the Berkeley Anthropology Department, and by Janet Roitman, Rijk van Dijk, Patsy Spyer, Rafael Sanchez, and Françoise Vergès. I am especially grateful to Paul Richards and Murray Last, and to Peter Geschiere and Wim van Binsbergen, for inviting me to present some of this material at seminars held in 1997 at University College, London, and Leiden University. Their comments and those of other seminar participants greatly enriched my thinking about the topics addressed in this chapter.

1 The February 1996 ballot, held ten years after the events analyzed in this chapter, was the first attempt to reestablish multiparty politics and state accountability in Sierra Leone in some twenty years a result of both internal popular demands and international pressure. Fifteen months later, the government elected in 1996 was ousted by a coup. However, in March 1998, it was reinstated to power, thanks to the military efforts of Nigerian-led West African troops.

2 For the relationship between notions of civility, civilization, and civil society, see Elias 1978.

3 Habermas's analysis of the rise of the bourgeois public sphere as a set of institutions that enabled the political participation of increasing numbers of citizens has also been criticized from the perspective of European and American history. The exclusion from the public discursive exchanges of the voices of women, the illiterate, the propertyless, slaves, and other significant portions of the population has always raised questions about the limits of actually existing democracy' (Fraser 1992, 110; see also Eley 1992; Ryan 1992). Even when these groups have gained access to this conversation, the shift away from an engagement with formal politics – signaled, for example, by the failure to exercise the right to vote – underscores the need to move beyond identifying who is 'legally eligible to participate' to reach an understanding of the changing forms and sites of the political (Schudson 1992, 147–48).

4 A high degree of control over results at the local level is possible in single-party states precisely because power tends to become more personalized, and patronage negotiations take place locally rather than on the national scene (see Hayward and Dumbuya 1985, 79). Throup (1993, 377–80) argues that in Kenya, too, single-party rule has not excluded electoral competition and real political change. In addition, Fauré (1993, 324–26) explores the diffidence of Ivoirian voters toward openly competitive electoral contests as a feature of African forms of political culture that directly challenges prevailing Western notions of democratization.

5 Chief Foday Kai was related to the village chief in Kpuawala. He was also a graduate of the prestigious Bo School, a former civil servant, and a recipient of the Order of the British Empire.

6 Foday Kai supported in his chiefdom the few weavers who could still make the older, complicated cloth patterns using only natural dyes, and he ensured that a younger generation was trained by them. He also supervised in his compound the training of dance groups in largely abandoned forms of performance. Foday Kai had represented Sierra Leone at a number of international cultural events in Nigeria (e.g., FESTAC 1977), the United Kingdom, and the United States, as well as being a regular lecturer for the Peace Corps and the international diplomatic community in Freetown. For his role as cultural broker and interpreter-inventor of his peoples' traditions for outsiders, he was once referred to as 'Mr. [Mende] culture' (Lamp 1987, 72). See James and Tarnu 1992 for Foday Kai's biography.

7 The notion of a transnational civil society deserves a more sustained discussion, which space limitations prevent me from undertaking here. Guyer (1994) explores its implications for Nigeria, and Basch, Glick Schiller, and Szanton Blanc (1994) discuss the role of US-based trans-national Asian and Caribbean communities in political and other developments in their home countries.

8 V.J.'s brother, the section chief, had gone on pilgrimage to Mecca several years ahead of Paramount Chief Dabo, and was thus himself an *Alhaji*.

9 *Mbeindo ngi navo nwjɔa nya ndee va. Daboisia, ti gbatɛngo, kɛ nya ta, ngulɔ mia a nya gbatea.*

10 The link between multipartyism and an oppositional ethnic politics was explicitly made by factions in the Sierra Leone civil war. In 1991, the Revolutionary United Front (RUF) – the main (non-Mende) rebel group in the civil war – launched its first incursions into Sierra Leone through Mende territory on the Liberian border and tried to stir up ethnic rivalries in the region through, among other things, the display of SLPP symbols. Though the rebels were unsuccessful in this effort (Richards 1995, 139), their move points to the likelihood that in the 1986 elections, the display by V.J.'s supporters of palm fronds could also be read as a sign that the APC faced a growing threat from a Mende opposition.

11 V.J.'s supporters drew parallels between their candidate's opposition to a corrupt government and Ndawa's (literally, 'big mouth,' 'big name') activities against the colonial administration. They made much of the fact that Dr Dabo had been sacked in 1984 from his ministerial post in social welfare and rural development because of financial irregularities. They also claimed that V.J. had stronger roots in the area because of his putative links to a famous indigenous lineage. However, the paramount chief could trace his own family's presence in this region for at least as long as V.J.'s. The P.C.'s father and grandfather had preceded him in the chiefdom's leadership, even though their family came during the nineteenth century from the Guinée–Sierra Leone border region.

12 For a discussion of the politics of masking and the masking of politics in Sierra Leone, especially under the APC regime, see Nunley (1987, 203–15).

13 During the civil war, for example, the resistance to clear-cut oppositions, and the effort to blur boundaries, gave form to the figure described by the Krio neologism, *sobel*, the soldier-rebel. Unable to distinguish between the attire or behavior of the government's military forces and their rebel enemies, the civilian population recognized the shifting boundaries between these purported opponents well in advance of the events that in 1997 brought just such a paradoxical alliance to power. The saying 'Soldiers by day, rebels by night' (Richards 1996b, 7) located the articulation of these identities in the relationship between day and night, open and covert action, in a dynamic of shape-shifting that has its antecedent in the Mende political imaginary in the figure of *ndɔgbɔsui* alluded to in connection with the 1982 elections in the Wunde region. More generally, *ndɔgbɔsui* is an anthropomorphic trickster, a shape-shifting figure common in Mende lore (see Harris and Sawyerr 1968).

References

Abraham, Arthur. 1978. *Mende Government and Politics under Colonial Rule: A Historical Study of Political Change in Sierra Leone, 1890–1937.* Freetown: Sierra Leone University Press.

Basch, Linda, Nina Click Schiller, and Cristina Szanton Blanc. 1994. *Nations Unbound: Transnational Projects, Postcolonial Predicaments, and Deterritorialized NationStates.* Langhorne, PA: Gordon and Breach.

Bayart, Jean-François. 1993. *The State in Africa: The Politics of the Belly.* Translated by M. Harper and C. and E. Harrison. London: Longman.

Bayart, Jean-François, S. Ellis, and B. Hibou. 1997. *La Criminalisation de l'état en Afrique.* Espace International. Paris: Éditions Complexe.

Castoriadis, Comelius. 1987. *The Imaginary Institution of Society.* Translated by K. Blamey. Cambridge, MA: MIT Press.

Chakrabarty, Dipesh. 1992. 'Postcoloniality and the Artifice of History: Who Speaks for "Indian" Pasts?' *Representations* 37:126.

Chalmers, Sir David. 1899. *Report by Her Majesty's Commissioner and Correspondence on the Subject of the Insurrection in the Sierra Leone Protectorate, 1898.* London: Her Majesty's Stationery Office.

Cohen, Abner. 1981. *The Politics of Elite Culture: Explorations in the Dramaturgy of Power in a Modern African Society.* Berkeley: University of California Press.

Comaroff, Jean, and John Comaroff, eds. 1993. *Introduction to Modernity and Its*

Malcontents: Ritual and Power in Postcolonial Africa, Chicago: University of Chicago Press.

Ekeh, Peter. 1975. 'Colonialism and the Two Publics in Africa: A Theoretical Statement.' *Comparative Studies in Society and History* 17: 911–12.

Eley, Geoff. 1992. 'Nations, Politics, and Political Cultures: Placing Habermas in the Nineteenth Century'. In *Habermas and the Public Sphere*, ed. C. Calhoun. Cambridge, MA: MIT Press.

Elias, Norbert. [1938] 1978. *The History of Manners*. Translated by E. Jephcott. New York: Pantheon.

Fauré, Yves. 1993. 'Democracy and Realism: Reflections on the Case of Côte d'Ivoire.' *Africa* 63 (3): 313–29.

Ferme, Mariane. 1992. 'Hammocks Belong to Men, Stools to Women: Constructing and Contesting Gender Domains in a Mende Village.' Ph.D. diss., University of Chicago.

Fraser, Nancy. 1992. 'Rethinking the Public Sphere: A Contribution to the Critique of Actually Existing Democracy.' In *Habermas and the Public Sphere*, ed. C. Calhoun. Cambridge, MA: MIT Press.

Fyfe, Christopher. 1962. *A History of Sierra Leone*. Oxford: Oxford University Press.

Geschiere, Peter. 1995. *Sorcellerie et politique en Afrique: La viande des autres*. Paris: Karthala.

Guyer, Jane. 1994. 'The Spatial Dimensions of Civil Society in Africa: An Anthropologist Looks at Nigeria.' In *Civil Society and the State in Africa*, ed. John W. Harbeson, Donald Rothchild, and Naomi Chazan. Boulder, CO: Lynne Rienner.

Habermas, Jurgen. [1962] 1989. *The Structural Transformation of the Public Sphere: An Inquiry into a Category of Bourgeois Society*. Translated by Thomas Burger with Frederick Lawrence. Cambridge, MA: MIT Press.

Hann, Chris. 1996. 'Introduction: Political Society and Civil Anthropology.' In *Civil Society: Challenging Western Models*, ed. C. Hann and E. Dunn. London: Routledge.

Harbeson, John W., Donald Rothchild, and Naomi Chazan. 1994. *Civil Society and the State in Africa*. Boulder, CO: Lynne Rienner.

Harris, W. T., and Harry Sawyerr. 1968. *The Springs of Mende Belief and Conduct*. Freetown: Sierra Leone University Press.

Haugerud, Angelique. 1995. *The Culture of Politics of Modern Kenya*. New York: Cambridge University Press.

Hayward, Fred. 1985. 'Changing Electoral Patterns in Sierra Leone: The 1982 Single-Party Elections.' *African Studies Review* 28 (4): 62–86.

Hayward, Fred, and Ahmed Dumbuya. 1983. 'Political Legitimacy, Political Symbols, and National Leadership in West Africa.' *Journal of Modern African Studies* 21 (4):645–71.

Hayward, Fred M. and Jimmy Kandeh. 1987. 'Perspectives on Twenty-Five Years of Elections in Sierra Leone.' In *Elections in Independent Africa*, ed. Fred M. Hayward. Boulder, CO: Westview Press.

Hutchinson, Sharon. 1996. *Nuer Dilemmas: Coping with Money, War and the State*. Berkeley: University of California Press.

James, F. B., and S. A. J. Tamu. 1992. *B. A. Foday-Kai: A Biography*. Freetown: People's Educational Association of Sierra Leone.

Kalous, Milan. 1974. *Cannibals and Tongo Players of Sierra Leone*. Auckland: Wright and Carman.

Kandeh, Jimmy. 1992. 'Politicization of Ethnic Identities in Sierra Leone.' *African Studies Review* 35 (4): 81–100.

Karlström, Mikael. 1996. 'Imagining Democracy: Political Culture and Democratisation in Buganda.' *Africa* 66 (4): 485–505.

Kilson. Martin. 1966. *Political Change in a West African State: A Study of the Modernization Process in Sierra Leone*. Cambridge, MA: Harvard University Press.

Kpundeh, Sahr John. 1995. *Politics and Corruption in Africa: A Case Study of Sierra Leone*. Lanham, MD: University Press of America.

Lamp, Frederick. 1987. 'Review of Radiance from the Waters: Ideals of Feminine Beauty in Mende Art, by S. A. Boone (1986).' *African Arts* 20 (2): 17–26; 72–74.

Little, Kenneth. 1965. 'The Political Function of the Poro,' part 1. *Africa* 35 (4): 349–65.

— 1966. 'The Political Function of the Poro,' part 2. *Africa* 36 (1): 62–71.

MacCormack, Carol P. 1983. 'Human Leopards and Crocodiles: Political Meanings of Categorical Ambiguities.' In *Ethnography of Cannibalism*, ed. P. Brown and D. Tuzin. Washington, DC: Society for Psychological Anthropology.

Mamdani, Mahmood. 1996. *Citizen and Subject: Contemporary Africa and the Legacy of Late Colonialism*. Princeton: Princeton University Press.

Marchal, Roland. 1993. 'Un Espace urbain en guerre: Les Mooryann de Mogadiscio.' *Cahiers d'Études Africaines* 332 (130): 295–320.

Mbembe, Achille. 1992. 'Provisional Notes on the Postcolony.' *Africa* 62 (l): 337.

Moore, Sally Falk. 1996. 'Post-Socialist Micro-Politics: Kilimanjaro, 1993.' *Africa* 66 (4): 587–606.

Murphy, William. 1990. 'Creating the Appearance of Consensus in Mende Political Discourse.' *American Anthropologist* 92 (l): 24–41.

Nunley, John W. 1987. *Moving with the Face of the Devil: Art and Politics in Urban West Africa*. Urbana: University of Illinois Press.

Rabo, Annika. 1996. 'Gender, State and Civil Society in Jordan and Syria.' In *Civil Society: Challenging Western Models*, ed. C. Hann and E. Dunn. London: Routledge.

Reno, William. 1995. *Corruption and State Politics in Sierra Leone*. Cambridge: Cambridge University Press.

Richards, Paul. 1995. 'Rebellion in Liberia and Sierra Leone: A Crisis of Youth?' In *Conflict in Africa*, ed. Oliver Furley. London: I.B. Tauris.

— 1996a. 'Chimpanzees, Diamonds and War: The Discourses of Global Environmental Change and Local Violence on the Liberia-Sierra Leone Border.' In *The Future of Anthropological Knowledge*, ed. H. Moore. London: Routledge.

— 1996b. *Fighting for the Rain Forest: War Youth and Resources in Sierra Leone*. London: International African Institute, in association with James Currey and Heinemann.

Ryan, Mary 1992. 'Gender and Public Access: Women's Politics in Nineteenth-Century America.' In *Habermas and the Public Sphere*, ed. C. Calhoun. Cambridge, MA: MIT Press.

Schudson, Michael. 1992. 'Was There Ever a Public Sphere? If So, When? Reflections on an American Case.' In *Habermas and the Public Sphere*, ed. C. Calhoun. Cambridge, MA: MIT Press.

Scott, D. J. R. 1960. 'The Sierra Leone Election, May 1957.' In *Five Elections in Africa*, ed. W. J. M. Mackenzie and K. Robinson. Oxford: Clarendon Press.

Simmel, Georg. 1950. *The Sociology of Georg Simmel*. Edited and translated by K. Wolff. Glencoe, Ill.: Free Press.

Spülbeck, Susanne. 1996. 'Anti-Semitism and Fear of the Public Sphere in a Post-Totalitarian Society: East Germany.' In *Civil Society: Challenging Western Models*, ed. C. Hann and E. Dunn. London: Routledge.

Throup, David. 1993. 'Elections and Political Legitimacy in Kenya.' *Africa* 63 (3): 371–96.

Vail, Leroy. 1989. 'Introduction: Ethnicity in Southern African History.' In *The Creation of Tribalism in Southern Africa*, ed. Leroy Vail. Berkeley: University of California Press and London: James Currey.

Woods, Duayne. 1992. 'Civil Society in Europe and Africa: Limiting State Power through a Public Sphere.' *African Studies Review* 35 (2): 77–100.

Zack-Williams, A. B. 1989. 'Sierra Leone 1968–85: The Decline of Politics and the Politics of Decline.' *International Journal of Sierra Leone Studies* I: 122–30.

Section 2.B
The City

FILIP DE BOECK
Kinshasa
Tales of the 'Invisible City' & the Second World[1]

Reference
Abridged version of a chapter in Okwui Enwezor et al. (eds)
Under Siege: Four African Cities. Freetown, Johannesburg, Kinshasa & Lagos
Kassel: Hatje Cantz Publishers, 2002

In 1997, while Brazzaville was busy bombing itself out of existence, and while rockets fired from Brazzaville's presidential place in the direction of Kinshasa fell on Kintambo and other riverine neighbourhoods, leaving tens of Kinois dead, historian Ch. Didier Gondola published his *Villes miroirs. Migrations et identités urbaines à Kinshasa et Brazzaville 1930–1970*. Gondola's book is a history of the twin cities of Kinshasa and Brazzaville, mirroring each other across the Congo river, like an imperfect materialization of the city of Valdrada which Italo Calvino describes in *Le citta invisibili* (1972). Translated into English as *Invisible Cities* (1974), Calvino tells the story of a Venetian traveller, Marco Polo, who diverts the aged Tartar emperor Kublai Khan with tales of the cities he has seen in his travels around the empire. Soon it becomes clear that each of the fantastic places that Marco Polo describes is really one and the same place, the city of Venice. The Kinshasa described here resembles Calvino's invisible Venice, for it also contains many cities in one. It is at once a city of memory, a city of desire, a hidden city, a trading city, a city of the dead, a city of signs, a city of words, an oneiric city, a city of utopia. And like Calvino's Venice and Gondola's twin cities, this Kinshasa too cannot be understood without reflecting upon reflection, upon reflecting realities, mirrors, images, imitation, imagination, and (self-) representation. This contribution presents Kinshasa as a vast mirror-hall. Starting from but drastically expanding Gondola's notion of mirroring cities, we seek to analyse the various levels of mirroring which fracture Kinshasa's urban world into a series of kaleidoscopic, multiple, but simultaneously existing, worlds. Each of these 'micro-cities' constantly reflects the others, though this reflection is not always necessarily symmetrical. Some of these cities, and some levels of mirroring between them, are more visible than others.

Above all, this contribution tries to capture Kinshasa's constant urge to move beyond the tarnish left upon the surface of its mirroring realities; the ways in which this city, sometimes playfully, sometimes desperately, but always with tremendous vitality, tries to break through the layers of dust and dirt, the palimpsests of colonization, de-, re- and neo-colonization that have settled upon its surface and have dulled, sometimes even destroyed, its lustre. Living in an urban reality stained by a film of increasing poverty, by the tears and blood drops of physical and symbolic violence, as well as by a pervasive sense of societal crisis and loss, Kinshasa's inhabitants struggle to reach beyond the fractures inflicted by the post-colonial world and the disjunctions at play in the myths of modernity *and* tradition. This is also where the metaphor of the mirror is pushed to its limits. Kinshasa does not merely reflect. It is not merely represented in the mirrors held up by pre-colonial pasts, colonialist modernities or nationalist myths. Certainly, to an important extent it is animated by the reflecting images of these imposed representations. Simultaneously, however, it resists, shatters, transforms and moves beyond all of those in often unexpected and surprising ways.

Paradigms of resistance against the hegemonies of state, money and market fail to capture fully the complexities of the realities lived by many in Congo today, nor do they manage to seize the dynamics of subversion by means of which the metaphor of the mirror comes alive in the urban world of Kinshasa. Both literally and figuratively, Congo's capital constantly smashes its own mirrors. At the same time, it never stops to piece itself back together. In ways that often leave the observer perplexed, the city constantly activates and undergoes the effervescent push and pull of destruction and regeneration. The incessant and chaotic crossing of the borders between these two forces somehow seems to generate the energetic source from which Kinshasa taps the power to embody, animate and sustain its own *eidos*, its own ongoing attempts at societal creation. In its most essential form, this power is operated by a frontier logic of mutation. It is, in a way, the power of the fetish. Like the fetish, the city of Kinshasa is a constant border-crossing phenomenon, resisting fixture, refusing capture. And like the fetish itself, like the magic activated through the mirror in the bellies of Congo's power objects, the city's moving force of mutation is generated in 'the slippage between the dominance and the subordination of the surface' (Davies 1998: 141; see also Spyer 1998). Mentally and materially, the city emerges in unstable space. It is a product of a profound mixture between different cultural itineraries and sites. Its content is composite and is generated through crossing various borders and mediating between different opposites. As such, it is also extremely well adapted to carry this mutant message, for it presents in and of itself a space of confrontation, mutation and movement. Out of the breccia of broken glass, the debris of its own pasts, the city thus feverishly transforms and continues. In a sustained effort to recreate and institutionalize itself, the city tirelessly re-energizes an ever-growing web of plural meanings and social imaginary significations.

The following sections provide a summary of the different mirrors in which Kinshasa is captured and authored by external gazes and representations. More importantly, however, they also set the stage to move beyond such identity play which reduces Kinshasa to the mere role of 'significant other', in an attempt to start understanding Kinshasa's originality, its internal struggle to contemplate and author its own identity.

Mirrors and models: The colonial speculum

One level of reflection through which Kinshasa is made to exist is quite obvious: it takes place in the European mirror of colonialism which invented and created the primitivist idea of the Congo and its counter-image, the urban landscape. The history of the creation and evolution of the city that is called Kinshasa today, from its origins as a small trade station, established by King Leopold's envoy Stanley upon his arrival in Ngaliema Bay on 1 December 1881, its subsequent rebirth as Léopoldville, capital of Belgian Congo, between 1908 and 1960, to the large city of at least 6 million people it has become now, is a trajectory that cannot be apprehended without taking into account the military, monetary, medical and moral dynamics of the colonizing context in which it emerged.

1961. Lumumba murdered, Congo in crisis. I was born in 1961, a post-colonial subject. I was born not in Congo, but in Antwerp, in a street named *Beschavingstraat*, 'Civilization Street'. Standing in the shadow of the Church of Christ King, our house was one of many similar houses in a new suburban housing-estate, erected after the Second World War. A couple of streets away, on a little square and opposite my grandparents' house, stood one of the only two houses that Le Corbusier built in Belgium. In 1961, this house, a 1926 realization, was still inhabited by its original principal, Mister Guiette, an Antwerp painter who, so my father tells me, also had two beautiful daughters. The house still exists, the daughters have gone. The post-war modernism of my childhood neighbourhood, a modest reprise of Le Corbusier's architectural ideals, reflected the optimism of that period.

Our own street ended on the *Tentoonstellingslaan*, 'Exhibition Avenue', close to what then still was the *Kolonielaan*, the 'Colony Avenue', which has undergone a name change since. The port of Antwerp was the umbilical cord which connected tiny Belgium to its giant baby of a colony. Yet, this was not the reason for all the colonial references in the street names of my early childhood neighbourhood. Only recently did I realize why the streets were so full of colonial memories. Going through some personal papers and documents of my grandmother's after her death, I found some photos of the World Exhibition that was held in Antwerp in 1930. No doubt the photos had been made by my grandfather, who worked in a small photo-shop in Antwerp in that period. An important section of the 1930 World Exhibition was dedicated to Flemish Art, appropriately housed in the Church of Christ King. On a plot next to this church, in the area where my childhood neighbourhood would be erected two decades later, stood an imposing, resolutely modernist, Congo pavilion in which Belgium's colonial oeuvre was proudly put on display. In line with a tradition that started with Universal Exhibitions at the end of the nineteenth century, including Tervuren's famous example of 1898, the 1930 Congo display also included a *village africain*. This 'African Village' consisted of an architecture that imitated the *style soudanais*, a vaguely Arabizing architectural style which never really existed as such in pre-colonial Congo, but which referred to a crucial element of the Leopoldian colonial mythology. In this mythological construction, the colonizing drive that was set in motion by King Leopold II and that swept through the Congo in the last decades of the nineteenth century, was invariably legitimated as a humanitarian struggle against 'Arab' slave traders such as the legendary Tippo Tip. The adobe style of the 1930 African Village provided an invented architectural commemoration of this era, which culminated in the *campagne arabe* of 1892–95 and similar events of the time, including that other, equally famous but slightly surreal, colonial founding myth, Stanley's rescue of Emin Pasha. Throughout the colonial period, the Arabizing style remained popular in Belgian Congo as well. The architecture of the colonial prisons that the Belgians erected throughout the country and which continue to be used today still bear witness of this colonial orientalism.

The 1930 African Village conveys the complexities and ambiguities that are inherent in the notion of 'place' as it existed in the colonial discourse and imagination. The image of Congo which was created in this Antwerp display, next to a Le Corbusier house of the same period, calls into being a completely imaginary reconstruction of an equally imaginary traditional Africa. Within the Exhibition display, this colonial reflection is mirrored in and juxtaposed by the 'modern' imperialist Congo pavilion and the Flemish Art in the equally imperialist Church of Christ King.

The Congo has, of course, always fascinated the Western imagination, from Conrad's *Heart of Darkness* to Naipaul's *A Bend in the River* and de Villiers' SAS pulp fiction airport literature, with titles such as *Panique au Zaïre* and *Zaïre adieu*, spectacularly racist cocktails of exoticism, sex, violence, intrigue and betrayal, with an African pin-up girl on the cover. In varying degrees, 'Congo' appears in these works of fiction as a powerful negative image of the Western Self, in which the West constantly projects all of its fears and fantasies. For example, in the wake of the 1995 Ebola outbreak in Kikwit, 500 km south-east of Kinshasa, a leading Belgian newspaper characterized the virus as symptomatic of a wild and undomesticated country. In the same way, Hollywood has associated the outbreaks of AIDS with the Central-African forest and phantasmagoric constructions of the ways in which the virus jumped from monkeys to Africans. The great discrepancy which is generated in the mirroring process between this topos, the Congo of the imagination, and the topicality of the physical Congo, which is rendered invisible by the strength of the imagined place, seems to go unnoticed by most. What the African Village of the 1930 World Exhibition reveals is precisely this rupture, this fault-line between representation and reality which is so characteristic of the problematic place of 'place' in the colonial and post-colonial contexts.

Throughout its emergence and gradual development, Léopoldville, as colonial speculum and as large-scale project in social engineering, grafted upon its urban geography and ecology many of the evolutionist oppositions that also underpinned the cultural construction of difference both in the colonial intervention and at home. The difference between metropolitan Prospero and colonial Caliban, between Self and Other, Culture and Nature, Rationality and Irrationality, Man and Woman, writing and speech, knowledge and ignorance, modernity and tradition, or peace and war, is constantly generated in this European speculation. It is this ideological configuration that underpinned to a large extent the ways in which the city was shaped and designed. It is also the same mirror that gives birth to Léopoldville's two reflecting halves, the western Ville and the indigenous Cité. In these complementary but opposing spaces qualities such as 'public' and 'private' acquire radically different meanings.

During the post-war period in which the modernist suburban housing-estate of my childhood years was built, Belgian modernism was also given a second life in Congo. In 1940, Léopoldville was home to some 50,000 inhabitants. At the end of World War II the number of inhabitants had doubled, to attain 200,000 in 1950, 400,000 at Independence and well over a million in 1970. In the early decades of the twentieth century, Léopoldville developed itself along the Kintambo–Kalina axis. Kintambo developed out of Stanley's early trading post and consisted of the city's oldest industrial and residential sites. Kalina, currently Gombe, developed into the capital's administrative area, housing the colonial administration's offices and residential villas. Gombe has very much kept that function today. Kintambo and Kalina were soon connected by a railroad. Around this axis gradually developed commercial centres and several *cités indigènes*, indigenous camps and settlements, inhabited by Congolese workers. On the Kintambo side, the labour camps arose along the river, in proximity with the industrial activities of that part of the city, its shipyards, metallurgy and other activities such as the confection industry of Utex Léo. On the Kalina side, a considerably larger space was set aside for the development of several indigenous neighborhoods, most notably Kinshasa, Barumbu and Lingwala.

Consisting of a large number of small *parcelles*, these neighbourhoods were laid out according to a well-ordered grid which continued the original ground-plan of an army camp that had been located there previously. These indigenous neighbourhoods, camps and, after the Second World War, *cités jardins*, consisted of houses that were either individually constructed and owned (and there existed a *Fonds d'Avance*/loan system to encourage such individual ownership) or they were built by colonial employers and companies. Here too, these neighbourhoods existed in close proximity with the administrative and residential centres of Léopoldville. Yet, they were consistently separated from these central areas by stretches of no man's land, by the main railroad (which also connected the city to the port of Matadi in the Lower Congo), as well as by a number of other *zones tampons* buffer zones, such as the city's botanical gardens, commercial zones, an ethnographic museum displaying indigenous life styles, a zoological garden, mission posts and army camps.

In terms of its spatial layout, the stretched-out booming urban conglomeration that Léopoldville was rapidly becoming thus emerged from the very beginning as a racially segregated city, with a strict demarcation line between a central white Ville, with its administrative and residential areas (Kintambo, Ngaliema and the current Gombe, later expanded into the residential neighbourhoods of Limete), and a 'peripheral' African city, the *cité indigène*.

On top of the racial lines of segregation that structured the city of Léopoldville, or Lipopo as the city was called by its Congolese inhabitants, the colonial economic demands and necessities also occasioned a demographic, strongly gendered, segregation. In the early decades of the Belgian Congo's existence, the colonial population mainly consisted of men. It was only very slowly that families, wives and children became an established fact of Léopoldville's urban social make-up. Hesitantly, they started to emerge in Léopoldville during the interbellum period, but it was only after the Second World War that wives and family became a standard part of the colonial city's social make-up. This demographic imbalance, however, was not a reality that characterized the lives of the white colonials alone. Before 1930, the male-female ratio in Léopoldville's indigenous neighbourhoods was three to one. At the end of the Second World War men still outnumbered women two to one, and special taxes were imposed on single women who were living in the *cités indigènes*. This reflected not only the colonial endeavour to control the city's growth rate, but also the simple fact that these indigenous *cités* mainly functioned as depots of cheap African labour, in which there was room neither for women nor the unemployed. Especially after the Second World War, in a vain attempt to diminish and contain the mounting social and political tensions in the city, the colonial administration developed a strict policy to clean up the streets of the city. Those without jobs were rounded up by the *Force Publique*, the colonial armed forces, and sent back to the interior. Paralleling the city's segregated spatial and demographic development, the *Force Publique*, strategically located in army garrisons throughout Léopoldville, was built along equally strict segregated lines, with a superstructure of Belgian officers on the one hand, and a body of Congolese recruits, mostly Bangala from the Congo's Equateur province, on the other. It is mainly these soldiers who became the driving force behind the development of Lingala, their native language, as the city's major *lingua franca*.

Despite a vast array of far-reaching colonial measures which aimed at restricting and controlling the rural migration to the city, Léopoldville kept expanding. In 1949, faced with the demographic explosion of Léopoldville and the increasing social unrest it engendered, the Belgian colonial administration started to implement a large urbanization program through a newly created office, the *Office de Cités Indigènes de Léopoldville* (OCIL). One of the office's realizations was the Renkin neighbourhood, named after Belgium's first Minister of Colonial Affairs. The Renkin neighbourhood formed the heart of what would become Matonge, later to become the vibrant core of Kinshasa's night life.

In 1952, the OCIL was succeeded by the *Office de Cités Africaines* (OCA). This office was created to better coordinate the government's response to the increasingly pressing needs of a rapidly growing city.[2] The goal OCA set for itself was ambitious: the construction of 40,000 new 'quality homes' throughout the colony over the next ten years. Of these new homes 20,000 would be built in Léopoldville alone. Between 1952 and 1960, the city thus expanded drastically, giving birth to an impressive number of new 'satellite' *cités* such as Banda-lungwa, Yolo Nord and Yolo Sud, Matete, Lemba, Ndjili and, finally, Kinkole (De Meulder 2000; see also de Saint-Moulin 1970; de Saint-Moulin and Ducreux 1969). Still, OCA's housing programme and urban planning efforts, impressive as they may appear today, fell short of providing a satisfactory solution to the city's enormous demographic expansion and increasingly chaotic character. The colonial government concentrated all of its efforts at urban expansion in OCA, while barring all non-governmental housing programmes and initiatives. The government would refuse, for example, to sell land to private companies to construct new homes for their employees. And yet, the rate at which the much needed new houses were constructed within the OCA programme was far too slow to bear up against the population growth. Worse even, many of the new houses remained empty because they were too expensive for Kinshasa's commoners. As a result, shantytowns and *bidonvilles* started to spring up everywhere across the city. The situation worsened during the first years after Independence. At first, the unfulfilled OCA plans continued to be realized, though at a much slower pace. This effort at continued urban planning was co-ordinated by the *Office National de Logement* (ONL) and financed by the *Caisse National d'Epargne et de Crédit Immobilier*. Gradually, however, the government started to abandon all efforts at urban planning. No longer restrained by government supervision, the shantytowns started to expand ever more to become the endless and still growing sprawl of popular neighborhoods, the vast peripheral city, the *zones annexes* of which Kinshasa consists today. In the process, the capital has expanded far beyond its colonial borders: towards the Lower Congo in a westernly direction, and in an easterly and southerly direction, over the hill range that used to contain the city before, towards the Bateke plateau and the Kwango. As a result of this unbridled growth, the city has grown away from its old colonial heart. This evolution was recently consolidated by the decision of President Laurent Kabila to order the building of a new major market square in Masina, in an attempt to alleviate the pressure on the old central market area near the Rue du Commerce. Its construction confirms the fact that the colonial city centre, which was also the geographic centre of the city during colonial times, long since ceased to be the geographic and cultural centre, and had become peripheral to the daily experience of the majority of Kinshasa's population.

It is in Camp Luka, Masina, Kimbanseke, Kingasani, Kisenso, Ngaba, Makala, large parts of Mont Ngafula and the many other similar *zones annexes* and *communes urbano-rurales* of post-colonial Kinshasa that the failure of modernist urban planning, as it was conceived by the colonial government and the early post-colonial state, was most clearly illustrated. It is here, also, that Kinshasa started to re-invent itself into the city that it has become today. The growth of this new Kinshasa has also marked a mental move away from the 'place' of colonialism (and this place is both a spatial reality and a language, French). It has, in other words, moved away from the mimetic reproduction of an alienating model of colonialist modernity, imposed by the colonial and the Mobutist state upon the city's population through a wide-ranging arsenal of physical and symbolic forms of violence. For the past four decades, the city has also moved away from the secular 'time of the (post-)colonial nation' and the official 'religious time' of the Catholic Church which accompanied these efforts at nation-building. It is in these increasingly numerous informal urban areas, with their complex patchwork of multiple local ethnic identities, that the city's inhabitants have started to re-territorialize the urban space, develop their own specific forms of what De Meulder has called 'proto-urbanism', and infuse the city with their own praxis, values, moralities and temporal dynamics. This process, which is perhaps better referred to as a form of 'post-urbanism', started at Kinshasa's margins and has now engulfed the city as a whole. Unhindered by any kind of formal industrialization or economic development, the city has by-passed, redefined or smashed the (neo-)colonial logics that were stamped onto its surface. It has done so spatially, in terms of its architectural and urban development, as well as in terms of its socio-cultural and economic imprint. Reaching across the formation period of high colonialism and its modernist ideals, Kinshasa is, to some extent, rejoining its earlier rural roots. Today, aided by an unabating political and economic crisis, the city is undergoing a large-scale process of informal *villagization*, in which a new type of agrarian urbanity and even a new type of ethnicity is generated (see also Devisch 1996).

For an external observer it is not always easy to read this new urban landscape. Related to the Western failure to reach beyond its blurred vision of a largely fictitious Congo is the development of a second form of cataract, which is becoming increasingly apparent in the incapacity of much of the academic discourse to grasp fully and make visible the changing realities in contemporary Congo and Kinshasa. Faced with worlds and interactions that no longer correspond to the social inter-weave as we tend to conceptualize and experience it, one becomes acutely aware that it is futile to explain some of the processes currently taking place in Congolese society by means of the standard vocabularies usually used by social and political scientists, economists, demographers and urban planners. Terms and concepts such as 'state', 'administration', 'government', 'governability', 'democracy', 'army', 'citizenship', 'law', 'justice', or even 'education' and 'healthcare' no longer seem to apply unequivocally to the realities usually covered by those terms.

Why is a building called 'national bank', 'university', 'state depart-ment', 'hospital', or 'school' when the activities which take place in it cannot be given standard meanings and realities usually covered by those words? In January 1995, for example, Belgian newspapers reported that the national bank's total stock of foreign currency amounted to US$ 2,000 and a handful of Swiss francs. Similarly, university professors today earn US$ 200 a month, if they are paid, that is, and most departments of Kinshasa's national university have not bought books, or produced a single doctoral dissertation, since the Zaïreanization of the early 1970s. What does it mean to be a city with an estimated six million inhabitants in which there is hardly any car traffic or public transport, for the simple reason that, at frequent intervals, there is not a drop of fuel available for weeks or even months? Why continue the social convention of referring to a bank-note as 'money' when one is confronted daily with the fact that it is just a worthless slip of paper? The withdrawal, in November 1993, of the IMF and the World Bank from the country attested to the fact that

Congo was no longer partaking in the formal world economy. But what is the use of distinguishing between formal and informal or parallel economies when the informal has become the common and the formal has almost disappeared?

For years now, Congo's 'second' or 'shadow' economy has become the first and virtually only one. For Kinois it has long since become a cliché to say that no economic model can explain how a city like Kinshasa survives. For the pousse-pousseurs (removal men, using push-carts), the quados (informal car-mechanics), the khaddafis (illegal vendors of fuel), the cambistes (money changers), taxi-drivers, shoe-shiners, night-watchmen and ligablos (street vendors) who daily experience in the flesh the continuing deterioration of their standards of living, and whose lives unfold in avenue misère, the common discourses of political, economic and other analysts and 'experts' are therefore totally devoid of sense. To them, Kinshasa-la-belle has long since become Kinshasa-la-poubelle, referred to as Koweit City rive gauche, Sarajevo or, more recently, Kosovo and Tchetchénie.

Mirroring Kinshasa's inhabitants' attempts at constantly renaming and thereby reclaiming their city, the colonial and post-colonial authorities invested a lot of energy in the construction of their vision of the urban space. The colonizing dynamics of naming and renaming the city and its composite parts are typical of both the colonial and the Mobutist period. During colonial times, not only the city's name, Léopoldville, referred to the colonial master but so did the names of many a neighbourhood: Belge I, Belge II, Bruxelles. Similarly, Mobutu stamped himself onto the city's map by renaming streets, buildings (Mama Yemo hospital, Stade Kamanyola), military camps and neighbourhoods (Cité Mama Mobutu, Camp Mobutu). These acts of name-giving illustrate the constant attempts at mastering the city, at producing domination, at defining place and encapsulating it in language. And yet, the names themselves immediately become sites of opposition against the official order.

The breakdown of the colonial city model and its local appro-priation, transformation and cultural reterritorialization had already started during the colonial period itself. In 1959, more than half of Léopoldville's population was under the age of eighteen, and of this large group, only half was schooled. In 1960, the capital, already over-populated, was flooded by another wave of youngsters who were fleeing from the rebellion and warfare in the interior (a process that is currently repeating itself). It is against this background of a decade of rising insecurity and socio-economic and political unrest that street gangs of youngsters without schooling or a salaried job started to make an appearance in the streets of Léopoldville.[3]

Between 1957 and 1959, in the same period in which the adminis-trative reform took place, six cinemas opened their doors: 'Sibika' in the Kintambo neighborhood, and 'Astra', 'Mbongo-Mpasi', 'Macauley', 'Moustapha' and 'Siluvangi' in the popular neighbour-hoods of Lingwala, Kinshasa and Barumbu. These movie theaters, which flourished all over the city except in the 'European' neighbour-hoods of Ngaliema, Léopoldville and Limete, soon became a favourite meeting place of Léopoldville's youth, especially those youngsters at the margins of the colonial urban order, at risk of being expelled by the authorities. Westerns in particular had a tremendous impact on the way in which the urban youth subcultures of that time chose to express themselves and became a decisive factor in the creation of Billism. In particular the image of the buffalo hunter and culture-hero Buffalo Bill, alongside other cowboys such as Pecos Bill, left a deep impression.[4] These cowboys provided ideal role models for the young Kinois, who started to imitate the appearance (blue-jeans, checkered shirt, neckerchief, lasso) and the tics of the Hollywood actors. After each movie, these young urban cowboys circulated on their 'bicycle-horses' to announce the message of the Western (*mofewana*, Lingala deformation of Far West), crying loudly *Bill oyee!*, upon which the bystanders would reply with *serumba!*.

As such, Billism appropriated and transformed the image of the cowboy-hunter to make it its own. Most of the members of these ludic groups of young urban 'terrorists', more generally known as 'The Spongers of the Far West' (*Les Ecumeurs du Far West*), lived on the margins of colonial society. The movement produced various competing youth gangs. Around 1957 most of these gangs, such as the 'Yankees of Ngiri-Ngiri', shaped up around leaders, most of whom were well-known local delinquents. These groups organized themselves in little territorial fiefdoms throughout the city (in Ngiri-Ngiri, Saint-Jean, Camp Luka, Bandal, Kintambo, Bandalungwa, Barumbu, Kinshasa and later Lemba, Ndjili, Matete, Yolo) and like sheriffs, they 'made the law' (*kodondwa*) and 'created order' (*tobongisa*, one of the Bills' slogans) in their neighbourhood, while stealing for a living and fighting over territory with neighboring gangs. Each territory thus had its chiefs and subchiefs, its ritual specialists known as *professeurs*, its own laws and rules, declared by the *maître* of each particular gang, its own systems of taxation (making other citizens pay for a safe passage through gang territory), and its own pass-time rituals, such as weight-lifting, gang-raping neighbourhood girls, or smoking marijuana. Billism also strongly focused on music and guitars. As such the movement was at the origin of the birth of multiple local orchestras, some of which evolved later into well-known bands, such as Zaiko. As such, Billism, mobilizing and channeling the social forces from the margin, greatly contributed to the establishment of one of the most powerful forms of expression in Kinshasa's flamboyant popular culture.

What distinguished 'the Bills' above all was the use of a particular argot, known as Hindubill, a mixture of French, Lingala, English and local vernacular languages. In a counter-hegemonic inversion, 'Hindu' refers to 'Indian', the cowboys' natural enemies (that is, the state agents). It also makes reference to the 'Indian' marijuana the Bills smoked. 'Hindu' possibly also betrays the influence of Hindi movies shown in the cinemas of Léopoldville during that period. This Indian cinematographic influence is partly responsible for the way in which the emerging figure of the Mami Wata – half woman and half fish, who promises access to wealth in return for human lives – has started to dominate the city's imagination since the 1960s. In Kinshasa's popular paintings, Mami Wata invariably appears as a white-skinned 'Indian' lady (and this in spite of the West African origin of the Mami Wata figure).

As the language of youth, Hindubill formed the hidden transcript of the youthful underdogs of Kinshasa who were excluded from education and salaried jobs and thus from the world of 'adults'. With Hindubill, the urban cowboys created their own modes of in- and exclusion. At the same time the persona of the Cowboy emerges as an emancipatory figure, representing the spirit of the coming Independence. The Bills played an important role in the lootings and the uprising that spread through Kinshasa in January 1959. The Bills also re-territorialized the city in yet another way, by renaming various areas, markets, schools, bars and other public spaces of the city, upon which they bestowed names such as Texas, Dallas, Casamar, Godzilla. This re-territorialization implied an explicit criticism of the Belgians' insufficient and segregationist urbanization of a too rapidly expanding Léopoldville. Undoubtedly, the Bills' practice of reclaiming and renaming parodied the colonizer's imperialist obsession with mapping and labelling, while at the same time playfully commenting upon the claims of the emergent nationalist movement.

From November 1960 onwards, with the mounting 'Congo crisis' and the increasing unrest throughout the country, many new youth gangs appear. These still made use of the vocabulary of the Bills but at the same time they increasingly shifted from the figure of the Cowboy to that of the Soldier, with references, for example, to the United Nations Blue Helmets, thereby reflecting in their vocabulary and organization the changing context of the period in which they emerged.

Billism laid the foundation for much of the contemporary urban youth culture. Kinshasa's cinemas have long since disappeared. Instead, films have become available through television, or they are watched in small neighbourhood video-theatres, where one usually pays for a full evening programme including clips of the latest Congolese hits and concerts, a movie à la Ninja or Rambo, some soccer and, to top it off, a porn movie. Yet, the way in which Western action movie hunters/warriors are captured and localized by Kinshasa's youth, but even more by the military, is reminiscent of the Bills in the 1950s. Zorro, Rambo, Superman, Terminator, Godzilla and the Power Rangers have become common role models for Kabila's *kadogos* (child-soldiers) and for the urban youth in general. Kinshasa's youth share with their forebears the same capacity at fracturing and re-inventing the urban public space. Street children in Kinshasa sing: 'It is said that water that sleeps does not move. The sleeping water only moves when one throws a stone into it.' Often, Kinshasa's youngsters are like such a stone, shattering the water's reflecting surface and sending ripples and waves through the pool in which Kinshasa beholds itself. They inscribe themselves in new temporalities. They also recycle and generate surprising, oftentimes embodied, cultural vocabularies and aesthetics. Now, as in the past, these feverishly reflect Kinshasa's social history while providing a subversive comment upon the banalization of violence, the militarization of society, the apocalyptic gale-force sound and fury of the city's constant religious transfiguration, and the material hardships in today's urban scape.

The village and the forest city

The growing ruralization of Kinshasa is a strong reminder of the fact that the capital has not only looked into the mirror of modernity to design itself, but that it has always contained a second mirror as well. This mirror is provided by the village, the rural hinterland that constitutes Kinshasa's demographic and ethnic make-up, the countryside that feeds Kinshasa, forms its natural backdrop, and exists in the city by way of contrast. It is this contrast that allowed the city to fashion itself as city, to define itself as *centre extra-coutumier* and, as marker of difference in opposition to the village, to place itself outside of the normative order of a rural and more traditional world that was – and often is – considered to be backward and primitive. And yet, at the same time, the construction of Kinshasa's urban space and identity has always remained a contested and dislocatory presence, a reminder of an artificial breach. In reality, this urban identity has constantly been invaded and formed by, blending with and depending on the village's traditions, moralities and pasts.

Three decades ago, someone like Henri Lefebvre, in his acclaimed work *The Production of Space*, could still, somewhat naively, write: 'Much as they might like to, anthropologists cannot hide the fact that the space and tendencies of modernity (i.e. of modern capitalism) will never be discovered either in Kenya or among French or any other peasants.' (Lefebvre, 1991 [1974]: 123). Lefebvre thereby continued the same long modernist tradition which underpinned the creation of *difference* in the colonial period, and which is characterized by its conceptualization of the world within a polarized framework opposing, for example, modernity and tradition, city and countryside, centre and periphery, 'warm' and 'cold' societies, culture and nature, male and female, the 'hard rationality' of liberal capitalism generated in the urban space and the 'soft irrationality' of a rural 'economy of affection', and so forth. However, the distinctions between urban and rural realities, between 'modern' and 'traditional' worlds, or between what is situated locally and what is considered to be global, can no longer be taken for granted. It is no doubt a perceptual error to concentrate exclusively on the centre, or the city, in order to understand the production of modernity (or the construction of, for example, 'modern' male African identity). Rather than to scrutinize the processes of modernity's construction from the metropole's perspective, it is also important to look at the fringes, at the periphery, at those sites, whether located in the rural countryside or in the city itself, where 'modernity' has not solidified but is a fluid and negotiable reality, an unfinished hegemony.

In the post-colony, moreover, categories such as 'centre' and 'periphery', or 'city' and 'village', and the string of qualities attached to them, have often themselves become states of mind rather than objective qualities of space. The way in which the urban and the rural are constantly deconstructed in the post-colony necessitates an imaginative theorizing of that reality. For example, whereas the space of the city has not only undergone a marked ruralization, it has also, and increasingly, become, in the collective social instituting imaginary, the space of the forest. The hunter's landscape, which is one of the potentially dangerous, frontier-like margins, is thus constantly mapped onto the urban, and thus 'central' landscape. Hence, Werrason, the current uncrowned king of Kinshasa's popular music scene, refers to himself as 'the king of the forest' (*le roi de la forêt*) and the 'chief of the animals' (*mokonzi ya banyama*). It is no coincidence that the bar, a most crucial site in the urban landscape, is often redefined as village, such as Village Syllo, with its pastoral setting, along the Avenue Lumumba, or Limete's Village Bercy. In the latter, the light bulbs are put inside Alladin lamps, which function as *pars pro toto* for the local, conjuring up the rural and the village. At the same time the notion of the village blends into an interesting palimpsest through a reference to an icon of the global western world, the Stade de Bercy in Paris, where a number of Kinshasa's orchestras gave concerts in recent years. Often also, the bar is conceptualized as 'forest'. In the social imaginary, the nocturnal environment of the bar is no doubt one of the most important locales in which the city most fully displays its 'urbanity' and modernity, and in which 'diamond-hunters', and others who have access to dollars track down and capture, through ostensive consumption of beer, women and consumer goods, their interpretation of the 'good life' as promised by and defined in their notion of 'modernity'.

It thus seems that, in Kinshasa today, modernity as exemplified by the city is not only contested or unfinished at its fringes, that is, the rural hinterland, but also in its very heart, the polis, where the local logic of hunting and gathering has infused the urban world, both metaphorically and practically, with its own moralities, its own ethics of accumulation, expenditure and redistribution, and its own specific pathways of self-realization. Especially for the urban young, the hunter provides a model of identification and a figure of success and eminence. It is no coincidence that it was precisely Buffalo Bill, a buffalo hunter, who became a culture-hero for Kinshasa's youngsters. Even today, the image of the hunter continues to have a strongly epistemic power. It offers the possibility of remaking both identity and place, and generating – to some extent at least – a social environment in the midst of chaos and change. For the 'children of Lunda' (*bana Lunda*) or 'the children who work money' (*basali ya mbongo*), the numerous youngsters who leave Kinshasa and other urban centres to travel hundreds of kilometers to the Angolan diamond fields of Lunda Norte, 'hunting' diamonds and dollars constitutes a crucial part of the active capturing of the urban space, for it allows them to refashion the city (and thereby 'modernity', the West, the *mundele* or 'white man') in their own terms, which are those of long-standing moralities, rooted in local rural pasts (see De Boeck 1999a/b, 2000). Congolese youngsters' engagement in more global economies of diamond export and dollarization is thus often shaped from an utterly local perspective and out of a memory that is rooted in the *longue durée*. Although memory and history in the urban context are of a specific kind and have undergone some radical transformations over the past decades, the expanding peripheral city is thus not without history, unlike Koolhaas's notion of the 'generic city' (Koolhaas, 1996). To conquer the city and shape their own moral and social economies in this urban space, the urban young tap into sources and routes of rural identity formation, thereby negotiating and reinventing the content and architecture of the intermediate world in which they find themselves. As such, the passage into Angola is a contemporary version of a much older strategy of self-realization, as hunter and warrior, in that it constitutes a veritable rite of passage, modelled upon the old *mukanda* circumcision ritual which is still practised in the countryside, and to which youngsters explicitly refer when they share and discuss their experiences in the Angolan diamond fields. It is important, however, to stress that the past (represented in the form of hunting logics, the village morality of capture and redistribution, the ultimately rural modes of self-making as hunter and/or warrior) which is thus carried into the urban present is *not* a static model. On the contrary, for the urban youth the past becomes, if not reflexively at least in practice, a source for active engagement with the present, in ways that give shape both to very creative and outgoing forms of collective imagination and to a constant invention of a future for tradition (as imagined, for example, by Kinshasa's musicians in their video clips, in which the persona of the 'traditional chief' is frequently re-enacted as a potent icon of power). More generally, rural 'folkloristic' music has been continuously recycled by urban bands such as Swede-Swede since the 1980s).

At the same time, the rural periphery has (once again) gained in importance. As elsewhere in the world, where processes of globalization are played out in a context of frontier expansion, the Congolese hinterland has become most central in the capitalist dynamics. Whereas the city has become peripheral and in some respects village-like, the bush is the place where dollars are generated, where the 'good life' is shaped and where villages transform into booming diamond settlements, where life focuses on money and the consumption of women and beer.[5] The little diamond boomtowns of Kahemba and Tembo, along the borderline between Congo's Bandundu province and the Angolan province of Lunda Norte, have become most central in capitalist dynamics and the dollarization of local economies. As such, the diamond traffic, and the phenomenon of dollarization which has followed in its wake, are also emblematic of a return to the Léopoldian economy of extraction that has marked the origin of Kinshasa and so many other cities throughout Africa. The political economy of the *comptoir* has always been colonial in its very essence. In the past it contributed a lot to the urbanization of the African material and mental landscape. The contemporary *comptoir* economy in Congo and Angola has continued to contribute a great deal to the frontier urbanization of places such as Mbuji-Mayi or

Fig. 1 Dry cleaner, Kinshasa
(© Marie-Françoise Plissart)

Fig. 2 Bodybuilding, Kinshasa
(© Marie-Françoise Plissart)

Tshikapa (in the Kasai), Kahemba and Tembo (in southern Bandundu), as well as the Kwango river diamond settlements in Angola, or the diamond 'ranches' around Kisangani. These local sites have become, in certain ways, globalized spaces, the economic and cultural dynamics of which are linked to many other different places on the globe that play a role in a semi-formal world-economy, from Luanda, Kinshasa, Brazzaville, Bangui and Bujumbura, to Antwerp, Bombay, Beirut, Dubai, Tel Aviv and Johannesburg. At the same time, these locally generated 'bush' dollars have also engendered the further development, revival, sometimes even gentrification, of certain areas in Kinshasa: Masina's *quartier Sans Fil*, Ndjili's *quartier Sept*, and some parts of Lemba, such as the more residential areas of Salongo and Righini.

Diasporic movement and the mirroring of modernity

The local creation of modernities leads us to a third mirror in which Kinshasa generates an image of itself, contemplates and reflects upon itself, and projects itself outwards. This mirror is situated in the context of the diaspora. Effectively barred from travelling abroad during the colonial period, the Congolese were quick to inscribe themselves in processes of increasingly intensive migration after

Independence. This mobility intensified and was accentuated by the gradual economic decline that started to manifest itself in the latter half of the 1970s and that reached mind-boggling dimensions towards the end of Mobutu's long and disastrous reign. The breakdown of the Zaïrean state and the increasingly harsh living conditions in Kinshasa and the country at large prompted a huge exodus.

Almost invariably, the first stop along the often difficult path of diasporic existence was Belgium, and even today the focal point of Kinshasa's diasporic mirror remains the neighbourhood of Matonge, situated in Brussels. In many respects this Belgian Matonge continues to be the social and cultural nexus of Europe's Congolese migration. It is named after one of Kinshasa's most vibrant neighbourhoods, the fast-beating heart of the city's night life and popular music scene, with its effervescent central square, *Rond Point Victoire*, with its night clubs and open air bars and *ngandas* (eating places), with its West African *commerçants* in their suave *boubous* robes, the proud descendants of the Coastmen who arrived in Kinshasa in the 1930s, with its freshly roasted *kamundele* goat meat, and its crowded *Djakarta* market, lit up by hundreds of little kerosene lamps at night.

Both the colonial mirror, the mirror offered by the village and the mirror activated by the diasporic movement constantly echo a deeper level of speculation. This underlying mirror is often a broken and deforming one, a mirror that reflects Kinshasa's complex relationship with the outside and the beyond of a more global, transnational world, with the real and imagined qualities of 'modernity' and of the wider, whiter, world of the West. Driving along Kinshasa's Bypass, as the road which leads from the *Rond Point Ngaba* to the *Echangeur* of Limete is named, the observant eye might notice a dry cleaner or *blanchisserie* ('whitener' in French), named *La Modernisation*, 'Modernization'. On the facade of the house, stuck into the white-washed cement, little shards of broken mirror form the letters of the word *Modernisation*. Not devoid of irony, mirroring modernity, assimilating to the West, and inscribing oneself in the project of what is, in the end, still a very colonialist modernity, is here shown for the white-wash operation that it has always been at heart. The colonial *évolué*, this prototype of Naipaul's *mimic man*, or Kinshasa's *mundele ndombe* the 'Black White', or Fanon's *peau noir, masque blanc,* or today's pale youngsters, whitened by disastrous 'beauty' skin products – all of these figures illustrate the processes of imitation and the creation of image embedded in this mirroring. To some extent, the young diamond hunters of Kinshasa have moved beyond the mimetic. But it remains a complex process to break the spell of this image in the mirror, the image of this 'African Europe' that colonial administrators, missionaries, expatriates and the elites of the post-colonial state held up to Kinshasa for so long as a model to aspire to.

In Congo, as elsewhere in Africa, the collective social imaginary concerning the West (referred to as Putu, Miguel or Mikili) is rich in fairy-tale images that conjure up the world of modernity, and the luxurious, almost paradisiacal lifestyle of the West. In Lingala, for example, Belgium is referred to as *lola*, 'heaven'. 'The West', as a topos of the Congolese imaginary, where one enjoys the benefits of endless sources of wealth for free, sums up all the qualities of the 'good life'. The life-style of a local rich urban elite and of the expatriate confirms the reality of this 'Idea of the West'. Also, rather than deconstructing this myth for the home front, people who live and undergo themselves the often harsh realities of life in the diaspora usually go to great lengths to deny this grim picture and to confirm the exactitude of the collective imaginary. Admitting that life in the West often is a life of poverty would not devalidate the 'topos of the Western Paradise' for those who remained behind on the home front. It would instead be interpreted as a sign of personal failure and weakness of the *mikiliste* who followed the trail of the diaspora. Rather than admitting that life in the diaspora is not that easy, Congolese living abroad therefore often prefer to send home pictures of themselves in front of a Mercedes, omitting to mention the fact that the Mercedes actually belongs to the neigbour. As such, Europe (and increasingly the United States, as the ultimate Land of Cockaigne or 'luilekkerland [Dutch – litt. Lazy-sweet-land], 'the Putu of the *banoko*' [the Uncles, that is, the Belgians]) continues to be framed in these positive terms. Europe is *malili*, 'cool', whereas Africa is *moto*, 'hot', full of suffering. For most, the ideal of Putu conjures up a world without responsibilities: 'Something is broke? Not to worry. Bring it to the white man and he will fix it' sang the late Pepe Kalle in one of his songs.

Nevertheless this myth of the West has got the moth in it. Another phrase of Pepe Kalle's goes as follows: *bakende Putu, bakweyi na désert*, 'they went to Europe, but landed in the desert.' The phrase conveys the demythologization of the Idea of Europe: those who left for Europe and are now living in the diaspora have discovered that life in Putu is in reality a desert, a life of poverty filled with problems concerning money, housing, visas, and so forth. Simultaneously, the phrase also conveys a second meaning: 'We Congolese started *en route* towards an insertion into a global ecumene of modernity, but we

never attained our goal. Somewhere along the way we ran out of fuel and had to land in the desert.' The world of modernity with its tempting promises of boundless consumerism embedded in a vision of an expansive capitalism in the service of the nation-state, has become the fool's paradise in which the Congolese nation is no longer capable of living. It is out of reach for those who do not partake in the lottery of politics, have salaried jobs, know how to access international organizations and businesses, or have access to diamond-dollars.

The blame for the impossibility of accessing this Western version of the 'good life', is not only ascribed to the excesses of the Mobutu era, but increasingly the blame is also laid on the doorstep of the West itself. 'When the Belgians left, they gave us Independence, but at the same time they threw the key to open the door to development into the ocean' is a frequently heard remark in Congo. One shop-owner of a *magasin* which recently opened its doors painted the following motto above the entrance: *A qui la faute? Chez le blanc!*, 'Who is to blame? The White Man!' As such, the motto translates a growing break away from the world of modernity as defined by the metropole, a definition which reduces an increasing number of people in Congo to a subaltern status as part of a swelling Third World proletariat.

For an ever-growing number of 'malcontents', the world of modernity as defined and propagated by the West and its agents – the state agent, the missionary, the development worker, the dwindling local urban elites – has indeed become an inaccessible chimera. Some observers have therefore interpreted *la grande fête de Kinshasa,* the wave of lethal and yet ludic lootings which swept through the city and demolished the country's economy in 1991 and 1993, as a radical break with the West. What was being demolished in the *pillage* were the icons of western modernity: fancy restaurants, supermarkets and industrial plants such as General Motors. Similarly, in 1997, Congo's new leaders, who to a large extent were recruited from the diaspora, were contemptuously nick-named *occasions d'Europe* upon their arrival in Congo. In other words: the members of this new ruling elite were perceived to be like second-hand cars. No longer wanted in Europe and the States where they could not obtain a steady position, they returned to Congo like *Bounties* (the brand name of a bar of chocolate with a coconut filling): black on the surface and white at heart. This second-rate, hybridized version of the West is the best one can get, but it never quite is the genuine article.

Although the tendency to turn away from the modernist position, in a true spirit of resistance against Western domination, is certainly there, this does not mean that people resist or reject modernity's promise of the good life itself. A painting by Chéri Samba, one of Kinshasa's most acclaimed artists, entitled *La femme et ses premiers désirs*, 'Woman and Her First Desires', shows the painter's own wife, Fifi, sitting in a bourgeois living room in Kinshasa, surrounded by the signs of her and her husband's status: refrigerator, television set, rotating fan, stereo chain, a cooking furnace (see Jewsiewicki 1995: 56, plate 13). These are the fruits, the bourgeois contents of modernity that everybody, in the end, wishes for. What people increasingly object to, however, is the ideological hegemony of modernity, the fact that the West imposes upon them, from above and from outside, its own definition of 'the good life'. Much of the cultural and political struggle in Congo today focuses on control over a politics of identity as self-representation, which implies that it is self-generated and self-constructed. To a large extent the arguments of identity today centre round the question of who represents whom, and to/for whom. Who is author, who is subject of representation? Recourse to colonial and post-colonial stereotypes is inevitable in situations where identities are at play.

A secret city of public words

Behind the garden city, the forest city and the village city lurks yet another city, an invisible but very audible city of whispers, of what Kinois call *les on dit*, of fleeting words, questions, harmful suspicions and treacherous accusations. The powerful and relentless production of gossip and rumour constantly runs through the city. Shamelessly, leaving no subject untouched, it spreads like a bush fire through all of Kinshasa's communities. Often a weapon of the weak, it enters the scene from the margin and takes over the whole city, pumping its words like blood through the veins and arteries of this giant urban body. The motor of Kinshasa's public life, the capillary bio-power of this Radio Trottoir, Radio Sidewalk, punctuates the city's heart-beat and constitutes its public eye (see Nlandu-Tsasa 1997). Uniting and dividing the city through the force of words, it generates the capital's urban mythologies, its aesthetics of laughter, its cultural repertoires and collective imaginaries; it creates its heroes and damages the reputation of its most powerful and prominent citizens. It amplifies itself in the columns of the numerous newspapers that have started to proliferate since the end of Mobutu's one-party system and that daily are read and commented upon collectively at several points throughout the city by the *parlementaires debout*, the 'politicians' of the street. Urban rumour solidifies in the paintings of Kinshasa's artists. It translates into the scripts of its popular street theatre and locally produced TV soaps. It echoes in the lyrics of Kinshasa's urban troubadours.

In spite of its formidable creative force, Kinois rarely have something good to say about their gossip mechanisms. Franco, the most prominent musician that the city ever produced, bitterly addresses *Radio Trottoir* in one of his songs: 'You sabotaged me, Radio Trottoir, You broke my marriage. With information that you spread around but did not even bother to verify. You broke my marriage with your gossip!' In a similar vein his contemporary, Tabu Ley, complains in a song: 'Gossip kills this city. Friends, you might hear something today, but try to see it with your own eyes before you start spreading illness for nothing.' The invisible space of rumour and gossip constantly fractures and reshapes the composite anatomy of the city's public and private spaces. It produces the awkward intimacy of a public secrecy, a crowded and promiscuous common living space, shared by all of the city's inhabitants. In colonial times, the qualities and characteristics of 'private' and 'public' held distinctly different connotations in the 'white' city and the indigenous peripheries. At sunset a curfew banned the Congolese from the European areas of town, and both sides retreated into the privacy of their own living areas, ignorant of and often uninterested in each others' lives. The neighbourhoods and houses where both worlds touched each other geographically were often the literally intermediate and blended worlds of *métissage,* of those who did not firmly belong to either space or crossed the social or racial lines that pervaded colonial society and thus had no fixed place in it. Mixed African-European households, mostly set up by Portuguese or Greek traders and shop owners, formed a buffer zone between African and European neighbourhoods. The colonials retreated into their residences, offices, clubs and restaurants, and restricted their contact with indigenous worlds to a functional minimum, in ways that were not much different from the life-styles of many expatriates in Kinshasa today.

Life in the African parts of town, on the other hand, was played out in the *parcelle* and in the street. The *parcelle* is a space that is typical of Kinshasa. Often surrounded by a wall and with an iron gate that demarcates its entrance, the *parcelle*, with its house or houses, and usually with its mango or palm tree and little garden of vegetables and crops, creates a small island of more or less private domesticity, in the shared intimacy of one's (extended) family and ethnic affiliations. In many areas of the city, though, the *parcelle* has been invaded by and lives in close proximity and symbiosis with the street. As such, many *parcelles* are rather 'public' private spaces. Simultaneously, Kinshasa also generates 'private' public spaces, such as the recreative and ludic places of the bar, the night-club, the hotel and the *nganda* (originally the retreat where fishermen rest after their work, but now the name given to 'formally informal' restaurants, often in the backyards of private homes). In these meeting points, men meet their friends, mistresses and concubines in an atmosphere of privacy and secrecy, and yet invariably also in view of all, within reach of *Radio Trottoir's* tentacles and subjected to the gaze of the public eye. The *phonie* is another place where private and public become interchangeable. Every neighbourhood has its small *phonie* enterprises, where one can enter into contact with otherwise unreachable friends and relatives in the interior of the country through radio wave communication. Often the *phonie* is also a meeting point for people from the same regional or ethnic background. Money matters, love affairs, marriages, births, divorces, illnesses, deaths and other private family matters are shouted into the microphone as well as into the ears of the neighbourhood's and indeed the country's *trottoirs*. In Kinshasa, the private life of the individual and the moralities generated by the collective gaze are constantly living in a sometimes uneasy, often contradictory cohabitation with each other.

Like many capitals around the world, Kinshasa has always been a narcissistic city, very much fascinated and preoccupied by the events of its own micro-cosmos. To an outsider who is unfamiliar with the city's inner argot, its signs and secrets, Kinshasa's urban codes therefore often appear difficult to crack. At the same time, Kinshasa constantly displays and puts itself on stage. Just like the city they live in, Kinois are extremely skillful at managing not just one but several individual identities at the same time. The constant negotiation between these individual and collective identities almost always takes place or is commented upon in the public sphere. Kinshasa exists in the public eye and through its public appearance. Nourished by the force of pretence, the *faire croire* and *faire semblant* that pervades the urban praxis, Kinshasa is essentially an exhibitionist city or, as Yoka says, *une ville-spectacle*, a spectacle city (Yoka 1999: 15). The urban aesthetics of display and public appearance are most clearly illustrated in the city's most private space, which is simultaneously also its most public theatre: the body. Outdoing Proust's Paris, Kinshasa is a city of *flaneurs* and idle strollers, a proudly sensuous city where bodies, both male and female, are constantly dressing up and taking themselves out into the dusty streets and alleys of each neighbourhood to be seen, to display themselves in feigned indifference to the public gaze; it is a city, also, where there are always eyes to see and behold, and where spectators constantly comment upon the outfit, the movement of hips and buttocks, the style of the hairdress, the whole bearing, appearance and *gabarit* of passers-by, their whole social skin and social skill. In fact, the eyes of the beholders offer a mirror which constantly reflects one's own social strength. In spite of, or maybe precisely because of its extreme poverty, Kinshasa's aesthetic regime of the body has turned into a veritable cult of elegance, culminating in the movement of the *Sape*, an acronym for *Société des ambianceurs et des personnes elegantes*, the Society of Fun Lovers and Elegant Persons. Started in the early 1980s around 'King of Sape' Papa Wemba, a popular musician, this movement escalated into real fashion contests and potlatches in which youngsters would display their European fashion designer clothes, in an attempt to outdo each other. Recently, this spirit of elegance has found a second breath in the flourishing context of Pentecostalist and other Christian fundamentalist churches, in which the city's new figures of success, its most famed preachers such as Fernando Kutino or Soni Kafuta, show off their Armani and Versace suits to their admiring and ecstatic followers, under the motto that 'one has to appear clean before God' (*Il faut être propre devant Dieu*).

Pushing the mirror metaphor to the limit of reflection and beyond, the religious transformation which Congolese society is currently undergoing has contributed to a reconfiguration, if not an obliteration, of the dividing lines between public and private space, as well as an increasing theatricalization of the city. This process goes hand in hand with an increasing star-ization of those who occupy the front stage, the *pasteurs* and musicians. The new *vedettariat* and *staromanie* in the popular music scene has given rise to new forms of violence. Not only does the music and its accompanying dance styles reflect, and reflect upon, the violence that pervades the city and Congolese society at large, but the frequent clashes between avid followers of rival bands have themselves become increasingly responsible for the quality of mounting insecurity in Kinshasa's public spaces. Home to street children and military, Kinshasa's main arteries, crossroads, markets, sport stadia and administrative sites have often become a social no man's land, governed by the predatory violence of the street. At the same time, the enchanting space of the church, with its new moral economies and its own forms of physical and symbolic violence, has swallowed and encompassed the space of popular culture. It has also claimed and drastically reconfigured the public space as such. In all corners of the city, and at all times of the day and the night, thousands upon thousands of Kinois gather to pray. In the process, the space of the church has become the city's main stage, a space of *témoignage* also, where people publicly bear witness of their sins and their conversion, where they display and act out their poverty or wealth, their misery or blessing, leaving no stone of their personal lives unturned, no intimate detail unmentioned. In the process, the religious dynamics in these churches have also thoroughly impacted on the private space and contribute to a radical restructuring of the social networks and moral and ethical matrices that constitute the family, kin relations and ethnic affiliations. Within the church context, the changed relations between the spaces of public and private space are indicative of deeper changes in the relationship between subjectivity and intersubjectivity in Kinshasa today. While presenting a vast effort to recreate a new, all-inclusive intersubjectivity on a moral basis, the religious praxis pushes aside the intersubjective moral model which has always been provided by 'the village', with its ethics of kin solidarity, reciprocity and gift logic. Paradoxically, this effort thus contributes to an increasing diabolization of social life as it has been lived until now.

The first and second worlds of Kinshasa

While taking into account these various levels which constitute Kinshasa's ecology today, there is yet another, and more fundamental, mirroring process that impacts on all the previous ones: that between the visible city of the 'first world' and of the day, and an invisible Kinshasa that exists in what Kinois themselves refer to as the nocturnal 'second world' or 'second city', an occult city of the shadow, as it exists in the local mind and imagination. 'If there can be a better way for the real world to include the one of images, it will require an ecology not only of real things but of images as well' wrote Susan Sontag (1978: 180). The urban scape of Kinshasa, its activities, its praxis, and its specific meaningful sites (the parcelle or compound, the

bar, the church, the street) should be read not only as geographical, visible and palpable urban realities but also, and primarily so, as a *mundus imaginalis*, a local mental landscape, a topography and historiography of the local Congolese imagination that is no less real than its physical counterpart, a 'second world' that is collectively shared by all social layers in Kinshasa, uniting its *beau monde* and its *demi-monde*.

In the autochthonous experience, daily life constantly uses the processes of mirroring and reflecting to make sense of itself. The activities of the day constantly include the world of the night, of the dream and of the shadow: to interpret the world of the living, a diviner opens up another space-time, another world, the world of ancestors, through a mirror, or by means of the unmoving surface of water in a gourd. Dreams are beacons in the night but they impact in very tangible ways on decisions one has to make during the day: whether or not to travel today, whether to meet so-and-so, whether to set out on a hunt or postpone it. The material realness of the mask, as image, as double, and as dancing representation of the dead, doesn't make the existence of the dead any less real. Rather, the mask *becomes, is, posits* the ancestor while simultaneously being a mask made of raffia and wood. 'To consider the obverse and the reverse of the world', writes Mbembe,

> as opposed, with the former partaking of a 'being there' (*real presence*) and the latter of a 'being elsewhere' or a 'non-being' (*irremediable absence*) – or, worse, of the order of unreality – would be to misunderstand. The reverse of the world and its obverse did not communicate with each other only through a tight interplay of correspondences and complex intertwined relations. They were also governed by relations of similarity, relations far from making the one a mere copy or model of the other. These links of similarity were thought to unite them, but also to distinguish them, according to the wholly autochthonous principle of simultaneous multiplicities. (Mbembe 2001: 144–45)

One of the main questions relates to the changes that seem to have appeared in the mechanisms operating this simultaneous multiplicity of the two different worlds that exist on each side of the mirror, and thus also in and through each other. In urban Congo, something seems to have changed in the slippage between visible and invisible, between reality and what we can call, for lack of better words, its double, its shadow, spectre, reflection, image, or *elili*, as it is referred to in Lingala.

What is it, then, that has affected the praxis and rhetoric of the image in Kinshasa today? Within the local experiential frame, rendered in Kinois' accounts of their lives and of their city, the double, this other, nocturnal ghost of a city which lurks underneath the surface of the visible world, somehow seems to have taken the upper hand. Today, mirroring the way in which the second or 'shadow' economy has taken over the first or formal economy, this other, 'second world' (*deuxième monde*), 'second city' (*deuxième cité*), 'pandemonium world' (*monde pandemonium*), or 'fourth dimension' (*quatrième dimension*, that is, one of the multiple 'invisible' worlds of what is referred to as *kindokinisme*)[6] increasingly seems to push aside and take over the first world of daily reality. 'The second world is the world of the invisible', says one inhabitant of Kinshasa, 'and those who live in it and *know* are those who have four eyes, those who see clearly both during the day and during the night. Their eyes are a mirror. A man with two eyes only cannot know this world. The second world is a world that is superior to ours. The second world rules the first world.' This, and many other similar accounts, seems indicative of the widespread feeling that what you see is not what you see (unless you have four eyes), and what is there is not what is 'really' there or, more important, is not what matters most. The seen and the unseen, it thus seems, no longer reflect, balance and produce each other in equal, and equally *real* ways. Somehow, the reverse has become more *ontological* than the obverse. It is no longer experienced as a similar but parallel reality, but, on the contrary, as the reality that has come to inhabit and overgrow its opposite. Symptomatic of this more general change is the invasion of the space of the living by the dead (see De Boeck 1998). A term which is currently used in Lingala to describe this new quality of mounting *Unheimlichkeit* and elusiveness of the world, is *mystique*. In the post-colonial *Afrique fantôme* that Congo seems to have become, it is increasingly frequent to designate people and situations as *mystique*, difficult to place, attribute meaning to and interpret.

This changed nature of the point of inflection between different but simultaneously real worlds, the change in the mirroring mechanisms of reflection and retroflection that constitute the passage between the obverse and the reverse of the world, heavily impacts on daily life in Kinshasa. For example, it continuously transforms the qualities and realities of what constitutes life and death, as well as the ways in which they relate to each other. Similarly, the changed relationship between obverse and reverse constantly promotes a religious transfiguration of daily reality. The incessant reinvention of the Congolese urban lived-in environment is not at all marked by a Weberian *Entzauberung*. It is, on the contrary, enacted and produced most strongly, not only in the 'enchanting' spaces of Christian fundamentalism that have taken over the city, but also in the frenzied and often obsessional production of discourses and practices surrounding witchcraft (and both are, of course, intimately related). In the process, the dynamics of witchcraft have undergone some dramatic changes. One of the most disconcerting phenomena that highlight this evolution is the central role that children are nowadays given in these newly developing witchcraft discourses and practices. In contemporary Kinshasa, thousands of children are implicated in witchcraft accusations, and often end up on the street as a result of this. As such, they find themselves at the heart of one of the most disturbing transformations in the Congolese societal *multi-crise*, namely the changing relationship between the world of the visible and the invisible, between life and death, or between reality and its double.[7] Commonly described as a 'dead society' (*société morte*), Kinshasa's street children, who to a large extent live during the night and often sleep, eat and live in places such as cemeteries, have come to embody the growing alienation of the order of the visible. They constitute a fulcrum between the processes of doubling and dedoubling and fully exemplify the permeability and interchangeability of the borderlines between day and night, living and non-living, public and private, or order and disorder (De Boeck 2000).

All of these changes are characteristic of some deeper alterations that Congolese society as a whole is undergoing. Without going into the historical roots of these changes here, this evolution may be summarized as a generalized crisis, situated in the Congolese capital's capacity for semiosis and semiotics, for observing and interpreting the syntaxis, semantics and pragmatics of the sign *as sign*. Not that Kinshasa's inhabitants do not know how to work with signs, or have stopped doing so – quite the contrary – one could even argue that Kinshasa is marked not by a lack but by a constant overproduction of leading sense, and that it is precisely this 'over-heating', this excess of the signifier, that leads to the crisis of meaningfulness. But it is also in the nature itself of the transcription of one reality into the other, and therefore in the nature of the representational, that the changes have ensconced themselves. In the process, something has happened to the relationship between image and reality. A change has occurred in the ways in which the representation and the represented reality relate to each other.

Applying a linguistic and sociological perspective to the daily scene in Kinshasa, one could say that the rupture between discourse, representation, action and structure is total. The urban reality has gradually turned into a world in which fact and fiction are interchangeable. In Kinshasa today, it is no longer possible to forget or deny the Saussurian arbitrariness of the sign, or the facticity of the social fact. What Taussig (1993) has termed the 'mimetic faculty', the capacity to pretend that one lives facts, not fictions, has often ceased to operate in an adequate way. To put it differently, there is a strong sense of what Baudrillard (1983) has termed the 'precession of simulacra', thereby pointing out the changing relations between the signifying 'real' and the representational 'imaginary', or the liquidations of all referentials. The common links and paths of transfers between signifier and signified, or between predicate and subject, have imploded or are subverted: what I have previously called the *faire croire* and *faire semblant* have often taken over from reality. In Kinshasa, as a consequence, more than anywhere else, there is no reality that is strong enough to resist language. Often, the discrepancies between signifier and signified allow for the generation of a specific kind of Kinois humour, enabling, for example, the *locataire* of an old and decrepit shack to refer to his dwelling as the *palais du peuple*, 'the people's palace', after the imposing parliamentary building of the same name which was constructed in the heart of Kinshasa by the Chinese. But in that specific Kinois language, the shifts are often less benign. Very often what poses as true is actually false, the lie becomes truth. As a result, to give but one example, the boundaries between legal and illegal are continuously shifting. Such shifts are operated by the widespread mechanism of reversibility that is constantly at work in the daily lives of most Kinois. Hence, also, as I noted earlier, the important place which this city attributes to appearance. Undoubtedly, this crisis of meaning that can be observed at all levels of Congolese society has profoundly alienating effects on both macro- and micro-levels of societal life.

But this sociological level only captures the more obvious effects of the crisis of meaning that may be observed in Kinshasa. On another, deeper, level, one could stand the argument on its head and say that Kinshasa's 'image-repertoire' does not so much suffer from a lack but rather from an excess of overlap between the signifying and the signified, or between the structures of the symbolic, the 'real' that resists language, and the level of the imaginary. At this level, the problem with notions such as 'fact' and 'fiction' is that they do not take into account the autochthonous experience of the realness of the double, but risk reducing it to something unreal, a mere 'fantasy'. But if, on the contrary, one takes the reality of the thing and its double seriously, one starts to see that the deeper crisis situates itself primarily in the changing functions and qualities of junction and disjunction (such as the disjunction between life and death), and hence of the role of the imaginary, which operates that disjunction or *dédoublement*. Much of the current Congolese societal crisis, the subjectivity of which is lived and experienced most strongly in precisely the urban locale, situates itself in this slippage. Put in a different way, the societal crisis in Congo essentially evolves around the containment, the struggle to reestablish control over an increasingly overflowing imaginary. And at the heart of this struggle lies the ever more problematic possibility of positing or 'siting' of the double (for example, death as the double of the living, or the double as the living and familiar figure of death). What may be observed here is, in a way, the *liquidation* of the double, the unwholesome coalescence of the reflecting sides into one, or the gradual take-over of one by the other. As such, in its more extreme forms, this process of liquidation operates a killing, a destroying of reality, an annihilation or *néantisation* of the world in its most essential structure. And through this liquidation, which produces Kinshasa as idol and as eidolon, the imaginary ceaselessly creates its own level of autonomy, with all of its excesses, its witchcraft, its diabolization of social life. This new 'siting' of the city's imaginary forms the undercurrent that reshapes the urban locale today.

Notes

1 This work is part of a larger collaboration between De Boeck and photographer Marie-Françoise Plissart which culminated in the publication of a book, *Kinshasa. Tales of the Invisible City*. Together with architect Koen Van Synghel, Filip De Boeck also curated an exhibition on Kinshasa for the 9th Architecture Bienniale in Venice, September 2004.
2 For a detailed history of colonial architecture in Léopoldville and Congo, see De Meulder 2000. Personal reminiscences of a rapidly changing city are offered by Kolonga Molei 1979. See also La Fontaine 1970.
3 Even before, between 1920 and 1940 small gangs of youngsters had made their appearance in the streets of Léopoldville. These gangs mostly recruited amongst the children of policemen and soldiers of the Force Publique.
4 Gondola (1997: 310) mentions in particular two films that introduced Buffalo Bill to the youthful Congolese audiences: the versions of Cecil B. de Mille (1936) and William Wellman (1944). Most popular, however, was *Pony Express* (translated as 'Le triomphe de Buffalo Bill'), made by Jerry Hooper in 1953, in which Charlton Heston played the much-appreciated part of Buffalo Bill.
5 The boomtowns of Tembo and Kahemba, in the administrative units of Kasongo-Lunda and Kahemba respectively, are a good example of these dynamics. In 1984, the *cité* of Kahemba officially counted 10,522 inhabitants (*quartiers* Kahemba, Mobutu and Sukisa). Ten years later the population of Kahemba had multiplied tenfold, with small aircraft flying in almost daily with goods and people from Kinshasa. Today the town of Kahemba is reducing in size again, due to the difficulties of accessing Angola since the end of 1998.
6 *Kindokinisme* is derived from the Lingala term *kindoki*, 'witchcraft'. The use of the neologism is significant in that it illustrates how the unpredictable transformations of reality constantly seem to require new conceptual frameworks.
7 *Le Potentiel*, 4 September 2000.

References

Baudrillard, J. 1983. *Simulations*. New York: Semiotext(e).
Calvino, I. 1974. *Invisible Cities*. New York: Harcourt.
Conrad, J. 1983 [1902]. *Heart of Darkness*. Harmondsworth, Middlesex: Penguin.
Davies, I. 1998. 'Negotiating African Culture: Toward a Decolonization of the Fetish'. In F. Jameson and M. Miyoshi (eds) *The Cultures of Globalization*. Durham, NC/London: Duke University Press.
De Boeck, F. 1998. 'Beyond the Grave: History, Memory and Death in Postcolonial Congo/Zaire'. In R. Werbner (ed.) *Memory and the Postcolony. African Anthropology and the Critique of Power*. London: Zed Books.
— 1999a. 'Domesticating Diamonds and Dollars: Identity, Expenditure and Sharing in Southwestern Zaire (1984–1997)'. In B. Meyer and P. Geschiere (eds) *Globalization and Identity. Dialectics of Flow and Closure*. Oxford: Blackwell.
— 1999b. '"Dogs Breaking their Leash": Globalization and Shifting Gender Categories in the Diamond Traffic Between Angola and DRCongo (1984–1997)'. In D. de Lame and C. Zabus (eds) *Changements au féminin en Afrique noire. Anthropologie et littérature. Volume 1*. Tervuren/Paris: Musée royal de l'Afrique Centrale/L'Harmattan.
— 2000. 'Le "deuxième monde" et les "enfants-sorciers" en République Démocratique du Congo', *Politique Africaine* 80: 32–57.
De Boeck, F. & M.-F. Plissart. 2004. *Kinshasa. Tales of the Invisible City*. Ghent: Ludion.
De Meulder, B. 2000. *Kuvuande Mbote. Een eeuw koloniale architectuur en stedenbouw in Kongo*. Antwerpen: Uitgeverij Houtekiet / De Singel.
de Saint-Moulin, L. 1970. 'Ndjili, première cité satellite de Kinshasa'. *Cahiers économiques et sociaux*, VIII (2): 295–316.
de Saint-Moulin, L. and M. Ducreux 1969. 'Le phénomène urbain à Kinshasa. Evolution et perspectives'. *Etudes congolaises* XII (4).
de Villiers, G. 1978. *Panique au Zaïre*. Paris: Plon.
— 1997. *Zaïre adieu*. Paris: Editions Gérard de Villiers.
Devisch, R. 1996. '"Pillaging Jesus": Healing Churches and the Villagisation of Kinshasa'. *Africa* 66 (4): 555–86.
Fanon, F. 1986 [1952]. *Black Skin, White Masks*. London: Pluto Press.
Gondola, Ch. D. 1997. *Villes miroirs. Migrations et identités urbaines à Kinshasa et Brazzaville 1930–1970*. Paris: L'Harmattan.
Jewsiewicki, B. 1995. *Chéri Samba. The Hybridity of Art*. Quebec: Ed. Esther A. Dagan.
Kolonga Molei. 1979. *Kinshasa, ce village d'hier*. Kinshasa: SODIMCA.
Koolhaas, R. 1996. 'La ville générique', *Architecture d'aujourd'hui* 304: 70–7.
La Fontaine, J. 1970. *City Politics. A Study of Léopoldville 1962–63*. Cambridge: Cambridge University Press.
Lefebvre, H. 1991[1974]. *The Production of Space*. Oxford: Blackwell.
Mbembe, A. 2001. *On the Postcolony*. Berkeley: University of California Press.
Naipaul, V.S. 1980. *A Bend in the River*. Harmondsworth, Middlesex: Penguin Books.
Nlandu-Tsasa, C. 1997. *La rumeur au Zaïre de Mobutu. Radio trottoir à Kinshasa*. Paris: L'Harmattan.
Sontag, S. 1977. *On Photography*. New York: Farrar, Strauss and Giroux.
Spyer, P. (ed.) 1998. *Border Fetishisms. Material Objects in Unstable Places*. New York/London: Routledge.
Taussig, M. 1993. *Mimesis and Alterity. A Particular History of the Senses*. London: Routledge.
Yoka, Lye M. 1999. *Kinshasa, signes de vie*. Tervuren/Paris: Institut Africain-CEDAF/L'Harmattan.

ABDOUMALIQ SIMONE
On the Worlding of African Cities

Reference
African Studies Review, 44, 2 (2001): 15–42

Worlding from below:
New domains of African urbanization

Placing African urban processes in a global dimension
At the heart of world cities theory is the elaboration of new spaces of transaction. These spaces open up conventional designations of scale and configure a new 'place' for places in an economy oriented around densities of knowledge creation and the generalization of control. Notions of world cities point to new economic capacities and infrastructures which construct, assemble, and channel flows of information, goods, and influences (Agnew and Corbridge 1998; Balibar 1995; Castells l996a; Taylor and Watts 1995; Leyshon and Thrift 1998). But perhaps more important, they constitute a way of

identifying and speaking about an arena of operation that is not limited simply to new forms of monopolization (Taylor 2000). For such notions may also precipitate new behaviors and positions for individuals and groups residing in cities apparently most marginal from these new economic capacities.

It is clear that African cities, with the possible exception of Johannesburg, are nowhere close to being world cities. Rather, they are largely sites of intensifying and broadening impoverishment and rampant informality operating on highly insubstantial economic platforms through which it is difficult to discern any sense of long-term viability. African cities have also been subject to substantial restructuring over the past decade. In line with normative orientations of governance, these changes have emphasized decentralization of formal political authority and responsibility, if not necessarily capacity and real decision-making power.

The assumption has been that decentralization facilitates the incorporation of local populations within a systematic 'stream' of urban development. As such, individuals and groups will then behave in line within a set of consensual and democratically deliberated objectives and procedures. Theoretically, this greater 'coordination' of behavior helps constitute a platform for increased investment, resource mobilization, and thus, economic development and job creation. But in many respects, the concentration on decentralization and the related production of urban infrastructure circumvents the broader issue of how discrete African cities can move toward greater long-term economic viability. There is limited conception about what real economies are potentially attainable. There is a limited conception of how the developmental trajectories of discrete cities are probably dependent upon expanding the possibilities of transurban interactions among African cities. A critical issue becomes how to elaborate complementarities and niche functions within a larger nexus of regional economic growth. Despite the power of their colonial antecedents, African cities have served as important frameworks for African societies to engage the larger political and economic world on their own terms. As Coquery-Vidrovitch points out, African cities were places for the 'integration of households into new networks of capitalist production; the invention of new webs of concepts and practices of land and land laws; new patterns of foodstuff consumption; new regulations governing social and political life' (1991:73).

Disrupting spatial coordinates: penetrations and inversions

In many respects, however, the operations of global economies make it nearly impossible for many Africans to continue functioning 'inside' their cities. A seemingly arbitrary circulation of the unknown has penetrated these cities. What makes people rich or poor, what accounts for loss and gain, and 'working assessments' of the identities of who is doing what to whom are viewed as more uncertain. As the 'insides' of African cities are more differentially linked to proliferating networks of accumulation and circulation operating at also increasingly differentiated scales, this uncertainty is 'materialized.' In other words, it takes the forms of specific bodies and identities, in which parts of bodies, as well as part-objects, specific locations, and built environments, are seen to embody particular forces of well-being and success.

Thus cities are overpopulated, not simply with people, but also with the forces of magic, spiritual invocation, sorcery, willfulness, and death. What had been the purview of the so-called bush now runs rampant through the city, and there is little recourse to effective mediation or clear boundaries. As a result, urban dwellers now find themselves forced to operate with a more totalizing sense of exteriority. This stems from the proliferation of multiple figures of interlaced territories that make it difficult for many to determine exactly 'where' they are and under whose jurisdiction. Localities are often reparceled into narrow enclaves due to internecine conflicts. Some states are essentially private actors. In other instances, private indirect governments elaborate new technologies of domination and new bases of property and social stratification. In some areas, religious networks constitute the 'real' public authority with sometimes no other scale but that of the world on which to operate (Mbembe 1999). As the material deconstruction of existing territorial frameworks leaves more Africans without coherent local and national arenas, a certain 'worlding' has been enforced in terms of where they see themselves operating.

Much of this 'worlding' is a state of being 'cast out' into the world. The capacity to maintain recognizable and usable forms of collective solidarity and collaboration becomes difficult. Modifying Bourdieu's (1990) reflections on habitus, these social activities can be viewed as crucial means through which localities, as social territories, are marked and are experienced as self-contained, almost 'organic' environments. Therefore, a sense of being encompassed, drawn into and acting upon a circumscribed world of commonality, is nearly impossible as the previously relied upon practices of forging social solidarity dissipate. Urban residents appear increasingly uncertain as to how to spatialize an assessment of their life chances – that is, where will they secure livelihood, where can they feel protected and looked after, where will they acquire the critical skills and capacities? When children across most African cities are asked about what they will do with their lives, the answer usually entails a life trajectory carried out far away from the place they consider 'home'. But the 'worlding' taking place is not only something that occurs by default. It is not simply the by-product of the implosion of urban Africa. To a certain extent, this 'worlding' is a process inherent in the very formation of African cities themselves. In other words, it involves the production of orientations to, and sensibilities about, the urban that seemed to posit that the salient features of urban life and its accomplishments were always also taking place somewhere else besides the particular city occupied. An uneasy mixture of external imposition and local redeployment of selective appropriations of that imposition shaped most African cities (Anderson and Rathbone 2000; Diouf 1998; Mabogunje 1990). As such, these cities exist in a universe of being rooted 'everywhere and nowhere'. But at the same time, they have an extensive history of being subject to often highly idiosyncratic compromises, social and economic arrangements that make them very 'localized' whatever the series of networks and external connections in which they 'participate'.

This is why African cities often appear to act in an incessant state of preparedness. They keep residents in an almost permanent state of changing gears and focus, if not location. Of course, there are quarters where most of the residents have spent their entire lives growing up, raising families, and devoted to the same occupation or way of life. But even these stabilities are situated in a larger arena in which social economies must be prepared to exert themselves with large measures of fluidity. Indeed, if you take the life stories of many households across the region, people have been prepared to migrate at a moment's notice, to change jobs, residences, and social networks with little apparent hesitation.

This sense of preparedness, the ability to be ready to switch gears, has significant implications for what residents think it is possible to do in place, in *the* place of the city (and also *in* place of the city). Households do display considerable determination and discipline to save over the course of many years to send children to school, to build a house, or to buy tickets so one or more members can migrate elsewhere. They are in a place; they demonstrate commitment to it. But at the same time, African cities operate as a platform for people to engage in processes and territories elsewhere.

The long period in which different versions of colonialism were in operation was, of course, critical to the shaping and present-day capacities of most African cities. But the importance of colonialism is not that it gave rise to cities in what was for the most part a rural continent. Rather, the crucial move was to shape urbanization so cities would act instrumentally on African bodies and social formations. They would act on them in ways that made various endogenous forms of, and proclivities toward, urbanization possible only within the context of an enforced engagement with the European world (Cooper 1996; Diouf 1998; Guyer 1995). The ways in which this 'urbanization for engagement' was accomplished and manifested varied in different settings and time periods according to the degree and kind of urbanization that preceded colonialism. It varied as well with the different ways in which distinct African societies used the creation of new cities and/or the transformation of precolonial ones for their 'own' objectives, however diffuse, coherent, varied, or contradictory they might have been (Clignet 1966; Rayfield 1974).

The present emphases on decentralization, local management, the exigencies of poverty alleviation, and regionally articulated local economic development are all in significant ways a reformulation of instruments used to evolve urban life according to the conditions that would ensure a very specific engagement with nonlocal worlds, and particularly, non-African worlds. This engagement necessitated not only the remaking of African identities and practices, but also the (hyper)visibility and crystallization of 'traditional' selves and social formations so that they could be the objective and concretized targets of remaking. A key method of such visibility was the resistance registered to the remaking itself, that is, the various ways in which bodies and groups refused to cooperate or assimilate with one or more aspects of the colonial enterprise. So cities could operate as arenas for the consolidation of a wide range of local practices, initiatives, and identities, but under conditions in which this consolidation was to be inextricably linked to its dissolution and remaking (Apter 1992; Aronson 1978; Augé 1999; King 1990).

What we find in the diverse trajectories of urban development throughout the sub-Saharan region is a large sense in which urbanization was grafted onto inhospitable domains. But once grafted, urbanization had a significant effect in terms of reordering territorial relations beyond the scope of the immediate territory of which it was a part. The extent of this reordering was limited, however. In all regions, and particularly across Central Africa, large swathes of territory remained outside of functional colonial control. Even in West Africa, Senegal, Cote D'Ivoire, the Gold Coast, and Nigeria contributed almost all of the region's recorded total economic output (Hopkins 1973). While cities primarily served to organize the evacuation of primary products, the ongoing development of this function opened up spaces for Africans to elaborate livelihoods outside of European supervised wage labor.

These opportunities derived largely from the configuration of other geographies, concretized through the movement of populations back and forth between urban and rural domains. Opportunities derived from the expanding transactions such movements were able to establish and into which they were able to draw increasing numbers of people – then going on to proficiently coordinate more complex networks of relationships among them. Without large amounts of consistently reliable material resources upon which to draw in order to provide some deepening infrastructure for these alternative spaces of livelihood formation, relations and practices had to be renegotiated continuously. The project of making something out of the city other than what was expected by a fuller incorporation in capitalist production led to a 'search' for different organizational forms and auspices under which to operate (Christopher and Tarver 1994; Salau 1979). Such practices increasingly depended on identifying loopholes and under-regulated spaces in changing colonial economies, compensations and alternatives that could potentially be appropriated by diverse actors with different agendas (Akyeampong 1997; Martin 1995; Ranger 1986; White 1990).

Fluidity thus remained both a fundamental strength and a weakness. These 'alternative' economic and cultural practices were unable to remake the city in ways that could serve the objective of expanding agricultural activities for the bulk of rural residents. Nor could they expand the integration of the bulk of the city and its residents into capitalist circuits. Instead, they acted as a limiting constraint, allowing people to urbanize relationships derived from ruralized solidarity and to identify possibilities of urban sustainability in 'undersupervised' rural domains. Thus urban Africa's pursuit of 'independent' agendas and aspirations took place largely in this 'closed' circuit, both intersecting with and running parallel to the narrow ways in which the overall urban economy was linked to global capital. Cities have been the places where Africans have most intensely engaged the conflicts precipitated by their own points of view, their political and economic practices, and their heterogeneous, often contradictory, representations of outside worlds.

Cities were also places where Africans' own strivings and deliberations about present and future ways of living were the most adamantly structured by the wavering demands of external powers. Regulating the city became a map for regulating the territory of colonial jurisdiction. During the colonial period, innovations derived from city living, although very much at work in the configuration of African urban spaces, also had to be put to work in rural areas outside the city, as well as in other cities both in Africa and abroad (Goerg 1998; Wright 1991). The effects brought about by this spreading of innovation were reincorporated into the city.

Developments in cities enabled the rural areas to produce and organize themselves in different ways. Increases in rural productivity allowed different kinds of consumption, and thus different kinds of social organization in the city. But people were also driven from the rural areas (Robertson 1997). Marginalized by the changes, they came to cities as places of refuge. This circuit frequently confounded clear divisions between the city and the country, or between one city and others. Yet the city's surrounding areas could never be a totally sufficient or satisfactory 'outside' – a friction-free place to target the accomplishments of the urban outside the 'city walls'. Those remaining in rural areas were often suspicious of whatever came from the city. They were often amenable to the distorted reassertion of customary authority and thus resisted this deployment of urban experience (Mamdani 1996).

Still, a certain urban connection to the rural goes beyond the exigencies of day-to-day economic survival or connections based on affection. The association of this connection is an acknowledgement of a cumulative African urban experience which requires the insertion of the rural in its midst, because the 'outsides' of the colonial city were sometimes the only available space in which the particular experiential wisdom of African urban residents could be enacted (Fetter 1976; La

Fontaine 1970). The rural areas sometimes could be places where the colonial gaze wasn't as strong; where urban Africans didn't always have to show a certain measure of compliance.

At the same time, engagement with colonizers was constant. In that constancy, negotiation and flexibility were necessary. Europeans and Africans had to 'borrow' incessantly from each other if they were to be engaged with each other. This was the case even where living and working spaces were segregated. More than perhaps other cities, colonial cities depended upon a multitude of shifting, highly localized, and fluid tactics in order to keep the engagement going. Despite all the overblown claims made on this concept, a certain urban hybridity was not only possible but also necessary.

The process of urban identity making and exchange was just that – a continuous process of making and exchanging. Yes, people had their identities. Different moral regimes, governance systems, and economic practices were associated with different quarters. But still residents from all walks of life 'tried out' different ways of being and doing things in the city. Regularities were sought and often institutionalized. Very little that was tried was completely discarded or given up. Operational memory was thus spatialized. In other words, African residents came to work out specific places and domains for being specific things, working out what were often contradictory needs and aspirations. There were places to 'keep tradition alive' and there were places to be 'modern,' places to be a 'kinsman' and places to be a cosmopolitan urban 'dweller' as well as more textured and subtle combinations of these primarily artificial polarities (Guyer and Belinga 1995; Pons 1969).

In some regions, the urban and rural are now inverted. The city is 'turned over' to the task of reestablishing modes of thinking and acting historically associated with the rural areas. Rural areas, particularly at the frontiers of national borders, become sites of urbanization. It is here that links to the global economy are frequently the most elaborated. Dollars rule, and telecommunications and air transport operate more efficiently than in many established cities. These urbanized frontiers are sites of highly exploitative relationships and excessive expenditures. They are highly contested and often violent terrain. But they also manifest ways of domesticating these economic arrangements that resonate with cultural memories of important values (Roitman 1998). These arrangements thus attain a sense of familiarity that enables them sometimes to usher in more effective mechanisms of social protection and distribution than have existed previously. The question then becomes how to relocalize these capacities back within the cities in 'terms of shifting lines of partial (translocal as well as local-global) connections and patterns of de- and re-territorialisation' (De Boeck 1998:803).

Despite the profound difficulties the majority of African urban residents face in piecing together livelihood on a daily basis, significant efforts are made, to engage the city as a resource for reaching and operating at the level of 'the world'. It is my contention that these efforts make up something more than attempts to shape a long-standing situation in which African labor exists as fundamentally delinked from any anchorage in the possibility of making local spaces productive. The 'worlding' is more than simply a state of being 'cast out' into the world as the 'homeless' or the marginal. Granted, there is little autonomy African societies can currently exercise in terms of ensuring a sufficiency of resources and participation in international economic transactions. Yet African cities continue to be places of experimentation for engagement, the terms of which are not exclusively fixed or determined in advance.

Configuring new urban domains

A new urbanized domain is also taking shape based on the entrenchment of specific circuits of migration, resource evacuation, and commodity exchange. Specific urban places, separated by marked physical and cultural distance, are being interpenetrated, in large part by the actions of African actors themselves. For example, cities as diverse as Mbuji-Mayi, Port Gentile, Addis Ababa, Bo, and Nouadibhou are being tied together through the participation of those who make them their base in an increasingly articulated system of countertrades involving mutual connections to Bombay, Dubai, Bangkok, Taipei, Kuala Lumpur, and Jeddah.

These circuits in turn 'spin out' and link themselves to the more conventional migratory paths of West and Central Africans to Europe, and increasingly the US, and East Africans to North America and the UK (Constantin 1996). Despite the fact that these circuits are organized around different commodities, a common profile has taken hold. Valuable primary commodities, such as minerals in particular, are diverted from 'official' national export structures into intricate networks in which large volumes of underpriced electronics, weapons, counterfeit currencies, bonds, narcotics, laundered money, and real estate circulate through various 'hands' (Hibou 1999; Egg and Herera 1998; Obervatoire Géopolitiques des Drogues 1999). The diversion can also include oil, agricultural products, and timber.

The elaboration of this domain is more than a matter of migrants seeking economic opportunity in the expanding service economies of the North and Southeast Asia or the purchase of cheap goods from urban markets in these regions. It is more than a dependence on remittances. Rather, an intricate framework for operating at a 'world level' is being created through individual travel, the cultivation of permeable boundaries through which goods and money can pass with minimal regulation, the incorporation of formal financial and political institutions within informal mechanisms of disposing goods and accessing markets, practices of dissimulation, and a willingness to take substantial risks.

This 'worlding' may be a constantly unstable and precarious practice, unable to substantially alter the positions and capacities of distinct African cities within a globalized urban network (Herbst 1996). Operations at this translocal level are limited to a small section of Africa's urban population. Nevertheless, the attempts on the part of various associations, syndicates, and networks to articulate themselves and to act within this 'worlded' domain are not insignificant in the everyday social life of many African quarters.

In many ways, this 'worlding' ensues from the ways in which spaces of incapacity and marginality can be linked to reconsolidating political and economic power through a density of knowledge-based transactions represented by an elite cadre of urban centers. In one dimension of this articulation, Castells (1996b) refers to Africa's 'perverse connections' to the global economy. Globalization entails speed, unimpeded capital flows, the hyperreality of credit and fiscality, and the amplification of microdynamics and characteristics as key elements to profit making. Accordingly, globalization provides new opportunities for economic and political actors to operate outside increasingly outmoded laws and regulatory systems.

African cities are especially available to these opportunities precisely because they appear to be outside effective control, and thus anything can happen. Certainly the complicity and the intrigue are enormous. In some contexts it would almost seem that a new modernist urban vision has succeeded in taking hold. Luxury staterooms in presidential palaces and peri-urban hovels in sewage-laden lagoons often seem linked with few mediations in the elaboration of intricate schemes involving various Mafia, missionaries, militants, and merchant banks (Duffield 1998). At one and the same time, segregation among discernible classes and groups becomes more entrenched and provisional informal collaborations between the segregated classes continue to grow.

Local 'corporate' bodies also come together, perhaps for one deal involving a sweeping array of characters and positions. Here entrepreneurship imitates the best in conspiratorial fictional intrigue. While the actual number of urban residents involved in these economies may be quite small, their importance grows in the popular urban imagination. These ventures are constantly talked about. Throughout neighborhoods, people speculate on how to participate in them or spawn new ones.

At the same time, this emphasis neglects the significant role that various associations are playing in terms of attempting to extend the reach of urban quarters. Religious brotherhoods and fraternities, ethnically based trading regimes, syndicates, and even community-based and multi-association operations are functioning with increasing scope (Diouf 2000; MacGaffey and Bazenguissa-Ganga 2000). Urban quarters not only serve as platforms for popular initiatives – waste management, microenterprise development, shelter provision, and so on – but readapt local modalities of cohesion and sociality to more regional and global frameworks.[1] Some localities, such as Nima (Accra), Obalende (Lagos), Texas-Adjame (Abidjan), and Grand Yoff (Dakar) reflect a strong relationship between the elaboration of local associations and the generation of new economic activities and resources. Here associations become important in configuring new divisions of labor. They help coordinate the cross-border small and medium-scale trade of individual entrepreneurs and work ways of pooling and reinvesting the proceeds of this trade to access larger quantities of tradeable goods, diversify collective holdings, and reach new markets.

In the North, the post-Fordist complexion of urban economic life leaves large areas of underregulated and underutilized spaces intact. There are warehouses, suburbs, and markets whose status may reflect their lack of functionality to the immediate local economic setting (Augé 1999). But in many instances they are being seized upon by African actors as sites for workshops and storerooms for artisan production to niche markets or as nodes in the transshipment of illegal commodities (Kesteloot 1995; Sassen 1999).

Who and what belongs where

The capacity to sustain, extend, and participate in this 'worlded' domain, however, is increasingly dependent on the expansion of highly localized and territorially rooted extraction activities. Many states are 'giving up' on economic modernization and focus almost exclusively on the extraction of resources. Many African countries are narrowing attention to those aspects of primary production which, regardless of volatile price fluctuations, seem to assure long-term demand. This usually means a concentration on gold, diamonds, and oil. Large-scale gold reserves have recently been identified in Tanzania, Niger, Guinea, Ethiopia, Burkina Faso, Mali, and (on and off) Senegal. While Uganda, Rwanda, and Zimbabwe have little gold and diamonds of their own, they are heavily engaged in the mineral business via their participation in the conflict in the Democratic Republic of Congo. Sudan, Chad, Mozambique, Equatorial Guinea, and Cameroon are making efforts to expand oil production widely.[2]

Such a reintensification of seemingly 'colonial-oriented' economies raises issues about belonging – who are the original inhabitants of specific regions and to whom does the site of oil, gold, timber, diamond, and emerald extraction belong? Diverse groups who have lived together for decades, if not longer, are treating each other as strangers. There are pressures on people to acquire land and assets, not in the areas where they may have lived all of their lives, but in their area of family origin. Disputes are breaking out across the continent as to who is a citizen and who has the right to vote where (Geschiere and Nyamnjoh 1998; Geschiere 1999).

But can these conflicts be reduced simply to fights over the disposition of particular places for their own sake? Are they only about what can be drawn into and developed within a specific place on the basis of controlling key natural resources? Rather, fights about belonging and the rights incumbent on belonging for access to resources may be more about what the control of these resources means to enhancing the possibilities for actors to operate on the level of the larger world (Fisiy 1999; Reno 1998; Richards 1996). The attempt may not be to bring territory under the singular control of a particular force, but to create as many possibilities of linking that territory to a plurality of allegiances and opportunities. This plurality would then enable local actors to feel that their operations in localized spaces are also conduits to or extensions of a much larger world (Lock 1999).

The fight is not so much over the terms of territorial encompassment or closure, but rather over maintaining a sense of 'open-endedness.' Narrow, seemingly parochial factions and groupings predominate in these conflicts. But the specific configuration of 'sides' is not so much directed toward defending specific turf. Rather, social units are honed to better manage shifting allegiances and participation in multiple exterior networks. Disruption and local conflict are a way of coming to the 'stage' of making a particular group visible and known (Lemarchand 1997).

If one spends significant amounts of time in African cities, it is hard not to notice the incessant sense of preparedness and readiness to switch gears. Households do display considerable determination and discipline to save over the course of many years to send children to university, to build a house, or to buy tickets so one or more members can migrate elsewhere. They are in a place; they demonstrate commitment to it. But at the same time, African cities operate as a platform for people to engage in processes and territories elsewhere.

The location of this 'elsewhere' has commonly been other cities, both within and outside the continent. Increasingly, it also includes various interiors – rural areas, borders, and frontiers. The interiors are also symbolic and spiritual. They concern geographies that are off the 'map' – demonstrated in popular descriptions of subterranean cities, spirit worlds, lucrative but remote frontiers. Cities not only straddle internal and external divides, national and regional boundaries, but also a wide range of terrain and geographies, both real and imaginary.

This is an enormous task given the ease with which multinational capital can directly penetrate the diamond regions, the timber forests, and oil shelves. It is an enormous task given the increasing chasm between life in most of the rural and peri-urban areas and in the rest of the world. Africa contains rural and urban areas that slip further away from the control of normative institutions and discourses, even though, at least theoretically, access to any point in any given territory is now more precise and possible. Accordingly, there is a constant stream of people moving in and out of, as well as among, the various quarters within the city. There are people who can no longer operate or position themselves in places where disorder is increasing. There are others who seek the relative invisibility of disordered places in order to pursue new opportunities. There are many moving back and forth among them.

African cities were largely constructed as points of contact – as places to organize the evacuation of resources and to construct mechanisms through which broader territories could be administered. While they continue to play this role in the postcolonial period, critical points of convergence and articulation with the global economy do, however, take place outside these functions. This means that the manner in which individuals act or behave at the interfaces or junctions with global economies – i.e., how they access and manipulate opportunities to acquire widely divergent volumes of extracted resources – occurs largely outside the conventions and moral economies of either village or urban-based contexts. But it also means that those individuals, working as renegade miners, diamond purchasers, smugglers, financiers, go-betweens, and agents of multinational corporations, are 'resocialized' by the multiple, often ephemeral, institutions that attempt to give some shape to these engagements and economic activities.

What I want to do in the rest of this article is to talk about one example of how processes of informalization 'free up' a wide range of actors to participate in an emerging, albeit limited, configuration of 'world level' transactions that emerge from the initiatives of Africans themselves. These initiatives are, of course, enjoined to and shaped by the circuits of economic transaction elaborated by more powerful economic institutions and monopolies. This 'freeing up' can significantly loosen the moral coordinates through which urban quarters might maintain a semblance of coherence and social cohesion. The dissolution of cohesion in turn can precipitate and extend urban-based conflicts about who belongs where to rural areas which often now constitute the most direct links to the global economy through extraction activities. Thus the greater reach and rescaling of local initiative possible through participation in gradually emerging translocal urban domains must be balanced by efforts to reinvent at least provisional modalities of social cohesion if the fight over resources isn't to keep actors within highly parochial and localized spaces of operation.

I will provide an example of how this process of juggling cohesion and opportunity takes place. For the ways social cohesion and opportunity are balanced are critical aspects of how Africans from different walks of life might participate in a kind of 'worlding' from below (Kayetekin and Ruccio 1998).

'Zawiyyah City' and reaching the larger world

The encouragement of movement
In the following, I present a brief sketch of a specific practice through which social cohesion and opportunity are balanced in an overall attempt on the part of specific African urban residents, with specific affiliations, to operate within a larger, more 'worlded,' space of economic transactions. The sketch is about African groups in Jeddah and is derived from information based on over two decades of work with various African-based Islamic welfare organizations in which I have been attempting to help urban quarters with sizable Muslim populations think through specific local development strategies. The sketch is a composite of both my own observations and information gathered from discussions with various actors involved in the processes described.

Within many Sufi traditions, the zawiyyah plays an important role as both a service to members of a specific 'brotherhood' and as an embodiment and facilitator of the translocal character of this affiliation. The zawiyyah is part lodge where accommodation for traveling 'brothers' is provided, part site where zikhr (worship) can be performed according to the practices of a particular brotherhood, and part referral agency, where information about various opportunities and resources can be accessed.

When a man joins a particular Sufi order (tariqa), he is obligated to take a wird, an oath of loyalty. The loyalty is directed not only to the order as an abstract framework of religious practice, but also to the leadership, the shaykh, and the hereditary right and passing on of this leadership. The order is thus anchored in an unyielding focal point of mediation between the earthly and the divine. The hierarchies involved are complex and textured, not simply an arrangement with the shaykh at the pinnacle and the rest of his followers in a position of devotion and access. But a strong sense of the equality of all before the shaykh does exist, and it enforces a practice by which the talibe (the followers) must be responsible for the welfare of each other. The zawiyya is the key institution through which this responsibility is expressed. For in travel, individuals are operating outside of the confines of their local anchorage and support systems. Temporarily freed from these domains, the zawiyya becomes the most salient place through which the sense of connection among members of the tariqa can be expressed and also mobilized for various forms of collective action.

In many cities throughout West Africa, the zawiyyah was an important site through which migrants could be incorporated into the city. They might be connected to preexisting economic activities as apprentices or laborers. They might be provided with some small sums of capital with which to launch small enterprises and in this way expand the network and diversity of economic activities engaged in by the order. At other times, they were provided with goods to sell back to their home regions as a means of strengthening both trade and religious links. Given the specific political circumstances, the zawiyyah could also be used as a site for the dissemination of political analysis and organization (Hiskett 1984).

These established places of hospitality and support implicitly encouraged travel. Increasingly, zawiyyah became centers through which travel was tracked. The monitoring was not so much geared toward keeping tabs on the activities of followers as it was intended to cultivate a means by which their movements could be used as a resource. After all, talibe staying at a particular lodge would talk about what they were doing and what they had seen. To the extent that their successes and opportunities would bring glory to the shaykh, and thus to themselves in the 'next life,' there was a strong impetus to engage fellow members of the tariqa in various projects and opportunities. The zawiyyah then became a circumscribed domain of publicity, a place where devotees could get a sense of the wide range of locations and activities in which the tariqa was involved. They could be stimulated to take on new activities and conceive and assess individual possibilities in the larger context of what the order was doing (Launay and Soares 1999).

Thus in Treichville, where I visited a Tidiane zawiyyah in 1993, a large world map was placed on a wall in one of the common rooms. On the map, hundreds of cities were circled with magic markers and 'tagged' with numbers. On a table below the map were heavily worn and numbered cardboard files corresponding to the numbers on the map. In these files were various lists of names of followers living in these cities with brief profiles of each one. Some of the profiles had been written by talibe who had passed through this particular zawiyyah over the years. Others were stories and notes compiled by guests about other followers whom they had met or learned about in the course of their travels. Still others were, in essence, photocopies of profiles that were compiled in zawiyyah in other locations. 'Profile' is a very rough designation for these documents; they were not prepared, compiled, or used in any systematic way, especially because many talibe are functionally illiterate.

What is significant about these notations is not so much their systematicity or use. Rather, they point to a practice of articulating discrete individual stories and activities into a larger network of interconnected pursuits and opportunities. What exists within the scope of these written records may only serve as a reminder to *talibe* of the possibilities of reciprocity and collaborative action. In some circumstances, these graphically apparent indications of networked activity may actually mask the nature of the 'real' exchanges and collaborations taking place. They may incite *talibe* to seek out interactions with fellow devotees in other places under the auspices of religious comradeship and a purported knowledge about what they might be doing, but where such interactions might lead and who they might involve are matters to be negotiated. At one level, the *turuq* seek to establish means through which collaborations and mutual support can be exercised among talibe who are strangers to each other – that is, to assert the viability of such cooperation. At the same time, they seek to fine-tune such collaborations in ways such that certain economic activities, especially those that are illegal in specific contexts, can be pursued by *talibe* who find a means to trust each other and use their different skills and histories.

Zawiyyah *and the advent of Islamic 'Modernism'*

Until the post-World War II period of African urban history, the *zawiyyah* remained an institution for all talibe despite their economic capacities and social status. But in the acceleration of urban modernization in the postwar period, and then in the postindependence period, the *zawiyyah* in many cities became primarily an institution for small traders and the poorer members of the *tariqa*. Wealthier followers developed new associations and networks. They joined or formed political parties, welfare organizations, business clubs, and built special mosques and schools, as well as Islamic institutes and centers. These institutions increasingly served as a base for consolidating the local and national power of specific *taruq*, but also for attracting funds from and learning about opportunities in the larger Islamic world, particularly the Gulf States.

The traditional *zawiyyah*, then, has been increasingly incorporated into the orbit of these new organizations and objectives. How this incorporation takes place, and the subsequent role of the *zawiyyah* in a new network of institutions and entrepreneurial activities, of course varies in specific urban and national contexts. There are also differences in the extent to which various *turuq* cooperate or compete with each other, according to their relative strength in particular regions. In northern Nigeria, Tidiane, Qaddriyyah, Bruhaniyyah, and Sanusiyya *turuq* have strong pockets of adherents in a context of enormous diversity of Islamic expression, institutions, and entrepreneurship. As such, cooperation often remains minimal. In Abidjan, where Muslims have made a concerted effort in recent years to become a more prominent sociopolitical force, different *turuq* have joined hands in many activities.

Despite the proliferation of new institutions, schools, mosques, enterprises, and political and cultural associations based on varying emphases on class, ethnic, and national distinctions, the relationships among Sufi-oriented institutions retain a large measure of the spirit of the *zawiyyah*. In other words, the ethos of how the *zawiyyah* has operated throughout hundreds of years is infused into the operational practices of Sufi *turuq* as a whole. These are *turuq* still dominated by the leadership position of the *shaykh* and the responsibilities of the talibe to take care of each other.

The rest of the Islamic world has maintained a largely ambivalent attitude toward the predominance of Sufism in West African religious

Fig. 1 Telephone centre in Bel-Air, Dakar (Photograph by Doran H. Ross, courtesy Allen F. Roberts & Mary Nooter Roberts)

practice. The orthodox Sunni *Wahabi* traditions which prevail in the Gulf are largely critical of this practice, viewing it as an essential deviation from the *Sunnah,* the way of the Prophet Muhammed and the normative frameworks of *Makhtab,* the guidelines informing religious activities. But in practice, a wide range of mutual engagements has ensued. With its large Muslim population and relatively fluid political and economic environments, West Africa is an important place of operation for the major Islamic powers. In the past two decades, particularly, reform movements emphasizing a more politicized role of Islam in national and international affairs have been active through various formations of the *Jebha Islamiyyah,* the Muslim Brotherhood. Various *shia* groupings based in Lebanon and Iran have used elements of the large Lebanese community in West African cities as nodal points in their political and economic operations. Through its well-endowed welfare association, *Dawa Islamiyyah,* the Libyans have also been extremely active in building mosques and schools throughout the region. They have funded a variety of political groups and have trained local leaders.

Urban West African communities have been the targets of sizable amounts of external funding, in part through an ongoing contestation among the major Islamic powers for predominance. While I was living in a Muslim household in Nima, a primarily Muslim quarter of central Accra, three of the sons were receiving money from different countries – Saudi Arabia, Iran, and Libya – to work as organizers in the community. Conflicts among local groupings with different external affiliations often became quite tense and competitive. Serious neighborhood disruptions, however, could still be tempered over long dinner conversations among the brothers at home. Loyalties shifted according to need. The kinds of ideological and political distinctions that external 'allies' sought to enforce were never deeply rooted in any community in which I lived. Additionally, substantial amounts of external assistance were capable of diversion. In another example from Accra, the Muslim Judicial Council bought and sold large stores of rice in 1990 with funds intended to develop new Islamic secondary schools in the country. I know this because I was called on to assist the council in framing a strategic development plan for these schools.

Agencies such as the African Muslim Agency, largely funded by Kuwait, were established to disseminate religious materials and support religious education in each African country. While much of the effort of this agency is indeed focused on such pedagogical activities, it has developed substantial business interests in many countries. Even some of the scholarships it offers for advanced religious and secular studies are 'sold' on the open market. Many Christian students pretend to be Muslims in order to be eligible for these. On the other hand, these 'converts' are frequently sought out by the various Muslim agencies themselves. For example, the African Islamic Institute in Khartoum is a large, well-endowed center of secondary and postsecondary education. It is well known that any student who does well here is likely to have opportunities for advanced professional training in the Gulf States. Many of the students from Nigeria and Ghana, particularly, are 'converts' who are subsidized by Gulf State entrepreneurs in exchange for their participation in a wide variety of illicit business ventures. The belief is that these 'converts' are freed from particular family and community obligations and are more amenable to taking risks. But as converted Muslims, they are also in many ways not viewed as 'real' Muslims, a view that prevails despite Islamic injunction which says that Muslims, whether they are born to Muslim families or not, can only be Muslims through taking the *shahada,* the profession of belief.

The African Islamic Institute is only one of a number of interrelated Islamic institutions and private corporations in the Gulf States. This network operates with significant scale and reach and includes institutions such as the Islamic Development Bank, the Saudi and Libyan versions of Dawa Islamiyyah, the Fahd Foundation, a venture capital operation, as well as a network of banks, construction firms, clearing houses, and import-export firms. The underregulated banking, customs, and market structures of most West African countries play an important role in the recirculation of money and commodities used by the Muslim Brothers, in particular, to launch repeated forays into financial markets with more capacity in Asia, Europe, North America, and Latin America.

The important point is not the existence of these Gulf-based economic operations, but the ways in which various *turuq* have sought to engage them in order to advance their own interests. Through a well-elaborated system of seminars, meetings, religious convocations, and, of course, the annual pilgrimage to Makkah for *haj,* West African Muslims have long been availed opportunities to travel to and throughout the Islamic world, particularly the Gulf States. As in the past, preparations for the *haj* can take many years. The pilgrimage involves a sizable investment of personal resources. Local savings mechanisms are usually relied upon in order to generate the resources needed to fulfill this obligation. The Saudi government allots a specific number of 'places' and requires specific plans for accommodation and travel on the part of national 'delegations'. This means that national organizing committees are formed. Payments are made to these committees for handling all the logistics of the pilgrimage, as well as negotiating who goes and under what circumstances.

Struggles over who controls these committees can be intense, for control means that large amounts of money are available to committees, usually for some time before the actual pilgrimage is made. There are frequently controversies over how these funds are used and invested prior to their deployment to cover the costs for national delegations. In Benin, for example, there have been repeated controversies over the extent to which haj funds have been used to cover a variety of precarious pyramid schemes. In other circumstances, the Tidiane *tariqa*, by organizing separate deals with the Saudi government, has been able to use *haj* funds to support various takeover

activities of European properties and companies by Saudi-based firms. These investments are made in return for a specific portion of the profits and access to employment opportunities and markets for the commercial interests of major Tidiane businessmen.

In recent years, some *turuq* have become heavily involved in the transshipment of narcotics, counterfeit currencies, credit cards, and other financial instruments. They have also organized bartered exchange on a large scale – where gold supplies, for example, are bartered for weapons, machinery, and vehicles. These economic concentrations require dispersed networks capable of plying distinct national regulatory environments – with differences in banking rules, customs procedures, and laws governing corporate formations and trade. The wide-ranging networks of *zawiyyah*, mosques, and Islamic centers scattered around the world can be appropriated as potential nodes in this specialization in 'unconventional' trade and economic activity.

Every year during the *haj*, there is a meeting of what is popularly known as the 'twelve tribes.' These twelve 'tribes' roughly correspond to (1) the major West and East African *turuq*; (2) syndicates based on personal loyalty to a major religious/business leader; (3) leading commercial families associated as patron or funder of a specific network of Islamic welfare and education institutions; and (4) various other actors tied to particularly large youth councils, haj committees, and even political parties. In saying that these 'tribes' roughly correspond, I have several dimensions in mind. First, the use of the notion of 'tribes' points to the arbitrary composition of these interest groupings. For example, Tidiane interests are not consolidated within the boundaries of a single grouping. The Tidiane tariqa is in actuality made up of many diverse figures, tendencies, and institutions. While acknowledging nominal loyalty to an overarching history and *shaykh*, the *tariqa* is much too large and dispersed to fall under a single administrative rubric. There are also many different economic interests and activities within discrete Tidiane networks. In part, this heterogeneity has to do with the very different situations and histories of various Tidiane orders in West Africa. But it also relates to deep divisions about the political, economic, and cultural orientations of Tidiane orders, not only across countries, but within them as well.

The notion of rough correspondence also reflects ebbs and flows of who talks to whom and who is willing to deal with whom, as well as the changing fortunes of particular businessmen and syndicates. For example, the Malian businessman and marabout Bameni Cissoko, who had amassed a fortune through highly suspect means, has lost most of it through a variety of legal troubles and visible efforts to become a major political actor within the West African region. The Patel family in Abidjan, once an important patron of politically oriented Islamic reform, has relocated much of its commercial activities out of the continent. Shaykh Mohammed Al-Amoudi is head of a Swedish consortium of thirty engineering and construction companies (Midroc Scandanavia), head of the ABV Rock Group, chief investor in the primary African ITC company World Space, the owner of Capitol Bank and the National Commerce Bank, and the owner of a sizeable amount of Ethiopia's economic assets. Al-Amoudi once was a prominent figure in these African networks but no longer plays an active role since moving back to Ethiopia several years ago to become the country's, and perhaps the continent's, major business investor.

In fact, it is never certain whether the designation 'twelve tribes' represents twelve discrete groupings at all. On the one hand, as I indicated before, *turuq* are religious brotherhoods that vary in terms of their cohesiveness and spread. Some remain almost exclusively mystical orders devoted entirely to religious revelation. Others are widely dispersed. They may maintain an overarching sense of a coherent religious identity, but how that identity is expressed and organized in specific national, political, and economic contexts can differ widely. On the other hand, the substantial investment made by normative Sunni Islam in Africa through various national and international agencies has had a significant effect in solidifying spaces of Islamic practice and organization outside of the *turuq*. This support has cultivated sizable networks of professionals, students, and entrepreneurs operating throughout the Islamic world. Different *turuq* now often seek affiliation and support from these networks as a means of gaining new opportunities, under the guise of proffering reform movements within the *turuq* themselves.

Various businessmen and entrepreneurs who operate as local agents of various banks and corporations based in North Africa, the Gulf States, and Malaysia, also intersect. Additional prominent players include large import enterprises, particularly those in Dubai and Bahrain, which have become important places for the acquisition of commodities and the 'cleansing' of money through commodity purchase. Often these businessmen and agents have little direct interest in the religious orientations of the *turuq* themselves but participate in them because they provide an advantageous framework for their economic activities. The leadership of the *turuq*, in turn, use their business expertise as a means of expanding their own economic capacity. But these configurations are by no means stable. On the other hand, there has been concern during the past twenty years about ensuring a stable access to the Gulf States.

Preserving Africa Jeddah

The 'twelve tribes' began as a way to deal with increasing concerns on the part of Saudi authorities that Jeddah was being overwhelmed by illicit African business activities. Saudis felt that the increasing African presence in several city quarters, such as Mahallet al-Yemen and Mahallet al-Shan, was changing the character of the city. To a large extent, the Saudis were looking for scapegoats to blame for the negative results of urban growth in the country's primary urban center. On the other hand, a variety of smuggling and illicit economic activities – from the scams surrounding the importation of so-called red mercury (with which Saudi rials were supposedly counterfeited), increased narcotics trafficking, and the use of the port of Jeddah to divert and repackage a wide range of commodities – were of purportedly increasing concern to the royal family. While Saudi commercial interests had long taken advantage of many of these activities, they had grown to a scale that was becoming increasingly visible. Given the exceedingly tight way in which Saudi society is organized, an unusual opportunity was provided to African interests in Jeddah to exert greater control in policing themselves.

What is particularly significant about this process is that the tradition of the *zawiyyah* was reappropriated as a primary reference point for actualizing such control. Competition among groups using Jeddah as some kind of commercial base, place of trade and exchange, or node in the transshipment of commodities could have been amplified. Instead, different interests, again roughly corresponding to the lines of demarcation mentioned earlier, began discussing mechanisms for keeping Saudi urban space available to their operations. In the course of these discussions – at first held through a variety of intermediaries – the interlocking relationships between *turuq*, nationally based commercial interests, transnational commercial operations of the different turuq, and common affiliations with discrete banking structures, religious propagation, and welfare institutions became increasingly clear. Like the function of the *zawiyyah* as a place for

hospitality, mutual support, and accountability, the 'twelve tribes' developed increasingly into a loose-knit council. This council was ready to accommodate 'travelers' from different regions, Sufi orders, and institutional affiliations in order to keep track of the activities of diverse Africans in Jeddah. It attempted to use an accounting of these activities as a means of maximizing the resourcefulness and opportunities available to different yet loosely configured interests and actors making up the 'twelve tribes.'

During the single opportunity I had in 1995 to witness these discussions, the primary focus was the situation in Jeddah. But discussion of Jeddah also led to a lengthy and often convoluted overview of the various political, economic, cultural, and religious dynamics at work in shaping the commercial interests and activities of these key religious and commercial leaders. There was little discussion of the details of specific businesses and commercial ventures, except as they related to specific problems that had to be solved in the behaviors of particular operations in Jeddah itself. There was no effort to prohibit specific activities, except if they posed an immediate and concrete risk to any member of the major interest groups or to their operations within a specific city or region. Instead, there was a complete accounting of what it was possible to do within a specific ministry, company, city, or country. The focus was on assessing what was possible and what was not possible. So if, for example, money laundering through Islamic commercial banks in Egypt was deemed not possible, it was assumed by all that, from that point on, no one would attempt to do so. Through this discussion of possibilities, specific activities were both inferred and disciplined.

Additionally, the different interest groups discussed areas of need: for cheaper transportation, government connections, labor, financing for deals, real estate investment, and even the need for various new infrastructures in their respective countries. Whether different interest groups could successfully keep open a space of operation in Jeddah was predicated on a practice of open-ended information exchange and identifying opportunities for collaboration among different African actors and interests. When such an exchange worked, it was used as evidence that a much broader level of collaboration might be possible.

But the primary objective – to ensure collaboration and to sustain the mixture of African strangers, travelers, and residents in Jeddah – never went beyond Jeddah. In other words, there was no obligation to try to transfer this *zawiyyah*-like practice of regulating African behavior in Jeddah to a larger scale. When the different interest groups operated with some consensus that collaboration was working well in Jeddah, however, this consensus provided a large measure of confidence for them to 'try out' collaboration of other kinds.

Rumor has it that the 'twelve tribes' have been crystallized into a major council of African 'Mafia' dividing up territories and sectors for increasingly expanding illegal trades. While such may well be the case, I have no way of verifying the truth of the rumors. But neither am I interested in the ways unconventional trade may be taking place. Rather, what I want to amplify from this sketch is the way in which Islam provides a vehicle for a mutual accommodation, however reluctant, awkward, and contested it might be, on the part of actors from substantially different cultural and political contexts. This mutual accommodation – of different actors and institutions paying attention to, adapting themselves, and often manipulating and using each other – provides a platform through which the specific commercial and political interests emanating from distinct African cities can be resourced and extended. This extension of scope and capacity beyond the confines of the particular African city faces competition and challenges when operating in another city, in this case Jeddah. Because of its combined religious and commercial significance, Jeddah comes to constitute an important site of African operations. A process unfolds in which there is an attempt to stabilize the interaction of the diverse characters and purveyors of those interests. The process entails Africans reaching deep into their traditions to take essential elements of a once important Sufi institution, the *zawiyyah*, to inform how such regulation might take place.

Throughout all of these deliberations, Islam remains a consistent reference point. What Islam may mean, however, to various African actors and institutions is, of course, not consistent in itself. Nevertheless, Islam remains an important platform on which many Africans of various capacities and walks of life attempt to access and operate at the level of a larger world.

In the example of Jeddah, we see how an historical modality of assemblage, deeply rooted in many West and East African societies, is given a new lease on life through its application outside of the continent. Here a tool that has long passed in urban Africa is treated as embodying some important principles for extending urban Africa outside the continent. While a vast world of unofficial economies is one of the few real opportunities for substantial wealth creation in the continent, these activities increasingly rely on cut-throat competition and have generated increased levels of insecurity and conflict. Here, many of the traditional tools and social institutions of reconciliation and cooperation simply don't work. But in efforts to secure an external base whereby actual or potential competitors at home can collaborate and reduce their vulnerabilities abroad, aspects of these same social institutions can potentially work to great effect. Such effectiveness instills greater measures of confidence that can then be reapplied to difficult dilemmas faced at home.

Conclusion

This article has attempted to sketch some dimensions through which African urban residents are attempting to elaborate a transurban, 'worlded' domain of operations. It has looked at several ways in which they try to balance the need to maintain some functional sense of local 'rootedness' while at the same time gaining access to opportunities that are more transnational, even global, in scope. Given just how increasingly precarious life in urban Africa has become, residents who share a quarter must often find ways of not locking themselves into fixed commitments with each other. They must pursue their own livelihoods and aspirations, but at the same time, they must engage each other in ways that maintain some semblance of local stability, interaction, and cohesiveness. A series of practices and institutions must be elaborated in order to balance these divergent, yet interconnected, needs. As such, they constitute pathways to operations on larger scales.

There is no uniform marginalization of African cities from global processes which accounts for the production of all the processes of informalization under way or the ways in which belonging and collaborative action are being reshaped. As in cities everywhere, different dimensions, institutions, and spaces within African cities are increasingly connected to aspects of cities around the world. This connection at a globalized urban scale is consolidated through a broad range of informational flows, financial transactions, and interinstitutional affiliations that are negotiated within transnational private arenas. This consolidation, emerging from highly informalized processes, is increasingly subject to new notions of legality, private standards, and norms which operate with substantial authority (Sassen 1999).

At the same time, Africans are not passive bystanders to these processes. Specific and long-standing traditions of social regulation and collective effort are being reworked as elements in elaboration of spaces of economic transaction, knowledge production, and cultural influence that are translocal and transnational. They are translocal and transnational in terms that, although subsumed to the constellations of power which define the prevailing dynamics of what is 'global,' reflect substantial African control. The notion of well-bounded communities of affection and cooperation, where local citizens all participate collectively in processes of governance capable of ensuring democracy and better livelihoods, may still resonate with the aspirations of the 'grassroots'. The conventional idea remains that African cities are largely made up of such well-bounded communities and that strengthening them is the key to development.

But these communities also point to ways of living and producing that become tenuous and ineffective within a globalized urban world. Therefore, the enclosure and sustenance of coherent local spaces increasingly depend on the capacity to secure effective individual and corporate engagements with the wide range of networks and flows that make up translocal domains. Local communities – either of affection or administration – cannot serve as places of self-containment or resistance without finding avenues to cross and interact with various scales and other spaces. But this is not just a matter of following new international norms, or of copying what other communities are doing. In adherence to a normative series of 'best practices,' localities 'announce' their irrelevance. It is important for communities to signal that they can be trustworthy partners or that they are safe bets for investment. But to a large degree, communities can usually only come to this larger stage by using terms and practices that emerge from their own aspirations and logic (Ranciere 1998).

There are actors and domains within almost all African cities which increasingly operate with substantial capacity, capitalization, and international scope. They do so in the contexts of a 'real power' constituted by imbricating multiple spaces of legality and illegality, formality and informality constantly pieced together and pulled apart. They also do so in the contexts of emerging 'legal' or 'normative' transnational arenas of economic transaction and control. The ability of African institutions to participate in these arenas seems, in part, to be a by-product of the very operations of informalization on larger scales.

How this corresponds to the now frequently brutal deconstruction of polity and community, such as is taking place in the Democratic Republic of Congo, Angola, and the Sudan, remains largely unknown. But the emergence of new financial instruments and trade regimes perhaps points the way to even more possibilities where a substantial history of 'worlding' from below can help shape new modalities of economic capacity. This capacity is sometimes set aside, sometimes complicit with, and sometimes set against the trajectories of African exclusion. These operations on larger scales, in turn, point the way to sectors and activities that might constitute the basis for new 'formal' economies.

Notes

[1] This is the conclusion of a broad range of initial field study reports under the auspices of the MacArthur Foundation/Council for the Development of Social Science Research in Africa Programme on Africa's Real Economies.

[2] See particularly *Africa Research Bulletin: Economic, Financial and Technical Series,* vol. 35, 1998.

References

Agnew, John A., and S. Corbidge. 1995. *Mastering Space: Hegemony, Territory, and International Political Economy*. London: Routledge.

Akyeampong, Emmanuel. 1997. 'Sexuality and Prostitution Among the Akan of the Gold Coast, 1650–1950.' *Past and Present*: 144–73.

Anderson, David M. and Richard Rathbone, eds. 2000. *Africa's Urban Past*. Portsmouth, NH: Heinemann; Oxford: James Currey.

Apter, Andrew. 1992. *Black Critics and Kings: The Hermeneutics of Power in Yoruba Society*. Chicago: University of Chicago Press.

Aronson, Dan. 1978. 'Capitalism and Culture in Ibadan Urban Development.' *Urban Anthropology* 7: 253–64.

Augé, Marc. 1999. *An Anthropology of Contemporary Worlds*. Stanford: Stanford University Press.

Balibar, Étienne.1995. 'Has 'The World' Changed?' In *Marxism in the Postmodern Age*, ed. Antonio Callari, Stephen Cullenberg, and Carole Biewener. New York: Guilford Press.

Bourdieu, Pierre. 1990. *The Logic of Practice*. Cambridge: Polity Press.

Carter, David M. 1997. *States of Grace: Senegalese in Italy and the New European Immigration*. Minneapolis: University of Minnesota Press.

Castells, Manuel. 1996a. *The Information Age: Economy, Society, and Culture. Vol. 1: The Rise of Network Society*. Cambridge, MA: Blackwell.

— 1996b. 'The Net and the Self: Working Notes to a Critical Theory of Information Society.' *Critical Anthropology* 16 (I): 9–38.

Christopher, A. J., and James D. Tarver. 1994. 'Urbanization During Colonial Days in Sub-Saharan Africa. In *Urbanization in Africa*, ed. James D. Tarver. Westport, CT: Greenwood Press.

Clignet, Remi. 1966. 'Urbanization and Family Structure in the Ivory Coast.' *Comparative Studies in Society and History* 8: 385–401.

Constantin F. 1996. 'L'informal International ou la Subversion de la Territorialite.' *Cultures and Conflicts* 21/22: 311–46.

Cooper, Fred. 1994. 'Conflict and Connection: Rethinking Colonial African History.' *American Historical Review* 95: 1516–45.

— 1996. *Decolonization and the African Society: The Labor Question in French and British Africa*. New York: Cambridge University Press.

Coquery-Vidrovitch, Catherine. 1991. 'The Process of Urbanisation in Africa: From the Origins to the Beginning of Independence.' *African Studies Review* 34 (I): 1–98.

De Boek, Filip. 1998. 'Domesticating Diamonds and Dollars: Identity, Expenditure, (1984–1997).' *Development and Change* 29: 777–810.

Diouf, Mamadou. 1998. 'The French Colonial Policy of Assimilation and the Civility of the Originaires of the Four Communes (Senegal): A Nineteenth-Century Globalization Project.' *Development and Change* 29: 671–96.

— 2000. 'The Senegalese Murid Trade Diaspora and the Making of Vernacular Cosmopolitanism.' *Public Culture* 12 (3).

Duffield, Mark. 1998. 'Postmodern Conflict: Warlords, Post-Adjustment States and Private Protection.' *Civil Wars* 1 (I): 65–102.

Egg, Johnny, and Javier Herera, eds. 1998. *Echanges Transfrontaliens et Integration Régional en Afrique Subsaharienne*. Paris: ORSTOM.

Fetter, Bruce. 1976. *The Creation of Elizabethville 1910–1940*. Stanford: Hoover Institution Press, Stanford University.

Fisiy, Cyprian. 1999. *Rural Land Management and Infrastructure Development in Cote D'Ivoire*. Washington, DC: The World Bank.

Geschiere, Peter. 1999. 'Geographies of Autochthony.' *CODESRIA Bulletin* 3/4: 85–86.

Geschiere, Peter and Francis Nyamnjoh. 1998. 'Witchcraft as an Issue in the 'Politics of Belonging': Democratization and Urban Migrants' Involvement with the Home Village.' *African Studies Review* 41 (3): 69–92.

Goerg, Odille. 1998. 'From Hill Station (Freetown) to Downtown Conakry (First Ward): Comparing French and British Approaches to Segregation in Colonial Cities at the Beginning of the Twentieth Century.' *Canadian Journal of Afican Studies* 31 (I): 1–31.

Guyer, Jane. 1995. 'Introduction: The Currency Interface and its Dynamics.' In *Money Matters: Instability, Values, and Social Payments in the Modern History of West Africa*, ed. Jane Guyer. Portsmouth, NH: Heinemann; London: James Currey.

Guyer, Jane, and S. Eno Belinga. 1995. 'Wealth in People as Wealth in Knowledge: Accumulation and Composition in Equatorial Africa.' *Journal of African History* 39: 91-120.

Herbst, Jeffrey. 1996. 'Responding to State Failure in Africa.' *International Security* 21 (3): 120-44.

Hibou, Béatrice. 1999. 'The 'Social Capital' of the State as an Agent of Deception.' In *The Criminalization of the State in Africa*, eds. Jean-François Bayart, Stephen Ellis, and Beatrice Hibou. London: James Currey; Bloomington: Indiana University Press.

Hiskett, Mervyn. 1984. *The Development of Islam in West Africa*. London: Longman.

Hopkins, A. G. 1973. *An Economic History of West Africa*. New York: Columbia University Press.

Kayatekin, S. A., and D. F. Ruccio, 1998. 'Global Fragments; Subjectivity and Class Politics in Discourses of Globalization.' *Economy and Society* 27 (I): 74–96.

Kesteloot, Christian. 1995. 'The Creation of Socio-Spatial Marginality in Brussels: A Tale of Flexibility, Geographical Competition and Guest-worker's Neighbourhoods'. In *Europe at the Margins: New Mosaics of Inequality*, ed. C. Hadjimichalis and D. Sandier. Chichester: John Wiley.

King, Anthony D. 1990. *Urbanism, Colonialism, and the World Economy: Cultural and Spatial Foundations of the World Urban System*. London: Routledge.

La Fontaine, J. S. 1970. *City Politics: A Study of Leopolduille 1962–63*. London: Cambridge University Press.

Launay, Robert, and Benjamin F. Soares. 1999. 'The Formation of an 'Islamic Sphere' in French Colonial West Africa.' *Economy and Society* 28: 497–519.

Lemarchand, René. 1997. 'Patterns of State Collapse and Reconstruction in Central Africa: Reflections on the Great Lakes Region.' *Afrika Spectrum* 32: 173–94.

Leyshon, Andrew and Nigel Thrift. 1998. *Money Space: Geographies of Monetary Transformation*. London: Routledge.

Lock, Peter. 1999. 'Military Downsizing and Growth in the Security Industry in Sub Saharan Africa.' www.idsa-india.org/an-dec8-10.html.

Mabogunje, Akin. 1990. 'Urban Planning and the Post-Colonial State in Africa: A Research Overview.' *African Studies Revieiu* 33: 121–203.

MacGaffey, Janet and Rémy Bazenguissa-Ganga. 2000. *Congo-Paris: Transnational Traders on the Margins of the Law*. International African Institute. London: James Currey; Bloomington: Indiana University Press.

Mamdani, Mahmood. 1996. *Citizen and Subject: Contemporary Africa and the Legacy of Late Colonialism*. Princeton: Princeton University Press.

Martin, Phyllis. 1995. *Leisure and Society in Colonial Brazzaville*. Cambridge: Cambridge University Press.

Mbembe, Achille. 1999. 'At the Edge of the World: Boundaries, Territoriality, and Sovereignty in Africa.' *CODESRIA Bulletin* 3/4: 4–16.

Observatoire Geopolitique des Drogues. 1999. *World Geopolitics of Drugs Report 1997–98*. Paris: OGD.

Pons, Valdo. 1969. *Stanleyville: An African Urban Community Under Belgian Administration*. London: International African Institute, Oxford University Press.

Ranciere, Jean. 1998. 'The Cause of the Other.' *Parallax* 1 (2): 25–31.

Ranger, Terence. 1986. 'Religious Movements and Politics in Sub-Saharan Africa.' *African Studies Review* 29 (2) : 1–69.

Rayfield, J. R. 1974. 'Theories of Urbanization and the Colonial City in West Africa.' *Africa* 44 (2): 163–85.

Reno, William. 1998. *Warlord Politics and African States*. Boulder, CO: Lynne Rienner.

Richards, Paul. 1996. *Fighting for the Rainforest: War, Youth and Resources in Sierra Leone*. International Africa Institute. London: James Currey; Portsmouth, NH: Heinemann.

Robertson, Claire C. 1997. *Trouble Showed the Way: Women, Men, and Trade in the Nairobi Area 1890–1990*. Bloomington: Indiana University Press.

Roitman, Janet. 1998. 'The Garrison-Entrepôt.' *Cahier d'études africaines* 150-52: 297–329.

Salau, Ademola. 1979. 'The Urban Process in Africa: Observations on the Points of Divergence from the Western Experience.' *African Urban Studies* 4: 27–34.

Sassen, Saskia. 1999. *Globalization and Its Discontents: Essays on the New Mobility of People and Money.* New York: Free Press.

Taylor, Paul J. 2000. 'World Cities and Territorial States Under Conditions of Contemporary Globalization.' *Political Geography* 19: 5–32.

Taylor, Paul J., and Michael Watts, eds. 1995. *Geographies of Global Change.* Oxford: Blackwell.

White, Louise. 1990. 'Bodily Fluids and Usufruct: Controlling Property in Nairobi.' *Canadian Journal of African Studies* 24: 418–38.

Wright, Gwendolyn. 1991. *The Politics of Design in French Colonial Urbanism.* Chicago: University of Chicago Press.

Section 2.C
Technology

BRIAN LARKIN
Degraded Images, Distorted Sounds
Nigerian Video & the Infrastructure of Piracy

Reference
Public Culture, 16, 2 (2004): 289–314

In Kano, the economic center of northern Nigeria, media piracy is part of the 'organizational architecture' of globalization (Sassen 2002), providing the infrastructure that allows media goods to circulate. Infrastructures organize the construction of buildings, the training of personnel, the building of railway lines, and the elaboration of juridicolegal frameworks without which the movement of goods and people cannot occur. But once in place, infrastructures generate possibilities for their own corruption and parasitism. Media piracy is one example of this in operation. It represents the potential of technologies of reproduction – the supple ability to store, reproduce, and retrieve data – when shorn from the legal frameworks that limit their application. It depends heavily on the flow of media from official, highly regulated forms of trade but then develops its own structures of reproduction and distribution external and internal to the state economy.

It is through this generative quality that pirate infrastructure is expressive of a paradigmatic shift in Nigerian economy and capital and represents the extension of a logic of privatization into everyday life. Piracy's negative characteristics are often commented on: its criminality, the erosion of property rights it entails, and its function as a pathology of information processing, parasitically derivative of legal media flows (Chesterman and Lipman 1988; Coombe 1998). Important as these questions are, the structural focus on legal issues tends to obscure the mediating nature of infrastructure itself. In the Nigerian case, this is seen most strikingly in the rise of a new video industry that makes feature-length films directly for domestic video consumption (see Larkin 2000; Haynes 2000; Ukadike 2000; Ukah 2003). This new industry has pioneered new film genres and generated an entirely novel mode of reproduction and distribution that uses the capital, equipment, personnel, and distribution networks of pirate media. These Nigerian videos are a legitimate media form that could not exist without the infrastructure created by its illegitimate double, pirate media.

In recent years, then, there has been a wholesale shift in which many entrepreneurs previously involved in the distribution of pirate material have switched to the reproduction and dissemination of legal media. The mass importation of foreign music and films brought about the capital and professional expertise that facilitated the rise of a local film industry. This wandering over the lines that separate the legal from the nonlegal has been a common experience for urban Africans, who have been progressively disembedded from the infrastructures linking them to the official world economy and instead have poured energy into developing informal networks – equally global – that facilitate traffic in economic and cultural goods outside the established institutions of world trade (Simone 2000, 2001; Bayart, Ellis, and Hibou 1999; Mbembe 2001).

In addition to generating new economic networks, piracy, like all infrastructural modes, has distinct material qualities that influence the media that travel under its regime of reproduction. Piracy imposes particular conditions on the recording, transmission, and retrieval of data. Constant copying erodes data storage, degrading image and sound, overwhelming the signal of media content with the noise produced by the means of reproduction. Pirate videos are marked by blurred images and distorted sound, creating a material screen that alters audiences' engagement with media technologies and their senses of time, speed, space, and contemporaneity. In this way, piracy creates an aesthetic, a set of formal qualities that generates a particular sensorial experience of media marked by poor transmission, interference, and noise. Contemporary scholars of technology returning to the Frankfurt school have stressed that technology's operation on the body is a key factor in producing a sense of shock – the complex training of the human sensorium associated with modern urbanism (Benjamin 1999; Crary 2000; Doane 2002; Hansen 1995, 2000; Kracauer 1995; Schivelbusch 1986). This work is crucial in understanding the phenomenological and cognitive effects of technology when it is working at its optimum. What is less discussed (but see Schivelbusch 1986; Virilio 2003) is how technology influences through its failure as much as through its successes. Yet the inability of technologies to perform the operations they were assigned must be subject to the same critical scrutiny as their achievements. Breakdown and failure are, of course, inherent in all technologies, but in societies such as Nigeria, where collapse is often the default state of technological existence, they take on a far greater material and political presence (see also Mbembe and Roitman 1995; Koolhaas et al. 2001).

Rather than elide pirate infrastructure by using it as a window into legal questions of intellectual property, I wish to foreground it. If infrastructures represent attempts to order, regulate, and rationalize society, then breakdowns in their operation, or the rise of provisional and informal infrastructures, highlight the failure of that ordering and the recoding that takes its place. By subjecting the material operation of piracy and its social consequences to scrutiny, it becomes clear that pirate infrastructure is a powerful mediating force that produces new modes of organizing sensory perception, time, space, and economic networks.

Infrastructure

Capitalism, as many thinkers from Marx to Henri Lefebvre and David Harvey have reminded us, is not separable from space but produces the spaces through which it operates. All regimes of capital depend on infrastructures – shipping, trains, fiber optic lines, warehouses – whereby space gets produced and networked. Cities, or social space itself in Lefebvre's (1991) terms, take on real existence through their insertion into networks and pathways of commodity exchange, and it is infrastructure that provides these channels of communication. Infrastructure is the structural condition of the movement of commodities, whether they are waste, energy, or information. It brings diverse places into interaction, connecting some while divorcing others, constantly ranking, connecting, and segmenting spaces and people (Graham and Marvin 1996, 2001; Sassen 2002).

Infrastructures were key to the first modern corporations, which were organized around the continuous circulation of goods, services, and information on a large scale (Mattelart 2000). As such they have been enormously influential by organizing territory, standardizing time, and innovating new forms of economic organization. The rise of new electronic communication has intensified these processes, in turn instituting their own effects on people's sense of time and distance and on their conceptions of the present and simultaneity (Kern 1983; Mattelart 1996; Schivelbusch 1986; Virilio 1997).

The difficulty here is that much of the work on the transformative effects of media on notions of space, time, and perception takes for granted a media system that is smoothly efficient rather than the reality of infrastructural connections that are frequently messy, discontinuous, and poor. Technologies of speed and the infrastructures they create have had a profound impact on countries like Nigeria, but it is painfully obvious to people who live there that they often do not work as they are supposed to. This does not simply reflect national poverty but rather is inherent in the functioning (and the threat of collapse) of all technological systems. What distinguishes poor countries is the systemic nature of these failures, so that infrastructure, or the lack of it, becomes a pressing economic and social issue and a locus of political resentment toward the failures of the state and state elites. At the same time, the creation of successful infrastructures sets in motion other types of flows that operate in the space capital provides and that travel the routes created by these new networks of communication. The organization of one system sets in motion other systems spinning off in different directions.

The corruption of infrastructure

Piracy's success lies in its own infrastructural order that preys on the official distribution of globalized media, thus making it part of the corruption of infrastructure. By *corruption* I mean the pirating of a system's mode of communication – the viruses that attach to other kinds of official or recognized movement. Technological infrastructure creates material channels that organize the movement of energy, information, and economic and cultural goods between societies but at the same time creates possibilities for new actions. In Nigeria, this can be seen clearly in the so-called 419 schemes.[1] Sending letters by fax and e-mail, 419 fraudsters claim to be a senior Nigerian official – a bank president, a petroleum minister, a relative of a dictator – and state that they urgently need to transfer a large amount of money out of the country (for an overview see Apter 1999; Hibou 1999). The recipients are told that if they agree to help, they will receive a percentage of the money. In this way, complete strangers are

Fig. 1 Alhaji B.K.'s video shop, Kano (© Brian Larkin)

lured into what the FBI has described as the most successful fraud in the history of the world – and one of Nigeria's main foreign currency earners. The 419ers target foreign businesses; they make use of international financial arrangements, such as bank accounts and international money transfers; and they depend on new communication technologies – first fax machines and now e-mail. It is a form of fraud that depends on a certain cosmopolitanism, on the internationalization of finance, and as a form of action it is inconceivable without the technological and financial infrastructure brought by Nigeria's oil boom. The oil monies of the 1970s and 1980s allowed for a deep penetration of corporate capitalism in Nigeria and created the professional and technological networks upon which 419ers prey. It also inaugurated the spectacular corruption that gives 419 letters believability to victims. The fraud pirates the discourses and procedures of capitalism but also requires its own infrastructure of communication. In this way, the very success of any infrastructural flows creates possibilities for their own corruption, placing in motion the potential for other sets of relations to occur and creating a ripple effect on movements of people, culture, and religion.

Like 419, piracy operates as a corruption of communications infrastructures that develops its own circuits of distribution using officially organized media. Films made in Hollywood and intended for distribution in an organized, domestic circuit are copied by pirates; sent to Asia or the Middle East, where they are subtitled; recopied in large numbers as videocassettes, video CDs (VCDs are the dominant technology for media storage in much of Asia), or DVDs; and then reshipped mainly within the developing world. In recent years, as Nigeria has become progressively disembedded from the official global economy (with the single exception of its oil industry), it has become ever more integrated into a parallel, unofficial world economy that reorients Nigeria toward new metropoles such as Dubai, Singapore, and Beirut (what AbdouMaliq Simone [2001] more broadly calls the 'worlding of African cities'. See also Bayart, Ellis, and Hibou 1999; MacGaffey and Bazenguissa-Ganga 2000; Mbembe 2001).

Let us take the example of the picture (Fig. 1) of the sign for Alhaji

B. K.'s video shop in the Kofar Wambai market in Kano, Nigeria.

Kofar Wambai is best known for the sale of thread used in the elaborate embroidery of the long Hausa gown, the *babban riga*. Whole tracts of the market are suffused in the bright colors of thread hanging from the stall doorways, but in one section are lane after lane of small shops specializing in the reproduction and wholesale distribution of audio- and videocassettes: Indian, Sudanese, Western, and Hausa music; Islamic preaching; and Indian, Western, and Hausa video-cassettes.

Cassette sellers at Kofar Wambai are represented by the Kano Cassette Sellers Recording and Co-operative Society Ltd. (Kungiyar Gawa Kai Ta Masu Sayar Da Kaset Da Dauka Ta Jihar Kano), a society whose headquarters is at Kofar Wambai but whose members spill out far beyond the confines of the market. The success of Kano's cassette reproduction industry is grounded in three developments: First, in 1981, the Motion Pictures Association of America (MPAA) suspended the distribution of Hollywood films to Nigeria. This was in response to the seizure of MPAA assets by the Nigerian government in an attempt to indigenize the control of Nigerian companies. Second, the oil boom of the late 1970s boosted consumption, allowing for the mass dissemination of cassette-based technologies. Finally, the longstanding position of Kano at the apex of wide-ranging transnational trading networks facilitated the quick exploitation of these possibilities and the forging of a distribution network that stretches over northern Nigeria and beyond. The subsequent rise of piracy means that far from disappearing, Holly-wood films have become available at a speed and volume as never before.

The everyday practice of piracy in Kano was based around the mass distribution of the two most popular drama forms, Indian and Hollywood films, and the reproduction of televised Hausa dramas and Islamic religious cassettes. Nearly all of those who might be described as pirates were at the same time involved in the duplication and sale of legitimate media, and the organization that emerged made Kano the regional distribution center for electronic media in northern Nigeria and the wider Hausaphone area (which covers parts of Chad, Cameroon, Benin, Ghana, and the Sudan). The system is this: the main dealers are based at centers in Kano, like Kofar Wambai market. They then sell to distributors in other northern cities, and these in turn supply smaller urban and rural dealers who provide goods for itinerant peddlers. The system is based on a complex balance of credit and trust; and although it depends, in part, on piracy, it has evolved into a highly organized, extensive distribution system for audio- and videocassettes. The success of this new form of distribution has not been lost on the government, which – though critical of piracy – has used cassette distribution as a way of spreading political messages.[2] As Alhaji Musa Na Sale, president of the cassette sellers association, told me, if something is popular, 'even the nomads will hear it'. The decentralized nature of this distribution system means that neither the government nor the association knows exactly how many people are tied to the industry, especially given its massive expansion with the rise of Hausa video films.

Hausa distributors have had to rely on Lebanese and Indian traders for access to foreign videos that were coming from the Persian Gulf. In the 1990s, these videos often had the distributor's name superimposed on the tape itself: for example, *Excellence Kano* for Hollywood films and *Al-Mansoor, Dubai* for Indian ones. Hollywood films were imported to Kano directly from the Middle East or trans-ported north from Lagos. Because of the great popularity of Indian films among the Hausa (Larkin 1997, 2003), Kano was and is the main clearinghouse for Indian films. This traffic is controlled by two primary distributors, both based in Kano. For many years the trade was routed through Dubai, and it was common to watch Indian films with advertisements scrolling across the bottom of the screen announcing 'Al Mansoor's video' followed by a long list of his many shops in Dubai, Abu Dhabi, and other parts of the gulf, along with their telephone, telex, and fax numbers. These videos often found their way to the Kano television station, CTV, where announce-ments for Al Mansoor's many video shops sometimes obliterated the Arabic and English subtitles at the bottom of the screen.

With the recent emergence of video CDs, the routes of the market for Indian film have changed considerably. According to one Indian distributor, the market is now oriented toward Pakistan, where VCD plants make high-quality dubs of Indian films. Master copies are shipped via DHL to Kano, where they are then transferred to tape and sold in bulk to Hausa distributors. I was told the gap between a film's release in India and its appearance in Kano could be as little as seven days.[3] American films are pirated through similar networks. They are copied illegally in the United States and shipped to Dubai or Beirut, often arriving in Nigeria while they are still on first-run release in the United States. One Jean-Claude Van Damme film I watched had Chinese subtitles superimposed over Arabic ones, providing a visible inscription of the routes of media piracy. Frequently US videos contain a message scrolling across the bottom of the film every few minutes stating: 'Demo tape only. Not for rental or sale. If you have rented or purchased this cassette call 1-800 NO COPYS (1-800-662-6787).[4] Federal law provides severe civil and criminal penalties for unauthorized duplication or distribution.'

Kofar Wambai is the apex of a formal, highly ordered system of reproduction and distribution for media goods in northern Nigeria and is one example of the ways in which media piracy generates new infrastructures of the parallel economy in Nigeria. It is part of a much larger process whereby the Nigerian economy has split between a traditional official economy oriented toward legal participation in the international division of labor and an unofficial economy, each one with its own infrastructures and networks, sometimes overlapping, sometimes opposed.

Piracy

Piracy is an ambivalent phenomenon in countries like Nigeria. It is widely feared by indigenous film and music makers as destructive of the small profits they make by way of intellectual property. It has had disastrous effects on indigenous music makers and contributes substantially to the erosion of the industry as a whole. Yet at the same time, many of these same people consume pirate media both privately and professionally. Piracy has made available to Nigerians a vast array of world media at a speed they could never imagine, hooking them up to the accelerated circuit of global media flows. Where cinema screens were once filled with outdated films from the United States or India, pirate media means that Nigerian audiences can watch films contemporaneously with audiences in New York or Bombay. Instead of being marginalized by official distribution networks, Nigerian consumers can now participate in the immediacy of an international consumer culture – but only through the mediating capacity of piracy.

Piracy is part of a so-called shadow (second, marginal, informal, black) economy existing in varying degrees beyond the law. It produces profits, but not for corporations, and provides no revenue for the state.[5] The second economy is untaxed and unmonitored and enjoys all of the benefits and precariousness of this location. Until recently, media infrastructures in Nigeria, from the construction of radio diffusion networks to the building of television stations, have usually been state controlled and organized around the fundamental logic of providing publicity for the state – indeed, of representing its progressivist, developmentalist logic (Larkin 2000). Piracy, by contrast, is based in unofficial, decentralized networks, and Nigerian video represents the migration of these networks into the mainstream. The rise of privatized media represents not so much an erosion of state power but a larger movement in which the shadow economy has reconfigured the state itself. According to US State Department figures, Nigeria is the largest market for pirate goods in Africa, and one estimate suggests that up to 70 percent of current Nigerian GDP is derived from the shadow economy, making it, in percentage terms, the largest such economy in the world, matched only by Thailand (see Schneider 2000; Simone 1998; Bayart, Ellis, and Hibou 1999; Mbembe 2001; Apter 1999). Figures such as these are always provisional and, like many statistics about Nigeria, often simulacral, being not so much a numerical reference to the actual state of affairs in Nigeria but rather a mimicking of rationalist representations of economies that are measurable. But in Nigeria, the second economy has grown to such a scale that no one really knows how to represent it. No one is sure how large the GDP is; no one can calculate the balance of payments or even the size of Nigeria's population (Bayart, Ellis, and Hibou 1999; Hecht and Simone 1994). Strong forces are at work to make sure that revenue streams from major industries, like oil, are obligingly opaque. Jean-François Bayart, Stephen Ellis, and Béatrice Hibou (1999) have argued that illegal activities in Nigeria (such as fraud, corruption, and the import and export of illegal oil, drugs, and videos) have grown to such a degree that they now form part of the routine operations of the state rather than a pathology outside of it. Nigerians have become famous within Africa and beyond for migrating as workers, importers, exporters, smugglers, drug carriers, and fraudsters. While the federal state continues to take part in the formalized ritual of the official economy, many Nigerians see a widening gap between it and the everyday reality of how Nigeria functions. Piracy is part of this larger reconfiguration of the Nigerian state and economy.

Ravi Sundaram (1999) argues that informal processes in Indian media ecology should be seen as a pirate modernity – a mode of incorporation into the economy that is disorganized, nonideological, and marked by mobility and innovation. This formulation nicely captures the ambivalence of piracy, refusing the simple equation that piracy is an alternative or oppositional modernity (though there are elements of this in people's justification that pirate media goods redress economic inequalities between developed and underdeveloped countries). Piracy is non-ideological in that it does not represent a self-conscious political opposition to capitalism – it is not a kind of tactical media (Garcia and Lovink 2001). But it is also worth stressing the high degree of formality that marks this 'informal' world. A focus on the mobility, innovation, and provisionality of piracy elides the fact that pirate networks are highly organized and determinative of other sets of relations.

Hausa video

In the 1990s, distributors who had been involved with the repro-duction and distribution of religious, Hollywood, and Indian cassettes began to turn their attention to Nigerian and especially Hausa-language videos. Nigerian videos are narrative, feature-length films

Figs 2–3 Alhaji B.K. in his shop in 1995 (above) and in 2002 (below) (© Brian Larkin)

produced in English, Hausa, or Yoruba (Haynes 2000; Ukadike 2000; Ukah 2003; see also Meyer 2003 and Wendl 2001).[6] They are not the kind of African movies usually screened at film festivals but rather are oriented toward popular audiences – meaning that their production and financing depends entirely on how well they perform in the marketplace. By 2001, over 3,500 films had passed through the Nigerian film and censorship board – dwarfing by many times the total number of Nigerian feature films. The films are produced in Yoruba, English, and Hausa, with English-language videos – commonly called 'Nigerian videos' – receiving the greatest investment and prestige and distribution to Ghana, Kenya, and as far south as South Africa. Hausa-language videos emerged in the mid-1990s, spurred by local drama troupes, disaffected television professionals, and popular Hausa-language authors seeking to make films of their books. In 2001 alone, two hundred Hausa videos were released, easily making this one of the most vibrant forms of African media.

Fig. 4 The jackets for Hausa films distinguish pirate from legal media
(© Brian Larkin)

Hausa films have distinguished themselves from southern Nigerian videos by de-emphasizing story lines about magic and the corruption of urban life, concentrating instead on themes of love. In this they draw heavily on the narrative and visual style of Indian films, especially in their use of spectacular song and dance sequences (Larkin 2000, 2003). The production of such a large number of videos has resulted in a small army of people working in the industry as editors, camera operators, directors, set designers, actors, composers, musicians, singers, and graphic designers as well as those involved in distribution and sales. At least three video magazines modeled after the Indian film magazine *Stardust* are in circulation, and, as with Indian films, there is a substantial local audio market based on the sale of movie sound tracks.[7] Hausa videos, which can sell anywhere from ten thousand to one hundred thousand copies, have come to dominate audio- and videocassette production, marginalizing – for the moment – foreign film and music distribution. Video rental shops that used to carry a mixture of many different cassettes are now dominated by Hausa films, and the shops themselves, along with video clubs (many of them illegal), have proliferated across the urban landscape.

Figures 2 and 3 show the office of Alhaji B. K., former vice president of the Kano Cassette Sellers Recording and Co-operative Society Ltd. In 1995, Alhaji B. K. specialized in recording religious cassettes that he dubbed in his studio/ shop in Kofar Wambai. Figure 2 shows the hardware and equipment involved in cassette distribution. The explosive market for Hausa video films transformed his business, so that by 2002 it was almost wholly devoted to the reproduction and distribution of Hausa films. Figure 3 shows his shop now: the dubbing facilities have been moved off-site, the audiocassette machines are gone, and the walls are lined with video jackets. His shop now functions primarily as a place to meet clients traveling to Kano. This transformation is common among most, if not all, distributors. Many still sell Indian and American films, of course; their sales do not seem to have suffered even though their proportion of the market has dropped with the unprecedented popularity of Hausa and Nigerian videos. The shift in businesses like this is indicative that, in the north, Hausa video films have fed off of the networks of piracy much as

piracy fed off networks of official media.

As Hausa film exploded in popularity, the style and shape of the video market changed considerably. Hausa videos have come to dominate the market, creating a huge demand that was not there previously.[8] Hausa video film production has become highly organized and regulated, with producers, distributors, and camera operators organized into their own professional associations. An established system of production, postproduction, and distribution has been put into effect: a producer puts up the initial money, finds a writer, director, and actors, and produces the film. Once the film is made, the editing complete, and the covers for the tapes printed, the film enters into a waiting list for release, which ensures that no more than six films come out per month. On the release date, the producer takes the film to one of the distributors in Kano and sells a master copy of the tape and several hundred copies of the jacket for about N50 (about 50 cents) each. The film sells for N250 (about $2.50) each. Intellectual property is vested not so much in the tape, which is the prerogative of the distributor, but in the jacket, which is created and controlled by the filmmakers themselves. The jackets for Hausa films – wraparound sleeves in which cassettes are inserted (see Fig. 4) – are the only way to distinguish pirate from legal media. The distributor covers the cost of the dubbing machines and the capital outlay and provides important access to the network of distributors. No money is paid to the producer until the film has been sold. Unsurprisingly, this system has been the source of considerable tension between producers and distributors, as it leaves producers carrying all the risks of failure. On at least one occasion, producers in the Kano State Filmmakers Association got together to threaten to boycott distributors in order to increase the price of the jackets.[9] Some filmmakers do exhibit films at the cinema, and others try to sell to television stations, but the economic heart of the industry is the exploitation of domestic video technology.

Video filmmaking, like many aspects of the informal economy, is a precarious and highly volatile business. The tension between distributors and filmmakers is indicative of a struggle for control over the industry, but both parties remain vulnerable to the leveling out of the market. The early boom period of Hausa and Nigerian videos – when it seemed that anyone could make money in the film industry – has passed. Now filmmakers say they have to work harder for less profit, and this has led to an exodus of key directors from the industry (especially in southern Nigeria and Ghana). The precariousness of the industry in the north also comes from increasing moral criticism of the films themselves, especially the contentious accusation that they are influenced by un-Islamic Indian films. This threat was heightened in 2001 when, following the introduction of sharia law in Kano State, all Hausa filmmaking was banned.

Filmmakers responded to the government's ban by organizing themselves under the Kano State Filmmakers Association, a formal interest group that could negotiate with the government. Because filmmaking was such a new phenomenon, most filmmakers were young (many in their thirties) and lacked ties to senior patrons allied with older forms of trade. Still, the association possessed several ways of exerting pressure on the government. First, magazines such as *Fim* argued that even Islamic states such as Iran had film industries, so that film was not inherently un-Islamic. Tabloids such as *Bidiyo* noted that sharia law was being applied only to filmmakers – there was no question of banning films from India, Hollywood, or southern Nigeria – and threatened to run popular actors and actresses against incumbent politicians. In a meeting with the Ministry of Information of Kano State, the association pointed out that when Zamfara State (the first state in northern Nigeria to turn to sharia law) banned prostitution, they supplied prostitutes with alternative forms of employment and that when they closed down cinema halls, they compensated the owners.[10] By this precedent, they argued, the Kano State government should now be responsible for the welfare of the producers, directors, actors, musicians, composers, writers, editors, and graphic designers employed in the film industry. Since the industry was so large and established, there was no way such compensation would be possible. As a compromise, the filmmakers proposed establishing a censorship board that would certify the Islamic and cultural acceptability of films but allow filmmaking to continue. When the proposal was accepted in March 2001 and the censorship board was put in place, one of its first moves was to ban mixed-sex song sequences in films.

The market for Hausa films has solidified, so that five main distributors now dominate the industry. Cassettes are dubbed in bulk and sold on a wholesale basis through wide-ranging networks forged when Hausa films did not yet exist. Kano, long important as a media center for Indian films and religious cassettes, is now the dominant center for the much larger market for Hausa films. Small distributors travel there from all over northern Nigeria, Chad, Cameroon, and Ghana. Hausa distributors have their own networks that are restricted almost wholly to the Hausa-speaking diaspora.

The roots of all Nigerian film (whether English, Hausa, or Yoruba) in piracy means that the physical quality and look of Nigerian video films has been determined by the formal qualities of pirate infrastructure. Piracy standardized a particular quality of reproduction; both filmmakers and distributors believe that while people like Nigerian videos, they will not pay higher prices for better image or sound quality. Because the new Hausa videos are dubbed using the same machines as pirate films, because they rely on the same blank cassettes and are distributed through the same channels, piracy has created the aesthetic and technical horizons for nonpirate media. It is this question of aesthetics to which I now turn.

The materiality of piracy

In his film *Kumar Talkies*, director Pankaj Kumar evokes the role of the cinema in small-town Indian life. In one scene, a group of men talk about going to watch films in the nearby city. The newness of the films there, the high quality of their reproduction, and the experience of moviegoing come to stand for a temporal and cultural difference between the town and the city. One man says that he doesn't watch films at home because he never gets to see the entire film. Kumar then cuts to the local cinema owner, who explains that this indeed is the case: in order to save electricity costs, he takes out a few reels from each film, imposing enormous jump cuts on the formal integration, slicing whole chunks of narrative from the audience's view. The big city, not surprisingly, becomes the place where this fracture can be repaired, where films are shown in their entirety, and where audiences do not have to confront their physical and cultural marginality every time they attend the cinema.

I have argued elsewhere (Larkin 1998–99) that media technologies do not just store time, they represent it. As Stephen Kern (1983) has written, different societies can feel cut off from history or excessively attached to the past – without a future or rushing toward one. Technology, especially the media, often provides the conduit for our experience of being 'inside' or 'outside' history. The materiality of media creates the physical details and the quotidian sensory uses through which these experiences are formed. In *Kumar Talkies*, the everyday operations of cinema houses provide a sign vehicle and

symbol for marginality and provincialism. In postcolonial societies, such as India or Nigeria, this sense is intensified due to the powerful link between technology and colonial rule, where modern technology was part of a civilizing mission of colonial power (Adas 1989; Mrázek 2002; Prakash 1999; Spitulnik 1998–99).

Breakdown

In Nigeria, the ubiquity of technological breakdown and repair imposes a particular experience of technology and its cultural effects. Contemporary urban theory, perhaps understandably, has been less quick to explore these cultural articulations, focusing instead on the reconfiguration of urban space brought about by new media. Paul Virilio, in a typically contradictory fashion, lobbies fiercely for both sides of the argument. On the one hand, he proclaims with dystopian excess that the immediacy of real-time technologies has fundamentally transformed our ability to understand time and space. Instead of being marked by duration or the unfolding of events in succession, time, he argues, is now exposed instantaneously (Virilio 1997, 2000). Events that take place at a distance are experienced immediately thanks to the telepresence brought about by real-time technologies. Speed here is the crucial dimension (see also Kern 1983). Speed conditions our experience of time, producing temporal compression and allowing us to act at a distance. Cities that used to be organized around entrances and exits – nodes that regulate the exchange of people and goods – have given way to the immaterial interface of information exchange. This is certainly the case in contemporary Nigeria, where a series of technological changes over the last ten years, including the rise of satellite television, the growing penetration of Internet culture, and the belated arrival of mobile phone networks, has created new technological portals through which Nigerians engage with one another and the world beyond.

The difficulty with this side of Virilio is his assumption that the experiential transformations he analyzes presume a stable, smoothly operating technological infrastructure. The transition he identifies is totalizing, penetrating homogeneously and organizing universally. It partakes of a world of fast-operating computers, clear-picture televisions, and constant telecommunication signals. But Virilio (2003) also notes that with the invention of the train came the derailment, and few thinkers have been as insistent as he is that the development of technology is tied to the development of catastrophe. My interest in technological collapse is somewhat different. It is not in extravagant spectacles like collapsing bridges or exploding space shuttles but in the small, ubiquitous experience of breakdown as a condition of technological existence. In Nigeria, cars, televisions, VCRs, buses, and motorbikes are often out of service. Even when they work, electricity supplies are unreliable and beset by power surges that damage consumer equipment. NEPA, the Nigerian Electric Power Authority, is famously known by the epithet 'Never Expect Power Always,' and phone lines are expensive and difficult to obtain. Poverty and the disorganization of the Nigerian economy mean that consumer technologies such as scooters and cars arrive already used and worn out. After their useful life in Belgium or Holland, cars are exported to Nigeria as 'new' second-hand vehicles.[11] After these vehicles arrive in Nigeria, worn parts are repaired, dents are banged out, and paint is resprayed to remake and 'tropicalize' them (see Verrips and Meyer 2001). This is, of course, a temporary state of affairs. Other parts expire, second-hand parts break down, while local 'innovations' and adjustments designed to make cars, televisions, and VCRs work fail. A cycle of breakdown, repair, and breakdown again is the condition of existence for many technologies in Nigeria. As a consequence, Nigeria employs a vast army of people who specialize in repairing and reconditioning broken technological goods, since the need for repair is frequent and the cost of it cheap (Sundaram 1999; Verrips and Meyer 2001).

Critical work on urbanism has argued that utopian theories of technology and urban transformation de-emphasize the fact that entire societies are excluded from the new information infrastructures (what Manuel Castells [1998] terms 'technological apartheid'; see also Castells 1996; Graham and Marvin 1996, 2001; Sassen 2002). These arguments recur somewhat in debates over the so-called digital divide and the division of the world into technological haves and have-nots. My difficulty with this move is with the dichotomizing logic it promotes and its assumption that the economic and cultural effects of new technologies are absent from 'disconnected' societies. The danger here is that this polemic looks through rather than at the object at hand and fails to examine the structuring effects that technologies and their failures – however dysfunctional – have in everyday life. Virilio's account of the experience of speed in contemporary urbanization is highly relevant to societies such as Nigeria, but perhaps not in the ways he imagines. There is no question, for instance, that new technologies have resulted in profound temporal acceleration for Nigerians. But the poor material infrastructure of Nigeria ensures that as the speed of Nigerian life increases, so too does the gap between *actual* and *potential* acceleration, between what technologies *can* do and what they *do* do. Thus, even as life speeds up, the experience of technological marginalization intensifies, and the gap between how fast society is moving and how fast it could move becomes a site of considerable political tension.

The poor condition of infrastructure and the ubiquity of breakdown bring about their corollary: repair as a cultural mode of existence for technology. This is a consequence of both poverty and innovation. Breakdown and repair structure the ability of subjects to use and be used by technologies and also these subjects' sense of time and place. The culture of repair rests on the experience of duration in the everyday use of technology. Breakdown creates a temporal experience that has less to do with dizzying, real-time global integration than with waiting for e-mail messages to open, machines to be repaired, or electricity to be restored. In Nigeria, all technologies are variously subject to a constant cycle of breakdown and repair; the promise of technological prosthesis is thwarted by the common experience of technological collapse. Each repair enforces another waiting period, an often frustrating experience of duration brought about by the technology of speed itself. The temporal experience of slowness comes as a consequence of speed-producing technologies, so that speed and acceleration, deceleration and stasis are relative, continually shifting states.

In Figure 2 we see the stringing together of cassette recorders used to dub audiocassettes in Kano. The covers – intended to protect the cassette while recording – have been ripped off for ease of ejection. Wires hang loosely, sometimes tangled in bunches; many machines have their casings broken, and all are exposed to the harmattan winds that deposit layers of dust on every surface of the city. Piracy depends on material modes of reproduction such as these. The operations of piracy create material effects on the storage and retrieval of data and sensorial effects on notions of space, time, culture, and the body. In Nigeria, the infrastructure for media, especially pirate media, is often marked by disrepair and noise.

Nigerian dealers in the legal and illegal reproduction of media record data on cheap tapes with low-quality machines. This informa-tion is retrieved for the most part through old VCRs, televisions, and cassette players marked by distortion and interference. Watching, say, Hollywood or Indian films on VCRs in Nigeria, where there is no official distribution of nonpirate media, means necessarily watching the dub of a dub of a dub. As the same dealers, using the same equipment and same blank cassettes, dub Hausa video films, the result is that the visual standard for pirate media remains in place. Pirated images have a hallucinogenic quality. Detail is destroyed as realist representation fades into pulsating, pure light. Facial features are smoothed away, colors are broken down into constituent tones, and bodies fade into one another. Reproduction takes its toll, degrading the image by injecting dropouts and bursts of fuzzy noise, breaking down dialogue into muddy, often inaudible sound. This distortion is often heard in the vibrating shrillness of the tape players used by *masu saida kaset*, itinerant cassette hawkers who travel around the city selling eclectic collections of music.

The quality of the tape player used by these cassette sellers is standard in Nigeria. As the seller travels, the cassette player blares out Indian film sound tracks, Islamic preaching, or Hausa songs at such a high volume that the signal degenerates into the pure vibration of the machine. In this, the machine actually mimics the sound of live musical performances in Kano, which often rely on the distorted amplification of microphones, loudspeakers, and portable generators.[12] This distortion affects many media in Nigeria. Film prints, for instance, arrive at the end of long, picaresque journeys that begin in the metropolitan cinematic centers of India or Europe and cross the cinema halls of many countries before reaching the Nigerian circuit. There, they are often shown until they literally fall apart. All are scratched and heavily damaged, full of surprising and lengthy jump cuts where film has stuck in the projector and burned. Although the image and sound of video are poor, Ghanaian video filmmaker Willy Akuffo has warned video makers against a nostalgia for the 'quality' of film that forgets how terrible film prints actually were. As a former projectionist, he had to deal with repairing burned film and refixing previous repairs that the prints had accumulated on their journey to Africa.[13] Likewise, the quality of video projection, with its low-resolution, ghostly images, can be highly variable depending on the age and condition of the equipment. In the poorer cinemas that converted to video in the mid-1990s, there were terrible problems with tracking and inaudible sound. The projected image often filled only a portion of the cinema screen or would be distorted into an hourglass shape. At other times, the corners of the image vibrated as if the screen were a photograph peeling off.[14]

The infrastructure of reproduction, like most contemporary infrastructures in Nigeria, is marked by cheapness, faulty operation, and constant repair. 'All data flows,' the media theorist Friedrich Kittler (1999: 14) reminds us, 'must pass through the bottleneck of the signifier,' and in so doing they are vulnerable to being 'engulfed by the noise of the real'. The 'real' here is precisely the fuzziness of cinematic images or the hissing of tape recorders – the noise produced by the medium of transmission itself as it encodes and disseminates data across space and time. Yuri Tsivian (1994) has termed this effect the 'semiotics of interference' and has analyzed the operation of early Russian cinema, arguing that the physical conditions of media exhibition – scratches on the film and noise and vibrations from projectors – became part of the 'message' of films themselves.[15] For Nigerians, the costs of consuming and producing world media require operating on the margins of technology. Distortion on an audio tape, like dropouts on a video or a slow connection to the Internet, are the material conditions of existence for media. While media infrastructure creates the reality of being ever more connected to a globalized world, it does so by emphasizing Nigerians' marginalization at the same time. Electricity blackouts, snowy television images, difficulties getting international phone lines, and distorted loudspeakers on cassette players all create a technological veil of semiotic distortion for Nigerians.

Some of this distortion is taken for granted, rendered invisible to people by its ubiquity. It is clear, for instance, that many of the most popular transnational media forms, such as sports, action films, wrestling, and Indian films, are highly visual and thus capable of overcoming both linguistic differences and audio degradation. But this degradation is rarely commented on. Instead, what these films evoke is the fantasy of other countries where deficiencies in infrastructure are believed not to exist. For many northern Nigerians, Saudi Arabia is a place where electricity always flows, where roads have no potholes, and where hospitals are of the highest quality – just as everyone in Europe and America is thought to own televisions and mobile phones.[16] These fantasies represent implicit and sometimes explicit critiques of the failures of the Nigerian state to provide basic infrastructures for everyday life. The breakdown of infrastructure provides a conduit for critiques of the state and of the corruption and ethnic favoritism of political elites (Verrips and Meyer 2001).

Conclusion

In his exhaustive study of the rise of print, the historian Adrian Johns (1998) argues that piracy, rather than being an aberration of an 'original' mode of text production, is central to the way print operates and spreads over time and space. The qualities we now associate with print – its fixity, guarantee of authorship, and commodity form – were not inherent in the technology but the result of a social compact, the institution of a technological order of reality. Johns is instructive in reminding us that, in many parts of the world, media piracy is not a pathology of the circulation of media forms but its prerequisite. In many places, piracy is the only means by which certain media – usually foreign – are available. And in countries like Nigeria, the technological constraints that fuel pirate media provide the industrial template through which other, nonpirate media are reproduced, disseminated, and consumed.

Piracy and the wider infrastructure of reproduction it has generated reveal the organization of contemporary Nigerian society. They show how the parallel economy has migrated onto center stage, overlapping and interpenetrating with the official economy, mixing legal and illegal regimes, uniting social actors, and organizing common networks. This infrastructure creates its own modes of spatiality, linking Nigeria into new economic and social networks. Piracy means that Nigerian media production and circulation no longer depend on the intervention of the state (colonial or postcolonial) but are captured by the logic of privatization and gradually extend over differing areas of social experience. Sundaram (1999: 61), writing about everyday electronic culture in India – self-trained programmers who build computers and servers by cobbling together second-hand computer parts – refers to this as 'recycled modernity,' one that is 'everyday in its imaginary, pirate in its practice, and mobile in its innovation'. Rem Koolhaas (Koolhaas et al. 2001) has recently explored a similar phenomenon in the collapse of traffic systems in Lagos, a city overwhelmed by an increase in cars and a lack of roads. There, jams and bottlenecks force detours through 'non-flow' areas, spreading traffic off the planned grids and expanding the motorable space of the city. As cars back up for longer periods of time, they create markets for

hawkers. Over time the markets get formalized, roadside mosques are marked out to service the workers, and new infrastructures emerge to paper over the inefficiencies of the old (see also Mbembe and Roitman 1995; Simone 2001; Verrips and Meyer 2001).

The infrastructure of reproduction created by piracy generates material and sensorial effects on both media and their consumers. Cheap tape recorders, old televisions, blurred videos that are the copy of a copy of a copy – these are the material distortions endemic to the reproduction of media goods in situations of poverty and illegality, and they shape the ways these media take on cultural value and act on individuals and groups. The dialectic of technological breakdown and repair imposes its own cultural experience of modernity, an alternative speeding up and stasis, and a world where gaps in space and time are continually annihilated and reinforced.

Notes

This essay was originally written for the conference 'Transmissions: Globalization, Technology, Media', organized by Patrice Petro and Tasha Oren at the University of Milwaukee, Wisconsin, and it benefited greatly from the response of participants there (a shorter version of this article appears in the conference volume of the same name). Earlier versions of this essay were presented also at the African Studies Association meeting, Columbia University's Boas Seminar, and the Media and the Future of Area Studies conference at New York University, and I would like to thank all respondents. Many of the ideas took shape in a graduate seminar I cotaught with Reinhold Martin. I would like to thank him and the graduate students in the class. I owe a huge debt of gratitude to those who introduced me to Hausa video and its media infrastructure, above all to Alhaji B. K. and Alhaji Musa Na Sale of the Kano State Cassette Sellers and Recording and Co-operative Society Ltd.; the directors Ado Ahmad, Tijani Ibrahim, and Aminu Hassan Yakasai; and the cultural activism of Ibrahim Sheme, Umar Farukh, and Abdalla Uba Adamu. I dedicate this essay to the memory of Aminu Hassan Yakasai and Tijani Ibraheem, two directors who pioneered Hausa video film. Finally I thank Meg McLagan, Birgit Meyer, and the *Public Culture* editorial committee for comments on the manuscript.

1   *419* refers to the section of the Nigerian criminal code that deals with cases of fraud. Criminals who engage in this type of crime are known as 419ers (Apter 1999).

2   After the Maitatsine riots of 1981, the Nigerian government circulated a video of the mass arrest of followers of the millenarian leader Maitatsine as a warning to other followers. Musa Na Sale, one of the most prominent cassette dealers working with traditional Hausa singers, said that he would meet with singers and *malams* (religious leaders whose teachings were sold on cassette) to instruct them as to 'what the government needs to talk about and what the government doesn't want.'

3   This could be true, but there is likely an element of boastfulness to this claim. In 1993 when distribution was still by cassette, I was told that films could arrive in Kano as little as seven days after their release in India. In 2002, I was told by the same distributor (but a different person) that the reason for the shift to VCDs was to increase speed and quality and that the problem with videos was that they could take up to a month or more to be received from Dubai.

4   This is now a number for information about new drugs.

5   Although, as Jonathan Haynes pointed out to me, governments do collect revenue through taxes on blank cassettes.

6   Ghana is the only other country in West Africa to have developed its own video film industry. Over time, there has been a cross-pollination between Ghanaian and Nigerian English-language videos, so that similar themes, genres, and cultural styles crop up in both.

7   Two of these magazines, *Mujallar Fim* and *Mujallar Bidiyo*, can be accessed online at www. kanoonline.com.

8   This trend is confirmed by Indian film distributors who told me their sales remained constant during the rise of Hausa films and that sales currently remained strong. Certainly, Indian films remain hugely popular among

Hausa filmmakers and continue to provide a source of inspiration, technical ideas, and narrative themes for Hausa films.

9 I was told on a number of occasions that many people in the video industry – distributors, editors, jacket designers, musicians, and actors – can make more money than producers, though many actors complain that they do not get paid until after the producer receives money from the distributor.

10 Ironically, perhaps, when filmmakers from Kano traveled to Zamfara to shoot a film, they were invited to the governor's mansion to meet Zamfara's first lady – a huge fan of Hausa video.

11 For an interesting comparative example, see the trade in second-hand clothing analyzed by Karen Hansen (2000). Also, Gerald Lombardi's 1999 study of computer use in Brazil includes a fascinating discussion of the informal (and illegal) market in phone lines that feeds off poor infrastructure.

12 Christopher Waterman (1990) points out that distortion by amplifiers became such an accepted part of live performance that musicians would intentionally destroy new loudspeakers to achieve the desired buzzing sound. I thank Andrew Apter for reminding me of this.

13 Birgit Meyer reminded me that Akuffo described this problem with poor film prints at a workshop organized by the International Study Commission of Media, Religion, and Culture (19–27 May 2000, Accra, Ghana).

14 Yet despite these problems, cassettes remain the more popular medium in northern Nigeria. In January 2002, when I asked Hausa video filmmakers why they had not switched to video CDs to distribute their movies, they pointed out that the technology was not yet widely available in the north, in part because damage to a VCD could ruin the entire disc, while damage to a tape created only passing moments of fuzziness.

15 James Ferguson (1999) makes an interesting but different argument on the role of 'noise' in globalization. Ferguson focuses on the traffic in cultural meanings, arguing that cities are culturally 'noisy' in that all sorts of forms of cultural flows clash and are available to urban dwellers. But Ferguson's (1999: 208) central question concerns 'which of the bits floating in the swirl of events does any given social actor bear.'

16 Writing about the cosmopolitan sexual relations between Hausa *yan daudu* (men who act like women) and men in Saudi Arabia, Rudolf Gaudio (1996) argues that when these *yan daudu* return from Saudi Arabia, they parade their sophistication and cultural savoir faire – part of which involves raving 'about the creature comforts that Saudi Arabia [has] to offer: telephones, air conditioning, a constant supply of electricity and running water. '"*Ba abin da babu*" they would say, "there's nothing that isn't there."' See also O'Brien 1999.

References

Adas, Michael. 1989. *Machines as the measure of men: Science, technology, and ideologies of Western dominance.* Ithaca, NY: Cornell University Press.

Apter, Andrew. 1999. 'IBB = 419: Nigerian democracy and the politics of illusion'. In *Civil society and the political imagination in Africa: Critical perspectives,* edited by John L. Comaroff and Jean Comaroff. Chicago: University of Chicago Press.

Bayart, Jean-François, Stephen Ellis, and Béatrice Hibou. 1999. *The criminalization of the state in Africa.* Bloomington: Indiana University Press.

Benjamin, Walter. 1999. *The arcades project.* Cambridge, MA: Harvard University Press.

Callaway, Barbara. 1987. *Muslim Hausa women in Nigeria: Tradition and Change.* Syracuse, NY: Syracuse University Press.

Castells, Manuel. 1996. *The information age: Economy, society and culture.* Vol. 1, *The rise of the network society.* Oxford: Blackwell.

— 1998. *The information age: Economy, society and culture.* Vol. 3, *End of millennium.* Oxford: Blackwell.

Chesterman, John, and Andy Lipman. 1988. *The electronic pirates: DIY crimes of the century.* London: Routledge.

Coombe, Rosemary J. 1998. *The cultural life of intellectual properties: Authorship, appropriation, and the law.* Durham, N.C.: Duke University Press.

Crary, Jonathan. 2000. *Suspensions of perception: Attention, spectacle, and modern culture.* Cambridge, MA: MIT Press.

Doane, Mary Ann. 2002. *The emergence of cinematic time: Modernity, contingency, the archive.* Cambridge, MA: Harvard University Press.

Ferguson, James. 1999. *Expectations of modernity: Myths and meanings of urban life on the Zambian copperbelt.* Berkeley: University of California Press.

Garcia, David, and Geert Lovink. 2001. 'The ABC of tactical media'. In *The public domain: Sarai reader 01,* edited by Sarai, the New Media Collective and Society for Old and New Media. Delhi: Sarai, the New Media Initiative.

Gaudio, Rudolf. 1996. 'Men who talk like women: Language, gender, and sexuality in Hausa Muslim society'. Ph.D. diss., Stanford University.

Graham, Stephen, and Simon Marvin. 1996. *Telecommunications and the city: Electronic spaces, urban places.* London: Routledge.

— 2001. *Splintering urbanism: Networked infrastructures, technological mobilities and the urban condition.* London: Routledge.

Hansen, Karen Tranberg. 2000. *Salaula: The world of secondhand clothing and Zambia.* Chicago: University of Chicago Press.

Hansen, Miriam. 1995. 'America, Paris, the Alps: Kracauer (and Benjamin) on cinema and modernity'. In *Cinema and the invention of modern life,* edited by Leo Charney and Vanessa R. Schwartz. Berkeley: University of California Press.

— 2000. 'The mass production of the senses: Classical cinema as vernacular modernism'. In *Reinventing film studies,* edited by Christine Gledhill and Linda Williams. London: Arnold.

Haynes, Jonathan, ed. 2000. *Nigerian video films.* Africa Series no. 73. Athens, OH: Ohio University Center for International Studies.

Hecht, David, and A. M. Simone. 1994. *Invisible governance: The art of African micro-politics.* Brooklyn, N.Y.: Autonomedia.

Hibou, Béatrice. 1999. 'The "social capital" of the state as an agent of deception, or The ruses of economic intelligence'. In *The criminalization of the state in Africa,* edited by Jean-François Bayart, Stephen Ellis, and Béatrice Hibou. Bloomington: Indiana University Press.

Johns, Adrian. 1998. *The nature of the book: Print and knowledge in the making.* Chicago: University of Chicago Press.

Kern, Stephen. 1983. *The culture of time and space: 1880–1918.* Cambridge, MA: Harvard University Press.

Kittler, Friedrich. 1999. *Gramophone, film, typewriter.* Stanford, CA: Stanford University Press.

Koolhaas, Rem, Stefano Boeri, Sanford Kwinter, Nadia Tazi, and Hans Ulrich Obrist. 2001. *Mutations.* Bordeaux, France: Arc en rêve centre d'architecture.

Kracauer, Siegfried. 1995. *The mass ornament: Weimar essays,* translated by Thomas Y. Levin. Cambridge, MA: Harvard University Press.

Larkin, Brian. 1997. 'Indian films and Nigerian lovers: Media and the creation of parallel modernities'. *Africa* 67, no. 3: 406–40.

— 1998–99. 'Introduction to Media technologies and the design for modern living: A symposium'. *Visual Anthropology Review* 14, no. 2: 11–13.

— 2000. 'Hausa dramas and the rise of video culture in Nigeria'. In *Nigerian video films,* edited by Jonathan Haynes. Africa Series no. 73. Athens, OH: Ohio University Center for International Studies.

— 2003. 'Itineraries of Indian cinema: African videos, Bollywood, and global media'. In *Multiculturalism, postcoloniality, and transnational media,* edited by Ella Shohat and Robert Stam. New Brunswick, NJ: Rutgers University Press.

Lefebvre, Henri. 1991. *The production of space.* Cambridge, MA: Blackwell.

Lombardi, Gerald S. 1999. 'Computer networks, social networks, and the future of Brazil'. Ph.D. diss., New York University.

MacGaffey, Janet, and Rémy Bazenguissa-Ganga. 2000. *Congo–Paris: Transnational traders on the margins of the law.* Bloomington: Indiana University Press; Oxford: James Currey.

Mattelart, Armand. 1996. *The invention of communication,* translated by Susan Emanuel. Minneapolis: University of Minnesota Press.

— 2000. *Networking the world, 1794–2000,* translated by Liz Carey-Libbrecht and James Cohen. Minneapolis: University of Minnesota Press.

Mbembe, Achille. 2001. *On the postcolony.* Berkeley: University of California Press.

Mbembe, Achille, and Janet Roitman. 1995. 'Figures of the subject in times of crisis'. *Public Culture* 7: 323–52.

Meyer, Birgit. 2003. 'Ghanaian popular cinema and the magic in and of film'. In *Magic and modernity: Interfaces of revelation and concealment*, edited by Peter Pels and Birgit Meyer. Stanford, CA.: Stanford University Press.

Mrázek, Rudolf. 2002. *Engineers of happy land: Technology and nationalism in a colony*. Princeton, N.J.: Princeton University Press.

Na Sale, Musa. 1995. Interview by author. Kano, July.

O'Brien, Susan. 1999. 'Pilgrimage, power, and identity: The role of the *hajj* in the lives of Nigerian Hausa *bori* adepts'. *Africa Today* 46, no. 3/4: 11–40.

Prakash, Gyan. 1999. *Another reason: Science and the imagination of modern India*. Princeton, N.J.: Princeton University Press.

Sassen, Saskia, ed. 2002. *Global networks, linked cities*. New York: Routledge.

Schivelbusch, Wolfgang. 1986. *The railway journey: The industrialization of time and space in the nineteenth century*. Berkeley: University of California Press.

Schneider, Friedrich. 2000. 'Dimensions of the shadow economy'. *Independent Review* 5, no 1.: 81–91.

Simone, AbdouMaliq. 1998. 'Urban social fields in Africa'. *Social Text* 16: 71–90.

— 2000. 'Going south: African immigrants in Johannesburg'. In *Senses of culture: South African culture studies*, edited by Sarah Nuttall and Cheryl-Ann Michael. Oxford: Oxford University Press.

— 2001. 'On the worlding of African cities'. *African Studies Review* 44, no. 2: 15–41.

Spitulnik, Debra. 1998–9. 'Mediated modernities: Encounters with the electronic in Zambia'. *Visual Anthropology Review* 14, no. 2: 63–83.

Sundaram, Ravi. 1999. 'Recycling modernity: Pirate electronic cultures in India'. *Third Text* 47: 59–65.

Tsivian, Yuri. 1994. *Early cinema in Russia and its cultural reception*. London: Routledge.

Ukadike, N. Frank. 2000. 'Images of the "reel" thing: African video-films and the emergence of a new cultural art'. *Social Identities* 6: 243–61.

Ukah, Asonzeh F.-K. 2003. 'Advertising God: Nigerian Christian video-films and the power of consumer culture'. *Journal of Religion in Africa* 33: 203–31.

Verrips, Jojada, and Birgit Meyer. 2001. 'Kwaku's car: The struggles and stories of a Ghanaian long-distance taxi driver'. In *Car cultures*, edited by Daniel Miller. Oxford: Berg.

Virilio, Paul. 1997. *Open sky*. London: Verso.

— 2000. *The information bomb*. London: Verso.

— 2003. *Unknown quantity*. London: Thames and Hudson.

Waterman, Christopher Alan. 1990. *Jùjú: A social history and ethnography of an African popular music*. Chicago: University of Chicago Press.

Wendl, Tobias. 2001. 'Visions of modernity in Ghana: Mami wata shrines, photo studios, and horror films'. *Visual Anthropology* 14: 269–92.

JOJADA VERRIPS & BIRGIT MEYER
Kwaku's Car
The Struggles & Stories
of a Ghanaian Long-Distance Taxi-Driver

Reference
In Daniel Miller (ed.) *Car Cultures*
Oxford: Berg, 2001, pp. 153–84

19.20.1996. Saturday. This morning we wanted to go to Accra, but on the road to the center I all of a sudden noticed that the temperature of the engine in our car (a Toyota Corolla Estate from 1985) was rising in such an alarming way, that we decided to immediately visit a workshop near our house in Teshie to let mechanics have a look at the problem. Well, they prepared us surprise after surprise. They spent hours trying to solve the mystery of the sudden rise in temperature – to no avail. Not only did the temperature remain disquietingly high, to our amazement and great annoyance our gasoline meter also started to indicate incredible things. The mechanics carelessly removed a particular part (the thermostat) and threw it away – for according to them we would not need it in Ghana anyway – replaced some old parts for new ones, and emptied and filled the radiator that many times that we seriously started worrying about their expertise and fearing for the 'life' of our car. When the friendly smiling gentlemen at last began to remove the radiator in order to clean it, because this surely would end all our technical problems, we told them to immediately stop their seemingly fruitless efforts, for we did not want to have our car completely ruined by them. They are real *bricoleurs*, who try to behave professionally without having the proper tools, but who evidently have no technical knowledge of cars. Pretenders. One just starts with something in the hope that it will work. If you trust these so-called specialists, in no time you will end up with a totally damaged car which hangs together with ironwire and adhesive tape! With each turn of their screwdriver not only its value decreases but also its usability on Ghana's roads, which are not 'car-worthy' anyway (diary fragment Jojada).

21.10.1996. Monday. Today we brought our Toyota to another workplace at Osu (Accra). When we came to collect our vehicle at five o'clock it was not yet ready, though we had been assured that this would be the case. I saw the car standing somewhere with the hood aloft. When I looked under it I got a shock. The radiator was replaced, the original fan removed and a kind of huge propeller attached to the engine block. When I angrily asked a mechanic what the hell had happened, he smiled and told me not to worry at all, because this strange propeller was a 'proper adjustment' to the climate in which our car now had to function. The original fans were too weak for the tropical circumstances, so everybody with a car like ours would sooner or later replace it by a strong one which would always be in operation, and do away with the thermostat, a useless and even dangerous part in these circumstances. We felt horrible and irritated, for once again the value of our car had gone down due to this so-called adjustment. The mechanic, however, tried to explain that we should be glad with it, for now our car was 'tropicalized' or 'baptized into the system', but we could not be glad at all. These people not only don't ask you anything, they also devaluate your property because they are *bricoleurs* and no real mechanics who respect an engine (diary fragment Jojada).

These two fragments from Jojada's diary show how shocked we were by the way in which Ghanaian car mechanics treated our more-than-ten-year-old second-hand car (for which we had just paid 7.6 million Cedis and which was praised by our Ghanaian friends and neighbours for its newness and beauty) when it had some minor technical problems.[1] These people really made us angry by their seemingly respectless and unprofessional approach towards the engine. However, as we eventually discovered, this approach was not an indication of their lack of technical knowledge, and our anger rather indicated our own ignorance and bias about cars, their upkeep and repair.

We visited Ghana, in the case of Birgit, to study Ghana's vibrant videofilm industry and, in the case of Jojada, to continue research on the artisanal fishery sector, and, like many anthropologists working in urban areas, had just bought a car in order to drive around. While initially we took the use of such a seemingly familiar thing as a car for granted in the same way as we did at home, our experience with mechanics made us understand that cars were an incredibly interesting, yet unduly neglected research topic. For that reason, Jojada gradually shifted his attention away from canoes and started a small odyssey through the realm of cars in Ghana. Though not focusing on cars directly, Birgit also realized the importance of car matters, both in films and for their audiences, and collected information about this. The motive behind these endeavours was to deal with our first, strongly negative impressions of car mechanics and electricians, and to give room to a gnawing feeling that these impressions were totally off the mark and appeared to reveal more about a Western fetishization of cars than about actual Ghanaian expertise with regard to vehicles. In order to understand the importance and meaning of cars in contemporary Ghana, we sought to find out how one obtains them, uses them and keeps them rolling on the often defective roads, how they are 'adjusted' or 'tropicalized,' how one repairs them with a minimum of tools and an often discouraging lack of spare parts, and what kind of perceptions of and stories about cars were circulating.

Our point of departure became a car which had appeared in the open space next to our house in Teshie just a few days before our car troubles started. This Peugeot 504, which looked like a heap of scrap-iron beyond repair, was nevertheless day in day out patched up by a young man and a few assistants. At the time we developed an interest in this vehicle, it was nothing more than a beautifully blue-sprayed body with the slogan *God Never Fails* on its back and a worn-out engine inside. To mention just a few glaring defects, it had no electrical wiring, the coverings of the doors and the seats seemed to have disappeared, the tyres were in a terrible condition and the exhaust pipe almost trailed on the ground. The man who invested so much time, energy and money turned out to be long-distance taxi-driver Kwaku A,[2] who together with his young wife and baby lived in two rented rooms nearby. Several months before, he had had a serious accident with his car and now he was trying to bring it back on the road again, for he desperately needed some income. Soon after we got in touch with Kwaku, we found out that the Peugeot 504 had been imported from the Netherlands in September 1991. To our surprise, we realized that it had crossed our path in Ghana before; we even had made a ride in it in the company of one of its former owners, a Dutch development worker whom we met during an earlier trip to Ghana. This Dutchman sold it somewhat later to a befriended South African doctor, who in his turn sold it to Kwaku, for the amount of $3000 in April 1994, on the condition that during one year he was to pay $250 per month to a certain Ghanaian woman.

This rather remarkable coincidence prompted us to write at least part of the 'biography' of Kwaku's car and to use it as an empirical entrance into the world of cars in Ghana. Soon after we met Kwaku, we therefore made an agreement with him: in exchange for all kinds of data, he would take Jojada on small trips and introduce him to relevant people and places to invest in the reconstruction of his beloved car, the 'God Never Fails',[3] so that he could start as a long-distance taxi-driver again. Kwaku initiated Jojada in the scarcely explored, thoroughly male domain of the car world in Ghana.

Given that all over the globe cars play a tremendously important role as means of transport and sources of power and prestige, it is surprising that they are so much neglected by anthropologists. When we started looking for anthropological work on cars and car-related matters, we realized that the few existing publications focus on very partial aspects. There is, for instance, some anthropological literature on drivers (with regard to America see Agar 1986; with regard to Africa see Field 1960; Jordan 1978; Peace 1988). These authors, how-ever, merely focus on social networks, contacts with passengers and other sociological topics, and pay virtually no attention to the car in its materiality. The same applies to anthropological studies of car slogans (e.g. Lawuyi 1988, Van der Geest 1989), which regard the mottos car owners choose to paint on their cars as a reflection to their world view. In his chapter on a ride in a Songhay bush taxi, Stoller, too, confines himself to a Geertzian symbolic analysis of 'the complex of Songhay bush taxi interaction' (1989: 69-84). We do not, of course, wish to deny the merits of approaching cars as vehicles of meaning (see also White 1993). But our point is that research should not be limited to symbolical approaches but should also address the more mundane and material aspects of cars in their use in everyday life.

It seems that, up until now, Kopytoff has pleaded in vain for more anthropological research on cars, conducted along the following lines:

> The biography of a car in Africa would reveal a wealth of cultural data: the way it was acquired, how and from whom the money was assembled to pay for it, the relationship of the seller to the buyer, the uses to which the car is regularly put, the identity of its most frequent passengers and of those who borrow it, the frequency of borrowing, the garages to which it is taken and the owner's relation to the mechanics, the movement of the car from hand to hand over the years, and in the end, when the car collapses, the final disposition of its remains. All of these details would reveal an entirely different biography from that of a middle-class American, or Navajo, or French peasant car (1986: 67).

It would lead too far to discuss the reasons for anthropologists' reluctance to write such 'auto'-biographies.[4] Certainly Otnes, in his reflection about the fact that social scientists pay so little attention to cars as objects,[5] hits an important point:

> A general reason ... is quite simply that much of sociological theory ... has a tacit but nevertheless a strong anti-materialist bias in which an artifact becomes a 'mere vehicle,' a mundane means of little substance or interest (1994: 50).

Next to this general anti-materialist bias, which has been opened up in anthropology only in the course of the last decade (e.g. Miller 1987, 1995), one may also notice a bias against modern technology. Resonating with a mistrust of technology propounded by Western intellectual tradition (expressed most explicitly by thinkers such as Max Weber and Martin Heidegger), in Africanist anthropology there still is a tendency of favouring the study of local, cultural traditions. While it may no longer be stated overtly that African drivers show a 'lack of "feeling" for machines', and that their allegedly defective attitude towards cars 'may be the result of a youth passed in a nonmechanic world' (Morgan and Pugh 1969: 608, quoted approvingly by Jordan 1978: 41), the view that Western technologies are foreign to and potentially disruptive of African culture is still lingering on.[6]

Paradoxically, in the practice of everyday life in Western societies, this anti-technological bias is accompanied by an uncritical attitude which just takes technology in general, and the car in particular, for granted. As the Dutch sociologist Van de Braak (1991: 50ff) has argued, there is a rift between production and use of cars. Consumers simply expect that a car keeps on rolling; only at the very moment when something is wrong does one realize how little one knows about car technology and quickly seeks help from a specialist, who, in turn, is expected to replace the necessary parts without changing the technological structure as such. This unquestioning stance, masked by blind confidence, can best be characterized as alienation (ibid.: 51).

In this chapter we seek to overcome the anti-material and anti-technological bias of our discipline, as well as the typically Western, taken-for-granted attitude towards cars which we appeared to reproduce in our reaction to the Ghanaian mechanics, and investigate cars in their mundane as well as symbolical, material-technological as well as spiritual dimensions. The foremost goal of this chapter, then, is to understand, by way of a detailed study of Kwaku's car, why and how cars in Ghana are culturally redefined or, as Ghanaians put it, 'baptized into the system,' 'tropicalized' or 'adjusted,' and to investigate how cars are kept in the system for periods Westerners usually deem technically impossible. On the basis of our necessarily tentative answers to these intriguing questions, we will briefly reflect on the car as a marker, and indeed, a vehicle of modernity. Before dealing with the vicissitudes of the Peugeot 504 it is necessary, however, to say something in general about Ghana's infrastructure, car trade, the Ministry of Transport and Communications, the insurance business, types of car use and (police) control.

Roads, customs and licences

Ghana is almost fully dependent on lorries and cars for the transport of goods and people, for it does not have an elaborate railway system.[7] Ghana's road network is most dense in the southern regions and least in the northern ones. Due to the bad condition of these roads, the reachability of particular places and areas often forms a serious problem. Highways exist only in, around and between big cities such as Accra and Tema. The rest consists of asphalted interregional two-lane roads, untarred country roads and bush tracks. The problem with many of these roads is that they are full of potholes, and therefore rather dangerous, especially in the dark, for outside the big cities lighting is almost always absent. Nowadays the government invests a lot in the maintenance and improvement of Ghana's road network, but it has not yet been able to bring the quality of the network to an acceptable level which matches its intensive use. For many Ghanaians, this is a constant point of criticism with regard to the state, which is regarded as unable to cater for the needs of drivers and travellers. As Ghanaian popular videomovies[8] indicate over and over again, good roads and beautiful cars are much cherished and figure as ultimate icons of modernity. There are endless scenes in which the camera takes the audiences on a mimetic ride through the beautiful highways and lanes of Accra – scenes which prompt audiences to loudly admire the beauty of the capital city, which eludes them in their everyday life, and which apparently can only be seen from the perspective of a smoothly-running limousine.

As Ghana does not have its own automobile industry, the country is fully dependent on the import of new and second-hand cars, trucks, lorries and busses from abroad. Until a few years ago, the import of used vehicles from European countries, for instance the Netherlands and Germany, was flourishing.[9] Lots of old vehicles, sometimes declared unroadworthy in these countries, were shipped to Tema where they could be collected by their owners (private persons, car dealers, or companies) after they had paid a certain amount of customs duties, including a so-called over-age tax. The latter kind of tax is considerable when a car is older than a particular number of years. One of the tricky things with the import of old cars is that the government tends, on the one hand, towards decreasing the age beyond which this tax has to be paid and, on the other, to increase this tax each year. The background of this policy is to muzzle the import of too many cars above a certain age.[10] For the Toyota Corolla we bought in 1996, the trader who imported it had to pay 50 per cent of

the C.I.F. Value, that is C 3.767.327.00, as over-age tax plus 10 per cent (or C 753.466.00) customs duty. Although a price of 7.6 million Cedis for a more than ten year old car that would cost no more than $500 in Europe may seem excessive, if we add to this the amount paid for it abroad, the costs of shipment and insurance, then it is understandable.

Against the background of such high prices for used vehicles, it is no wonder that people struggle to keep them on the road as long as possible. Many people get into serious debt with relatives and friends in order to get their certificate of payment of custom duties in Tema harbour, without which certificate registration by the Vehicle Examination and Licensing Division is simply impossible. These problems frequently occur in the case of cars shipped by expatriates to relatives in Ghana, or cars bought on trips abroad by Ghanaians without sufficient knowledge of the latest tax rules and regulations.

After an imported car has been released, more obstacles have to be overcome before one can finally drive it. Officially, a vehicle has to be technically examined by state officials, for without such an examination one will not get a licence number. Getting such a number may be a difficult affair, if one does not know the right official and/or one has not enough money to ease one's way through the bureaucratic channels. Therefore car owners often let others go through the time- and money-consuming procedures at the licensing offices. In and around these offices are found many 'agents' – who make a living by offering their services in getting the proper registration documents within reasonable time. As in the Cameroonian situation described by Mbembe and Roitman (1996), here too the official bureaucracy is seconded by its 'fake parallel', and only through particular 'ways of doing' can one access the necessary documents. The amount of money agents demand for their knowledge of the proper procedures and how to circumvent them, for instance by offering officials they know (or work with) small 'gifts', can be rather high, but worth the cost, especially if one is in a hurry. A government decree in 1996, that every car owner had to reregister his or her vehicle before a particular date, resulted in a bonanza not only for these agents but also a host of others, such as the insurance people, the producers of licence plates, the sellers of all kinds of car accessories, the owners of small repair-shops and vulcanizers, whom one can regularly find in the direct vicinity of a licensing office. The final step in obtaining the formal right to drive the car after the certificate of roadworthiness and a licence number are obtained is to insure one's vehicle. Even without the documents mentioned, the police may be lenient in exchange for 'presents'. So the 'adjustment' of the car as a mechanical process is accompanied by similar adjustments in the cultural norms of Ghanaian bureaucracy and commerce.

Public transport

When one wants to travel in Ghana, one travels by car. Though the state maintains particular bus lines between big cities with rather good material, this kind of public transport is of minor importance compared to the private sector. Ghanaians travel within and between cities with private taxis and *trotros* (derived from the threepence charge one once had to pay for a ride). Formerly these *trotros* or *Mammy lorries* were Bedfords, which were imported in great numbers from Britain as complete vehicles between 1948 and 1959 and thereafter C.K.D, that is 'Completely Knocked Down', to be assembled in Tema until 1966, when this type of lorry was banned (cf. Kyei and Schreckenbach 1975: 8). These characteristic vehicles, almost all with evocative slogans in the front and at the back, which for more than three decades

Fig. 1 Gye Nyame repairshop (courtesy Tobias Wendl)

Fig. 2 God First repairshop (© Jojada Verrips)

dominated the image of traffic flow on Ghana's roads, packed with passengers and all kinds of goods such as yams, fish, fowl and fruits have almost all disappeared now. Nowadays, the transport of persons and their goods is mainly by passenger cars and station wagons made into short- and long-distance taxis, as well as with all kinds of delivery vans, ingeniously transformed into small busses, and ordinary busses. The passenger cars are painted yellow at the front and back of each side and have a small black shield which indicates the name of the car owner, the maximum amount of passengers, etc. The long-distance

cabs (mostly Peugeot station wagons, but also small and big busses) normally also have such a shield, but they are not painted in a specific manner. Instead they almost always have painted slogans, such as *Sea never Dry, Don't Kiss the Horror* or *God Never Fails* (cf. Kyei and Schreckenbach 1975; Date-Bah 1980; Van der Geest 1989).[11]

In a big city like Accra the apparent chaos hides an order in which many drivers work in turns on particular trajectories between stations, use fixed charges and belong to unions with elaborate rules and regulations. The unions often run (rented or owned) stations[12] and supervise the admission of new taxi-drivers on the basis of such criteria as experience, knowledge of a trajectory, state of the vehicle and the possession of the proper documents. After having been accepted as a new member, one has to pay income and welfare tax as well as booking and union fees. Not all taxi-, *trotro-* and big bus-drivers own their vehicles. Many of them drive for relatives or other private persons, who often live abroad. It is exactly this practice which forms a frequent source of troubles. Common complaints by the owners, for instance, are that their drivers do not maintain the vehicles properly and, still worse, do not stick to the financial agreements made with them but instead keep too much money for themselves. Conversely, drivers complain about owners' greediness, their inclination to attribute any technical fault to the driver, and their general indifference towards the hardships involved in the job.[13] These potential conflicts notwithstanding, driving a taxi or *trotro* is considered a respectable business, which not only conveys prestige, but often earns more money than one can get through other jobs. Therefore becoming a driver, and possibly a car owner, is aspired to by many young men.[14] Our neighbour Kwaku was one of them, and he even managed to get his own car exceptionally fast. His case shows that the high hopes vested in vehicles do not always materialize and that driving an old Peugeot between Accra and Takoradi may be a heavy, almost unbearable burden.

Struggling with 'God Never Fails'

Kwaku was born in Teshie,[15] where his father (a Ga) worked as a carpenter. As he did not like to stay in the family house after his mother's (a Fanti) death, he ran away from home at the age of 13; first to Labadi (the neigbouring Ga village which has became absorbed by Accra) where he became a driver's mate, and later to Takoradi (Western Region) where he started living with his mother's sister's husband. After a few years he returned to Labadi where he became a mechanic's apprentice, for he loved cars and later wanted to have his own workshop, but the buying of tools turned out to be an unsurmountable obstacle.[16] He got his driving licence and earned some money by driving around his elder brother, a rather successful businessman. Then he obtained a job as a driver for a hotel owner in Accra. While working for this man in the early 1990s, he became acquainted with the South African doctor Henry H. and his Dutch friend Klaas W., the development worker. Through the doctor he obtained his first taxi, a Datsun, which he bought for C 457.000, a rather low price at the time (September 1992). Since he only possessed C 107.000, Kwaku had to borrow the rest from his friend, whom he very quickly paid back in monthly installments of C 25.000.[17] Very soon after he got it, Kwaku gave the car to a driver to exploit it for him in the morning; he himself used it during the night. Because of troubles in the hotel – the owner and his wife did not understand where Kwaku's money came from and accused him of theft – he left the place for the doctor's house and became his 'houseboy'. Though Kwaku invested much money in the maintenance of the old Datsun, he still earned a ot with its exploitation, at least enough 'for the house' and for his expensive marriage with Rose in March 1994.

He managed to organize a wedding many young people dream of (and which forms a recurring, characteristic feature of popular video movies): the bride was wearing a white gown, the ceremony took place in church, and there was a reception afterwards. Through this church wedding – in the Apostolic Church of Ghana to which Rose and her family belong – the marriage became officially registered. Many young women want to persuade their boy friends to make such an arrangement, which is also much favoured by Ghana's booming pentecostal charismatic churches (cf. Meyer 1998), because official registration makes it legally impossible for the husband to take a second wife. As Mr and Mrs, Kwaku and Rose commanded much respect from neighbours when they moved to their beautifully painted two-room apartment in Teshie: a modern, Christian couple with a comparatively fine income. While Kwaku was very proud of having been able to marry in such a way, he also felt that many people, especially in his own family, would envy them and seek to spiritually destroy their happiness.

And indeed, soon after the wedding, Kwaku got into trouble, when for unknown reasons the car burnt out. He managed, however, to sell the heavily damaged vehicle for a higher price than he bought it for. In April 1994 his employer and friend Henry sold the Peugeot 504 he had bought from the Dutch development worker to Kwaku. This time the price was considerably higher, that is $3000, to be paid in monthly installments of $250 into the bank account of the doctor's Ghanaian girlfriend, who was to remain the official car owner until the payment had been settled.

Kwaku started to invest in the car immediately after he got it. He transformed it into a comfortable long-distance taxi with which he began to transport passengers and goods between Accra and Takoradi. His home base became a station in Kaneshie owned by a local cooperative (the Kaneshie Co-operative Association) where he joined an independent local group of Peugeot drivers (not yet resorting under the Ghana Private Road Transport Union [GPRTU] of the Trade Union Congress [TUC] working on this lucrative trajectory. In order to be able to maintain his car well, he first bought the body of an old Peugeot 504 for C 200.000, and somewhat later also the engine for C 500.000. He left both in Takoradi to cannibalize them just in case the need might arise. This is a common practice among long-distance drivers who mostly work with rather old and worn-out material.

For ten months Kwaku drove without many problems and therefore earned a decent living and had a good time with his then pregnant wife.[18] But then an endless series of troubles with the car started, which eventually made Kwaku decide to become a good Christian again, for these problems almost ruined their life. It all started in February 1995 with three flat tires in a row, each at a place where there was water at both sides of the road – incidents which worried Kwaku a lot, for 'this could be no coincidence'. He visited a church elder, an old lady, who told him to fast for seven days. Yet he did not stick to her advice and on April 13, on his way back to Accra, he had the first serious accident with his Peugeot near Malarn junction not far from Takoradi. He needed almost three months to get the damaged car back on the road again. Though the insurance company paid him C 500.000, he still needed to borrow money from relatives. Fortunately the doctor, who had left Ghana for some time, appeared on the scene again. In August he hired Kwaku and his car to travel, and this reduced Kwaku's debt to 1.2 million Cedis.

But from then on the car became a real nuisance, a money-

Fig. 3 Inside of 'God Never Fails' (© Jojada Verrips)

devouring monster. Kwaku's diary in which he meticulously recorded any event related to his car – his autobiography, so to speak – contains entry after entry on disturbingly knocking bearings, malfunctioning cylinders, an out-of-order crankshaft, a leaking radiator, etc. Time and again he had to make embarrassing trips to uncles in order to borrow money from them, which they sometimes refused. He even considered meeting the church elder again to pray for him, so that his predicament might end. In spite of all these technical problems, Kwaku managed to pay off part of his debt. On April 13, exactly one year after his first accident, he had a serious second one.

I thought that I and my passengers would die. I really felt there is something behind, so that I cannot pay the money, so that she will get the car. So let us pray over things and stop joking. (...) I was reporting to her that the car was not working properly and asked her to give me some money. She said I had to go and come. I did that three times, but she did not give me the money I asked for.

Fig. 4 Kwaku and his yellow-sprayed 'God Never Fails' in 1999 (© Jojada Verrips)

> Then I decided to borrow the money elsewhere. I have not been at her place anymore. (...) The thing has become a sort of pressure on me. I want to get rid of Mary and transfer the car to my own name.

From then on Kwaku did not pay Mrs Mary P. for a long time. At the time we met him in September 1996, he still owed her C 600.000; and had stopped paying her since that April after he had had his second serious accident with the car. He believed that she was behind it – that is, that she had used some destructive 'spiritual' means – because she wanted to get the vehicle back. Since his car was seriously damaged and moreover showed more technical shortages with every day, he decided to stop making trips to Takoradi and back and to invest all the money he could borrow in slowly repairing his vehicle. He even used the capital (C 200.000) his wife had accumulated in order to start a trade. This, of course, put tremendous pressure on their relationship, especially since Rose had become pregnant again. They had frequent quarrels, and not much was left of the image of the modern, better-off couple they had given before. Rose often stayed with her own parents, and expected Kwaku to become a better husband – a project he himself assented to in discussion, but could not always live up to because of his allegedly quick temper.

Kwaku now became a regular visitor to repair-shops in Teshie and all over Accra. He cleverly used his elaborate network to recruit a whole series of specialists, from sprayers to electricians, who could help him in bringing his car back to life again. Sometimes, however, these people caused more problems than they solved. Once a welder worked so carelessly that the electric wiring of the Peugeot caught fire and was partly destroyed. This is no small wonder, for welders, who usually work without protecting their eyes, are not used to removing inflammable material in their direct environment. When something happens they simply use a small plastic bottle with water to extinguish a fire. In this case to no avail, with the result of a damage of C 60.000 of which the unlucky welder could only pay C20.000 immediately.

At the time we developed a serious interest in Kwaku's car, he and a befriended electrician were busy installing new wiring (see Fig. 3)

But they could not properly test it, for the Peugeot's battery urgently needed to be repaired or, still better, replaced. The problem was not to find a battery repair-shop, which abound in Accra, but the money needed to repair it. In these shops, one repairs, refills and recharges for a price dependent upon the number of plates in a battery.[19] It is here that our financial involvement in the revival of Kwaku's car began, for we decided to help him buy a new battery in exchange for information. But this proved hopeless, for the vehicle was in bad shape. To list only a few of the technical problems, the shock-absorbers were weak and needed to be refilled with oil, the radiator and the fuel pump were leaking, the bearings were knocking, the cylinders, pistons and crankshaft were worn out, the starter often did not work, the fanbelt was damaged, the gearbox looked dangerous, no meter on the dashboard was working and almost all of the fuses were fixed instead of replaced by new ones.[20] As Kwaku used to say: 'The body is nice now, but the inside is not good.'

In order to make the inside better, so that he could start his business again, he did what so many of his colleagues would do in similar circumstances. He fell back on using all kinds of locally invented 'adjustments' and, when these would no longer work, on buying secondhand or even new spare parts. Since original parts are often unavailable in Ghana or much too expensive, one frequently makes do with cheap imitations of an inferior quality produced in countries such as Nigeria and India. Since even these copies are rather expensive, the common practice, however, is to first pay a visit to one of Accra's many markets, for example at Kaneshie, where old engines are cannibalized and a wide variety of second-hand parts are offered. In these areas one can also find a host of small workshops where old parts, which are usually thrown away in Western countries, are most ingeniously 'revitalized' or utilized to repair engines. In the machine-shop God First Engineering Works, for instance, the walls of old cylinders are turned into 'new' ones to be placed in engine blocks with worn-out linings (see Figs 1 and 2). Here one is confronted with a tremendously rich sort of technical knowledge and practice, which came into existence due to a shortage of money and hence of means and parts. This is backed by an impressive degree of inventiveness.[21]

Kwaku is a master in using technical 'adjustments'.[22] For example, he replaced the two-chamber carburettor of his old Peugeot with a one-chamber one in order to save petrol. The air inlet was not original any longer, but consisted of a piece of pierced tin. A lot of gaskets and rubber parts, such as bushings, were 'indigenous', that is, cut out of old tubes and tyres. The art of recycling these materials is practised with a minimum of tools by a small army of highly skilled masters and their apprentices. All the fuses in the Peugeot were repaired with copper wire, because original ones could not be found or were too expensive. At several places nails were used as lock pins. Some rubber tubes were fixed with iron wire, whereas others which evidently were out of use were closed with old sparkplugs, butterfly nuts or even pieces of wood.

Next to these directly visible 'adjustments', there were a series of hidden ones. In order to prevent the knocking of some worn-out main bearings in the engine block, Kwaku had put pieces of greasy paper between them and the crank-shaft. Instead of using a special spring, his distribution chain was held in its proper place with a piece of copper pipe. He had raised the oil level in his shock-absorbers beyond normal so that he could drive more comfortably on roads full of potholes. He more than once asserted that in case of an emergency situation, he would not hesitate to temporarily use soap-suds instead of brake fluid. A more careful inspection of 'God Never Fails' would certainly have revealed more technical 'adjustments'. Similar ones and others, such as the huge propeller-like fan put in our car, could be observed in other vehicles.

It is important to realize that this widespread 'tropicalization' of motorcars in Ghana (as well as in many other African countries) not only rests on a thorough knowledge of how engines work, but also and especially on a rather unique type of knowledge of how one can keep old ones working in a situation of limited goods. People like Kwaku not only have to cope with a shortage or lack of spare parts, they often do not have the proper tools to repair their vehicles, and for that reason they often involve their bodies in ways that compensate for the lack of such tools. For Kwaku it was almost normal to suck petrol out of his tank in order to clean certain car parts or to use his tongue to feel if his battery was still charged. And since the gasoline, oil and temperature gadgets had stopped working long ago, on his trips between Accra and Takoradi he constantly tried to figure out by listening and smelling, whether his car was still going strong.

Only a few garages in Accra are equipped with sophisticated instruments to repair cars, for example those of big dealers, but they are too expensive for ordinary people like Kwaku. In contrast to the often poorly equipped workshops of many mechanics[23] – who like to advertise themselves as, for instance, 'gearbox doctors' – these garages look like sophisticated 'hospitals' for machines. It would be wrong, however, to presume that the workshop mechanics on the one hand, and the employees of these modern 'hospitals' on the other, represent respectively an inferior and a superior approach to the car. They share a thorough knowledge of how this pre-eminent specimen of modern technology works and can best be kept working under the given circumstances, but differ in the way they are able to treat it when it refuses to function properly. At this point mechanics and people like Kwaku show an incredible inventiveness based on a perception of the car, more especially the engine, as a thing or an object which technically can be dominated and domesticated. And they need this, for old cars constantly confront their users with new problems to be solved.

Kwaku, for instance, managed to get his car back on the road in the middle of November, but was faced with a serious breakdown of his engine less than a month later. On a trip from Accra to Takoradi his crankshaft became loose, as a consequence of which at least one connecting rod of a piston was totally spoiled and others seriously damaged. In the meantime he had earned a little bit of money, but not enough to easily overcome this new disaster. We left Ghana when he was struggling to find an additional sum of money to the one we 'borrowed' him. But he was successful, for in 1999 he was still on the road between Accra and Takoradi with 'God Never Fails', this time sprayed yellow, and had managed to pay off his debt to Mary and finally become the official owner (see Fig. 4).

Though it seems as if mechanics and people like Kwaku 'will fix everything and bring it back to life again', this does not mean that their perception of cars, especially engines, and how they (dys)-function is merely technical. Here one enters the fascinating area of the beliefs, images and lore with regard to these material objects. Just like the canoes used in the artisanal fisheries, they very often are seen and treated as a kind of beings with a will of their own, who can get hurt and die and therefore have to be carefully protected against all kinds of evil influences. To make things more complex, most drivers, as is also the case in Western societies, tend towards a strong identification with their vehicles, that is, with already semi-anthropomorphized material objects (cf. Verrips 1994).[24] At times they feel so much one with their car, that what happens to these 'beings' also happens to them. And though drivers know that many cars are old and therefore

Fig. 5 The blessing of Kwaku's car in 1996 (© Jojada Verrips)

run more risks of collapsing than new ones, that accidents occur as a consequence of bad road conditions, overloading, speeding and the use of alcohol,[25] they nevertheless want to have an answer to such pressing, classical questions as why a car collapses or gets involved in an accident at a particular time and place, so that income is lost.

We will start by describing some of the practices or rituals to protect cars from collapsing and getting involved in accidents and then present some of Kwaku's stories about why such things happen. Apart from painting slogans of the type *God Never Fails* on their cars, drivers often also use stickers saying, for instance, *I am covered by the blood of Jesus* or *I will make it in Jesus name*. Next to this kind of protective formulas on and in their cars, Christian drivers often ask their pastor and church elders to pray over their vehicles, so that they will be protected against the influence of evil forces or Satan. Muslim drivers also visit their malams to pray over their cars, so that they will be protected against evil. Some of them even go so far as to park the car in front of a malam's house so that it will not be stolen.[26]

Kwaku himself went through a protective Christian ritual just before he started making long distance trips between Accra and Takoradi again: '… we prayed that whatever ties there were on the car with evil, God should burn them. Seeking for the blood of Jesus Christ.' When he was about to take his car back on the road in November 1996, he invited us to accompany him to the *Apostolic Church* one Sunday. In order to mark his good intentions and high hopes for the future, he attended church together with Rose after quite a long period of absence. After the service the pastor and a number of church elders blessed the car through prayers (see Fig. 5). When we told him in the course of our discussion about this ritual that we did not attend church at home, Kwaku said that he could appreciate that, as he himself had not been a churchgoer in the past. 'But, he said, 'you don't have juju [black magic]. But we here, we have it here, and we have to protect ourselves against it and the only way to do it is through the Holy Spirit.' Clearly, Christianity is regarded as generating power and protecting people against evil forces.

Kwaku, however, did not assume that such rituals would protect him against all kinds of troubles, for he explained:

It is protected, but not that nothing will happen to it. Against evil forces and unwanted accidents, but not against technical failure. The car is old. Technical failures are caused by lack of mainte- nance. It is essential that you grease it. It is like our own bodies, you have to put grease in the joints. If the pastor prayed over it, there still should be oil, water, all what is necessary. Like a body you have to feed it.

This statement notwithstanding, he often talked about evil forces spoiling totally worn-out parts of his car. For him, in everyday life technical and supernaturally caused failures were entangled, so much so that a clear-cut boundary between the two domains could not be drawn. In any case, he started each journey with a silent prayer because he believed that regular praying and listening to what God said to him while under way were important ways to avoid all sorts of trouble. He was also convinced that living according to Christian rules might yield luck on the road and a decent income.

Kwaku told us many stories about the use of *juju* to protect cars and drivers. According to him, there were many non-Christian – but also 'nominally' Christian – (taxi)drivers who had hidden special things, such as particular beads or pieces of (bloodstained) cloth, under the hood or the pedals, in the steering wheel or even the engine in order to drive safely and earn a lot of money with their trade. He especially feared (truck) drivers from Nzima in the Western region, for some of them were supposed to have very strong magical powers

… which make that, if the car is gonna crash you might not find them anymore, the drivers. They might be somewhere else. (…) It is just like an air bag. As soon as you get the impact, the airbag will explode to the one steering. That's how it is, as soon as the accident comes, he vanishes.

But according to Kwaku 'most of the drivers have got a kind of protection which they might not tell. Not for vanishing or disappear- ing, but sometimes it protects them from evil forces.' In spite of all these protective measures, drivers every now and then are confronted with these forces and their destructive influence. They might manifest themselves, for example, in suddenly broken engines, mysterious flat tyres, and more or less serious accidents. In Kwaku's view, and much in line with the stance of the pentecostal-charismatic churches, all these evil forces come from the realm of the Devil, who was sacked from heaven by God and dragged along all demons (cf. Meyer 1999b), and

are called upon by envious or greedy persons to afflict cars and their owners. There are many stories circulating around spiritual pacts made between local priests and their clients, which involve killing others spiritually through car accidents, or even offering a whole car as a blood sacrifice in exchange for personal gain (cf. Meyer 1995). Other stories are about strange beings roaming about in the night, and seek- ing to distract drivers' attention so that their car will perish. Kwaku told us that he had often seen such beings along the roadside, but that as a result of his faith in God he had always managed to get through.

Due to the presence of witches among the passengers, a car may become 'strong' 'stiff' or even stop all of a sudden at a certain place, so drivers believe.[27] Kwaku experienced this several times; once, for instance, when he had Hausa people from Ivory Coast in his car who carried cola and a strange bag with them:

I was coming from Takoradi and as soon as I got to the big bridge, the car couldn't go anymore. I turned back, then I drove fine. I returned back again, it couldn't go again. So I drove to the station and dropped them to the next car. (…) I didn't understand it. In certain traditions cola means something. Maybe they are having something of a dead person, the hair or the nails. If your car is not that type of car, it can't go.

There are also many stories about the ghosts of persons who either died in a car or were transported in it to be buried, which prevent automobiles from functioning properly. Kwaku told us, for instance, how the ghost of his deceased stepmother stopped the very small car in which he and some of his relatives were travelling to her burial.

We saw oil coming out, smoke, so we stopped. The driver was complaining 'why?', nothing was wrong with the car. The woman wanted us to be comfortable and knew the car that they brought was very big, a lot of space. So the body was put into that car, then we had more space. It was two hours to the village where we were going, in the Volta Region.

In order to prevent this kind of trouble, one often pours libation at mortuaries when collecting a corpse and ritually purifies cars in which people died by accident.[28]

But it is not only envious outsiders who may cause technical breakdowns and accidents. Kwaku, for instance, was afraid that jealous uncles might poison him and spoil his car because of his relative success as a long distance taxi-driver. He also suspected one of his father's wives of seeking to spiritually spoil his business, because she was jealous that he – 'just a small boy' – could own a car. In dreams and visions, he every now and then 'saw' how envious 'witches' used his car spiritually, and the next day he felt that the car was tired and run- down. It was, however, very difficult to recognize them, for in his visions – about which his pastor and a prophet said that they were justified – they were using different people's faces. Nevertheless he was pretty sure that there were close relatives who wanted to destroy him and his car. His experiences with witchcraft – here, too, the 'dark side of kinship' (Geschiere 1994) in the sense that he saw himself as a target of his relatives' envy – formed one of the reasons why he would not like to live in the family house and felt in constant need of protection.

Conclusion

By now it may be clear that our initial anger and amazement about the treatment of our Toyota, which we found increasingly embarrassing as our research proceeded, reflects a particular Western way of dealing with cars. At least in our experience at home, car repair is a specialized yet centralized affair. Like many car owners, we take the technological dimension of cars for granted and simply trust that, regular maintenance at the garage provided, everything works. In case something might go wrong, we would never dare to touch the engine of our VW ourselves and rather leave it to the care of expensive specialists, who do not admit snoopers at the workplace. And, afraid to get stranded somewhere along the road, we are prepared to follow the mechanics' advice to replace all sorts of parts even before they break down, or alternatively to buy a newer car when maintenance of the old one becomes too expensive. All this pinpoints a rather ignorant and, in a sense, alienated attitude towards car technology.[29]

How different are things in Ghana where there are great numbers of different specialists for various aspects of cars, where parts will only be replaced after they broke down, and where even lay people have an admirable working knowledge of motors and can easily engage in technical debates with the mechanics. The distance between the realms of repair and use, so characteristic of Western societies, is blurred. On the whole, it appears that the engine commands much less awe. People easily and pragmatically take it apart, and even rig up self-made spare parts from improper materials in order to make it work again. This self-assured pragmatism is diametrically opposed to Western images of the impact of technology in Africa and urges us to pay more attention to how machines – not only cars, but also phones, computers, cameras and so on – are used, maintained and repaired in everyday life.[29]

If the car, as many authors suggest (e.g. Mbembe and Roitman 1996: 160), is one of the main markers of modernity, then Kwaku's struggles with *God Never Fails* can certainly reveal important features of African ways of dealing with modernity. The key term, of course, is 'adjustment' – a process not imposed from above as in the case of the IMF's Structural Adjustment Programmes, but emerging in the practice of everyday life. 'Adjustment', as we experienced ourselves, becomes necessary as soon as a car enters Ghana and becomes 'part of the system'. This involves ingenious technological changes as well as more or less elaborate spiritual measures. The background of these endeavours, of course, is poverty and scarcity, and it would be naive to merely celebrate them as expressions of cultural creativity. At the same time, at least with regard to the situation described here, there is no reason to subscribe to a pessimistic notion of all-pervasive crisis which speaks through Mbembe and Roitman's account of the Cameroonian situation in general, and their representation of the (middle-class) car as a 'broken down machine' which has been reduced to 'a figurative object' (ibid.: 161) in particular. Kwaku's story reveals a tremendously powerful will and capacity – at least on the part of ordinary people – to keep the engine working by all means, even at a time when the West tends to forget Africa as much as its old, cast-off cars.

Notes

We dedicate this chapter to our friend and colleague, the medical sociologist Dr Kodjo Senah, who taught us as much about cars as about Ghanaian society, and with whom we had so many wonderful rides in his Lion (an old Peugeot 505). The research on which this essay is based has been made possible partly through the generous financial support of the Netherlands Foundation for the Advancement of Tropical Research (WOTRO). We would like to thank Marleen de Witte for transcribing our interviews with Kwaku and Daniel Miller for valuable editorial comments and suggestions.

1 In September 1996, 1000 Cedis were the equivalent of Hf 1,00, and about US $0.50. Due to inflation, the Cedi has been losing value to such an extent that in September 1999, C 3400 were exchanged for $1.00. When we expressed the wish to buy a car, our Ghanaian friends strongly advised us not to get a car which had been 'in the system' for some time already, but rather a secondhand one directly imported from Europe. Despite their sometimes considerable age, such cars are regarded as 'new'.

2 We use pseudonyms for all persons featuring in this chapter.

3 According to Kwaku he painted the slogan *God Never Fails* on the Peugeot, because God had listened to his fervent prayers to influence the previous owner in such a way that he would give or sell his car, which he had stored away for some time, to him.

4 Though Van der Geest even quotes Kopytoff's valuable call in a footnote, he does not take up the gauntlet, for he also deals with cars in a rather superficial way and does not show how they undergo what he tersely calls a 'cultural redefinition' (Van der Geest 1989: 35).

5 Sociologists, too, only paid scanty attention to cars. For notable exceptions see Lupton (1999), Otnes (1994), Van de Braak (1991).

6 Cf. Van Binsbergen (1999), who develops this argument with regard to ICT, and pleads for more research on Africans' use and perception of computers.

7 The only railway which can be said to play a role of some significance is the one between Accra and Kumasi. But in comparison with transport by lorry and car, railway traffic does not mean very much. Though Ghana does use navigable rivers and lakes, especially Lake Volta, waterways are not optimally used for the transport of goods and persons, on the contrary. As a citizen of a country in which transport over water is tremendously important, and as an anthropologist who once did fieldwork among Dutch bargees (Verrips 1990a and b), Jojada often wondered why inland navigation is so underdeveloped in Ghana.

8 The Ghanaian video-film industry emerged in the mid-1980s. Instigated by the fact that the state-owned film industry had not been able to produce feature films for years, local, untrained producers took up ordinary video-cameras and made their own films. These movies, which are closer to the soap-genre than to artistic 'African film', visualize stories and experiences from everyday life. They became tremendously popular and are screened in all the major cinemas. Cf. Meyer 1999a.

9 Cars liked very much in Ghana as well as in other African countries are Peugeots. Nowadays they do not reach Ghana over land any longer. Due to the political situation in countries such as Algeria it is too dangerous to drive used cars through the Sahara with the goal of selling them in West African countries for a much higher price than the one paid in Europe.

10 This discouraging policy of the government seems to be successful, for the number of really worn-out and dangerous cars and lorries in Accra's streets in the early 1990s was considerably higher than in the mid-1990s.

11 We also collected in and around Accra a great number of (English, Ga, Twi and Ewe) slogans on cars used for public transport. Hand-painted ones are increasingly being replaced by slogans made of adhesive letters and stickers. Many refer to a Christian background of the driver and/or owner. Islamic ones, such as *Insha Allahu* and *Allahu Wakidu*, are rather rare.

12 At the long-distance stations one often finds a ticketseller, porters, and an overseer or stationmaster who regulates which car will get the next ride and makes sure that the drivers stick to the rules and fares. This system of turns is rather complex and may cause serious conflict between the drivers of 'home' and 'away' cars. Another source of conflict, this time with the passengers, is the extraordinarily high fares drivers sometimes ask on busy Friday evenings for a ride from Accra to other places. The newspapers every now and then publish complaints about this type of 'Friday evening travel roguery'.

13 In 1996, drivers using an ordinary cab had to pay the owner C 15.000 on each day of the month. In 2000, the amount is C 30.000 (the increase reflects both inflation and higher prices for gasoline). Each month, drivers receive back two days' pay, and are allowed to keep the extra money made. If the owner lives abroad, the money often has to be paid to a relative, who puts the money in a particular bank account. Car repairs made necessary through old age or accidents form a constant source of dispute between drivers, owners, and their representatives. The popular soap-like TV series *Taxidriver* (produced by *Village Communications*, and broadcast by GBC in 1999) depicts this type of conflict. In a comic vein, the series figures the daily experiences of TT, a Ga taxidriver, with his, sometimes rather weird,

customers, the arrogant Asante car owner, car mechanics, policemen, and Christian prophets.

14 In this respect little has changed since Field's observation, made forty years ago, that '[a]mong young men, particularly illiterates, there is no more widespread ambition, nor one more often achieved, than to drive, and if possible own, one of the thousands of passenger car lorries that raven about the roads' (1960: 134).

15 Teshie was originally a Ga fishing village in the immediate neighbourhood of Accra. In the course of the twentieth century, Teshie grew in size and accommodated an ever-increasing number of persons from other Ghanaian peoples (above all Asante, Ewe, and Muslims from the North) working in Accra. While the old village centre near the coast is still inhabited by Ga fishermen and their families, the newer parts are multi-ethnic. The area where we stayed, and where Kwaku also lives, consisted of a mixture of (rundown) middle-class homes, and compound houses, in which separate rooms were rented to different tenants.

16 With cars as in many professions, the apprentice system is still in operation in Ghana. When a boy wants to become car mechanic, electrician, welder, sprayer, vulcanizer or rubber spare part cutter, to name just a few specializations, he has to become an apprentice in the workshop of a master. In exchange for money and *Akpeteshie* (locally distilled gin) he will usually be trained for four years. Only after having been an apprentice, chief apprentice and assistant, can a young man become master himself. All this time he merely gets 'chop money' and has to serve his master. Officially it is strictly forbidden to offer one's services for money to others without the master's consent, but in practice this happens frequently.

17 This is no small wonder, for the contract contained a clause in which it was stipulated that the car would be the property of the doctor again, if Kwaku would only once forget an installment.

18 A trip with seven passengers from Accra to Takoradi or vv. brought Kwaku plus/minus C 15.000 net. Together they paid him C 38.500 (C 5.550 each), but he had to deduct from this C 18.000 for petrol, C 1.500 booking fee, C 1.000 welfare fee and C 1.000 union tax. Because gas was cheaper than petrol, Kwaku preferred to use this type of fuel, but often he could not because of problems with the gas installation in his car.

19 The more plates the higher the price. In 1996 the price of repairing, for example, a 12-volt battery with 19 plates was C 17.500 and refilling plus recharging C 11.500. As in almost all small workshops in Ghana, in battery repairshops environmental pollution is the order of the day: acids are just poured on the ground,

20 In this connection it is interesting to take note of the results of an official German test of vehicles in Kenya (cf. *Süddeutsche Zeitung Magazin* 11.12.98), which showed they all suffered from at least fifty technical shortages. According to the official Kenyan documents, however, some of them were technically OK. We realize that, of course, an examination of cars according to Western standards may be problematic because it fails to acknowledge local technical ingenuity. Certainly there are a great number of 'adjustments' which have no negative impact on safety, although they may still be unacceptable for Western technicians. At the same time, it has to be acknowledged that the line between 'adjustments' and lack of maintenance as a result of poverty may be thin at times. In our view, there are no grounds for an exaggerated cultural relativism, because lives are at stake.

21 Strikingly the introduction of the car did not entail the development of an indigenous Ga, Twi, or Ewe terminology for its parts and their working. Almost all the terms used by drivers and mechanics are English ones.

22 Cf. Stoller who remarks in a chapter on a Songhay (Niger) bush taxi: 'Each taxi, of course has a driver, someone who has obtained his driver's permit and who knows very well how to repair automobile engines' (1989: 73). It is striking, however, that although his anthropology emphasizes the relevance of the senses, he does not say anything about the ways in which such a vehicle is perceived and treated by drivers. Kwaku constantly referred to how he used his senses (especially his ears and nose) to find out how his car was functioning. Striking in this connection were his expressions: 'I felt a smell' or 'I heard a scent'.

23 See Van Dijk (1980: 228 ff) who made similar observations about repairshops in Ouagadougou.

24 We found that, in a sense, this field was much easier to grasp than the technological dimension. This does not only stem from the fact that here we touch on common grounds for anthropologists, but also from our own everyday experiences with the representation of and meaning attached to cars in Western societies. Certainly many car advertisements in our own society speak to potential buyers' desire to identify, or better still, be identified with his or her car.

25 In general the number of accidents on Ghana's roads tends to disquietingly increase just before and after Christmas, when many people travel in often overloaded vehicles. It is also in this period that one hears more about molesting and even lynching of drivers who caused serious accidents.

26 We did not hear of rituals performed by groups of drivers in order to protect them while being on the road. In Nigeria, however, cabdrivers are used to collectively bring blood sacrifices to Ogun, the god of steel whom they consider to be their patron.

27 Passengers and other drivers were not the only possible agents of witch-craft: His wife also feared that beautiful Fanti women on one of his trips to Takoradi would bewitch him so that he would not return to her.

28 Kwaku told us that it was not unusual to purify polluted cars with seawater at the beach because it was supposed to be very powerful. He, however, would not go there, for the seaside was also associated with the Devil and Mami Water (cf. Meyer 1999c).

29 Who hasn't heard the familiar stories about the tractors brought to Africa as a means to further development, which just break down and stop functioning because of a lack of spare parts and knowhow? It would be worth examining whether the dysfunctioning may be due to other than technological factors.

References

Agar, M.H. (1986), *Independents Declared. The Dilemmas of Independent Trucking*. Washington, DC: Smithsonian Institution Press.

Dat-Bah, E. (1980), 'The Inscriptions on the Vehicles of Ghanaian Commercial Drivers: A Sociological Analysis'. *Journal of Modern African Studies* 18 (3): 525–31.

Field, M.J. (1960), *Search for Security. An EthnoPsychiatric Study of Rural Ghana*. London: Faber & Faber.

Geschiere, P. with C. Fisiy (1994), 'Domesticating Personal Violence: Witch-craft, Courts and Confessions in Cameroon'. *Africa* 64 (3): 321–41.

Jordan, J.W. (1978), 'Role Segregation for Fun and Profit. The Daily Behaviour of the West African Lorry Driver'. *Africa* 48 (l): 30–46.

Kopytoff, I. (1986), 'The Cultural Biography of Things: Commoditization as Process'. In: A. Appadurai (ed.), *The Social Life of Things. Commodities in Cultural Perspective*. Cambridge: Cambridge University Press, pp. 64–91.

Kyei, K. G and Schreckenbach, H. (1975), *No Time To Die*. Accra: Catholic Press.

Lawuyi, O.B. (1988), 'The World of the Yoruba Taxi Driver. An Interpre-tative Approach to Vehicle Slogans'. *Africa* 58 (l): 112.

Lupton, D. (1999), 'Monsters in Metal Cocoons: "Road Rage" and Cyborg Bodies'. *Body & Society* 5(l): 57–73.

Mbembe, A. and Roitman, J. (1996), 'Figures of the Subject in Times of Crisis'. In P. Yaeger (ed.), *The Geography of Identity*. Ann Arbor: University of Michigan Press, pp.153–86.

Meyer, B. (1995) '"Delivered from the Powers of Darkness." Confessions about Satanic Riches in Christian Ghana'. *Africa* 65: 236–55.

— (1998), '"Make a complete break with the past." Memory and Postcolonial Modernity in Ghanaian Pentecostalist Discourse'. *Journal of Religion in Africa* XXVII (3): 316–49.

— (1999a), 'Popular Ghanaian Cinema and "African Heritage"'. *Africa Today* 46(2): 931–14.

— (1999b), *Translating the Devil. Religion and Modernity Among the Ewe in Ghana*. IAL Series. Edinburgh: Edinburgh University Press.

— (1999c), 'Commodities and the Power of Prayer. Pentecostalist Attitudes Towards Consumption in Contemporary Ghana'. In: B. Meyer and P. Geschiere (eds), *Globalization and Identity. Dialectics of Flow and Closure*. Oxford: Blackwell, pp. 151–76.

Miller, D. (1987), *Material Culture and Mass Consumption*. Oxford: Basil Blackwell.

— (ed.) (1995), *Worlds Apart. Modernity through the Prism of the Local*. London and New York: Routledge.

Morgan, W.B. and J.C. Pugh (1969), *West Africa*. London: Methuen.

Otnes, P. (1994), *Can we Support Ourselves by Driving to Each Other? Collective and Private Transportation: How the Automobile has Affected Us, What Collective Transportation Does Differently, and Why. A Chreseological Suite in Eight Movements*. Oslo: Institute of Sociology.

Peace, A. (1988), 'The Politics of Transporting'. *Africa* 58 (l): 14–28.

Stoller, P. (1989), *The Taste of Ethnographic Things. The Senses in Anthropology*. Philadelphia: University of Pennsylvania Press.

Van Binsbergen, W. (1999), 'ICT and Intercultural Philosophy. An African Exploration'. Paper Presented to the Seminar 'Globalization and the Construction of Communal Identities', Leiden, February 2000.

Van de Braak, H. (1991), *Een wild dier. De auto als lustobject*. Amsterdam: Uitgeverij Balans.

Van der Geest, S. (1989), 'Sunny boy": chauffeurs, auto's en Highlife in Ghana'. *Amsterdams Sociologisch Tijdschrift* 16 (l): 20–39.

Van Dijk, M.P. (1980), 'De informele sector van Ouagadougou en Dakar. Ontwikkelingsmogelijkheden van kleine bedrijven in twee Westafrikaanse hoofdsteden'. (Ph.D. Thesis. Amsterdam: Free University).

Verrips, J. (1990a), 'On the Nomenclature of Dutch Inland River Craft'. *MAST* 3(l): 106–19.

— (1990b), *Als het til verloopt … Over binnenschippers en hun bonden 1898–1975*. Amsterdam: Het Spinhuis.

— (1994),'The Thing Didn't "Do" What I Wanted'. In J. Verrips (ed.), *Transactions. Essays in Honor of Jeremy Boissevain*. Amsterdam: Het Spinhuis, pp. 35–53.

White, L. (1993), 'Cars out of Place: Vampires, Technology, and Labour in East and Central Africa'. *Representations* 43 (Summer): 2–50.

Section 2.D
Modernity's Enchantment

ISAK A. NIEHAUS
Witch-hunting & Political Legitimacy
Continuity & Change in Green Valley, Lebowa 1930–91

Reference
Africa, 63, 4 (1993): 498–529

Over the past two decades the press has reported on hundreds of Lebowa residents being tried by South African courts for executing witches. A survey of these reports points to the involvement of prominent political personages in several cases of witch-hunting. During December 1983 chieftainess Ramaredi Chuene, sister of the late Dr Phatudi (Lebowa's former Chief Minister), and 227 members of her chiefdom, near Lebowakgorno, were charged with stoning a Mrs Nkuna to death. Previously eighteen *dingaka* (diviner-herbalists) had accused Mrs Nkuna of sending lightning that struck a hut (*Rand Daily Mail*, 24 April 1984). Between April and May 1986 forty-three 'necklaced' 'bodies were uncovered in shallow graves, dongas and bushes in three Sekhukhuneland villages. This discovery occurred in the wake of what has been described as a 'civil war' between the Sekhukhuneland Youth Organisation and security forces. The dead were allegedly victims of a campaign to eliminate 'collaborators' and witches. One man described how he had seen his wife burnt to death while youths sang 'freedom songs' (*Sunday Times*, 20 April 1986).[1] In June 1987 two Lebowa Legislative Assembly members were acquitted on charges of 'terrorism' after they had called for the elimination of tribal rule and the removal of witches. These charges related to events around Bushbuckridge, where thirty-six suspected witches were killed (SAIRR, 1988: 907).

This article investigates the nature of the involvement of Lebowa's chiefs, Comrades[2] and Legislative Assembly members in witch-hunting. At the level of anthropological theory, I suggest that the witchcraft complex should be viewed primarily as an attempt by ordinary villagers to deal with undeserved misfortune. In this context, I argue, diverse actors found it politically convenient to involve themselves in attempts to identify and punish witches in their quest to attain legitimacy. The ethnographic material presented derives from the Lebowa village of Green Valley. Fieldwork was conducted over a period of twenty-four weeks during 1990 and 1991. Information does not pertain to the period of fieldwork alone. Through life histories, the retrospective memories of informants and oral traditions I aim to reconstruct changes in witchcraft accusation and witch-hunting in Green Valley, through time, since the 1930s. My approach is thus primarily diachronic.

Witchcraft, politics and anthropological theory

The political significance of witchcraft has been a prominent focus of much anthropological literature. Witchcraft accusations have been seen as exceptionally useful instruments in local and national power struggles. Harris (1974) argued that witches provide a scapegoat for frustrations which originate elsewhere. He saw the European witch craze of the sixteenth and seventeenth centuries as an attempt by the nobility and clergy to mystify exploitation by convincing the poor that their troubles lay with imaginary witches, 'The principal result of the witchhunt system', he wrote, 'was that the poor came to believe they were victimized by devils instead of princes and popes' (1974: 247). He contended that this 'drew the poor further and further away from confronting the ecclesiastical and secular establishment with demands for the redistribution of wealth and levelling of rank' (1974: 239).

Other analysts have viewed witch-hunting as an attempt to intimidate political opponents. Mitchell (1956) and Marwick (1965) saw accusations as marking competition for headmanship. Steadman (1985) proposed that the aim of New Guinea witchhunters is to generate fear. The public punishment of witches, he argued, communicates the accusers' willingness to use violence to protect their interests and to dispose of future offenders who threaten those interests. Among the Hewa of Papua New Guinea, Steadman observed, witch-hunters killed members of nearby flooring and roofing groups against whom they bore grievances. The punishment of witches thus presents a test of power between corporate groups. In future competition for resources, there was a readiness among those intimidated to submit to the interests of the intimidators, It is not influential men in these groups, who pose the primary threat, who are killed as witches, but rather weak, vulnerable individuals who reside with them. Killing strong men, or those likely to be defended by them, is extremely dangerous. Steadman insisted that people are killed as witches, rather than as political opponents, because supernatural accusations are not verifiable or disprovable and are therefore appropriate 'where the reality of the crime is irrelevant'. He reported that Hewa witchhunters are *always* uncertain of evidence to justify their accusation. The 'witchcraft idiom' also provides an excusable motivation for reestablishing relations where there is a possibility of future cooperation.

Rowlands and Warnier (1988) and Geschiere (1988) have viewed sorcery as lying at the heart of political processes in Cameroon. In a one-party system, where village communities lack the capacity to express political dissent, sorcery constitutes a 'popular mode of political action'. Its manipulation is a reaction against the offensive behaviour of elites and constitutes an integral local strategy of equalising wealth. In Cameroon, power, wealth and success are viewed ambiguously as the result of occult powers. Should villagers experience misfortune or die, the powerful or wealthy may be accused of sorcery. Yet villagers are reluctant to accuse benevolent members of the elite. This set of beliefs thus places rich people under constant pressure to redistribute resources. Members of the urban political elite with connections with a village of origin 'face redistributing a sizeable part of his/her wealth to the direct benefit of the village or being threatened by sorcery'. They are 'expected to put their position in the state apparatus or party to good use, to provide their villages with roads, a school, a dispensary, etc. and their kin with salaried jobs' (Rowlands and Warnier 1988: 130).

Such attempts to unravel the complex relationship between witchcraft and political processes have seldom been theoretically satisfactory. This is evident in the inability of Harris (1974) and Steadman (1985) to account for the acceptance of witchcraft accusations by non-accusers. Harris fails to show how the poor came to accept a. belief which apparently went so strongly against their interests. Steadman's account is also marked by inconsistent logic. He questions explanations of witch-killing which assume that the killers believe in witches, even although the accuracy of such assumptions can not be verified' (1985: 112). Yet, he insists, the 'idiom of witchcraft' is powerful enough to mobilise wide support for the killing of 'innocent' individuals who may be distant relatives of some killers and their supporters (p. 116).[3]

Analysts seem over-zealous in viewing witchcraft accusations as a direct form of political action. Models exaggerate what Cohen (1979) calls the 'instrumental' dimension of witchcraft as a symbolic formulation and do emphasize its 'intrinsic-existential' dimensions. Hammond-Took (1981: 83) warns that witch beliefs do not merely express social relations, but are a set of beliefs and practices in their own right which structure chaotic experiences so that the world can be made meaningful. In this context witchcraft presents a personalized conception of evil which enables people to explain, diagnose and compensate for unmerited misfortune.

An adequate account of witch-hunting in Lebowa should ideally take cognizance of these considerations. Krige (1947: 8) provides some useful clues to the political potential of witch beliefs when she writes:

since evil operates through the medium of human beings it can also be brought under human control. The parts assigned to the characters, the witch and the sorcerer, presuppose a just world,

ordered and coherent, in which evil is not merely outlawed. bu can be overcome by man-made techniques. In the result men fee secure and the moral order is upheld.

It is possible to transcend negative views of witch-hunting as a cover attempt to mystify subordinates or to intimidate political opponents Instead, the involvement of political actors in witch-hunting can be seen as a positive and creative attempt to eliminate evil and thereby perform an essential social service. Engagement by political actors ir the management of misfortune presents a potent source of politica legitimacy. Although they cannot undo the crime of witchcraft. they can protect the innocent from future misfortune by neutralizing the witch. This view is central to Willis's (1970) account of the witch-cleansing cults of central Africa. 'African witch-cleansing cults,' he writes, 'go so far as to inaugurate the millennium, the age of bliss ... in which pain, disease, untimely death, violence and strife, war and hunger will be unknown' (p. 133). This perspective more fruitfully illuminates ethnographic material on the politics of witch-hunting in Green Valley, Lebowa.

Green valley: witch beliefs and their social setting

Green Valley is situated in the Mapulaneng area of the Transvaal lowveld. It is a fairly large village which comprises eight residential locations and had an estimated population of approximately 20,000 in 1990. One of the most notable demographic features of Green Valley is the great ethnic diversity of its inhabitants. Despite official identification of Green Valley with the North Sotho Pulana, many of my informants identified themselves as Pedi, Kone, Pai, Roka, Kgaga, Lobedu (Sotho); Hlanganu, Tshangana (Tsonga); Ndebele, Swazi and Zulu.

Green Valley has a rich and varied political history. Since 1919 it has been the political centre of the Setlhare chiefdom.[4] The chiefdom derives its name from *kgôsi* Setlhare Chiloane – the grandson of Maripe Mashile, who in 1864 led the Pulana in their defeat of Swat invaders at the battle of Moholoholo (Ziervogel, 1954: 107). In 1919 Green Valley was scheduled for exclusive African occupation. Older informants said that when *kgôsi* Setlhare returned from Europe, where he had participated in the First World War, he purchased the land from the South African government. He reportedly asked all subjects to contribute money, or cattle for the purpose. Subsequently households paid annual rent to Mr McBride – an agricultural officer employed by the South African government – for the right to reside, cultivate land and let stock graze in Green Valley. In 1948 the Setlhare chiefdom was incorporated into the Bushbuckridge Trust Land and placed under the authority of a Bantu Affairs Commissioner. Green Valley now became the reception site for hundreds of households relocated from the eastern Transvaal countryside. During the early 1950s Bantu Authorities were introduced to the lowveld: the Setlhare chiefdom became a Tribal Authority and the Bushbuckridge area a Regional Authority. This undermined chiefly autonomy.

In 1960 a 'betterment' scheme was implemented in Green Valley which reordered existing residential arrangements. Households in the village were relocated to demarcated sites in clearly defined residential locations. As a result of these removals nearly all households lost their fields. Stock limitations of ten cattle per household were also imposed. These removals destroyed subsistence agriculture and undermined the role of chiefs in conserving and allocating land. These difficulties were complicated by problems surrounding chiefly succession in Setlhare: from 1956 to 1989 the chieftaincy was occupied by regents who lacked the respect accorded to proper chiefs. In 1973 the Bush-buckridge Trust became part of the Lebowa 'homeland'. This event was almost unnoticed by Green Valley's residents. It did not affect the material circumstances of their lives or alleviate the local 'authority crisis'.

Since 1986 the political void left by the demise of chiefly rule came to be filled by the Comrades. In 1986 the Brooklyn Youth Organisation (affiliated to the South African Youth Congress) was established. This placed youths in the forefront of the political struggle. Attempts by the Comrades to improve village water supplies and roads were popularly approved. Yet older residents resented the intimidatory tactics which marked consumer and school boycotts. Such resentment led to the formation of the Sofasonke Civic Union. A bloody conflict between Sofasonke and the Comrades culminated in the burning of many homes and several murders. By 1990 most signs of Sofasonke activity had ceased. With the unbanning of the African National Congress (ANC) a Green Valley Civic Association, dominated by adult ANC supporters, was formed to solve 'community problems'.

Through time an elaborate system of witch beliefs has developed in Green Valley which presents itself as a *bricolage* of ideas drawn from Sotho, Tsonga and Nguni traditions. This system is used to account for the occurrence of many otherwise inexplicable instances of misfortune, ranging from issues affecting the entire community (sudden quarrels among friends, pestilence among cattle, crop failures, or drought) to more individual concerns such as untimely death and disease. The deaths of young people and those resulting from suicide, lightning, motor car accidents or being trampled by cattle may be attributed to witchcraft. Snake bites, vomiting blood, abdominal pain, loss of appetite, paralysis of the limbs, swollen ankles or legs, infertility, insanity, convulsions and epileptic fits may also be accounted for in these terms.

Witches (*balôi*) personify the 'standardised nightmare' of villagers. They are perceived as fundamentally evil men and women, motivated by envy and greed to harm fellow humans. Male witches are regarded as most potent, although women are thought to resort to witchcraft more often. Most witches are believed to be middle-aged or elderly people. Babies may be born as witches. Yet they are thought capable of using their power only upon reaching mature years. Witchcraft is allegedly practised by poor people or wealthy individuals with no visible means of income. A Christian remarked that he thought 'Witches are the offspring of the devil. They are guided by the satanic spirit'. Although the identity of witches is said to be secret, they are alleged to know each other, and to meet at night to perform their evil deeds. Witches, I was told, went about naked and were credited with supernatural abilities such as flying and entering through the roofs of houses. They were believed to bewitch people through the use of herbs or poisons and/or by sending familiars (*dithuri*) to perform evil errands for them.

Informants said that, prior to the 'betterment' removals of 1960, witches in Green Valley solely used poisons. One man commented, 'The old Pulana and Shangaan witches did not know anything about familiars. Only recently did they start using them. That is because they bought them from the Zulu people in Durban.' In the past the crocodile's brain was perceived as the most potent of all poisons. It was thought to cause migraine and to crack a victim's brain.

Other poisons are *sejêso* and *sefôlô*. *Sejêso* is a slow poison which causes abdominal pains, suffocation and TB. *Sefôlô*, when placed on paths, causes those who step on it to develop swollen legs and cancerous boils. It is also said to cause motor vehicle accidents. Witches are believed to conduct lightning by manipulating material objects rather

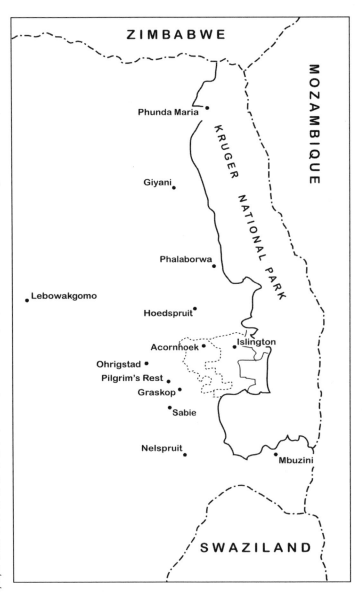

Fig. 1 The eastern Transvaal

than by sending lightning birds (see Hammond-Tooke, 1981: 99). This required the cooperative effort of at least two witches. Whilst the woman stands shaking an African tray containing a mirror, peacock feathers and a hammer, the man ascends into the sky. From the sky he uses a mirror to search for a victim, descends with the natural lightning, kills his victim with a hammer and sets her or his house alight with witches' fire.

The group of familiars includes the baboon (*tšhwène*), owl (*šibiri*), snake (*nôga*) and cat (*katse*). Witches have a peculiar relationship with familiars. It was suggested that familiars emanated from the witches' stomach or that witches themselves could metamorphose into

Fig. 2 The Mapulaneng/Mhala District

familiars. Baboons were most commonly used to perform errands such as stealing money, beating victims to death or causing unwanted abortions. Witches were also thought to make use of zombies (*ditlôtlwane*), *tokolose* and *mamlambo*. Zombies are the living dead, obtained by hypnotizing humans or resurrecting corpses. Zombies are usually kept in valleys and may be used to plough the witches' field at night, to steal money for them or to work on the Witwatersrand and send remittances. Zombies sometimes form a train at night by holding hands, with the witch as locomotive. Witches are said to send the *tokolose*, which can change its sex at will, to rape women or to have sex with men and castrate them. The *mamlambo* is a snake which changes into a woman or man and has sexual intercourse with the witch. 'Like a vampire,' I was told, 'the *mamlambo* demands blood'. To satisfy this need the witch has to slaughter a cow or a child to feed it. The *mamlambo* was described as greedy and possessive. It may prevent its keeper from marrying or killing his or her spouse.

Ethnographies of the Transvaal Sotho often distinguish between 'Witches of the day' who use poisons and 'witches of the night' who keep familiars (Hammond-Tooke, 1981: 96; Krige and Krige, 1943: 250; Monnig, 1967: 71). Informants did not deem this distinction significant and saw witches as capable of performing both types of witchcraft. Moreover, they believed that herbs could transform into familiars such as a snake, *tokolose* or *mamlambo*. A more significant distinction was drawn between *ngaka balôi* (witch herbalists), who sell poisons, *balôi* who have inherited the lust to harm and kill from their mothers, and *balôi kêndla*, who merely buy poisons to cause harm. Informants also spoke of *maemae* (ritual murderers), who aim to attain wealth by using medicines made from human genitals, nails, skin and tongue.

Chiefs and witches, 1930–56

Until 1956 Green Valley was characterised by a high degree of agricultural self-sufficiency, networks of reciprocal co-operation between domestic units, and by stable chiefship. In this context witchcraft was seen as a threat to the entire community. Witchcraft accusations were managed by chiefs and the punishment of witches often reaffirmed group solidarity (Douglas, 1970: xxvi).

Prior to 1948 the residential pattern in Green Valley was one of scattered homesteads. Households were able to meet most subsistence requirements from their fields, which were as large as they could cultivate. Although yields varied a great deal, some farmers reported harvests of up to ninety bags of mealies – enough to fill two large sheds – plus thirty bags of sorghum. No stock limitations were imposed, and cattle herds varied from fifteen to over 150. Rural production also contributed towards the payment of rent. By selling one cow households were able to pay for the grass and dip of all other stock. Migrant labour remittances were of secondary importance in income generation. Many men said that they became migrants solely to purchase clothes. In large households brothers took turns to migrate, and men migrated as seldom as once every five years. Nearly all migrants from Green Valley were employed at the Transvaal Gold Mining Company (TGMC) in Pilgrim's Rest. They worked nine-month contracts, travelled to Pilgrim's Rest on foot, and earned about five 'bob' a day. Retrospective perceptions of this period were clouded by a myth of a carefree and affluent past. Yet informants recalled years of severe hardship. During 1933, 1937, 1939 and 1941 most mealie fields in Green Valley were destroyed by drought, *difênêfênê* (cutworm) and plagues of locusts. During 1939, which saw the worst of these droughts, maize surpluses were soon exhausted and people were forced to queue at the general shop in Acornhoek to buy rations. In a stampede by anxious buyers at the shop a child was trampled to death. In each of these years labour migration peaked.

Agricultural production required close cooperation between men and women and elaborate networks of reciprocity between households. During crucial periods of the agricultural cycle more labour was required than could be met by even the largest households. *Matsêma* (work parties) were held for tasks such as ploughing, hoeing, harvesting, sorghum threshing, the cutting of thatching grass and housebuilding. On these occasions women brewed beer and invited neighbours to work at their home or in their fields on a reciprocal basis. I was told that 'nobody refused to come unless they had serious problems at home'. Hoeing, planting groundnuts and cutting thatching grass were considered women's tasks; uprooting trees, ploughing and housebuilding those of men. Such gender divisions were never strictly enforced. Other tasks such as cultivation and sorghum threshing were not gender-specific. *Matsêma* are remembered as festive occasions.

Neighbourly cooperation extended beyond *Matsêma*. Men built homes for widows in return for beer. Neighbours regularly borrowed donkeys and sledges to transport produce to Acornhoek. During times of severe drought residents of Green Valley could *šikêla* (visit to ask for maize) at Manyeleti, Sand River, Bedford and Islington. According to this custom villagers were obliged to give a bag of their surplus mealies to visiting kin and to sell bags to non-kin for £1. Residents of these villages, in turn, visited Green Valley to *šikêla*. Informants could not recall any inter-household conflicts over land and mentioned that this was because fields did not encroach upon each other. Conflicts were largely between individuals and arose from drunkenness or disputes over women. Such squabbles were usually settled through a ritual known as *ho tswa relano* (reconciliation). Disputing parties each brought a chicken, cooked the birds on a common fire, and shared the meat.

The incorporation of Green Valley into the Bushbuckridge Trust Land undermined agricultural self-sufficiency in the village. Politically the trust was placed under a Bantu Affairs Commissioner and Bantu Authorities (introduced during the early 1950s). Residents resented these changes, particularly the greater powers granted to agricultural officers employed by the trust. They did not understand why they were forced to take goats to the dipping tanks. 'We lost many goats there and had to carry their carcasses from the tanks on sledges.' In 1951 large numbers of cattle died during a foot-and-mouth disease epizootic. Nearly all households reported stock losses. Informants were furious about the measures taken to deal with the crisis. Green Valley was placed under quarantine and no stock were allowed to enter or leave the village. Agricultural officers rounded up all cattle to inject them in their tongues and burn the carcasses of dead cattle to ensure that nobody ate the meat. An elderly man expressed widely shared sentiments when he said, 'The only reason our cattle died was because the whites came here with their injections. We know how to treat our cattle. Many *dingaka* around here could have given them medicines that would have effectively cured them.'

From 1948 Green Valley became the reception site for hundreds of displaced households. Harries (1989, 104) draws attention to several factors which stimulated a flow of Africans from white-owned farms on to trust land during this period. They include legislative measures restricting the number of labour tenants and 'squatters' on white-owned farms, increased use of insecticides and mechanisation of production methods. Many farms west of Green Valley were purchased by the South African forestry department, and former tenant households were forced to move on to trust land. To accommodate the incoming households three residential locations were established in Green Valley during 1955 and fields were limited to the size of one morgen (2.1 acres). Few households were capable of harvesting more than six bags of mealies on these new fields. Migrant labour remittances had become indispensable to household survival. Migrants now worked twelve-month contracts, and many sought employment on the Witwatersrand.

Under Setlhare Chiloane (1914–45) and his son Jon Mabalane Chiloane (1946–55) chiefly rule conformed to what Sansom (1974a: 137–47) describes as the 'Western' pattern characteristic of the South African inland plateau, in which administrative functions and resource regulation were centralised under chiefly authority. Chiefs heard disputes in their *kgôrô* (court) and directly controlled access to the means of production by allocating land to households. Moreover, chiefs ensured a patterned use of resources by declaring open and closed seasons. Informants recalled that nobody was allowed to plough before chiefs announced the beginning of the season. Similarly, they could commence harvesting only after chiefs had performed the rite of the first fruits.

Sansom (1974b: 260) argued that, because the power of Western chiefs was immanent in the system of allocating resources, chiefly rituals did not emphasise the ruler's uniqueness. Fieldwork underlined these observations. Unlike the position among the Lobedu, rituals did not legitimate the power order by investing chiefs with semi divine characteristics (cf. Kertzer, 1988: 4654). Indeed, a member of the royal family recalled that Chief Sedhare seldom attended any public gatherings. Rather than emphasizing the role of the chief himself, rituals constructed and reconstructed, the *môsate* (royal kraal) as the political centre – defined by Geertz (1983: 122) as 'a point where leading ideas come together with leading institutions to create an arena in which the events that most vitally affect its members' lives

take place'. Rituals aimed, for example, at making rain, at ridding the land of cutworm, and at publicly punishing witches, were organized from the *môsate*. They involved popular participation and confirmed the chiefdom's 'organic unity'.

Chiefs summoned *dingaka* to the *môsate* when cutworm invaded Green Valley's fields. Herbalists cleansed the land by sprinkling medicines at the corners of all fields and burning grass from each field in a bonfire. Thereafter the chief's *dintona* (subordinate political officers) assembled about 100 children who were in their pre-puberty years to the *môsate* and issued them with bottles containing ash and cutworms. At daybreak the children emptied the bottles into the river Klaserie and shouted, 'Worms! Worms! Go back to Phalaborwa!' Informants firmly believed in the efficacy of this rite. One man recalled, 'One or two days after the children returned the worms disappeared entirely. You could see them crawling away.'

Rain-making rites were conducted annually in August, before the first spring rains were expected. These rites were performed only by the chiefdom's official rainmakers. *Kgosi* Maripe appointed Ngwa Photo and her husband Mphau Sekgobela to this prestigious position. It was later inherited by their sons Makonti and Makhwela. In August all household heads were summoned to the *môsate* and asked to make donations in cash and kind to the rainmakers. The rainmakers then left for (the Lobedu queen) Mojaji's country to purchase rain-making medicines. Upon their return pre-puberty children were called to collect dry grass from the fields and given drops of rain-making medicine. From here they moved to sleep at the river Klaserie. The next morning they entered the river, threw medicines into the water and shouted 'Rain! Rain!'. Rainmakers promised the chief that as the children returned it would rain. Older informants said thunderless clouds usually assembled within hours of the ritual. 'Sometimes it rained so heavily that we would be unable to plough.'

Informants recognized that rainmaking rites could be unsuccessful. It was widely believed that the blood of a pangolin (*kgwara*), an aborted foetus not properly buried in cool river sand and a human corpse which lay in the open veld could prevent rain. Witchcraft was also invoked as an. explanation for the failure of rainmaking rites. Herbalists, envious of the chief's official rainmakers, were said to render these rites ineffective by placing *šibêka* medicines on the veld. They reportedly wanted residents to pay them to remove the medicines.

The Sekgobela rainmakers blamed the drought of 1939 on witches. On their advice Chief Setlhare summoned a diviner to the *môsate*. The diviner sniffed out Sinkelele, a middle-aged farmworker and herbalist, as the one responsible. The accusation was popularly approved. Sinkelele, who lived in a shanty on the northern outskirts of Green Valley, had previously been expelled from the neighbouring Moletele chiefdom for using *šibêka*. An old man recalled:

> We all knew that Sinkelele was a witch, Even the children. If he entered your home and you refused him beer your beer lost its colour and became tasteless. If you quarrelled with him and you walked away you'd find a baboon a few metres away. Even in broad daylight. Then you ran like hell. He was full of tricks, but never killed anybody.

At Chief Setlhare's court Sinkelele was threatened with death unless he confessed and showed the villagers his medicines. Sinkelele reportedly took the witch-hunters to an isolated place where they discovered a grass broom hanging from a tree. Underneath the tree were pieces of clay pot with distinctive marks. Informants believed that as the broom swung it chased away the rain clouds. They recalled that all grass, shrubs and bush around the tree were dry. As a punishment Sinkelele was tied to a tree stump and a huge fire built around him. This, I was told, was 'to make him feel the heat which he caused us to endure'. The medicines found at Sinkelele's home were also burnt in the fire. Sinkelele was released and expelled from Green Valley.

In 1941 a *pitsô* (meeting) was called when locusts invaded Green Valley's mealie fields, very little rain fell and cutworms destroyed the remaining crops. At the chief's *kgôrô* teams of men were organized to search the village for *šibêka*. The witch-hunters returned with Karatsane, a herbalist and master of a local initiation lodge. Karatsane was accused of hanging a goatskin, which he smeared with *šibêka* medicines, near the river. *Kgôsi* Setlhare also ordered a fire to be built to punish him

The year 1954 was the last time a Green Valley resident was accused of preventing rain. He was Phiri, a herbalist and initiation master, who was apprehended by a *ntona* of chief Mabalane. Phiri was also accused of stealing an antelope horn and medicines from the Sekgobeta rainmakers, conducting lightning, and of killing an initiate at the lodge of another initiation master. Phiri confessed and removed his medicines only after he had been punished. Phiri was allowed to remain in Green Valley after he had promised chief Mabalane never to practise witchcraft again.

All those publicly accused of witchcraft were newcomers to Green Valley. Sinkelele and Karatsane were both immigrants from Phalaborwa. There is no sense in which the accusation of these people can be seen as a chiefly attempt to intimidate political opponents. They rather reflect the perception of Phalaborwa as a hot, dry and impoverished area where beggars, witches and ritual murderers resided. Hall writes of Phalaborwa, 'it seems unlikely that agriculture was ever a prosperous process in this harsh landscape, "a thoroughly unpleasant place to live"' (1987: 68).

Chiefs Setlhare and Mabalane also mediated in the case of private accusations or witchcraft between members of different households. People who suspected their neighbours of practising witchcraft were obliged to report this to the *kgôrô*. Both the accuser and the accused were required to leave five cattle for safe keeping at the *kgôrô*. The chief then appointed three witnesses – one for each party and a third to represent himself to consult a *mungôma* (diviner) at Phunda Maria (near Venda), An informant explained, 'Only the best *mungôma* who are special and perfect were permitted to sniff witches.' I was also told that because *mungôma* feared retaliatory action against them by the family of the accused they were prepared to point out witches only when granted permission by the chief. If the accused was pronounced to be a witch his trousers and shirt were cut and his head shaven in a rough manner. The accuser could then collect the cattle from the *môsate*. If the accused was found not guilty he blew a goat's horn as he entered the village to proclaim his innocence. He could then collect the cattle in compensation for having been wrongly accused. Witches were never killed and were seldom expelled. One informant remarked, 'Their punishment was to be exposed. Everybody went around announcing that this was a witch and shouted at them.'

Private accusations of witchcraft did not occur frequently. Only two informants recalled that their relatives were taken to Phunda Maria. Both were proclaimed innocent. A woman who developed paralysis of her arm blamed the family who wanted to marry their son for hiring a 'thug from Phalaborwa' to bewitch her. Although she reported the matter to the chief's *ntona*, and he summoned the 'witch' to the *kgôrô*, the man fled.

Throughout this period the power of witchcraft was viewed ambivalently. Occasionally *ngaka balôi* were said to use their power to punish those who engaged in unsociable behaviour and to practise vengeance magic. Herbalists were often asked to place *tawana* (*ndzawana* in Tsonga) medicines on people's household items and livestock. These medicines were believed to cripple thieves, make their eyes turn red and cause them to suffer from insomnia. Informants also said that the thunderbolts of *ngaka balôi* struck only thieves. One man remarked, 'During the days of *kgôsi* Setlhare there was no such thing as theft. The thieves were scared that they'd be bewitched. The *ngaka* were the policemen of the people.' Where victims deserved being bewitched those suspected were not accused. During the 1930s Trigane, a herbalist, was said to have sent lightning which killed a girl at the women's initiation lodge. Her mother reportedly requested Trigane to strike her co-wife, who, she said, had stolen her bridewealth money. When Trigane threw the divination dice he told her someone from her own house had stolen the money. Yet the mother insisted that he should strike the thief. An elderly informant remarked about the incident, 'Those people killed themselves.'

Political instability, relocation and witchcraft, 1957–86

During the late 1950s and early 1960s the form of witchcraft accusation, witch-hunting, the control thereof and the very conception of a witch were radically transformed.

During these years the power and autonomy of chiefship, were eroded to such an extent that Setlhare's chiefs dissociated themselves from witch-hunting. Effective chiefly rule was undermined by wider structural processes and by local particularities of chiefly succession. With the introduction of Bantu Authorities Setlhare's chiefs were no longer accountable solely to their subjects, but also to the magistrate, Bantu Affairs Commissioner and Regional Authority in Bushbuckridge.[5] With the greater responsibilities granted to white agricultural officers employed by the trust, the role of chiefs in regulating agricultural activities, conserving and allocating land diminished.

In 1956 Chief Mabalane was succeeded by Elson Sekganyane, his eldest son. Sekganyane was very unpopular. He was described as a chief who saw himself as enlightened, who scorned Pulana traditions, sjambokked people at his *kgôrô* and was an alcoholic. The chief's right-hand man recalled, 'He always roamed around as if he was insane. Commissioner Paulsen told me to look after him like a herdboy. Once I even had to handcuff him,' Sekganyane never summoned rainmakers to the *môsate*. Instead, he arranged prayer days in times of drought, to which all local priests were invited. Sekganyane died in 1959. Before his funeral, his subjects called a *pitsô* to discuss the circumstances surrounding his death. At the meeting it was alleged that the chief's body was full of burn marks and that he had been bewitched. Men apprehended Maboye, a herbalist, and took him to a *mungôma* at Phunda Maria. The *mungôma* pronounced Maboye guilty of prescribing a herbal concoction which had turned the chief into an alcoholic, made him insane and eventually killed him. Upon Maboye's return an angry crowd stoned him to death. Informants said that in response to this event the magistrate prohibited witchhunting and banned all *pitsô*.

Sekganyane's heir was a toddler when his father died and Masinyane Chiloane – the fourth son of Setlhare's first house – was appointed to deputize as a regent in his absence. In 1962 Masinyane was assaulted with an axe. He became mentally retarded, no longer spoke properly and was deemed unfit to rule. Masinyane was replaced by Senone – the eldest son of Setlhare's third house. Senone's wife recalled that he lacked the status of former chiefs and was constrained in his duties by the Bantu Affairs commissioners. The commissioners appointed *dintona* on his behalf. They also called *pitsô* at which Senone merely interpreted their words; he spoke Afrikaans exceptionally well. Important disputes were brought before the magistrate's court rather than the chief's *kgôrô*. She also recalled that, after Senone had argued with his brothers over the subdivision of residential sites and fields, he relinquished his position and left Green Valley. Senone returned upon the insistence of the commissioners, but only after his brothers had apologised to him.

After his death in 1969 Senone was replaced by a third regent, German Chiloane – Sekganyane's younger brother. Many informants said that they respected Chief German. One man described him as 'a man among men'. He said that the chief himself listened to all cases brought before the *kgôrô* and turned a blind eye to many official regulations. 'He never had a grudge against anybody. Many people set up businesses without a licence, but he never troubled them. He also never collected any money from us.' Chief German died in a motor car accident in December 1989.

As the ability of chiefs to control witchcraft accusations progressively declined, residential relocations during this period generated severe social tensions within and between different households. From 1960 a second 'betterment' scheme was implemented in Green Valley, The village was subdivided into residential, arable and grazing land. Eight locations were established and 410 residential sites were marked out.[6] Agricultural officers of the trust relocated households on to these sites and imposed limitations of ten cattle per household. These removals effectively destroyed the last remnants of subsistence agriculture. All households lost the fields which they had cultivated prior to relocation. Out of fifty-three households sampled, only three were granted half-morgen plots in compensation.

Relocation eroded the networks of reciprocal cooperation which had been built up between neighbouring households in Green Valley over decades. *Matsêma* disappeared entirely. Many informants described their new neighbours as complete strangers. One woman commented, 'You were lucky if you had good neighbours. When you found yourself sitting next to people you disliked, there was nothing that you could do about it.' I heard many reports of cattle destroying neighbours' gardens and of theft and murder. These tensions are expressed in some of the names given to locations. A location in which many murders occurred was called Kgapa Madi (Sotho for 'scooping blood') and another, Budlaya Bongolo (Tsonga for 'killing donkeys'). Here a man had killed his neighbour's donkey when it wandered into his kitchen and drank from a pot of beer.

The demise of subsistence agriculture has placed women in a powerless and precarious position. Through working in the fields women made the most important contribution to household diets. After relocation they became almost completely reliant upon the remittances of migrant men. Apart from divination and hawking there were few economic activities to compensate for this loss. There have been exceptionally few wage-earning opportunities for women in and around Green Valley.

'Betterment' removals have also had a profound effect upon generational relations. In the absence of migrant fathers, mothers and grandparents found it hard to discipline children. Boys no longer herded cattle and were free to attend school more regularly. This enhanced children's status *vis-à-vis* their illiterate parents. Since 1960 generational relations in the village have been characterized by 'cohort dissonance'. Rosaldo (1980: 110–20) uses the concept of a cohort to denote individuals who share a collective identity and a sense of life's possibilities by virtue of having come of age together and sharing formative historical moments when crucial life choices are made.

Green Valley's youths have little insight into events during times of agricultural self-sufficiency which shaped the lives of elders. Likewise youths are confronted by vexing situations unknown in the world their parents inhabited.

In this new context witches were no longer perceived as threatening the entire Green Valley community. Indeed, informants suggested that all *šibêka* medicines disappeared during the removals. Witchcraft came to be seen as directed solely against individuals and individual households. Accusations of witchcraft tended to occur more frequently than before. These tendencies reflect the rapid erosion of community sentiments and increased tensions within and between households. Nine of the fifty-three individuals whose life histories I recorded claimed to have been bewitched between 1957 and 1986. Two were women who accused their husbands. In all other instances in-laws or neighbours were suspected. The conception of a witch also broadened. Witches were perceived as no longer working evil through the use of medicines and poison alone, but also by sending familiars. This transformation was probably because Green Valley residents began to consult Stimela, a *mungôma* based in Giyani, who employed a different explanatory framework from that of the *mungôma* at Phunda Maria. The change had important implications. Their association with mythical animals dehumanized witches and exaggerated their antisocial nature. This conception also legitimised exceptionally violent methods of punishment.

Of the nine individual witchcraft cases only one led to an open accusation. This outcome can be accounted for in terms of the expense and inconvenience of consulting a *mungôma*. Moreover, Sansom (1972) argues that in setting out to accuse others individuals put themselves at risk. He also points to the difficulty accusers face in obtaining support from the public. In this respect people felt betrayed by local authorities. Women who saw themselves as the victims of witchcraft were seldom able to mobilize such support. In 1975 Mrs R. L.'s husband, a migrant in Graskop, absconded and married a second wife without her consent. In 1978 he returned to Green Valley and asked her to be reconciled with him. However, Mrs R. L. discovered that he had hidden herbs in his jacket pockets. Although she reported this to the Tribal Authorities, officials refused to attend to the case. Mrs C. E., a widow, experienced great tensions with her neighbour when she was relocated to Pelindaba. 'He used to climb on top of the roof of his *lapa* (kitchen) and scream at me whenever he was drunk. Sometimes he even came to my house, kicked my pots, and teased me.' When she developed abdominal pains and severe constipation in 1984 Mrs C. E. thought he had bewitched her. In fear of her life, she moved to Budlaya Bongolo. Here she became an active member of the Zion Christian Church.

Victims who successfully mobilized others to support their accusation could do so only because the alleged misdeeds were deemed plentiful and horrific.
[…]

Comrades and witches, 1986–90

During the 1980s political processes in Green Valley were drastically transformed. The political void left by the erosion of chiefship came to be occupied by national liberation movements and the Comrades. Teachers and activists from the Witwatersrand were prominent in the formation of many organizations associated with the United Democratic Front (UDF) in Mapulaneng. They were supported by the brothers Matsikitsane and Segopela Mashile, who, as members of the Lebowa Legislative Assembly, used their prominent position to further popular causes.[7] In the Shatale township the Mapulaneng Crisis Committee, Shatale Youth Congress, Student Representative Councils (SRCs) and Teachers' Associations were established. These bodies aimed to maintain law and order. They patrolled the township streets at night and formed a court to mediate disputes.

In April 1986 a mass meeting was held in Green Valley to discuss local problems. At the meeting the Setlhare Crisis Committee and Brooklyn Youth Organization were established. The Setlhare Crisis Committee proved unable to survive police repression. It met on only three occasions. By May all its active members had been detained. The Brooklyn Youth Organization proved more resilient and attracted a large following among male youths. They organized from Green Valley's schools and held meetings late at night. As such, youths were placed in the forefront of the political struggle. One young man recalled, 'Before 1986 youngsters played soccer, danced and stabbed each other, but now we started mobilizing the masses'.

This political pre-eminence of youths reflected developments throughout South Africa at the time. Bundy (1987) describes the political education of students during the 1980s as nationwide and spectacularly rapid. He explains it in terms of a number of interrelated processes. Foremost was accelerated growth in the number of children and young adults and a substantial expansion in black schooling, despite the glaring defects of black education. In the context of the South African economic crisis, this meant mounting unemployment among the young. High-school leavers, he argues, 'have been thrust on to the labour market at precisely the moment that it is contracting; many are too highly educated for cheap or unskilled labour …' (p. 312). The impact of unemployment and prospective unemploy-ability has been a spur to radicalism.

Like the Cape Town student movement described by Bundy the involvement of the Brooklyn Youth Organization in local educational issues provided the framework for wider forms of community action. Initial campaigns focused on the schools. Through a series of class boycotts, students demanded an end to the annual payment of R80 'school building fees' and called for the introduction of SRCs, free books, and an end to corporal punishment. Although several student leaders were arrested, teachers conceded student demands during 1988. School fees were reduced and SRCs established. Through other campaigns they confronted white businesses and the Tribal Authorities, which they perceived as exploitative. During 1986 Com-rades organized a stay-away on May Day and launched a boycott of a Bushbuckridge supermarket. They laid concrete slabs in the streets to force workers to stay at home and confiscated consumer goods. In 1987 the Brooklyn Youth Organization called upon villagers not to pay annual site taxes (R1), and service rents (R15, for water and graveyard maintenance) to the Tribal Authority offices. By this time the activities of Tribal Authorities had almost ground to a halt. Although Nkotobola – the son of Chief Sekganyane – was nominated to replace Chief German, he had not yet been officially installed by the Lebowa government. At least three residential locations in Green Valley were without *dintona*.

In a cultural context where authority is associated with age the Brooklyn Youth Organization faced a severe legitimation crisis. Many of their actions were explicitly aimed at gaining acceptance among village adults. By fiercely opposing the notorious *psianga* youth gang the Comrades gained considerable moral credibility. *Psianga*[8] carried out a reign of terror from Cottondale. In Acornhoek they wrung the necks of chickens, destroyed groceries, kidnapped and raped women. *Psianga* also beat children and burnt a furniture shop in Green Valley. The Comrades apprehended several *psianga* members, sjambokked

them and burnt their homes. Moreover, the Comrades negotiated with a nearby saw mill to provide safe transport for its employees and formed squads to escort commuters home at night. They regularly organized marches to the Acornhoek police station to demand the more effective provision of infrastructure such as piped water, roads and the installation of electricity.

The Comrades also came to play an important role in the politics of public morality. In so far as they exercised control over ambiguous aspects of public morality, their actions resembled those of the rural Welsh youth groups described by Peters (1972). Welsh youths exhibit seemingly anti-social behaviour such as removing gates, cutting shapes in cornfields and thrusting hens down chimneys. However, Peters does not regard such acts as anti-social. Rather, he sees them as condemning the pride of immoral individuals. Most adults tacitly approve of them. They are regarded as a way of teaching those who display arrogance, or engage in improper courtship and inappropriate sexual relations, a lesson. Peters suggests that criticism of such individuals in fact originates with adults. Adults also sustain anonymity by ascribing these actions to the young, rather than to specific individuals. Institutions controlled by adults such as law, religion and kinship lack flexibility in dealing with such ambiguous social relations. Institutionally, adults are unable to control, for instance, associations between local girls and stranger men, or to punish adultery. By delegating the responsibility of moral control to youths the adult community is able to maintain its integrity. Youths are jurally minors, with a limited sense of externality. 'The ignorance of immaturity gives the youth group the irresponsible freedom to act; maturity traps adults into the measured responsibility of inaction' (Peters, 1972: 135).

In a similar way the Brooklyn Youth Organization intervened in the morally ambiguous field of witchcraft.[9] Local youths dedicated themselves to eliminating this evil. In 1986 the Comrades called a series of meetings and asked people attending to name those they suspected of being witches. Names which were popularly approved were recorded on a list. Thereafter, disciplinary teams were formed to punish the witches. Although women were forbidden to attend the meetings, youths sought the active participation of adult men. Of meetings in Brooklyn, which were presumably attended by many Green Valley residents, Ritchken (1987: 1) writes, 'The most enthu-siastic accusers were the older, unemployed men. They would refer to previous occasions when witches were identified, but the witch would then bribe the chief or the *ntona* and remain within the community.' In Mapulaneng the scale of these witch-hunts was enormous. Between April and May 1986 more than 150 people were accused of witchcraft and attacked by youths. At least thirty-six of the suspected witches were killed. Informants said that most witch killings occurred in Kasteel and Brooklyn. In Kasteel youths necklaced a man after lightning had struck a young girl and burnt a pensioner whom they suspected of keeping a *tokolose*. They also killed a wealthy *ntona* who sold coffins and was suspected of being a ritual murderer. A baboon apparently ran from his bedroom when his house was burnt. In Brooklyn three women pensioners were accused of keeping zombies and sjambokked to death (Ritchken, 1987: 11).

Informants were very hesitant to talk about the effects of the 1986 witch-hunt in Green Valley. I learnt that youths stoned an elderly Botshabelo woman to death. Previously neighbours had accused her of witchcraft, but she had been pronounced innocent by a *mungôma* in Giyani. Comrades also burnt homes in Budlaya Bongolo. One of the accused was Mr M. B., who had arrived from Ohrigstad in 1971 and set himself up as a *ngaka*. Here customers visited him day and night to collect medicines. Neighbours were surprised when a leader of the

Brooklyn Youth Organization came to his home, accused him of murdering people with *sefôlô*, and blamed him for the death of a girl in Kgapa Madi. Mr M. B. claimed to be innocent and said he could not be blamed for what others did with potent herbs. During the evening Comrades attacked his home, smashed the windows and threw a home-made petrol bomb inside. The bomb, however, failed to ignite. During the evening Mr M. B.'s household fled to Cottondale. The next day his son-in-law came to the home with a truck to collect all furniture and possessions.

During 1988 and 1989 Comrades conducted witch-hunts in Tsakane and Mapalene. In Tsakane a young girl's corpse was found in a dam. It was claimed that her sex organs and nails had been cut. Comrades collected donations from Tsakane residents, rounded up suspects and took them to a *mungôma*, who identified four as witches. Youths allegedly planned to kill them, but dispersed when police intervened. In Mapalene Comrades consulted a *mungôma* after a man had died of poisoning. Upon their return they summoned a meeting and played a cassette recording with the voice of the *mungôma* which blamed a man and woman for his death. Both were heavily sjambokked and taken to hospital. Police arrested three young men in connection with the incident. Two were released on bail. The third was imprisoned for a period of eighteen months.

The Brooklyn Youth Organization did not attain unqualified legitimacy among adults through these campaigns. Their actions evoked a mixed response. Some migrant labourers were grateful. They commended the courage of the youths in apprehending witches and commented positively upon the disappearance of *psianga* and upon the reductions in school fees and taxes. Others – notably women, the unemployed and pensioners – criticized their tactics as intimidatory. A woman *ngaka* mentioned that, during the witch-hunts, 'my trainees all got rid of their medicines and joined the churches'. Likewise the leader of a *segôkgô* dance group said her team disintegrated in the wake of political unrest. Indeed, some older people feared that they could become the victims of witch-hunts. One woman remarked; 'I'm very scared of those who go around singing at night. We always feel threatened by the Comrades. Years ago members of our family could sleep outside when it was hot. Now we can't. I'm even afraid of you.'

There are several reasons for the distrust and resentment of the Comrades. Bundy (1987) observes that, although the Cape Town youth movement alluded to the desirability of a common political cause with their parents, the involvement of workers was 'conspicuously absent' in the uprisings of 1985. He points to youth militancy, a political perspective of immediatism and naive underestimation of the state's resources as likely reasons. An immediate anticipation of victory, he argues, easily results in demoralization. These factors were certainly applicable to the Brooklyn Youth Organization. However, most adult criticisms were not of broader political strategy, but rather of the manner in which Comrades intervened in witchcraft accusations. Although suspicions of witchcraft may well have originated among adults, it was the youth who decided to act and who determined the nature of the punishment. Criticisms were thus, not of witch-hunts *per se* but of improper procedures used to identify witches and of exceptionally violent methods of punishment. Elders told me how Comrades arrived with sjamboks to disrupt night vigils and told mourners not to eat meat because it would encourage neighbours to bewitch one another. Violent methods of punishment also had the effect, as Foucault (1986: 9) observed of torture as a European public spectacle, of making punishment seem equal in savagery to the crime itself and of making the tortured an object of pity. The Brooklyn Youth Organization was dominated by a cultural ethos of youthful

masculinity which valued aggression and fearless bravery. One informant pointed out the similarity between participation in the struggle and men's initiation (*ngôma*). 'There you become a man. When you are from the *ngôma* you won't reveal any secrets when the police capture and torture you because you have already experienced torture.' Members said that elders and women did not play an active part in the movement because they feared confronting the police.[10]

The actions of Green Valley's youth presented a direct challenge to adult authority. This differs from the situation in the Welsh countryside, where the institutional strength of the community remained vested with adults (Peters, 1972: 120). Comrades described elders as politically ignorant, and saw them as hampered by their inability to speak English. One Comrade said that elders 'have old-fashioned ideas and are scared of the whites. They think they [whites] are God'.

During October 1989 adults who supported the Tribal Authority, councillors of the late Chief German and school principals, established the Sofasonke ('We die together') Civic Union to oppose the Comrades politically.[11] Sofasonke held regular meetings in Brooklyn and Green Valley. In November Sofasonke burnt seven homes in Brooklyn and killed three Comrades. They also fired upon a car driven by Matsikitsane Mashile. Informants said they were surprised that Sofasonke were allowed to hold meetings openly during the national state of emergency and that no police action was taken to apprehend the killers. Members of the Brooklyn Youth Organization retaliated by necklacing a man alleged to have been a Sofasonke agent.

On 28 January 1990 Nelson Ramodike, Chief Minister of Lebowa, with representatives of the South African Council of Churches and of the UDF, met Comrade and Sofasonke leaders to discuss the violence. The next day Ramodike made an urgent appeal for peace at a Green Valley high school. Yet, that very night, several houses and cattle were burnt and a Comrade leader was seriously injured. Comrades retaliated by killing the principal of the German Setlhare High School in Brooklyn – a co-founder of Sofasonke. Over the Easter weekend a 15-year-old schoolgirl, the sister of a Comrade leader, was butchered to death. Violence subsided only after a Lebowa Police riot squad had arrested twenty Comrades and five Sofasonke members. Throughout the conflict Sofasonke remained an elusive organization, with little overt support in Green Valley. An elderly informant adequately summarized feelings when he said, 'It has been much worse since Sofasonke have been around. They said they were better than the Comrades, but they also killed people.' During the fierce conflict between the Comrades and Sofasonke no victims were identified as witches.

The unbanning of the ANC in February 1990 led to greater political stability in Green Valley. Soon a permanent ANC office was established in Acornhoek. In August a Green Valley Civic Association, with four block committees, was formed to solve community problems and to mediate in local disputes. A Women's League was established and the Brooklyn Youth Organization became directly affiliated to the ANC Youth League. These changes allowed greater adult participation in political structures and made local bodies directly accountable to the ANC's regional office in Nelspruit. One ANC member commented, 'In the past the sjambok was always the answer. Today there is freedom of speech. Because we operate more openly our parents have also begun to understand our policies.'

The Christmas witch-hunt, 1990–91

Between 23 July and 3 August 1990 nine Green Valley residents died. Six young men, including members of a local football team, died in car accidents. An elderly man committed suicide, and the corpse of a woman was found outside her home with stab wounds. On Saturday 4 August five funerals were conducted at the Kgapa Madi graveyard. As mourners left the graveyard they were addressed by a leader of the Brooklyn Youth League who was also a prominent ANC political educationist. He spoke through a loud-hailer, saying that death is very painful.

> If five people die every week more than twenty will die in a month. If things go on like this we'll all die... You yourself may be the next ... The priests should pray to God to stop these deaths. If these deaths are man-made the ministers should pray that the witches must stop. The witches think they are safe because I told my Comrades to stop burning them.

Some elderly mourners voiced their agreement and shouted, 'Tsamayang balôi ('Away with witches!').

During the December holidays of 1990 a witch-hunt commenced. Over a fortnight thirty-four people were identified as witches in four of Green Valley's locations. The witch-hunt was novel in that it involved wide community participation. Although Comrades were the most prominent witch-hunters, they were assisted by many adult residents. A member of the Youth League remarked that most meetings were called not by the Comrades but by the community (badudi). 'They just needed the help of the Comrades – their sons.' Here the participation of local youths approximates to the role Peters (1972) ascribes to Welsh youth groups. By allocating blame for un-merited misfortune, and publicizing personal affairs, the Comrades were vital to the creation of a sphere of public morality. The vast scale of the witch-hunt dramatically linked scattered individual concerns, coordinated the actions of local groupings and gave them a distinctive public flavour.[12]

Kgapa Madi. On 20 December residents of Kgapa Madi. where one of the deceased soccer players had lived, called a meeting to discuss the cause of his death. Donations of R2 were collected from those who attended and used to consult a *mungôma* in Giyani. However, the *mungôma* was reluctant. to assist them. Some informants said that this was because a witch had disrupted the meeting with medicines. A second meeting was called after a youth had committed suicide. His corpse was found hanging from a tree by a noose made from his shirtsleeves. Here it was decided to send delegates to consult a powerful *mungôma* at Mbuzini, near Swaziland. Upon their return the delegates relayed that the *mungôma* had informed them that the young man's own relatives had bewitched him and that he required R1,700 to sniff the witches. A traffic official arranged for additional collec-tions to be taken. Comrades compiled a list of approximately thirty suspects and forced them to accompany them to Mbuzini by bus.

Upon their return the delegations displayed seven people whom the *mungôma* had pointed out as witches. They included S. M., the deceased soccer player's *malome*, who was accused of laying *sefôlô* medicines on the road where the car had crashed. He was said to have worked with B.O., who was furious when the young man divorced her daughter. H. C. and his wife, R. C., were accused of bewitching his stepson – the young man who had committed suicide. The son was known as having been rude and disrespectful towards his stepfather. Three other Kgapa Madi residents (B. D., F. I. and S. O.) were also said to keep zombies. The accused were instructed to climb on top of the bus, confess to the crowd, and tell them who had helped them to bewitch their victims, Some 'witches' swore at the crowd. Others were more cooperative and, between them, identified six other Kgapa Madi residents as witches.

When the meeting had dispersed Comrades searched the homes of the accused. Youths suspected B. D. of keeping zombies under his coalburning stove, dug beneath it and found a piece of decayed meat. B. D.'s refusal to eat the meat was taken as evidence that it was human flesh. Thereafter they proceeded to demolish the homes of the witches and to evict them. Many fellow household members of the witches supported these acts. S. O.'s husband asked the Comrades not to demolish his house, as it did not belong to his wife, and vowed to chase her away, The Comrades consequently demolished her room only. The daughter-in-law of another witch told me that she planned to divorce her husband. In other cases kin sought to protect the accused. The children of several accused disputed the accusations. They took a list of all witch-hunters to the Acornhoek police station and reported the matter to high-ranking ANC officials. Regional ANC leaders told the youths to halt the demolitions and allow the accused to return to Kgapa Madi. With the exception of four witches, who fled to Phalaborwa, all the accused had returned to Kgapa Madi by January 1991.

Kiyelane. Two incidents preceded the Kiyelane witch-hunt. On Sunday 18 November a Standard 5 pupil died in the Garankuwa hospital after complaining of a headache and vomiting blood. On Friday 14 December a migrant returned home with his Christmas bonus and stopped overnight at a local shebeen. On Saturday morning he was found naked and confused in a fruit store. The migrant discovered that his salary, identity papers and savings and account books were missing, and could not recall what had happened. The migrant's son reported the incident to fellow Comrades. Kiyelane residents met on an open stretch of land to discuss the problem of witches. Both incidents were commented upon and it was decided that those responsible would be apprehended.

After intensive investigations, four people were brought before a meeting on Saturday 29 December and accused of witchcraft. L. A. and his wife, B. A., were accused of selling poisoned beer to the migrant. Comrades found a bottle of termite poison in their home and alleged that the couple had poured it into the beer they sold. They were also said to have rinsed beer glasses with brake fluid to intoxicate their customers and enable them to pick their pockets. Y. N. was accused of poisoning her nephew – the Standard 5 pupil. On the night of his death she had reportedly woken his father and told him, 'don't worry. The boy is well where he is.' Y. N.'s son confirmed that she was a witch. He accused her of killing his brother. and of causing his father to desert the family. N. K. was accused of keeping a snake. During 1988 her grandson struck a young boy with his fist. The boy died immediately. She was alleged to have doctored him with medicines.

As the proceedings were getting under way, armed policemen arrived to disperse the Comrades. During the evening L. A. and B. A. sought refuge at the home of a senior member of the Civic Associa-tion and N. K. fled to the neighbouring homeland of Gazankulu. The next day the witch-hunters reassembled. They loaded Y. N.'s possessions on two trucks and removed her to Violetbank.

Tsakane. On Christmas day a 5-year-old boy from Tsakane disappeared. All next day residents searched for the child, without success. Towards evening a meeting was called at the Tsakane sports ground and it was decided to consult the *mungôma* at Mbuzini. The *mungôma* was also asked to rid Tsakane of witches, who had plagued the location since 1988. Donations of R20 were collected from local inhabitants.

The boy's parents suspected that D. P., a shebeener who was living with her white boyfriend, had kidnapped the child. On Thursday 27

December D. P. and several other suspects were forced to board the bus. When the bus returned at 9 p. m. on Sunday eight witches were presented to Tsakane residents. The *mungôma* confirmed that D. P. was a ritual murderer and pointed out seven other suspects. N. B. who was said to ride a white horse at night, and was blamed for killing his lover's husband, was put forward as the leader of Tsakane's witches. They were accused of keeping familiars, sending a *tokolose* to rape young women, killing their relatives, disrupting meetings of the Tsakane block of the Civic Association. and burying a human brain under the gate of Chief German's *kgôrô* to stupefy him. Tsakane's witches were detained until 7 January, when, along with those of Mapalene, they were brought to the Green Valley sports ground.

Mapalene. During 1990 three Mapalene residents committed suicide: a housewife and a pensioner hanged themselves. and a young boy shot himself. Suspicions of witchcraft heightened when tombstones in the graveyard were painted. On 4 January 1991 Mapalene residents met to discuss these events. At the meeting it was said that only the graves of those who had committed suicide had been painted. This, I was told, was done by witches, to prevent the spirits of the deceased from troubling them. R4,000 was collected to finance a trip to Mbuzini. Thirty suspects were rounded up and told to board the bus, which departed at 7.30 a.m. on Saturday. About fifty witnesses accompanied them.

When the bus returned a large crowd gathered and demanded to see the witches. A member of the ANC Women's League recalled that regional ANC leaders instructed local officials to protect the witches and their property. The officials asked the driver to keep the witches inside the bus and allow only witnesses to alight. The witches were called upon to address the crowd only when everyone was seated. Comrades blamed the nine witches for all the deaths in Mapalene and for desecrating the tombstones. They were said to keep familiars and to poison their neighbours. One woman was accused of bewitching the uterus of her daughter-in-law, causing her to be pregnant for seventeen months and to abort. Another woman reportedly bought a baboon from a *ngaka balôi* which she wanted to send to Johannesburg to fetch her son, who had absconded. She proved unable to control the baboon, however, and it killed two of her neighbours. As the witches were speaking the crowd became hostile and started throwing stones and empty beer cans at them. In reaction to this tense situation ANC officials told the crowd that the witches would address them at the Green Valley sports ground the following day. They asked the witches to board the bus and transported them to the Acornhoek police station for their own safety.

On Monday 7 January ANC officials collected Tsakane and Mapalene's witches from the police station and brought them to the sports ground. They assured the station commander that they would protect the witches. The meeting was attended by over a thousand people. At the meeting a Brooklyn Youth League leader said the Green Valley community did not want unnatural deaths. He then instructed the witches to fetch their medicines and burn them in front of the crowd. Although the witches complied the crowd became very antagonistic. ANC officials were thus compelled to transport the witches back to the police station by bus. Youths followed the bus on foot, gathered outside the police station gates and shouted for the witches to come out. Eventually a Lebowa Police riot squad dispersed the crowd with tear gas, rubber bullets and sjamboks.

Green Valley's witches remained in the police station for two weeks before they could resume residence in the village. During this time ANC and Civic Association officials addressed a series of meetings in all locations. They urged residents not to harm the witches and instructed Youth League marshals to protect them.

The Green Valley witch-hunt certainly resembled earlier witch-cleansing cults in central Africa (cf. Richards, 1935; Marwick, 1950; Willis, 1968, 1970). It was organized with the explicit aim of ridding Green Valley of misfortune and presented a ritual drama involving wide participation. However, the Green Valley witch-hunt differed from the others in important respects. Willis sees a sense of social renewal and reincorporation as the general outcome of witch cleansing. This, he suggests, involves the collective consumption of anti-witchcraft serum, after which witches resume their places in the community. 'Supposedly, a new and morally regenerated life then begins for everyone' (1970: 131). Willis's view does not portray the ambiguity and contestation which characterized the Green Valley witch-hunt. It also underplays the violation, anguish and terror of witch-hunting.

Local ANC officials whom I interviewed firmly believed in witches. A local member of the Women's League who said, on radio, that she did not believe in witches told me that the statement did not reflect her true views. 'I only said that to prevent havoc.' Their general impression was that sufficient action had been taken in forcing the witches to burn their medicines. They saw the killing of witches as untenable, as it would trigger harsh police retaliation and would anger regional ANC leaders. They also feared that if witches were expelled they could assist vigilante groups to annihilate the Comrades.

Other informants were sceptical of the effectiveness of the mild treatment the witches had received. One informant mentioned that, even if the herbs had been burnt, 'they can look for other rubbish and continue witching'. Another said that he had lost 'all confidence' in the ANC and argued that ANC officials protected the witches because D. P. and her son were ANC members. Unchecked by the ANC, the Green Valley youth would certainly have expelled the witches, allowing no hope of return.

Yet there can be little doubt that the majority of Green Valley residents approved of the eventual outcome of the witch-hunt. Under adult control, Comrades nonetheless exercised a legitimate role in the politics of public morality. The witch-hunt dramatized their power to influence the outcome of local events and communicated their willingness to eliminate evil. Such considerations outweighed any political benefits which could be attained from manipulating the witch-hunt in a cynical attempt to eliminate, or intimidate, political opponents as the analysis of Mitchell (1956), Marwick and Steadman (1985) would lead us to believe.

[...]

Conclusion

In this article I have sought to take the perceptions informants themselves have of witches seriously. The reality of such beliefs, as an intellectual attempt to explain, manage and compensate for undeserved misfortune, cannot be lightly dismissed as an 'idiom' which masks ulterior motives. From this perspective it can be argued that the involvement of political actors in witch-hunting can best be understood as an attempt to eliminate misfortune, perform a valuable social service and thereby attain political legitimacy. I have argued against simplistic interpretations of witch-hunting as an act aimed at eliminating or intimidating political opponents.

Despite important changes in the forms of witch beliefs and in patterns of witchcraft accusation, there have been remarkable continuities in its political implications through time. From 1930 to 1957 witches were perceived as threatening the livelihood of the entire

Green Valley community. In this context witch-hunts, which were aimed at restoring fertility to the land, reaffirmed the solidarity of villagers, and constituted the royal kraal as the symbolic centre of the chiefdom. Impoverished herbalists, blamed for using *šibêka* medicines, were not associated with political opponents of Setlhare's chiefs.

In the post-relocation years witches were viewed as threatening individuals and individual households. From 1986 Comrades exploited public perceptions of the South African government as protecting witches, They gave powerless individuals the necessary public support to accuse neighbours and kin as witches. Although many elderly people indeed felt intimidated by the Comrades it can he argued that this was a consequence of, rather than a motivating factor for, witch-hunting. In making accusations youths sought the active cooperation of village adults. It is notable that members of Sofasonke were killed not as witches but as political opponents. An analysis of the Christmas witch-hunt of 1990/91 underlines many of these observations. Green Valley residents were willing to incur considerable expense to see that the correct witches were identified. Methods of identification were dramatically convincing and the witches identified represented diverse political affiliations.

There are several reasons why the accusation of witches who are associated with mystical forces of evil may bear greater political potential than those associated with opposing political factions. It establishes a moral opposition between the witchhunter and the forces of evil which is not otherwise possible. Second, witch beliefs also deal with the perennial human problems of death and misfortune, which are a more compelling force in motivating people to action than purely political obligations. In other words, people are more likely to be active participants in a hunt for those who they hold responsible for endangering their harvest or the death of their child than to recite praise poems to a chief or to celebrate May Day. Third, by posing a generalized threat to the community rather than to any particular section of it, witches constitute a multivocal symbolic formulation. Many different actors, with diverse beliefs, could identify themselves with the witch-hunt. Here its political potential lies precisely in the multiple and diverse meanings associated with the witches.

Notes

1 See Anderson (1990) for a comprehensive analysis of the Sekhukhuneland witch killings.
2 Informants drew a clear distinction between the Comrades and adult office beaters of national liberation movements such as the UDF and ANC. The term *BaComrade* was used solely to refer to the members of political movements such as the Sekhukhuneland, Shatale and Brooklyn Youth Organisations. I retain this emic distinction.
3 Steadman's (1985) model may be of limited applicability to the African context, To a large extent the model relies upon evidence from Occania. where witches are believed to direct their destructive energies outside their own group. In the African situation witchcraft accusations characteristically 'occur only between persons already linked by close social bonds' (Marwick, 1970: 280).
4 Other villages in the Setlhare chiefdom include Brooklyn, Arthur's Seat. Rooiboklaagte, Craigburn and Dingleydale.
5 See Comaroff's (1974) insightful analysis of the implications of this process for chiefship among the Tshidi of Bophuthatswana.
6 The locations in Green Valley are Kgapa Madi, Budlaya Bongole, Kiyolane, Tsakane, Maripe, Mapalene, Crossroads, Pelindaba and Botshabelo.
7 Ritchken (1987) argues that, as the leaders of tenant struggles against the use of child labour by the Hall & Sons farming enterprise, the Mashile brothers have been closely aligned with the ANC since the 1950s. With the banning of the ANC they were jailed on charges of 'sabotage'. They were released

in 1963 but deported to the Ciskei and Transkei respectively. With the establishment of Lebowa in 1973 Segopela returned to Mapulaneng and was elected to the Lebowa Legislative Assembly in 1978. Matsikitsane returned in 1978 and was elected to the Legislative Assembly in 1983. In Mapulaneng the Mashile brothers made Ministers accountable for bureaucratic inefficiencies and took local issues to the highest authorities.
8 The name *psianga* ('rebel' in Tsonga), I was told, is derived from Mozambique's Renamo movement.
9 There are historic parallels between the actions of Green Valley's Comrades and those of guerrillas during the Zimbabwe war. Lan (1985: 167) writes that witch-finding was one of the most controversial techniques used by guerrillas to gain the support of villagers. As guerrillas entered the villages they attentively listened to complaints of witches and would interrogate them. 'The guerrillas' explicit and aggressive policy against witches was the final turn of the key in the lock. The doorway to legitimate political authority was wide open' (p. 170).
10 Women were underrepresented in local ANC structures. During 1990 there were only two women on the twelve-member executive of the Green Valley Civic Association. However. by February 1991 both had quit. One was accused of being a ritual murderer. The other's husband forbad her to attend meetings. Two members of the Mapalene block of the Civic Association were women, as were only four of the twelve Maripe High School SRC members. These figures are surprising, given high rates of male absenteeism and the ANC's commitment to gender equality.
11 The name possibly derives from the Sofasonke Party of James Sofasonke Mpanza a popular leader of squatter movements in the Witwatersrand during the 1940s. After being converted to Christianity Mpanza became an opponent of the Communist Party (French, 1982). Subsequently the name has been associated with conservative political groupings in the Witwatersrand.
12 See Kertzer's (1988: 214, 56–76) discussion of ritual's politically integrative functions.

References

Anderson. R. L, 1990. 'Keeping the Myth Alive: justice, witches and the law in the 1986 Sekhukhune killings'. BA honours dissertation, Johannesburg: Department of History. University of the Witwatersrand.
Bundy, C. 1987. 'Street sociology and pavement politics: aspects of youth and student resistance in Cape Town, 1985', *Journal of Southern African Studies* 13 (3), 303–30.
Cohen, A. 1979. 'Political symbolism', *Annual Review, of Anthropology* 8, 87–114.
Comaroff, J. (1974) 'Chiefship in a South African homeland', *Journal of Southern African Studies* 1 (1), 36–51.
Douglas, M. 1970. 'Introduction: thirty years after Witchcraft, Oracles and Magic', in M. Douglas (ed.), *Witchcraft Confessions and Accusations*. London: Tavistock.
Foucault, M. 1986. *Discipline and Punish: the birth of the prison*. Harmondsworth: Penguin.
French, K. 1982. 'Squatters in the forties', *Africa Perspective* 21, 28.
Geertz, C. 1983. 'Centres, kings and charisma', in *Local Knowledge*. New York: Basic Books.
Geschiere, P. 1988. 'Sorcery and the state: popular modes of action among the Maka of southeast Cameroon', *Critique of Anthropology* 8 (1), 35–63.
Hall, M. 1987. *The Changing Past: farmers, kings and traders in southern Africa*. Cape Town: David Philip.
Hammond-Tooke, W. D. 1981. *Boundaries and Belief: the structure of a Sotho world-view*. Johannesburg: Witwatersrand University Press.
Harries, P. 1989. 'Exclusion, classification and internal colonialism: the emergence of ethnicity among the Tsonga-speakers of South Africa', in L. Vail (ed.), *The Creation of Tribalism in Southern Africa*, Berkeley, CA: University of California Press.
Harris, M, 1974. *Cows, Pigs, Wars and Witches: the riddles of culture*. New York. Random House.
Hausse, P. In 1988. *Brewers, Beerhalls and Boycotts: a history of liquor in South*

Africa. Johannesburg: Ravan Press.

Heald, S. 1986, 'Witches and thieves: deviant motivations in Gisu society', *Man* 21 (1), 657–8.

Kertzer, D. 1998. *Ritual, Politics, and Power*. New Haven, CT: Yale University Press.

Krige, E. and J. 1943. *The Realm of a Rain Queen*. London: Oxford University Press, for the International African Institute.

Krige. J. 1947. 'The social functions of witchcraft', *Theoria* 1, 8–21.

Lan, D. 1985. *Guns and Rain: guerrillas and spirit mediums in Zimbabwe*. London: James Currey.

Marwick, M. 1950. 'Another modern anti-witchcraft movement in east central Africa', *Africa* 20 (1), 100–12.

— 1965. *Sorcery In its Social Setting*. Manchester: Manchester University Press.

— 1970. 'Witchcraft as a social strain-gauge', in M. Marwick (ed.), *Witchcraft and Sourcery*. Harmondsworth: Penguin.

Mitchell, J. C. 1956. *The Yao Village*. Manchester: Manchester University Press.

Monnig, H. 1967. *The Pedi*. Pretoria: Van Schaik.

Peters, L. 1972. 'Aspects of the control of moral ambiguities: a comparative analysis of two culturally disparate modes of social control', in M. Gluckman (ed.), *The Allocation of Responsibility*. Manchester: Manchester University Press.

Richards, A. 1935. 'A modern movement of witch-finders', *Africa* 8 (4), 448–61.

Ritchken, E. 1987. 'Comrades, Witches and the State: the case of the Brooklyn Youth Organization'. Unpublished paper, African Studies Institute, University of the Witwatersrand.

Rosaldo, R. 1980. *Ilongot Headhunting, 1883–1974: a study in society and history*. Stanford, CA: Stanford University Press.

Rowlands. M. and Warnier, J. 1988, 'Sorcery, power and the modern state in Cameroon', *Man* 23 (1), 118–32.

Sansom. B. 1972. 'When witches are not named', in M. Gluckman (ed.), *The Allocation of Responsibility*. Manchester: Manchester University Press.

— 1974a. 'Traditional economic systems', in W. D. Hammond-Tooke (ed.), *The Bantu-speaking Peoples of Southern Africa*. London: Routledge.

— 1974b. 'Traditional rulers and their realm', in W. D. Hammond-Tooke (ed.), *The Bantu-speaking Peoples of Southern Africa*. London: Routledge.

South African Institute of Race Relations. 1988. *Survey of Race Relations in South Africa*. Johannesburg: SAIRR.

Steadman, L. 1985. 'The killing of Witches'. *Oceania* 56 (2),106–23.

Willis, R. 1968. 'Kamcape: an anti-sorcery movement in southwest Tanzania', *Africa* 38.

— 1970. 'Instant millennium: the sociology of African witch-cleansing cults', in M. Douglas (ed.), *Witchcraft Confessions and Accusations*. London: Tavistock.

Ziervogel, D. 1954. *The Eastern Sotho*. Pretoria: Van Schaik.

FRANCIS NYAMNJOH
The Convert
Act One, Scene III & Act Two, Scene III

Reference
Francis B. Nyamnjoh, *The Convert, A Two-Act Play*
Gaborone: Mmegi Publishing House, 2003, pp. 11–17 and 29

From the introduction by David Kerr

This play tackles the theatrically attractive but ethically complex issue of Christian fundamentalism … the play revolves around the Ultimate Church of Christ and the four main characters affected by it. The audience is given a deftly sketched picture of a corrupt world beyond it, lacking in spiritual or community values. We see the corruption in the hopeless task the girl Charity has 'chasing files in an ocean of shacks in the Ministry of Money'. It is also hinted in the difficulty Damien faces trying to climb the educational ladder, seeking 'spillovers of sexually transmitted marks'. More widely, we feel the anomie which haunts the lives of young people, so many of whom are totally disillusioned with life that police have to guard the city lake from suicide attempts.

In this context it is hardly surprising that young people like Charity, and eventually Peter, find a sense of solidarity, self-esteem and community identity in the fellowship of born-again Christianity. Nyamnjoh presents this process in a subtle manner. The characterization, for example, is remarkable for its avoidance of any obvious protagonist; the audience is allowed no clear character with whom to identify. The four main characters, Pastor, Damien, Charity and Peter have both virtues and flaws, each providing insights into ways the consumer-oriented materialism of modern life impacts upon African spirituality and community values.

Act One Scene III

(*Once more members of the Ultimate Church of Christ have congregated in their hall of worship. With them are many new people who have come to be born again or simply to satisfy their curiosity. Those to be born again are vomiting their transgressions and dedicating themselves to Jesus. There is the Pastor and the Chorus. Also present are Charity (dressed completely in white) and Damien. During the Altar Call some come forward and confess their sins. With every song, there is spontaneous dancing and clapping of hands in accompaniment.*)

Pastor: We have heard sad stories of hell; our sinful brothers and sisters have confessed their world is the devil's lair. Let's beseech Christ's intercession. Let's bar for them the gates of hell and lead them up the narrow path; that they may benefit from the salvation that is ours.

Chorus: The way to hell is broad and tarred; to its right is the narrow path rough with stones and tough to climb. Let's be governed by our faith. Let's kill the desires of the flesh. Let's be well and truly born again. (*Singing*) 'I have a reason to praise the Lord...'

Pastor: It's truly, truly sad to think how deep in evil they've sunk; using Christ to promote Satan. Which is a hideous crime sponsored by churches we know only too well; churches that claim to be as old as our Saviour. Join us to smile in triumph like Christ who bravely conquered Satan as did David to Goliath.

Chorus: Let's fight on, as did David; let's swing his sling to bring down the Anti-Christs who blaspheme our Lord in public and in private.

Pastor: The mass defections say it all, that the flock has found in us the true torchbearers of eternal life. We must not relent the fight to oust evil and crush its life essence.

Chorus: Let's keep our doors open; for day and night in thousands they come to ask, seek and knock; that from evil we may deliver their souls – souls for long imprisoned by churches that claim to be of Christ.

Pastor: We've heard them confess one and all; they've renounced Satan without fear and have promised to heed God's call. Does one of us have any testimony to make that shows we were sinners just as well, long before we discovered Christ and the joy of being born again in Him?

(*Charity puts up her hand first, and the coordinator asks her to come forward and tell her tale*)

Charity: Before I knew Christ three years back, I was the biggest sinner-girl in town.

Chorus: Alleluia. Praise the Lord.

Charity: I liked MCing parties, what every girl loves doing. I cherished going out with handsome guys for pride's sake, to challenge my friends, to prove that I was tough. I was very popular, attracting pot-bellied men with big wallets and flashy cars, torturing them and then sending them back to tell the story of their disgrace by a woman of substance.

Chorus: Alleluia. Praise the Lord.

Charity: I abused my flesh in every way as I thought myself queen of the world. I smoked cannabis, downed beer, took strong drinks, visited medicine men and adorned myself with charms and amulets; I bought the latest dresses in fashion and chased after men to make money. As the most famous girl in town, I drove in the latest cars – Mercedes, BMW, Pajero, Hyundai, you name them. I frequented the best chicken-parlours and sampled the thickest wallets in hotels of exceeding comfort. Nothing ever pricked my conscience that what I did was at all wrong. For I was always in time to confess my sins on Saturday in preparation for Sunday mass, where I was a permanent and privileged communicant. For I knew the priests with some of whom I smiled deep.

Chorus: The devil at work. What a devious creature.

Charity: Then, most suddenly, most unexpectedly, I began to reap what I sowed: my beauty began to wilt. I had used bleaching creams without knowing of their ugly and harmful side effects. I had hopped into bed with Tom, Dick and Harry, paying scant attention to the ills of lust. Fear took hold of me. But that was just the beginning. I failed my finals in college and my parents died of grief. My *sugar daddies* fled when my beauty retired. For a year or two I was drained by pain, humbled by hunger and mastered by fear. But then came a glimmer of hope from an angle I least expected.

Chorus: Alleluia. Praise the Lord.

Charity: Jesus Christ offered me his bosom and tendered me the key to his heavenly mansion. I seized it with vigour and joy; for I thought I was lost, but I had been found. May the Lord be praised.

Chorus: Alleluia. Praise the Lord.

Charity: Today I know better.

Chorus: Alleluia. Praise the Lord.

Charity: I know that Knowing married men, mining devious wallets or fornicating with soutanes, is ba-aaaddd. Having pre-marital sex is unthink-aaable. Nature tells you this is wrrrong. To be a sex hungry youth is to offend your God. That I know thanks to Jesus.

Chorus: Jesus is great. Praise the Lord.

Charity: Today I have discovered the Ultimate Church of Christ and taken my distance from peddlers of sin. I'm freed at last of the hypocrisy of the past. The church that used to be mine, I know no more. For, by condoning sin, it made Godliness look like something abstract, an illusion!

Chorus: Alleluia. Praise the Lord.

Charity: Go up to the mountains, do not remain in the plains or you'll be consumed. Praise the Lord.

Chorus: Alleluia. Amen.

Charity: And today I can proudly say to every tempting lecher: 'Heh! Don't touch. I'm God's anointed. I'm Jesus Embassy where no devil dares. For Jesus is my champion, the only one.' Praise the Lord. (*Bounces back to her seat, thumbs up*)

Chorus: Alleluia. Praise the Lord. Christ is the Prince of Light; the Generator of hope – friend to the fallen lord of Eden. Come to Jesus and be satisfied, for neither adultery nor fornication, nor polygamy can satisfy you. Alleluia. Praise the Lord.

Pastor: (*Intones a song*) 'Amazing Grace, how sweet the sound...'

Chorus: (*Sing*) Amazing Grace, how sweet the sound
That saved a wretch like me
I once was lost but now am found
Was blind but now I see.

Pastor: We were once lost, but now are found; we were once blind, but now can see. Let's stay steadfast in our faith, let's be Christ's guerrillas on earth.

Chorus: Alleluia. Praise the Lord. (*Singing*) 'Come to Jesus and be satisfied. Amen...'

Pastor: Let's wage a holy war of words, let's use our wit to win the war, let's champion the cause of those the world rejects.

Chorus: Alleluia. Praise the Lord.

Pastor: Today's sermon is titled: *God, sex, and man*. It is especially prepared for our new brothers and sisters.

Chorus: May they see the light of God through your words.

Pastor: Let's start with the following questions: Do you know that you were specially created? Do you know that your creator loves you specially? Do you know that your sexual capacity is a sign of this love? And do you know that this gift is meant to do you good and not to destroy you?

Chorus: From sister Charity's testimony we find the answers.

Pastor: Praise the Lord. You must be guided by the Bible which we may aptly term God's Handbook of Advice against Vice. These questions are fundamental. The way to the Lord is narrow, rough and tough. We must be wary of how we lead our lives, particularly our sex lives; for it is here that we are most tempted and most victimized.

Chorus: May the good Lord disarm our lust and blunt our fantasies, so that recklessness finds no refuge in us.

Pastor: There are two important questions we should always ask ourselves whenever we want to entertain a sexual relationship: is this relationship permitted and approved by God? Does it promise eternal happiness to you, others and the world? These questions would constantly remind us that God hates fornication, adultery, homosexuality and masturbation.

Chorus: Alleluia. Praise the Lord.

Pastor: We must also avoid sinful thoughts. Matthew 5:28 says it all: *Everyone who looks at a woman lustfully has already committed adultery with her in his heart.* [NIV]

Chorus: It doesn't become us, God's anointed, to sin in any way.

Pastor: Avoid reading immoral books and magazines, stop watching immoral films. Wriggle not to *Soukous, Bikutsi, Kwasakwasa, Dombolo, Zengué*, or *Kwaito*, nor melt in the arms of *Zouk*, no matter how tempting.

Chorus: The devil finds easy prey in wriggling or melting souls.

Pastor: Keep away from illicit caresses, thirsty kisses and starving bottoms.

Chorus: In Jesus we trust. Alleluia.

Pastor: Dear brothers and sisters in Christ, kindly abstain from these vices for your own good. The Bible is very clear on the fate of those who persist in their sins. Join me to read what Revelation 21: 8 says on this:

Chorus: (*Open their Bibles and read out*) *But as for the cowardly, the* *faithless, the polluted, as for murderers, fornicators, sorcerers, idolaters, and all liars, their lot shall be in the lake that burns with fires and sulphur, which is the second death.* [NIV]

Pastor: None of us here wants to die again in this manner. We all want to inherit the Kingdom of God. But to be on our guard we should listen to I Corinthians 6: 9–10, which reminds us with the words:

Chorus: (*Open their Bibles and read out*) *Do you not know that the unrighteous will not inherit the Kingdom of God? Do not be deceived; neither the immoral, nor idolaters, nor adulterers, nor sexual perverts, nor thieves, nor the greedy, nor drunkards, nor revilers, nor robbers will inherit the Kingdom of God.* [NIV]

Pastor: But we should not despair; we should not tremble with fear. God is forgiving as long as we would listen to him. After all, has he not done so much for us already? Doesn't John 3:16 tell us all?

Chorus: *For God so loved the world that he gave his only son, that whoever believes in him should not perish but have eternal life.* [NIV]

Pastor: Though our new brothers and sisters have sinned and fallen short of God's glory, Christ would always answer when they ask, give when they seek, and open when they knock. Thus let's all strive to live in Christ for, as II Corinthians 5:17 says:

Chorus: *Therefore, if anyone is in Christ, he is a new creation; the old has passed away, behold the new has come.* [NIV]

Pastor: Stand up all, let's pray to the Almighty that he may forgive our new brothers and sisters of their sins and take them into his Kingdom.

Chorus: (*All stand and spread out their hands in prayer*). Praise the Lord. Alleluia.

Pastor: Lord God, some of us here present have sinned in our thoughts, words and deeds. We believe that Jesus died on the cross for us. We believe in him as our Saviour and Lord. Forgive our new brothers and sisters their sins and heal them of their ailments. Grant them too your fatherhood and send your Holy Spirit to live within them just as you have done for us your children. Grant us the power to follow your footsteps to eternity. We thank you for hearing our prayer and for answering it here and now. Amen.

Chorus: Alleluia. Let's sing and praise the Lord our God, let's get mad with joy, let's rush afield and bring home the lost flocks.

Pastor: Remember, brothers and sisters, the open gate at the end of the road through which each must go alone. And there, beyond, is a light we cannot see, our Father claims His own, finds happiness and rest.

Chorus: There is comfort in the thought that a Loving God Knows Best.

Pastor: (*Intones a song*) 'There is life and joy...'

Chorus: (*Sing*) There is life and joy over there... Over there... There is life and joy over there... Over there... There is life and joy over there... Over there ... Over there ... Over there.

(*Tithes and offerings*)

Pastor: Now is your time to prove to God Almighty that you appreciate the good things He has done for you. Remember, as always, that your giving is an open door to your prosperity. Keep your coins aside, and put your papers in that basket. Dip your hands right into the bottom of your pockets, and give big to the Lord who cherishes a cheerful giver. Give big, so that your effort may be used to win more souls to God the ultimate giver. (*Intones a song*) 'Give, it shall come back to you...'

Chorus: (*Sing*) 'Give, Give, Give, it shall come back to you ... Give, Give, Give, it shall come back to you ... good measure, pressed down, and shaken together, and running over, shall men give into

your bosom ... For with the same measure that ye mete withal it shall be measured to you again...'

(*Other luring songs are sung as tithes and offerings proceed. Every now and again there is an outburst of someone speaking in tongues. There is dancing and clapping as well. An elder is appointed to say a prayer for the offerings, after which the coordinator makes a few announcements and closes the session.*)

Elder: Lord God, we call upon you, to free these gifts of all evil, envy or bitterness, so that they may become harmless to our Pastor and his family whom you have elected to communion with you. In Jesus name we pray.

Chorus: Amen. We've lit a lamp and searched our souls. Not a shred of evil, envy or bitterness in them have we found.

Elder: Praise the Lord.

Chorus: Amen.

Pastor: Go home with joy and hope. Be wary and tread with care, for the devil is omnipresent. He never fails but tries again. And since we know not with the flesh, let's better avoid than overcome temptation. Live in communion with Christ till we meet again. Continue your evangelization crusade and await reward in the world hereafter; for we are not of this world.

Chorus: Christ will light our way; he will guide us away from evil, and will crush our enemies. He is our shield against Satan and his men.

Pastor: (*Intones a song*) 'Allelu, Allelu, Alleluia... '

Chorus: (*Singing*) Sing Alleluia, Sing Alleluia, Sing Alleluia ... Jesus Christ has conquered Satan... Sing Alleluia, Sing Alleluia, Sing Alleluia....

(*They all go out of the hall singing.*)

CURTAIN

Act Two Scene III

(*It is past midnight. The Pastor is in bed sleeping. From time to time he cries and talks out in his sleep.*)

Pastor: Nooooo!... Nooooooooo! ...

Pastor: Help! ... Help! ... Help! ...

Pastor: Please! ... Please! ... Please! ...

Pastor: Don't let me fall! ... Nooooooooo!

Pastor: Hold meeeee! .... Snakes! ... Snakes!... Scorpionnnnns!

Pastor: I've done nothing wrong...

Pastor: My hands are clean...

Pastor: Go away ...

Pastor: Leave me alone ...

Pastor: Nooo! ... I'm not thirsty ...

Pastor: Take the blood away...

Pastor: Don't let the dog loose...

Pastor: Noooooooooooooooooooo! ... Snakes! ... Scorpions! ... Stones!... My head! ... I'm deeeeeeeeead! (*wakes with a start, sweating profusely and shaking like a reed in a river. He rushes to the mirror holding his head like someone bleeding, but doesn't see any wound.*)

Pastor: Thank God I'm not bleeding ... What a nightmare...

Pastor: That young man dripping blood and full of hate ... what did he say his name was? ... (*Tries hard to remember but fails*)

Pastor: The air is heavy. (*Sighs.*) The devil lurks in our midst. I feel its coarse hands at work.

(*He sits on the bed for a while, his head in his hands, deep in thought. Finally, murmuring inaudible words of prayer, he gets back into bed, dejected.*)

CURTAIN

ALLEN F. ROBERTS & MARY NOOTER ROBERTS
Aura & Icon in Contemporary Senegal

Reference
Introduction from *A Saint in the City: Sufi Art of Urban Senegal*, Los Angeles: UCLA Fowler Museum of Cultural History, 2003, pp.21–41

It's so hard to be a saint in the city – Bruce Springsteen

Dakar is a boldly visual city. Images abound, despite – or perhaps because of – the fact that Senegal is a largely Muslim country. The focus of this volume is upon the visual culture of the Mourides, a Senegalese Sufi movement centered upon the life and teachings of a local saint named Sheikh Amadou Bamba – also known by the honorific 'Serigne Touba' – who lived from 1853 to 1927 (Fig. 1).[1] Mouride visual culture includes abstract acrylic paintings on canvas and other 'art' – as that term is generally understood in the West – but it comprises a far wider range of popular expression: from devotional icons to murals, advertising images to apotropaic drawings that protect and heal, cosmological architecture to idiosyncratic attire, illustrated Web sites to souvenirs for tourists.[2] Indeed, visual culture is 'an arena' in which meaning is constituted and 'images, sounds and spatial delineations are read on to [*sic*] and through one another, lending ever-accruing layers of meanings and of subjective response to each encounter' we have with them (Rogoff 2000, 28).

Of particular interest is 'the centrality of *usefulness* in [the] popular visual culture' of everyday life (Morgan 1998, 24, our emphasis) – that is, how images are instrumental to solving problems and meeting needs. We shall also consider those circumstances in which 'the visual is contested, debated and transformed as a constantly challenging place of social interaction and definition' of identity (Mirzoeff 1998, 6). Two terms, *aura* and *icon*, are points of reference for the visual dynamism of Senegal, for they allude to how sacred images convey a blessing power called *baraka* (or *barké*). As Mouride visual artists will explain through the pages to follow, *baraka* helps people to address the misfortunes, contestations, and transitions of everyday life.

Visual culture is the manifestation of *visuality* in daily life, as well as in its epiphanal moments.[3] Visuality is a specific way of looking and because of the strength of their faith, Mourides possess what Richard Davis calls a 'devotional eye' (1997, 38). Visuality is therefore a 'cultural *system*' to borrow the famous phrase of Clifford Geertz, for 'symbols … synthesize a people's ethos – the tone, character and quality of their life, its moral and aesthetic style and mood – and their world-view – the *picture* they have of the way things in sheer actuality are' (1979, 79, our emphasis). It is important to recognize that synthesizing symbols need not produce passive pictures, for as Victor Turner (1970, 22) taught, symbols can instigate action. Indeed, the agency of *baraka* available through Mouride images shapes events and practices. Such processes will be investigated here to redress a deficiency that David Freedberg has perceived in the literature of representation in which images may be described, 'but the relations between how they look and why they work are almost entirely passed over' (1989, 135).[4]

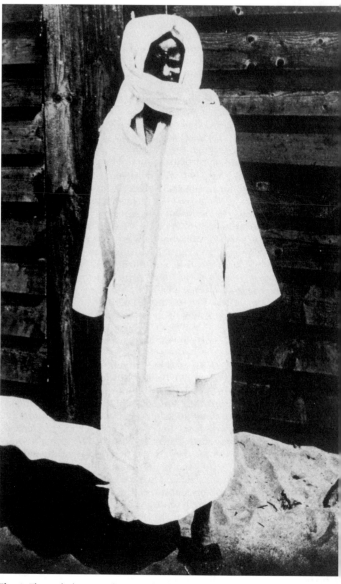

Fig. 1 The only known photograph of Sheikh Amadou Bamba was taken in 1913 by French authorities and published in a colonial compendium (Marty 1917: 222). Although the negative can no longer be found, the photo has led to an explosion of devotional imagery in recent years (Photo from a microfilm of the Marty book, in public domain)

'Mouride' is a French spelling for the Arabic term *Murid* (pl. *Muridiyya*), meaning 'disciple' or 'novice'; and Mouridism is a Sufi movement steeped in the mystical teachings of a particular saint – in this case, Sheikh Amadou Bamba.[5] As such, Mouridism shares a great deal with orthodox Islam but also differs from it in significant ways.[6] Like all religious terms, *Sufism* is difficult to define, in large part because it is so 'self-consciously esoteric' (Ernst 1997,139).[7] The word self is probably derived from the Arabic term for 'wool' with reference to the woven robes of the first generation of Muslim ascetics (B. Mbacké 1995, 91). Many Muslims around the world consider Sufism to be 'the inner dimension of Islam, and [it] has been neatly described as "the Science of the Heart"' (Netton 1992, 246) with reference to the numerology, astrology, and other intellectual pursuits its adepts have developed so highly (see Tall 1995), matched by the deep, selfless reflection that Sufism promotes. As Serigne Touba himself asserted, Sufism is 'the best of sciences in which a man can pass his entire life' (Bamba 1984, v. 628).

Sufism is a situated knowledge and localized practice, for its 'paths' (tariqa) lead to Paradise through the teachings of particular saints who lived in particular places at particular times. There are four principal Sufi Ways in Senegal: the Qadiriyya (of which Amadou Bamba was originally a member), the Tijaniyya, the Layens, and the Mourides.[9] It is estimated that there are some four million Mourides, most of whom self-identify as Wolof and speak the Wolof language. Yet as a Muslim movement, Mouridism cuts across ethnicity, and indeed, because Islam has been practiced in Senegal for so many generations, ethnicity is not as pronounced as it may be in some parts of Africa.[10]

Mouridism may have much in common with other Sufi movements in Africa (see Vikør 2000) and elsewhere in the world (Shah 1990), but it also possesses its specificity, developed over time because of local cultural and historical factors.[11] For example, Adriana Piga notes that Bamba, as 'a profound expert in popular Wolof religiosity,' may have 'consciously and wisely' stressed that Muhammad was a respected elderly man capable of resolving all controversies within the community,' so as 'to establish a rapport between Islamic values and those of Wolof social structure' (2002, 88).

Similarly, the saints around whom different Sufi orders have been created may share some characteristics, but each is different as well. The term *saint* is the most common English translation of *wali Allaha* – an 'intimate' or 'friend of God' in Arabic (Cornell 1998, xviii). Given that many English speakers will be most familiar with how the word *saint* is understood in Roman Catholicism, care must be taken to situate the word within its own philosophy, relationships, and practices, both for Sufis around the world and more specifically for Mourides of Senegal.[12]

Amadou Bamba revealed his saintly relationship to God in the first couplet of his most celebrated ode (Bamba n.d. 1, v. i):

Jaawartou bil – fourqâni rabbiyal – Mouhine.
Malaktou nafsiya wa zahzahtoul – Lahine.[13]

These are lines so enticingly rhymed that Mourides say they 'demand' to be sung, as they are by many people for hours at a time as they work and pray. The verses are Serigne Touba's affirmation that 'Thanks to the Quran, I have been able to approach my Lord. I have mastered my soul, and I have distanced the cursed one (Satan).' Such purity and proximity to God are among the factors that lead Mourides to recognize Amadou Bamba as a saint. Indeed, *Jaawartou* (the ode, or *khassaïd*, in question) is felt to possess so strong a blessing (*baraka*) that it is considered a 'Passport to Paradise'. If someone is fortunate enough to have a copy of the Saint's passport poem upon his or her person at death, surely God will lift that soul to Heaven.

Mouridism is one of the most distinctive aspects of contemporary Senegalese social life. Indeed, it would be impossible to understand how the republic's 'brisk and vigorous democracy' (NPR 1998) makes it 'a beacon of hope ... in a troubled region' (Wallis and Caswell 2000) without fully appreciating this, its most economically and politically influential Islamic movement. Mouridism links all secular and sacred

activities. Senegal also has 'a long tradition of amicable and tolerant coexistence between the Muslim majority and the Christian ... and other religious minorities' (CIR 2000; Ndiaye 2002, 606); and political scientist Leonardo Villalón (1995) holds that the country's striking stability can be directly attributed to the unusual balance of power between the Senegalese government and the Mourides and other religious orders (see also Biaya 1998). In the midst of Africa's current turmoil, Senegal peacefully elected long-time opposition candidate Abdoulaye Wade as its president. A devoted Mouride, Wade is affectionately called 'le Président de la Rue Publique' (*rue publique*, or 'public street,' is a pun on *république*). Since Mr. Wade's election, the country has taken on new significance in negotiations concerning international peace and economic recovery (Onishi 2002a).[14]

Aura and the power of images

The remarkable capacity of visual arts to *actively* instigate powerful actions and responses has been addressed by a number of scholars in recent years, among them Robert Plant Armstrong in his signal work *The Affecting Presence* (1971), Donald Cosentino in *Sacred Arts of Haitian Vodou* (1995), David Freedberg in *The Power of Images* (1989), Wyatt MacGaffey in *Power and Astonishment* (1993), and Robert Farris Thompson in *Face of the Gods* (1993). Numerous studies of Byzantine icons and related Christian works have broached similar issues, for it has long been recognized in such fields that icons possess a living presence and exercise powers over and for their beholders. Hans Belting's (1994) landmark study of the dynamic attributes of Byzantine icons is a deep investigation of the relationship between image and viewer. An interesting complement is David Morgan's incisive explanation of the active nature of Protestant imagery in contemporary American life and of how images structure devotion. As Morgan writes, 'to have an image of Christ that listens, an image that returns one's gaze or watches over one, is to have a Christ who is not simply represented by the picture, but is in some sense presented in it. Contemplation of this image is an encounter, an act of visual piety' (1998, 57). Such work exemplifies the important 'move ... from looking at cultural artifacts as reflective to perceiving them as constitutive' that has profoundly marked discourse on representation since the 1980s (Rogoff 2000, 8). Such positions will prove pertinent to understanding the processes of Mouride visual culture and the underlying visuality according to which they are produced.

Mourides state that images of Amadou Bamba and his family are active sources of potency and power (Figs 2, 4). The images offer protection, prosperity, benevolence, healing, and reversal of misfortune. It is common to see Mourides touch reproductions of Serigne Touba's photograph to their foreheads, or kiss wall murals to receive his blessing. Indeed, the Saint's image possesses powers akin to (but interestingly different from) those of Byzantine icons, Hindu 'god-pictures,' or popular images of Roman Catholic saints, for it is alive with active blessing.[15]

Mourides describe the power of images as *baraka* from the Arabic, or *barké* as the word is borrowed into Wolof, The term refers to 'benedictions' (*barakat Allah*), and is closely associated with the divine grace (*fadl*) mentioned frequently in the Quran (Chebel 1995, 67).[16] In west Africa, *baraka* 'bestows physical superabundance and prosperity, and psychological happiness' (Triaud 1988, 53), and it 'has come to designate the aura surrounding a saint, his power, his sanctuary, his miracles. his blessing. or his tomb' (Chebel 1995, 67). Whenever Mourides describe divine or mystical attributes of Amadou Bamba, they speak of his *baraka*.[17] Like many West Africans, Mourides hold that

Fig. 2 The image of Amadou Bamba informs passersby that the owner of this auto-parts shop is a Mouride while the *baraka* conveyed by the saint's image blesses them. Touba is the name of the pilgrimage city in east-central Senegal where Bamba is buried (Photo by AFR and MNR, Dakar, 1994)

Fig. 3 The artist/activist Yelimane Fall uses paintings such as this one called 'Work' and signed MF for Messenger of the Faith, to instruct urban youth about self-reliance through the teachings of Amadou Bamba. Written blessings incorporated into the work include the Basmallah and one for servants of God (Photo by Don Cole, Fowler Museum at UCLA x 99.51.6)

baraka is inherited by the direct descendants of a holy man (Brenner 1984, 69), which immediately suggests political forces and intrigues.

Baraka is a form of divine intervention available through visual imagery. As David Morgan asserts, 'the first thing to learn about the popular piety to which ... images appeal is that, for most people, it is more important to cope with an oppressive or indifferent world than to resist or subvert it. Thus, the theology of the sublime and sovereign Deity is subordinated by many believers to an apparatus of intercession' (1998, 23–24).[18] 'Sacred images can provide this very sort of "apparatus", for their 'popular iconography is thoroughly "interested", "engaged", functional, and extrinsically purposive' (Morgan 1998, 25). In other words, visual culture can help people address and resolve everyday problems.

The complexities of *baraka* are such that Clifford Geertz has argued that in Morocco, it is 'one of those resonant words that it is better to talk about than to define.'[19] *Baraka* 'encloses a whole range of linked ideas: material prosperity, physical well-being, bodily satisfaction, completion, luck, plenitude.... [and it makes] the proposition (again, of course, wholly tacit) that the sacred appears most directly in the world as an endowment – a talent and a capacity, a special ability – of particular individuals' (Geertz 1971, 33). Geertz would avoid any sense that *baraka* is like the mana of Polynesia or some sort of spiritual 'electricity,' and instead suggests that it is

> personal presence, force of character, moral vividness. Marabouts have *baraka* in the way that men have strength, courage, dignity, skill, beauty, or intelligence.... It is a gift which some men have in greater degree than others, and which ... marabouts have in superlative degree. The problem is to decide who (not only ... among the living, but also among the dead) has it, how much, and how to benefit from it. [Geertz 1971,44][20]

From Geertz's musings it is not difficult to understand why some have debated whether or not *baraka* should be translated as 'charisma,' as that concept and force is understood through Christian theology and Weberian sociology (Cruise O'Brien 1988b). As Jean-Louis Triaud (1988, 53) asserts, *baraka* shares much with charisma but differs from it insofar as *baraka* is necessarily associated with sainthood and can be conveyed to and inherited by others. In our opinion, the term *aura* comes closer to the Mouride concept of *baraka* than charisma seems to.[21]

Aura is from the Greek and means 'breeze' or 'breath' (OED 1982, 565), and *baraka* may be 'the spiritual breath that emanates from the Prophet and finally from God' of which Adriana Piga writes so eloquently (2002, 92). *Aura* is also sometimes used to refer to the inherence of power and presence within a work of art (Freedberg 1989), for 'in the auratic experience the object becomes human, as it were' (Foster 1988, 197), and possesses the capacity to produce a response, bestow well-being, and protect its viewers. Through the theorizing of Walter Benjamin and the debates his work has engendered, *aura* has also come to be associated with the 'authenticity of a thing ... [and] the essence of all that is transmissible from its beginning, ranging from its substantive duration to its testimony to the history which it has experienced' (Benjamin 1988, 221). When Benjamin wrote that 'to perceive the aura of an object we look at means to invest it with the ability to look at us in return' (1988, 188), he might have been speaking of a Mouride sense of *baraka*. Furthermore, that an object with *aura* has 'weight, opacity and substance' and 'never quite reveals its secret[s]' (Baudrillard 1983, 22–23) also echoes Mouride sentiments. Above all else, Mourides feel that *baraka*/aura does things: it works, changes, and helps.

Bamba's portrait lives in the multiplicity of images produced through countless media (Fig. 3). It is important to realize that sacred imagery for other, better-known religions can be understood and deployed in similar ways, witness how the image of the Virgin of Guadalupe adorns T-shirts, dashboards, the walls of Chicano businesses, and the very bodies of those who have themselves tattooed (see Brading 2001). The Saint's aura is maintained even when his images are handmade in series or mechanically produced as tourist art, photocopies, or Web pages. Despite their seeming alienation from the aura of images as Benjamin sought to define the concept, such portraits in such media provide an active presence through which the Saint's blessing encourages and protects his devotees.

An important nuance should be stressed here: images of the Saint are *produced* rather than *reproduced*, and they *present* rather than *represent*, for each time an artist creates an image (and many state that Bamba guides their hands as they do), an *inherence* of the Saint as experienced through his *baraka* results, to borrow a term from David Freedberg (1989). All instances are particular, even when what may seem to be the same image is produced many times by an artist. As the Mouride artist Assane Dione puts it, every time he paints the Saint's portrait he 'pierces' it further, to learn new truths. And active blessing is available because, in some sense, every portrait *is* the Saint.

The physical relationship that Mourides share with images of Amadou Bamba and the people closest to him establishes an intimate, bodily association between Mourides and the holy ones whose *baraka* they seek. As David Morgan notes, 'those who venerate the saint or Savior of popular images bring broken bodies to be mended, shattered nerves and sick children to be healed. The body of the believer is explicitly engaged' as one *beholds* a portrait of the Saint (Morgan 1998, 31). 'Behold' also implies transaction as one 'grasps' the aura of Amadou Bamba in order to use it to one's benefit. As Kay Turner has written, a sense of suffering, whether one's own or that of others, 'can impel active affiliation with the embodied Divine. After all, it is the loneliness of suffering, felt in such a real way through the body, either physically or emotionally, which creates the need for relationship to other bodies, including divine bodies' (K. Turner 1999, 118). Turner is writing specifically of the impact of sacred images upon women, and gender may influence how Mouride women and men understand and interact with images (see Coulon 1988); yet life is difficult for almost *all* Mourides, and the suffering of the Saint provides them with a means of embodying their own senses of anxiety and loss. A hagiographical 'fellowship' with images results.[22]

Social scientists might assert that human agency underlies the experience of aura. From such a perspective, one may *believe* that

Fig. 4 The holy man Serigne Modou Faye sits in his devotional sanctum graced by works by Assane Dione, one of his followers. Four sons of Amadou Bamba are depicted, their images bringing God's blessing (*baraka*) to those gathering in the tiny room to hear sermons or to seek Serigne Faye's healing (Photo by AFR and MNR, Dakar, 1999)

saints, holy places, relationships, and sacred objects possess *baraka*, but these are predispositions, intentions, and imaginings rather than 'realities'.[23] Such perspectives can bear useful fruit (e.g., Hardin and Arnoldi 1996), and we recognize that the visual culture we would understand is shaped by religious values, epistemological frameworks, and ontological premises; but for this book we choose a different path, following the call of Rowland Abiodun (1990) to put the 'African' back into 'African Art.' Based upon research conducted with Mouride guidance since 1994, our understanding is that *baraka* is divine efficacy. Such an assertion may verge on the '*baraka*-as-electricity' perspective that Geertz would eschew, yet after hearing many Mourides explain how transformative *baraka* can be, especially through the powers of writing and as directed through mystical devices of healing and protection, it is difficult not to accept such an explanation as its own frame of reference (Fig. 4). That is, regardless of whether or not those espousing a Cartesian sense of science would accept such views, we choose to present Mouride visuality as closely as we can to the manner in which we have been led to understand that many Mourides themselves would prefer to present it.

The 'visual overload' of contemporary Dakar

That Dakar is a very visual city is not surprising, for as the capital of the Republic of Senegal, its citizens participate in globalizing styles and forces as avidly as anyone elsewhere in the world (see, for example, Mustafa 2001a or Fall et al. 1998). They also experience the extraordinary 'visual overload of everyday life' that seems to typify today's world (Mirzoeff 1998, 8). Yet Senegal is an overwhelmingly Muslim country, and a question immediately presents itself. Aren't images prohibited by Islam? First hints that they are not appear as soon as one catches a taxi into Dakar from the outlying airport. In all likelihood the trunk and bumper of the cab will bear stickers depicting turbaned and robed African men, and more pictures of them will

Fig. 5 A panel from the factory mural of Pape Samb ('Papisto') near the port of Dakar depicts Amadou Bamba and his ardent follower Ibra Fall flanked by the Kaaba of Mecca, the infamous Slave House of Gorée Island, and a lion standing for the saint's courage but also as the mascot of the Senegalese national soccer team (Photo by AFR and MNR, Dakar 1999)

adhere to the dashboard and the periphery of the windshield. Some of these gentlemen have kindly demeanors, some seem stern, but the one most frequently seen can hardly be seen at all, for his face is shrouded in mysterious shadow. Recognizable by his virtual absence is Sheikh Amadou Bamba.

Written exhortations like *Begue Bamba* (Love Bamba!), *Mouridoulahi* (God bless the Mourides!), *Touba* (the sacred city where the Saint is buried), and *Dieuredieuf Serigne Touba* (Thank you, Master of Touba!) accompany the images on the cab. These provide a first glimpse of a transcolonial cosmopolitanism that is discrepant from what one encounters elsewhere in the world (cf. Clifford 1997, 36; Lionnet 2000), for it is very explicitly based upon particular forms of spirituality. The sayings are written in Roman letters rather than Arabic script, present phrases in Wolof, include Arabic loanwords, employ French orthography, and may include mystical puns. For example, Wolof linguists would write 'thank you' as *jëre-jëf*, whereas the fairly homophonous *Dieuredieuf* of the taxi bunk provides its own blessing by explicitly repeating the French word *Dieu*, or God. As the ornamented airport taxi suggests, Dakar is a city of images and texts.

To reach downtown hotels from the airport, one follows broad, anonymous avenues that suddenly plunge into urban commotion. Colorful minibuses clogging the road have so many photographs, stickers, and paintings on them that they seem like altars on wheels. Stores and workshops crowd the streets, many bearing wall paintings of Amadou Bamba, always shadowy of mien. Here, hubcaps for sale surround a huge image of the Saint, delineating the obscurity of his face (Fig. 2). There, a haunting portrait overlooks a parked car. A sign for a fastfood shop selling lamb kebabs shows Serigne Touba standing impassively beside a tethered sheep. Bread kiosks portray him too, as do plumbing and tailor and cobbler and TV repair and all manner of other small businesses and informal work shops.[24] Crossing inner-city working-class neighborhoods with evocative names like La Médina,[25] Patte d'Oie (Goose Foot), and Gueule Tapée (Smacked in the Mouth), one finds innumerable depictions of Bamba's mysterious

obscurity. Glass paintings, posters, lithographs, drawings, photocopies and portraits of him executed in many other media are likely to be found inside these same dwellings, and some are places of such visual intensity that we have dubbed them 'imagoriums' (Fig. 4).

So, who was and *is* Amadou Bamba? What is the impact of his haunting image – how does one gain the Saint's *baraka*, or blessing, from it? How can one understand the proliferation of his portrait vis-à-vis the antipathy toward imagery avowed by many Muslims, including some Mourides? How do images of the Saint provide a 'Passport to Paradise' to those who follow his righteous path? And how does his image contribute to post- or transcolonial refabulation of urban spaces in Senegal and around the world? These are among the questions to be broached here.

The life of a saint

'Islam in Africa is nearly as old as the faith itself' René Bravmann (2000, 489) reminds us, and a mere century after the Prophet Muhammad's death in 632 C.E., Islam had already been brought across the Sahara from northern Africa and was being practiced in trading towns of the Sahel.[26] Growth of the religion has been phenomenal, and by the turn of the twenty-first century, one of every eight Muslims in the world hails from sub-Saharan Africa, while one of every three sub-Saharan Africans is Muslim (Kane and Triaud 1998, 7). Yet despite these enormous numbers, sub-Saharan African Islam has not received the scholarly attention one might expect, and mainstream volumes on global Sufism (e.g., Schimmel 1975; 1994) generally ignore African contributions altogether (Bravmann 2000, 491).[27]

Muslim ideas and practices were introduced to what is now Senegal by the tenth century (Hiskett 1994, 107). Islam was important to Wolof royalist politics, and fifteenth-century European visitors 'were impressed by the role of Muslims in the courts of Wolof chiefs [and kings] as secretaries, counselors, and divines [sic]' (Levtzion 2000, 78). In the eighteenth century, Sufism was brought across the Sahara and 'impregnated Sub-Saharan Islam with new influences', spiritual technologies, and paths to divinity (Kane and Triaud 1998, 12). And in our own days, circles of Sufi learning continue to inform human movement throughout West Africa and across the Sahara to the Mediterranean.

Ocean trade has also connected Senegal to other parts of the world for many centuries. Lying at the westernmost point of the African continent, Senegal is the first sub-Saharan country encountered as one sails southward 'around the bend' from Europe. Senegal has long been a threshold between the Americas and Africa as well, and the fortifications and infamous 'Slave House' of Gorée Island lying just off Dakar provide poignant reminders of the transatlantic slave trade (Fig. 5).[28] Muslims from what is now Senegal were among the first slaves brought to the Americas. 'Literate, urban, and in some cases well traveled, the Muslims realized incomparable feats in the countries of their enslavement' (S. Diouf 1998, 1). To underscore the point, Manning Marable writes that 'faith and spirituality have always been powerful forces in the histories of people of African descent. Central to that history is Islam' (quoted in S. Diouf 1998, back cover).[29]

Over the course of the millennium that Islam has been practiced in Senegal, it seems that records and oral vestiges of earlier Wolof religion have been lost and that long ago 'even magic became the prerogative of Muslim clerics' (Levtzion 2000, 79). A fusion of Islamic and non-Islamic practices called *dyabar* (*jabar*) in Wolof is of vital importance to daily life, however, especially in healing and related performance practices. Islam in Senegal has always differed from the religion as it has been adopted and adapted elsewhere in West Africa, especially regarding the emphasis given to marabout holy men (Levtzion 2000, 77), and this factor, above all, contributes to what is distinctly different about Wolof – and, even more particularly, Mouride – visual culture.

Amadou Bamba was born in the village of Mbacké, Senegal, in 1853. His father was Mame Mor Anta Saly and his mother Mame Diarra Bousso. His own Arabicized name was Ahmed ben Muhammad ben Habib Allah, but his father named him 'Bamba' after the locale from which one of his own Quranic teachers hailed (Thiam 1999; Hamoneau 1998, 41–55). Mourides, however, often say that the first syllable of 'Bamba' is 'really' ban, the Wolof word for 'clay,' thus underscoring the primordial calling that the Saint would fulfill (Anon. 1998).

Bamba is said to have been different from other infants, for he never cried, insisted on staying in that part of his home given to prayer, and showed extreme repugnance if an activity prohibited by Islam should occur in his presence (B. Mbacké 1995, 15). His youth was marked by its 'miraculous intensity' of Quranic study, and he was soon recognized as a devout scholar, a masterful poet, as someone who 'rarely forgot anything,' and as one who 'found pleasure in perpetual physical and intellectual work... In giving to the Sheikh the wisdom of his youth, God conducted Himself as he had toward His infallible Prophets and His well-protected Allies' (B. Mbacké 1995, 17–18, 20, 32).

As he grew, Bamba 'followed the traditional peripatetic pattern of scholarship and Sufi affiliation,' David Robinson tells us, and even as 'the student gave way to the teacher,' he continued to read avidly and seek spiritual training from those more profoundly educated than he (Robinson 2000, 212). The Saint 'regarded education as the main weapon in his struggle to save the souls of the masses' (Babou 2002, 152), and he soon became known as a man of profound faith who emphasized charity, humility, piety, peaceful coexistence, and above all, the hard labor necessary to feed one's family.[30]

Late nineteenth-century Senegal was marked by political turmoil, as the centuries-old transatlantic and trans-Saharan slave trades ended and several small but influential kingdoms were brought under French colonial dominion. Serigne Touba's piety and sacralization of work proved especially apposite in the late nineteenth-century transition from a feudal political economy to colonial capitalism. 'Those who had been closely associated with the courts of the old states, the ceddo or warrior class, and those who had been the chief victims of the raids and violence of those states ... found a new framework in the Mourides and a form of Islam compatible with their own background' (Robinson 1991, 150). Sufism, with its stress upon strong bonds between taalibés (followers) and marabouts, or 'holy men,' like Bamba, provided 'an Islamic handbook to the production of charisma' and ideology, and a structure of adaptive practice in early colonial years (Cruise O'Brien 1988b, 4). People began submitting to Amadou Bamba in great numbers through a self-abnegating principle called njébbal.[31]

While some Senegalese Muslims called for holy war against the French, the Saint professed that the only jihad he would lead would be against the venality (nafs) of his own soul (Dièye 1997, 17–18).[32] Indeed, Serigne Touba was a lifelong pacifist who, as one admirer said, carried a pen, not a gun (Cruise O'Brien 1975, 54). Yet although he derided those who would engage in holy war except as 'spiritual combat' to find salvation within themselves, the French colonial administration found Bamba to be 'surreptitiously revolutionary' (Dumont 1975, 34). With prodding by colonially appointed chiefs and informers enjoying the fruits of favor (Searing 2002, 79 and passim), the Saint was sent into what would stretch to seven years of

Fig. 6 A reverse-glass painting by Mor Gueye portrays Amadou Bamba praying on the waters as he was sent into exile by French colonial authorities. The Archangel Gabriel assists the saint as fish come for blessing and angels halt the ship's progress. This miracle gives Mourides courage in difficult circumstances (photo by Don Cole, Fowler Museum at UCLA, x99.13.13)

exile (1895–1902) in the French Equatorial African colony of Gabon, followed by four years in Mauritania and long house arrest in Senegal (see Robinson 2000, 214–22).

The intention of the administrators was to diminish Bamba's prestige and bring an end to the 'intolerable' state within a state created by his avid following (see Coulon 1985). Only later would the colonial officials realize that for Senegalese Muslims, this exile echoed the Prophet's flight from Mecca (Makkah) to Medina in 622, which marked the advent of Islam. Thus it helped to confirm Bamba's status and stature as a saint. Furthermore, it was just prior to and during his exile in Gabon that Amadou Bamba performed his greatest miracles (karamat in Arabic) When he wrote of praying on the waters, calming a ravenous lion, and repeatedly escaping the cruel plots of his French captors, he proved himself a saint according to Sufi criteria (see Schimmel 1994, 128, 193); and his humility – even to the point of denying the significance of such acts – only reinforced this assessment of him, as did his own writings describing the secrets God and the Prophet had revealed to him during his tribulations (Bamba n.d.; Fig. 6).

In all naïveté, the French created a sacred martyr, for 'a combination of suspicion and antagonism towards Muslim leaders, coupled with the secular influence of the colonial state, effectively transformed Islam into a grassroots ideology of opposition to colonialism' (C. Stewart 1997, 57; fig. 26). Indeed, as David Robinson suggests, 'the French, much more than Bamba and his followers, created the resistance and the image of resistance' (1991, 150). During his last years, in fact, Serigne Touba accommodated and actively collaborated in the colonial agenda (Robinson 2000). Robinson is quick to caution, however, that Bamba or others who acted similarly should not be dismissed 'as "sell outs" according to a polarization into "resistors" and "collaborators," but rather [they] should be seen as persons who sized up their historical contexts and chose their options in rational ways' (Robinson 1997, 156). Reflecting such sentiments, Senegalese President Léopold Sédar Senghor could later laud Serigne

Touba as an 'apostle of Négritude,' and more recent political writers have considered him one of the greatest Senegalese *résistants* who, '1400 years after Muhammad (may His name be praised)/ Re-illuminates the saintly heavens!' (M. Wade 1991, 52).

Visual hagiographies in transcolonial Senegal

In *The Idea of Africa*, V. Y. Mudimbe writes that the monolithic memory of colonial life in places like Senegal is fracturing into a kaleidoscope of 'often particularist memories competing with each other' (1994, 140). This refers to the postcolonial moment, of course, informed by postmodernist challenges to master narratives, positivist assumptions, and hegemonic arrogance. Options have been opened and alternatives aired. Yet a *revolution* has not occurred in the way Thomas Kuhn (1996) sought to define that term, for most frequently, factions wish to usurp but then enjoy power and privilege rather than changing the system more fundamentally (see Doy 2000). For this reason, Françoise Lionnet (2000) has suggested that the term *trans-colonial* may be more appropriate than *postcolonial* for understanding such conflicted circumstances.

Transcolonial removes us from an ultimately false dependency upon temporal perspective. After all, what will happen after 'post-whatever?'[33] 'Trans-' speaks to both spatial and relational approaches and 'takes the form of networks among sites marked differentially by the imperial project and the colonial will to power' (Lionnet 2000, 31).[34] The term has other advantages, for it allows one to gain a sense of the constant movement of individuals and groups that characterizes contemporary life in Africa and elsewhere in the world (see Clifford 1997); it assists in developing an understanding of the inexorably shifting 'process geographies' that link different parts of the world (Appadurai 2000, 7); and it therefore helps overcome any static 'myth of continents' that hinders study of cultural dynamics (Lewis and Wigen 1995).[35] 'Transcolonialism' also facilitates the understanding that many aspects of Senegalese political economy created or en-hanced during the colonial period – as well as many tactics developed to counter colonial hegemony – continue to be useful and used in the decades after Senegalese Independence in 1960.

The image of Amadou Bamba has proven especially apt in meeting the demands of such political and expressive ferment. Though a figure of the colonial period, the Saint stands for hard work, perseverance, and both resistance and accommodation in today's circumstances of difficulty and want, bringing his promise of miraculous transformation to bear upon the most intractable problems of everyday life (see A. Roberts 1996). As factions within the African city create their ever-changing senses of themselves, memory must be reconfigured and given thrust and purpose through new 'myths' and heroes (Fig. 7).

Having passed away in 1927, Bamba's is a recent life, and his followers are still discovering new information and ways to understand Serigne Touba's lessons. Some elderly people remember seeing him, and they are much sought after by those wishing to hear stories from such proximate sources, for they gain Bamba's blessings by doing so. Indeed, following the perspectives Mourides share with Sufis the world over, one can expect that revelations and exegeses will continue as long as the Mouride movement exists (cf. Cruise O'Brien 1988a). Of particular interest here is the role that visual hagiography plays in such creative processes.[36]

Hagiography is an active process of identity formation located in conceptual space somewhere between memory and history. That is, hagiography retains origins as diffuse as memory, yet it is as purposeful and politically driven as history.[37] Hagiography causes and/or permits adherents to become swept up in a saint's biographical narrative in such a way that their own lives seem extensions of the saint's. As Edith Wyschogrod (1990) asserts, saints' lives do not merely exist, they are constructed and reconstructed endlessly, ensuring that they are forever perpetuated in a 'sacred present' (Searing 2002, 93) that is con-tinuously grafted onto the pure potentiality of a remembered past.

A single photograph of Amadou Bamba exists, taken in 1913 (Marty 1917, 222; see Fig. 1). All subsequent depictions in a great many media by a great many hands are derived from this one source. The Saint's face is so shadowed that it presents little if any trace of personality or emotion, and it is therefore nearly devoid of individ-ualistic particularity – except insofar as this very peculiarity is what is recognized as the Saint's portrait and no one else's. The image has an especially pronounced timelessness as a consequence, yet as Bogumil Jewsiewicki asserts, 'the act of looking reinserts the image in time,' bringing it to bear on the viewer's present concerns and reflections (1996, 19; see also Kratz 2002, 119).

Through the visual epistemology practiced by Mourides, the image of Amadou Bamba is both a cipher and a sign, and its pro-nounced ambiguity is conducive to the mirroring of hagiography. Mourides use the term *mirror* to refer to how they see themselves in Serigne Touba's portrait, and in the words of the artist Mor Gueye, such reflection occurs even as he himself paints the image. Similar metaphors abound in Sufism outside of Senegal, for 'the mirror (*mazhar*) of signs reflects the visible and announces the invisible,' while the speculation that Sufism encourages 'consists of polishing the mirror of the soul' (Hirt 1993, 39, 64).[38]

Visual and narrative hagiographies of Amadou Bamba, his mother Mame Diarra Bousso and his devoted promoter Sheikh Ibra 'Lamp' Fall are ongoing and draw upon a number of sources for analogies. Christianity is one, and there is reason to believe that Mame Diarra Bousso shares Marian traits. Similarly, a Mouride sense of the Saint's love merges with how Jesus is understood by Senegalese Christians. Muslims revere Jesus as a Prophet discussed at length in the Quran, of course, although their understanding of His relationship with God differs from that of Christians (see Corrigan et al. 1998). Nevertheless, the prophetic model of Jesus is available to Mourides for hagio-graphical extension to the Saint. The small minority of Senegalese Christians include the late Léopold Sédar Senghor, a hero of African independence, the first president of the Republic of Senegal, and a most vocal spokesman for international humanism. It can be assumed that he and other Senegalese Christians have provided a context of dialogue in which similarities between Christianity and Islam have been explored and developed.

Icons, iconoclasm, aniconism

Mouridism illuminates the far-reaching impact of Islam in Africa and the ways it has become intertwined with indigenous cultures for more than a millennium. An issue essential to the present study is the creative tension between universalist Islam and its local adaptations, especially with regard to the use or avoidance of visual imagery. As Clifford Geertz has put it, 'Islamization has been a two-sided process. On the one hand, it has consisted of an effort to adapt a universal, in theory standardized and essentially unchangeable, and usually well-integrated system of ritual and belief to the realities of local, even individual, moral and metaphysical perception. On the other, it has consisted of a struggle to maintain, in the face of this adaptive flexibility, the identity of Islam not just as religion in general but as the particular directives communicated by God to mankind through the preemptory prophecies of Muhammad' (Geertz 1971,14).

With this 'struggle' in mind, some scholars have proposed that universalist Islam with a capital 'I' be opposed to localized 'islams' with lower case 'i's'. Robert Launay notes how loath most Muslims would be to accept such a position and takes the more general stance that 'Islam does not exist apart from the specific beliefs and practices of diverse individuals in particular communities at precise moments in historical time' (1992, 5–6). Such a statement could just as easily be applied to Catholicism or any other multiethnic, transnational religion, of course. Further complicating an understanding of how Islam has been and is practiced in Senegal is the French colonial policy dubbed *Islam noir*, meant to define differences among African and other Muslim communities for divide-and-conquer strategic advantage (see Robinson 1997 and 2000; Triaud 2000). One may conclude that 'Islam itself is a process' that is both historically and culturally dynamic, as Louis Brenner (1997, 492) tells us, and that Mouride arts demonstrate how a culture adapts a major world religion to its own local historical circumstances and aesthetics through a 'blending of belief and ... artistic imagination' (Bravmann 2000, 489).

Differences between universalist and localized Islam are especially evident with regard to the place of imagery in everyday life (see, for example, Kirker 1992). Many Muslims – including some Mourides – believe that Islam has lacked figural traditions throughout its long history and that images are forbidden; yet Islamic art representing human subjects has flourished in many places up to and including our times. Well-known examples are illuminated manuscripts and miniature paintings from the thirteenth through the fifteenth century produced by Mogul, Persian, Ottoman, and related cultures (Binney 1973; Grabar 2002); North African lithographs and other popular arts featuring sacred subjects in wide use today (Starrett 1995); and contemporary popular paintings from Egypt that joyfully celebrate fulfillment of the pilgrimage to Mecca (Parker and Neal 1995).[39] These days too, political photographs are in constant public display, even in the strictest of contemporary Muslim states such as Iran; witness a front-page Reuters photograph from the *Los Angeles Times* of 5 June 2001 that shows men near Tehran celebrating the twelfth anniversary of the death of Ayatollah Ruhollah Khomeini in front of his towering portrait.

The Quran makes no mention of imagery at all, and any sense that images are to be shunned is based upon the 'tradition ... of the sayings and doings of the Prophet' called the Hadith (Netton 1992, 90), recorded after the death of Muhammad in 632 C.E. (Grabar 1987, 72). Oleg Grabar asserts that the 'puritanical' reaction to imagery that many have come to assume characterizes all Islam was the product of a complex history or interaction between early Muslims and the Christians and Jews in whose midst Islam arose. 'Precise historical circumstances, not ideology or some sort of mystical ethnic character, led to the Muslim attitude.... It is indeed very likely that Judaic thought and arguments played an important part in the formation of a doctrine against images' among Muslims, even as early Islam sought to define itself vis-à-vis the icon-rich Byzantine Empire (Grabar 1987, 93–4).[40]

More generally, 'a constant in the history of the arts', Grabar tells us, has been 'a typologically definable attitude that sees and understands any representation as somehow identical with that which it represents.... The peculiarity of the Muslim attitude is that it immediately interpreted this potential magical power of images as a deception, as an evil' (Grabar 1987, 95). One can nonetheless take issue with Grabar for calling this a 'Muslim' attitude because of variation within the expanse of early Islam he seeks to describe. While

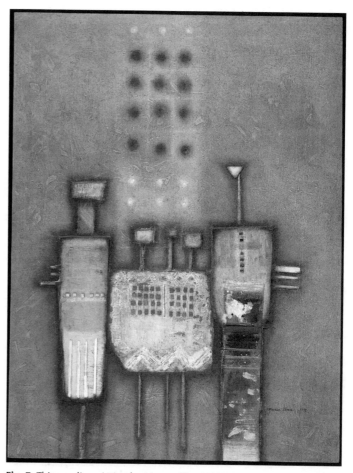

Fig. 7 This acrylic painting by Moussa Tine (1998) incorporates plywood to depict a Mouride family receiving a shaft of *baraka* blessing from on high (130 x 100.5 cm, private collection, photo by Don Cole, Fowler Museum at UCLA)

peasants considered images of vital talismanic assistance and elites often collected Christian and other images as decorative *objets d'art*, it was those of the 'literate middle' between these politico-economic extremes who provided the moralistic texts eschewing visual representation of living beings (Grabar 1987, 97).

A complementary hypothesis would be that overattention to figurative representation by Islamicist art historians has obscured full understanding of the significance of equally engaged, coeval arts. Whatever the reasons may have been for aniconic sentiments among influential early Muslims, basic human needs were ever present, and if they could not be met by images, they must have been – as they still are – met by other devices. The development of algebra, geometry, astrology, and related sciences by early Muslim scholars is, for example, justly celebrated (see Lawlor 1982), but the fact that these were *applied* as well as intellectually stimulating sciences may be overlooked. Then as now, these and other complex symbolic systems are 'technologies of enchantment' and 'enchantments of technology,' as

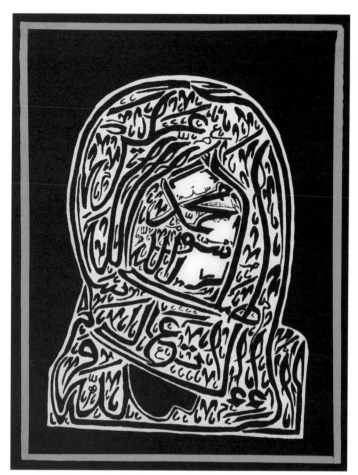

Fig. 8 Serigne Gueye, son of noted artist Mor Gueye, has created his reverse-glass painting as a calligram based upon the bust of Amadou Bamba. Following Sufi mystical principles, the saint's image is effaced to become the Word of God, suggesting proximity and blessing (Photo by Don Cole, Fowler Museum at UCLA, x99.56.30)

the late Alfred Gell (1994) had it, in that they actively challenge and perfect one's being in the world.

Given the ways that Mourides and many other Muslims 'write the body' and perceive numerical relationships even as they paint photo-realist portraits of saints, boundaries between 'realist' and 'abstract' depiction of humans may be more blurred than many have assumed.[41] (Fig. 8). Indeed, 'realism' is in the eye of the beholder, for what may appear to be photorealist portraits can be understood very differently through a Mouride visual epistemology. David Freedberg is correct in asserting that 'the will to image figuratively – and even anthropomorphically – cannot be suppressed,' even by Muslims (Freedberg 1989, 54–55).[42] The Mouride artist 'Papisto Boy' reflects something of this view when he passionately holds that 'one must not adore an image (*dessin*), as we are told in Islam; but in the case of Amadou Bamba, it is not an adoration, it is something divine, it is an obligation.'

A final point concerns the use of photography in Muslim cities from Tehran to Dakar. Whether or not photography is subject to the same restrictions that many Muslims would impose upon other forms of visual representation has been the subject of much scholarly discussion and many legal opinions in the Muslim world. As Annemarie Schimmel notes, 'the fascination with "group photos" and videos in the Islamic world seems quite unexpected in the iconoclastic atmosphere' of conservative Islam (1994, 34). However, what is not clear from the Islamic scholarship we have consulted – including that of Schimmel – is whether contemporary theories of photography (including cross-cultural work like that of Christopher Pinney [1997]) are being consulted when such assertions are made.

Conclusions: visual culture and the inscription of memory

Amadou Bamba exalted and sanctified hard work, and his image, based upon the aforementioned single photograph taken in 1913, is depicted on the walls of workshops, junkyards, homes, and businesses. An explosion of urban imagery occurred in the late 1980s, due to political agitation by young people reacting to the shortcomings of their central government. Through a movement called Set/Setal street names were changed, old monuments were removed and others created, murals were painted throughout the city; and Dakar was profoundly changed to reflect local values, hopes, and heroes. It is by no means a coincidence that this same moment gave birth to vibrant rap and hiphop in Wolof, inspired by music from the United States (Benga 2001; Mbodji 2002), nor that other subversive forms of expression emerged then and continue to develop at an ever-accelerating pace. These range from popular dance to new forms of dress and modes of adornment (Biaya 2002). Transcolonial Senegal is undergoing constant refabulation; a new cultural topography is being created through inscription of an updated imaginary.[43] Portraits of Serigne Touba have figured importantly in this vibrant collage, and the Saint has emerged as an 'alternative figure in nationalist memory' standing for and promoting both 'a rupture in postcolonial memory' and a 'new modernity' (M. Diouf, personal communication, 1995).[44]

Mourides find ways to cope and thrive in the life and lessons of the Saint, not only for activities of informal-sector economics but also for their many international export/import businesses rapidly extending around the globe. When paintings of Serigne Touba grace the outer wall of a home, business, or a sprawling inner-city junkyard, a simple site of activity is transformed into a *place*, endowed with the 'distinct potencies' of connotative significance (Casey 1987, 186).[45] Such 'places of memory' (*lieux de mémoire*) become the basis for social identity constantly negotiated with the world. While contemporary political economy may be the context for such action, it is the active impact of the image of Amadou Bamba – its aura – that articulates the dynamic nature of Mouride visual culture.

Notes

[1] There are many introductions to Islam such as Elias 1999 and Tayob 1999, to which readers may wish to turn for general information about the religion. The purpose of the present book and the exhibition that has been written to accompany it is to discuss the visual culture of a specific Muslim movement in Senegal and its diaspora, rather than to discuss Islam as a whole.

[2] 'Visual culture' as we employ the phrase follows the attempts at definition of an emerging field of inquiry different from Eurocentric 'good eye' Art History (Shohat and Stam 1998, 27), while sharing the concern that the anthropological term *culture* carries its own academic baggage (see Poole

1997, 8). Much of what we shall discuss is 'popular' culture, and that said, we further recognize that 'the concept of the "popular," as Pierre Bourdieu (1983) observed, is always ambiguous because it comes to us inscribed with the history of political and historical struggles. It is a site of contested evaluations' (Barber 1997, 3). As Néstor García Canclini would add, most dangerous of all is the tendency to commoditize collective memory as 'popular culture', for an *unequal appropriation* of cultural capital produces an 'exotic representation of the state of backwardness that industry reduces to the condition of a curiosity for the sake of tourists' (1993, 22, vii, original emphasis). For further discussion of the use of 'popular culture' as a concept to explain contemporary Senegalese expression, see Katchka 2001, 17–23.

3 Hal Foster (1988) presents the contrast between vision (the biological event of seeing) and visuality (how what one sees is interpreted, according to one's cultural particularities). Robert Nelson (2000) has assembled essays applying such perspectives to a wide range of world artistry through an equally wide range of periods – including Mouride arts in Roberts and Roberts 2000.

4 As Jeremy Coote and Anthony Shelton have concurred, 'why art objects should function as they are supposed to do, how in fact they do ... and why and how they are vehicles of meaning are questions more often ignored than asked, and more asked than answered,' in part because of the distinct marginalization of art as a subject of interest within the greater discipline of Anthropology (1994, 3).

5 Aliaa El Sandouby suggests that the term *Mouride* may be more nuanced, for 'in explaining the nature of the relationships between the *wali* and his disciples (*muridin*), the mystic philosopher Ibn Arabi uses the Quranic context to find legitimacy ... [for Sufism]. Ibn Arabi finds a divine authorization for the will (*irada*) of the *muridin* to seek His Face (*yuridun wajh-allah*), and from the verb chosen by God here: "*yuridun*" (seek, strive, yearn for) comes the word "murid." As the Quran (6:52) states, "Send not away those who call on their Lord morning and evening, seeking His Face." In this way, the asceticism of the *murid* would lead to the tangible connection with the Divine, the ultimate aspiration of seeking His Face' (Aliaa El Sandouby, personal communication, 2002). Implicit in the word *Mouride*, then, is a yearning for visualization of God.

6 The term *orthodox* is problematic because it is so perspectival, yet there is no central authority determining dogma or what is 'correct' for all Muslims. Orthodox becomes an especially politically charged term as powerful authorities seek to impose their particular visions of what is appropriate, or are accused of doing so by others who feel that they are 'right' instead. For African examples of how Sufism differs from more 'orthodox' and reformist movements, see the essays of Westerlund and Rosander (1997) and Kane and Triaud (1998). Our purpose is to present the proudly distinctive heritage of Mourides as reflected in their visual culture; we pass no judgment upon, nor do we ourselves in any way intend to participate in, debates about reform within Islam as it might be applied to Mourides or anyone else.

7 An immense literature introduces and explains the history, beliefs, and practices of worldwide Sufism, as outlined in Shah 1990, Ernst 1997, and other sources listed in our bibliography. It is instructive to note how infrequently African Sufis are mentioned in such texts, and an avowed purpose of the present research is to take a step toward rectifying such neglect. It may be noted that over the past forty years in the United States, what is sometimes called 'New Age Sufism' has departed from Islamic Sufism, especially insofar as non-Muslims may participate; see <http://usinfo.state.gov/usa/islam/pwili300.htm> offered by the U.S. State Department to enlighten citizens about Islamic practices in the United States after the tragedies of 11 September 2001. Ernst reviews both 'traditional' Islamic Sufism as practiced in the United States and Sufism understood as 'a universal spirituality beyond the limits of religion' (1997, xx). The Golden Sufi Center of Inverness, California <www.goldensufi.org>, might be described as a site of New Age Sufism. Our discussion of Senegalese Sufism may share values and other elements with American movements such as these, but in this book our interest is to understand *Mouride* visual culture on its own terms.

8 Such a definition of the word Sufi is common knowledge among Islamic

scholars, but it is significant to find that Serigne Bachir (Bassirou) Mbacké (1895–1966), who was a Mouride scholar and son of Amadou Bamba, wished to present such commonalities to his Senegalese readers. His text was completed in 1932 in Arabic, translated into French by Khadim Mbacké (a researcher at the Institut Fondamental de l'Afrique Noire in Dakar), and published in 1995. Amadou Bamba himself wrote about the precepts and practices of Sufism in his poetic work *Massalik-al-Jinan* (1984, vv. 602–61), describing Sufism as 'an individual divine obligation'; see also Hamoneau 1998, 73–88. Adriana Piga asserts that 'the authority and influence' of Sufi orders in Senegal have 'no equivalent in any sub-Saharan African nation' (2002, 34).

9 Sufi movements local to Senegal or found elsewhere in West Africa are introduced in K. Mbacké 1995, the essays of Robinson and Triaud 1997, and Vikør 2000. The Tijaniyya, a Sufi movement brought to Senegal from Morocco and Algeria, is presented in Triaud and Robinson 2000. The Qadiriyya is 'the oldest Sufi *tariqa* [order] and the one that produced all the others' and was founded by Abdel Qadir al-Jilani, who lived from 1077 to 1166 C.E. (Hamoneau 1998, 46). Layens (Laayène, from the Arabic Ilahiyyiin, 'People of God') are a Senegalese movement largely of Lebou (Lebu) ethnicity living in greater Dakar; see Piga 2002; K. Mbacké 1995; and <wwwcresp.sn/EcoYofFlEcoMusee/Siteweb/intro.htm>.

10 Important ethnic groups of western and central Senegal include FulBe (Fulani or Pulaar), Tukulor, Sérèer, Djola, Sóninke, Saraxulle (Sarakolé), and especially Wolof. One might expect more specific attention to the ethnicity of Mourides than will be found in this book, given the ethnic focus of most writing about Africa including some of our own (see Roberts and Roberts 1996); but the personal and collective identity; financial aid, and above all the ethic of Mourides helping other Mourides to create micro-businesses as they were once helped themselves fulfills some functions that ethnicity does elsewhere (see Repetti 2002). The late Tshikala Biaya (1998) provided a useful overview of the place of ethnic hybridity in Mouride politics as well as a comparison between Mouride nationalist politics and those of Luba peoples of southeastern Congo/Kinshasa whom we have also studied. On the place of Mouridism in growing Wolofization, see Piga 2002, 221–25. Boubakar Barry (1998) documents the historical coherence of the greater Senegambian region of which Mouride cosmopolitanism is a part. Thanks to Dr Wendy Wilson Fall for discussion of these points.

11 James Searing (2002, xxix) wisely calls for more comparative religious study in Africa, through juxtapositions of, say, the Mourides of Senegal with the Shembe Nazareth Church of KwaZulu Natal. Adepts consider themselves fervent Muslims and Christians, respectively, while adapting their practices to local culture and history. It would also be fruitful to compare Senegalese Sufi movements with grassroots religious movements elsewhere in the world – whether Sufi or not – to escape the spurious sense that social life occurring in one place in Africa can only be relevant to social life somewhere else in Africa. Given that Mouridism arose in circumstances of colonial oppression, what commonalities might it have with recent religious history in Bosnia, Guatemala, or inner-city Chicago?

12 Like Catholic saints, *wali Allah* arise through popular acclaim; but Islam possesses none of the hierarchy and dogma of Roman Catholicism, and so *wali Allah* are never officially sanctioned as Catholic saints are by the Vatican. Furthermore, some Islamic scholars resist the term *saint* because it has been used as the translation of words from Arabic, Farsi, Urdu, and other languages, thus absurdly reducing the complex diversity of the roles and relationships implicit in such terms (Aliaa El Sandouby, personal communication, 2002). As imperfect as saint is in Muslim contexts, the fact that so many Mourides use the French word *saint* to refer to Amadou Bamba leads to our usage in the present volume.

13 Wolof is written in Arabic as well as Roman script, and the orthography here is French, as it appears in popular tracts translated into French and published in Senegal.

14 For a discussion of Senegalese politics through the first year of Abdoulaye Wade's presidency (2000–2001), see the essays of *Le Sénégal contemporain* edited by Momar-Coumba Diop (2002), and especially those of Linda Beck, Aminata Diaw, Sheldon Cellar, and Mamadou Mbodji.

15 For a presentation and discussion of contemporary Hindu 'God pictures,'

see Larson, Pal, and Smith 1997. Useful comparison can be drawn between the ways that Mourides understand the power of images of Amadou Bamba and the ways that Hindus interact with 'God pictures' through *darśan* and being seen by a deity (see Eck 1998; Inglis 1999). For Hindus, 'icons form an important point of entry of God into the world' and 'become the point of access (and ultimately of transcendence) for human devotees' (Davis 1997, 31). Such comparisons are even more intriguing when the visual subject is a saint like Shirdi Sai Baba (c. 1842–1918), who illustrates 'how fuzzy the boundaries between Hindus and Sufis can sometimes be' in India, in that he offered both *darśan* and *baraka* and accepted Hindu *puja* offerings while dwelling in a mosque (Rigopoulos 1993, 7, 69, 82). We intend to explore such parallels and contrasts of visualities and the visual hagiographies they promote in future research and conferencing.

16 According to the *Encyclopedia of Islam* (1999), *baraka* is only used in plural (*barakat*) in the Quran and can be translated by 'beneficent force, of divine origin, which causes superabundance in the physical sphere and prosperity and happiness in the psychic order.' Naturally, the text of the Quran (*kalâmu-llâh*) is charged with *baraka*. God can implant an emanation of *baraka* in the person of his prophets and saints: Muhammad and his descendants are especially endowed therewith. These sacred personages, in their turn, may communicate the effluvia of their supernatural potential to ordinary men, either during their lifetime or after their death, the manner of transmission being greatly varied, sometimes strange. God, however, can withhold his *baraka*. Among agricultural peoples, *baraka* is recognized in cereals, causing them to multiply miraculously. *Baraka* is to be met with, here and there, attributed to the most diverse objects. Already in the Quran, 'the olive tree and the 27th Ramadan are *mubârak* .... [and] the rather obscure *tabârakalâh* (Quran 47:1) is commonly used as a prophylactic against the "evil eye."' This mainstream explanation concurs with the sense of *baraka* among Mourides more than one might expect, given the localized practices of the latter.

17 *Mysticism* is another term that is difficult to pin down because of its wide fan of usage across many different religions. It may be considered an 'interior pilgrimage' (Turner and Turner 1978, 7), in that one plumbs the depths of one's soul to find divinity. As Serigne Bassirou Mbacké (a son of the Saint) put it, 'mysticism and religious law come from the same source. The only difference between them resides in the fact that mystics attach more importance to the minute scrutiny to which they submit their souls and consciences, and to the practices aiming to assure their rectitude through reception of grace and the concentration of all interest upon God' (B. Mbacké 1995, 91). Titus Burckhardt (1995, 21–27) provides a usefully general discussion of Sufism and mysticism.

18 Morgan is writing about Protestant imagery, and especially as it is understood and used by Evangelical Protestants of the midwestern United States. That his statements addressing the visual piety of people from, say, rural communities in Iowa may be extended to facilitate an understanding of urban Sufis in Senegal is further proof that comparative and cross-cultural religious perspectives are needed to understand how visual culture 'works'.

19 Trade links and human movement have long made Morocco and Algeria sources of religious inspiration for Senegalese; Geertz's research in Morocco is of direct relevance to the present discussion as a consequence.

20 Marabout, meaning 'a holy man' (Netton 1992, 162), is a term that 'in turn derives from a root meaning to tie, bind, fasten, attach, hitch, moor. A "murabit" is thus a man tied, bound, fastened to God, like a camel to a post, a ship to a pier, a prisoner to a wall' (Geertz 1971, 43). One is reminded of the similar sense implicit in the English word *religion* based upon its Latin root *religare*, 'to bind fast' (Soukhanov 1993,1525). Eric Ross explains further nuances of *marabout*, for 'the French word is itself a corruption of a Spanish word, originally from the Arabic plural *il-murâbitún* '"people of the *ribât*"'. The *ribât* was a tenth century institution: a fortified rural outpost on the frontiers of Islam (along the Byzantine march, along Morocco's Atlantic coast – hence the city of Rabat) where young men would volunteer to 'hold the line' (Cornell 1998, 33). These outposts became the prototypes of subsequent Sufi institutions (often called *zâwiyyah* in Africa). The *ribât* also served as the prime institution for the Sanhaja religious reform movement at the origin of the Almoravid dynasty

(al-murâtitún – those of the *ribât*), whence the term passed through Castilian into French. The French first used the term in Algeria to designate both individual living Sufi sheikhs and the shrines and saints' tombs that dotted the countryside. They then exported the term to their other Muslim colonies' (Eric Ross, personal communication, 2002). For a discussion of colonial usage of the term *marabout* and the consequent hesitation some scholars have in using it, see Triaud 1997, 11–16.

21 We make this choice with trepidation because of the extensive use of the term *aura* in New Age and related practices. A brief browse of Amazon.com on 5 May 2002 produced 499 book titles that include *aura*, referring to 'righteous aura,' 'energetic wisdom,' 'how to see your aura in 60 seconds,' 'celestial perception,' 'the color of your aura.' 'psychic warriors.' 'aura-reading and subliminal persuasion,' 'aura-imaging photography,' and many more applications of the word. These engaging topics are *not* our subject here, as we consider the particular visuality of Mourides. Still, although such usage may have been what Geertz was alluding to in denying that *baraka* is spiritual 'electricity,' there may he cross-cultural similarities worthy of investigation.

22 Gaston Bachelard's consideration of a 'fellowship with objects' (1991, 157) is applied to African art and material culture in Roberts and Roberts 1997, 7.

23 It may also be that what the late Alfred Gell called 'methodological atheism' (borrowing the phrase from Peter Berger) is sometimes at play, as a 'principle that, whatever the analyst's own religious convictions, or lack of them, theistic and mystical beliefs are subjected to sociological scrutiny on the assumption that they are not [and cannot be] literally true. Only once this assumption is made do the intellectual manoeuvres characteristic of anthropological analyses of religious systems become possible' (1994, 41).

24 Much more could be said of Mouride participation in the informal economy of Senegal that 'eludes state control and regulates itself according to its own profit circulation and redistribution rules' for 'home-based, craft-type activities requiring minimal capital and low professional qualifications' (Repetti 2002, 46, 58). An excellent study by Massimo Repetti found that while over 70 percent of the population of Dakar between the ages of twenty and twenty-nine receive no wages, more than thirty thousand 'microbusinesses' produce significant income, most of which 'is immediately invested within the social network' supporting very large numbers of persons at some minimal level of subsistence (Repetti 2002, 45–46; see also Piga 2002, 401–12). See A. Roberts 1996 for a discussion of how many Mourides understand their participation in the informal sector according to models provided by the life and lessons of Amadou Bamba.

25 Eric Ross notes that while contemporary Senegalese may assume that La Médina is named for the holy city in Saudi Arabia where the Prophet is buried, a sinister Orientalist irony remains in French colonial history. 'The French started using "La Médina" in north Africa to designate the old walled cities, as opposed to their new "modern" ones. By the time they occupied Morocco they had implemented a policy of segregating the "Arab" Médina from the "*Ville Nouvelle*" for political as well as perceived health reasons (the "indigenes" ["natives"] were to live their way unperturbed in the old 'medieval' Médinas, while the Europeans and the "*évolués*" were to demonstrate the benefits of modem living in the *Villes Nouvelles*). When bubonic plague devastated Dakar in 1914 colonial administrators attempted to replicate the north African model. They created a "Médina" for the '*indigènes*' a safe distance from [what was then constructed as the "modem" city of] Dakar' (Eric Ross, personal communication, 2002).

26 The Sahel lies just south of the Sahara and extends from the Atlantic Ocean to the Red Sea. It is characterized by the arid climate, scrubby vegetation, and difficulties of human existence that are to be found, for example, in rural Arizona and New Mexico. Most of Senegal lies in the Sahel with the exception of the southwestern lands of the Casamance that begin the forested ecology of coastal West Africa.

27 Both Islam and Christianity as practised in Africa deserve more scholarly attention than they have received, for they have been ignored due to a romantic sense that they were introduced to the continent and are therefore not 'traditional' African religions. Given that the Prophet sent a party of eighty family members and followers to Ethiopia around 615 C.E. in

what is sometimes called the 'First Hegira' (Hijra) in order to avoid persecution in Mecca, one might argue that Islam *began* in Africa (see Hamoneau 1998, 27). That Islam has been observed in parts of West Africa for well over a millennium leaves one wondering how long a practice has to be in place to he considered 'indigenous' (see Ross 1994). The same could be said for Christianity, practiced in Ethiopia since the fourth century C.E. if not earlier. Robert Launay (1992) offers a usefully straightforward discussion of these matters in the introduction to his book.

28 The importance of Gorée Island and more specifically of its 'Slave House' have been debated of late; see D. Samb 1997. Regardless of how Western historical records may be interpreted, Gorée has emerged as a critically important *lieu de mémoire*, especially for African Americans seeking to visit – both physically and spiritually – the places transited by their ancestors; see Caswell 2000; Ebron 2000; and hooks 1995, 71–73. As Catherine Coquery-Vidrovitch (1999, 382–83) writes, even if Gorée never served the purposes now ascribed to it, it is evocative of places that once did. Its increasing importance to cultural pilgrims, including Western heads of state and the Pope, and its designation as a UNESCO World Heritage Site since 1978 reinforce Gorée's claim to significance (see Camara 2000).

29 Muslim contributions to early colonial life in the Americas are a subject of current study; see Gomez 1998 and 1994, and R. Turner 1997, for discussion and relevant bibliography.

30 The history and bibliography of Amadou Bamba's life are accessibly presented in Babou 2002; Barry 1998; M. Diouf 1990; Klein 1998; Piga 2002; Robinson 2002; Searing 2002; Sy 1969; and Villalón 1995. Broad but somewhat dated views are also available in such works as Cruise O'Brien 1971; Copans 1998; and Creevey 1970. Important hagiographies of Amadou Bamba include B. Mbacké 1995 and M. Wade 1991.

31 See Villalón 1995, 119–21; Piga 2002,92–100; and Cruise O'Brien 2002; however, Cheikh Anta Babou (2002, 153) suggests that 'the apparent total submission of Murid [Mouride] disciples to the will of their *shaikhs* [spiritual leaders] claimed by adherents to the Muridiyya, and conveyed by the literature appeared to be a simplification of the complex relationships between marabout and disciples.'

32 *Jihad* is 'struggle' and by no means necessarily refers to 'holy war'.

33 We are reminded of the modem supermarkets and larger 'hypermarkets' of Dakar. What will one call a store even more vast than the latter?

34 The active sense of the word *transcolonial* comes from the prefix 'trans-' that connotes 'across, on the other side, beyond'; 'through'; and 'change, transfer,' as in words such. as *transaction, transient, transfer, transitive, translate, transport, transpose,* and *transverse* (Soukhanov 1993, 1899). See Ranger 1996 for a discussion of the use of 'postcoloniality' in African studies.

35 African application of Appadurai's dynamic concept 'process geography' is presented in A. Roberts 2000. We are currently working with Africanist historian Edward Alpers to elaborate such ideas in a consideration of the Indian Ocean World linking eastern Africa with peoples of the islands and rim, all the way to India and beyond. Senegalese Mourides led by the late Serigne Adboulaye Dièye have established intercultural and ecumenical devotional groups in both Réunion and Mauritius that we intend to study in future.

36 Judging from Yahoo.com browsed on 5 May 2002, 'visual hagiography' is emerging as a useful phrase for describing a wide array of expression ranging from ancient Chinese Buddhism <www.aasianst.org/absts/1995abst/ china/csesslo6.shtm> and a twelfth–century illuminated life of Saint Cuthbert <www.utppublishing.com/detail.asp/TitleD=2116)> to the teaching of theology at Oxford University <wwwtheology.ox.ac.uk/news/openday/shtml>, photographs of Stalin <wwwutoronto.ca/scrap/reviews. html>, and the images accompanying a boxed set of John Lennon CDs <http:// popculturecorn.com/music/issues/jan99/review-johnlennon.html>.

37 Memory and the making of history in central African societies have been explicit topics of our previous research, writing, and exhibitions; see Roberts and Roberts 1996.

38 The word *sign* in these sentences is meant to carry both semiological and mystical senses, for God's will is revealed in signs – *aya* in Arabic, and a loanword in Wolof that refers to Quranic verses. See Schimmel 1994; Fal et al. 1990, 37. The term *cipher* is also intriguingly appropriate to a

description of Bamba's face, for while it may refer to a code or some similarly arcane and enigmatic system, its etymology also refers to both 'the Arabic system of numerical notation' and to 'the mathematical symbol (0) denoting absence of quantity, zero' (Soukhanov 1993, 346). Some Mourides consider the image of Amadou Bamba to be composed of numbers and therefore a source of numerical symbolism, and from a Sufi perspective, 'zero' may connote the sum of all entities rather than an absence, as in the sacred void of a mosque's *Mihrab*, for instance, where one encounters God Almighty.

39 'Hajj paintings' have been created throughout Egypt for more than a century, although they are more a rural than an urban art. The pilgrim him or herself is often portrayed in explicit detail, as are many other persons significant to Muslim history or the particularities of the Hajj (Parker and Neal 1995). The resulting murals can be quite spectacular and stand as an interesting parallel to the Senegalese arts discussed here; indeed, comparative study of popular Islamic arts such as these could be of great heuristic value.

40 Issues of Islamic iconoclasm are reviewed and an excellent bibliography provided in Flood (forthcoming). Our thanks to Dr. Z. S. Strother for providing a prepublication copy of this paper to us.

41 We have written elsewhere of how the Western tendency to collect 'realistic' figurative arts may preclude full understanding of how geometrical or other more 'abstract' arts can refer to human qualities and characteristics and even be wholly 'anthropomorphic.' See Roberts and Roberts 1996, 156, 175, and passim.

42 Perhaps the ultimate example of 'the will to image' is a 'photograph' of the Prophet Muhammad as a winsome young boy that we have seen several times in Dakar. The photo appears to be many generations removed from a drawing or perhaps a highly retouched photograph of someone, and our guess is that it comes to Senegal from north Africa as does a great deal of popular Islamic material and visual culture.

43 In 'refabulation,' old places are endowed with new meaning; see A. Roberts 1996 for related examples of Mouride culture-building. See also Repetti (1999) and Mustafa (2001b) on the creation of new topographies for the urban imaginary in Dakar; the essays and photo montages of the issue of *Revue noire* called 'Africa Urbis' (Mulin 1999) for other cases on the continent; and Spivak (1988, 4) for theoretical discussion of how the 'functional change in a sign system' such as is implied in refabulation can be 'a violent event'.

44 Writing of the 'refabulation' of Dakar and of a 'new imageric collage' in urban interstices of course implies that there have been previous constructions during the colonial period and times previous to it. Catherine Coquery-Vidrovitch (1999) discusses the imposition of a particularly French sense of *lieux de mémoire* as colonial authorities created both the city of Dakar and its 'official' ambiance through erection of monuments and creation of holidays and related events. As she says, African residents of these same places acted to create their own oppositional places and activities, in part according to models from their own cultures, in part through mimesis of colonial practice.

45 These and related ideas concerning place memory are developed and applied to central African ethnography in Roberts and Roberts 1996.

References

Abiodun, Rowland. 1990. 'The Future of African Art Studies: An African Perspective.' In *African Art Studies: The State of the Discipline* (no stated editor), 63-89. Washington, DC: National Museum of African Art, Smithsonian Institute.

Anonymous. 1998.'Le Mouridisme déborde le cadre confrérique.' *Dakar soir*, special issue (June): 3.

Appadurai, Arjun. 2000. 'Grassroots Globalization and the Research Imagination.' *Public Culture* 12, no. 1: 1–19.

Armstrong, Robert. 1971. *The Affecting Presence: An Essay in Humanistic Anthropology*. Urbana: University of Illinois Press.

Babou, Cheikh Anta. 2002. 'Brotherhood, Solidarity, Education, and Migration: The Role of the *Dahiras* among the Murid Muslim Community of New York.' *African Affairs* 101: 151–70.

Bachelard, Gaston. 1991. 'Lamplight.' In M. Jones (ed.), *Gaston Bachelard, Subversive Humanist: Texts and Readings*, 157–60. Madison: University of Wisconsin Press.

Bamba, Amadou. n.d. *Jaawartou*. Translated from Arabic to French by Papa K. Seck. Dakar: Lamp Fall Dabo.

— 1984. *Massalik-al-Jinan Huqqa-L-Bukau*. Translated from Arabic to French by Serigne Same M'Baye. Dakar: Dar el Kitab.

Barber, Karin. 1997. 'Views of the Field: Introduction.' In *Readings in African Popular Culture*, edited by Karin Barber, 1–12. Bloomington: Indiana University Press; Oxford: James Currey.

Barry, Boubakar. 1998. *Senegambia and the Atlantic Slave Trade*. New York: Cambridge University Press.

Baudrillard, Jean. 1983. *Simulations*. New York: Semiotext(e).

Belting, Hans.1994. *Likeness and Presence*. Chicago: University of Chicago Press.

Benga, Ndiouga. 2001. 'Dakar et ses tempos: Significations et enjeux de la musique urbaine moderne (c. 1960-années 1990).' In Momar-Coumba, Diop (ed.), *Le Sénégal contemporain*, Paris: Karthala.

Benjamin, Walter. 1988. *Illuminations*. Edited by Hannah Arendt. New York: Random House.

Biaya, T. K. 1998. 'Le pouvoir ethnique-concept, lieux de pouvoir et practiques contre l'Etat dans la modérnité africaine: Analyse compare des Mourides (Sénégal) et Luba (Congo-Zaire).' *Anthropologie et sociétés* 22, no. 1: 105–35.

— 2002. 'Culture du loisir et culture politique.' In Momar-Coumba, Diop (ed.), *Le Sénégal contemporain*. Paris: Karthala.

Binney, Edwin, III. 1973. 'The Arts of the Book.' In Pratapaditya Pal (ed.), *Islamic Art: The Nasli M. Heermaneck Collection*. Los Angeles: Los Angeles County Museum of Art.

Bourdieu, Pierre. 1983. 'Vous avez dit populaire?' *Actes de la Recherche en sciences sociales* 46: 98–105.

Brading, D.A. 2001. *Mexican Phoenix, Our Lady of Guadeloupe: Image and Tradition Across Five Centuries*. New York: Cambridge University Press.

Bravmann, René. 2000. 'Islamic Art and Material Culture in Africa.' In Nehemia Levtzion and Randall Pouwels (eds), *The History of Islam in Africa*. Athens, OH: Ohio University Press.

Brenner, Louis. 1984. *West African Sufi: The Religious Heritage and Spiritual Search of Cerno Bokar Saalif Taal*. London: C. Hurst & Co.

— 1997. 'Becoming Muslim in Soudan Français.' In D. Robinson and J.-L. Triaud (eds), *Le temps des marabouts*. Paris: Karthala.

Burckhardt, Titus. 1995. *Introduction to Sufism*. London: Thorsons.

Camara, Abdoulaye. 2000. 'Senegal: Institutional Aims and Objectives – The Musée historique de Gorée. In C. Ardouin and E. Arinze (eds), *Museums and History in West Africa*. Washington DC: Smithsonian Institution Press; Oxford: James Currey.

Casey, Edward. 1987. 'Place Memory.' In *Remembering, A Phenomenological Study*. Bloomington: Indiana University Press.

Caswell, Nim. 2000. 'Tourism: Seasoned Section Seeks Divinity.' *Financial Times*, 13 November: ii.

Chebel, Malek. 1995. *Dictionnaire des symboles musulmans: Rites, mystique et civilization*. Paris: Albin Michel.

CIR (Committee on International Relations, U.S. House of Representatives). 2000. 'Annual Report, International Religious Freedom 1999 in Accordance with Section 102 of the International Religious Freedom Act of 1998' (February): 69–70.

Clifford, James. 1997. *Routes: Travel and Translation in the Late Twentieth Century*. Cambridge, MA: Harvard University Press.

Coote, Jeremy, and Anthony Shelton.1994. 'Introduction.' In *Anthropology, Art, and Aesthetics*. New York: Oxford University Press.

Copans, Jean. 1980. *Les marabouts de l'arachide: La confrérie mouride et les paysans du Sénégal*. Paris: L'Harmattan.

Coquery-Vidrovitch, Catherine. 1999. 'Lieux de mémoire et occidentialisation.' In J.-P. Chrétien and J.-L. Triaud (eds), *Histoire en Afrique: Les enjeux de mémoire*. Paris: Karthala.

Cornell, Vincent. 1998. *Realm of the Saint: Power and Authority in Moroccan Sufism*. Austen: University of Texas Press.

Corrigan, John, Carlos Eire, Frederick Denny, and Martin Jaffee. 1998. *Readings in Judaism, Christianity, and Islam*. Upper Saddle River, NJ: Pre tice Hall.

Cosentino, Donald. 1995. 'Imagine Heaven.' In *Sacred Arts of Haitian Vod* edited by Donald Cosentino, 24–55. Los Angeles: UCLA Fowler Museu of Cultural History.

Coulon, Christian. 1985. 'Prophets of God or of History? Muslim Messia Movements and Anti-Colonialism in Senegal.' In W. Van Binsbergen a M. Schoffeleers (eds), *Theoretical Explorations in African Religion*. Londc Routledge and Kegan Paul.

— 1988. 'Women, Islam, and Baraka.' In D. Cruise O'Brien and C. Coul (eds), *Charisma and Brotherhood in African Islam*. Oxford: Clarendon Press

Creevey (Behrman), Lucy. 1970. *Muslim Brotherhoods and Politics in Seneg* Cambridge, Mass.: Harvard University Press.

Cruise O'Brien, Donal. 1971. *The Mourides of Senegal*. London: Oxfo University Press.

— 1975. *Saints and Politicians: Essays in the Organization of a Senegalese Peas Society*. London: Cambridge University Press.

— 1988a. 'Charisma Comes to Town: Mouride Urbanization, 1945–198 In Donal Cruise O'Brien and Christian Coulon (eds) *Charisma a Brotherhood in African Islam*. New York: Oxford University Press.

— 1988b. 'Introduction.' In *Charisma and Brotherhood in African Islam*, edit by Donal Cruise O'Brien and Christian Coulon, 1–31. New York: Oxfo University Press.

— 2002. 'Le talibé mouride: La soumission dans une confrérie religieu sénégalaise.' In D. Cruise O'Brien, M.-C. Diop, and M. Diouf (eds), *construction de l'Etat au Sénégal*. Paris: Karthala. (Translation of the Engli version originally published in 1969, with an additional note).

Davis, Richard. 1997. *Lives of Indian Images*. Princeton: Princeton Universi Press.

Dièye, Cheikh Abdoulaye. 1997. *Healing of America*. Vacoas: Mauriti Printing Specialists, Ltd.

Diop, Momar-Coumba, ed. 2002. *Le Sénégal contemporain*. Paris: Karthala.

Diouf, Mamadou. 1990. *Le Kajoor au XIXe siècle: Pouvoir ceddo et conqu coloniale*. Paris: Karthala.

Diouf, Sylviane. 1998. *Servants of Allah: African Muslims Enslaved in t Americas*. New York: New York University Press.

Doy, Gen. 2000. *Black Visual Culture*. New York: I. B. Tauris Pubs.

Dumont, Fernand. 1975. *La pensée religieuse d'Amadou Bamba*. Dakar: L Nouvelles Editions Africaines.

Ebron, Paula. 2000. 'Tourists as Pilgrims: Commercial Fashioning of Tran atlantic Politics.' *American Ethnologist* 26, no. 4: 910–32.

Eck, Diana. 1998. *Darsan: Seeing the Divine Image in India*. 3d ed. New Yor Columbia University Press.

Elias, Jamal. 1999. *Islam*. Upper Saddle River, NJ: Prentice Hall.

Encyclopedia of Islam. 1999. *Encyclopedia of Islam*. CD-ROM ed., v.1. Leiden (The Netherlands): Brill.

Ernst, Carl. 1997. *Sufism: An Essential Introduction to the Philosophy and Pract of the Mystical Tradition of Islam*. Boston, MA: Shambala.

Fal, Arame, Rosine Santos, and Jean-Léone Doneux. 1990. *Dictionnaire wolc français suivis d'un index français-wolof*. Paris: Karthala.

Fall, N'Goné, Jean-Loup Pivin, Khady Diallo, Bruno Airaud, and Patri Felix-Tchicaya. 1998. 'Oumou Sy, Sénégal.' *Revue noire* 27, theme issu 'Special mode/African Fashion': 80–85.

Foster, Hal. 1988. 'Preface.' In Hal Foster (ed.), *Vision and Visuality*. DIA A Foundation 'Discussions in Contemporary Culture' 2. Seattle: Bay Press

Freedberg, David. 1989. *The Power of Images: Studies in the History and Theory Response*. Chicago: University of Chicago Press.

García Canclini, Nestor. 1993. *Transforming Modernity: Popular Culture Mexico*. Austen: University of Texas Press.

Geertz, Clifford. 1971. *Islam Observed: Religious Development in Morocco a Indonesia*. Chicago: University of Chicago Press.

— 1979. 'Religion as a Cultural System.' In William Lessa and Evon Vo (eds), *Reader in Comparative Religion*. New York: Harper and Row.

Gell, Alfred. 1994. 'The Technology of Enchantment and the Enchantment Technology.' In J. Coote and A. Shelton (eds), *Anthropology, Art, ar Aesthetics*. New York: Oxford University Press.

Gomez, Michael. 1994. 'Muslims in Early America', *Journal of Southern Histo*

60: 671–701.

Grabar, Oleg. 1987. *The Formation of Islamic Art*. Rev. and enlarged ed. New Haven: Yale University Press.

Hamoneau, Didier. 1998. *Vie et enseignement du Cheikh Ahmadou Bamba, fondateur de la voie soufie mouride*. Beirut: Les Editions Al-Bouraq.

Hardin, Kris, and Mary Jo Arnoldi. 1996. 'Introduction: Efficacy and Objects.' In Mary Jo Arnoldi, Christraud Geary, and Kris Hardin (eds), *African Material Culture*. Bloomington: Indiana University Press.

Hirt, Jean-Michel. 1993. *Le miroir de Prophète: Psychanalyse et Islam*. Paris: Bernard Grasset.

Hiskett, Mervyn. 1994. *The Course of Islam in Africa*. Edinburgh University Press.

hooks, bell. 1995. *Art on My Mind: Visual Politics*. New York: The New Press.

Inglis, James. 1999. 'Master, Machine, and Meaning: Printed Images in Twentieth-Century India.' In Ruth Phillips and Christopher Steiner (eds), *Unpacking Culture: Art and Commodity in Colonial and Postcolonial Worlds*. Berkeley: University of California Press.

Jewsiewicki, Bogumil. 1996. 'Presentation.' *Cahiers d'études africaines* 36, no. 1–2: 7–24.

— 1999. 'Congolese Memories of Lumumba: Between Culture Hero and Humanity's Redeemer.' In *A Congo Chronicle: Patrice Lumumba in Urban Art*, 79–92. New York: Museum for African Art.

Kane, Ousmane, and Jean-Louis Triaud. 1998. 'Introduction.' In Ousmane Kane and Jean-Louis Triaud (eds), *Islam et islamismes au sud du Sahara*. Paris: Karthala.

Katchka, Kinsey. 2001. 'Putting Art in Place: Exhibiting Community and Cultural Policy in Twentieth-Century Senegal.' Ph.D. diss., Indiana University, Department of Anthropology.

Kirker, Constance. 1992. "This Is Not Your Time Here.' Islamic Fundamentalism and Art in Sudan.' *Issue: A Journal of Opinion* (U.S. African Studies Association) 22, no. 2: 5–11.

Klein, Martin. 1998. *Slavery and Colonial Rule in French West Africa*. New York: Cambridge University Press.

Kratz, Corinne. 2002. *The Ones That Are Wanted: Communication and the Politics of Representation in a Photographic Exhibition*. Berkeley: University of California Press.

Kuhn, Thomas. 1996. *The Structure of Scientific Revolutions*. 3rd ed. Chicago: University of Chicago Press.

Larson, Gerard, Pratapaditya Pal, and H. Daniel Smith. 1997. *Changing Myths and Images: Twentieth-Century Popular Art in India*. Bloomington: Indiana University Art Museum.

Launay, Robert. 1992. *Beyond the Stream: Islam and Society in a West African Town*. Berkeley: University of California Press.

Lawlor, Robert. 1982. *Sacred Geometry: Philosophy and Practice*. London: Thames and Hudson.

Levtzion, Nehemia. 2000. 'Islam in the Bilad al-Sudan to 1800.' In Nehemia Levtzion and Randall Pouwels (eds), *The History of Islam in Africa*. Athens, Ohio: Ohio University Press; Oxford: James Currey.

Lewis, Martin, and Karen Wigen. 1997. *The Myth of Continents: A Critique of Metageography*. Berkeley: University of California Press.

Lionnet, Françoise. 2000. 'Transnationalism, Postcolonialism or Trans-colonialism? Reflections on Los Angeles, Geography, and the Uses of Theory.' *Emergences* 10, no. 1: 25–35.

MacGaffey, Wyatt. 1993. *Astonishment and Power*. Washington, DC: Smithsonian Institution Press.

Marty, Paul. 1917. *Etudes sur l'Islam au Sénégal*. 2 vols. Paris: Ernest Leroux.

Mbacké, Bachir (Bassirou). 1995. *Les bienfaits de l'Eternel ou, La biographie de Cheikh Ahmadou Bamba Mbacké*. Dakar: Imprimerie Saint-Paul.

Mbacké, Khadim. 1995. *Soufisme et confréries religieuses au Sénègal*. Etudes islamiques 4. Dakar: Imp. St Paul.

Mbodji, Mamadou. 2002. 'Le Sénégal entre ruptures et mutations: Citoyennetés en construction.' In Momar-Coumba Diop (ed.), *Le Sénégal contemporain*. Paris: Karthala.

Mirzoeff, Nicholas. 1998. 'What Is Visual Culture?' In Nicholas Mirzoeff (ed.), *The Visual Culture Reader*. New York: Routledge.

Morgan, David. 1998. *Visual Piety: A History and Theory of Popular Religious Images*. Berkeley: University of California Press.

Mudimbe, V. Y. 1994. *The Idea of Africa*. Bloomington: Indiana University Press.

Mulin, Amédé, ed. 1999. 'African Urbis.' *Revue noire 31*, special issue.

Mustafa, Hudita Nura. 2001a. 'Oumou Sy: The African Place, Dakar, Senegal.' *Nka: Journal of Contemporary African Art* 15 (winter): 44–46.

— 2001b. 'Ruins and Spectacles: Fashion and City Life in Contemporary Senegal.' *Nka: Journal of Contemporary African Art* 15 (winter): 47–53.

Ndiaye, Augustin. 2002. 'Une minorité confessionnelle dans l'Etat laïc: Point de vue d'un chrétien.' In Momar-Coumba Diop (ed.), *Le Sénégal contemporain*. Paris: Karthala.

Nelson, Robert. 2000. 'Descarte's Cow and Other Domestications of the Visual.' In Robert Nelson (ed.), *Visuality before and beyond the Renaissance*. New York: Cambridge University Press.

Netton, Ian. 1992. *A Popular Dictionary of Islam*. London: Curzon Press.

Nooter, Nancy. 1984. 'Zanzibar Doors.' *African Arts* 17, no. 4: 34–39, 96.

NPR (National Public Radio). 1998. Reporting on President Bill Clinton's visit to Senegal in April.

OED (*Oxford English Dictionary*). 1982. *The Compact Edition of the Oxford English Dictionary*. 2 vols. New York: Oxford University Press.

Onishi, Norimitsu. 2002. 'Senegalese Loner Works to Build Africa, His Way.' *New York Times* (April 10): A3.

Parker, Ann, and Avon Neal. 1995. *Hajj Paintings: Folk Art of the Great Pilgrimage*. Washington, DC: Smithsonian Institution Press.

Piga, Adriana. 2002. *Dakar et les ordres soufis: Processus socioculturels et développement urbain au Sénégal contemporain*. Paris: L'Harmattan.

Pinney, Christopher. 1997. *Camera Indica: The Social Life of Indian Photographs*. Chicago: University of Chicago Press.

Poole, Deborah. 1997. *Vision, Race, and Modernity: A Visual Economy of the Andean Image World*. Princeton: Princeton University Press.

Ranger, Terence. 1996. 'Colonial and Postcolonial Identities.' In R. Werbner and T. Ranger (eds), *Postcolonial Identities in Africa*. London: Zed Books.

Repetti, Massimo. 1999. 'Segnare la citta.' *Africa e Mediterraneo* 1: 19–21.

— 2002 'Social Relations in Lieu of Capital.' *Social Dimensions in the Economic Process* 21: 43–59.

Rigopoulos, Antonia. 1993. *The Life and Teachings of Sai Baba of Shirdi*. Albany: State University of New York Press.

Roberts, Allen. 1996. 'The Ironies of System D.' In C. Cerny and S. Sheriff (eds), *Recycled, Reseen: Folk Art from the Global Scrap Heap*. New York: Harry Abrams for The Museum of International Folk Art, Santa Fe.

— 2000. 'First Word: Is "Africa" Obsolete?' *African Arts* 33, no.1: 1, 4, 6, 8–9, 93–4.

Roberts, Mary, and Allen Roberts. 1996. *Memory, Luba Art and the Making of History*. Munich: Prestel for the Museum of African Art, New York.

— 1997. *A Sense of Wonder: African Art from the Faletti Family Collection*. Seattle: University of Washington Press for the Phoenix Art Museum.

— 2000. 'Displaying Secrets: Visual Piety in Senegal.' In R. Nelson (ed.), *Visuality before and beyond the Renaissance*. New York: Cambridge University Press.

Robinson, David. 1991. 'Beyond Resistance and Collaboration: Amadu Bamba and the Murids of Senegal.' *Journal of African Religion* 21, no. 2: 149–71.

— 1997. 'An Emerging Pattern of Cooperation between Colonial Authorities and Muslim Societies in Senegal and Mauritania.' In D. Robinson and J.-L. Triaud (eds), *Le temps des marabouts: Itinéraires et stratégies islamiques en Afrique occidentale française v. 1880–1960*. Paris: Khartala.

— 2000. *Paths of Accommodation: Muslim Societies and French Colonial Authorities in Senegal and Mauritania, 1880–1920*. Athens, OH: Ohio University Press.

Rogoff, Irit. 2000. *Terra Infirma: Geography's Visual Culture*. New York: Routledge.

Ross, Eric. 1994. 'Africa in Islam.' *International Journal of Islamic and Arabic Studies* 11, no. 2: 1–36.

Samb, Djibril, ed. 1997. 'Gorée et l'esclavage: Actes du séminaire sur "Gorée dans la traité atlantique: Mythes et réalités.' *Initiations et etudes africaines* 38. Dakar: Institut Fondamental de l'Afrique Noire (IFAN) and l'Université Cheikh Anta Diop de Dakar.

Schimmel, Annemarie. 1975. *Mystical Dimension of Islam*. Chapel Hill: University of North Carolina Press.

— 1994. *Deciphering the Signs of God: A Phenomenological Approach to Islam.* Albany: State University of New York Press.
— 1999. *My Soul Is a Woman: The Feminine in Islam.* New York: Continuum.
Searing, James. 2002. *'God Alone Is King': Islam and Emancipation in Senegal. The Wolof Kingdoms of Kajoor and Bawol,* 1859–1914. Portsmouth, NH: Heinemann; Oxford: James Currey.
Shah, Idries. 1990. *The Sufis.* New York: Anchor Books.
Shohat, Ella, and Robert Stam. 1998. 'Narrativizing Visual Culture: Towards a Polycentric Aesthetics.' In N. Mirzoeff (ed.), *The Visual Culture Reader.* New York, Routledge.
Soukhanov, Anne, ed. 1993. *The American Heritage Dictionary of the English Language.* 3d ed. Boston, MA: Houghton Mifflin.
Spivak, Gayatri. 1988. 'Subaltern Studies: Deconstructing Historiography.' In R. Guha and Gayatri Spivak (eds), *Selected Subaltern Studies.* New York: Oxford University Press.
Starrett, Gregory. 1995. 'The Political Economy of Religious Commodities in Cairo'. *American Anthropologist* 97, no. 1: 51–68.
Stewart, Charles. 1997. 'Colonial Justice and the Spread of Islam in the Early Twentieth Century.' In D. Robinson and J.-L. Triaud (eds), *Le temps des marabouts.* Paris: Karthala.
Sy, Cheikh Tidiane. 1969. *La confrérie sénégalaise des Mourides.* Paris: Présence africaine.
Tall, Cheikh Ahmad. 1995. *Niche des secrets: Recueil d'arcanes mystiques dans la tradition soufie (islamique).* 2d ed. Dakar: published by the author.
Tayob, Abdulkader. 1999. *Islam: A Short Introduction.* Oxford: Oneworld.
Thiam, Serigne Médoune. 1999. 'Qui était Khadim?' *Touba, Mensuel islamique d'informations générales, d'analyses et de réflexions* (June): 5.
Thompson, Robert Farris. 1993. *Face of the Gods: Art and Altars of Africa and the African Americas.* Munich: Prestel for the Museum for African Art, New York.
Triaud, Jean-Louis. 1988. 'Khalwa and the Career of Sainthood: An Interpretive Essay.' In *Charisma and Brotherhood in African Islam,* edited by Donal Cruise O'Brien and Christian Coulon, 53–66. New York: Oxford University Press.
— 2000. 'Islam in Africa under French Rule'. In N. Levtzion and R. Pouwels (eds), *The History of Islam in Africa.* Athens, OH: Ohio University Press; Oxford: James Currey.
— 1997. 'Introduction'. In D. Robinson and J.-L. Triaud (eds), *Le temps des marabouts.* Paris: Karthala.
Triaud, Jean-Louis and D. Robinson (eds) 2000. *La Tijâniyya – Une confrérie musulmane à la conquête de l'Afrique.* Paris: Karthala.
Turner, Kay. 'The Power of Images: Embodiment and Identification'. In *Beautiful Necessity: The Art and Meaning of Women's Altars.* London: Thames and Hudson.
Turner, Richard. 1997. *The Forest of Symbols.* Ithaca, NY: Cornell University Press.
Turner, Victor. 1970. *The Forest of Symbols.* Ithaca: NY: Cornell University Press.
Turner, Victor, and Edith Turner. 1978. *Image and Pilgrimage in Christian Culture.* New York: Columbia University Press.
Vikor, Knut. 2000. 'Sufi Brotherhoods in Africa'. In N. Levtzion and R. Pouwels (eds) *The History of Islam in Africa.* Athens, OH: Ohio University Press.
Villalón, Leonardo. 1995. *Islamic Society and State Power in Senegal: Disciplines and Citizens in Fatick.* New York: Cambridge University Press.
Wade, Madike. 1991. *Destinée du Mouridisme.* Dakar: Côté West Informatique.
Wallis, William, and Nim Casswell. 2000. 'Beacon of Hope Shines Bright in a Troubled Region', *Financial Times,* 13 November.
Westerlund, David, and Eva Rosander. 1997. *African Islam and Islam in Africa: Encounters Between Sufis and Islamists.* Athens, OH: Ohio University Press.
Wyschogrod, Edith. 1990. *Saints and Postmodernism.* Chicago: University of Chicago Press.

Section 2.E
New Figures of Success: Beyond the Modern?

Justin-Daniel Gandoulou & the *Sapeurs* of Brazzaville

In 1984 Gandoulou published his first and highly intriguing study of young African dandies – *les Sapeurs*[1] – in Paris: young Congolese from Brazzaville who came to Paris to realize their dream of dressing up in the latest style in order to impress their fellow men (and women). Especially striking is the highly ritualized character of their culture: a sequence of fixed phases, their own forms of celebration, their own language.

The first fragment is from Gandoulou's 1984 study in Paris and succinctly describes the disappointments and the endurance of a *Sapeur* trying to realize his dream in *Paname* (their code name for Paris). The other fragments are from his later 1989 study that is based on subsequent research in Brazzaville and deals with the *descente* – that is, the return – of successful *Sapeurs* to Brazzaville where they need to dazzle their countrymen.

While the phenomenon of the *Sapeurs* attracted wide interest throughout (francophone) Africa and also in France, none of Gandoulou's writings are as yet available in English. We are, therefore, particularly happy to include an English translation of these earlier texts in this reader. Gandoulou's highly imaginative and original research into this spectacular subculture merits broader attention.[2]

JUSTIN-DANIEL GANDOULOU
Between Paris and Bacongo
& Dandies in Bacongo
(trans. by Modeste Kemetia & Peter Geschiere)

Reference
Excerpt from Justin-Daniel Gandoulou, *Entre Paris et Bacongo,* 1984, Paris: Centre Pompidou

[pp. 17–18]

'…You see, when I got out of the plane at Roissy-Charles-de-Gaulle, nobody came to welcome me. Although I had never been to France before, I knew Paris very well. I even brought a subway ticket from Brazzaville. Upon arrival at Roissy, I took a taxi without asking any inquiries from anybody (because I did not want people to know that I had never been to France). In the taxi, I uttered just one phrase: *Place de la République.* I was wearing a yellowish outfit which Domy sent me right from Paris. I was not just anybody!

When we came to *Place de la République*, I immediately recognized the place since I had already seen it on the pictures my friends used to send me from Paris. On the sidewalk, there was a group of people who were all fashionably dressed. I told myself: Oh! So I am really at Paname; they are all fine. I know that when they see me they will all think that I have been living in France for a long time. Anyway, I was neither looking like a "peasant", nor like a *ngaya*.[3] I was holding nothing else apart from my travelling bag. Without stopping on the sidewalk, I went straight to the MEC. I was surprised: what a building, I said to myself. I was a bit disappointed. However, I went upstairs to meet my friend Domy. Since then, I live with him and five other guys. We manage like that all the same. In the beginning, I was sleeping on a piece of cardboard on the floor. But this lasted only for a while, for I finally found an old mattress in the street not far from the *Place de la République*. After all, the most important thing is to spend the night. Besides, I don't want to spend money carelessly. Hey! I have other preoccupations. But certainly not "to work like a Turk", day and night. That is not me. At the moment I am preparing for a trip to Brazzaville next July. Therefore, my *gamme* (collection of outfits) must be complete by then.

I have been living in MEC for one year now and I quite like it because there is some *ambiance*. But at times unbelievable things happen here...You see, at times, at 5 am, cops come up to look for someone we do not know. That is what is not good about this place. Apart from this, one feels at ease: we don't pay rent and we try to manage to pay the electricity bill. Well, the house is pretty dilapidated, maybe that is what is annoying … However, we are fine here.'

Reference

Excerpts from Justin-Daniel Gandoulou, *Dandies à Bacongo: Le culte de l'élégance dans la société congolaise contemporaine*, 1989, Paris: L'Harmattan, pp. 11–13, 69–74, 87–9, 98–101, 105–17

[pp. 11–13]

'It is a tradition, madam, we are born like this. My father was like this and my grandfather too. We can only be like them. I may even say that if we have acquired this mentality, it is because, you see, our parents and grandparents worked with the Whites. So they were...how can I say it, during the colonial period, they worked with the Whites. Well, Whites used to dress well. Therefore, they tried to imitate the Whites a little bit. When the Whites left, they continued to dress neatly, that is, in the European style. Of course, we the children have now inherited it... like father, like son. Like you, you speak French; you have never been taught French. This is because you are born in a society where French is spoken and you are bound to speak French. If I am dressed like this, it is because my father was like this. I cannot help it. It is a pretty sight, you see; we look nice like this. We must reject ugliness, you see...

'Let me point out that you French people, you smoke a lot. You smoke tobacco, and yet you do not cultivate it. But you smoke it. Why then do you smoke it, do you have it at home? You just do it, but why? It is the same thing! We come to your country, we work here and we were colonized by the French. We acquired some habits, we are obliged to be well dressed. It is a way of

expressing oneself. Jamaicans plait their hair. Congolese want to be neat, that's all...'

You know, nice feathers make a beautiful bird...'

(Extracts from a radio programme on 'Fashion-conscious youths' titled *L'Oreille en coin* on France-Inter, June 1984)

This study is a sequel to an earlier one – *Between Paris and Bacongo* [4] – which was based on a marginal aspect of African emigration in France, especially by Congolese – what may be called 'adventurous emigration'. This concerns only young men, most of them uneducated and jobless. Remember that the Adventurer is a *Sapeur* and that emigration means adventure. *Sapé* is the past participle of the verb *saper*, derived from *la Sape* which gives these people the common name of *Sapeur*. *Sape* is a slang word which means dress with the connotation of prestigious elegance and the latest fashion. For the *Sapeurs* and the Adventurers, this word refers also to '*La Société des Ambianceurs et des Personnes Élégantes*' (SAPE = Society of Merry-makers and Elegant People). *La Sape* is the facade for a particular system of values.

In other West and Central African countries as well, there are young migrants – just like the *Sapeurs* – who want to go abroad and who stand out by their refined and expressive way of dressing. However, the emigration of the Congolese *Sapeurs* is the product of a particular region and ethnic group, with popular and urban roots. Moreover, it is backed by a specific sub-culture characterized by specific socio-cultural factors. Thus, this type of emigration is at the same time specific and representative of a wider phenomenon.

The meeting of Western and Congolese cultures created a new dynamic culture which left a mark on the attitude and lifestyle of the Congolese. The latter try to identify and adapt to the new forms of behaviour and new ways of living. Apparently, they want to look like a European, or at least appropriate some of the essential and prestigious qualities which, according to him, make the latter superior.

Is the *Sapeur* phenomenon not one of the indirect consequences of this cultural shock observed since the Congolese society was opened up to the West? However, it is worth mentioning that present-day *Sapeurs* situate themselves at some distance from this cultural shock. Clearly, many things have changed in the meantime. Yet, one must note that the behaviour of these *Sapeurs* is not neutral. After all, *Sapeurs* may be young but they inherit a situation which does not depend only on them.

The question is, why does Congo, in particular, exude such a phenomenon that seems to manifest itself as typically 'Western'? This country is neither richer nor more developed than other African countries... One might suggest that it is due to the Congolese economic dependence on the former colonial power. But it is clear that all these countries depend economically on the former colonial power. One might also think that the lifestyle of these *Sapeurs* is simply the product of a process of acculturation. Undoubtedly, these are precarious assertions. It is therefore difficult to understand why specifically Congo produced such a phenomenon which, apparently, will not fade away in the foreseeable future. Indeed, the present socio-economic, socio-political and socio-cultural environment in Congo seems to favour the perpetuation of the *Sapeurs*' life-styles. But how does it have this effect? Does it operate directly or indirectly?

This study also intends to show how some people – the *Sapeurs* – in a certain situation try to achieve certain things by behaving in a rational way. Depending on their resources, their personal capacities and their present expectations, they adopt appropriate attitudes and develop corresponding strategies. They provide answers and innovate. They create a situation, rituals, etc. – in short, a sub-culture – that they have not foreseen as such themselves, which does not specifically match their intentions, and which in turn conditions them. It may thus be interesting to try and understand the internal dynamics of this group and its networks – forms of behaviour, strategies and practices of re-appropriation, diversion and transfer of original functions and meanings, or even the redefinition of meaning…

My main concern in this study is to attempt to answer a general question which is twofold. On the one hand, is it possible to understand why the *Sape* (and its sub-culture) emerged from Congo and what specific elements played a role in this? On the other hand, at the level of individuals, how do young Bacongo adapt themselves to the new culture of the *Sape* to such an extent that they desperately want to emigrate?

Readers should note that I will use the term 'Adventurer' to refer to a *Sapeur* who has emigrated; 'Parisian' for an Adventurer – initiated into *la sape* – who has come back to the country after a journey to Paris; and finally *Sapeur* for those who still want to make the trip.

[pp. 69–74]

b) La Descente-frime (The flamboyant/parading return)

Remember that the emigration to Paris as a daily preoccupation of the *Sapeur* is backed by a double objective. There is first, the initiation into the art of *La Sape* and how to build up a stock of outfits bearing the labels of 'Great Designers.' This is followed by either the *descente-frime* (the 'showing-off return') or the *descente-tentative d'intégration sociale* (the 'social-integration-attempt return'). The 'showing-off return' differs from the second one by its initiation aspect and its 'social status' dimension characterized by a kind of schizoid socio-centrism and auto-reference, since the Adventurer moves in a world of suspense, floating above an objective social reality.

When emigrating, the *Sapeur* leaves behind him his young friends. They expect him to succeed in his initiation, like other *Sapeurs* who have already made the trip before him. Moreover, before leaving for Paris, the *Sapeur* reassures his friends that they will not be disappointed. He becomes some sort of ambassador of his 'neighbourhood', especially of his circle of close friends. Therefore, he has no right to relent in his effort or to fail. Henceforth, he bears a heavy psychological responsibility which he will only get rid of the day he 'returns' – on condition that he does indeed satisfy the needs of his friends. This is why many *Sapeurs* do everything possible to stick to their adventurous plans, even when they are confronted with harsh Parisian realities. They also know that, once their fixed objective is achieved, they will be overwhelmed on their return to Brazzaville by all the ostentatious praise and celebration with which their friends will receive them – as a kind of splendid gratification. Any emigrant-to-be is aware of this:

> The Parisians (*Grands*) really bring us joy when they come back, in spite of the difficulties they face there in Paris (if there are any difficulties at all). But their ways of being, behaving and doing *la Sape* please me. They are very successful. And that is why, when I go to Paris, I must come back here and live what they enjoy when they return. I mean glory, *succès-foule*....[5]

After the initiation in Paris, the return constitutes the moment that is so much awaited by both the *Sapeur* and his friends back in Brazzaville. It is the culmination, the consecration as a *Grand*, an accomplished *Sapeur*, considering that the last verdict will be given in Brazzaville. Thus, on the eve of his return, the news of his coming spreads among his closest friends, and at times even beyond this circle.

The panegyrists come from among his closest friends and other acquaintances. Among the *Sapeurs*, such a praise-singer is called *nkélo*. The *Sapeur* contributes to this himself, for he will have sent either a letter, or a tape to his friends: 'I am coming, you won't be disappointed. *Vrai biahu gamme ya fuluka yéna*.[6] You should all come and welcome me at the Maya-Maya airport,[7] in shorts.' The *Sapeur* who is returning is well aware of his former situation which was in general a precarious one. Since his dream has come true, he must adopt attitudes which symbolize his 'success'. This is the time to affirm his individuality to the not yet initiated *Sapeurs* and also to show to the non-*Sapeurs* that he now belongs to a higher social rank and that one has to reckon with him. So there is a lot of showing off at such moments. Although he is aware of the fact that he doesn't have the assets on which objective social success can be based, he must keep up appearances, as is indicated by the following story about a *Sapeur*:

> The day after his arrival, Sadi woke up a bit late. After taking his bath, he 'dressed up to the nines'[8] and the first thing he did was to go round Bacongo: Biyoudi, Barrière, Pacha, Marché Commission, etc. There was a party that weekend (the lifting of a mourning) at the *Maison du Combattant* in Bacongo. He had succeeded in getting an invitation. This was the biggest occasion he was to attend since his return. He had to make many people talk about him; some of the guests were from among the upper ten. So Sadi had himself *sapé à la mort* (dressed to kill) – *na tiya tuanso*.[9] He waited until the majority of the guests were seated before he walked in towards the centre of the dance floor followed by his *Mazarin*[10] who was carrying his documents. He strode majestically, pretentious as he was, his arms crossed on his back, his head well perched on a straight neck; his eyes seemed to be lifted slightly as if he was observing the sky, but from time to time, he turned his head right and left as if he was following the movement of a fly. In fact he tried to give himself the allure of a respected man, a *Grand Monsieur*, who discreetly recognizes his peers while at the same time ignoring them. When he reached the centre of the floor, he stood for a while and turned 90° degrees. Then absent-mindedly, he pulled up his trousers by the belt and talking to himself said: 'Hey! Yes, I have really arrived.' Meanwhile, the *Mazarin* was waiting in a corner. Sadi walked up to him and asked him to go and fetch a girl he had just noticed in the hall: 'Young man, go and call that girl in blue. Tell her that I am from Paris and that I live there.' The young man obeyed; unfortunately, he did not return with an immediately positive result. But he made it clear that he would try again some other time. It is worth specifying that Sadi was wearing a *m'kaka wa buyeza, wa mfuba, na basse ya* Weston croco, of Bordeaux colour.[11] Then, sitting down on a chair, he crossed his legs so as to let people see his Weston pair of shoes and Pierre Cardin socks. During the twenty minutes spent at the party, he danced only once with a young lady who was sitting at the same table with them (with him and the *Mazarin*). His special and captivating way of dancing obliged other dancers to sit down and watch him dancing, some with a lot of pleasure and others with condescendence. He would stop dancing for a few seconds just to admire his shoes and wipe them with a handkerchief which he removed from his pocket like a magician. Before continuing to dance, he stopped a second time, admired his Westons and said to himself: 'Ah! Westons, *ngé té bu tudidi ga. Ntsia myéla tama kué se ko, mameh?*[12] Just before the song was ending, he sat down for a

minute and waited until everybody was seated again. Then, he stood up and left, followed by his *Mazarin*. He removed a bunch of keys from his pocket and started shaking it. In doing this, he was giving the impression that he owned a car.[13]

Back in Brazzaville, the *Sapeur*, who lives an ascetic life in Paris so as to save money for buying clothing, becomes a 'big spender'. But he must also, and more importantly, exhibit his outfits. In other words, he must valorize himself by exhibiting external signs of wealth and social success. It is through such an arsenal of signs that his chosen milieu and the rest of the population will appreciate and classify him as being among the people who have succeeded socially in life and deserve respect in society. Thus, the *Sapeur* becomes a passionate visitor of certain public places and leisure areas where prominent people usually meet. In order to re-affirm the image they want to show to society – that is, to show off – some *Sapeurs* do not hesitate to hire cars. Others prefer to hire a 41S moped (which is now popular among the Congolese youths of Brazzaville) from young *Sapeurs*-to-be or from non-*Sapeurs*. Once they are on the moped, they opt for a special position which is very characteristic of the *Sapeur*: sitting on the saddle, the legs are spread wide in an exaggerated manner and their heels are placed on the edges of the pedals. The hands holding the handlebars are well stretched out so as to push the chest in. On the head which they keep completely stiff, most of the time they wear dark *cadres*[14] resting on the nose so as to exhibit their light (pawpaw colour) complexion. For *Sapeurs* generally, a walk is still as admirable as a moped ride. This is the best way to make oneself noticed by others. And a *Sapeur* who is in *diattance* [15] on the road gives himself more rights than a bike rider, as far as their highway code is concerned. Cars give way, if they don't simply stop their engine, when the guy is showing off. Anyway, during *diattance*, he ignores everything around him, since he wants people to notice himself alone. Of course, drivers as well as pedestrians stop to admire him. And since this is what he wants, he does enjoy it.

Once they get to Paris, they immediately start thinking of returning home and some do so quite quickly. This shows the interest they attach to the 'return'. Some *Sapeurs* arrive in Paris and think of going back after six months or a year. When one has an idea of the costs of the *gamme* (stock of outfits – the least expensive varies between 15,000FF and 20,000 FF), one can hardly be surprised, given the socio-economic situation in France at present, that they have recourse to immoral or illegal means. Most of them take one to three years to prepare well for their return. All of them are obsessed with the desire to go back home and show that they have not only changed, but more importantly, that they live their life and enjoy the prestige that their new status as *Grand*, total *Sapeur* and 'Parisian' confers upon them.

As a matter of fact, the *Sapeur*'s dreams and his social imaginary circle around a twofold scene. One is the initiation journey to Paris, focused on the acquisition of a stock of outfits; the other is the return to Congo which marks the moment of apotheosis, of consecration. As to the first scene, the social imaginary breaks in contact with reality and disappears, giving way to this reality which becomes contradictory and unbearable. As to the second, in contrast, there are no obstacles; it is the scene of the glory with which the *Sapeur* is covered, provided he meets the expectations of his own milieu and a number of shameful secrets from his Parisian life are not disclosed to the people at home. Throughout his stay, he will excel in showing off, and people will talk a lot about him. This is very gratifying: 'That is true, *bia ka néti, bia mpé kazébi. Allez za bazé. Allures zé nandi.*'[16] Thus, showing off is a way to win (back) social consideration. It is true that when he is *bien*

sapé, full of *allure* and proud of himself, he will be served with respect and be duly considered whenever this is necessary. At times even, conscious and proud of his new situation, he will exaggerate. He behaves as if he wants to take his revenge because he has been denied access for so long to this kind of gratifying situation. For before he leaves Paris, he tells his peers: '*Faut nzié nab a wisa baboons.*'[17] It is therefore necessary to understand that 'the showing-off return' is the fulfilment of the initiation course of the *Sapeur*. The motto of a *Sapeur* may be 'see Paris and die', yet he cannot deprive himself of this *descente-frime*; he has to return at least once. It is only after this that he can devote himself to other social and cultural activities, and even 'free himself'. This showing-off return imposes constraints from which the Parisian cannot escape when he is going back. For example, changing one's outfits regularly or making one's presence noticeable in the social and leisure circles of the *Sapeur* is seen as indispensable; but just as crucial is that on these occasions one must have the means to offer drinks to friends. It will be clear, therefore, that 'the showing-off return' requires serious preparation, both financially and for the necessary stock of outfits. There is a striking difference here with Western habits and the way they shape everyday relationships between people; there, for instance when one invites a friend (man or woman) to go out, each one may settle his/her own bills. However, in Brazzaville, on all occasions the person who invites must systematically settle all bills. So when 'a Parisian' invites friends or takes one or several of his girl-friends out for a drink, the principle is that he settles the bills: 'it is the man who pays.' He is permanently scrutinized by his friends. And the slightest 'mistake' he makes has serious effects. People do not hesitate to make remarks like: '*Grand, m'samu ka mi tama kué gâni ko! Ngé affaires za fua. Faut vutu kué kadi kuna, mbo wa landi vutu kuiza.*'[18]

A few years ago, a billboard was put up near the Total market of Bacongo on which every day or week the names of 'Parisians' were written down who had distinguished themselves in the *Sape* and the *frime* (showing off) – in order of merit. A mark was added to each name. Thus people could follow regularly who were the best in this competition… This type of competition is organized by the circle of *Sapeurs*-to-be (who have not yet emigrated) and their sympathizers, but it has its echoes even in the circle of 'Parisians' in Paris. This again contributes significantly to the promotion of adventurous emigration. Only after spending some time exhibiting his stock of outfits, may the *Sapeur* think seriously about living a normal life in society. The 'social-integration-attempt return' which we will discuss in subsequent paragraphs, can be considered one of the possible ways out for which the *Sapeurs* hope. For it should be noted that, even if it is possible to remain a *Sapeur* for a long time, a man cannot remain 'Parisian' all his life.

[pp. 87–9]

Section 2: *Sapeurs*: Longing for the Journey

How to become a Sapeur

In most cases, *Sapeurs* are young people from a modest social background with limited economic prospects.[19] In socio-cultural respects, they do not benefit from the same advantages as other youths who come from the elite in power. These young fellows who left school often quite early and are unemployed cannot expect a helping hand from their parents who themselves often lack both financial means and the influence to impose themselves on or even bribe some civil servant in national education (in order to get their children promoted to the next class, 'buy a certificate for them' or re-integrate them into the school system after their being dismissed).[20] Concerning the job market, the same handicaps play a role, in an even more pronounced form, as a result of the economic situation of the country. The future thus appears bleak to these youths. Yet, like their comrades from less modest backgrounds, they also aspire to social success. Unfortunately, they don't have the same chance of attaining this.

While some – especially youths from a modest social background who have to look after themselves – try to imagine strategies that might grant them social recognition, others (the 'daddy's boys') have nothing to worry about. Their parents take care of their future and their social success by different means. They need not put on their father's suit to be respected in society; it suffices to bear his name and enjoy the privileges of the function and social status that go with it. When need arises, simply introducing oneself as 'the son of Mr X' draws the attention of people to you. But there is another way of gaining social consideration without uttering a word – that is, by exhibiting material means. These youngsters – at least some of them – go out in their parents' cars (in Congo, a car is still considered a sign of luxury and prestige), or ride powerful motorcycles given to them by their parents – all elements that generate social consideration in this country. When tribalism or regionalism – and the nepotism that they engender – are superimposed upon these social inequalities it makes things worse.

Finally, in view of these manifest handicaps, youths from modest social backgrounds have no other choice for attempting to gain, nonetheless, social consideration and prestige, than to try to look like members of the dominant classes of Congolese society. We will return to this later.

Table 1 Situation and place of residence of parents and place of residence of the boys interviewed

Initial letters of names	Position of parents		Place of residence of the parents	Place of residence of the boys
	Father	Mother		
NT[21]	Salaried worker	Housewife	Brazzaville	Brazzaville
B	Retired worker	Housewife	Brazzaville	Brazzaville
Y	Trader	Deceased	Brazzaville	Brazzaville
K	Farmer	Farmer	Rural area	Brazzaville
M	Deceased	Farmer	Rural area	Brazzaville
B[22]	Taxi driver	Market trader	Rural area	Brazzaville
G	Farmer	Farmer	Rural area	Brazzaville
C	Retired primary teacher	Housewife	Brazzaville	Brazzaville
NG	Deceased	Deceased	Rural area	Brazzaville
S	Trader	Market trader	Brazzaville	Brazzaville
ND	Bricklayer	Market trader	Brazzaville	Brazzaville
MB	Retired customs agent	Seamstress	Rural area	Brazzaville
K	Carpenter	Deceased	Brazzaville	Brazzaville

Thus, any game of appearances that these youths from modest social backgrounds – who want to be called *Sapeurs* – play in order to stand out in society, is in order to seek social recognition. *Sapeurs* are

not born; they are made. All depends on the social environment in which someone grows up; and also on the personality of the individual. But once one has joined the circle of *Sapeurs* with their complex system of values, you can either remain or leave. It is worth mentioning the different conditions one has to meet in order to join the *Société des Ambianceurs et de Personnes Élégantes* (SAPE). Firstly, there is the action or influence of the *Sapeur* on the non-*Sapeur* subject.[23] When a young man lives near a group of *Sapeurs* or frequently visits them, one can expect, unless he is of very strong character, that he will at least sympathize with some of their ideas before himself adopting completely the heavy burden of values of the SAPE milieu. On top of the direct influence that the environment has on him, he also exposes himself to all sorts of daily pressures: his *Sapeur* companions will regularly laugh at him, level cutting remarks, trying to make him believe that he is a non-entity, a *ngaya* (the *Sapeurs* also often say *tsukuta*). This is to make him adopt the system of values that are particular to the society of the *Sapeurs*. In fact, when he can no longer withstand his friends' mockery, he will end up by giving in to the pressure.

When we talk of influence, we are referring especially to the spontaneous admiration for the sub-culture of the *Sapeurs* – notably for their exploits and the *succès-foule* (total success) they have with the girls – among the *ngaya*.

> I have many *Sapeur* friends (both girls and boys). I got personally interested in the *Sape* because it pleased me. I used to see these *Grandes* (girls) who dressed very fashionably; they had a 'total success' with the boys (both *Sapeurs* and non-*Sapeurs*). I was wondering if I could be like them one day – that is, enjoying this pleasure of seducing people and being seduced too. All this flattered me so much that I finally put myself on to it. It is wonderful, you know…'

as a *Sapeur* girl in Bacongo told us. However, we should note that influence should not be considered a sign of passivity or a fundamental inclination of a social actor who allows himself to be manipulated. The actor is here a subject capable of pursuing his/her intentions. The non-*Sapeur* accepts being subjected to the influence of the *Sapeur* because he believes apparently that the latter has precious information at his disposition, with regard to the situation that confronts them both.

[pp.98-101]
c) Means of existence
One of the everyday problems which *Sapeurs* (migrants-to-be) face, like their 'Parisian' peers, is their lack of regular means of existence because they don't have a job. An obvious question is to what extent they can still appeal to lineage or family solidarity, as an African reality.

We have to make a distinction here. On the one hand, we have 'Intello-*Sapeurs*' (intellectuals) who, because of their level of education, have relatively good relations with their families; and, on the other, jobless *Sapeurs* who abandoned school and have relatively precarious relations with their families. It should be noted that most of them are minors[24] who generally live with their family. However, those who abandoned school, given the often precarious nature of their relations with their family, tend to lose some advantages like daily meals. Parents with modest social means may invest in the education of those of their children who appear to have a better future. This does not mean that once a child abandons school, he will no longer get any attention from his parents. As a well-known Congolese adage says '*Muna ka ba losa kâ woko.*'[25] But it is true that the majority of African parents see their children as a kind of potential

Figs 1 & 2 *Sapeur* in Paris (courtesy J. D. Gandoulou)

insurance or social security. The longer a child studies, the better (although educational failure does not necessarily mean failure in life, because there are people who succeed in life without having any diplomas). In short, the truth is that parents become less attentive to children who abandon school. So tensions may arise, since the parents refuse to supply the children's essential needs (food and some pocket money). Thus, those of the *Sapeurs* who left school early prefer to spend most of their time either with their friends who are in the same situation, so that they can try to manage together, sharing whatever food they find; or they try to manage individually, by having themselves invited by other friends whose parents still look after them; or they simply seek refuge in the houses of *Grands* [26] with whom they have good relations thanks to the small services which they render from time to time. It should be added that *Sapeurs* are generally

attentive young people and full of respect for these *Grands*. Because of this, they easily get help when they are in need. Therefore, when daily problems arise, they often get solved. Some people may despise them and call them names such as *délinquents*, but others admire them and do not hesitate to come to their aid.

As far as outfits are concerned, it should be recalled that the parents' economic situation is such that neither the educated nor those who abandoned school can expect any help for expenses for clothing. After all, outfits are very expensive. Even if parents wanted, they would not be able to help, given that a pair of Weston shoes (the cheapest) costs about 30,000FCFA (600FF) while the SMIG (minimum wage) in Congo is 23,000FCFA (470FF) a month. To the *Sapeur* this particular need to dress well is as preoccupying as food. Moreover, he must also make sure that he has some pocket money because, being *bien sapé*, he will be able to seduce girls who will be eager to go out with him, but only on condition that he will pay for everything. To overcome this, *Sapeurs* have different possibilities. They do paid jobs, especially in the informal sector. Many of them sell cigarettes. At present in Brazzaville, especially in Bacongo, there is no street without a cigarette kiosk, where sometimes also some non-perishable food (tinned food, for instance) is sold. Some of them sell local newspapers (*Mweti, Etumba, Le Stade, La Semaine*) or French magazines (*Paris-Match, Elle, Lui*) which they pick up in big hotels and from planes stationed at the airport. Others are occasional photographers during weekends (using 'polaroid' cameras), making the tour of night clubs and dance-bars. Like their peers in Paris, *Sapeurs* in Brazzaville pretend not to know that manual labour can be a source of income. But contrary to the 'Parisians', when they do it nonetheless, they go to great lengths to hide this. In Brazzaville, when a *Sapeur* carries crates at Beach (the name of the river port), he will make sure that nobody knows about it. The same thing happens when he is working at the seaport of Pointe Noire[27] or in other economic centres in Congo. They do it sporadically.

Since they know that in Paris some jobs, such as in the iron industry, painting, building, welding, etc. are relatively easy to get, they are interested in doing them in Brazzaville as apprentices, in preparation for their imminent journey to Paris, but also to survive and provide for their daily needs. As apprentices, they are not well paid, sometimes even not at all. In this case they can only depend on the odd jobs that they do without their patron knowing. Smarter guys do relatively well. Let us not forget those who experiment as taxi drivers, generally without licences despite the risk that this entails. They only travel certain routes in order to avoid the police; and this greatly reduces their daily income since they can only take their clients to certain destinations. There are also those who depend on their girlfriends who either do petty trading in the market or trade between Brazzaville, Kinshasa and the hinterland; or the girls work at hairdressers' saloons; or some go out with *Grands Messieurs* as mentioned earlier. Sometimes, as *ndengésé* (messengers), the boys may receive subventions, although as *indicateurs* (informers) for the state's intelligence services they hardly get any recompense at all. Yet, some say that many of these young men in Bacongo live from spying and denouncing. Lastly, some – but they are few – have parents who still have some means and who are willing to help out, up to a certain degree. They are also the less scrupulous ones who often refuse to economize. In need, they do not hesitate to *subtilize* (pinch) their parents' money: '...*na mana mona ample mu nzo mpé, ntsidi nkuntu nkatudi.*'[28] Such practices, condemned by society as immoral, are commonplace to *Sapeurs* who claim to find it almost moral. Thus, they use all sorts of euphemisms when they talk about such acts. For example, they say *katula* when they refer to stealing.

For unemployed *Sapeurs* in particular one can only speak, in view of the above, of living from day to day. But this kind of life is not synonymous with poverty. It is also a life style. In the hierarchy of needs, there are clear priorities; the *gamme* (stock of outfits) comes first and the rest in second position...

[pp. 105–117]

The Ritualized Party

Among the *Sapeurs*' sociability and leisure activities, the most important event remains the ritualized party, central to which is a more or less implicit challenge (to which we will come back below). The party is either an anniversary of a club or of one of its members, or a *boum*[29] on the initiative of the club or its members. Its organization and programme follow a series of norms which confer on it a ritual value.

The ritual's tests

The ritual really starts from the moment a minimal quorum is present. There are a series of well-defined factors, acts and tests on the basis of which a party and consequently its organizers are appreciated. The first test is the presentation of the stars of the day (or night) to the public by a panegyrist. This presentation is just a pretext to display outfits to the guests who in fact constitute the judges. This goes beyond the simple exhibition of outfits as a sign. It is also a test to pass in front of this cognizant audience who are also involved in this new field of signification. The second test is the degree of spontaneity and courage of the intimate *copine* (girlfriend)[30] who has to kiss the *Sapeur* publicly on the mouth (*avances za mante*), showering him with presents. He must also receive kisses and presents from other acquaintances – boys and girls alike. This is because the number of presents received counts, just as the talents of his friends in praising his *gamme* (outfits) and complimenting him also count. The *Sapeur*, on his part, must exhibit his talents for the *frime* (showing off) before and during the dance to a piece of music of his choice. The role of the *copine*[31] in this test counts as much as the outfit, for it goes without saying that a *Sapeur* must have a girlfriend. Finally, the third test is that of the general lively atmosphere of the party. As determinant as the first two tests, this one, of course, requires *savoir faire* and necessarily material means, especially financial ones, but also the ability to bring both prominent figures from the *sapeur* milieu and a sufficient number of girls to the party. These are crucial elements for prestige and success. In other words, just as the presence of numerous prominent *Sapeurs* honours the party and raises its prestige, so an abundance of girls testifies to the success of the club with the latter.

When these factors (sign elements) come together, it seems there is no reason why one cannot speak of the party in terms of success.

The sociability and leisure circuits of the *Sapeurs* – especially the scope and type of social relations that are developed – make this milieu relatively closed, entertaining a network of quite particular relations and forms of communication.

Organizing the party

Once the idea of a party is conceived after long deliberations during a meeting, the club unanimously fixes the organizational details. They also agree upon the amounts to be contributed. Then comes the appointment of the members of the organizing committee which is generally made up of a *président-directeur général (P-DG)*, a *directeur-général (DG)*, a *président-directeur de la Sape (P-DS)*, a *président-directeur d'organisation (P-DO)*, and finally a *sécrétaire général*. If the club consists of more than four members, each president has a vice-president. Each member has specific tasks, but the P-DG supervises everything because he is the *patron*. The one who contributes the highest amount is automatically appointed P-DG. If the other members are supposed to contribute, for instance, 10,000 F, he will contribute 15,000F or 20,000F. He is seconded in his responsibilities by the DG, whereas the P.-DH (or the P-DS) ensures the completeness of the *gamme* (outfit) of each member. The Secretary General takes care of the finances. The P-DG supervises, but the P-DO organizes. He is, so to say, the pivot of the whole affair. Another meeting is held to take stock once all contributions are in. Then, the P.-DG and the P-DO meet the manager of a dance-bar to discuss the material conditions of the organization and the programme of the party (renting of the hall,

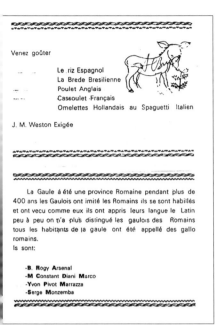

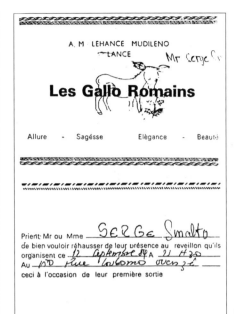

Fig. 3 Invitation card (courtesy J. D. Gandoulou)

prices of drinks, music, etc.). If the party is a *boum* or an anniversary, the price of the hall will be around 30,000F; but if it is a Christmas Eve Party, it may be 50,000F. During these negotiations, the manager of the dance-bar generally asks for a formal permit to hold the party, usually to be issued by the vice-mayor of the *arrondissement*. If this has not been obtained, the party may be interrupted by the police who are called *ngongi* by the *Sapeurs*. When both sides come to an agreement, the manager issues a receipt to the organizers as a go-ahead sign. After this, the P-DG and the P-DO look for someone from inside or outside their group who will conceive the *nkélo*[32] and the design of the invitation card before they go and see the printer. There are a number of printing presses that particularly attract them because of their reasonable prices, such as *Imprimerie Angèle* at Mpissa, *Papeterie Marie* at Bacongo, *Timbre Poity* at *Plateau des quinze ans*, etc. It is to be noted that the more bombastic the *nkélo* text is – often peppered with Italian words – the better, even if the text as a whole becomes impossible to decipher to the point that people think one needs to be a *Sapeur* to be able to read it. In fact, this abundant use of Italian phrases and labels on the card highlights how closely the *Sapeurs* try to follow the history and development of Italian fashion – Italy being seen as the cradle of *la Sape*. They certainly do not forget French phrases and labels, for Paris is notably still the global centre of *la Sape*. Concerning the dispersed use of phrases in Lari, especially at the end of the text, this signals the importance of this local language in their everyday speech, in comparison with other Congolese languages. Because, as they emphasize, the *nkélo* as a means of expression does not exist in any other Congolese language than Lari. After the invitation cards have been collected from the printer (between 100 and 150 cards), they are distributed among members of the club. Everybody takes about twenty or more, which he hands out to potential guests. Cards are not given to just anybody; generally, they make sure that the cards are given only to 'distinguished' guests, that is, eminent *Sapeurs* – *têtes d'affiche* of the milieu. This is important because the mere fact that such a personality will be attending the party gives a plus to it, making

people talk about is as a success. This is an honour for the club. Thus, it can happen that even an intimate friend or brother will not get an invitation just because he is a *ngaya* (a 'square', with no feeling for the *Sapeurs* and their taste for elegance). If it is a new club, each member will move about with a card pinned on his shirt and go to places where his peers usually come together. The aim is to let people know about the new club. In addition to cards, the party is also advertised in the *Sapeurs* milieu through a word-of-mouth publicity campaign. Between the time the party is announced and its eve, all invitees as well as the organizers are in a frenzy to get together their *gamme* (outfits) to wear. This is the period when all day long young men roam the streets of Brazzaville and Bacongo in particular, with bags in their hands, looking for a waistcoat to borrow or a pair of Weston shoes. 'I can go and see, for instance, a *Grand* and tell him: '*Mu septembre fête tu sâ donc bu fuanakané muna ntangu muna wa ku nkotesa m'kaka wa mfunda wow u niku mona na wo, wu ku toma ka.*'[33] This goes on until the young man concerned has put his *gamme* together. Generally, everybody manages quite well. They are obliged to succeed if they want to avoid disgrace by their friends. Moreover, the invitation card is often very clear on this issue.[34]

A few hours before the party starts, the organizing committee – sometimes with the help of the manager of the bar – begins to re-arrange the hall. Tables and chairs or stools are generally arranged one behind another round the dance floor – whether it is rectangular or circular – making sure that they leave out a small section of honour reserved for the stars of the party. Drinks are kept in a refrigerator behind the bar while the music system is put in a separate cabin or also behind the bar.

Enter the artists

At the appointed time, guests arrive one after another. Generally, they arrive two or three hours after the starting time indicated on the invitation card, in the company (or not) of their *copines*, in this case mostly *Sapeuses* (female *Sapeurs*). Meanwhile, the organizers, fashionably dressed as appropriate, wait impatiently in a separate room for the quorum to be attained, until it is finally time for the presentation and they can, one by one, triumphantly enter and parade before an equally impatient, but also critical and cognizant, audience. Impossible to make a premature public appearance – the trick is to create and maintain mystery and suspense. But this does not deprive the audience of the pleasure of chatting while sipping some syrup or fruit juice that is served accompanied by soft (in most cases foreign) music. At the same time, a large crowd outside, made up of curious onlookers, sympathizers of the milieu (Sapeurs-to-be), and even Sapeurs who were not invited but want to profit from the crowd to show off, besiege the entrance of the dance-bar. In order not to block the access to the hall, the crowd carefully leaves a path where guests can pass. Where dressing – réglage – is concerned, the crowd is a severe judge, even if they (apart from the Sapeurs who are also there) do not necessarily know the subculture. This means that when guests enter the path to the door, they become the objects of remarks that can be quite nasty if their outfits are not in order: 'Oh, ngé kala kuaku, za fuaza zé, pantalon na ceinture ka zi ta dia ko,'[35] but also of encouraging comments when the réglage impresses. Sometimes when the outfit is absolutely inadequate, the crowd can be so severe that someone may angrily step forward and drag a guest out of the path with an unconsciously skilful gesture and without a word, as if the victim has committed a crime. This brutal act highlights how serious the crowd of sympathizers is about the SAPE system of values. In many respects such a crowd is the breeding ground of future Sapeurs guaranteeing the reproduction of their proud Society.

Every man his strategy

While some guests, with an air of importance and a firm stride, are already moving towards the hall, others are more preoccupied with how to make themselves noticed and wait for the last moment to arrive. For anonymity should be avoided at all costs. It sometimes happens (as a young man X, whom we followed, did) that a Sapeur (that is, one who is a guest) carefully peeks from his house for the right moment. He will send his errand boy to take the temperature in the hall and among the crowd of curious onlookers. The boy has to report on the climate and on the ambiance, but also on who is dominating the scene by his Sape and allure so as to allow the Sapeur (still at home) to take the necessary precautions in order to avoid unpleasant surprises or even being humiliated. The errand boy will run to and fro between the hall and the residence of the Sapeur. Sometimes, he comes to reassure him: 'Ah Grand, bob u we, bu kué duka gana m'samu vrai gana.'[36] But sometimes, he tells him to wait; it all depends on how things will go because people are still arriving: 'No Grand, limbo kuaku, gamme za tiya zékuna mbo zi ku fua ou bien soba gamme.'[37] According to the appreciation of his scout, the Grand may change his outfit once or twice until the scout comes to reassure him. When the appreciation remains negative and the Sapeur has tried all his outfits, he has to choose between staying away or playing his last card by going to borrow another outfit from a Sapeur who was not invited to the party. In most cases, he does everything to go, for staying away is a confession of defeat – it means a lack of gamme (outfit), za fua zé, as signalled on the invitation: 'In case of absence, lack of outfit.' Determined to go, the Sapeur stands once more before the mirror to make sure that the réglage is all right. His little scout adds compliment after compliment: 'Grand, it is okay,' pointing his thumb to the sky. Then the 'count-down' begins. The Grand leaves his house and moves towards the street while the boy showers praises on him. Before setting off – the Sapeurs call it démarrage ('the take-

off') – he pulls his trousers up so that his belt reaches his navel to bring out his prominent belly and buttocks (which stand out even more thanks to 'military shorts' worn under his trousers). Then, he readjusts his shirt in his trousers at the back.[38] Finally – last gesture - shoulders forward, and feet firmly on the ground, he is then on his way. He walks elegantly, balancing his shoulders and legs in simultaneous and rhythmic movement, his feet pointed outwards - Charlie Chaplin style – so that his heels are pushed down, his face protected with dark glasses, which stand out all the more because of his fair, paw paw complexion, carefully maintained. His arrogance coupled with his walk – Sapeurs call it diattance – and his allure, draw the looks, sometimes admiring, sometimes wondering, of the people he meets on his way, but he confronts them with clearly studied indifference. Thus it happens that he can ignore his best friends under such circumstances.

When he turns up at the party, his is saluted by his supporters' applause. He then enters the hall, diagonally crossing the dance floor with his head slightly raised; pretending to be completely indifferent he does not look at anyone. Meanwhile, the other guests seem to have their eyes glued to him. At the middle of the floor, he stops for a while, looks around and takes off his maffioso glasses with one hand with the other, he takes a handkerchief from his pocket to wipe his face. Before taking his place among his peers, he puts back his glasses, taps several times with one foot on the ground and then, with his two hands, he pulls up his trousers again to his navel. Once seated with his legs crossed, carefully exposing his multicoloured Pierre Cardin socks and Weston shoes, he places his hands on his knees, starts whistling before agilely snapping his thumbs in time with the tapping of his foot. When the waiter offers a glass of fruit juice, he answers with a dignified voice accompanied by a hand gesture: 'No, thanks. That's kind of you.' No gesture is accidental. Everything is done to remind people of the personality of a respected grand Monsieur. Throughout the party, he does not stop repeating these gestures and attitudes.

Staging the spectacle

This is the long-awaited moment. The quorum is there. Then a presenter or panegyrist designated by the organizers steps forward, up to the dance floor. Generally this person will be an excellent orator and therefore not just chosen at random. The first condition is to be versed in the demanding values of the Société des Ambianceurs et de Personnes Élégantes. The speaker will order the DJ to stop the music and call the few invitees who are still outside to come in. Increasing suspense creates relative silence. After a word of introduction to thank the guests for coming, he starts the occasion formally with the presentation of stars of the show. One after one, he calls up the P-DO, the P-DG, the P-DH, the SG etc., accompanying each call by a panegyric (nkélo) in which he systematically enumerates ex professo all the items of the outfit of the person concerned including the different labels, the complexion (make-up, if it is the case), and the exploits the individual has already to his credit in the Sape. There is necessarily some exaggeration (as is also evident on the invitation cards), since the intention is to draw the guests' attention to the star of the moment and also to glorify him, so that the audience will appreciate him all the more and talk about him, and through him talk about the party. It is the same as selling an article; sometimes, the star is attributed qualities he does not have. While the panegyrist is praising the great man, the girlfriend of the latter enthusiastically comes forward and kisses him on the mouth (avances za mante), before handing him a present. Other acquaintances also come and kiss him while offering him presents and making remarks about him to add to the panegyric: 'Eh za bazé, bima *bia mupia, gamme ya tiya.*'[39] The present has a symbolic value. It is given to affirm the specific relationship between the giver and the receiver. The object itself carries no meaning apart from the relationship that it establishes.

On this subject, one can mention the *malaki* of the Bakongo described by G. Balandier[40] which links two or more groups for an ostentatious consumption of goods that sometimes leads to wastage. The author specifies that this practice

> …forms a system of total gifts in the sense of Marcel Mauss. It functions under the sign of ostentation, extravagance and rejoicing: the rules oblige one to give more than one has received on a similar occasion, more goods to consume, more commodities and more entertainment.[41]

Apart from the relations it establishes among the groups present, the consumption of food and drinks has no particular significance. These practices

> … create or strengthen social links while revealing latent antagonisms and rivalries in prestige. … [they] rest on the same dialectic which consists in converting the actual or potential conflict into a relation of cooperation and alliance; an ambiguous relationship into one of friendship; and contested prestige into recognised prestige.[42]

Indeed, some *Sapeurs* profit from the party and the presentation of gifts to manifest their antagonisms and rivalries by giving, for example, empty packets or bottles of perfume filled with water as presents. Jean Baudrillard adds that:

> What we notice in the symbolic object (the present, but also the traditional, ritual or artisanal object) is that it is not only a concrete manifestation of a total relationship of desire (ambivalent, and total because it is ambivalent); we can perceive also through the singularity of the object, the transparency of social relations in the context of a dualistic or an integrated group relationship.[43]

After the presentation of gifts, the star comes on to the floor. The presenter makes another sign to the DJ to play the music the star has chosen, often specifically a solo part with a good beat, called *chauffé*. The *Sapeur* (the star of the evening) displays a few dance steps with a lot of *frime* but without the least drop of sweat, the applause of all, and then again takes his seat.

He may continue showing off, in order to have his picture taken alone or with his *copine* or his friends. The same scenario is followed for all the stars of the party. After all the presentations, everybody takes his seat again. Once more the stars accompanied by their girlfriends go back on the floor and dance to the beat of a band like Zaiko or Papa Wemba to open the floor for all. This is then the beginning of the party.

Servants return to their duties. Guests drink, dance, show off, mooch and play love games in public in a way that was hitherto unusual and forbidden by tradition. The intention is not to promote a certain moral 'liberalization', but rather to show the audience that one shares is intimate with the other person; it may be also a way to scare off other *Sapeurs*. Those whose advances are fruitful do not hesitate to leave the party half way to go and complete them elsewhere, no doubt in different ways. It sometimes happens that, by some cunning means, intruders[44] sneak into the hall, alone or in company. Mostly without a partner, they hope to flirt with a girl and take her home; but often they leave alone, quite bitter. The *Sapeur* milieu is hard in this sense,

since seduction is one of the fixed components of the subculture of the *Société des Ambianceurs et de Personnes Élégantes*. Some *Sapeurs* deliberately come to parties on their own, not because they have any intention to seduce, but because they are afraid that their girlfriends will be 'seized'. There are also guys who go to parties alone for this specific reason, but many girls do the same. *Sapeurs* call them *bongabala* (*fille libre*/good-time girl).

While other guests (those who wait till the last moment to come out) are arriving at the hall, the dancing reaches a climax and some *Sapeurs* try to flaunt everything they are wearing ('the dance of the labels'). Some dances like reggae, disco or funk are not popular with the *Sapeurs*. Their almost exclusive preference is for rumba and its *chauffé*[45] as it is played notably by some young bands like Zaiko Langa Lnga, Choc stars, Victoria or Viva la musica de Papa Wemba. The *Sapeur* is a skilful and elegant dancer who takes great pleasure in dancing, almost as much as in dressing fashionably. It is indispensable if one wants to give a thrilling show to the spectators. For a *Sapeur* it is impossible to dissociate dancing from fashion and consequently from a party. Both are elements that spice up the daily life of a *Sapeur*. Both are corner stones of his attractiveness and integrating elements of his personality. Since dancing occupies such an important place in daily activities, it is not mere distraction. It is a form of expression, a language that claims freedom which manifests itself in the *Sapeur*, sooner or later, breaking with traditional morals, at least as far as the erotic dimension is concerned. This explains their strong attachment to the rumba; to them it has two sides, the first, during which the two partners dance close to each other (offering a suitable opportunity to seduce); and the second during which the two partners separate and dance solo. This erotic aspect of the dance, questioned by the traditional morality as expressed by the adults, can be assimilated to the *fête* (party) in the full sense of the word. As Jean Duvignaud writes: 'It (*la fête*) places man in close touch with a world without structure or code, a world where its forces hold sway, the great moments of subversion.'[46] In other words, *Sapeurs*, while dancing, play with the rules of traditional morality. This explains (next to their extravagant dressing) why adults keep their distance, avoiding the places – notably dance- and café-bars – attended by *Sapeurs*.

A special ambiance

Throughout the party, a dense atmosphere prevails of showing off, exposure, duelling and competition, sometimes manifest, sometimes latent. Often, one has the impression of watching a fashion parade. Everybody, except the *copines*, has put on Weston shoes: '*Lacet ou mpasula ya Weston, basse ya nkatu ou ya croco.*'[47] Outfits are generally either in *huile* (oil) or *gaba* or *mfunda* or even *makahutsu*. Others are in *nuyeza* or similar fabrics, complete *n'kaka* or *demi-dakar*.[48] Tergal (a form of nylon) is absolutely not allowed. In this ambiance, every form of behaviour aimed at singularizing the individual is allowed. Everybody shows great imagination in order to get themselves noticed.

The party offers the opportunity for people to express old rivalries or new ones that come up during the festivities. In most cases, they are provoked by slander related to girlfriends or outfits. Such rivalries are expressed through showing off, taking on certain allures – *miéla*[49] – and through *la Sape* in general. It is about who is the best dressed guy, with the most striking allure; since fighting is forbidden, this is the only means to settle the score. Apart from people with inside knowledge (close friends), only the most perspicacious among the guests may notice on the spot that there is a confrontation going on between two opponents. This can last throughout the party. Each gesture or action by an opponent will be considered not as neutral, but rather as a challenge to the other. Often it is attributed a special meaning. But the most humiliating act which a *Sapeur* can inflict upon his opponent, in order to show his superiority, is to step on the tip of the other's shoes. This means *ngé za fua zé*[50] – 'your place is not here.' It is reminiscent of a teacher reading a poorly written assignment which infuriates him; the teacher's most likely reaction is then to get a red pen and cross out the whole piece of work or in any case the part in question. This is certainly not a gratuitous analogy since to go that far a *Sapeur* must be convinced that he is much better *sapé* (dressed) or that his opponent's shoes cannot stand the comparison with his own. Sometimes people go and change only to come back and challenge an opponent.

All this highlights the importance of shoes in the attire of a *Sapeur*. For any outfit, he will be sure to put on fashionable shoes. Note that this is an asset of such great importance that the *sapeurs* invest amounts of money with which one could buy a piece of land in Congo.[51] Most *Sapeurs* are aware of this, and this is the reason they pay so much attention to their shoes and take so much care of them. So, it is not exceptional for a *Sapeur* in Paris to put his shoes in a safe. But it seems that this relative importance the *Sapeurs* give to their shoes is not peculiar to them; it is everywhere in Congolese society. All Congolese know the particular story of the politician in disgrace who was stigmatized as rich and scandalous, not because of the numerous bars of gold in his house, but rather because of the number of pairs of shoes.

While all kinds of encounters are taking place, beams of light and flashes from cameras highlight people dancing closely together or showing off their outfits. This brings us to the role of a particular person, one of the rare non-*Sapeurs* who is always present at parties and highly solicited by all: the photographer. Sometimes, he comes at the request of customers and sometimes on his own initiative. He is one of the keystones of the manifestation. His work, the photos, serve to immortalize the events, especially the euphoria of the *Sapeur bien gammé* and *bien alluré*. The photo is the concrete proof afterwards – to be sent to whoever will want to know – that one is or has been a *Sapeur*, and consequently used to wear this or that piece of clothing with this or that prestigious label. This concrete proof is all the more important to the *Sapeur* since after the party he must return the outfits that do not belong to him to their owners.

The end of the party

The end of the party is marked by the gradual departure of all those who feel that their ambitions have been realized, either regarding amorous conquests (*Katula fille*)[52] or as far as the *frime* (showing off) is concerned; they may prefer to leave stealthily and continue the party elsewhere. There are also those who wisely go home because of tiredness. Taking advantage of this progressive emptying of the hall, the onlookers see their chance to get in, one after the other, to enjoy the last moments of the party and to give their comments on the spot. They exchange general impressions about the party before coming to their overall verdict. These impressions will spread the next day by word of mouth throughout Bacongo (among *Sapeurs* and non-*Sapeurs*) so that those who were not there will be informed about the ambiance that prevailed and which *Sapeurs* stood out in which respect. After everybody (including the last onlookers) has left, the organizers – the stars of the party – stay for a few moments to settle things with the bar manager (the re-arranging of the place, the cleaning up etc.) before leaving. Often, they, like many others who attended the party, may not go home straightaway. Since they have dressed fashionably,

they want to take full advantage of the outfits they borrowed by continuing their showing off in their usual dance-bars. Next morning, they can either exchange the outfits between each other or wear the same ones to continue parading throughout Bacongo, sometimes even going beyond the limits of the neighbourhood – *ni mo kua tu kue déké*[53] – just to be seen. They parade the main streets, pay surprise visits to friends (*Sapeurs* and others) who they do not usually visit, even if it means walking long distances or going to places they do not know that well. All this is just to be noticed – 'Did you see me?' Finally, it is time to return the borrowed outfits.

For various reasons, notably because of their precarious situation, *Sapeurs* enjoy fostering relationships inside and outside their group; indeed they are often very good at this.

Notes

[1] Here, as in the translated text above, we prefer to leave the term *Sapeur* untranslated, just like the key words of their subculture (*frime* – showing off; *gamme* – stock of outfits). Where necessary we added an approximate translation. We wish to express special thanks to Professor Gandoulou for his permission to translate these texts and also for providing a few photographs from his private collection.

[2] See for a more recent impression of the *Sapeurs'* world a film on the musician Papa Wemba in Paris, *The Importance of Being Elegant*, by George Amponsah and Cosima Spender (Brussels and Paris 2004). Papa Wemba is from Kinshasa (present-day Democratic Republic of Congo, the former Belgian Congo). Brazzaville, the birth-place of *la Sape*, where Gandoulou did his research, lies opposite Kinshasa on the Congo river and is the capital of the Republic of Congo (the former French Congo).

[3] A young man not initiated into the world of the *Sapeurs*, and without taste or elegance.

[4] See the first fragment above.

[5] This was the refrain of a famous song by Papa Wemba.

[6] 'I am bringing original outfits.'

[7] The Brazzaville International Airport (Congo).

[8] *Bien sapé* or *bien gammé*.

[9] Sadi dressed very fashionably with all the self-assurance, *savoir-faire* and respectability that went with his new status of a *Grand*.

[10] The word *Mazarin* – the name of a minister of Louis XIV – is appropriated by the *Sapeurs*. For them, it refers to the 'little one' (*Sapeur* or not) who runs the errands of a *Grand*.

[11] Sadi was wearing a green linen suit and a Weston pair of wine-coloured crocodile leather shoes.

[12] 'Hey! Westons, you did everything to reach this place. How are you coping, *mameh*?' (This is an idiomatic expression derived from *maman*).

[13] Owning a car in Congolese society is still considered an external sign of wealth.

[14] This word means glasses in the *Sapeurs'* jargon

[15] This means to walk like a *Sapeur*.

[16] 'That is true, he brought back nice clothes. He has taste. That is good. Woow, this is going well. He has allure (showing off).'

[17] 'I have to go and convince them.'

[18] '*Grand*, your *affaires* are not going well. You should go back to where you came from [Paris] and then come back here again' [suggesting that he is not well initiated into *la Sape*].

[19] See Table 1.

[20] These practices have become almost common among parents who have the necessary means and connections – that is, people from the dominant ranks of Congolese society.

[21] Divorced parents.

[22] Divorced parents.

[23] Especially in Bacongo two boys out of three will become *Sapeur* and one girl out of three (personal estimate).

[24] Children between 13 and 18 years.

[25] Congolese adage in Lari (local language) which means 'one cannot

²⁶ Here *Grand* refers to an elder who has certain material assets at his disposal.
²⁷ Congo's economic capital with a seaport
²⁸ 'If I have the opportunity to steal in my parents' house, I will not hesitate.'
²⁹ Surprise party.
³⁰ In the *sapeur* milieu, people use the term *fille*, even when they express themselves in Lari (local language). In order to avoid confusion we prefer to translate *fille* simply by *copine*. When the *Sapeuses* (female *Sapeurs*) speak about their lovers, they use the word *garçon*.
³¹ Here, *copine* (girl) is used in its general sense of a female – that is, a young person of the feminine sex.
³² Here, *nkélo* refers to the text on the invitation card which is of course directly related to the panegyric (see Figure 3).
³³ We are organising a party in September and I hope you will help me with your best suede suit – which looks so good on you – and which I see you wear so often.
³⁴ They might write on the invitation card: 'Absence means lack of outfit, *kué na buma kô* (you are nothing).'
³⁵ 'Hey you! You may go back home because your trousers do not match your belt. Your *réglage* does not fit.'
³⁶ 'Ah Grand, the way you are dressed, it will go very well when you get there.'
³⁷ 'No Grand, do not bother, drop it. There are very beautiful outfits there. This will not work; or else change your *gamme*.'
³⁸ The action of tucking the shirt in the trousers.
³⁹ 'Ah it fits, a beautiful new outfit.'
⁴⁰ See G. Balandier, *Sociologie actuelle de l'Afrique noire*, Paris: PUF, 1982 (4th edition), p.507.
⁴¹ See the description of a *malaki* in G. Balandier, *Afrique ambiguë*, Paris: Plon, 1957, p. 149.
⁴² J. Baudrillard, 'La génèse idéologique des besoins', *Cahiers internationaux de sociologie*, XLVII, 1969: 47
⁴³ Ibid.
⁴⁴ This mostly concerns people who have stayed on at the entrance; it is difficult to send them away once they have managed to get into the hall, since there is the risk that they will then talk badly about the party in order to discredit it.
⁴⁵ This is the most rhythmic part of the music during which each partner dances – in principle – alone.
⁴⁶ J.Duvignaud, *Fêtes et civilisations*, Genève: Éd. Weber, 1973, p. 41.
⁴⁷ Weston shoes with laces, low shoes, Weston mocassins or low shoes made of crocodile skin.
⁴⁸ 'Oiled' gaberdine, either in suede or leather, or else linen; a whole costume or in different combinations.
⁴⁹ Arrogance, *frime*, pride that is complemented by ostentatious indifference.
⁵⁰ 'Hey you – you look ridiculous.'
⁵¹ Here we should be careful since the price of land fluctuates greatly.
⁵² 'Seize a girl' – here the term *fille* (girl) should be taken in its common sense (person of the female sex).
⁵³ We are in a mood to parade (*frime*).

BASILE NDJIO
Evolués & Feymen
Old & New Figures of Modernity in Cameroon[1]

Reference
Unpublished paper

In his seminal book about the expectations of modernity in the Zambian Copperbelt, James Ferguson contends that the economic recession of the late 1980s has swept away the dreams of prosperity and better life that many Zambians shared at the time of the booming mining industry in earlier decades. This economic decline would have turned the modernist optimism into an overwhelming sense of despair, suffering, fear and panic, for which Ferguson (1999) uses the term 'abjection'. Since its publication in 1999, Ferguson's *Expectations of Modernity* has triggered passionate debates among scholars (see *Politique Africaine* 2001). While some pointed out that his book seems to limit the experience of modernity in post-colonial Africa to a general feeling of 'distress' and 'disconnection' from the mainstream of the global economy, others rather accuse him of practising an 'ethnology of tragedy and decline' (see Sichone 2001).

My research on *feymen* tells us another story about the expectations of modernity in contemporary Africa. These *feymen* – as young professional swindlers and successful urban tricksters are commonly called in Cameroon – manage to accumulate considerable wealth through the practice of *feymania* which implies swindling, hoodwinking and financial deceptions. The example of these formerly marginalized urban youths who have achieved the transformation of rags to riches in a short timespan and without the aid of the post-colonial powers, runs contrary to Ferguson's pessimistic account of the experience of modernity in the Zambian Copperbelt. Indeed, the success-story of these young Cameroonian *feymen* is a good illustration of the ambivalent character of what we call 'modernity' in post-colonial Africa, which straddles pessimism and optimism, despair and hope, disenchantment and enchantment. It thus demonstrates that, in sub-Saharan Africa, the experience of modernity is not only reducible to pure tragedy as a misreading of Ferguson's *Expectations of Modernity* might suggest.

This study stresses the millennial dimension of modernity in post-colonial Africa. It is about the extraordinary ability of marginalized urban youths in Cameroon to invent new opportunities for enrichment that enable them to get round the conditions of liability and exclusion which many have been experiencing since the late 1980s (see Jua 2003; Konings 2006; Ndjio 2001). Since the mid-1990s the concepts of *feymania* and *feymen* have become key metaphors for referring to new forms of enrichment and other subversive economic practices that contravene state laws and international economic regulations; they also serve to designate former disenfranchised urban youths turned nouveaux riches.

The main argument developed in this contribution is that the idealization of *feymen* by many Cameroonian youths helps us understand the social, political and economic mutations that Cameroon has been going through since the early 1990s. More importantly, the *feymen* phenomenon permits us to apprehend the shift in the social imaginary of success and power in this country. For today there is an increasing tendency among Cameroonians to prefer financial elites, who often lack social and cultural capital, to politico-bureaucratic elites who are devoid of financial resources. This is also manifest in the general propensity to associate success and social prestige with the accumulation of financial resources, and especially the extravagant consumption of the products of Western technologies. This, according to Michael Rowlands (1989), has become the ultimate touchstone for assessing one's rate of success or confirming one's upward mobility. In other words, the popular glorification of both *feymania*-related activities and *feymen* gives us an indication of how the 'material culture of success' (Arnoldi et al. 1996; Rowlands, 1996) has taken a dramatic turn in contemporary Cameroon, as in many sub-Saharan African countries (see also Banégas and Warnier 2001).

Through the case study of one prominent *feyman* from Yaoundé, this text will show that successful 'criminal' entrepreneurs who bring into play a resourceful and inventive spirit have become the embodiment of people's modernity expectations in this country. They have become role models for many disenfranchized Cameroonian youngsters who tend more and more to idealize both their exceptional promotion and extravagant lifestyle. More importantly, the study will demonstrate that these celebrated conmen, who have hardly any school diplomas, have today supplanted the post-independence *évolués* (educated elites) who formerly incarnated the mythology of modernity in Cameroon.

The old mythologies of modernity

At the AEGIS conference of June 2005 at the School of African and Oriental Studies in London a panel was organized on the theme of 'Modernity in Africa'. During the passionate discussions that followed the presentation of various contributions, both participants and panellists agreed that it was not easy to provide a consensual definition of the complex and elusive notion of 'modernity'. Scholars, among them prominent anthropologists who had worked extensively on issues related to modernity in contemporary Africa, may have become perplexed about the vicissitudes of the modernity project and its mythology, but African post-colonial rulers and their subjects were less so – at least during the first decades after Independence (c. 1960). Indeed, right from the beginning of the decolonization process in the mid-1940s up to the early 1990s, there seemed to be a consensus between the newly emerging class of native elites and their populations on what I will call, after Jean-François Lyotard (1984), 'the meta-narratives of modernity'. To them it seemed to be characterized as the Enlightenment which colonization had brought to backward Africans through colonial administrators, Western missionaries, traders, teachers and development experts. One of the refrains of the original version of the Cameroon national anthem stated, '*Cameroun, berceau de nos ancêtres; autrefois, tu vecus dans la sauvagerie et peu à peu tu sors de ta barbarie*' (Cameroon, cradle of our forefathers, in the past, you lived under savage condition, but now you emerge little by little from this barbarism). This more or less embodied the natives' perception of modernity as the liberation from obscurantism, and emancipation from the tyranny of tradition.

This modernist ideology went along with the strong belief that only Western education could help the natives move from barbarism to civilization. What the French colonial administration referred to as '*l'école moderne*', in opposition to '*l'école traditionnelle*,' exemplified this sublimation of Western schooling, not only as the passport to civilization, but also as the sanctioned path of upward mobility and social recognition (see Martin 1982). The modern school I came to know in my youth was a place where the natives were taught not only to feel uncomfortable with their customs, but also to get rid of them, since they were devaluated and considered backward. Western

civilization was brought to the people in its idealistic representation that deliberately concealed its imperialist project, as Edward Said has brilliantly demonstrated in his book *Culture and Imperialism* (1993). In Francophone countries for instance, the natives were subjected to an education system which not only created a fantastic myth about France and reproduced her imperial view about Africans, but also stressed the superiority of her civilization over African culture. The main purpose of instruction, also since Independence, consisted of civilizing or modernizing the natives – that is, making them assimilate the highly valorized French culture which allegedly would enable them to enjoy the benefits of modernity. In other words, post-colonial teaching in Africa, which was modelled on the syllabus of the French colonial system, aimed above all at making the natives *petits Gaulois à la peau noire*.

Thus, they were trained to know a great deal more about French history, geography and literature than they did about their own society or environment. They had, for instance, to learn how to sing *La Marseillaise*, and more importantly, to speak and write correctly in French – a language of crucial importance to the native elites who aspired to take over colonial power because it heightened what Friedrich Nietzsche (1966 [1887]: 201) would have called the 'pathos of distance' between civilized and uncivilized. Similarly, they had to familiarize themselves with French *bonnes manières* and civilities which affected their lifestyle, as well as reshaped their identities. They had to eat, walk, dress, think and behave like middle-class Frenchmen from Paris. As an exhibition of colonial photos organized in Yaoundé in March 2006 showed, African *évolués* were educated to become deracinated peoples who were out of touch with their own environment.

In many francophone countries, the sublimation of education often led to the constitution of the '*temple du savoir*' which was imagined as a space where the natives would achieve their cultural transmutation. This was the case with Cotonou in Benin whose *Quartier Latin* strove to replicate the spirited Parisian intellectual life of the 1950s and 1960s, as also with Dakar and Saint Louis in Senegal. In Cameroon, Yaoundé, as the political and administrative capital of the country, embodied for a long time this space of knowledge. This city which housed most academic institutions in the country became known as *la ville des évolués*, because a significant number of its inhabitants were civil servants or bureaucrats. Likewise, the hill on which the *Université de Yaoundé* (then the only university in the country) was established, was named *La colline du savoir* (hill of knowledge). Somehow, Yaoundé, with its training schools and university, was the place where young educated Cameroonians from all regions of the country strove to achieve their *quête du savoir* (quest for knowledge).

The celebration of education found its expression in official slogans such as, *L'école: notre avenir et la porte vers le bonheur* (School: our future and the gate to happiness) or *L'éducation: La voie royale vers le développement et le progrès du pays* (Education is the royal road to development and progress of the country) or *Éduquer la jeunesse, c'est former les leaders de demain* (Educating youth is preparing tomorrow's leaders). This official ideology which made education not only the alpha and omega of social promotion, but also a glorious struggle for the emancipation of the natives, penetrated even modest families like mine. People like my parents were made to believe that only the success of their progeny in school could help them escape the marginalization they were experiencing as second-class citizens. As far as I can remember from my adolescence, the rare moments I was severely punished by my father were when I was missing from school or when he caught me playing football with my peers, while I should be studying. Like many of my childhood mates, I wanted to be a football player. This passion for football which at that time was seen by the elders as the activity of thugs or 'lost children', inevitably put me in conflict with my parents, especially my father who rather wanted me to become a *long crayon*, as educated elites are commonly called in Cameroon.

Through 'discipline and punishment' –. to paraphrase Michel Foucault (1979) – my father, like most of my schoolteachers, thought that he could make me acquire the much sought-after Western knowledge. Though he was barely educated and could easily fall into the category of what the folks derisively called *school long time* (uneducated fellow) or *imbouc* (illiterate), my father was highly interested in school, for he strongly believed that *sans l'école, tu n' es rien dans la vie* (without school you are nothing in life). His desire to see me doing better in school was motivated by the importance that disenfranchized populations then attached to education and (university) diplomas, especially prompted by the accomplishment of some of my relatives who at that time were the only young men from the neighbourhood to graduate from the university. Their academic achievement which was the basis of their social promotion as senior bureaucrats working in Yaoundé, reverberated on my entire family which was now well-known in the neighbourhood, and even beyond, as the '*famille des intellectuels*' (family of intellectuals).

Like the post-independence native bourgeoisie who, as Frantz Fanon (1966) pointed out, evolved within the same universe of discourse dominated by Western culture, my father, too, valued modern education, and especially university diplomas. This was because he saw them as a guarantee of the natives' headway towards evolution and emancipation, and as a proof of their mastery of the highly valorized Western culture that marked the social distinction between the 'primitive' and the 'civilized', the rulers and the ruled, the elites and the masses, the powerful and the powerless, etc. Possessing diplomas, especially university degrees, was of importance to the natives because both the colonial and post-colonial administration had made diplomas the much sought-after commodities with which one could bargain for access to the state. To put it simplistically, diplomas were seen as highly valuable resources that helped the educated natives achieve their accumulative project, insofar as they enabled them to claim access to state resources through salaries, rents and other remunerations (see Mbembe and Roitman 1995; Mbembe 2001). That is why, until the late 1980s when the economic depression had not yet induced the demise of the former welfare state nor downgraded many African states to the position of highly indebted poor countries, the *évolués* were the embodiment of success, prestige and power. More importantly, they incarnated the expectations of modernity in post-colonial Africa (Ndjio 2001, 2006).

Evolués: an ethnography of fallen idols

It is almost impossible to narrate the enlightenment story of modernity in post-colonial Africa without referring to the former heroes of knowledge who were popularly known in Francophone countries as *évolués*. In the colonial understanding, the term encompassed all educated natives who had in common their share of Western knowledge. These enlightened Africans generally set themselves apart from other natives by a certain type of behaviour and the self-conscious adoption of a distinctive system of ethical values and philosophical beliefs which not only celebrated intellectualism, mannerism and artificiality, but also made a play on the mimicry of the Western way of life idealized as the marker of modernity. By *évolués*, I

mean in general the educated natives who had accomplished the feat of becoming strangers to themselves and to their own people by accepting to suppress their own culture in favour of Western civilization. Thus, the term makes allusion to the natives who essentially lived on what can be termed the economy of cognition and expertise – that is, on the commodification of their knowledge to the post-colonial state which in days past offered them high remuneration. More specifically, it refers in this study to those educated Africans who, up to the late 1980s and early 1990s, were placed at the top of the hierarchy of power in the modernist, (post-) colonial order of things, because in particular this class of modernizing elites 'lived in collaboration with western culture, and against their own people', to quote Edward Said (1993: 298). No wonder that it was to these accommodating educated elites that the colonial administration handed over power when circumstances forced it to grant 'Independence' to its former colonies. A country such as Senegal provides a good illustration of the social ascendancy that the *ku jàng ekool* (educated elites) enjoyed when the modernist mythology had not yet lost its splendour. These people, who in the past dominated the national economy and the political landscape, played a decisive role in the construction of the post-colonial state and the transformation of this country into what Christian Coulon (1999: 69–83) aptly calls '*la République des lettrés*'.[2] In this republic of learned people where the possession of Western education conditioned access to financial and material resources, those who lacked this Western culture were either excluded from the post-colonial public sphere or denied access to state resources (see Ndjio 2005). This was the case for a large segment of the population who were treated as second-class citizens, because they constituted what the politico-bureaucratic elites disdainfully called *illettrés*, *ignorants*, *analphabètes* or *villageois* – terms which made reference to illiteracy and backwardness.

In Cameroon and in many other sub-Saharan African countries, the white-collar elites commonly known as *fonctionnaires* (civil servants) were until recently the iconic figures of post-colonial *évolués* who took over from the colonial powers when most African states became independent in the early 1960s. Moreover, up to the late 1980s, these bureaucrats embodied the old mythologies of modernization which, as discussed earlier, sublimated the accumulation of Western knowledge. Unlike illiterate peasants and uneducated urban dwellers whose living conditions have changed little since the colonial period – due to their exclusion from state resources – this segment of the population that benefited most from the *cameroonisation* of the administration, and from the official ideology which made Western education the reliable route for social climbing, experienced rapid social promotion (see Martin 1982). Indeed, up to the late 1980s and early 1990s, young Cameroonians who graduated from prestigious training schools such as ENS (teacher training school), ENAM (advanced school of administration and magistracy), EMIA (military academy), ENSPT (advanced school of post and telecommunication), ENTP (advanced school of public works) or CUSS (medical school) were assured to move in a short time from being a 'small man' to being a 'big man'. This was because their possession of the highly valued Western knowledge, symbolized by their university diplomas, gave them access to one of the many lucrative posts in the expanding civil service and public sector almost automatically. Thus, university degrees provided them with the means for securing higher salaries and the privileges attached to their function (free lodging, service car, health insurance, allocations of bank credits, etc.). For example, up to the late 1980s, a junior secondary school teacher, engineer or medical doctor could earn between 4 and 5 million FCFA a year,[3] while a manual worker who worked at least 12 hours per day could hardly secure 500,000 CFA per annum.

With such financial assets, a young *fonctionnaire* could not only achieve his modernity dreams, he could also easily pay back his 'communal debt' (Marie, 1997) to those of his relatives who had supported his studies at the time he was still economically dependent. Moreover, these financial resources enabled him to enjoy an outstanding position in society. One of my former secondary school teachers, who is struggling today, recalled with nostalgia the good times when a *fonctionnaire* could wear designer clothes, own a nice car or live in a comfortable house. As he explained to me during a discussion we had in November 2004 in Yaoundé:

> It is a pity that young people like you did not experience the good times of Ahmadou Ahidjo [the first Cameroonian President who ruled the country from 1960 to 1982] when the *fonctionnaires* were treated like princes by the state. The large majority of civil servants lived in a comfortable house, because they enjoyed a housing allowance, and when they were transferred to another town, the government allocated to them a travel allowance. I still remember that, when I was appointed to Maroua [in the Far-North Province] after my graduation from the teacher training school in 1981, the government offered me a substantial amount of money and a return plane ticket for my relocation. I even used part of this money to buy a plot of land in Yaoundé. At that time, one was proud of being a *fonctionnaire*, because the *fonctionnaires* enjoyed a social prestige. People had high regard for us not only because we were the *évolués*, but also because we had financial means. For example, when I went to ask for my wife's hand, her parents cordially welcomed me when they learned that I was a *professeur de lycée* (secondary school teacher). They knew that with what I earned, I could offer a decent life to their daughter. They were proud of having a son-in-law who was a senior civil servant. At that time, I lived in a beautiful house and owned a smart car.

As a result of their relatively high standard of living, the *fonctionnaires-évolués* were looked upon by many Cameroonian youths as role models. For many people, achieving their modernity dreams meant becoming a *haut fonctionnaire* (senior bureaucrat) – a term which was generally associated with power, money and respectability. For example, young Bamileke from the western region of Cameroon, who left 'their beautiful Bamilekeland for Yaoundé', as André-Marie Tala, the renowned Cameroonian singer, pointed out in his beautiful song *Je vais à Yaoundé*, were not only in search of 'a better life' in the city of the *évolués*. Through this exile, they were also striving to fulfil their dreams of becoming a senior bureaucrat. For this was the obsession of many youths of that period, as Santerre and Mercier-Tremblay (1982) emphasize. In those days, especially when the relative prosperity of the local economy placed the post-colonial state at the centre of the production and distribution of wealth, families dreamt of having their own *haut fonctionnaire* who could make the state resources flow towards them. The high esteem and respect that the bureaucratic elites enjoyed in those days, found justification in the fact that, at that time, they symbolized what many Cameroonians imagined as success, prosperity, self-confidence and a better life. To paraphrase a retired civil servant from Yaoundé, who has now become a taxi-driver: a *fonctionnaire* was a *millionaire*. That is why families, even from the underprivileged classes, did their best to send their children to school, hoping that they too could become a senior civil servant later. All the sacrifices that parents made and the regime of discipline that their children were submitted to, aimed above all at making them

become a *grand type* ('big man'). I still remember the conversation that I had with my father when I got admitted to the university in 1989:

> My beloved son; now that you have obtained your *baccalaureat*, I hope that you understand that I did not mean to harm you when I was harsh with you. If I sometimes mistreated you, it was because I wanted your success in school. I wanted you too to become *quelqu'un* (important person). Thank God! You are on the right track. I have no doubt that very soon, you will complete your studies and find a good job in the public sector. You will probably earn a high salary like all those who have gone to the university.

However, already by this time the Cameroonian government was no longer able to provide job opportunities to the growing number of university graduates, so that the sole prospect that university diplomas now offered to young Cameroonians from underprivileged backgrounds was long-term unemployment. But, my father saw the *évolués-fonctionnaires* as models of accomplishment. Yet for many disappointed youths, they had already become nothing but fallen heroes who looked like relics of a social and economic order that was falling apart as a result of the demise of the welfare state.

Post-modern conditions in post-colonial Africa

If at first in post-Independence Africa modern developments seemed to coincide with the dreams of the heroes of independence who depicted the continent and its people as moving forward, or with the sublimation of what Robert Young (1990) calls 'white mythologies', the present post-modern conditions rather correspond with people's pessimism about their continent that is now viewed by many as an archipelago of unhappiness, or depicted as a place of anxiety, distress and despair.

Acknowledging the propensity of many Africans to turn to derision all the meta-narratives that (post-)colonial rule has striven to impose as truths beyond dispute (see Bayart et al. 1992), one can say that the post-modern condition is also accompanied in sub-Saharan Africa by what Jean-François Lyotard (1984) termed 'incredulity' towards such overarching narratives. The first incredulity is towards the ideology that formerly imagined the (post-) colonial state as the centre of production and more or less equal distribution of wealth – its premise being that only the post-colonial state could provide economic security and job opportunities to a large number of its active population, and that, outside the state apparatus, there were no 'alternative pathways in upward mobility', to quote Nantang Jua (2003: 19). The general distribution of the 'national cake' to the state's various clients and the *salarisation* of the society which, according to Achille Mbembe (2001: 75), 'enabled the rulers to require submission and obedience of their subjects', reinforced these mythologies about the post-colonial state.

The second scepticism concerns the (post-) colonial educationist ideology of earlier days which presupposed a connection between education and social promotion, making the possession of Western knowledge the key to success and prosperity. Thus, the established system granted status only to the *fonctionnaires-évolués* (see Schilder 1994). One illustration of the current distrust of the modernist project and its great narratives about education is the belief prevailing among young Africans that 'study and erudition are useless, and that prestige without wealth is only false prestige, for one cannot turn French into Francs' – as Tsakala Munikengi and Bongo-Pasi (2004: 94) maintain for young Congolese from Kinshasa. Filip De Boeck (2001) similarly mentions the case of young diamond diggers from the southwest of the Democratic Republic of Congo and north Angola, who strongly believe that these precious stones shun intellectuals, and that, in order to succeed in life, you need neither diplomas nor an academic background.

But not only disillusioned Congolese and Angolan youths share this pessimistic view about schooling and Western knowledge. In a country such as Cameroon, the devaluation of education is reflected today in the popular saying, 'L'école ne paie plus aujourd'hui au Cameroun' (schooling no longer pays off in Cameroon). In this country, the depreciation of schooling has led to a general contempt for longs crayons (as the educated elite are commonly known in Cameroon). For example, one successful trickster from Douala whom I interviewed in 2003, during my field research on the nouveaux riches, made this critical reflection about university diplômés:

> When I see all these young men who have graduated from the university being forced to sell cigarettes or drinking water on the streets to make ends meet, or these doctas [holders of a doctorate] who have worn down their backsides on the school bench, walking under the tropical heat because they cannot afford a taxi, I cannot help asking myself if it is worth being a long crayon in this country.

As a poor long crayon, I myself have experienced the disdain that families now manifest towards their educated elites who lack financial means. On the occasion of the funeral of my maternal grandfather in Tonga, my mother's native village in the western region of the country, each member of the family had to contribute money to meet the huge expenses that such events require. One of my mother's younger sisters was disappointed by the fact that my contribution and that of my uncle who is a university professor hardly exceeded 100, 000 FCFA (less than $200). So she made these comments:

> The main problem with our family is that we only have longs crayons who are sabitou [he who knows all], but have nothing in their pocket. You are all teachers, medical doctors, university professors, engineers, etc, but you are poor fellows. What is the point of being an intellectual, if you are not even able to offer a decent funeral to your parent? Honestly, I don't see what is your usefulness to our family. Do I need to remind you that your young brother, who is not a long crayon like you [she referred to our cousin who is a successful feyman], offered alone 1.5 million FCFA [nearly US$ 3,000], in addition to ten cases of champagne and fine French wine. If we were not lucky enough to have such a vrai type (affluent person) to spare us the shame that you were about to inflict on the entire family, the funeral of the parent of grands intellectuels like you would have looked like a funeral of poor villagers.

Unlike what Jean-François Lyotard (1984) maintains in general, the 'incredulity toward meta-narratives' in post-colonial Africa is less the result of a general progress in the sciences than the consequence of the sustained economic depression that many sub-Saharan African countries have been experiencing since the late 1980s and early 1990s. Not only has this economic crisis swept away the modernist millenarian mythologies that in the past provided people with optimism, self-confidence and rosy expectations about their future; it has also twisted their aspiration into resignation, as many are now facing a tragic downturn in their lives (Ndjio 2006). This is the case of young diplômés and other university graduates whose chance of finding a permanent job in the formal sector, and most notably in the public

service, has been narrowed by the drastic adjustment policies that most African countries have been compelled to endorse willy-nilly. This is also the case for civil servants. In 1993, for instance, those who were lucky enough to retain their jobs in a context of massive lay-offs as a result of the closing down or privatization of many state-owned enterprises, saw their salaries being reduced by more than 60 per cent (see Jua 2003). With the transformation of their formerly high incomes into what many Cameroonians now derisively call the salaire insuffisant et difficilement acquis (insufficient and hard-to-earn salary: a word-play with SIDA, the French acronym for AIDS), most civil servants and bureaucrats[4] are now living in a state of clochardisation (destitution), which makes many feel nostalgic about the good old days.

For example, when in November 2004 I again met my secondary school teacher mentioned earlier, I was disconcerted by his destitution. This formerly self-assured man, who commanded deference and respect from his students, was now a mere shadow of his former self. Draconian structural adjustment programmes imposed by international trustees, which led to two consecutive salary cuts in the public sector in 1993, had moved the man whom we affectionately called Grand Prof from the privileged group of bureaucratic elites to the contemptuous category of urban proletariat. The stunning setback in his life had shattered the confidence he formerly had in both himself and the post-colonial state. Moreover, the hardship and distress that Grand Prof, like many other fonctionnaires-évolués who were not connected to barons of the ruling CPDM regime and state officials, has been going through since the early 1990s, had led him to repudiate the modernist philosophy on education, and its ethical principles that professed devotion, honesty, integrity and honour.

However, and this is the main outcome of my research, the loss of prestige and the decline in social prominence of the fonctionnaires, as a result of the pauperization of most of them, have coincided with the emergence in the early and mid-1990s of a new class of nouveaux riches. These might be termed 'post-modernist elites' in contrast to the former 'modernist notables'.

Feymen: post-modernist elites

As in many African countries, the post-modern condition in Cameroon is associated with a shift in the social imaginary of success and power (see Politique Africaine 2001). The popular revision of the canons of social accomplishment is especially prompted by the rise in this country of new forms of wealth that seem to resuscitate among Cameroonians the modernist optimism of the past. This is because most of the nouveaux riches are former car-cleaners, sauveteurs (hawkers), nangaboko (street children), attaquants (small-time criminals) or tacleurs (touts) of the Douala or Yaoundé central market, who were excluded from state resources and marginalized in the society. In many respects, feymen embody the figures of self-made men whose stunning economic success reassures many disenfranchised Cameroonian youths that one does not necessarily need to be a long crayon or to have good political connections, in order to become economically successful.

In the popular literature, the term feymen refers to wheeler-dealers, confidence tricksters and professional swindlers who essentially live on the criminal economy that has been made popular in Cameroon as feymania. Through the 'art of composition' – to quote Garas (now 45 years old), a prominent feyman who pretends to be one of the initiators of feymania-related activities in Cameroon – cunning young tricksters manage to extort huge amounts of money from their victims who are often top-ranking politicians, or wealthy businessmen, both locals and foreigners. Dominique Malaquais (2001a: 102–5) mentions, for instance, the case of Donatien Koagne – the most famous and successful Cameroonian *feyman* – and his acolytes who succeeded between 1992 and 1995 in defrauding millions of US dollars from several African Heads of State and Western executive managers (see also Ndjio 2006, especially chapters 4 and 5). Through 'fantastic' accumulation of wealth and ostentatious exhibition of riches, some successful *feymen* now rival the bureaucratic elites' display of grandeur and notability. Moreover, the efforts of these tricky businessmen to gain reputation and social recognition on the basis of riches, and their ability to command deference and respect from other groups as a result of their wealth, challenge the established system that has so far emphasized the centrality of the post-colonial state in the process of accumulation and distribution of riches.

Indeed, *feymen*'s strategies of accumulation signal the mutations that have taken place in the post-colonial classical pathways to accumulation since the mid-1990s. The brief case study of Sengat, a prominent *feyman* from Yaoundé, not only furnishes a striking example of a formerly underprivileged youth who has moved from rags to riches in a short time span; it also highlights the radical change that *feymen* and other post-modernist elites have brought about in the mode of access to wealth and power in post-colonial Cameroon.

Sengat is a young *feyman* (36 years old) who comes from a humble Bamileke family from the western region of the country. The family immigrated to Yaoundé in the late 1950s. In 1986, Sengat left secondary school after only two years to fend for himself. By 1988, he had started in petty trade, selling cigarettes and candies in front of the Abbia cinema in Yaoundé. His goods were displayed in a small kiosk that he rented from a friend. As he found it very difficult to earn a livelihood in this business, he switched to the second-hand clothes trade; thanks to his personal contacts, his good head for business and his entrepreneurial spirit, he was able to quickly establish a reliable customer circuit. He was very astute, exploiting the tastes and desires of his customers who were mostly young men from the middle-class he came to know when running his kiosk. After a few months of trading, the profit was already sufficient to enable him to set up his own stall outside the Yaoundé central market and to increase his stock,. For about two years, his business was going well until all his goods were stolen.

However, this mishap did not stop his efforts to earn more money. Instead, he took advantage of his connections with some young *tacleurs* and *attaquants* (hawkers) from the Yaoundé central market who were involved in the *bizness* (unlawful activities), to enter into several smuggling networks. Initially, he was a member of a network specializing in selling stolen clothes which generally operated in small groups of four or five individuals. His partners who were working in shops owned by Lebanese, Pakistani and Syrian wholesalers or wealthy Bamileke merchants, smuggled goods from their patrons, and handed them over to him. His role was to sell these stolen goods and share the benefits with his associates. The deal brought him in much higher earnings than he earned when he was engaged in legal activities. But the arrest of several of his suppliers, and the saturation of the *bizness* as a result of the involvement of many young *tacleurs* and *attaquants* from the market, ended up forcing him to retire from this unlawful activity, and try his luck in another *bizness*. So by 1991, he was engaged in a network of counterfeiting and deception, selling forged passports and visas, fake import-export licences, and other official documents provided by some traffickers with whom he worked. For example, passports were sold for FCFA 30,000 and visas

to Western Europe or the United States for between FCFA 500,000 and FCFA 800,000. Most of his numerous customers were young people who wanted to travel to Europe or the United States, while anti-immigration laws implemented by most Western countries made it very hard to get a visa in their embassies in Cameroon. For a brief period (1991–2), Sengat and his accomplices successfully organized confidence tricks that enabled them to extort money from many *dupes*.[5] Moreover, he succeeded in running away to France, before being arrested by the police. Some of his victims were local businessmen and close relatives of government officials from whom the would-be *feyman* allegedly extorted several FCFA million.

Once in Paris, Sengat joined a group of young Cameroonian traffickers mostly operating in the Rue Guy Môquet and in neighbourhoods like Château d' Eau and Château Rouge alongside the *mikilistes* and *sachistes* (petty traffickers) from Congo-Brazzaville and the former Zaire (see MacGaffey and Bazenguissa-Ganga 2000). Most of his *bizness* partners were young Bamileke migrants who originated from New-Bell in Douala, and from Madagascar and Nkongkana in Yaoundé. He started his clandestine activities in the French capital by stealing goods from department stores and shopping malls, and then selling them in the cafés, restaurants, clandestine bars, beauty salons and stores of Château d'Eau and Château Rouge where many Africans congregated. For more than a year, this traffic was his main means of livelihood, though he did not make substantial profits. He then decided to venture into drug trafficking, stealing luxurious cars, counterfeiting credit and telephone cards, and money forging. By 1994, he had become one of the wealthiest *attaquants* of Château d'Eau and Guy Môquet and was now respectfully called *Président*. At that time, he already distinguished himself by his style of dressing, and among his circle of acquaintances and girlfriends one could count many well-known African singers based in Paris. Those who sang his praises or mentioned his name in their songs were regularly showered with money and gifts.[6]

Thanks to his success in dubious businesses, the former hawker had acquired wealth and notoriety that later helped him to set up an effective ring of deception with his *chindas* (courtiers or henchmen) throughout Western Europe. According to an informant, a Paris-based *feyman* who was once a member of this ring of tricksters, Sengat achieved one of his best coups in September 1993, when he and his accomplices reportedly swindled FF8 million from a wealthy Jewish merchant who owned a big shop in Rue Barbès. The same year, with the help of a *brancheur* (contact man), he extorted BF5 million from two Flemish diamond traders in Antwerp, and BF500,000 from a well-off Zaïrian businessman who owned a restaurant at Matongé, a neighbourhood in Brussels which is famous for its many African shops and restaurants. On coming back to Paris, the *feyman* organized a lavish party in a luxurious hotel at the *Place de la Défense*, in order to celebrate his success. He allegedly spent about a month in this five-star hotel, before making a triumphal return to his home country where his numerous admirers welcomed him like a national hero, especially because he brought back home several fancy cars. The former abandoned child turned nouveau riche later invited several well-known Congolese singers for a huge live concert. All these artists and their suites were lodged at the Hilton Hotel, the most expensive hotel in Cameroon, at his expense.

I first met Sengat in December 1995 when I was working in *Caesar's Palace*, a casino owned by Pierre Kwemo, another renowned *feyman* from Yaoundé, who is now a Member of Parliament on the ticket of the Social Democratic Front (the main opposition party in Cameroon). The young nouveau riche was living at that time in a suite at the Hilton hotel where the casino was located. Prior to this meeting, I already knew the *feyman* by reputation because his extravagant lifestyle – acquiring the latest Ferrari or offering 200 bottles of French champagne in one night – was regularly on the front page of many local newspapers. The notorious trickster was not only a regular customer of the casino; he was also a compulsive gambler who helped keep the casino afloat, since he regularly lost huge amounts of money, sometimes up to FCFA 10 million in one night. His financial power now enabled him to enjoy an easy life, and especially to compete with the political-bureaucratic elites in what Arjun Appadurai (1986) has called 'tournaments of value'; that is, in the display of grandeur and wealth in the form of expensive cars, large houses, jewellery and other luxurious items, as well as in lavish contributions to ritual celebrations, such as funerals, weddings and birthdays.

This example, which is far from being an isolated case, shows that, unlike the modernist notables, who were mostly state-based bureaucrats whose fate depended above all on the caprices of the post-colonial regime, the post-modernist elites of today owe their success above all to their ability to seize the opportunities for quick enrichment provided by the present 'millennial capitalism' (Comaroff and Comaroff 2000). Striking is their capacity to circumvent the post-colonial state in getting access to financial and material resources, and thus to free themselves from state paternalism. Their desire to bypass the post-colonial state has led many *feymen* especially to operate exclusively in what Janet MacGaffey (1991) calls the 'second economy' outside the formal circuits of the national economy, thus giving priority to 'alternative modes of accumulation', to use Geschiere and Konings' term (1993). In so doing, they 'break state laws and regulations which they dismiss as unacceptable', as MacGaffey (1991: 12) put it when discussing illegal traders and criminal businessmen from the former Zaire (see also De Boeck, 1999, 2001). The most radical among these adventurous entrepreneurs even tend to seek accumulative opportunities outside their home country. Wealth derived from this unconventional economy enables some successful professional swindlers not only to plagiarize and surpass the lavish and ludicrous lifestyle of the politico-bureaucratic elites, but also to appropriate the latter's code of prestige and insignia of power. In short, their success in *feymania*-related activities allows many marginalized youths to participate in what Filip De Boeck (1999: 970) characterizes as an 'economy of ejaculation' that formerly only benefited the post-colonial comprador bourgeoisie (see also Nyamnjoh 2000).

Feymen: new role models for the Cameroonian youth

Today, many young Cameroonians, especially marginalized youths in poor districts of Douala and Yaoundé, dream of becoming a successful *feyman*. Like many affluent urban tricksters or professional swindlers, they too aspire to wear expensive clothes, drive fancy cars, live at luxurious hotels, distribute money to their destitute fellows and make the whole neighbourhood come to life. Some of these nouveaux riches have become 'illustrious sons of the soil' who need to be protected by their community from 'dangerous outsiders' and 'jealous people'.[7] They have also become widely admired role models for young Cameroonians among whom trickery is now seen as a noble form of activity, and deception as a national sport (see Hibou 1999: 105).

For example, during field research I undertook in 2003 in Kassalafam, my childhood neighbourhood, I was amazed by two things: firstly, the tremendous popularity of the local conmen who were celebrated in popular songs,[8] as *des modèles* and *valeurs sures* (reliable role models), or as *les gens de l'espoir* (people who bring hope). Despite the misfortunes of some of them,[9] the image these *feymen* generally conveyed was that of having achieved happiness, a good life and prosperity. The esteem the locals had for these professional swindlers was perceptible in the stories they liked to tell each other about their wealthy neighbourhood fellows. Such stories were almost always about spectacular *coups* carried out abroad, unimaginable fortunes amassed in a short span of time, the squandering of money in luxurious hotels or casinos, or enjoyment in smart nightclubs with beautiful girls. They were also about these young nouveaux riches owning the most expensive limousines in town or building impressive mansions in gentrified residential areas. In this overpopulated neighbourhood, as in other poor districts of Douala, it was even common to see young men wearing a T-shirt with the portrait of one of the successful conmen, or simply adopting the famous *feymen* look which Malaquais terms 'ghetto glamour' (Malaquais 2001a: 109; see also 2001b).

Some local *feymen* even patronized their own fan club which gathered several hundred young men from the neighbourhood. For example, in June 2003, I had the opportunity to take part in a popular meeting organized by a fan club whose members were welcoming Gnacos, a well-known *feyman* from the neighbourhood. The then 27-year-old *feyman*, affectionately called 'Boss' or 'President' by his admirers, had just bought a new Mercedes 600, and intended to drink to his new acquisition with his young neighbours. During this gathering, the *feyman*, who allegedly was flush with *petro-dollars*,[10] offered FCFA 3.5 million to his supporters for a drink. That day, the neighbourhood was in a fever of excitement, as men and women of different ages were drinking, dancing, shouting or making fun of each other. For instance I heard a young lady, who had been drinking all night long, say to her neighbour who was complaining about her being so noisy, that he was 'a *pauvre type* (poor man) who could not even offer a bottle of beer to his friend'. She went on to remind the middle-aged man who was a college teacher, that '*Vauriens* (people of no substance) like him should keep their mouth shut, because they were not *des vrais gens comme des feymen* (important people like *feymen*) who made the whole neighbourhood come to life.'

Secondly, I was struck by the appealing effect the *feymen's* success had on the imagination of the local youths. Indeed, many young men from Kassalafam seemed to model their own identities on the *feymen's* extravagant *habitus*. For example, young people from this neighbourhood who wanted to be considered a *vrai type* or a *don gah* ('real' man or woman) by their fellows generally pretended to be a *feyman* or a *petite* (mistress) of a successful *feyman*. This performance entailed their having to become what young Congolese call *sapeurs*: people who flaunt their appearance by wearing expensive fashionable clothing (cf. Gandoulou 1989 and this volume). It also meant the lavish distribution of bottles of beer and presents to the neighbourhood lads, or the unsparing spending of money in bars, nightclubs and *circuits*, or the exhibition of a number of *belles petites*. This hedonistic behaviour was not only regarded as the sign of 'savoir-vivre', but equally as the major marker of success and prosperity.[11]

Yet, what struck me most in the course of my investigation was the strong desire of many youngsters from the neighbourhood to follow in their *modèles'* footsteps, and to embrace a *feymania* career as well. The attraction of the young Kassalafam residents to *feymania*-related practices was partly prompted by the fact that the wealthiest and the most respected families in the area were those whose sons were successful *feymen*. For example, on my return to the place in autumn

2002, I was surprised to find that a number of families from the neighbourhood had considerably improved their living conditions, and were now living in a modern house equipped with either a cable TV or a new television with a DVD player attached. The sitting rooms of these houses were regularly full in the evenings or at the weekends, as relatives from neighbouring compounds gathered to watch movies or some popular Brazilian soap opera. In many cases, these families owed their improvement to their new rich sons whose extraordinary promotion provided the locals with optimism and self-confidence about their future, although many of them were still experiencing hardship and poverty.

This was the case of one of my close neighbours whose sons' success in *feymania*-related activities had made them one of the most important and influential families in the area. A luxurious house surrounded by an impressive fence had replaced the decaying hovel where the family used to live in the past. The success of the two *feymen* also reverberated on their mother (an old widow) who enjoyed great social prestige with her peers, and so was regularly assailed by requests from her neighbours who had trouble making ends meet. For example, many women from the neighbourhood usually called her *manveu* (chief's mother or first wife), or referred to her as *la mère des hommes bien* or *des richards*, that is, a 'lucky mother' whose children had turned their lives into a success. I still remember the snatches of conversation I picked up by chance between the old lady and a group of women from the neighbourhood who told her that she was lucky to have all her children in Europe, who could send her 'big money' every time she was in need, or enable her to 'cross the ocean' (travel overseas). One of the women expressed her wish that her sons too could travel to the West and come back with money and big cars. Each time the wealthy sons paid a visit to their mother, accompanied by their *métisse* girl-friends, neighbours would rush into the house to admire these successful young men. Many of the onlookers wished they had a son, sibling, fiancé or in-law of this particular stature.

Teenagers were particularly impressed by the *feymen*'s high-powered cars, which they nicknamed 'Michael Knight', in reference to the famous American television series, the *Nightrider*, in which the main character drives a high-tech black Corvette. For example, I witnessed three young boys hotly discussing the capabilities of the two *feymen*'s sport cars that were parked in front of their mother's house. Two of them were teasing the third boy named *Petit Vieux*, for not having a close relative who owned such a car. His response was: 'When I become a *feyman*, I will have my own *bolide* [high-speed car] too.' He added: 'My car will be even fancier than those of Bernard Tapi and Gnacos [the *feymen*'s nicknames]. I will own a private jet in which I will travel all over the world with my friends and my family.' At that point, the other two kids stopped making a fool of *Petit Vieux* and instead engaged with him in dreaming about becoming *feymen*. One of the teasers, Kiki, also associated *feymen* with owning expensive cars, living in impressive mansions and wearing fashionable clothes. 'When I become a *feyman*, I will have everything,' he said. Here an interesting twist of events took place as the second boy, Jojo, vehemently protested: 'That is not fair; because if you have everything, it means that we will have nothing.' In doing so, he was clearly articulating the communal discourse concerning selfish *feymen* who are perceived as not adhering to the principle of sharing. Kiki, knowing the negative stigma associated with this aspect of *feymen*, replied: 'Don't worry, I will give you something since you are my friends.' Clearly, the ambition of many of the youth of my area to become *feymen* was associated with their dream of travelling to Europe

or North America, the alleged Promised Land, where one can attain the benefits of global capitalism.

Critical questions that follow from the above are: what makes *feymen* so attractive or popular with the weaker socio-economic categories? What kind of expectancies do they convey today? I venture here three suggestions that, however, do not foreclose other propositions.

Firstly, *feymen* or successful urban tricksters are admired for their ability to accumulate wealth without the aid or approval of the post-colonial state, even though the latter claims in Cameroon, as in many other African countries, the 'legitimate' right to decide which of its citizens will or will not get access to state and non-state resources. Indeed, *feymen* are people who successfully evade the official clientelist system and get rich without having to perform 'the dance of collaboration' (Rush 1990) with the ruling CPDM regime, or engage in patrimonial relationships with the men in power.

Secondly, many Cameroonian youths hero-worship international swindlers and other smooth criminals, because of their capacity to contest the present globalization process that only exacerbates the impoverishment of the large majority of Africans through economic, cultural and political exclusion (see Bayart 1994, Comaroff and Comaroff 2000; Nyamnjoh, 2000). Little wonder that Cameroonian con artists who are cunning enough to deceive middle-class Westerners are generally viewed as taking their revenge for all the injustice and exploitation Africans have been experiencing over a *longue durée*. In the inner cities of New-Bell and Madagascar, their successful swindling operations in the West are often celebrated as the victory of the wretched of the earth over the rich and powerful Westerners.

Thirdly, successful swindlers seem to be so popular today because they are the iconic figures of the new modalities of wealth creation. These fantastic modes of accumulation in times of economic crisis and marginalization of the poor have become for many African youths the only means to achieve their modernity expectations. Comaroff and Comaroff (2000) use the expression 'occult economy' to translate what is popularly known in Cameroon as *feymania*. More interesting is that these new forms of accumulation challenge the official mode of access to riches, especially the postcolonial state's ideology which has so far associated economic success and social promotion with possession of social and cultural capital controlled by the regime. Indeed, unlike the classical route to enrichment, which rested on education, training, degrees, hard work, patience, and skill, these new forms of wealth rather rely on chance, courage, recklessness and risk. The general feeling that prevails today among the youths is that you do not need to be a *long crayon* to become rich. After all, the nouveaux riches whom many people look upon as their role models are not the *diplômés*. Symptomatic of this predominant social imaginary that devaluates or plays down schooling and diplomas, is the increase in Cameroon of what Janet Roitman (2005, also this volume) has called the 'bush economy' which enables some marginalized youths to rectify the situation of liability that impinges on their lives.

In this country where many people are still obsessed with the ideas of change, prosperity and success, *feymania*-related practices, like the 'bush' or the 'occult economy', offer the underprivileged the expecta-tions of access to instantaneous riches that could transform their desperate conditions. Acknowledging, for instance, the success stories of some formerly idle young men from the neighbourhood, who are now riding in limousines or putting up in five-star hotels, provides people with hope about their future, despite their miserable condi-tions. Moreover, it enhances their conviction that poverty and misery

– which have become commonplace for many people – are just a temporary phase of hard times, that might soon go away.

Conclusion

What this study has shown is that the most noticeable manifestation of the post-modern condition in Africa, and particularly in Cameroon, is not only the popular distrust of the modernist meta-narratives which formerly mythologized the post-colonial state as the unavoidable centre of wealth production and distribution, or the official educationist ideology which promoted (and continues to promote) Western education and the possession of diplomas as the only way to upward mobility. In contemporary Cameroon, post-modernity also goes along with a fundamental change in the social imaginary of success, prestige, social achievement and recognition. Whereas in the past, the educated bureaucratic elites – or what the French colonial lexicon called *les évolués* – embodied prosperity and power, as well as symbolizing what Cameroonians imagined were models of accomplishment, today these formerly privileged social groups have become fallen idols. The loss of their grandeur and respectability coincided with the emergence by the mid-1990s of a new category of nouveaux riches commonly known as *feymen* who, through an economy of swindling and deception, managed to get access to wealth from which they were formerly excluded by the post-colonial system because of their lack of the right type of cultural capital. The stunning economic success of these formerly marginalized youths, and more importantly, their ability to create wealth in times of economic depression and marginalization of the poor by the regime in power, has made them into role models for many Cameroonian youths, especially those from underprivileged backgrounds.[12]

Notes

[1] An earlier version of this paper was presented at the AEGIS conference held at the School of African and Oriental Studies in London: 28 June–1 July 2005. I would like to express my gratitude to both the Executive Board of the Amsterdam School of Social Science Research for financing my trip to London, and WOTRO (Netherlands Foundation for the Advancement of Tropical Research) for its financial support to my research. I also wish to extend my thanks and recognition to Peter Geschiere, Peter Pels and Birgit Meyer whose insightful remarks and comments helped me improve the form and content of this text. Moreover, I drew a wealth of inspiration from the works of James Ferguson, Francis Nyamnjoh, Dominique Malaquais, Michael Rowlands, Achille Mbembe and Filip de Boeck. As usual, I benefited from stimulating discussions with Eileen Moyer.
[2] See also Banégas and Warnier, 2001: 5–7.
[3] 1 \$= 550 FCFA at the time of writing.
[4] Except those who occupy a really high position in the public sector, which gives them an opportunity to misappropriate state resources.
[5] According to our informants, one of the tricks consisted in selling the same visa to several customers.
[6] It is said that the popular Congolese singer Koffi Olombide's successful song, *Papa Bonheur* (1994), in which the singer praised an open-handed *feyman*, was dedicated to Sengat.
[7] According to Bongmba Kifon (2001: 48), some customary leaders from the Grassfields region of Cameroon have passed a rule making it an offence to try and use witchcraft against an elite who is supposed to bring financial resources to his homeland.
[8] See La Piro de Mbanga: *Don't lefam Tara* (Don't give up my brother); *Suffer go finish* (Suffering will end soon), Guy Lobe: *Foa no ba sick* (Poverty is not illness).
[9] During my stay in that neighbourhood, I attended the funeral of two young *feymen* who had been shot in Indonesia. Two other *feymen* from the locale were reportedly arrested in Taiwan, as they were trying to deceive some local businessmen.
[10] It was said that the young *feyman* had just come back from a successful *front* in the United Arab Emirates where he allegedly extorted US\$ 1.8 million from a local banker.
[11] For a comparison with young diamond diggers from Angola and Democratic Republic of Congo, see de Boeck, 1999, 2001.
[12] However, as I have shown in a previous study (see Ndjio 2006), people's perception of *feymen* is ambivalent, for those who are keen to idealize their extraordinary economic success are the same people who tend more and more to associate their dazzling fortune with what many Cameroonians now refer to as *mokoagne moni* or 'magic money', more precisely wealth acquired through occult means involving the ignoble trade of the bodies of innocent victims by some mystical organizations to which the nouveaux riches allegedly belong. Thus people's admiration for these 'new figures of success' is always mixed with fear and suspicion.

References

Appadurai, A. ed. 1986. The *Social Life of Things. Commodities in Cultural Perspective.* Cambridge: Cambridge University Press.
Arnoldi, M.J., Ceary, C.M., and Hardin, K. L., eds. 1996. *African Material Culture.* Bloomington: Indiana University Press.
Banégas, R. and Warnier, J.-P. 2001. 'Nouvelles figures de la réussite et du pouvoir.' *Politique Africaine*, 82: 5–23.
Bayart, J-F. ed. 1994. *La Réinvention du capitalisme.* Paris: Karthala.
Bayart, J.-F., Ellis, S., and Hibou, B. 1999. *Criminalization of the State in Africa.* Oxford: James Currey.
Bayart, J-F, Mbembe, A. and Toulabor, C. 1992. *Le Politique par le bas en Afrique noire: Contributions à une problématique de la démocratie.* Paris: Karthala.
Bongmba Kifon, E. 2001. *African Witchcraft and Otherness: A Philosophical and Theological Critique of Intersubjective Relations.* New York: State University of New York Press.
Comaroff, J. and Comaroff, J. L. 2000. 'Introduction' in J. and J.L. Comaroff, eds, *Millennial Capitalism and the Culture of Neoliberalism,* special issue, *Public Culture,* 12(2): 291–343.
Coulon, C. 1999. 'La tradition démocratique au Sénégal: Histoire d'un mythe.' *Studia Africana,* 10: 69–83.
De Boeck, F. 1999. 'Domesticating Diamonds and Dollars: Identity, Expenditure and Sharing in Southwestern Zaire (1984–1997).' In B. Meyer and P. Geschiere, eds, *Globalization and Identity: Dialectics of Flow and Closure,* Oxford: Blackwell, pp.177–211.
— 2001. '"Garimpeiro" Worlds: Digging, Dying and Hunting for Diamonds in Angola.' *Review of African Political Economy,* 28 (90): 549–62.
Fanon, F. 1966. *The Wretched of the Earth.* Trans. Constance Farrington. New York: Grove Press.
Ferguson, J. 1999. *Expectations of Modernity: Myths and Meanings of Urban Life on the Zambian Copperbelt.* Berkeley: University of California Press.
Foucault, M. 1979. *Discipline and Punish: The Birth of the Prison.* Translated by Alan Sheridan. New York: Vintage/Random House.
Gandalou, J. D. 1989. *Dandies à Bacongo: le culte de l'élégance dans la société congolaise contemporaine.* Paris: L'Harmattan.
Geschiere, P. and Konings, P., eds. 1993. *Les Itinéraires d'accumulation au Cameroun/ Pathways to Accumulation in Cameroon.* Paris: Karthala.
Hibou, B. 1999: 'The "Social Capital" of the State as an Agent of Deception, or the Ruse of Economy Intelligence.' In J.-F. Bayart, S. Ellis, and B. Hibou, eds. *Criminalization of the State in Africa.* Oxford: James Currey: pp. 69–113.
— ed.2004. *Privatising the State.* Trans. J. Derrick. London/Paris: Hurst & Company/CERI.
Jua, N. B. 2003. 'Differential Responses to Disappearing Pathways: Redefining Possibility among Cameroon Youths.' *African Studies Review,* 46 (2): 13–36.
Konings, P. 2006. 'Bendskin' Drivers in Douala's New Bell Neighbourhood.' In P. Konings and D. Foecken, eds. *Crisis and Creativity: Exploring the*

Wealth of the African Neighbourhood. Leiden/Boston, MA: Brill, pp. 46–65.

Lyotard, J-F. 1984. *The Post-modern Condition: Report on Knowledge,* trans. Geoff Bennington and Brian Massumi. Minneapolis: University of Minnesota Press.

MacGaffey, J. ed. 1991. *The Real Economy of Zaire. The Contribution of Smuggling and Other Unofficial Activities to National Wealth.* London: James Currey.

MacGaffey, J., and Bazenguissa-Ganga, R. 2000. *Congo-Paris: Transnational Traders on the Margins of the Law.* Oxford/Bloomington: James Currey; Indiana University Press, in association with the International African Institute.

Malaquais, D. 2001a. 'Arts de feyre au Cameroun', *Politique Africaine,* 82: 101–18.

— 2001b. 'Anatomie d'une arnaque: *feymen* et *feymania* au Cameroun', *Études du CERI,* 77: 1–24.

Marie, A. 1997. 'Les avatars de la dette communautaire: crise des solidarités, sorcellerie et procès d'individualisation (itinéraires abidjanais).' In A. Marie et al., eds, *L'Afrique des individus. Itinéraires citadins dans l'Afrique contemporaine (Abidjan, Bamako, Dakar et Niamey).* Paris: Karthala, pp. 249–328.

Martin, J.-Y. 1982. 'Sociologie de l' enseignement en Afrique Noire.' In R. Santerre and C. Mercier-Tremblay, eds, *La quête du savoir: Essais pour une anthropologie de l'éducation camerounaise.* Montréal: Presses de l'Université de Montréal, pp. 545–79.

Mbembe, A. 2001. *On the Postcolony.* Berkeley: University of California Press.

Mbembe, A. and Roitman, J. 1995. 'Figures of the subject in times of crisis.' *Public Culture,* 7(2): 323–52.

Memmi, A. 1965. *The Colonizer and the Colonized.* Trans. Howard Greenfield. New York: Orion Press.

Moyer, E. 2003. 'In the Shadow of the Sheraton. Imagining Localities in Global Spaces in Dar es Salaam, Tanzania.' PhD Dissertation, University of Amsterdam.

Ndjio, B. 2001: '*Feymania* in Cameroon: Hidden Ways of Enrichment and Alternative Visions of Modernity.' Paper presented during the international conference on the 'Genealogies of modernity' organized by the ASSR/University of Amsterdam, 27–30 August.

— 2005. '"Carrefour de la Joie": Popular Deconstruction of the African Post-colonial public sphere.' *Africa,* 75(3): 265–94.

— 2006. 'Feymania: Magic Money, New Wealth and Power in Contemporary Cameroon.' PhD Dissertation, ASSR/University of Amsterdam.

Nietzsche, F. 1966 [1887]. *Beyond Good and Evil: Prelude in Rhymes and an Appendix of Songs,* trans. Walter Kaufmann. New York: Vintage Books.

Nyamnjoh, F. 2000. 'For Many are Called but Few are Chosen: Globalisation and Popular Disenchantment in Africa,' *African Sociological Review/Revue Africaine de Sociologie,* 4 (2): 1–45.

Politique Africaine. 2001. 81, March: 177–45.

Roitman, J. 2005. *Fiscal Disobedience. Anthropology of Economic Regulation in Central Africa.* Princeton and Oxford: Princeton University Press.

Rowlands, M. 1989. 'Material Culture of Success: Households and consumption in Bamenda.' In P. Geschiere and P. Konings, eds. *The Political Economy of Cameroon, Historical Perspectives/L'économie politique du Cameroun, perspectives historiques.* Leiden: African Studies Centre: 503–23.

— 1996. 'Consumption of an African Modernity.' In M. J. Arnoldi, C. M. Ceary and K. L. Hardin, eds, *African Material Culture.* Bloomington: Indiana University Press, pp. 188–213.

Rush, J. 1990. *Opium to Java: Revenue Farming and Chinese Enterprise in Colonial Indonesia, 1860–1910.* Ithaca, NY: Cornell University Press.

Said, W. E. 1993. *Culture and Imperialism.* London: Vintage.

Santerre, R. and Mercier-Tremblay, C. (eds). 1982. *La Quête du Savoir: Essais pour une anthropologie de l'éducation camerounaise.* Montréal: Presses de l'Université de Montréal.

Schilder, K.1994. *Self-esteem, State, Islam and Mundang Ethnicity in Cameroon.* Leiden: ASC, Research Series.

Séraphin, G. 2000. *Vivre à Douala: L'Imaginaire et l'Action dans une ville africaine en crise.* Paris: Karthala.

Sichone, O. 2001.'Pure Anthropology in a Highly Indebted Country.' *Journal of Southern African Studies* 27 (2): 369–79.

Tsakala Munikengi and Bongo-Pasi, M. S. W. 2004. 'The Diploma Paradox: University of Kinshasa between Crisis and Salvation.' In T. Trefon, ed. *Reinventing Order in the Congo: How People Respond to State Failure in Kinshasa.* London: Zed Books, pp. 82–98.

Weber, M. 1958 [1920]. *The Protestant Ethic and the Spirit of Capitalism.* New York: Scribner's Press.

Young, R. 1990. *White Mythologies: Writing, History, and the West.* London: Routledge.

JANET ROITMAN
A Successful Life in the Illegal Realm
Smugglers & Road Bandits in the Chad Basin[1]

Reference
Unpublished paper

As in other parts of Africa and elsewhere, many people living in the Chad Basin have recourse to unregulated economic activities and even theft in order to make a living. Despite the difficulties inherent in such livelihoods, the risks run, and the recourse to illegal practices, those who live such lives often associate them with forms of personal and social success. However, contrary to their own perceptions and explications of their lives and their livelihood, commentary and analysis of these people's activities tend to be trapped in stark oppositions. These latter interpretations by outside observers are concerned, for the most part, with the utility of unregulated commerce, its relationship to the state and to market capitalism. On the one hand, smugglers and road bandits evade state regulatory authority and thus are said to be a problem for economic development, since they deprive the state of important revenues. Often depicted as part of a residual economic realm, they are also often condemned for their failure to adhere to modern, capitalist logics that necessitate a rational-legal bureaucracy and predictable economic behaviour. On the other hand, as part of the so-called informal economy, unregulated economic networks are sometimes presented as nascent capitalism, being manifestations of capitalist behaviour freed from the bonds of state interventions and state clientelist networks.[2] This article offers a look at the lives and practices of the actors of unregulated commerce in order to dispel both of the above-stated views. As the actors themselves explain, their work takes place in an ambivalent space, being both outside the purview of state interventions (they evade economic regulatory authority) and national jurisdictions (they transgress the law) and yet essential to the very reproduction of the state (as a source of new rents) and the national economy (as a source of added value and incomes). Likewise, while these actors aspire to what they call 'modern life', as a figure of success, the definition of such a life is not over-determined; its referents are multiform, often embracing, for example, both 'the West' and 'Islam' in one and the same breath. This article will attend to that disposition, or the representation of 'modern life' as a mode of success fashioned with reference to seemingly contradictory representations of the sources of wealth, the nature of wealth, and the means to economic and social mobility. Those working in the realm of unregulated commerce in the Chad Basin, whose conversations with me are the basis of this text, view themselves as figures of success despite the conditions under which they work and their status as illegal economic operators.[3] They describe this success, or social and economic mobility, in terms of the ability to find or invent work and to accumulate wealth, which is correlated with the desire for economic security.

Modern life

Often associated with the right to engage in commerce regardless of means, those who smuggle petrol on the Nigerian–Cameroonian border describe their activities as part of 'democratization', since 'anyone can participate' and, moreover, their supply keeps gas prices low, thus aiding the impoverished consumer. And yet this call for the right to accumulation and consumption is not merely an appeal for the 'freedom of the market' against a predatory or parasitic state. More subtle than that crude contrast, this claim is in many ways an attempt to dismantle exclusionary references to 'democracy' and to *'la vie moderne'* (modern life). Indeed, the people I knew in the Chad Basin referred to *'la vie moderne'* (modern life) as opposed to 'modernity'.[4] I prefer to take up their expression because the term 'modernity' issues out of a particular reading of Western history and Western philosophy, which is in many ways irrelevant to my interlocutors. This is not to say that modernity, as a concept, can only be considered with respect to Western history or contemporary debates in Western political philosophy or theory. As has been argued elsewhere, the non-Western world was fundamental to, and even inherent in, the very genealogy of modernity.[5] These two terms – 'the West' and the 'non-West' – were produced as objectified categories and as the fundamental referents of a binary metaphysics both in and through imperialism. The history of modernity is not Western nor is it coterminous with the West; its genealogies are multiple in both geographical and temporal terms. However, the idea that there are 'multiple modernities', as is often said today, runs the risk of generating a narrative account of modernity that is ever more homogeneous, modernity becoming an increasingly inclusive and even standardizing category (Prakash 1990, and see Mitchell 2000). As Tim Mitchell writes,

> Modernity, like capitalism, is defined by its claim to universality, to a uniqueness, unity, and universality that represent the end (in every sense) of history. Yet this always remains an impossible unity, an incomplete universal. Each staging of the modern must be arranged to produce the unified, global history of modernity, yet each requires those forms of difference that introduce the possibility of a discrepancy, that return to undermine its unity and identity. Modernity then becomes the unsuitable yet unavoidable name for all these discrepant histories. (2000: 24)

An unsuitable name because, in the apt words of Bruno Latour (1993), 'We have never been modern': the claim to universality and unity always fails, as does the distinction between the material and the immaterial, or between reality and representation. Nonetheless, and uniquely for the purposes of the present paper, modernity is not only a manner of apprehending the real; it is also a matter of living-in-the-world (Asad 2003: 14). To my mind, the most pertinent point is made by Talal Asad when he says,

> The important question, therefore, is not to determine why the idea of 'modernity' (or 'the West') is a misdescription, but why it has become hegemonic *as a political goal*, what practical conse-

quences follow from that hegemony, and what social conditions maintain it. (2003: 13, his emphasis)

The answers to these questions lie in the genealogies of the very concept of modernity, as well as the interrogation of the processes and social arrangements that give rise to the conceptual binaries (West, non-West) with which it articulates and through which 'modernity' is enunciated.

This inquiry into the social conditions that serve to produce and maintain 'modernity' as a political project is beyond the scope of this paper. The conversations with people in the Chad Basin reproduced herein are utterly insufficient as reflections of this matter of living-in-the-world, and yet Asad's assumption of modernity as a political-economic project, or as a 'series of interlinked projects', does speak to the political nature of claims to modernity reflected herein. As we shall see below, the imagined spaces of 'modern life' are myriad, as one might expect. There is no uniform principle governing discourse on modern life in the region of the Chad Basin, in the respective nation-states of Cameroon and Chad, or in the community of unregulated traders and smugglers depicted herein. Nevertheless, the statements and assertions made by those I spoke with do reflect the point that 'modernity' or 'modern life' is a regulative political concept.[6] The concept-metaphors associated with this claim to modern life include both state regulation in the face of increased physical and economic insecurity as well as the possibility of engaging in economic exchanges that allow access to regional and international markets. At times, these claims are evidently contradictory. And yet they reflect the terrain from which a successful life in these countries is best pursued: on international borders, by engaging in unregulated commerce, and through emergent realms of economic regulation.

Sites of accumulation: 'Hollywood, Insh'allah'

Until about the mid-1980s, in the Chad Basin, as in most other parts of the world, 'the nation-state', 'economic development', and 'democracy' have prevailed as the preeminent signifiers of 'modern life'. But this changed as impoverishment, indebtedness, and increased factional fighting and warfare have accompanied the rather disingenuous process of political and economic liberalization on the African continent. Hence 'austerity' has become a predominant emblem of post-industrial society in Africa, as elsewhere (cf. Comaroff and Comaroff 2000, Ferguson 1999). And since international donors have made multiparty elections the condition of continued financing, 'democracy' is no longer taken to be a sign of the affluent society. In many parts of Africa, it has led to the militarization of society, where large parts of many countries have come under military jurisdiction or even militarism, where violence is generalized as a political procedure.[7]

In this context, those who participate in the unregulated economy in the Chad Basin maintain, quite rightly, that they have not made significat gains from the trappings of 'modern life', which include education, health care, employment in industrial and service sectors, and consumption – as well as the right to a passport or access to a stable, convertible currency. Today, their references to 'the market' and to 'democracy' are capricious; they refer simultaneously to a proliferation of repertoires that now give sense to these regulatory concepts. These include the discourses of Christian independent church movements and Islamic missionary movements; the narrative of economic development associated with non-governmental organizations or the state bureaucracy; the visions of freedom put forth by human rights organizations, newly established political parties, and community-based religious associations; and so forth. The coexistence of these various institutions and discourses has given rise to what *seem to be* combinatory approaches to 'modern life' when considered from the point of view of the teleology of modernity, with its references to religion versus secularism or the West versus the rest. However, if considered outside the logic of that teleology, these various social arrangements and political or economic institutions can be seen as participating in emergent global assemblages (Ong and Collier 2005), which, in the context described herein, both inform and give rise to particular conceptions of 'the market', 'democracy', 'modern life', and 'success.' In that sense, global assemblages circumscribe or materialize emergent material, collective and discursive relationships. In their recent critical reading of processes of globalization and the significance of 'the global', Ong and Collier explain that,

> In relationship to 'the global,' the assemblage is not a 'locality' to which broader forces are counterposed. Nor is it the structural effect of such forces. An assemblage is the product of multiple determinations that are not reducible to a single logic. The temporality of an assemblage is emergent. It does not always involve new forms, but forms that are shifting, in formation, or at stake. (2005: 12)

This formulation is helpful insofar as it highlights the study of a contemporary situation in terms of identifiable trajectories of change and transformation, hence permitting definition and evaluation of the problems that these transformations pose for those involved. This is what is 'at stake': the political claims made in the name of 'modern life' or, more generally and more ambitiously, the ways in which 'modernity' might be represented and/or questioned as a political project in the sense intended by Talal Asad. The emergent quality of these infrastructures and discursive forms is such that these domains are sites for the articulation – or problematization – of individual and collective situations and dilemmas in the contemporary world (Ong and Collier 2005: 2, Rabinow 2003, Latour 1993).

As conversations reproduced herein suggest, both economic security and national sovereignty are increasingly circumscribed as nodal points for questions about the means to success in the contemporary world and what it means to live a modern life. Those interrogations, debates, and modes of evaluation arise from composite referents (Christianity, Islam, humanitarianism, human rights, and so on), which inform judgements about the sites and sources of wealth, desired forms of wealth, and legitimate modes of appropriating wealth. Spontaneous and random conversations or interviews with young men involved in the unregulated trade in petrol in northern Cameroon, Nigeria, and Chad give insight into those views. At the illegal 'Boston City' street-side petrol selling post in Maroua, Cameroon, a group of young men refer to their state of affairs with reference to underspecified associations between wealth, desire, and empowerment:

> Boston City is a big city in the United States. We chose this name in order to attract clients and so that they can locate us quickly. For us, Boston simply means petrol. We wrote Boston City simply to say to people that we sell gas. We chose a city in the United States because we want to fight against the economic crisis like Americans; we want to gather our courage to forge ahead.[8]

Another young illegal petrol seller united apparently disparate signifiers (Hollywood, *insh'allah*) in his elaboration of his selling post, called 'Hollywood':

To start with, Hollywood is one of the great cities of the United States and I hope you're aware of the ambiance that reigns there. A lively city at all hours, twenty-four hours a day; rich, pretty to live in. To me, Hollywood is money, cleanliness, wealth in general. Thanks to the resources I have from selling gas, I would like – Insh'allah [if God permits] – to make my entourage, my neighborhood, a Hollywood... It's my dream, it's a point of reference.[9]

In Maroua, as in many other parts of the world, the imaginings of wealth and 'modern life' are mediated through both irreverent gangsta rap and the reverent *mujjahiddin*, often at one and the same time. In this sense, young illegal petrol sellers, who procure their wares at the frontier garrison-entrepôts and from militia-led cross-desert caravans, are reflections of the cosmopolitan subjects of late twentieth-century cultural production. In this young man's terms – 'Insh'allah' – Islam wills the realization of the capitalist dream, or the riches of Hollywood; it is not construed as the antithesis of the West. The young man who ran the Hollywood selling post's nickname is Alhadji Petel (Little Alhadji), a title that signifies success in Islam and in the local Muslim merchant society. *Alhadji* (*El Hajj*) is the title given to one who has made the pilgrimage to Mecca. In many parts of the Sahel, this is a sign of wealth and has come to signify a successful businessman, whether the religious excursion has been undertaken or not (refer to Grégoire 1991 and 1992).

No doubt, Islamic society is deemed by some as the very site of capital formation. In the 'Koweit City' selling post:

> I sell every day and the gas does not stop. Provisioning is permanent and I earn considerable profits. Like Kuwait, where they say the oil wells never end, I think of my locality as a center of permanent provisioning. Kuwait City is wealth. I posted this sign high because I dream of becoming rich one day...When you say 'gas' or 'petrol' you make direct allusion to countries like the United States, the USSR, Saudi Arabia, and Kuwait. That's why I chose Kuwait as a model.[10]

The billboard marking the busy intersection where provisioning is permanent reads: '*Koweit City. Droits de l'homme.*' ('Kuwait City. Human Rights.'), referencing the power of oil and the oft-admired stance of Saddam Hussein in the face of Western power, as well as the presumed association between profits and democracy ('oil' and 'human rights'). But the correlation between the latter two is not evident in the Chad Basin.[11] Despite the instatement of multiparty politics and the recent laying of an oil pipeline through Cameroon and Chad, profits have flowed neither from the vote nor from the blossoming of human rights organizations concerned with environmental issues in the region.

When I asked the illegal petrol vendor at the 'Koweit City' post why he chose this place of war – which Kuwait was at the time – he responded that he was 'not alluding to war, but only to becoming rich'. Others, however, identified explicitly with embattled locales in the geopolitically-defined world of Islam. Thus 'Welcome to Baghdad' ushers clients into one garrison of gas:

> I like this name because, before, Baghdad was a beautiful capital. Baghdad was destroyed during the Gulf War; that really bothers me. I would like this capital to be rebuilt quickly. The Americans are the cause of this destruction; they owe Saddam Hussein help...If I ever have the means, I hope to go there one day.[12]

This is highly reminiscent of what people have to say about the once resplendent capital of Cameroon, Yaoundé, which lies in the south; and the dilapidation, decay and destruction that have scarred other northern towns as well (cf. Mbembe and Roitman 1995). Indeed, the petrol sellers work illegally in front of dusty trees or at sordid crossroads under the constant threat of confiscation by the police or fiscal authorities, exactions by underpaid military personnel or local administrators, and theft without recourse to official complaints. This inspired the informal Association of Petrol Sellers to dub one spot 'Sarajevo-Bosnia':

> We chose this name because to be a petrol seller you must first be a strong and resistant guy since you spend the whole day, and often the nights, selling. You don't rest. And if someone attacks us, we can respond en masse to the attack. We wanted to post that to show you that the petrol sellers aren't weak; they can fight like the people in Sarajevo.[13]

In keeping with an economy of war and physical, if not explicitly political, defiance, another Sarajevo exists because:

> It's a site of war and here, where I sell petrol, I see a lot of miracles. I say miracles because, day and night, I witness lots of accidents... And late at night, the police come to take the taxi-motorcycles from the young people by force. Often they even rape the girls who pass by. For me, Sarajevo means disorder, trouble, noise. If they can take people's belongings by force and if one ends up fighting incessantly in a place, don't you see that I'm right to choose a place of war like Sarajevo?[14]

It is not insignificant that these young men refer to the icons of urban violence and war, which are sometimes valorized either in terms of empowerment in the periphery or as modes of attaining social mobility associated with a realm beyond the periphery. Their claims about the status of particular communities in the global economy – Islam, the West, sites of war, sites of capital accumulation — are not construed in terms of opposing poles. Their composite referents inform judgements about the sites and sources of wealth, desired forms of wealth, and legitimate modes of appropriating wealth. In that sense, the illegal petrol sellers' remarks register efforts to negotiate 'modern life' in a time of austerity, but they also contest, with recourse to varying referents, present and increasingly problematic modes of redistribution and alienation. 'War' has become a wide-spread paradigm for understanding the demise of specific metaphors and historical institutions that once regulated communities (e.g. economic development, national progress, social welfare), the generalization of certain modes of appropriation (e.g. seizure, debt), and the rise of their associated figures of authority (e.g. militias, renegade customs officials, foreigners) (see Roitman 2005).

The predicament of success

A successful life is signified by wealth creation associated with far-flung and unduly affluent localities, such as Hollywood and the Gulf States, and the capacity to withstand hardship and potential physical violence. Success is wealth, as they say, but wealth creation pre-supposes particular questions about physical and economic security, questions that are being asked in Cameroon today. It is not insignificant that the illegal petrol sellers, who are, for the most part, young, undereducated men, have formed a formal association for what is often deemed 'informal' economic activity. This initiative is indicative of their self-consciousness as economic agents as well as their desire to integrate the world of officialdom. Defiant in their physical resistance to adverse conditions, they are nonetheless not necessarily resisting

capitalism, integration into the world economy or the state.

But, as always, this desire for integration and legality is ambivalent, as is illustrated by other actors in the realm of unregulated trade and commerce, such as the until-recently illegal and unregulated taxi-motorcyclists, who also have their own professional associations in Cameroon. In the late 1990s, the Cameroonian fiscal authorities sought to capture this lucrative domain by legalizing the taxi-motorcycles through a series of regulations.[15] The latter included a new tax (*l'impôt libératoire*), a driver's licence, vehicle registration, vehicle insurance, a vehicle inspection sticker, *la carte bleue*, a parking permit, and a custom's receipt for imported motorcycles. Drivers are now supposed to paint the motorcycles yellow, and wear helmets and gloves, none of which I have ever seen. Most young taxi-men do not pay these myriad impositions. But this is not because they do not have the means, since most taxi fleets are financed by merchants, gendarmes, police, prefects, and even governors. The motorcycle-taximen – who are often referred to as *les attaquants* (the attackers) or *les casquadeurs* (the cascaders) – simply refer to a different register of appropriations which, ironically, often involves the very same people who are responsible for and collect official taxes. In response to criticism for not having paid his official taxes, one young motorcycle-taximan, a member of the *Association des moto-taximen* of Ngaoundéré, declared:

> We pay our taxes every day! Whether we have all the right papers for the motorcycle or not, we pay taxes to the police and gendarmes. In fact, it's become a reflex. The policemen of Ngaoundéré don't stop me anymore. I'm an old hand in the moto-taxi business. I've driven moto-taxis for people in high places, for men in uniform [who are owners of fleets of clandestine motorcycles]. Furthermore, often even when the police don't stop me, I go to them to pay the tribute (in monetary sense). My older brother initiated me. He is a *djo*, someone who knows all the secrets, all the strings. He told me that, with the police, it's not enough to go tell them that they are big men (*les grands*); you have to show them. It's like with the traditional chief, the *lamido*. The *lamido* doesn't work but he has a lot of money because people come to give it to him. The *lamido* doesn't ask anything of his subjects. His subjects come to give him envelopes out of respect and they also pray to Allah to give him long life. Since the policeman is also a chief – in fact, we call him 'chief' (*chef*) – you have to go towards him even when your papers are in order, especially when you are in order.[16]

During the same conversation, another moto-taxi driver added:

> People enter into the police force because they know that it pays. But it's not necessarily the monthly salary; there are a lot of 'asides' (*à côtés*). The police and the moto-taximen, we're partners. We know that if we are disposed to giving them a bit of money from time to time, we can work together. Together – that is the police and the moto-taximen – we exploit illegality. Even when you have all your papers in order, you're in illegality because the motorcycle is illegal. Not even 15 per cent of the motorcycles are painted yellow. We have imposed our vision of things on the authorities. The police themselves close their eyes; they can always find an infraction to ticket. That way, they have money for beer. Today, we have representatives at each crossroads, leaders who negotiate with the administration when there are problems. We parade in front of the authorities during national festivities, they solicit us during election campaigns. We've become an integral part of

society through the force of resistance. That's power. So that the system can continue to function properly, it's important that there are people in violation because, if everyone was in line with the law, the authorities – the police – wouldn't gain their share and then they would suppress the motorcycles on the pretext that they cause accidents, that we are hoodlums, etc. Today, maybe we are hoodlums, but we are hoodlums who help sustain families and contribute to the wellbeing of agents of the force of law. Long live the tolerant police (*la police compréhensive*)![17]

This young man's comments speak to the displacement of 'the salary' as a foundational source of wealth, the preeminent means of accumulation, and the most generalized form of redistribution.

Historically, or since the time of national independence in Cameroon, redistribution has occurred nationally through salary payments that have been ensured via external financing (Bayart 1979, 1989). These have underpinned the burgeoning civil service and parastatal sectors, providing the material means for national distribution and the construction of dependency relations through patronage networks and extended families. As everywhere, the salary system structures social stratification.[18] However, following in the traces of the colonial state, the Cameroonian postcolonial state has been the nexus of the great majority of salaried activity. Therefore, since the salary creates relations of dependency and debt between the state and recipients (and their dependants), it is constitutive of, and reflects, a particular notion of citizenship. In Cameroon, salaries are most often construed as 'privileges' as opposed to simple remuneration for productive activity. This is evident to anyone who has witnessed the pleadings of those who arrive, day after day, for months on end, at the barred windows of the public offices where salaries (might, eventually) be distributed. This perception of the salary as a privilege and not a right is the combined result of the deployment of the salary as part of a disciplinary apparatus establishing relations of dependency and indebtedness between the state and its subjects, as well as historical understandings of the relationships that bind wealth, work and the state (Mbembe and Roitman 1995).

Today, the salary is no longer an inherent aspect of an apparatus establishing and ensuring the basis for economic accumulation, social ascension and economic redistribution. The salary once constituted *le fonctionnaire*, the lynchpin figure in a system of economic transfers and social hierarchy. Today, a successful life must be envisaged outside of the bounds of the certificates and diplomas that once consecrated the *évolués*, the latter being the gatekeeper status for entry into the civil service, that ultimate haven of economic security. Today, a successful life must be imagined according to other itineraries of accumulation (Geschiere and Konings 1993). Unregulated commerce is one realm in which possible futures are fashioned. This is attested to by the petrol sellers and moto-taximen, but it is also manifest in the itineraries and practices of, for instance, the *feymen*, who now make up a significant diaspora, suggesting the possibility of an emergent African middle class developing across the bounds of national states and outside the bounds of national regulatory authority (see Ndjio this volume, but see also Malaquais 2001). Not entirely novel, working on or across international borders and eliding state fiscal regulatory authority has nonetheless come to be an increasingly significant mode of social mobility. This manner of livelihood signifies a certain success (beating the odds, outdoing conditions of physical and economic insecurity) and is associated with certain imagined spaces of 'modern life', be they Hollywood, the Gulf States or Johannesburg (the imagined and real eldorado of *feymania*). But life-outside-the-bounds is not equivalent to

a conscious mobilization for political resistance to the state (in the name, for instance, of fundamental transformations in economic or political policy). As one of the moto-taximen said above, 'We've become an integral part of society through the force of resistance.' This concern with economic and social integration prevails.

Indeed, when pushed on the question of the relationship between the world of traffickers and the state, the efficacy of the former as an economic domain is usually underscored, as is the mutually constitutive nature of unregulated commerce, on the one hand, and the state, on the other. This point is exemplified by remarks made by the young moto-taximan, who commented on resistance above:

Q: So traffickers steal from the state since they don't take the paths – I mean the roads – that the state has created for the movement of men and goods. They don't pay their taxes either. So doesn't the trafficker go against the social order since we pay taxes to finance schools, hospitals – collective services and social services?
R: That's just talk. Ahidjo and Ousmane Mey, didn't they massacre the Arabes Choas of Dollé, who wanted a school?[19] Didn't the Arabes Choas of Dollé pay their taxes, that is, since independence? Villagers who pay their taxes, do they get free medicine? Do they give schoolbooks to peasants' children? When people want to justify the embezzlement of funds, they should find other arguments. Taxes aren't for social services, they are for the personal works of leaders. It's like the right to passage that the men of the *lamido* take from those who do transactions on the river [Logone], or like the duties (*les droits*) that fishermen pay. It's a matter of tradition. We pay without seeking to know where the money goes.
Q: So you don't pay taxes because you don't know where the money goes?
R: Taxes, we pay them since now there is the *impôt libératoire*.
Q: Yes, but the impôt libératoire is for those who have a well-defined activity, a classified activity that corresponds to a well-defined tax. What is the profession indicated on your card?
R: Unemployed.
Q: But you just said that you're a cross-border merchant! Isn't that a job?
R: Yes, of course, but it's many temporary jobs. All of us here, we do many things at once: we sell gas, medicines, motorcycles, hardware – that we buy for ourselves or for those who send us across the border.
Q: Arms are part of hardware and drugs are part of medicines?
R: Are you trying to ruin our conversation?
Q: We're talking about traffic.
R: Arms and drugs are the affairs of those who've recently come into the traffic – knowledgeable traffickers, people who act on command (*commandement*), who have networks to sell their medicines. The people who are accused of doing this type of trafficking, or who steal vehicles and attack expatriates, are well-placed people. We see them with luxurious cars that they sell quickly to get another one. They're always traveling, they have houses even though we don't know exactly where they work. Those are the people who create problems for modest people like us, who work outside the rules, of course, but we don't harm anyone. Arms are for aggressions and killing. Drugs destroy. The petrol we sell is to move people around, to help the moto-taximen work. The motorcycles we bring [from Nigeria] contribute to economic development. The motorcycles keep young people from begging and stealing. They have a future thanks to the motorcycles. And, in Kousséri, there are no taxis. The functionaries who don't have cars – like most of them – take the

moto-taxis to work. Without the motorcycles, there would be no regular attendance at work; people would always go late. School kids who live far away would always be late and even absent. During the rainy season, people wouldn't go to work under the pretext of clouds. Without the moto-taxis, women would walk long distances with children on their backs. So, are the moto-taxis useful or not?
Q: The state should thank you, then.[20]

Another young man, who works on the borders in unregulated trade, confirmed such opinions, arguing:

We struggle in domains that force you to circumvent the law – with all the risks. For example, we sell contraband petrol and medicines, etc., which are officially forbidden. But what do you expect? Often those who are supposed to see that people respect the law are our sponsors; they give us our original financing. A customs official who finances a petrol smuggler is not going to attack him [the smuggler] or the protégés of his colleagues! And without us, the work of the policeman, the customs official, the taxman, the head of the gendarmes, would have no interest for those who do it. Thanks to us, they have no financial problems.... [President] Paul Biya says that you have to beware of people who talk about change (*le changement*), without saying clearly what must be changed. Us, we're the solution to the crisis. Whether you like it or not, it's better to be a trafficker than unemployed. We send money to our parents. We pay school fees for our little brothers. We contribute to our sisters' wedding preparations. Some of us have even gotten married with our own resources. None of us here have ever gone to prison. When we have a problem with the gendarmes, we negotiate. When we have problems with the customs service, we negotiate. That way, government officials compensate their low salaries and don't go on strike.[21]

The utility of livelihoods conceived and pursued through engagement in unregulated trade and commerce is apprehended as a matter of economic and social integration: these young men argue that such activities allow the official or state system to perpetuate itself since they devise new modes of social mobility and socio-economic redistribution. Contrary to analysis of these activities as part of an 'informal economy', as noted in the introduction to this paper, here utility is not evaluated in terms of whether or not these economic activities contribute to capitalism. Likewise, relations to the state are not portrayed by those involved as either a matter of conscious political resistance, on the one hand, or the espousal of extant political regimes and policies, on the other. Perhaps, in that regard, these livelihoods do imply a certain critique of binary categories, a form of subversion that transpires when dichotomies such as 'formal/informal' are shown to be irrelevant in practice. Either way, successful life and modern life involve interrogations of such categories ('formal/informal', 'the market', 'the state'), indicating that both 'success' and 'modern life' are not unproblematic signifiers. The problem of livelihood is quite often articulated in terms of economic insecurity – either with respect to the conditions under which one must establish the means to accumulate wealth and to access 'modern life', as the petrol sellers made clear, or with respect to the ways in which one responds to those conditions, as we saw for the moto-taximen. Although we are constantly reminded of the dire economic conditions prevailing on the African continent today, this reference to economic insecurity does not go without saying. In the Chad Basin, the predicament of livelihood and success is not necessarily conceived in terms of spiritual insecurity (see Ashforth 2004) or in terms of alleged foreign threats that harbour political insecurity (see *Politique africaine* 2003 on Côte d'Ivoire; Geschiere and Nyamnjoh 2000 and Ceuppens and Geschiere 2005 on autochthony). While economic insecurity is surely experienced in relation to those other forms of existential uncertainty, references to economic insecurity in the context described herein are typically spoken of with reference to the risk and likelihood of being subject to violent appropriations. The latter is discerned as a critical predicament, and is thus a topic of political and ethical reflection for those working the borders in the Chad Basin today.

Notes

[1] I would like to thank and pay special tribute to the late Hamidou Bouba and the late Yerima Issa, a nephew and his uncle, both witnesses to the conversations published herein and both victims of disease in their early twenties – a testimony to the non-universal nature of modernity and its failure to become an effective form of practice.

[2] These two positions represent the standard approaches to the 'informal economy' from within the disciplines of economics and political economy. For critical discussion, cf. Roitman 1990 and 2005; and Elyachar 2003 and 2005.

[3] The Chad Basin is a vague geographical concept. I use it here to refer to what are today northern Nigeria, northern Cameroon, Chad, and the Central African Republic. I lived in this region during various extended periods from 1992 to 2002, conducting research on the borders of these various nation-states with particular attention to ongoing transformations in the exercise of economic regulatory authority. Research was undertaken with the support of the SSRC-MacArthur Foundation Program on Peace and Security Fellowship; the Ciriacy-Wantrup Fellowship of the University of California-Berkeley; and the MacArthur Foundation Program on Global Security and Sustainability.

[4] While elaboration of the term is important, a definition of modernity is meaningless: 'modernity' is not a 'thing,' but rather a highly unstable referent. A formal definition would only serve the purpose of examining its teleology, which is not the aim herein.

[5] This argument has been made by many scholars and critics. The seminal reference is, of course, Edward Said's *Orientalism* (1978). See also, among others Spivak 1988 and 1993, Rabinow 1989, Memmi 1991, Mitchell 1991 and 2000, Said 1993, Gilroy 1993, Stoler 1995, Cooper and Stoler 1997, Anderson 1998 and Chakrabarty 2000.

[6] Spivak (1993) gives a most forceful account of 'modernity' as a regulative concept, insisting on the point that political claims are 'tacitly recognized as coded within the legacy of imperialism: nationhood, constitutionality, democracy, socialism, even culturalism. In the historical framework of exploration, colonization, decolonization, what is being *effectively* reclaimed is a series of regulative political concepts, the supposedly authoritative narrative of the production of which was written elsewhere, in the social formations of Western Europe. They are thus being reclaimed, indeed claimed, as concept-metaphors for which no *historically* adequate referent may be advanced from postcolonial space...' (1993: 48, and see 13–14).

[7] On militarization versus militarism as a mode of political action, refer to Mbembe 1990. On militarism and similar political claims, read Richards 1996, esp. Chapter Seven.

[8] Maroua, northern Cameroon, October 1993.

[9] Maroua, northern Cameroon, October 1993.

[10] Maroua, northern Cameroon, October 1993.

[11] This is a particularly apt moment to point that out since oil around Lake Chad and in southern Chad is now the subject of much heated debate. The World Bank is financing the construction of a pipeline from southern Chad, through the entire length of Cameroon, to the port of Kribi on the Cameroonian coast. This immense project has been stalled due to criticism from environmental and human rights groups, mostly represented by NGOs, but also associated with Chadian organizations and the armed

opposition movement in southern Chad.
[12] Maroua, northern Cameroon, October 1993.
[13] Maroua, northern Cameroon, October 1993.
[14] Maroua, northern Cameroon, October 1993.
[15] This legalization was both fiscally and politically motivated, the taxi-motorcycle drivers having been at the forefront of a movement dubbed *incivisme fiscal* by state authorities. See Roitman 2005 for elaboration.
[16] December 2001, Ngaoundéré, Cameroon.
[17] December 2001, Ngaoundéré, Cameroon.
[18] The centrality of salary payments in cycles of debt, redistribution, and reciprocity is examined in the case of the Ivory Coast by Mahieu 1989. For commentary on this same dynamic (and its crisis) in Europe, cf. Théret 1992.
[19] See Issa (1997) on the Dollé massacre of 1979.
[20] Kousseri, Cameroon, 23 December 2001.
[21] Touboro, Cameroon, 23 November 2001.

References

Anderson, Perry. 1998. *The Origins of Postmodernity*. New York: Verso.

Asad, Talal. 2003. *Formations of the Secular. Christianity, Islam, Modernity*. Stanford, CA: Stanford University Press.

Ashforth, Adam. 2004. *Witchcraft, Violence, and Democracy in South Africa*. Chicago: University of Chicago Press.

Bayart, Jean-François. 1979. *L'Etat au Cameroun*. Paris: Presses de la fondation nationale des sciences politiques.

— 1989. *L'Etat en Afrique*. Paris: Fayard.

Ceuppens, B. and P. Geschiere. 2005. 'Autochthony: Local or Global? New Modes in the Struggle over Citizenship and Belonging in Africa and Europe', *Annual Review of Anthropology*, 34: 385–409.

Chakrabarty, Dipesh. 2000. *Provincializing Europe. Postcolonial Thought and Historical Difference*. Princeton, NJ: Princeton University Press.

Comaroff, Jean and John Comaroff. 2000. 'Millennium Capitalism: First Thoughts on a Second Coming', *Public Culture* 12: 291–343.

Cooper, Fred and Ann Laura Stoler, eds. 1997. *Tensions of Empire: Colonial Cultures in a Bourgeois World*. Berkeley: University of California Press.

Elyachar, J. 2003. 'Mappings of Power: The State, NGOs, and International Organizations in the Informal Economy', *Comparative Studies in Society and History*, vol 45, 3: 571–605.

— 2005. *Markets of Dispossession. NGOs, Economic Development, and the State in Cairo*. Durham, NC: Duke University Press.

Ferguson, James. 1999. *Expectations of Modernity: Myths and Meanings of Urban Life on the Zambian Copperbelt*. Berkeley: University of California Press.

Geschiere, Peter and Piet Konings, eds. 1993. *Itinéraires d'accumulation au Cameroun*. Paris: ASC Karthala.

Geschiere, P. and F. Nyamnjoh. 2000. 'Capitalism and Autochthony: The Seesaw of Mobility and Belonging', *Public Culture* 12, 2: 423–53.

Gilroy, Paul. 1993. *The Black Atlantic: Modernity and Double Consciousness*. Cambridge, MA: Harvard University Press.

Grégoire, Emanuelle. 1991. 'Accumulation marchande et propagation de l'Islam en milieu urbain: Le cas de Maradi (Niger). *Islam et sociétés au sud du Sahara* 5: 43–55.

— 1992. *The Alhazi of Maradi: Traditional Hausa Merchants in a Changing Sahelian City*. Boulder, CO: Lynne Rienner.

Issa, Saibou. 1997. 'L'Impact de la crise tchadienne sur le Nord-Cameroun: 1979-1982'. Mémoire de maîtrise en Histoire. FALSH, Université de Yaoundé I.

Latour, Bruno. 1993. *We Have Never Been Modern*. Cambridge, MA: Harvard University Press.

Mahieu, Régis. 1989. 'Principes de l'économie africaine'. *Revue Tiers-Monde* 30: 725–53.

Malaquais, Dominique. 2001. 'Arts de Feyre au Cameroun', *Politique africaine* 82, June: 101–18.

Mbembe, Achille. 1990. 'Pouvoir, violence et accumulation', *Politique africaine* 39: 7–24.

Mbembe, Achille and Janet Roitman. 1995. 'Figures of the Subject in Times of Crisis', *Public Culture* 7: 323–52.

Memmi, Albert. 1991. *The Colonizer and the Colonized*. Boston, MA: Beacon Press.

Mitchell, Timothy. 1991. *Colonizing Egypt*. Berkeley: University of California Press.

— ed. 2000. *Questions of Modernity*. Minneapolis: University of Minnesota Press.

Ong, Aihwa and Stephen Collier, eds. 2005. *Global Assemblages. Technology, Politics, and Ethics as Anthropological Problems*. London: Blackwell.

Politique africaine 89, March 2003.

Prakash, Gyan. 1990. 'Writing Post-Orientalist Histories of the Third World: Perspectives from Indian Historiography,' *Comparative Studies in Society and History* 32, 2, April: 383–408.

Rabinow, Paul. 1989. *French Modern. Norms and Forms of the Social Environment*. Cambridge, MA: MIT Press.

— 2003. *Anthropos Today*. Princeton, NJ: Princeton University Press.

Richards, Paul. 1996. *Fighting for the Rain Forest: War, Youth and Resources in Sierra Leone*. London/Portsmouth, NH: James Currey/Heinemann.

Roitman, Janet. 1990. 'The Politics of Informal Markets in Sub-Saharan Africa', *The Journal of Modern African Studies* 28, 4, December, pp. 671–96.

— 2005. *Fiscal Disobedience. An Anthropology of Economic Regulation*. Princeton, NJ: Princeton University Press.

Said, Edward. 1978. *Orientalism*. New York: Pantheon.

— 1993. *Culture and Imperialism*. New York: Knopf.

Spivak, Gayatri. 1988. 'Can the Subaltern Speak?' in C. Nelson and L. Grossberg, eds, *Marxism and the Interpretation of Culture*. Basingstoke: Macmillan.

— 1993. *Outside in the Teaching Machine*. New York: Routledge.

Stoler, Ann Laura. 1995. *Race and the Education of Desire: Foucault's History of Sexuality and the Colonial Order of Things*. Durham, NC: Duke University Press.

Théret, Bruno. 1992. *Régimes économiques de l'ordre politique*. Paris: Presses Universitaires de France.

Index